Human Resource Management

Theory and practice

Human Resource Management

Theory and practice

second edition

John Bratton and Jeffrey Gold

MACMILLAN
Business

First published 1999 by
MACMILLAN PRESS LTD
Houndmills, Basingstoke, Hampshire RG21 6XS
and London
Companies and representatives
throughout the world

ISBN 0–333–73207–3 hardcover
ISBN 0–333–73208–1 paperback

A catalogue record for this book is available
from the British Library.

This book is printed on paper suitable for recycling and
made from fully managed and sustained forest sources.

10 9 8 7 6 5 4 3 2 1
08 07 06 05 04 03 02 01 00 99

Editing and origination by
Aardvark Editorial, Mendham, Suffolk

Printed and bound in Great Britain
at The Bath Press, Avon

After a few years away from their MBA programs,
most managers report that they wish they had focused more
on people management skills while in school.

Margaret Wheatley,
Leadership and the New Science, 1994, p. 144

Contents

part five
Employee and Industrial Relations

List of tables

List of figures

About the authors

John Bratton is Associate Professor, at the University of Calgary, Alberta, Canada, where he teaches HRM and Leadership on the Master's in Workplace Learning. He has taught HRM and Industrial Relations at Leeds Business School, Leeds Metropolitan University, England and the University College of the Cariboo, British Columbia, Canada. Before commencing his academic career, he completed an apprenticeship and worked in the engineering industry. His research interests focus on the politics of technology and workplace learning. He is co-author of *New Technology and Employment* (1981) and author of *Japanization at Work: Managerial Studies in the 1990s*.

Jeffrey Gold is Senior Lecturer in Human Resource Management at Leeds Business School, Leeds Metropolitan University, England. He has written numerous articles on human resource development and is a member of the Human Resource Development Unit within Leeds Business School.

Preface

The field of human resource management is one of the most dynamic and challenging areas for European managers. The turbulent business climate, caused by increased global price competitiveness, changing technologies, changing employment legislation, and changing workforce composition is challenging managers to utilize their employees more effectively to gain competitive advantage. In recent years there have been significant practical developments with increasing numbers of private and public sector organizations adopting HRM initiatives alongside downsizing and 're-engineering' the organization. The change towards more knowledge-based work and the growing acknowledgement that workers are the key to sustainable competitive advantage have strengthened the case for 'new' human resource management initiatives.

In academia, new human resource management books (Townley, 1994; Storey, 1995; Legge, 1995) have been published since we produced the first edition of *Human Resource Management: Theory and Practice*. Increasingly, HRM scholars have emphasized strategic aspects of HRM, adopted new perspectives and critically examined the new theoretical frameworks or HRM models. An important theoretical development which supports the central tenets of HRM is the integration of strategic management, organizational development, and adult learning to create a resource-based theory of competitive advantage. In addition, empirical-based data has been gathered, analysed and published on the extensiveness of HRM practices in North American and European organizations.

This second edition builds on the success of the first edition by incorporating these latest ideas, theories and research findings in HRM, to provide a comprehensive overview of HRM theory and a close examination of developing HRM practices. Like the first edition, it includes mini-cases and examples that describe HRM practices in Europe and elsewhere. All the material retained from the first edition has been edited for improvements in style and references have been updated. New in this edition is a chapter which focuses on strategic HRM and examines new evidence on the HRM–organizational performance link. New also is a discussion on workplace learning in Chapter 10 and issues in international HRM are considered in the final chapter.

Human Resource Management: Theory and Practice, Second Edition, has been written specifically to fulfill the need of introductory undergraduate and graduate courses for a rigorous analysis of human resource management. For some time there has been a tendency of undergraduate textbooks on personnel/human resource management to be much more prescriptive than analytical. The purpose of *Human Resource Manage-*

ment: *Theory and Practice*, Second Edition, is to provide our readers with a comprehensive knowledge and understanding of the latest relevant theories, practices, and functional activities of human resource management.

Academically rigorous and practically relevant, this book gives a comprehensive coverage of contemporary theories and concepts in key human resources activities such as recruitment and selection, appraisal, training and development, rewards management and employee relations. We have based the structure and contents on our own teaching, consultancy and research experience in HRM, and on current research findings and literature in the field. *Human Resource Management: Theory and Practice*, Second Edition, has been written for the European audience, but it draws examples and literature on HRM from Canada, the United States and other countries. This helps readers to compare international developments in HRM and to develop a broader understanding of HRM issues and practices.

Pedagogical features

Human Resource Management: Theory and Practice, Second Edition, includes a number of features that help the learning process:

Chapter outline and **Chapter objectives.** Each chapter opens with a topic outline and a set of learning objectives to guide the reader through the material that follows.

'HRM in practice' boxes. These are strategically placed in the chapter to help illustrate current developments or practices in HRM.

Diagrams and tables. Some of the conceptual material is presented by graphic diagrams. The aim is to help the reader to visualize the key elements of the theory being discussed. Data are presented to facilitate interpretation of key trends in HRM.

Theory and practice. This book bridges the gap between those books that are primarily theoretical and the textbooks that discuss what the personnel manager does, or should be doing (the prescriptive approach). This book is both theoretical *and* prescriptive. It reviews and discusses HRM concepts and includes up-to-date references on HRM scholarship. It also has a practical orientation — the 'how to' activities of HRM. For example, it discusses how to recruit and select and how to design training programmes.

Chapter summary and **Discussion questions.** All chapters end with a summary, a list of key concepts, a set of discussion questions to test readers' understanding of core concepts and to facilitate classroom or group discussion.

Further reading. All chapters end with references for further reading to provide elaboration of topics discussed in the text.

Chapter case study. Each chapter includes a case study to facilitate application of the theoretical material in the text and to help the reader appreciate the challenges of managing people at work, followed by questions or a task.

Glossary. A glossary is provided at the end of this book to help the reader review and define the key terms used in the text.

Bibliography. A bibliography provides the student with a comprehensive list of sources/works cited in the text.

Index. At the end of the book an index is included to help the reader search for relevant information and make this book a valuable resource for completing assignments or projects.

We are confident that the incorporation of new material and these pedagogical features will continue to make *Human Resource Management: Theory and Practice,* Second Edition, a valuable learning resource. We are also confident that this book will encourage the reader to question, to doubt, to investigate, to be sceptical and to seek multi-causality when analysing the problems and challenges of managing labour.

The plan of this book

This book is divided into five major parts. These parts are, of course, interconnected but, at the same time, they reflect different focuses of study. *Part one* introduces the nature and role of HRM and addresses some of the controversial theoretical issues surrounding the HRM discourse. It also examines the notion of strategic HRM and explores various strategic issues. *Part two* reviews the external contexts that affect human resource management policies and actions inside the organization. Changes in organizational structures, job design and employee health and safety are also examined in this section. The discussion in *Parts one* and *two* provides the context of HRM and prepares the groundwork for *Parts three* to *five.*

Parts three and *four* examine the key HR practices that comprise the HRM cycle illustrated in Figure 1.2: selection, appraisal, human resource development, and rewards. Several writers have reported how each of these four areas is back in vogue. The use of the assessment centre and psychological tests measuring personality appears to be on the increase (see Chapter 7). Performance appraisal methods, both among non-manual and manual workers, is growing in organizations on both sides of the Atlantic (see Chapter 8). In the area of reward or compensation management, employers have been moving towards a more individualist approach to the wage–effort bargain: merit pay, for instance, is increasingly replacing the traditional practice of the rate for the job (see Chapter 9). Human resource development is seen by theorists as a vital component, if not the pivotal component, of the human resource management model (see Chapter 10).

In *Part five* we address some of the developments in communications and employee relations. There is evidence that organizations are devoting more resources to employee communication programmes and introducing employee involvement arrangements (see Chapter 11). In the area of industrial relations, the traditional 'pluralist' or 'Donovan' model is undergoing change (see Chapter 12).

Acknowledgements

This textbook was originally inspired by our teaching and research at Leeds Business School and the University College of the Cariboo, Canada.

In writing the second edition of the book we would particularly like to thank the reviewers, and the instructors who adopted the text, for their valuable comments on the first edition. We endeavoured to incorporate their insights and criticisms to improve this edition. We would like to thank all the students we have taught in human resource management and industrial relations modules at Leeds Metropolitan University, the University College of the Cariboo, and the University of Calgary, who provided us with helpful comments on the learning material. We would like to thank Carolyn Forshaw for reading the manuscript in draft and applying her critical eye, thereby reducing the number of errors in the book and improving the style. We would also like to thank the 14 anonymous referees of the second edition for their helpful comments on earlier drafts of the manuscript. We are also grateful for the professional advice and support shown by our publishers, Nicola Young and Sarah Brown, throughout the project. John Bratton would like to recognize the assistance of Tanya Stevenson and the library and support staff at the University of Calgary. Jeff Gold would like to thank Stuart Watson, John Hamblett, Les Hamilton and Rick Holden at Leeds Metropolitan University for their inspiration in difficult times.

People Managment, from which some of the case studies in this book are taken, is the magazine of the Institute of Personnel and Development, with a circulation of 80 000 every fortnight. It is sent to all IPD members, and is available to non-members on subscription. For details, and a sample copy, contact *PM* by phone, on 0171-880 2214, or fax on 0171-880 6200.

The authors and publishers are grateful to the following for permission to reproduce copyright material:

National Institute of Economic and Social Research for Figure 3.2 and Tables 3.2, 12.1, 12.3, 12.5 and 12.7 from the *National Institute Economic Review*.

Sage Publications for Table 3.3 and 3.5 from G. Standing, 1997, Globalization, labour flexibility and insecurity: the era of market regulation, *European Journal of Industrial Relations*, **3**(1): 7–37.

Blackwell for Figure 1.4 by D. Guest, 1997, *Journal of Management Studies*, **25** and 12.1

by McLoughlin and Gourley, 1992, from the *Journal of Management Studies,* **29**: 675 and Figure 12.2 by Hyman, 1997 from the *British Journal of Industrial Relations,* **35**: 323.

Allyn & Bacon for Figure 11.4 from *Organizational Communication* by W.W. Neher.

IRC Press for Figure 12.3 from *The Canadian Workplace in Transition.*

MCB University Press for Figure 10.3 in *Effective Training* by P. Bromley from the *Journal of European Industrial Training,* 1989, **13**(7): 6.

John Wiley & Sons for Figures 1.2, 2.4, 2.5, 6.4 and 10.1 from *Strategic Human Resource Management.*

Phillip Alan Publishers for Figure 4.5 from A. Warde 'The future of work', *Social Studies Review,* September 1989, **5**(1).

Personnel Psychology, **41**: 65 for Figure 10.6 by Baldwin, T.T. and Ford, K.J. (1988) Transfer of training: a review and directions for future research.

People Management for HRM in Practice 1.1, 2.1, 3.2, 4.1, 4.2, 5.1, 6.1, 6.2, 7.1, 7.2, 8.1, 9.1, 9.2, 10.2, 11.1, 11.2, 12.1 and 12.2.

Personnel Management Plus for HRM in Practice 9.3, 11.3 and 12.3.

The Department of Trade and Industry for Tables 12.2 and 12.6 from *Workplace Industrial Relations in Transition.*

Every effort has been made to trace all the copyright holders but if any have been inadvertently overlooked the publishers will be pleased to make the necessary arrangements at the first opportunity.

List of abbreviations

ACAS	Advisory, Conciliation and Arbitration Service		MNC	Multinational Corporations
AEEU	Amalgamated Engineering and Electrical Union		MSF	Manufacturing, Science and Finance Union
CAC	Central Arbitration Committee		NAFTA	North American Free Trade Agreement
CBI	Confederation of British Industry		NUT	National Union of Teachers
CNC	Computer numerically controlled (machine tools)		OECD	Organization for Economic Cooperation & Development
CWU	Communication Workers Union		PBR	Payment by Results
EU	European Union		PCS	Public and Commercial Services Union
EEF	Engineering Employers' Federation		PRP	Performance Related Pay
EOC	Equal Opportunities Commission		QWL	Quality of Working Life
ERM	Exchange Rate Mechanism		SEM	Single European Market
ETUC	European Trade Union Confederation		SIHRM	Strategic International Human Resource Management
EWC	European Works Councils		SHRM	Strategic Human Resource Management
GDP	Gross Domestic Product		SMT	Self-managing Teams
GMB	General, Municipal Boilermakers' Union		SRSC	Safety Representatives and Safety Committee
GPMU	Graphical, Paper and Media Union		TGWU	Transport and General Workers' Union
HRD	Human resource development			
HRP	Human resource planning		TQC	Total quality control
HSC	Health and Safety Commission		TQM	Total quality management
IPD	Institute of Personnel and Development		TUC	Trades Union Congress
ILO	International Labour Organization		USDAW	Union of Shop, Distributive and Allied Workers
IMF	International Monetary Fund			
JCC	Joint Consultative/Consultation Committee		WHO	World Health Organization
JIT	Just-in-time		WIRS	Workplace Industrial Relations Survey (UK)

part one

The Nature of Human Resource Management

chapter one

The human resource management phenomenon

John Bratton

Successful corporate leaders recognize that their competitive edge in today's market place is their people. They also acknowledge that few organizations know how to manage human resources effectively, primarily because traditional management models are inappropriate in our dynamic work environment.[1]

In the reengineering corporation… hiring and promotion, development and deployment, are all now far too important to be left to Human Resources or Personnel alone.[2]

If anybody had to be the last person here, I would have bet on the Personnel Manager.[3]

Chapter outline

Chapter objectives

After studying this chapter, you should be able to:

1. Explain the role of human resource management in organizations.
2. Summarize the major activities associated with human resource management.
3. Describe the history of human resource management.
4. Explain the theoretical debate surrounding the HRM model.

● Introduction

This book is concerned with the management of people at work. The quotations opening the chapter provide insights into how the field of labour management is viewed by business executives, practitioners and academics in the 1990s. They also suggest that the ways in which organizations choose to manage their employees are in a state of transition. Labour management practices have assumed new prominence in the 1990s as concerns persist about global competition, the internationalization of technology and the productivity of workers. It is argued that these market imperatives require work organizations to adjust their system of managerial control to allow for the most effective utilization of human resources. Business executives, practitioners and academics argue that the traditional approaches to managing workers are inappropriate and 'can no longer deliver the goods' (Betcherman *et al.*, 1994, p. 2). To enlist workers' full potential and to produce behaviour and attitudes considered necessary for competitive advantage requires three aspects of managerial control to change: organizational and job design, organizational culture, and personnel policies and techniques. Thus, the developing managerial orthodoxy now posits the need for 're-engineering' of organizations towards 'flat' hierarchical structures, an enlargement of job tasks and job autonomy, ideally centred around work teams. Further, it is suggested that senior management can direct and inspire workers through the management of the more intangible aspects of the workplace, such as beliefs, norms of behaviour and values. In the jargon of the managerial theorists this is referred to as 'corporate culture'. In addition, the new orthodoxy asserts the need to recruit, develop and reward workers in ways which create a sustainable commitment to organizational goals and to ensure a 'high-performance' organization.

It is this third dimension to managerial control, personnel policies and techniques that is associated with the shift in the late 1980s from orthodox personnel management to the 'new' human resource management (HRM) paradigm (Beer *et al.*, 1984; Guest, 1990). The seminal book edited by John Storey, *New Perspectives on Human Resource Management* (1989), generated extensive debate about new labour management practices and the nature and ideological significance of the 'progressive' human resource management (HRM) paradigm. This theoretical discourse, and apparent enthusiasm for a new approach to managing workers, is not a British phenomenon. The paradigm shift to the HRM model from the orthodox personnel management approach, and the ensuing debates among academic observers, have taken place on both sides of the Atlantic, and in many other countries. However, the theoretical debate has been particularly fierce in Britain (Storey, 1995). There is one point that most academics do agree on; the new HRM model is, in part, a product of both the political ideology and the new economic order of the late 1980s, evidenced by the rise of radical Conservative governments headed by Margaret Thatcher in Britain and Ronald Reagan in the USA. Indeed, the 1980s are seen by many observers as a watershed in human resource management. The result, among other things, has been to change radically the way British and North American management deal with their workers and their unions.

The HRM paradigm has been good for academics. In the UK, business schools have renamed their departments and courses and established new university chairs in human resource management. The HRM 'cottage industry' has spawned a spate of books and articles advocating, analysing or contesting the concept, philosophy and significance of human resource management. In addition, two prestigious journals –

the *Human Resource Management Journal* and the *International Journal of Human Resource Management* – have become well established in the field. The literature presents 'hard' and 'soft' versions of HRM. The 'hard' version emphasizes the term 'resource' and adopts a 'rational' approach to managing employees; that is, aligning business strategy and HR strategy, and viewing people as any other economic factor, as a cost that must be controlled. The 'soft' HRM model emphasizes the term 'human' and thus advocates investment in training and development and the adoption of 'commitment' strategies to ensure that highly skilled and loyal employees give the organization a competitive advantage. For some, the HRM model represents a distinctive approach to the organization of work and the management of the employment relationship that fits with the new economic order (Beer *et al.*, 1984; Betcherman *et al.*, 1994). For others, the emerging body of literature about the HRM paradigm heralds the beginnings of a new theoretical sophistication in the area of management formerly called personnel management (Boxall, 1992). The HRM model has its detractors. It is identified by a number of scholars as a manipulative form of management control that represents a renaissance of a unitary (non-union) style of management (Wells, 1993); that is, a cultural construct concerned to manufacture acquiescence to corporate values (Keenoy and Anthony, 1992) and that plays a central role in 'constituting the self' and controlling the workforce (Townley, 1994). Grant and Oswick (1998) emphasize the deep divisions among HRM practitioners concerning the personnel management versus HRM debate. Classifying HRM practitioners into three groups, 'believers', 'atheists' and 'agnostics', they conclude that many practitioners who believe in HRM have had their faith 'installed' by the Institute of Personnel and Development (IPD). The IPD is characterized as 'an unwitting preacher' encouraging practitioners to believe in something that is unproven in reality. In recent times the HRM model, both among its advocates and its detractors, has come to represent 'one of the most controversial signifiers in managerial debate' (Storey, 1989, p. 4).

Within the mushrooming literature on HRM, it is possible to discern, by the late 1990s, a 'second wave' of critiques. This second-wave HRM 'agenda' has four distinct themes of significant analysis and debate. The first theme has been the attention given to the significance of the economic and social context in shaping and reshaping the HRM arena. The second theme of critical discourse has focused on the links between HRM and organizational performance. The third theme has refocused attention on structural organizational forms and organizational relationships. Finally, the fourth theme in the HRM discourse has examined the related ideas concerning 'knowledge' and learning in the workplace (Mabey *et al.*, 1998, pp. 2–3). This text examines most of the themes in this second-wave agenda, but it is necessary to emphasize that our choice is selective and, as such, represents our own particular perspective to HRM.

While the new HRM model, with its proactive approach towards labour management, envisions the human resource specialist as an 'architect' and an intellectual partner on the management team (Tyson and Fell, 1986), the HRM movement has not all been in one direction. The drive to improve performance and to pursue 'excellence' has, in many companies, produced leaner (and some would add, meaner) 'flatter' structures. Such experimentation in organizational design has placed greater emphasis on the role of the line manager, with non-specialists devoting more of their time to personnel and related activities (Millward *et al.*, 1992). Moreover, the philosophy of 're-engineering' (Hammer and Champy, 1993) provides argument for those advocating the elimination of HRM as a specialised function (Storey, 1995). An earlier re-engineering guru, Richard Schonberger, argued that HRM specialists were irrelevant. He expressed it like this: 'The fat is non-productive staff, which not only is expensive but actually is an obstacle to fast response and the pursuit of actions done for the good of the whole organization' (1982, p. 197). Our approach rejects the notion of 'one best way' as will be shown below. This chapter examines the theoretical debate about the nature and significance of the new HRM paradigm. To make sense, however, of the HRM discourse and determine whether it actually heralds a new theoretical model or is merely a repackaging of old ideas, it is important to examine the history of personnel/HR management.

● The history of human resource management

The foundation of modern HRM emerged from several interrelated sources. These include conflict management associated with the tensions and contradictions which are inherent in the employment relationship, the increased specialization of labour related to the growth in the scale of work organizations, the scientific approach of management to managing people, the 'empire building' activities of the specialists, and the employment-related law of the last three decades.

The genesis of personnel management

The history of human resource management has reflected prevailing beliefs and attitudes held in society about employees, the response of employers to public policy (for example, health and safety and employment standards legislation) and reactions to trade union growth. In the early stages of the Industrial Revolution in Britain, the extraordinary codes of discipline and fines imposed by factory owners were, in part, a response to the serious problem of imposing standards of discipline and regularity on an untrained workforce (Mathias, 1969). In the 1840s common humanity and political pressure began to combine with enlightened self-interest among a few of the larger employers to make them aware of alternative ways of managing their workforce, other than coercion, sanctions, or monetary reward.

In Britain and North America increasing numbers of employers were accepting responsibility for the general welfare of their workers in the 1890s. In Britain, a number of philanthropic employers began to develop a paternalistic care and concern for their employees. Such employers tended to be strongly nonconformist in belief. From the 1890s Quaker employers, for example, Cadbury and Rowntree, began to emphasize welfare by appointing 'industrial welfare' workers and building model factory villages. It was estimated that by 1914 there were probably between 60 and 70 welfare workers in Britain (Farnham, 1990, p. 20). Paternalistic employer policies were more evident in North America and Germany. In the USA, Henry Ford's autoplant, for example, established a 'Sociological Department' to administer personnel policies which were a concomitant of the '$5 a day' remuneration package. In 1900, large German companies like Krupp and Seimens were highly paternalistic (Littler, 1982). Over time, industrial welfare workers developed into the modern personnel/human resource management specialist.

World War I (1914–18) gave an added impetus to industrial welfare activities. To deal with the haemorrhage of skilled labour, many women were induced to enter industry for the first time. One outcome of this shift in employment was greater concern for workers' welfare in industrial work. By 1918 about 1000 women supervisors had been appointed to observe and regulate the conditions of work and, based upon experiments during World War I, the relationship between welfare and efficiency was established (Pollard, 1969). In a 'tight' labour market and when employee cooperation is at a premium, the main role of the industrial welfare worker can be characterized as a 'caring' one. The expansion of capacity during the war was achieved largely by longer hours of labour and more intensive work, better equipment, better management and better workshop organization (Pollard, 1969). Changes in workshop design were often associated with the spread of premium bonus systems (PBS) and were the first stirring of systematic management. The development of complex new payment systems meant that large organizations had to create a centralized wages department which further boosted the role of personnel management (Littler, 1982). World War I also saw the emergence of the industrial relations function, in its modern sense, in Britain. In 1919 two organizations, the Welfare Workers Association and the North Western Area Industrial Association, amalgamated to form a new body, the Welfare Workers Institute (WWI), with a membership of 700 (Farnham, 1990).

The inter-war period is traditionally characterized as years of economic depression, with high levels of unemployment and severe hardship for large sections of the community. This traditional view has its origins in the highly visible 'hunger marches' and in some of the literature of the period itself: Greenwood's novel, *Love on the Dole* (1933), Orwell's *The Road to Wigan Pier* (1937), and Lewis Jones' two books, *Cwmardy* (1937) and *We Live* (1939). In the early 1970s a new thesis recognized there were periods of cyclical depression and recovery in the inter-war period. In the 1920s and 30s, three developments began to influence the internal practices of organizations and the way employers viewed their human resources: rationalization, Taylorism, and the human relations movement. In the inter-war years, rationalization in Britain had a limited meaning; it referred to large-scale horizontal mergers of companies, plus the application of scientific methods of management and control. The shift towards corporate capitalism provided a rationale for a separate and specialist personnel department to take responsibility for effective management of people. Both scientific management and a derivative, the Bedaux system (see Littler, 1982), increased the importance of the 'controlling' personnel function. Another important development was the human relations movement. The Hawthorne experiments, pioneered by the American Elton Mayo and other researchers, were the driving force behind the movement. Advocates of this perspective on people in organizations were highly critical of Taylorists' 'economic rationality', and they advised managers to integrate employees into the organization. These developments help explain the rise in membership of the Welfare Workers Institute (renamed the Institute of Industrial Welfare Workers in 1924) from 420 in 1927, to 759 members in 1939 (Farnham, 1990).

World War II (1939–45), like World War I, immediately precipitated an increased demand for materials and labour. Between 1939 and 1943, Britain mobilized no fewer than 8.5 million insured individuals (18 per cent of the total population) for the armed forces, auxiliary forces, and the munitions industries. The war fostered an increased demand for human resource specialists as the human relations approach was embraced by many organizations anxious to maximize labour productivity and foster industrial peace. Farnham (1990) explains that personnel officers, as they were increasingly called, were seconded to munitions factories to establish personnel departments and to educate institutions to provide training programmes. In 1943 there were nearly 5500 personnel officers in factories employing over 250 employees, or three times as many as in 1939. The pattern of personnel management activities and industrial relations bequeathed by the extraordinary arrangements of wartime mobilization therefore contained the beginnings of the personnel management orthodoxy. Moreover, unlike welfare activity at the end of World War I, personnel management continued to grow in importance in the post-war period.

Personnel management: an established orthodoxy

After the war the personnel profession emerged stronger than ever and its members, and academics who studied the field, began to establish a new orthodoxy. In 1946 the Institute of Labour Management changed its name to the Institute of Personnel Management (IPM). It is argued that the name changes reflect a gender dimension to the discipline. The change from the Institute of Industrial Welfare Workers in 1924 to the Institute of Labour Management was influenced by concern that the term 'welfare' projected a feminine image among the growing and influential male membership (Townley, 1994). In post-secondary educational institutions, personnel management and industrial relations became mandatory courses for most business students (Pitfield, 1984). The development of the personnel management function after World War II must be seen against the backcloth of public policy and the pressure for workplace collective bargaining.

The post-war Labour government was committed to greater intervention in the economy; 'to combine a free democracy with a planned economy' (Coates, 1975, p. 46). The Labour government's commitment to full employment led to a growth of collective bargaining, and government agencies began to take a more active interest in the functioning of the labour market. The change of government after 1951 did not change the general pattern emerging in the British economy. The Conservative cabinet was anxious to prevent widespread industrial conflict and to encourage industrial peace through conciliation, mediation and arbitration (Crouch, 1982). Since 1960, public policy on issues affecting personnel management has not followed a steady trend. There have been vast fluctuations as one government has succeeded another, or as a government has revised its approach to regulating the employment relationship partway through its term of office. There is no doubt, however, that government intervention encouraged the rise of a substantial corps of personnel management and industrial relations specialists.

In the 1960s and 70s laws were passed that affected personnel management activities: the Contract of Employment Act 1963, the Redundancy Payments Act 1965 and the Industry Training Act 1964. In the 1970s, the Equal Pay Act 1970, the Sex Discrimination Act 1975, the Employment Protection Act 1975 and Employment (Consolidation) Act 1978 were the main pieces of legislation relating to the promotion of sexual equality and standards in employment. Further, in the area of compensation management, successive Conservative and Labour governments blew 'hot and cold' towards voluntary or statutory income policy. Similar developments can also be observed in North America.

In the 1960s British industrial relations was the focus of intense political controversy over the allegedly intolerable level of strikes. These developments were investigated by the Donovan Commission (1965–68). A central argument of the Donovan Commission was the conflict between the formal system of industry-level bargaining and the informal system of workplace or organizational bargaining: 'Britain has two systems of industrial relations', reported the Commission (1968, p. 12). The Commission also argued that the growth in the size of organizations had brought specialization in management: 'From a tiny band of women factory welfare officers in 1914, personnel managers have multiplied to well over ten thousand today, most of them men; and the scope of the job has greatly increased' (1968, p. 25). The Commission's recommendation that management should develop joint procedures for the speedy and equitable settlement of grievances is associated with a rise in professionalism among personnel managers.

It is outside the scope of this chapter to analyse why the profession became dominated by men. But in explaining the development and importance of personnel management, Clegg makes a revealing comment on the relationship between the rise of workplace bargaining and the personnel management function: 'productivity bargaining... was widely welcomed by personnel managers because it extended their function into the fabric of the business – the improvement of profitability' (Clegg, 1979, p. 100). A feminist explanation is offered by Townley (1994). She argues that gender was a dimension in the relative employment opportunities in the workplace, as 'soft' training positions went to women and senior industrial relations negotiating positions devolved to men. The current debate on personnel and HRM is also heavily gendered: 'Put bluntly, the focus of HRM – an agenda, in the main, prescribed by men – has been 'important' men in one field (academia) talking to, reflecting and reporting on 'important' men in another (business)' (Townley, 1994, p. 16).

Changes in public policy mark an important phase in the development of British personnel management, a shift towards a more legalistic control of employment relations. Further, the new legislation had an impact on the personnel manager's job. New collective and individual employment provisions greatly amplified the status and power of the personnel management function in organizations because the personnel specialist was expected to give expert advice and take on new executive responsibilities (Clegg, 1979). The growth of the personnel management function within British work organizations was reflected in the increased number of personnel specialists. The quantitative growth in the professional personnel function is provided by IPM membership data and workplace industrial relations survey data. Farnham shows that between 1956 and 1989, IPM membership rose from 3 979 to 35 548 (1990, p. 24). A decade after the Donovan Report, Brown (1981) and his colleagues found that 46 per cent of the manufacturing establishments sampled had personnel officers with some responsibility for 'dealing with trade unions'; the comparable 1966 figure was 38 per cent. The status and the importance an organization attaches to personnel management can be gauged by whether or not that function is represented on the board of directors. One survey (Millward *et al.*, 1992) found that slightly fewer personnel management specialists were represented on the board in 1990 than in 1984.

To summarize, personnel management takes place within a context of change. Its evolution has been significantly influenced by the dual pressures of public policy and the rise of workplace trade unionism and collective bargaining. It was during the late 1980s, however, that the term human resource management emerged in Britain. As we discuss later in this chapter, the change from personnel to human resource management is not just a matter of semantics. Moreover, the change did not happen in a political and economic vacuum; it reflected an ascendency of a new political ideology and the changed conditions of national and global capitalism. Further, if we accept a feminist critique, the gender dimension has also shaped the way personnel management has been constituted as a subject for study.

HRM in practice 1.1

Rail firms shunt 'old BR way' into sidings

The privatised train operators are now focusing on customer care, core competencies and culture-change courses

BY NEIL MERRICK People Management

Great North Eastern Railway (GNER) which operates trains between London and the north-east, celebrated its first birthday earlier this month by announcing that it would spend an extra £1 million on training over the next four years.

The investment, taking the company's annual training budget to £1.25 million, will allow it to place extra emphasis on customer service and to introduce core competencies for managers.

Twenty 'on-board coaches', will work alongside inspectors, caterers and other staff to assist them in meeting new delivery standards. 'Traditionally, managers have told employees what to do,' said Victoria McKechnie, the firm's HR development manager, who worked with many members of the coaching staff when the line was owned by British Rail. 'The idea of appointing coaches is to create a peer group on board the trains that will help to enhance customer service.'

GNER, which is owned by Sea Containers, manages 12 main-line stations based as far apart as Peterborough and Dunbar. About half of its 2 600 employees deal with customers daily, at the stations, on trains or over the telephone.

Some of the new money will be spent on a management training programme, which is being introduced in July to coincide with a new performance management system. The course will revolve around 12 core competencies, including teamworking, creativity and building relationships, that were proposed by managers.

According to McKechnie, the 'old BR way' of sending people on training courses has been abandoned in favour of coaching, mentoring and secondments. Managers and other employees are, with the assistance of the training department, responsible for identifying and meeting their own training needs.

> **'It is absolutely critical that, if a train breaks down, the people left in control know what they are doing.'**

Midland Main Line (MML), which runs trains between London and the East Midlands, is organising a 'Winning the Future' programme, under which all 600 employees who have direct contact with customers or fill support roles will attend a two-day programme focusing on culture change. About 300 maintenance staff will take part in similar events at their depots.

MML, privatised in April 1996, spends about £800 000 per year on training. Barry Brown, customer services direc-

tor, hopes that events focusing on culture and attitude change will be held annually, with all staff spending up to five days away from the workplace.

'It's the hearts and minds of front-line managers that have got to change,' he said. 'They are a pivotal influence on the staff below them.'

Richard Greenhill, an IPD vice-president and a partner with the Bacon & Woodrow consultancy, which has worked with six of the 25 new train operators, believes that training is encouraging employees to review traditional roles. 'People can organise themselves more effectively if they are prepared to be flexible and cross boundaries that they didn't cross previously,' he said.

Anglia Railways, privatised in January, has expanded its customer service programme to cover all its 650 staff. The company has also introduced a training scheme for telesales and ticket-office staff. Among the areas covered are proactive selling, such as asking a customer if they want to upgrade to first-class travel. 'In the past, railways have not been very good at selling themselves,' said Peter Meades, Anglia's communications manager.

Laurie Harries, spokesman for the RMT, said that the rail workers' union had always argued for better customer service training, but it was concerned that the rail operators might go too far in ending demarcation. The RMT is opposing proposals under consideration by a Railtrack working party that would see guards spending more time collecting money from passengers, rather than performing other duties.

'They want to make safety secondary to revenue-raising,' Harries said. "It is absolutely critical that, if a train breaks down, the people left in control know what they are doing.'

● The field of human resource management

The term 'human resource management' has been subject to considerable debate in Britain. As Storey (1989, 1995) notes, the concept is shrouded in managerial hype and its underlying philosophy and character is highly controversial because it lacks precise formulation and agreement as to its significance. Nonetheless, we obviously need a definition of the subject matter if we are to analyse and understand HRM practices. We will define the subject as:

> That part of the management process that specializes in the management of people in work organizations. HRM emphasizes that employees are critical to achieving sustainable competitive advantage, that human resources practices need to be integrated with the corporate strategy, and that human resource specialists help organizational controllers to meet both efficiency and equity objectives.

Naturally, our broad definition of human resource management would be incomplete without further explaining what we mean by such terms as 'human resources' and 'management'. First and foremost, people in work organizations, endowed with a range of abilities, talents and attitudes, influence productivity, quality and profitability. People set overall strategies and goals, design work systems, produce goods and services, monitor quality, allocate financial resources, and market the products and services. Individuals, therefore, become 'human resources' by virtue of the roles they assume in the work organization. Employment roles are defined and described in a manner designed to maximize particular employees' contributions to achieving organizational objectives.

In theory, the management of people is no different from the management of other resources of organizations. In practice, what makes it different is the nature of the resource, people. One set of perspectives views the human being as potentially a creative and complex resource whose behaviour is influenced by many diverse factors originating from either the individual or the surrounding environment. Organizational behaviour theorists, for example, suggest that the behaviour and performance of the 'human resource' is a function of at least four variables: ability, motivation, role perception and situational contingencies (McShane, 1995). Another set of perspectives emphasizes the problematic nature of employment relations: the two interrelated problems of 'control' and 'commitment' (Watson, 1986). The human resource differs from other resources the employer uses, partly because individuals are endowed with varying levels of ability (including aptitudes, skills and knowledge), with personality traits, gender, role perception and differences in experience, and partly as a result of differences in motivation and commitment. In other words, employees differ from other resources because of their ability to evaluate and to question management's actions, and their commitment and cooperation always has to be won. In addition, employees have the capacity to form groups and trade unions to defend or further their economic interest.

The term 'management' may be applied to either a social group or a process. The term 'management', when applied to a process, conjures up in the mind a variety of images of managerial work. Management may be seen as a science or as an art. The image of management as a science is based on the view that experts have accumulated a distinct body of knowledge about management which, if studied and applied, can enhance organizational effectiveness. This view assumes that people can be trained to be effective managers. Classical management theorists set out to develop a 'science of management' in which management is defined in terms of planning, organizing, commanding, coordinating and controlling'. In this classical conception, management is regarded as primarily concerned with internal affairs. Another set of perspectives on the role of management emphasizes that an organization is a purposive miniature society and, as such, power and politics are pervasive in all work organizations. By power we mean the capacity of an individual to influence others who are in a state of dependence. Organizational politics refers to those activities that are not required as part of a manager's formal role, but which influence, or attempt to influence, the distribution of resources for the purpose of promoting personal objectives. Robbins asserts that 'Politics in organizations is simply a fact of life. Those who fail to acknowledge political behaviour ignore the reality that organizations are political systems' (1991, p. 415). As Alvesson and Willmott (1996) observe in their critical study of management, the political quality of the management practice is 'denied' or 'trivialized'. These authors add that although individual managers might privately question the moral value and integrity of their actions:

> Caught in the maelstrom of capitalist organization, managers are pressured to emulate and reward all kinds of manipulative and destructive behaviours (1996, p. 39).

There is no doubt that much managerial energy and activity is linked to the political arena in which individuals manipulate, compete and cooperate in cabals and alliances (Mintzberg, 1983).

An alternative image of managerial activity is to view management as art. This implies that managerial ability and success depends upon traits such as intelligence, charisma, decisiveness, enthusiasm, integrity, dominance and self-confidence. The practical implications of this are quite different from the 'management as science' approach. If management is equated with specific traits associated with successful styles of leadership, it would provide a basis for selecting the 'right' individual for managerial positions in the organization. Managerial skills can be developed but cannot be acquired by attending business schools! In other words, if management is an art, managers are born. The science-versus-art discourse is not an arid academic debate, given public and private expenditure on management education and training.

The theme of control in organizations provides yet another view of the role of management. From this perspective, managerial control is the central focus of management activity. According to this approach managers seek to control the labour process by deskilling workers using scientific management techniques and new tech-

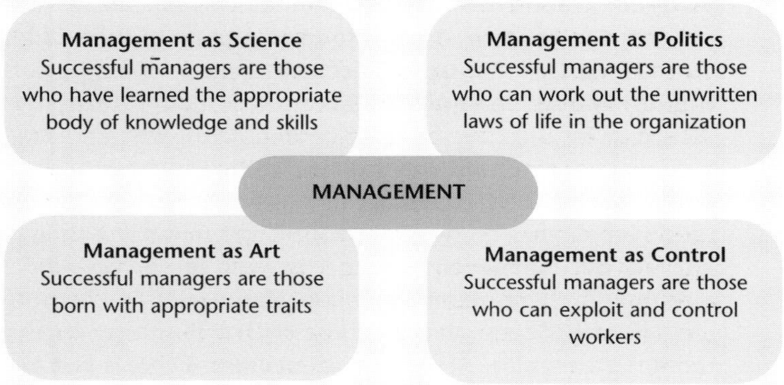

Management as Science
Successful managers are those
who have learned the appropriate
body of knowledge and skills

Management as Politics
Successful managers are those
who can work out the unwritten
laws of life in the organization

MANAGEMENT

Management as Art
Successful managers are those
born with appropriate traits

Management as Control
Successful managers are those
who can exploit and control
workers

Figure 1.1   Management as science, art, politics and control
Source: Adapted from Watson, 1986

nology. This approach to management has come to be associated with the seminal work of Harry Braverman (1974) and the labour process school to which his work has given rise. This perspective, which builds upon Marx's analysis of industrial capitalism, views work organizations as hierarchical in structure, where human beings are exploited and where managerial practices and technology are designed to control people: 'organizations are structures of inequality and control', assert Littler and Salaman (1984). Not surprisingly this approach has attracted much criticism (for example, see Kelly, 1985). In searching for the meaning of management, Watson's (1994) ethnographic study focuses attention on how managers shape both themselves and their subordinates through communicating values to be shared throughout the organization. He argues that management is inherently a 'social and moral activity... a human social craft. It requires the ability to interpret the thoughts and wants of others – be these employees, customers, competitors or whatever – and the facility to shape meanings, values and human commitments' (1994, p. 223).

Perhaps the most sensible way to approach the debate of what management is, is by recognizing that management is indeed both an art and a science and that, at the same time, it is involved in both political behaviour and control. Drawing on the work of Watson (1986), these four different perspectives on management are summarized in Figure 1.1.

Taken together, these four distinct images suggest that those who attempt to define and describe the management process should find ambiguities (and conflicts) of meaning. In essence, management is that group of individuals responsible for bringing together people and resources to produce goods or services (Watson, 1994). Collectively, managers are traditionally differentiated horizontally by their functional activities and vertically by the level at which they are located in their organizational hierarchy. Today the hierarchy is flattening and, as a result of information technology and re-engineering, the development of managers is more horizontal than vertical (Champy, 1996).

In recent years, the term 'human resources' has been adopted as an alternative to 'personnel' management. We would suggest there are at least four reasons for this. First, the vocabulary of management, like language as a whole, is not immune to fashion. With a growing awareness among practitioners and scholars of using gender-neutral language, human resource has been adopted by some to avoid gender-biased phrases such as 'manpower administration' and 'manpower planning'. Second, the term may be used because, for both practitioners and management scholars, it has come to denote a fundamentally different approach to the management of people in work organizations. Personnel management is to be directed mainly at the organization's employees, recruiting, training and rewarding them, and is portrayed as a 'caring' activity. It is concerned with satisfying employees' work-related needs and dealing with their problems (Torrington and Hall, 1987). In contrast, both the 'hard' and 'soft' versions of HRM are portrayed as a central business concern which is more proactive and integrated into corporate management. There is also less emphasis on formal and collective modes of management–employee relations, and a tendency to shift to a more informal individualistic orientation (Storey, 1989, 1992). Third, as the term becomes more fashionable it is increasingly being adopted by practitioners to describe that component of the management process concerned with the employment relationship. For example, many companies advertise for human resource management officers and managers when until recently these positions would have been titled 'personnel'. Many educational institutions and academics have changed the curriculum and book titles to reflect the trend towards redefining this management activity. The Institute of Personnel Management (IPM), in the 1980s, debated at conference changing the title of the house journal from *Personnel Management* to *Human Resource Management*. The IPM has also sponsored a new university chair, notably in 'human resource', not in 'personnel' management. Finally, drawing on Huczynski's (1996) and Jackson's (1996) analysis of 'management gurus', the term is attractive to many managers because the rhetoric of HRM provides an authoritative 'script' to create a sense of order and legitimacy to help them manage their existence. We have chosen to adopt 'human resource management' principally for the first two reasons.

● Human resource management activities

Human resource management is a body of knowledge and a set of practices that define the nature of work and regulate the employment relationship. HRM covers the following five functional areas:

- *Staffing*: the obtaining of people with appropriate skills, abilities, knowledge and experience to fill jobs in the work organization. Pertinent practices are human resource planning, job analysis, recruitment and selection.
- *Rewards*: the design and administration of reward systems. Practices include job evaluation, performance appraisal, and benefits.
- *Employee development*: analysing training requirements to ensure that employees possess the knowledge and skills to perform satisfactorily in their jobs or to advance in the organization. Performance appraisal can identify employee key skills and 'competencies'.
- *Employee maintenance*: the administration and monitoring of workplace safety, health and welfare policies to retain a competent workforce and comply with statutory standards and regulations.

Table 1.1 Ranking of HRM activities of general managers and HRM specialists, 1990 (percentages)

	All managers	Designated HRM managers	Other managers spending 25 per cent or more of their time on HRM matters
Staffing/HR planning	41	20	46
Recruitment	39	55	41
Training	38	24	45
Negotiating contract	27	44	20
Job evaluation	12	8	14
Reward management	10	7	6
Industrial relations procedures	8	18	8
Discipline cases	4	9	3

Source: Adapted from Millward et al., 1992

● *Employee relations*: Under this heading may be a range of employee involvement/participation schemes in union or non-union workplaces. In a union environment, it also includes negotiations between management and union representatives over decisions affecting the employment contract.

The activities HRM managers undertake vary from one workplace to another and might be affected by such factors as the size and structure of the organization (for example, single or multi-establishment organization), the presence or not of trade unions, and senior management's philosophy and employment strategy. Larger workplaces are more likely to employ at least one HRM or personnel specialist. Large organizations might divide HRM activities among several managers: one specialist for recruitment and selection, one for employee training and development and another for negotiating and administrating the collective agreement.

It is ten years since the HRM discourse began in the UK. How does the HR function in the UK look after a decade in which the HRM model has been debated and disseminated? Clearly there have been changes in the profile of the HR function over the last ten years. Sisson (1995) says that HR managers spend much less time dealing with trade unions now than was the case in the 1980s. There is growing evidence of non-HRM specialists taking on responsibility for key HRM functions. In 1990, 82 per cent of non-HR managers reported having responsibility for training and employee development (Millward et al., 1992, p. 32). But, contrary to forecasts by some observers, the HR task has not turned into a peripheral function and 'fears about a decline in the numbers and influence of personnel managers appear to have been equally groundless' (Sisson, 1995, p. 105). Table 1.1 depicts the ranking of activities, based on amounts of time spent on particular matters, undertaken by designated HR managers and non-specialist managers. The most substantial preoccupation of designated HR managers was recruitment, while, for the non-specialist, training was a significant preoccupation.

Human resource management practices are highly interrelated. Suppose, for example, senior management decides to redesign an assembly line by combining tasks and giving production workers additional responsibilities. As Chapter 4 will show, such changes in job design will impact on selection, rewards and training activities. A company that changes its manufacturing strategy by introducing 'cellular' or 'self-managed' teams will have different recruitment and selection priorities to a company that uses traditional assembly line production employing unskilled operators. Significant changes in job design will also require formal training and learning. In addition, if the company chooses to combine tasks and instill greater employee autonomy, an alternative reward system may have to be designed to encourage employee cooperation and commitment. These sets of human resource activities are designed to match individuals to organizational tasks, to motivate the workforce, and to deal with conflicts and tensions at work. HRM practices, therefore, aim to achieve two sets of objectives: improve employee performance and enhance organizational effectiveness.

To appreciate the full significance of these HRM practices it is important to recognize that HRM functions within the organization at two levels (Watson, 1986). At the first level, HRM activities are concerned with recruiting, motivating and developing competent employees. Hence, selection procedures are designed to supply the organization with employees with knowledge, abilities, and skills pertinent to their role within the organization. HRM activities then motivate the workforce by providing employees with satisfactory pay, benefits and working conditions. HRM professionals also develop individuals to ensure that they possess the knowledge and skills necessary to be effective employees.

Many academic observers of work organizations recognize that conflict between individual employees, within teams or between management and employees is inevitable and can enhance, rather than decrease, performance (Carsten De Dreu and Van De Vliert, 1997). Stephen Robbins (1991), an organizational theorist, distinguishes between functional and dysfunctional conflict. The former supports the goals of the work group and improves its performance. Richard Hyman (1989), an industrial relations theorist, identifies two types of workplace conflict: organized and unorganized. When a group of employees engage in planned action (for example, a strike) to change the source of discontent, it is referred to as organized conflict. When employees respond to discontent or a repressive situation by individual absenteeism or individual acts of sabotage, it is referred to as unorganized conflict. It is estimated that managers spend more than 20 per cent of every working day in some form of conflict-management activity. This brings us to the second level: HRM has responsibility for conflict management. HRM specialists are involved in a range of interventionist activities designed to alter the level and form of conflict that inevitably arises in work organizations. Ensuring that conflict does not hinder organizational performance is a central HRM role. So far we have focused on the meaning of management and the practical contribution HRM practices makes to the functioning of the modern work organization. We now turn to the major debates surrounding the HRM model.

● Human resource management: a new orthodoxy?

As we discussed earlier in this chapter, the notion of a HRM model is controversial. The debate centres on two fundamental questions. First, what is meant by the term 'human resource management'? For some, HRM represents a new approach to managing the labour process. For others, the term HRM is simply a relabelling and repackaging of 'progressive' personnel management. Noon (1992) argues that to reconceptualize HRM as a theory is to raise its status and deny its history. Legge (1989, 1995) and Blyton and Turnbull (1992) point out that the HRM model remains an elusive concept and contains contradictions and paradoxes. Detractors view HRM as rhetoric to disguise the consequences of deregulation and downsizing: 'a mask for the less acceptable face of the enterprise culture' (Keenoy and Anthony, 1992; Legge, 1995). Many of the key elements of the HRM model are drawn from organizational behaviour theories, such as motivation, leadership and team building. How should this model be viewed? How does it differ from the traditional personnel model? Is 'strategic' HRM a rupture from the prescriptive personnel management literature and the beginnings of a new theoretical sophistication (Boxall, 1992)? If, as some observers have argued, there is nothing particularly distinctive about the HRM model, or if it simply gives a greater prominence to organizational behaviour concepts, then HRM is just a change in style of presentation, or 'old wine in a new bottle.' Clearly, the meaning of the term is elastic and the literature reveals 'hard' and 'soft' versions of HRM (Legge, 1989, 1995). The second area of the debate focuses on the empirical data on the number of organizations allegedly adopting the new HRM model. What is the nature and extent of change in HR practices which give expression to the core concepts of HRM? Early studies suggested that the extensiveness of HRM was limited in both the USA and the UK (Storey, 1989; Guest 1991). However, the most recent studies provide prima facie evidence of 'a remarkable take-up' of HRM-type practices by large British businesses (Storey, 1992, 1995). Another aspect of the debate concerns the question of values. As Storey (1995) puts it, 'is HR generally a good thing or a bad thing? Should whatever progress it makes be applauded or denounced?' (p. 23). Clearly, there is a critical body of academic literature concerning the precise meaning and significance of the 'new' HRM model and the aim of the remaining part of this chapter is to examine the theoretical and empirical dimensions to the HRM debate that have pervaded managerial thinking and practice in the post-industrial organization.

What is human resource management?

Turning to the first area for debate, the conceptual, it is evident from reviewing the literature that the meaning and theoretical significance of HRM is contested. The 'soft' version of HRM emphasizes the importance of high commitment, workplace learning and enlightened leadership. Most normative HRM models, whether US or British, assert that the organization's 'human resources' are valued assets, not a variable cost, and emphasize the commitment of employees as a source of competitive advantage (Legge, 1989). Assumptions about the nature of human potential and the ability to tap that potential are based on organizational behaviour theories posited by such writers as Maslow (1954) and Herzberg (1966). The notion that commitment and performance can be enhanced by leadership style is based on the high-trust assumptions of McGregor's Theory Y (1960). By contrast, the 'hard' version of HRM emphasizes the calculative, quantitative and strategic management aspects of managing the workforce in a 'rational' way (Storey, 1989). A number of HRM scholars develop a particular HRM model to demonstrate analytically the qualitative differences between conventional personnel management and HRM (see, for example, Beer *et al.*, 1984; Fombrun *et al.*, 1984; Guest, 1987; Hendry and Pettigrew, 1990; Storey, 1992).

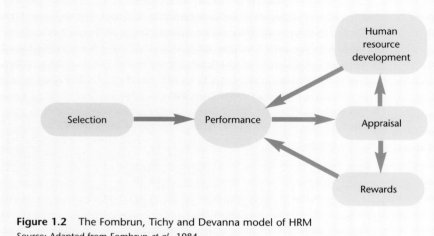

Figure 1.2   The Fombrun, Tichy and Devanna model of HRM
Source: Adapted from Fombrun *et al.*, 1984

The Fombrun, Tichy and Devanna model of HRM

The early HRM model developed by Fombrun *et al.* (1984) emphasizes the interrelatedness and the coherence of human resource management activities. The *human resource management cycle* in their model consists of four key constituent components: selection, appraisal, development and rewards (Figure 1.2). These four human resource activities aim to increase organizational performance. The weakness of the Fombrun *et al.* model is its apparent prescriptive nature with its focus on four key HRM practices. It also ignores different stakeholder interests, situational factors and the notion of management's strategic choice. The strength of the model, however, is that it expresses the coherence of internal HRM policies and the importance of 'matching' internal HRM policies and practices to the organization's external business strategy (see Chapter 2). The HRM cycle is also a simple model that serves as a pedagogical framework for explaining the nature and significance of key HR practices and the interactions among the factors making up the complex fields of human resource management. As we progress through the book, we will refer to the HRM cycle to explain the relationship of each individual HRM function to other HRM practices.

The Harvard model of HRM

The analytical framework of the 'Harvard model' offered by Beer *et al.* consists of six basic components:

1. situational factors
2. stakeholder interests
3. human resource management policy choices
4. HR outcomes
5. long-term consequences
6. a feedback loop through which the outputs flow directly into the organization and to the stakeholders. The Harvard model for HRM is shown in Figure 1.3.

The *situational factors* influence management's choice of HR strategy. This normative model incorporates workforce characteristics, management philosophy, labour market regulations, societal values and patterns of unionization, and suggests a meshing of both 'product market' and 'socio-cultural logics' (Evans and Lorange, 1989). Analytically, both HRM scholars and practitioners will be more comfortable with contextual variables included in the model because it conforms to the reality of what they know: 'the employment relationship entails a blending of business and societal expectations' (Boxall, 1992, p. 72).

The *stakeholder interests* recognize the importance of 'trade-offs', either explicitly or implicitly, between the interests of owners and those of employees and their organizations, the unions. Although the model is still vulnerable to the charge of 'unitarism', it is a much more pluralist frame of reference than that found in later models.

Human resource management policy choices emphasize that management's decisions and actions in HR management can be appreciated fully only if it is recognized that they result from an interaction between constraints and choices. The model depicts management as a real actor, capable of making at least some degree of unique contribution within environmental and organizational parameters and of influencing those parameters itself over time (Beer *et al.*, 1984).

The *human resource outcomes* are high employee commitment to organizational goals and high individual performance leading to cost-effective products or services. The underlying assumption here is that employees have talents that are rarely fully

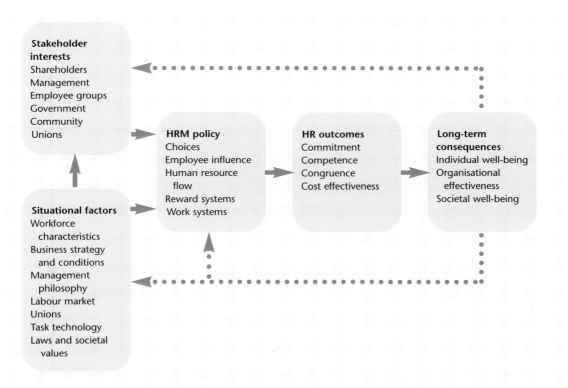

Figure 1.3 The Harvard model of HRM
Source: Beer *et al.*, 1984

utilized at work, and they show a desire to experience growth through work. Thus the HRM model takes the view that organizations should be designed on the basis of the assumptions inherent in McGregor's Theory Y (Guest, 1990).

The *long-term consequences* distinguish between three levels: individual, organizational and societal. At the individual employee level the long-term outputs comprise the psychological rewards workers receive in exchange for effort. At the organizational level increased effectiveness ensures the survival of the organization. In turn, at the societal level, as a result of fully utilizing people at work, some of society's goals (for example, employment and growth) are attained. Guest (1990) argues that the central themes of HRM are contemporary manifestations of the so-called 'American Dream': 'a kind of rugged entrepreneurial individualism reflected in and reinforced by a strong organizational culture' (1990, p. 391). A strength of the Harvard model is the classification of inputs and outcomes at both organizational and societal level, creating the basis for a critique of comparative HRM (Boxall, 1992). A weakness of the model is the absence of a coherent theoretical basis for measuring the relationship between HRM inputs, outcomes, and performance (Guest, 1997).

The sixth component of the Harvard model is the *feedback loop*. As we have discussed, the situational factors influence HRM policy and choices. Conversely, however, long-term outputs can influence the situational factors, stakeholder interests and HRM policies. The feedback loop in Figure 1.3 reflects this two-way relationship. There is no doubting the attractiveness of the Harvard model. It clearly provides a useful analytical basis for the study of HRM. The model also contains elements that are analytical (that is, situational factors, stakeholders, strategic choice levels) and prescriptive (that is, notions of commitment, competence, and so on) (Boxall, 1992).

The Guest model of HRM

David Guest (1989, 1997) has developed a more prescriptive theoretical framework, reflecting the view that a core set of integrated HRM practices can achieve superior

Figure 1.4 Stereotypes of personnel management and human resource management

	PM compliance	HRM commitment
Psychological contract	Fair day's work for a fair day's pay	Reciprocal commitment
Locus of control	External	Internal
Employee relations	Pluralist Collective Low trust	Unitarist Individual High trust
Organising principles	Mechanistic Formal/defined roles Top-down Centralised	Organic Flexible roles Bottom-up Decentralised
Policy goals	Administrative efficiency Standard performance Cost minimisation	Adaptive work-force Improving performance Maximum utilisation

Source: Guest, 1987

Figure 1.5 The Guest model of HRM

HRM strategy	HRM practices	HRM outcomes	Behaviour outcomes	Performance outcomes	Financial outcomes
Differentiation (Innovation)	Selection		Effort/ motivation	High: Productivity	Profits
	Training	Commitment		Quality Innovation	
Focus (Quality)	Appraisal		Cooperation		
Cost (Cost-reduction)	Rewards	Quality	Involvement	Low: Absence	ROI
	Job design			Labour turnover Conflict	
	Involvement	Flexibility	Organizational citizenship	Customer complaints Labour turnover	
	Status and Security				

Source: Guest, 1997

individual and organizational performance. Before we discuss the model, we need to discuss how, according to Guest, HRM differs from orthodox personnel management and to identify the major assumptions or stereotypes underpinning personnel and HRM (see Figure 1.4). Human resource management, according to the stereotypes shown in Figure 1.4, is distinctively different from orthodox personnel management because it integrates human resources into strategic management, it seeks behavioural commitment to organizational goals, the perspective is unitary with a focus on the individual, it works better in organizations that have an 'organic' structure, and the emphasis is on a full and positive utilization of human resources. Implicit in the contrasting stereotypes is an assumption that HRM is 'better'. However, as Guest correctly states, 'this fails to take account of variations in context which might limit its effectiveness… human resource management can most sensibly be viewed as an approach to managing the workforce' (1987, p. 508).

The central hypothesis of Guest's model is that if an integrated set of HRM practices is applied in a coherent fashion, with a view to achieving the normative goals of high commitment, high quality, and task flexibility, then superior individual performance will result. It also assumes that this will result in superior organizational performance. The 'Guest model' has six components:

1. an HRM strategy
2. a set of HRM policies
3. a set of HRM outcomes
4. behavioural outcomes
5. a number of performance outcomes
6. financial outcomes.

The model is shown in Figure 1.5. The model acknowledges the close links between

HRM strategy and general business strategies: differentiation, focus, and cost (see Chapter 2 for further discussion on these competitive strategies and linkages). The 'core' hypothesis, however, is that HRM practices should be designed to lead to a set of HRM outcomes of high employee commitment, high-quality employees, and highly flexible employees. Like Beer *et al.*, Guest sees high employee commitment as a vital HRM outcome, concerned with the goals of binding employees to the organization and obtaining behaviour outcomes of increased effort, cooperation, involvement, and organizational citizenship. High-quality employees refers to issues of workplace learning and the need for the organization to have a capable, qualified and skillful workforce to produce high-quality services and products. Flexibility is concerned with ensuring that workers are receptive to innovation and change and, using Atkinson's (1984) terminology, have functional flexibility. The right-hand side of the model focuses on the link between HRM and performance. According to the model, only when all three HRM outcomes – commitment, quality, flexibility – are achieved can we expect behaviour change and superior performance outcomes. Again, as Guest (1989, 1997) emphasizes, these HRM goals are a 'package' and each is necessary to ensure superior performance and financial outcomes depicted on the right-hand side of the model. He argues that: 'Only when a coherent strategy, directed towards these four policy goals, fully integrated into business strategy and fully sponsored by line management at all levels is applied will the high productivity and related outcomes sought by industry be achieved' (1990, p. 378). According to Guest, HRM policies are concerned with more than 'good' selection or training: 'they are intended to achieve the human resource management policy goals' (1989, p. 49). A key issue here is the distinctiveness of HRM practices: 'it is not the presence of selection or training but a distinctive approach to selection or training that matters. It is the use of high performance or high commitment HRM practices' (1997, p. 273). In other words, HRM practices differ from orthodox personnel management practices in that they aim to engender commitment in the employment relationship.

A number of conceptual issues associated with the model are recognized by Guest (1989, 1997). The first issue is that the values underpinning this HRM model are predominantly employee-orientated and unitarist. With the emphasis on long-term individual and corporate growth and pay related to individual performance, the role of trade unions within HRM has been questioned. Bramham (1989), for example, claims that there is a contradiction between the HRM organization culture and traditional trade unionism. He argues that collectivist culture, which has been the central tenet of trade unionism, poses a considerable problem for a firm pursuing a human resource management strategy. He goes on to posit, 'The HR company holds its employees in such high regard that exploitation would be *inconceivable* [our emphasis]' (p. 114). Guest (1987) recognizes that implicit in the HRM model is marginalization of trade unions; 'There is no recognition of any broader concept of pluralism within society giving rise to solidaristic collective orientation' (p. 519).

The second conceptual issue in the Guest model concerns the status of some of the concepts. The notion of 'commitment' is, argues Guest, 'a rather messy, ill-defined concept, but more importantly the empirical evidence has stubbornly failed to show the expected link between high commitment and high performance' (1987, pp. 513–14). A central feature in the HRM model is the explicit link between HRM and performance. But this raises the problem of deciding which types of performance indicators at individual, group, and organizational level to use in order to establish these links. We need careful statistical controls to assert cause and effect, otherwise the analysis may overstate the influence of HRM practices by including a whole range of non-HRM variables (see Chapter 2).

A strength in the Guest model is that it clearly maps out the field of HRM and classifies the inputs and outcomes. The model is useful for examining the key goals usually associated with the normative models of HRM: strategic integration, commitment, flexibility and quality. Guest's constructed set of theoretical propositions can also improve our understanding of the precise nature of HRM and the nature of the link between HRM and performance and can be empirically tested by survey-based and case-study based research. It has been argued elsewhere that its weakness is that it defines HRM as a particular managerial *style*. What might be more useful is a more holistic approach that studies employment relationships in their broadest sense, focusing on the 'management of labour' (Adams and Meltz, 1993), incorporating managers and non-managers, and covering an array of management styles. In this understanding, a number of discrete HRM strategies or 'models' can be adopted by senior management towards distinct groups of workers or 'internal labour markets' *within* the firm. Accordingly, within each workforce group, HRM incorporates a range of techniques including recruitment and selection, appraisal, rewards, and training and development (Friedman, 1977; Osterman, 1987; Boxall, 1995). Other critics have observed that Guest's model may simply be an 'ideal type' towards which Western organizations can move, thus positing 'somewhat unrealistic conditions for the practice of human resource management' which must subsequently be relaxed (Keenoy, 1990, p. 367). It may also make the error of criticizing general managers and HR practitioners for not conforming to an image academics have constructed for them (Boxall, 1992). Further, it presents the HRM model as inconsistent with collective approaches to managing the employment relationship (Legge, 1989). HRM could be consistent with either individual or collective approaches, although a strong corporate culture can conceal the use of collective controls by presenting the employment relationship in individualized terms (McLoughlin and Gourlay, 1992).

The Warwick model of HRM

This model emanates from the Centre for Corporate Strategy and Change at the University of Warwick and with two particular researchers, Hendry and Pettigrew (1990). The Warwick model draws heavily from the Harvard framework to extend the analysis of HRM and has five elements:

1. outer context
2. inner context
3. business strategy content
4. HRM context
5. HRM content (Figure 1.6).

The model takes cognizance of HRM business strategy and HRM practices, the external and internal context in which these activities take place, and the processes by which such change take place, including interactions between changes in both context and content. The strength of the model is that it identifies and classifies important environmental influences on HRM. Hendry and Pettigrew's research focused on mapping the context, identifying an inner (organizational) context and an external (wider environment) context and exploring how HRM adapted to changes in context.

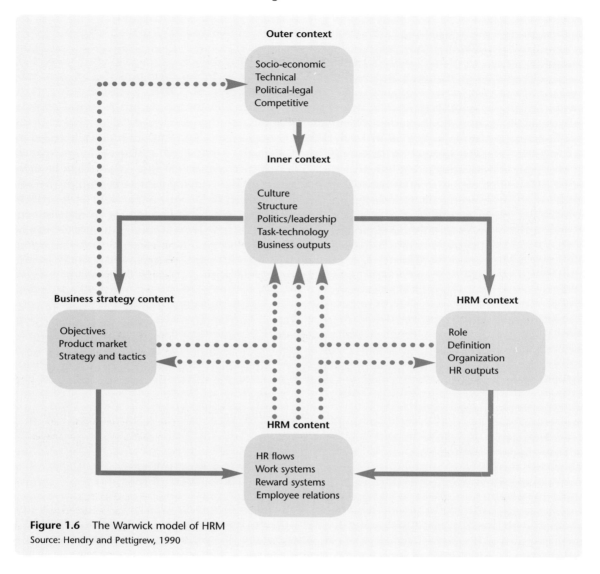

Figure 1.6   The Warwick model of HRM
Source: Hendry and Pettigrew, 1990

This model, argue Hendry and Pettigrew, provides 'better descriptions of structures and strategy-making in complex organizations and of frameworks for understanding them [which] are an essential underpinning for analyzing HRM' (1990, p. 35). While the implication is that those organizations achieving an alignment between the external and internal contexts will experience superior performance, a weakness of the model is that the process whereby internal HRM practices are linked to business output or performance is not developed.

The Storey model of HRM

The 'Storey model' is derived from the speculative accounts of what the HRM para-

Figure 1.7 The Storey model of HRM

	PIR and HRM: the differences	
Dimension	Personnel and IR	HRM
Beliefs and assumptions		
Contract	Careful delineation of written contracts	Aim to go 'beyond contract'
Rules	Importance of devising clear rules/mutuality	'Can do' outlook; impatience with 'rules'
Guide to management action	Procedures/consistency control	'Business need'/ flexibility/commitment
Behaviour referent	Norms/custom and practice	Values/mission
Managerial task *vis-à-vis* labour	Monitoring	Nurturing
Nature of relations	Pluralist	Unitarist
Conflict	Institutionalised	De-emphasised
Standardisation	High (for example 'parity' an issue)	Low (for example 'parity' not seen as relevant)
Strategic aspects		
Key relations	Labour–management	Business–customer
Initiatives	Piecemeal	Integrated
Corporate plan	Marginal to	Central to
Speed of decision	Slow	Fast
Line management		
Management role	Transactional	Transformational leadership
Key managers	Personnel/IR specialists	General/business/line managers
Prized management skills	Negotiation	Facilitation
Key levers		
Foci of attention for interventions	Personnel procedures	Wide-ranging cultural structural and personnel strategies
Selection	Separate, marginal task	Integrated, key task
Pay	Job evaluation; multiple fixed grades	Performance-related; few if any grades
Conditions	Separately negotiated	Harmonisation
Labour-management	Collective bargaining contracts	Towards individual contracts
Thrust of relations with stewards	Regularised through facilities and training	Marginalised (with exception of some bargaining for change models)
Communication	Restricted flow/indirect	Increased flow/direct
Job design	Division of labour	Teamwork
Conflict handling	Reach temporary truces	Manage climate and culture
Training and development	Controlled access to courses	Learning companies

Source: Storey, 1992

digm might consist of and from the literature on the 'standard moderns' (see Chapter 12). The model demonstrates the differences between what Storey termed the 'personnel and industrials' and the HRM paradigm. His model also has four parts:

1.　beliefs and assumptions
2.　strategic aspects
3.　line management
4.　key levers (see Figure 1.7).

The prevailing beliefs and assumptions of HRM, as pointed out by Guest (1987), are unitarist. According to the stereotypes depicted in Figure 1.7, HRM attempts to increase trust and employee commitment and aims to go 'beyond the contract'. The strategic aspects of Storey's model shows HRM central to corporate planning. The third component, line management, gives HRM specialists a 'transformational leadership' role in the organization. Evidence from 'core' companies suggests that general managers and line managers have emerged in almost all cases as the key players on HR issues. The key levers are shown on the lower portion of Storey's model and are issues and techniques strongly featured, explicitly or implicitly, in discussions of HRM. Storey found considerable unevenness in the adoption of these key levers (performance-related pay, harmonization of conditions and the learning company). The model was used to devise a checklist of 25 key HRM variables to quantify the degree of movement from one approach to the other in fifteen 'core' organizations (Storey, 1992).

HR versus personnel management

This review of some of the critical literature on HRM suggests that while similarities exist between the normative HRM models, whether US (for example Beer *et al.*) or British (for example Guest) and those of personnel management, there is a qualitative difference between HRM and traditional personnel management. First, that part of the management process labelled HRM is, in theory at least, integrated into strategic planning; as Hendry and Pettigrew (1990) state, 'the strategic character of HRM is indeed distinctive' (p. 36). Second, the HRM model emphasizes the importance of 'transformational leadership' (Tichy and Devanna, 1986) in the work organization. The purpose of leadership is to create a 'vision' and an working environment that generates worker commitment, innovation, change and 'self-renewal' at all levels of the organization. In most HRM models senior or corporate management are given prime responsibility for cultural leadership. Third, the role of line management is given a different emphasis in HRM; much greater stress is placed on line managers' responsibility of coordinating and directing *all* resources, to generate commitment and enthuse subordinates to innovate. To put it another way, HRM is too important for corporate success to be left to HR specialists. Fourth, the new HRM paradigm implicitly and explicitly emphasizes the importance of workplace learning at the individual and organizational level so that innovation and adaptation becomes 'systemic' (Beer and Eisenstat, 1996). On this point, the case study by Rinehart *et al.* (1994) provides a valuable reminder of viewing the HRM rhetoric with some caution. If Rinehart *et al.*'s research can be taken as typical, HRM innovations derived from the Japanese manufacturing model provide little opportunity for workplace learning: 'Cost reduction, not human development, is the goal of Kaizen' and, consequently, there was 'no genuine movement toward the unification of mental and manual labour' (Rinehart *et al.*,

1994, p. 171). Fifth, HRM assumes a non-union or a unitary frame of reference: thus 'there will be no place in a company's HR strategy of those who threaten the continuity of the organisation by attacking its basic aims', asserts Bramham (1989, p. 118). The 'hard' HRM model suited the ideological stance of Reagan and Thatcher (Legge, 1989). In a nutshell, the normative HRM models represent a renaissance of unitarism or a non-union labour strategy. Finally, the new HRM model appealed to corporate America because of national sentiment; in contrast to the 'Japanese management model', it was 'Made in America'. According to Guest, 'It [HRM] is American, optimistic, apparently humanistic and also superficially simple. In short, it has rediscovered elements of the American Dream. Fitting in with the political values of the Reagan years, this was a powerful message' (1990, p. 379).

These differences in emphasis suggest that HRM is a proactive central strategic management activity that is different from traditional personnel management with its implied passive connotations. However, the focus on proactive management also reflects the various exigencies of global price competition and technological change. Both Legge (1995) and Storey (1989, 1995) make insightful observations when they suggest that what may be of more significance is not the message, but the messenger; HRM represents the 'discovery of personnel management by chief executives' and the message itself has not changed but it is 'being received more seriously'. Over the last decade, HRM has taken on an increasing theoretical significance as it has become part of the wider sociological debate concerned with new management paradigms variously labelled post-Fordism, Toyotism, Japanization, re-engineering and the learning organization. The core argument of this chapter is that it is legitimate to define HRM as a particular approach to the management of the employment relationship with a distinctive set of HR policies and practices designed to produce specific outcomes: to secure the greater commitment of employees and improve organizational performance.

● Paradoxes and contradictions in human resource management

The more critical evaluations of HRM models expose internal paradoxes and contradictions. Paradox involves ambiguity and inconsistency, two or more positions that each sound reasonable yet conflict or even contradict each other. Paradox is inherent in HRM, similar to what Charles Dickens ([1859] 1952) wrote in *A Tale of Two Cities*:

> It was the best of times, it was the worst of times, it was the age of wisdom, it was the age of foolishness, it was the epoch of belief, it was the epoch of incredulity, it was the season of Light, it was the season of Darkness, it was the spring of hope, it was the winter of despair, we had everything before us, we had nothing before us, we were all going direct to heaven, we were all going direct the other way... (p. 21).

HRM contains ambiguities or paradoxes at several levels (Watson, 1986; Legge, 1989). At one level, ambiguity exists over the nature of the HR practitioner's authority. There is often ambiguity as to whether recommendations from HR departments are, in fact, recommendations or are instructions disguised as professional advice (Watson, 1986). A second area of ambiguity is that related to the nature and focus of HR responsibility. In essence, HRM practitioners are considered 'staff' rather than 'line' employees since they provide specialized, legal and professional advice to operations or production 'line' managers. The HR specialist is meant to give an HR perspective to senior and line managers, while managing people is not the exclusive concern of the specialist. HRM inheres in any managerial role. If, on the one hand, the HR manager over-emphasizes the specialist function and her or his expertise, the other managers may abdicate their HRM responsibilities and, in turn, lose touch with their subordinates and become less effective leaders. If, on the other hand, they underplay or marginalize their own specialized service, they may be ignored by the rest of the management team or see their responsibilities taken over completely by other managers.

At another level, there is ambiguity with regard to whether the main role of the human resource professional is a 'caring' or a 'controlling' one (Watson, 1986). Townley (1994), in her Foucauldian analysis of HRM, argues that HRM practices produce knowledge about work activities and employees' behaviour which enables the workforce to be more easily governed. A whole battery of HRM practices are designed to make employees more 'governable' and to bring order and stability to organizational life, but HRM practices can also develop into sources of disorder or instability. Watson calls this the 'paradox of consequences' (1986, p. 183). The notion of the 'paradox of consequences' refers to the fact that management's actions often have unintended consequences. Thus, for example, the paradox contained in the prescriptive advice to managers which encourages leaders to 'gain control by giving it up' (Champy, 1996). Another paradox can be identified when an individual performance-based reward has the result of increasing individual performance but, simultaneously, reducing a work group's synergy (Bratton, 1992).

The different forms of production paradigms themselves contain a number of contradictory tendencies that present familiar challenges for the firm adopting the progressive HRM model. The shift from Taylorist job designs to more integrated 'craft'-based work is a central strategy of the new HRM model. Not only can more high-quality, high value-added customised products be turned out under these new work structures, but 'multiskilled' workers are not as easy to replace and potentially possess greater bargaining power. Such job designs create a high-dependency relationship which can shift the balance of worker (and their unions)–management power (Wilkinson and Oliver, 1990). The regime of empowered and 'skilled' labour has a second 'double-edge' from the point of view of management: how to organize work so that workers' cooperation and commitment is maximized while, simultaneously, building systems of control that subordinate workers. Creating an organizational culture that fosters commitment and using microprocessor-based technology are two control strategies associated with the lean production paradigm. As Belanger et al. (1994) posit, 'the generation of commitment is seen not as a dissolution of conflict between management and worker but as a particular control strategy' (1994, p. 7). The study by Bratton (1992) of the application of new technology in work teams illustrated how workers paradoxically had more autonomy, while at the same time experienced tighter managerial control as a result of detailed monitoring by a MIS system; a process he referred to as 'computer-controlled-autonomy'. The 'paradox of consequences' suggests that because of persistent and fundamental continuities in the post-industrial labour process, there is no such thing as the 'right' human resource strategy, system or technique and that, whatever systems are adopted, they will have to be regularly modified or replaced as their internal tensions and contradictions appear.

Karen Legge's (1995) incisive critique of the HRM phenomenon identifies further ambiguities and tensions in the 'soft' and 'hard' HRM models. As such, she contrasts the 'rhetoric' and 'reality' of HRM where, for example, the rhetoric that asserts 'we are *all* managers now' due to 'empowerment' conceals the legitimate question as to whether a social group holding privileges and material returns far in excess of the new 'management stakeholders' can hold on to power: 'Paradoxically, then, a rhetoric adopted to enhance managerial legitimacy might prove the thin end of the wedge for at least some of its advocates' (1995, p. 56). Lyon and Glover (1998) contrast the HRM rhetoric on continuous investment in workplace learning with the reality of 'HRM's organizationally sponsored ageism' which, they argue, has adverse effects on older employee's involvement in workplace learning and employment security.

One notable feature of much of the HRM literature is the tendency for the research and debate on the HRM model to be gender blind. More recently, however, there has been more interest in the gender implications of HRM models (Dickens, 1994, 1998). Within that interest, Dickens has suggested that the HRM model 'might be at odds with the promotion of equal opportunities' and that the gender equality assumption in the HRM model, which emphasizes the value of diversity and individual learning and development, is part of the rhetoric rather than the reality. Theoretically, one of the most important consequences of gender analysis in the HRM approach is its power to question research findings and analysis that segregates studies of HRM from those of gender divisions in the labour market (Dex, 1988), patriarchal power (Witz, 1986), issues of workplace inequality (Philips and Philips, 1993) and 'dual-role' work–family issues (Knights and Willmott, 1986; Platt, 1997). More importantly, however, including the development of gender in the study of the HRM model has a potential to move the HRM debate forward by examining the people who are deemed to be the 'recipients' of HRM theory and practice (Mabey *et al.*, 1998).

The critical HRM literature also exposes some familiar contradictions inherent in the phenomenon of HRM. Exposing the tensions and contradictions here is meant to be positive, since it should make readers sceptical of the simplistic and evangelical teachings of management consultants offering 'quick fix' solutions to complex workplace issues. Godard (1991) identifies a number of contradictions underlying the new HRM paradigm due to the nature of the capitalist employment relationship. When people enter the workplace, they enter a contractual exchange whereby their behaviour is directed by controllers towards the achievement of specific tasks. As Godard (1991) argues, legally, workers 'alienate' themselves from the right to control the labour process and, consequently, workers have 'little objective reason to develop more than an instrumental orientation to their work' (p. 381). The wage–effort employment contract places an obligation both on the employer and the worker; in exchange for a wage, paid by the employer, the worker is obligated to perform an amount of physical or intellectual labour. The essence of the labour market is that workers *sell* their labour and seek to *maximise* their wage. To the employer, wages and benefits are a *cost* that negatively impacts on profit and therefore needs to be *minimized*. Thus, the wage–effort contract is inherently conflict prone as the logic makes the reward to one group the cost to the other (Hyman, 1975).

The 'effort' side of the contract also generates tensions and conflict because it is inherently imprecise and indeterminate. The contract permits the employer to buy a *potential* level of physical or intellectual labour. The function of management therefore is to transform this potential into *actual value-added* labour. HRM is about narrowing the gap between workers' potential and actual performance or, as Townley explains:

personnel practices measure both the physical and subjective dimensions of labour, and offer a technology which aims to render individuals and their behaviour predictable and calculable... to bridge the gap between promise and performance, between labour power and labour, and organises labour into a productive force or power (1994, p. 14).

Further, workers have the ability to evaluate, to question, and to resist management's actions; they also have the capacity to form organizations in order to defend or further their economic interests. In sum, these apparent contradictions have the potential to impact negatively on organizational performance.

● How extensive is human resource management?

Turning to the second area for debate, the empirical, how extensive is HRM? Judging from the plethora of articles and books (including this one) on HRM it would be easy to conclude that contemporary North American and British industry is practising 'new' HRM. But, what systematic evidence exists to confirm that innovative HRM practices have been, or at least are about to be, the new and preferred approach by North American and British managers? The answer to the question, of course, depends on the definition of 'innovative'. The term 'innovative HRM practices' is interpreted in different ways by researchers. For some practitioners and academics, it refers to greater employee autonomy or empowerment such as work teams. For others, it means the 'individualization' of the employment contract and new rewards systems such as pay-for-skill. Others interpret innovative HRM practices as a change in workplace 'culture' that is difficult to measure. When evaluating the evidence about the extensiveness of HRM we need to be aware of the methodological issues and challenges. The perceptive student will also note that different research designs (for example case studies versus surveys) have their own particular strengths and limitations. Guest (1990), Storey (1995) and Ichniowski *et al.* (1996) evaluate the empirical evidence from case studies and surveys to assess the diffusion of the practice of HRM in the USA and the UK. A study by Betcherman *et al.* (1994) surveyed major Canadian companies. The picture emerging from case studies and survey evidence is apparently one of considerable innovation in the use of HRM techniques to increase productivity and employee involvement in operational-level decision making, but hitherto, the new HRM model has not been adopted as a 'full system' across North America or the UK.

Case studies can represent an in-depth analysis of practising HRM. But, a decade ago, the evidence from cases on the extent to which HRM was practised was limited. The total number of detailed cases cited (ignoring the possibility of double-counting) to substantiate the claim that US industry was moving towards the HRM paradigm (what Guest refers to as 'the regular core') was estimated to be only 123. In the early period of the HRM debate the overexposure of a relatively small number of cases gave the impression that more change was taking place than was really the case. Over the last decade, research findings present a different picture. A significant number of important UK businesses have adopted HRM practices (see for example HRM in practice 1.1). A major UK study found 'extensive take-up of HRM-style approaches in... mainstream organizations' (Storey, 1992, p. 30). And, among high technology companies, another study provides evidence of some take up of HRM-style practices defined in terms of an emphasis on individual modes of job regulation and of high degrees of strategic integration (McLoughlin and Gourlay, 1992). Ichniowski *et al.* (1996) discuss a number of longitudinal case studies conducted in US establishments which document the changes from traditional employment practices to sets of 'innovative' HRM practices. Bratton's (1992) longitudinal case studies raise questions about whether the adoption of individual HRM practices, such as self-managed work teams, job flexibility and worker participation on the shopfloor, constitutes the introduction of the HRM model and whether HR managers really are the new corporate heroes. At Oil Tool Engineering and Flowpak Engineering the HR managers became redundant, and the line managers were given responsibility for personnel functions and became closely associated with the new work structures and HR practices. These two cases are reinforced by Millward *et al.*'s (1992) survey evidence. Storey (1995) also observes that the philosophy of 'reengineering the corporation' (Hammer and Champy, 1993) downplays the importance of human resource management as a specialist function.

Postal surveys can provide a useful 'snapshot' of management practices and evidence of the extensiveness and influence of HRM. The large-scale survey, however, can only measure restricted dimensions of management practice and therefore the derived data tends to produce results that underscore continuity in management practice. A 1986 survey found that between 1981 and 1986, 38 per cent of the US organizations surveyed had changed the departmental title. Of these changes 81 per cent had been to the human resource title. Also, the change often led to an increase in status reflected in the change in title of the head of the function from director to vice-president and from manager to director (Guest, 1990). The title change might simply be 'a symbolic gesture' with policies continuing much as before or the change in language might be a possible statement of intent (Guest, 1990). An interesting finding from Millward *et al.*'s large-scale survey is that in 1990 the vast majority of UK specialists had 'personnel' in their titles, less than 1 per cent of specialist managers being called 'human resource' managers (1992, p. 29). Among major Canadian companies survey information reveals only a minority has adopted the new HRM model; 'the large majority of Canadian firms still follow traditional approaches to human resource management', assert Betcherman *et al.* (1994, p. 58). Osterman's (1995) national cross-industry survey of American establishments is a recent and comprehensive study and presents information on the adoption of innovative HRM practices. Survey evidence showed that a 'clear majority' of USA business establishments have adopted at least one HRM innovation. For example, sixty-five per cent had adopted contingency rewards systems, defined as the presence of gain-sharing, pay-for-skills, or profit sharing. At the same time, however, US business establishments 'rarely adopt bundles' of new HRM practices. In other words, although individual work practice innovations are quite prevalent in most US establishments, the HRM model or 'systems' of innovative HRM practices are relatively exceptional.

The tendency to adopt individual innovative HRM practices is also common in UK organizations. Since 1990 an increasing number of British managers have introduced some sort of employee involvement programme and there is incontrovertible evidence of a renaissance of 'individualism' and a fall in the importance attached to 'collectivism' in the management of the employment relationship (Millward *et al.*, 1992). Sisson argues that some key concepts and practices associated with HRM are taking root in UK workplaces (1993, pp. 203–5) and the growth of contingency pay is cited as a symbolic desire by British employers to change towards 'individually-orientated' cultures (Bacon and Storey, 1993). Similarly, Marginson *et al.* (1993) reported significant change in employment management practices. Among establishments surveyed,

54 per cent had increased employee communication and involvement, as defined in terms of quality circles or problem-solving groups. Many of these HRM techniques could exist within either an HRM or a traditional personnel management model, depending both upon circumstances and strategic choice (Keenoy, 1990; Bratton, 1992). Using Legge's (1989, 1995) terminology, the adoption of *individual*, rather than 'bundles', of HRM practices may constitute the diffusion of the 'hard' HRM model with its focus on increasing labour productivity and cost-minimization.

Evidence that would support the argument that organizations have adopted the 'hard' HRM model is increased integration of HRM planning into strategic business planning. Three studies strongly suggests that 'a coherent human resource strategy, including an early strategic input on human resource issues, is found in only a small minority of those organizations that may be making some use of human resource management techniques' (Guest, 1990, p. 387). Little evidence of the strategic integration of HRM policies with corporate plans was found by Storey (1992, 1995). In the European Union, Brewster and Smith (1990) report that 'in many organizations human resource strategies follow on *behind* [our emphasis] corporate strategy rather than making a positive contribution to it' (1990, p. 37). They also found that HR specialists tend not to have a seat at the strategic table. For example, in the UK only 50 per cent of respondents claimed that the individual responsible for HR personnel is involved in the development of the corporate strategy from the outset. This observation affirms Sisson's (1995) point that the HR profession remains largely made up of 'clerks' and 'contract managers': the number of HR 'architects' in the highest levels of decision making is small.

Chapter summary

In this introductory chapter we have provided an overview of the dynamic field of human resource management. We have examined its history, from so-called welfare management to human resource management. The major concern of this chapter is with theories and perspectives. The emphasis has been on understanding competing normative HRM models rather than on HRM practice itself. We have discussed some of the major contributions of management theory in order to consider whether human resource management now represents a new orthodoxy. Certainly the language is different. Although most of the theories underpinning the HRM model and the techniques of HRM can be found in either organizational behaviour or leadership textbooks of two decade ago, on balance, we consider that the 'soft' HRM model, does represent a new approach to labour management which emphasizes that people, empowered and continuously learning, are central to organizational strategic performance.

On the second dimension to the debate, the extensiveness of HRM, recent case studies and survey evidence support the argument that HRM has established a secure foothold in US and UK post-industrial work organizations. But, as we noted earlier, there are methodological challenges and the significance of the data is open to different interpretations. The implementation of *individual* HRM practices can be interpreted as evidence for the 'hard' HRM model. The difficulty of measuring the key components of the 'soft' HRM model would support the argument that this model is 'a shallow rooted plant' (Legge,

1995, p. 338). Challenges to the new HRM orthodoxy come not only from within its own theoretical ambiguity that the 'HRM model is itself not a coherent, integrated phenomenon… it is in reality a symbolic label, behind which lurk multifarious practices, many of which are not mutually dependent upon each other' (Storey, 1995, p. 14), but also from the new political context. The election of 'New' Labour offers the prospect of changing the climate of workplace employment relations and subsequently strengthening the appeal of a 'European HRM model' that recognizes state and trade union involvement in the regulation of the employment relationship (Brewster, 1993, 1995). By examining the theoretical and empirical issues we have had the opportunity to discover how contesting perspectives complement and negate each other, and to gain insights into the discourse that surrounds the field of human resource management.

Management practice is characterized by power; the ability to influence others' behaviour. By virtue of the power that managers hold, the variations in organizational design, relations between managers and employees, and HRM practices will be largely shaped by senior management. Accordingly, the HRM discourse should be considered within the wider debates about strategic choice and constraints and the variability of management style. The strategic choice theory, popularized by Kochan *et al.* (1986) to account for changes in managerial industrial relations theories in the 1970s and 80s, can provide much insight into why certain HRM practices are adopted and implemented and why HRM practices vary so much from one employer to the next. The most important feature of the strategic choice theory is its focus on the capacity of senior management to make choices regarding the design of work and the management of employees. Management style refers to the preferred way of managing employees. Traditionally, in the industrial relations literature, management style is composed of two dimensions: individualism and collectivism (Purcell, 1987). Individualism centres on the types of HRM practices concerned with rewarding and developing employees to fully utilize each employee's capacity and role in the workplace. At the low end of the individualism axis are employers who view employees as a 'commodity' and a cost that should be minimized; this style approaches the 'hard' HRM model. At the high individualism end of the axis are those employers who recognize employees as being critical to organizational success and invest in people; this style approaches the 'soft' HRM model. The collectivism dimension of management style describes the way management deals with trade unions. Both theory and practice suggest that the individualism/collectivism dimensions cause variations in the mix of individual and collective approaches to workplace relations and these different approaches are typically associated with different competitive strategies. For example, a 'low individualism' management style is more likely to be found in firms employing relatively large numbers of unskilled workers and operating in a market where low unit cost is important. A 'high individualism' style, on the other hand, is most likely to be found in companies employing a relatively large number of skilled workers and where the product or service requires high diagnostic or problem-solving skills (Purcell and Ahlstrand, 1994). It is important to understand that management can choose from a variety of strategies and styles (see Chapters 11 and 12). The empirical evidence suggests that the vast majority of work organizations have not adopted the HRM model, others have adopted only elements of the model, and others have emphasized different features of the model to build a high performance workplace. For example, some firms emphasize investment in workplace learning as a building block to high commitment/performance; others have chosen a sophisticated reward system and job security (Guest, 1997). Furthermore, within the *same* company, management may adopt different styles for different categories of employee. For highly skilled or professional workers, a 'soft' HRM model may be adopted, while relatively easy-to-recruit unskilled employees experience a 'low individual' style. Conditions in the external labour market will therefore be another factor determining management style, policies and practices. What is important to recognize is that there are a number of possible configurations of HRM policies and practices, which will account for variability of management strategy and style. Finally, we should add a warning that theoretical models, at best, provide only a crude representation of *actual* workplace relations and the complex phenomenon known as human resource management.

Key concepts

Welfare management
Personnel management
Human resource management
Unitary perspective

Management
Scientific management
Human relations school
Japanization

Discussion questions

1. What role does human resource management play in organizations?

2. Explain the development of the human resource management profession. Account for the gender structure of the HR function in the UK.

3. To what extent is HRM different from conventional personnel management or is it simply 'old wine in new bottles'?

Further reading

Beer, M., Spector, B., Lawrence, P. R. *et al.* (1984) *Managing Human Assets*, New York: Free Press.
Dickens, L. (1998) What HRM means for gender equality, *Human Resource Management Journal,* **8**(1): 23–45.
Grant, D. and Oswick, C. (1998) Of believers, atheists, and agnostics: practitioner views on HRM, *Industrial Relations Journal,* **29**(3): 178–93.
Guest, D. (1990) Human resource management and the American dream, *Journal of Management Studies,* **27**(4): 377–97.
Legge, K. (1995) *Human Resource Management: Rhetorics and Realities*, Basingstoke: Macmillan.
Storey, J. (ed.) (1989) *New Perspectives on Human Resource Management*, London: Routledge.
Storey, J. (1992) *Developments in the Management of Human Resources*, Oxford: Blackwell.

Building High Performance Teams

Servo Engineering was founded in 1897 to manufacture an improved miner's safety lamp. Over the last fifty years the company has developed as a leading manufacturer of commercial vehicle components. In 1965 Servo Engineering became a subsidiary of Zipton Holding Ltd, which merged in 1977 with American Ensign. This multinational company has manufacturing plants in the UK, USA and Germany. In 1998 the UK group had four sites in the UK.

Between 1994 and 1998 the company replaced over half its conventional and numerical control machines with computer numerical control. In 1995 the firm organized production into six 'self-managed teams' (SMT). The SMTs were product-centred; for example, one SMT would manufacture a whole component such as vacuum pumps or air compressors. Each SMT operated as a miniature factory within the larger factory. Each SMT had sufficient machinery to complete the majority of the manufacturing stages. Processes outside the scope of the SMT were subcontracted, either to another SMT, or to an external contractor. The number of workers in each SMT varied between 12 and 50. The SMT operated a three-shift system: 6 am to 2 pm, 2 pm to 10 pm, and 10 pm to 6 am. The division of labour within the SMT is shown below. The 'SMT supervisor' had overall responsibility for the SMT. The product coordinator's job was to ensure the supply of raw materials and parts to meet SMT production targets. The 'charge-hand' acted as progress-chaser. Below the supervisory grades was a hierarchy of manual grades reflecting different levels of training, experience and pay. For example, the 'setter' was apprentice-trained and was paid a skilled rate to set up the machines for the semi-skilled operators. Semi-skilled workers received little training. In total, the firm employed 442 people. Two unions were recognized by the firm for collective-bargaining purposes: AEEU and MSF. The AEEU was the largest union at the factory; it had 200 members out of a total of 351 manual workers, a union density of 56.9 per cent.

The personnel manager at the factory was George Wyke, who had worked for the company for 25 years. Prior to becoming the personnel manager, he was an AEEU shop steward. He had no formal personnel management qualifications. The company gave SMT leaders considerable discretion for employee relations. To quote George Wyke:

> What the STM system has done as far as man-management [sic] is concerned, it has pushed that responsibility further down the chain, into the SMTs. So where somebody wants disciplining, they don't say to the personnel manager: 'I want to sack this bastard. What can I do to get rid of him?' They know what they have got to do. The only time they will come to me is to seek advice on whether they are doing it right or wrong.

Although levels of unemployment were high in the area, the company had difficulty recruiting 'good' people at its factory in Yorkshire. Also, absenteeism and turnover were high, as shown below.

Absenteeism	1998	Turnover Rates
5.3	January	34.4
5.7	February	20.4
8.0	March	27.5

The apparent low level of commitment among manual employees can be explained in two ways. First, shop stewards and workers expressed considerable discontent over the bonus scheme; the standard time allowed to complete a particular task was not considered adequate to earn a 'decent' bonus. Second, the way the SMTs were designed resulted in operatives performing narrow, repetitive tasks, closely supervised. The personnel manager, George Wyke, is due to retire this Christmas. The plant manager, Elizabeth Bell, has been concerned for some time over employee relations in the factory and the management style of George Wyke and some of the SMT leaders. Elizabeth Bell has decided to seek an external candidate to replace the incumbent personnel manager. Gleaning through the advertisements in newspapers and journals she also decided to drop the term 'personnel' and advertise for a 'Human Resource' Manager.

(Source: Adapted from 'The Motor Components Company: Japanization in Large-batch Production', in Bratton, J. (1992) *Japanization at Work*, London: Macmillan).

Questions

1. Describe the main features of George Wyke's approach to HR management. How does Wyke's approach differ from the stereotype HRM approach?

2. Discuss the contribution an HRM professional could make to the company.

Notes

1. Anthony, P. and Norton, L. (1991) Link HR to Corporate Strategy, *Personnel Journal*, April, p. 75.
2. Champy, J. (1996) *Reengineering Management: The Mandate for New Leadership*, New York: HarperBusiness, p. 36.
3. Joe Greenwood, *AEU Convener*, quoted in Bratton, 1992, p. 139.

chapter two

Strategic human resource management

John Bratton

If a global company is to function successfully, strategies at different levels need to inter-relate.[1]

Throughout the first half of our century and even into the early eighties, planning – with its inevitable companion, strategy – has always been a key word, the core, the near-ultimate weapon of 'good' and 'true' management. Yet, many firms, including Sony, Xerox, Texas Instruments, …have been remarkably successful… with minimal official, rational, and systematic planning.[2]

Chapter outline

Chapter objectives

After studying this chapter, you should be able to:

1. Explain the meaning of strategic management and give an overview of its conceptual framework.

2. Describe the three levels of strategy formulation and comment on the links between business strategy and human resource management.

3. Explain the two models of strategic HRM, the matching model and the resource-based model.

4. Comment on the various strategic HRM themes of re-engineering, workplace learning, trade unions and leadership.

5. Explain the methodological difficulties of measuring the link between HRM practices and organizational performance.

Introduction

In the first chapter we examined the theoretical debates on the nature and significance of the new HRM model, in this chapter we explore various strategic issues associated with HRM. Just as the new HRM model is contested, so too is the notion of strategy. So before we look at some of the issues associated with the strategy–HRM concept, this chapter first examines strategic management concepts and framework and explores the links between business strategy and HRM. The second part of the chapter considers the problems associated with the 'strategy' element of the term 'strategic HRM' (SHRM) and some issues associated with strategic HRM. The third part concentrates on the HRM–organization performance link and the presumption that the workplace innovations associated with the new HRM model actually make a difference to organizational performance. This chapter addresses a number of questions, some essential to our understanding of how post-industrial organizations work, which the new HRM paradigm raises. How do 'big' corporate decisions impact on HRM? Does the evidence suggest that firms adopting a 'strategic' HRM approach experience superior performance? There is a common theme running through this chapter; much of the academic work points out that there are fundamental structural constraints that attest to the complexity of implementing the new HRM model.

Strategic management

The word 'strategy' was first used in English in 1656 and comes from the Greek noun 'strategus', meaning 'commander in chief'. The development and usage of the word suggests that it is composed of *stratos* (army) and *agein* (to lead) and in its military context means 'to produce large-scale operations' (Aktouf, 1996, p. 93). The *Oxford Dictionary* defines strategy in terms of 'generalship'. In a management context, the word 'strategy' has now replaced the more traditional term, long-term planning, to denote an activity that top managers perform in order to accomplish

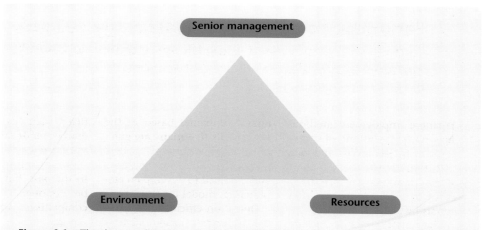

Figure 2.1   The three traditional poles of a strategic plan
Source: Adapted from Aktouf, 1996

an organization's goals. Wheelen and Hunger (1995, p. 3) define strategic management as 'that set of managerial decisions and actions that determines the long-run performance of a corporation'. Aktouf (1996) takes a similar view when he sees strategy as the maintenance of a 'vision of the future' that is constantly updated by data on both the internal and the external environment. Other definitions emphasize the achievement of performance goals: 'A strategy is a specific pattern of decisions and actions that managers take to achieve an organization's goals... For most if not all organizations, an overriding goal is to achieve superior performance... [Therefore] a strategy can often be defined more precisely as the *specific pattern of decisions and actions that managers take to achieve superior organizational performance*' (Hill and Jones, 1998, pp. 3–4). Strategic management is considered a continuous activity, undertaken by the upper echelon of the organization, that requires constant adjustment of three major interdependent poles: the values of senior management, the environment, and the resources available (see Figure 2.1). Strategic management emphasizes the necessity to monitor and evaluate environmental opportunities and threats in the light of an organization's strengths and weaknesses. Hence, any changes in the environment and the internal and external resources must be monitored closely so that the goals pursued can, if necessary, be adjusted. The goals should be flexible and open to amendment, subject to the demands and constraints of the environment and what takes place in the status of the resources.

Model of strategic management

We are the blind people and strategy formation is our elephant. Since no one has had the vision to see the entire beast, everyone has grabbed hold of some part or other and 'railed on in utter ignorance' about the rest (Mintzberg *et al.*, 1998).

HRM in practice 2.1

Japanese forced into HR strategy rethink

Japanese companies based in the UK are reforming local workplace practices to stay ahead in the global economy

BY JENNIE WALSH People Management

Japanese employment methods may have revolutionised organisations in the 1970s and 80s, but the demands of today's global markets are forcing a rethink, according to a new report by Arthur Andersen.

The report, which focuses on the personnel practices of Jap-anese companies based in the UK, reveals that many are grappling with the conflict between corporate values and culture, and the need to develop an employment model for the future.

Operation efficiency – Japanese industry's *raison d'etre* – achieved by pioneering prac-tices such as total quality management and continuous improvement, has provided significant competitive advantages in the past, but may no longer be enough to beat off competition, according to the report.

Japanese firms are now having to focus on developing and retraining local employees, moving from seniority-based pay to performance-related and locally set pay, and implementing more effective appraisal and communication systems.

Almost half of those surveyed did not have a defined grading structure, and the majority of these did not have an HR department. There is still a tendency for head offices in Japan to dictate or significantly influence the level of pay and benefits for UK employees.

Many companies are unwilling to replace existing job titles because this might 'upset traditional structures and hierarchies', although there is a strong consensus about the need to remove 'glass ceilings' for local staff and an acute awareness of equal opportunities issues.

'There is a tradition of lifetime employment, where employees work in all areas and get to know about every aspect of the business,' said Robert Hodkinson, author of the report. 'But that can hinder creativity and there is now a recognition of the need to change. On the whole, there has been a tendency to imitate rather than innovate.'

There is still a tendency for head offices in Japan to dictate or significantly influence the level of pay and benefits for UK employees.

Nikko Securities, the Japanese securities house, recently announced that London is taking over from Tokyo as the headquarters of its international operations. It has also installed Michel de Carvalho as head of international operations – the most senior position a European executive has ever achieved in a Japanese financial institution.

'Nikko is very much a Japanese company,' a spokesman said. 'But to provide the best level of service to our European clients we have to recognise that language and cultural differences exist, and so we have joint Euro-Japanese personnel at senior levels.'

Mark Hutchings, personnel manager at Sanyo Electric, pointed to Nissan's early approach to employing local nationals as key to its success.

'Nissan gave local nationals a chance to manage immediately. The problems experienced by other Japanese companies, including Sanyo, were largely because we didn't do that. Success does seem to be measurable by the extent to which local nationals are involved in management.'

In the descriptive and prescriptive management texts, strategic management appears as a cycle in which several events follow and feed upon one another. The strategic management process is typically broken down into five events or steps:

1. organization's direction
2. environmental analysis
3. strategy formulation
4. strategy implementation
5. strategy evaluation.

Figure 2.2 illustrates how the five events or steps follow and interact. At the corporate level, the strategic management process includes activities that range from appraising the organization's current mission and goals to strategic evaluation.

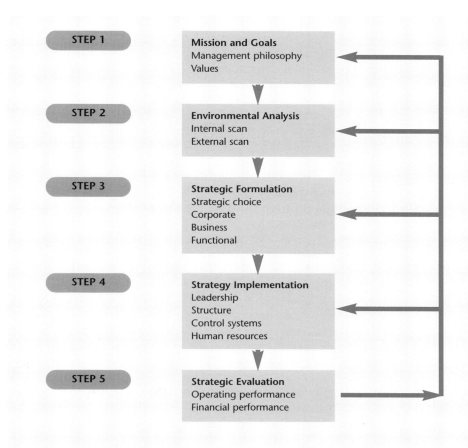

STEP 1

Mission and Goals
Management philosophy
Values

STEP 2

Environmental Analysis
Internal scan
External scan

STEP 3

Strategic Formulation
Strategic choice
Corporate
Business
Functional

STEP 4

Strategy Implementation
Leadership
Structure
Control systems
Human resources

STEP 5

Strategic Evaluation
Operating performance
Financial performance

Figure 2.2   The strategic management model

The first step in the strategic management model begins with senior managers evaluating their position in relation to the organization's current **mission and goals**. The mission describes the organization's values and aspirations. It is the organization's *raison d'être*, and indicates the direction senior management is going. A goal is a desired future state that the organization attempts to realize (Daft, 1998, p. 46). **Environmental analysis** looks at the internal organizational strengths and weaknesses and the external environment for opportunities and threats. The factors that are most important to the organization's future are referred to as strategic factors and are summarized with the acronym SWOT, meaning Strengths, Weaknesses, Opportunities and Threats. **Strategic formulation** involves senior managers evaluating the interaction of strategic factors and making *strategic choices* that guide the organization to meet its goal(s). Some strategies are formulated at the corporate, business, and specific functional level such as marketing and HRM. The use of the term 'strategic choice' raises the question of who makes decisions in work organizations and why they are made (McLoughlin and Clark, 1988). The notion of strategic choice also draws attention to strategic management as a 'political process' whereby strategic choices on issues such as resources are taken by a 'power-dominant' group of senior managers within the organization. Child (1972) affirms this interpretation of the decision-making process when he writes:

> [W]hen incorporating strategic choice in a theory of organizations, one is recognizing the operation of an essentially political process, in which constraints and opportunities are functions of the power exercised by decision-makers in the light of ideological values (Child, 1972 and quoted in McLoughlin and Clark, 1988, p. 41).

In a political model of strategic management, it is necessary to consider the distribution of power within the organization. According to Purcell and Ahlstrand (1994), we must consider 'where power lies, how it comes to be there, and how the outcome of competing power plays and coalitions within senior management are linked to employee relations' (p. 45). The strategic choice perspective on organizational decision making makes the discourse on strategy 'more concrete'; it also provides important insights into how the employment relationship is managed.

Strategy implementation is an area of activity that focuses on the techniques used by managers to implement their strategies. In particular, it refers to activities which deal with leadership style that is compatible to the strategies, the structure of the organization, the information and control systems, and the management of human resources. Leading management consultants and academics (see Champy, 1996; Kotter, 1996) emphasize strongly that leadership is the most important and difficult part of the strategic implementation process. **Strategy evaluation** is an activity in the strategic management process that determines to what extent actual change and performance matches desired change and performance. The strategic management model depicts the five main activities undertaken by senior managers as a rational and linear process. However, it is important to note that it is a *normative* model. That is, it shows how strategic management *should* be done and hence *influences* managerial processes and practices, rather than describes what is actually done by senior managers (Wheelen and Hunger, 1995). As we have already noted, the notion that strategic decision making is a political process implies a potential gap between the theoretical model and reality.

⬤ Hierarchy of strategy

Another aspect of strategic management in the multidivisional business organization concerns the organizational level to which strategic issues apply. Conventional wisdom identifies different levels of strategy: (1) corporate, (2) business, and (3) functional (see Figure 2.3). These three levels of strategy form a hierarchy of strategy within a large corporation. In different companies the specific operation of the hierarchy of strategy might vary between 'top-down' and 'bottom-up' strategic planning The top-down approach resembles a 'cascade', where the 'downstream' strategic decisions are dependent on higher 'upstream' strategic decisions (Wheelen and Hunger, (1995).

Corporate-level strategy describes a corporation's overall direction in terms of its general philosophy towards growth and the management of its various business units.

Such strategies determine the type of businesses a corporation wants to be in and what business units should be acquired, modified or sold. This strategy addresses the question *what business are we in?* Devising a strategy for a multidivisional company involves at least four types of initiatives:

- Establishing investment priorities and steering corporate resources into the most attractive business units.
- Initiating actions to improve the combined performance of those business units that the corporation first got into.
- Finding ways to improve the synergy among related business units in order to increase performance.
- Decisions dealing with diversification.

Business-level strategy deals with decisions and actions pertaining to each business unit. The main objective of a business-level strategy is to make the unit more competitive in its marketplace. This level of strategy addresses the question *how do we compete?* Although business-level strategy is guided by 'upstream' corporate-level strategy, business unit management must craft a strategy that is appropriate for their own operating situation. In the 1970s, Michael Porter (1980) made a significant contribution to our understanding of business strategy by formulating a framework that describes three competitive strategies: low-cost leadership strategy, differentiation strategy, and focus strategy. The low-cost leadership strategy attempts to increase the organization's market share by emphasizing low unit cost compared to competitors. In a differentiation competitive strategy, managers try to distinguish their services and products – such as brand image or quality – from others in the industry. With the focus competitive strategy, managers focus on a specific buyer group or regional market.

Miles and Snow (1984) also made an important contribution to the strategic management literature. These authors identified four modes of strategic orientations: defenders, prospectors, analysers, and reactors. **Defenders** are companies with a limited product line and the management focus on improving the efficiency of their existing operations. Commitment to this cost orientation makes senior managers unlikely to innovate in new areas. **Prospectors** are companies with fairly broad product lines that focus on product innovation and market opportunities. This sales orientation makes senior managers emphasize 'creativity over efficiency'. **Analysers** are companies that operate in at least two different product market areas, one stable and one variable. In this situation senior managers emphasize efficiency in the stable areas and innovation in the variable areas. **Reactors** are companies that lack a consistent strategy–structure–culture relationship. Thus, in this reactive orientation, senior management's responses to environmental changes and pressures tend to be piecemeal strategic adjustments. According to Miles and Snow, competing companies within a single industry can choose any one of these four modes or types of strategies and adopt a corresponding combination of structure, culture, and processes consistent with that strategy in response to the environment. These strategic choices help explain why companies facing similar environmental threats or opportunities behave differently and why they continue to do so over a long period of time (Wheelen and Hunger, 1995). In turn, the different competitive or business strategies influence the 'downstream' functional strategies.

Functional-level strategy pertains to the major functional operations within the business unit, including research and development, marketing, manufacturing, finance, and human resources. Typically, this strategy level is primarily concerned with maximizing resource productivity and addresses the question *how do we support the business-level competitive strategy?* The three levels of strategy – corporate, business, and functional – form a hierarchy of strategy within a large multidivisional corporation. Strategic management literature emphasizes that the strategies at different levels must be fully integrated. The need for integration has been explained like this:

> If a global company is to function successfully, strategies at different levels need to interrelate. The strategy at corporate level must build upon the strategies at the lower levels in the hierarchy. However, at the same time, all parts of the business have to work to accommodate the overriding corporate goals (F.A. Maljers, Chairman of the Board of Unilever, and quoted by Wheelen and Hunger, 1995, p. 20).

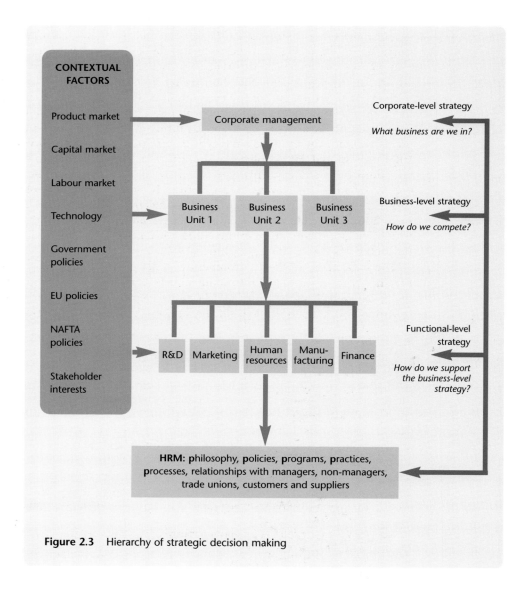

Figure 2.3 Hierarchy of strategic decision making

Business-level strategy and HRM

Strategic management texts emphasize that each level of strategy forms the strategic environment of the next level in the corporation. At the functional level, human resource management strategy is implemented to facilitate the business strategy goals. An HR strategy can be defined as 'The pattern that emerges from a stream of important decisions about the management of human resources, especially those decisions that indicate management's major goals and the means that are (or will be) used to pursue them' (Dyer, 1984, p. 159). Dyer's definition draws attention to the dynamic nature of strategy because strategy is conceived as a pattern in a *stream* of decision making (Boxall, 1992). HRM strategy is closely linked to business strategy. The nature of the links between HRM strategy and business strategy has received much attention in the literature. A range of business–HRM links have been identified and classified in terms of a proactive–reactive continuum (Kydd and Oppenheim, 1990), and in terms of environment–human resource strategy–business strategy linkages (Bamberger and Phillips, 1991). In the 'proactive' orientation, the HRM professional has a seat at the strategic table and he or she is actively engaged in strategy formulation. In Figure 2.3, this type of proactive model is depicted by the two-way arrows on the right-hand side showing both downward and *upward* influence on strategy. At the other end of the continuum is the 'reactive' orientation, which sees the HRM function as fully subservient to corporate and business-level strategy, and corporate and business-level strategies ultimately determining HRM policies and practices. Once the business strategy is determined, without the involvement of the HRM professional, HRM policies and practices are implemented to support the chosen competitive strategy. This type of reactive orientation would be depicted in Figure 2.2 by a *one-way downwards* arrow from business to functional-level strategy. In this sense the practice of strategic HRM is concerned with the challenge of matching the philosophy, policies, programs, practices and process, the 'five Ps', in a way which will stimulate and reinforce different employee role behaviours appropriate for each competitive strategy (Schuler, 1989).

The importance of the environment as a determinant of HRM policies and practices has been incorporated into some models. Extending strategic management concepts, Bamberger and Phillips' (1991) model depicts links between three poles: the environment, human resource strategy and the business strategy (see Figure 2.4). In

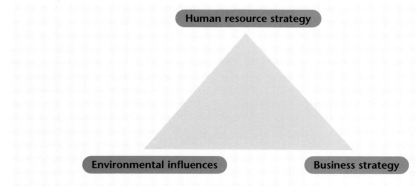

Figure 2.4 Environment as a mediating variable for HRM strategies
Source: Bamberger and Phillips, 1991

the hierarchy of the strategic decision-making model, the HRM strategy is influenced by contextual variables such as markets, technology, national government policies, EU policies and trade unions. Purcell and Ahlstrand (1994) argue that those models that incorporate contextual influences as a mediating variable of HRM policies and practices tend to lack 'precision and detail' of the precise nature of the environment linkages and 'much of the work on the linkages has been developed at an abstract and highly generalized level' (p. 36).

In the late 1980s, John Purcell made a significant contribution to research on business HRM strategy. Drawing on the literature on 'strategic choice' in industrial relations (for example Thurley and Wood, 1983; Kochan *et al.*, 1986) and using the notion of a hierarchy of strategy, Purcell (1989) identifies what he labels 'upstream' and 'downstream' types of strategic decisions. 'Upstream' or 'first-order', strategic decisions are concerned with the long-term direction of the corporation. If a first-order decision is made to take over another enterprise, for example, a French company acquiring a water company in southern England, a second set of considerations apply concerning the extent to which the new operation is to be integrated with or separate from existing operations. These are classified as 'downstream' or 'second-order', strategic decisions. Different HRM approaches are called 'third-order' strategic decisions because they establish the basic parameters of labour management in the workplace. In theory, wrote Purcell, 'strategy in human resources management is determined in the context of first-order, long-run decisions on the direction and scope of the firm's activities and purpose... and second-order decisions on the structure of the firm' (1989, p. 71). In a major study of HRM in multidivisional companies Purcell and Ahlstrand (1994) argue that what actually determines human resource management policies and practices will be determined by decisions at all three levels and by the ability and leadership style of local managers to follow through goals in the context of specific environmental conditions. Case study analysis has highlighted the problematic nature of strategic choice model building. Colling (1995) emphasized that the conception of strategic choice exaggerates the ability of organizations to make decisions independent of environmental contexts in which they do business. Further, the notion that a high-wage and empowering HRM strategy follows from an 'added-value' competitive strategy is more problematic in practice: 'added-value strategies do not preclude or prevent the use of managerial control over employees... [and] few companies are able to operationalise added-value programmes without cost-constraints and even fewer can do so for very long' (1995, p. 29). Much of the strategic human resource management (SHRM) literature has focused on two aspects of the strategy debate, the integration or '*fit*' of human resource management strategy with business strategy and the '*resource-based*' model of strategic HRM. The next section takes a critical look at these influential SHRM models.

● Strategic human resource management

Although the roots of the strategic literature on HRM are in 'manpower' [sic] planning, it is the normative HRM models developed in the 1980s that made the strategic concept central to research productivity in this area (Cappelli and Singh, 1992). In the 1980s, scholars attached the prefix 'strategy' to the term human resource management and the notion of 'strategic integration' became prominent in the HRM literature. Interest among practitioners in linking the strategy concept to HRM can be explained by the pressure to enhance the status of HRM professionals within companies (Purcell and Ahlstrand, 1994) at a time when 're-engineering' is questioning the need for HRM specialists in a 'flatter' organizational structure.

One key feature of Beer *et al.*'s (1984) model of HRM is *strategic integration*'; in particular the need to establish a close two-way relationship or 'fit' between the external business strategy and the elements of the internal HR strategy: 'An organization's HRM policies and practices must fit with its strategy in its competitive environment and with the immediate business conditions that it faces' emphasize Beer *et al.* (1984, p. 25). Drawing upon Beer *et al.*'s analytical framework, Guest posits that typically strategic planning emphasizes the quantitative aspects of finance, marketing and production and gives less attention to the qualitative dimensions of the post-industrial organization, such as values, culture and power. Consequently, the implementations of strategic business plans become more problematic if the human resources component is not an integral part of the strategic planning process:

> Because they are the most variable, and the least easy to understand and control of all management resources, effective utilization of human resources is likely to give organizations a significant competitive advantage. The human resource dimension must therefore be fully integrated into the strategic planning process (Guest, 1987, p. 512).

The concept of integration has three other aspects: the integration or 'cohesion' of HR policies and practices in order to complement each other and to help achieve strategic goals, the internalization of the importance of HR on the part of line managers and, third, the integration of all workers into the business to foster commitment or an 'identity of interest' with their organization. The basic proposition developed here is that if these forms of integration are implemented, workers will be more cooperative, flexible and willing to accept change, and, therefore, the organization's strategic plans are likely to be more successfully implemented. In this section we examine the nature of the relationship of one element of integration, the strategic planning–HRM link. This approach to strategic HRM is referred to as the 'matching' model. We also examine an alternative view of strategic HRM; the 'resource-based' model.

The matching strategic HRM model

The underlying premise of this influential model is that high-wage countries in the western hemisphere can only gain competitive advantage through adopting Michael Porter's (1980, 1985, 1990) generic 'low-cost' or 'differentiation' strategy. Further, each Porterian competitive strategy involves a unique set of responses from workers or 'needed role behaviours' and a particular HRM strategy that might generate and reinforce a unique pattern of behaviour (Schuler and Jackson, 1987; Cappelli and Singh, 1992). Thus, the practice of strategic HRM is concerned with the challenge of matching the philosophy, policies, programs, practices and process, the 'five Ps' (see Figure 2.3), in a way which will stimulate and reinforce different employee role behaviours appropriate for each competitive strategy (Schuler, 1989). Similarly, each type of Miles and Snow's (1984) competitive strategies – 'defender', 'prospector' and 'analyser' – will require that an organization's HRM polices and practices should be configured and managed in a way that is congruent with each particular strategy.

The publication of Fombrun *et al.*'s *Strategic Human Resource Management* (1984) generated early interest in the 'matching' model. Devanna *et al.*'s framework chapter in this book argued that 'HR systems and organizational structure should be managed in a way that is congruent with organizational strategy (p. 37). This is similar to Chandler's (1962) distinction between strategy and structure and his often quoted maxim that structure follows strategy. In the Devanna *et al.* model, human resource management strategy and structure follow and feed upon one another and are influenced by environmental forces (Figure 2.5). This basic model constituted the 'bare bones of a theory' on SHRM (Boxall, 1992).

The notion of 'fit' between an external competitive strategy and the internal HRM strategy is a central tenet of the HRM model advanced by Beer *et al.* (see Figure 1.3). The authors emphasize the analysis of the linkages between the two strategies and how each strategy provides goals and constraints for the other. There must be a 'fit between competitive strategy and internal HRM strategy and a fit among the elements of the HRM strategy' (Beer *et al.*, 1984, p. 13). Any inconsistency in internal HRM practices will likely lead to 'role conflict and ambiguity that can interfere with individual performance and organizational effectiveness' (Schuler, 1989, p. 164). There is some theorization of the link between product markets and organizational design and approaches to labour management. So, for example, a firm manufacturing large-batch products in a market where low cost is critical will, Beer *et al.* argue, need to develop a different approach to managing its workforce than a firm manufacturing small-batch, customized products where quality is a key success factor. HRM is seen to be 'strategic by virtue of its alignment with business strategy and its internal consistency'

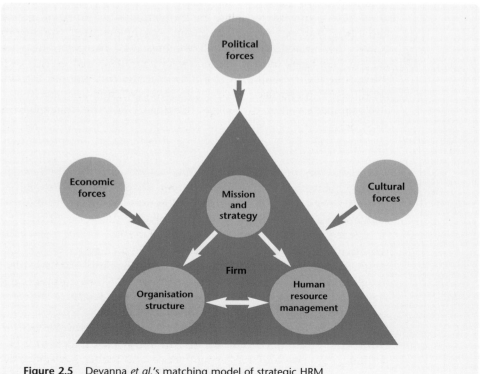

Figure 2.5 Devanna *et al.*'s matching model of strategic HRM
Source: Devanna *et al.*, 1984

(Boxall, 1996). In the matching model, the relationship between business strategy and HRM strategy is said to be 'reactive' in the sense that HRM strategy is subservient to 'product market logic' and the corporate strategy. The latter is assumed to be the independent variable (Boxall, 1992; Purcell and Ahlstrand, 1994). As Miller (1987) emphasizes:

> HRM cannot be conceptualized as a stand-alone corporate issue. Strategically speaking it must flow from and be dependent upon the organization's (market oriented) corporate strategy (cited in Boxall, 1992, p. 66).

Limitations with the matching model

The matching model can be critiqued both on conceptual and empirical grounds. In the first area, the conceptual, the matching model is predicated upon the rational view of strategic decision making grounded in clearly definable predispositions and acts of planning, choice and action. That is, the third-order or 'internal' strategy – a carefully planned approach to how people at work are to be deployed, developed, motivated and controlled – is derived from first-order or 'external' strategy – a chosen approach of competing in the marketplace. In other words, it assumes that organizational controllers act rationally. But, as many critical organizational theorists attest, strategic decisions are not necessarily based on the output of rational calculation. The assumption that business-level strategy and HRM strategy has such a logical linear relationship is questionable given Whittington's (1993) work on strategy. His two axes model has four perspectives on strategy – 'classical', 'evolutionary', 'processual', and 'systemic' – thereby complicating the notion of aligning business strategy and HRM strategy. What perspective on strategy is being adopted when writers make normative statements that HRM should 'fit' the business strategy? As Legge (1995) emphasizes, the notion of aligning business strategy and HRM strategy only applies to the 'classical' approach (the supreme goal is profitability and rational, top-down strategic planning is the means to achieve it) to strategy. Thus, the 'act of *consciously* matching HRM policy to business strategy is only relevant if one adopts the rationalistic 'classical' perspective on strategy (p. 103). The 'decision process' model and the 'political process' model appear to provide a more fruitful approach into strategic decision making. Proponents of the two models argue that managerial rationality is limited by lack of information, time and 'cognitive capacity' and, adding to the management milieu, management is a highly competitive process, in which managers fiercely compete for resources, status and power. Rather than viewing strategic choices as the outcome of rational decision making, Johnson (1987) opines that:

> Strategic decisions are characterized by the political hurly-burly of organizational life with a high incidence of bargaining, a trading off of costs and benefits of one interest group against another, all within a notable lack of clarity in terms of environmental influences and objectives (cited in Purcell, 1989, p. 72).

A second problem is with the prescriptive validity of the model. Some HRM theorists have questioned whether the fit metaphor is necessarily a desirable goal to achieve. In periods of market turbulence and financial stringency there is a tendency for corporate management to improve profitability by downsizing, decentralizing decision making and applying more demanding performance outcomes at the unit level. As Purcell (1989, 1995) argues, this, in turn, encourages similar trends in HRM and industrial relations strategies. A multidivisional company pursuing a strategy of acquisition, asset stripping, and downsizing might 'logically' adopt a set of HRM strategy that includes compulsory lay-off and a compensation system based on short-term performance results. In such a case, the business strategy and HRM strategy might 'fit', but as Legge points out, these HRM policies 'although consistent with such a business strategy, are unlikely to generate employee commitment' (1995, p. 126). In other words, achieving the goal of 'close fit' of business and HRM strategy can contradict the core 'soft' HRM goals of commitment, flexibility and quality. Further, senior managers are pragmatic and the potential for contradictions abound in the work arena. Work organizations may adopt a 'soft' version of HRM for white-collar managerial staff, which is consistent with its business strategy, while simultaneously pursuing a 'hard' version of HRM for blue-collar workers, which might undermine the commitment of the latter.

To further pursue the question whether a matching of business and HRM strategies is necessarily desirable, Boxall (1992, 1996) argues that 'excessive fit' can be disadvantageous to gaining competitive advantage. It can make a company inflexible and incapable of adapting quickly to the external environment: '[managers] need to respond appropriately to a *range* of competitive conditions'. He goes on to state that, 'The fit metaphor is an unfortunate one in an age when flexibility and the need for rapid learning in organizations have become perceived as such major virtues' (1992, pp. 68–9). Finally, a close alignment of HRM policies and practices with business strategy might be 'impractical' owing to the personality traits of managers; it 'assumes a rigidity of personality and a stereotyping of managers that is untenable, as well as an unrealistic precision in the selection process' (Legge, 1995, p. 127).

A third problem centres on underlying structural variables in profit-driven economies which seriously undermine the notion of strategic integration. Purcell's (1995) work, for example, demonstrates how the imperatives of the marketplace and 'rational' managerial decisions limit the adoption of the matching paradigm. He argues that when a financial-control mode of management and short-term investment criterion dominates, it tends to drive out long-term HR investment at the workplace and 'destroy' the basis of HRM as part of corporate strategy. He also notes that multidivisional companies are not monolithic; a range of possible patterns of corporate strategy is possible. It is, however, worth noting that the companies adopting a financial-control model, 'substantially out-perform the industry average' and, consequently, are viewed favourably by the capital markets. As the 1990s continue to be marked by short-term financial expediencies in the Anglo–North American capital markets, this trend makes the adoption of non-economic and intangible values characteristic of the 'soft' HRM paradigm as part of a corporate strategy improbable. The implications of Purcell's (1989) incisive analysis of the integration model is that, however inspired managers might be by the progressive HRM paradigm, there are contradictory 'structural tendencies' at work that will constrain management implementing this model. In addition, the matching model is essentially 'unitary' and it tends to assume that workers are unproblematic and will comply with management's perception of the 'needed role behaviours'. Advocates of tight fit between business and HRM strategies tend to ignore the realities of the workplace and the possibility that workers and their unions might influence strategic planning (Boxall, 1992, 1996).

In the second area for debate, the empirical, there are two related hypotheses: the first asks whether HRM strategies are in fact related to business strategy; the second question asks whether organizations that manage to achieve a 'tight fit' actually experience superior performance. The second and more challenging question, we address later in this chapter. As far as the first empirical question, it is evident that both survey-based research and case studies have generated only limited empirical support for the matching paradigm (Boxall, 1992, 1996; Legge, 1995). Jackson *et al.*'s (1989) survey study of 267 firms found some support for the proposition that firms pursuing an innovative strategy seek to develop HRM practices for blue-collar workers that are 'broadly consistent with that thrust', but that HRM practices varied with technology, industrial sector, organizational size and structure, and workplace unionism (cited in Boxall, 1992, p. 67). The study does not *disprove* the matching model of strategic HRM, but 'it provides few answers' (Jackson *et al.*, 1989, p. 782). Marginson *et al.* (1993), in a survey study of large UK companies failed to find an explicit link between HRM strategy and business strategy. Similarly, Purcell and Ahlstrand's (1994) study of multidivisional companies found that HRM issues are 'rarely taken into account' in the formulation of corporate strategies. Downie and Coates' (1994) survey study of Canadian firms reported that HRM is taking on somewhat 'more strategic importance', but provided little evidence to substantiate the notion of strategic integration. The study found that Canadian HR managers are 'often outside the decision-making circle'. Peck's (1994) survey study of the relationships between 'strategy, HR policies and the employment relationship' in 45 American firms concluded that the relationships between the three are 'more complex than previously assumed' (1994, p. 729). The case study of US steel mills by Arthur (1992) does provide some evidence of a fit between a low-cost business strategy and cost-reducing HRM practices, but the associations are 'far from perfect' (Pfeffer, 1994, cited in Boxall, 1996, p. 63). As a review of the literature makes clear, the fit metaphor has proven to be both conceptually and empirically elusive. The upshot is that aligning business and HRM strategies is a complex process and we lack detailed data provided by longitudinal case studies to demonstrate the relationship between business strategy and HRM strategy. We turn now to the second approach to strategic HRM, the 'resource-based' model.

The resource-based model

The resource-based model of SHRM draws attention to the strategic value of the workforce and to the issues of workplace learning. Thus it appears to embrace a 'soft' view of human resource management. The genesis of the resource-based model can be traced back to Selznick (1957) who suggested that work organizations each possess 'distinctive competence' that enables them to outperform their competitors, and to Penrose (1959) who conceptualized the firm as a 'collection of productive resources'. She distinguished between 'physical' and 'human resources', and drew attention to issues of learning including knowledge and experience of the management team. Moreover, Penrose emphasized, what many organizational theorists take for granted, that organizations are 'heterogeneous' (Penrose, 1959, cited in Boxall, 1996, pp. 64–5). More recently, Barney (1991) has posited that '*sustained* competitive advantage' (our emphasis) is not achieved through an analysis of its external market position but through a careful analysis of the firm's skills and capabilities; characteristics which competitors find themselves unable to imitate. Putting it in terms of simple SWOT analysis, the matching model emphasized the strategic significance of external 'Opportunities' and 'Threats', the resource-based perspective emphasizes the strategic

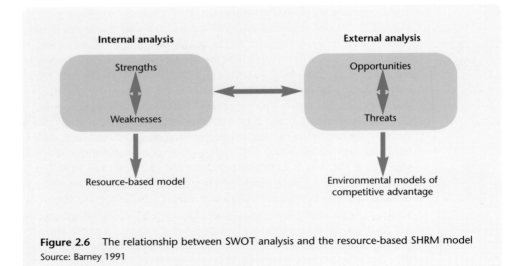

Figure 2.6　The relationship between SWOT analysis and the resource-based SHRM model
Source: Barney 1991

importance of internal 'Strengths' and 'Weaknesses'. This model, summarized in Figure 2.6, suggests that work organizations achieve sustainable competitive advantages by 'implementing strategies that exploit their internal strengths, through responding to environmental opportunities , while neutralizing external threats and avoiding internal weaknesses' (Barney, 1991, p. 99).

Barney argues that four characteristics of resources and capabilities are important in sustaining competitive advantage: value, rarity, inimitability and non-substitutability. From this perspective, the collective learning in the workplace by managers and non-managers, especially how to coordinate workers' diverse knowledge and skills and integrate diverse information technology, is a strategic asset that rivals find difficult to replicate. Figure 2.7 summarizes the relationship between resource heterogeneity and immobility, value, rareness, imitability, and substitutability and sustained competitive advantage. Amit and Shoemaker (1993) make a similar point to Barney when they emphasize the strategic importance for managers to identify, *ex ante*, and marshal 'a set of complementary and specialized resources and capabilities which are scarce, durable, not easily traded, and difficult to imitate' to enable the company to earn 'economic rent' (profits). Thus, according to the resource-based SHRM model, 'the value of the firm's strategic assets extends beyond their contribution to the production process' (p. 37).

It depends on a wide range of characteristics, including inimitability, limited substitutability, overlap with strategic industry factors and scarcity, and varies with changes in the relevant set of strategic industry factors. Amit and Shoemaker's multi-dimensional framework is useful because it recognizes the dynamic nature of strategy and takes into account the existence of power and conflict in shaping (and potentially subverting) strategy when they state that:

Owing to uncertainty, complexity, and conflict (both in and outside the firm), different firms will employ different strategic assets, without any one set being provably optimal or easily imitated. At best, managers can devise heuristic solutions that navigate

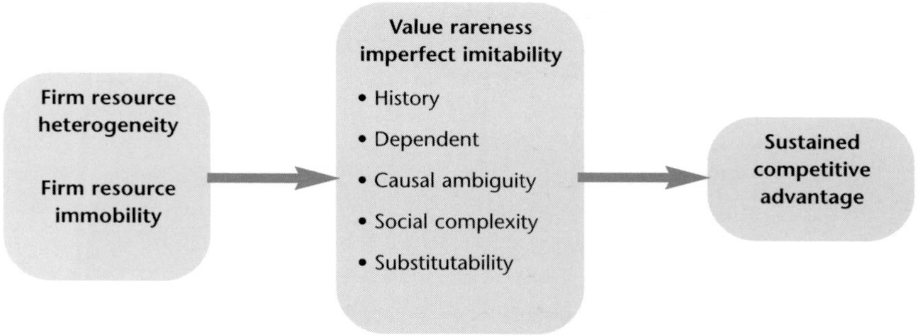

Figure 2.7 The relationship between resource endowments and sustained competitive advantage
Source: Barney 1991

between the numerous cognitive and affective biases characteristic of humans and organizations (1993, p. 44).

Cappelli and Singh (1992) envision a coming 'marriage' between business strategy and HRM strategy based on the mutual recognition of the sustainable competitive advantage that skilled employees potentially create for the post-industrial organization. As Cappelli and Singh go on to discuss, this means that 'competitive advantage arises from firm-specific, valuable resources that are difficult to imitate' (p. 186). The strategic significance of HRM, Cappelli and Singh argue, is when HRM specialists demonstrate how, by developing valuable, non-transferable skills, HR impacts positively on long-term organizational performance. Similarly, Kamoche (1996) argues that when the two dimensions of 'human resource competencies' and the 'firm's core competencies' are aligned the 'full value of this synthesis is realizable' (p. 226). John Purcell (1995) builds on Cappelli and Singh's work to offer a more optimistic scenario than that offered in his 1979 study. He argues that the organization's human resource assets can make the potential contribution of strategic HRM 'immense'. The role for internal HRM strategy is to avoid becoming enmeshed in short-term, decentralized financial–control models characteristic of most American, Canadian and UK multi-divisional companies. Instead, the strategic role for HRM is to develop 'horizontal' long-term strategies which place a 'premium' on the human resources and which 'emphasize intangible, learning, and skill transfer and the reduction in transaction cost' (Purcell, 1995, p. 84). The message for corporate HRM executives, argues Purcell, is clear; they have to demonstrate that the progressive HRM paradigm is invariably associated with improved organizational economic performance: 'The challenge for human resource management is to show a link between policy, practice and organizational outcomes that is meaningful to the corporate board' (p. 84). As we discuss later in this chapter, there now appears to be sufficient survey and case study evidence available to demonstrate a positive relationship between HRM and performance (Ichniowski *et al.*, 1996).

Limitations with the resource-based model

How should we evaluate the resource-based model? As with the contingent matching approach, the resource-based approach to strategic HRM can be critiqued on both conceptual and empirical grounds. One problem is that the term itself, 'resource-based' appears to mean different things to different authors. Some competing terms include 'distinctive competence' (Selznick, 1957), 'dynamic capabilities' (Teece *et al.*, 1990), 'core competencies' (Prahalad and Hamel, 1990), 'human resource competencies' and the 'firm's core competencies' (Kamoche, 1996) and so on. The definitions range from narrow specific interpretations to very broad descriptions and are 'sometimes tautological; resources are defined as firm strengths, and firm strengths are then defined as strategic resources; capability is defined in terms of competence, and competence is then defined in terms of capability' (Nanda, 1996, p. 100).

The prescriptive message of the resource-based approach is based upon the familiar assumptions in McGregor's (1960) 'Theory Y' – that workers have talents which are rarely fully utilized in the workplace – and could therefore be seen as no more than 'good intentions and whistling in the dark' (Guest, 1990, p. 392). The prescriptive validity of the resource-based approach has been questioned by some theorists. For some, this perspective on strategic HRM makes the mistake it accuses the matching model of making; 'it seems to be ascribing preeminence to the inside-out perspective of strategy' (Nanda, 1996, p. 103). The practitioner literature, however, warns against ignoring the strategic relevance of both external and internal factors and calls for a 'dual' focus on market analysis and organizational capabilities.

Another problem with the resource-based SHRM model stems from its implicit acceptance of a unitary perspective of the post-industrial workplace in which goals are shared and levels of trust are high. As is the case with the matching model, advocates of the resource-based SHRM perspective omit the dynamics of workplace trade unionism in the strategic equation. However, writers typically recognize the importance of workers' contribution to the labour process, knowledge and skills, synergy, proactive leadership, encouraging innovation and stimulating learning processes and, in contrast to the matching approach, it is a dynamic model of strategy. A comprehensive theory of strategic HRM would be 'pluralist' and incorporate worker interests within the nexus of the firm. As Boxall (1996) correctly acknowledges 'we must incorporate an adequate theory of employment relations into the theory of strategic HRM' (1996, p. 68).

Finally, what empirical support is there for the resource-based SHRM model? To date, the literature reports that empirical studies have lagged behind this model of strategic HRM. In relation to the question of empirical support Nanda (1996) makes a pertinent observation: 'While the analysis has been sophisticated at macrotheoretic level, it stands relatively unsupported by microtheoretic foundations on the one side and empirical verifications on the other' (Nanda, 1996, p. 97). The premise underlying the resource-based approach to strategic HRM is that sustainable competitive advantage or above average performance is derived from workplace learning: 'it is a firm's ability to learn faster and apply its learning more effectively than its rivals, that gives it competitive advantage' (Hamel and Prahalad, 1993, cited by Boxall, 1996, p. 65). This makes training and employee development a vital if not pivotal component of strategic HRM. In Britain and Canada however, the general record of workplace training is 'dismal'. Ashton and Felstead (1995) assert that there has been no systematic evidence of a transformation of training activity in British companies. In addition, Anglo–North American managements have placed more emphasis on non-standard employment and reducing labour costs and, explicitly or implicitly, have de-emphasized employment security, which would suggest a limited acceptance of the resource-based approach as it applies to HRM (Boxall, 1996). In Canada, Betcherman *et al.*'s (1994) survey study reported that 'the large majority of firms do not take a systematic, forward-looking approach to training; roughly 20 per cent appear to have a training budget and about 15 per cent have a formal training plan' (1994, p. 36). When faced with the various exigencies of global price competition, the majority of Anglo–North American companies have opted for a Porterian low-cost strategy and a market-driven HRM strategy to minimize investment in human resources. The consequences of a low-cost strategy in a free-market global economy leads to second-round effects on the workforce. Line managers, clerical and manual workers realize that their jobs are more insecure, and that their employers are compelled to be increasingly aggressive on employment relationship matters; that in turn affects workers' commitment to the organization and the value they place in upgrading their skills. Thus, a market-driven 'hard' HRM strategy can perpetuate a low-skill, low-wage economy. Despite consultants and senior business executives' protestations it would appear that much of the 'soft' HRM practices have been put back on the shelf.

Dimensions of strategic HRM

In addition to focusing on the validity of the matching and the resource-based SHRM models that have just been discussed, researchers have identified a number of important themes associated with the notion of strategic HRM that are briefly discussed here and, with the exception of leadership, more extensively in later chapters. These are: re-engineering organizations and work (see also Chapter 4); leadership; workplace learning (see also Chapter 10); and trade unions (see also Chapter 12).

Re-engineering and strategic HRM

Both 'hard' and 'soft' normative models of HRM emphasize the importance of organizational and job redesign. As we previously mentioned, much of the literature on the 'soft' HRM model is concerned with job design that would encourage the vertical and horizontal compression of tasks, worker autonomy and self-control or accountability. A new buzz word for the redesign of work organizations is 'business process re-engineering' (BPR).

Under capitalism the transformation of work organization has a long history (see for example Littler, 1982), so Hammer and Champy (1993) did not invent the process, but they certainly gave it a new name 're-engineering' and popularized the concept with over 2 million copies of their book sold worldwide since it was published in 1993. Hammer and Champy define BPR as:

> [T]he fundamental rethinking and radical redesign of business processes to achieve dramatic improvements in critical, contemporary measures of performance, such as cost, quality, service, and speed (1993, p. 32).

Hammer and Champy argue for a new approach to organizational design, work processes, and management. First, the hierarchy of the corporation is 'flattened' as many middle-management positions give way to 'enabling' information technology and self-managed work teams. Second, work is redesigned into self-managed teams and managerial accountability is shifted to the 'front line': 'Whatever supervisory capacity those middle managers might have had now passes to the people who work in teams or have become increasingly more self-managed' (Champy, 1996, p. xv). Third, information technology is a 'critical enabler' that allows organizations to do work in 'radically' different ways. Fourth, senior management make an 'unwavering' commitment to radical change, including cultural change, set ambitious goals, and initiate the re-engineering process. The elimination of many middle-management positions, the vertical and horizontal compression of job assignments, and self-managed work teams draws attention to 'strong' leadership and corporate culture, and the critical role of HRM. In essence, BPR puts the HRM techniques that seek to make workers' behaviour and performance more congruent with the organization's culture and goals. Finally, re-engineering as a social construct, displays the inherent power of corporate leaders to shape and define reality, not unlike what Machiavelli ([1513] 1961) wrote in *The Prince*: 'it is far better to be feared than loved... fear is strengthened by a dread of punishment which is always effective' (p. 52–3). Champy's notes that: 'capitalism is a system that quite literally works on fear... the only way to persuade many folks to undertake a painful therapy like reengineering... is to persuade them that the alternative will be even more painful' (1996, p. 49). Champy's candid observation reveals the 'darker side' to re-engineering and further tensions between 'hard' and 'soft' HRM models. The 'hard' version of HRM might be a necessary prerequisite before the 'soft' version of HRM can work in the re-engineered workplace.

Leadership and strategic HRM

The concept of managerial leadership permeates and structures the theory and practice of work organizations and hence the way we understand SHRM. In the management texts, leadership has been defined in terms of traits, behaviour, contingency, power, and occupation of an administrative position. Most definitions reflect the assumption that leadership involves a process whereby an individual exerts influence upon others in an organizational context. Leadership is by nature dialectical: it is socially constructed through the interaction of both leaders and followers (Smircich and Morgan, 1982). After a comprehensive review of the leadership literature, Yukl (1998) affirms that any definition of leadership is 'arbitrary and very subjective' and goes on to define leadership as:

> [T]he process wherein an individual member of a group or organization influences the interpretation of events, the choice of objectives and strategies, the organization of work activities, the motivation of people to achieve the objectives, the maintenance of cooperative relationships, the development of skills and confidence by members, and the enlistment of support and cooperation from people outside the group or organization (1998, p. 5).

Yukl's definition, while emphasizing many aspects of 'people skills', tends to be focused upon the dynamics and surface features of leadership as a social influence process. More critical accounts of leadership tend to focus upon the hierarchical forms to which it gives rise, power relationships, and the gender dominance. As such, it is argued that leadership is not simply a process of behaving or a process of manipulating rewards, it is a process of 'power-based reality construction' (Smircich and Morgan, 1982). Most of the leadership research and literature tends to be androcentric in nature and rarely acknowledges the limited representation of ethnic groups and women in senior leadership positions (Townley, 1994). Within the literature, however, there is a continuing debate over the alleged differences between a manager and a leader. For example, Bennis and Nanus (1985, p. 21) proposed that 'managers are people who do things right and leaders are the people who do the right thing'. Kotter (1990, 1996) proposed that managers develop plans whereas leaders create a vision and a strategy for achieving the vision. Further, Kotter proposed that managers and leaders differ in their methods for promoting their agenda. Managers *organize* and engage in a process of *controlling* and *problem-solving*, while leaders engage in a process of *alignment* and seek to *motivate* and *inspire*. Clearly, an individual can be a manager without leading, and an individual can be a leader without being a manager (for example an informal group leader or elected trade union leader). Kotter argues that a balance of management and leadership is necessary for a work organization to operate effectively.

The concept of leadership is a central building block of the 'soft' HRM model's concern with developing a 'strong' organizational culture and building a high level of worker commitment and cooperation. For Guest (1987), the current interest in alternative leadership paradigms in the 1980s, variously labelled 'transformational leadership' (Tichy and Devanna, 1986), 'charismatic leadership' (Conger and Kanungo, 1988), 'self-leadership' (Manz and Sims, 1989), or 'principle-centred leadership' (Covey, 1989, 1990) can be explained by understanding the prerequisites of the resource-based SHRM model. Managers are looking for a style of leadership that will develop the firm's human endowment and, moreover, generate employee commitment, flexibility, innovation and change. Of the many management gurus, Peter Senge (1990, p. 340) makes the most explicit link between strategic HRM, workplace learning, and leadership when he writes that 'leaders are designers, stewards, and teachers' and that a learning organization will remain only a 'good idea, an intriguing but distant vision' until the leadership skills required are more readily available. Thus, it would seem that a key constraint on the development of a resource-based SHRM model and a 'learning organization' is leadership competencies. Barney (1991) emphasizes that the resource-based SHRM requires leaders that develop the organization's 'rare and non-substitutional' human assets. Unlike technology assets, organizations cannot readily purchase human sustainable competitive advantages on the open markets and therefore 'managers are important in this model, for it is managers that are able to understand and describe the economic performance potential of a firm's endowments. Without such managerial analyses, sustained competitive advantage is not likely' (p. 117). The integrative theoretical of leadership and strategy developed by Nahavandi and Malekzadeh (1993) depicts the organizational leader to be 'key' to both the formulation and implementation of competitive strategy. If we accept Nahavandi and Malekzadeh's hypotheses, it would seem plausible that leaders who are 'open and participative' and 'challenge-seekers' are more likely adopt a 'soft' SHRM model to match the high risk 'prospector' and 'differentiation' competitive strategies, than leaders who desire 'control' and are 'challenge-averse' and focus on 'defender' and 'cost' leadership strategies. In the popular management literature, Hammer and Champy (1993), in *Reengineering the Corporation*, make a similar point when they argued that leadership is critical in the re-engineering processes: 'most re-engineering failures stem from breakdowns in leadership' (p. 107). Kotter (1996) also argues that the 'engine' that drives change is 'leadership, leadership, and still more leadership' (p. 32).

In essence, the 'transformational' leader extols to employees the need for working beyond contract for the 'common' good. This leadership style emphasizes the importance of vision building and the ability to communicate this vision and, simultaneously, enthuse subordinates to make their vision a reality: 'to innovate, to change and indeed to conquer new frontiers in the marketplace or on the shop floor' (Guest, 1990, p. 393). In contemporary parlance, the transformational leader is empowering workers. However, to go beyond the rhetoric, the transformational model shifts the focus away from the hierarchical nature of work organizations, control processes, inherent conflicts of interest between leaders and the led, and innate power relationships, towards the individualization of the employment relationship, and the development of individual leadership qualities or traits that might lead to gender and racial stereotyping of leadership traits (see Alvesson and Billing, 1992; Wajcman, 1996). Even though the new leadership paradigms emphasize 'shared leadership' and empowerment among 'core' workers, they represent a 'unitary' frame of reference on employment relations and are squarely aimed at 'bottom-line' results (Legge, 1995). The general assumption is that 'enlightened' leadership will result in higher productivity and effectiveness. Later in this chapter we will elaborate and expand on the HRM–leadership–performance linkages.

Workplace learning and strategic HRM

Within most formulations of strategic HRM, employee development has come to represent a key 'lever' that can help management achieve the substantive HRM goals of commitment, flexibility and quality. Beer *et al.* (1984, p. 85) muse that 'employee development is a key strategy for organizational survival and growth'. Others have argued that investment in employee development has become a 'litmus test' of whether or not employers have adopted the HRM model (Keep, 1989). In recent years, many academics and corporate leaders have been attracted by the concept of the 'learning organization' (Cohen and Sproull, 1996), 'management learning' (Burgoyne and Reynolds, 1997) or the more encompassing term, 'workplace learning' (Spikes, 1995). Workplace learning is an interdisciplinary body of knowledge and theoretical inquiry that draws upon adult learning and management theory. In practice, it is that part of the management process that attempts to facilitate work-related continuous learning at the *individual*, *group* and *organizational level*. For workers and managers alike, the assumptions about workplace learning capture the essence of the American Dream, the opportunity for progress or growth at work based on individual achievement (Guest, 1990). Workplace learning occupies centre stage in the 'soft' resource-based SHRM model. Individual, team, and organizational learning can strengthen an organization's 'core competencies' and thus act as the engine for sustainable competitive advantage.

From a managerial perspective, it is suggested that an organization's investment in workplace learning acts as a powerful signal of its intentions to develop its 'human assets'; this can help develop commitment to the organization rather than compliance. The pursuit of worker flexibility through workplace learning is discussed extensively by observers as a lever for sustainable competitive advantage: the ability to learn 'faster' than competitors (Dixon, 1992). Most advocates of Japanese or 'lean' production systems emphasize the importance of investing in human capital and the processes of workplace learning (for example Schonberger, 1982; Womack *et al.*, 1990). And Kochan and Dyer advise those firms adopting a 'mutual commitment' strategy to gain competitive advantage to make the necessary investment in their workforce and adopt the concept of *lifelong learning* (our emphasis, 1995, p. 336). The relationship between learning and worker commitment, flexibility, and quality have also been subject to much comment in the literature.

There is a growing body of work that has taken a more critical look at workplace learning. Some of these writers, for example, emphasize how 'cultural control' can be reinforced through workplace learning (Legge, 1995) and how the training of 'competencies' can render work more 'visible' in order to be more manageable (Townley, 1994). Coopey (1996) challenges the academic entrepreneurs such as Peter Senge, *The Fifth Discipline* (1990). Coopey argues that workplace learning theory assumes a unitarist perspective in which goals are shared and largely ignores conflict stemming from inherent tensions in the employment relationship, that power is omnipresent in work organizations, and that political activity by organizational members is likely to impede learning. He goes on to argue that the likely effect of workplace learning is to strengthen the power of senior management, those at the 'apex of the organization'. At the level of rhetoric, underpinning notions of 'high quality', 'flexible specialization' and functional flexibility, is the assumption of a well-trained 'high quality workforce' (Legge, 1995). However, empirical data show that in most Anglo–North American companies there is a growing trend in 'non-standard' forms of employment (for example part time and contractors). If these data are correct and we accept the plausible insight that 'peripheral' workers tend to receive the lowest level of training (Ashton and Felstead, 1995), there would appear to be a gap between the theory and practice of strategic HRM models.

Trade unions and strategic HRM

In the literature the new HRM model is depicted as 'unitary'; it assumes that management and workers share common goals, and differences are treated and resolved rationally. According to the theory, if all workers are fully integrated into the business they will identify with their company's goals and management's problems, so that what is good for the company and management is perceived by workers as also being good for them. Critical to achieving this goal is the notion of worker 'commitment' to the organization. This HRM goal has led writers from both ends of the political spectrum to argue that there is a contradiction between the normative HRM model and trade unions. In the prescriptive management literature, the argument is that the collectivist culture, with its 'them and us' attitude, sits uncomfortably with the HRM goal of high employee commitment and the individualization of the employment relationship including individual contracts, communications, appraisal and rewards.

Much of the critical literature also presents the new HRM model as inconsistent with traditional industrial relations and collective bargaining, albeit for very different reasons. Critics argue that HRM policies and practices are designed to provide workers with a false sense of job security and obscure underlying sources of conflict inherent in employment relations. According to Godard, historically a major reason for managers adopting 'progressive' [HRM] practices has been to avoid or weaken unions. However, he does concede that 'it would also be a mistake to view progressive practices as motivated solely or even primarily by this objective' (1994, p. 155).

Yet other industrial relations scholars, taking a more traditional 'orthodox pluralist' perspective, have argued that independent trade unions and variants of the HRM model cannot only coexist but are even necessary to its successful implementation and development. They argue that trade unions should become proactive or change 'champions' actively promoting the more positive elements of the 'soft' HRM model. Such a union strategy would create a 'partnership' between management and organized labour which would result in a 'high-performance' workplace with mutual gains for both the organization and workers (Betcherman *et al.*, 1994; Guest, 1995; Verma, 1995). What is clearly apparent from a review of the literature is that this aspect of the HRM discourse has been strongly influenced by political–legal developments and the decline in trade union membership and power in the US and UK over the last two decades. Therefore when you read Chapter 12 and the literature, it is important to remember that the debate is set in the contextual developments in the USA and Britain.

HRM and organizational performance

Although most HRM models provide no clear focus for any test of the HRM–performance link, the models tend to assume that an alignment between business strategy and HRM strategy will improve organizational performance and competitiveness. The resource-based SHRM model assumes a simple causal chain of 'soft' HRM policies of empowerment, team working and workplace learning → employee commitment → synergy → improved organizational performance. This 'involvement–commitment cycle' is the reverse of the vicious circle of control organizational theorists discussed in the early 1980s. A core assumption of this approach is that committed workers are more productive. The importance of commitment to organizational efficiency and competitiveness is emphasized by Beer *et al.* (1984): 'Increased commitment can result not only in more loyalty and better performance for the organization, but also in self-worth, dignity, psychological involvement, and identity for the individual' (1984, p. 19). In the late 1990s, demonstrating that there is indeed a positive link between HRM and performance has become '*the* dominant research issue' in the HRM field (Guest, 1997). Leaving aside the problem of securing worker commitment, how valid is the proposition that the resultant behaviours, as depicted in Figure 1.5 (Chapter 1), lead to improved individual and, in turn, organizational performance outcomes? In the rest of this chapter, we will explore the issue and problems of assessing the effects of the new HRM initiatives on organizational performance. The dominant empirical questions on this topic ask: Do we have a clear theoretical basis for classifying HRM practices? What types of performance data are available to measure the HRM–performance link? Do 'commitment-type' HRM systems produce above-average results than 'control-type' systems? Do work organizations with a better 'fit' between HRM practices and business strategy have superior performance (Cappelli and Singh, 1992)?

Measuring the links between labour issues and economic performance is well established in the field of industrial relations. For example, numerous empirical studies have monitored the impact of unions on wages and productivity. Although the 1960s and 70s saw research on the effects of such management initiatives as employee involvement schemes on various outcomes (attitudes, job satisfaction and productivity), Purcell wrote that if it were possible to prove that 'enlightened or progressive' HRM was invariably associated with higher productivity and lower costs 'life for the... HRM executive would be easier'. As it is, there is little conclusive evidence (1989, pp. 72–3). A similar point is made by Legge (1995, p. 196) when she comments on the absence of 'few, if any, systematic evaluations' of 'high commitment' management practices on organizational performance. Guest (1997) examines the weaknesses in the current theoretical HRM models with regard to the HRM–performance link. There are still gaps in our knowledge, but North American scholars, using analytical techniques from the field of industrial relations, have recently provided important information on these empirical questions. Much of this research has been spurred on by the debates around the relative merits of Japanese management and the new HRM paradigm. American academics Ichniowski *et al.* (1996) give a detailed review of some of the methodological challenges researchers face in identifying the linkages between HRM practices and performance and review the findings from a body of US research using different research designs. Betcherman *et al.* (1994) provide evidence on the HRM–organizational performance relationship using Canadian data. Both Betcherman *et al.* and Ichniowski *et al.* argue that in spite of the hard methodological challenges, the research evidence suggests that innovative HRM practices can increase organization performance. Before reviewing the findings, let us look at some of the methodological challenges with this type of research.

Methodological issues

There are two main types of workplace research designs, surveys and case studies. Surveys of establishments provide a vast amount of quantitative data that can test theories and permit a statistical analysis of HRM practices and performance. However, given the nature of the research instrument, a mail questionnaire, the results cannot hope to provide an accurate picture of the subtleties and intricacies of the way work is structured and *actually* performed, and the dynamics of the employment relationship. Case studies, on the other hand, can provide rich data on workplace activities and can be useful for suggesting hypotheses. Case studies provide for the opportunity to test the accuracy and source of the information. For example, a mail questionnaire asking respondents to indicate, in quantitative terms, the direction and extent of changes in skills resulting from self-managed work teams, can best be done by researchers gathering data from managers *and* workers affected. This raises another important point about the choice of research design. The information from mail questionnaires tends to be biased because the data are generated from one source, typically personnel managers. The obvious concern is that if there is only one respondent per establishment, 'any idiosyncratic opinions or interpretations of the questions can distort the results' (Ichniowski *et al.*, 1996, p. 309). The value of talking both to managers and workers is emphasized by Nichols (1986): 'a study which systematically samples both managers and workers is always likely to provide at least some snippets of information that rarely surface in other accounts and to suggest different lines of interpretation' (quoted in Bratton, 1992, p. 14). Case studies have their limitations. It is questionable how far researchers can generalize from case study results. Whatever the research design, the data might not provide a full account of HRM–organizational performance, because the selection bias operates against studies in badly managed work organizations.

Measuring the HRM–organizational performance relationship is problematic for researchers for other reasons: first, databases tend to estimate individual HRM practices, rather than an entire 'system'. Second, research on the outcomes of new HRM practices requires management participation and, moreover, disclosure of commercially sensitive information on performance indicators that many managers are unwilling or unable to provide to an independent researcher. The researcher has therefore to use 'intermediate' performance indicators such as accident, absenteeism and grievance rates. Third, a key element in the regression equation, innovative HRM practices, is based on subjective judgements. Researchers and respondents might define a 'self-managed team' in different ways, with or without a 'supervisor' or team 'leader'. Guest (1997) suggests that the expectancy theory of motivation provides a basis for developing a more coherent rationale about the HRM–performance link. Expectancy theory focuses on the link between motivation and theory. In essence, it proposes that individual superior performance is contingent upon high motivation plus possession of the necessary skills and abilities and an appropriate role and understanding of that role. According to Guest, 'It is a short step to specify the HRM practices that encourage high skills and abilities... We therefore have a theory which links HRM practices to processes that facilitate high individual performance' (p. 268). A fourth challenge is how to isolate external variables. For example, exchange rates can significantly affect financial outcomes (see Figure 2.5), which makes it difficult to measure accurately the impact of HRM practices. This problem is also recognized by Guest (1997) when he states: 'We also need a theory about how much of the variance can be explained by the human factor' (p. 268). Even if relevant indicators are made available to the researcher and the external variables are isolated, the problem of identifying the causal links remain a challenge. Do certain HRM practices lead to superior performing firms or do superior performing firms adopt certain HRM practices? In short, the implication of HRM choices for organizational performance is difficult to quantify with complete confidence. A combination of both survey and case studies probably provides the greatest confidence about the direction and magnitude of the performance effects of the new HRM practices. 'The key to credible results', write Ichniowski et al., 'is creating a collage of studies that use different designs with their own particular strengths and limitations' (1996, p. 312).

Research findings

The work by Ichniowski et al. reviews a diverse body of research on the HRM–firm performance link and the research by Betcherman and his Canadian colleagues further provides new evidence on the subject. Longitudinal case studies, in a Californian-based auto assembly plant and a US paper mill, document the reconfiguration of traditional work structures to the 'team concept' and subsequent improvements in productivity and quality performance. A cross-sectional comparative case study of two clothes factories found that 'team-orientated' work structures produced a 30 per cent advantage in overall production costs over a traditional work structure. Of the case studies examined, over 75 per cent of those that reported changes in economic outcomes also reported that these were positive. The results do need interpreting with some caution. The performance measures differ across studies and so are not comparable. Further, access to performance data may suggest that the more successful firms are overrepresented (Ichniowski et al., 1996). The findings from four **intra-industry** studies – steel making, automobile assembly, clothes manufacture and metalworking – show that different work configurations and worker empowerment arrangements associated with the new HRM model have superior output and quality performances. Of particular interest is Arthur's (1994) investigation into the performance effects of two labour management taxonomies: 'control' (traditional personnel management) and 'commitment' (new HRM). His regression results indicate that, at least in the context of a high-tech mass production plant, commitment-type HRM practices were 'associated with both lower scrap rates and higher labour efficiency than control'-type HRM practices (Arthur, 1994, p. 683). Second, *integrated* HRM innovations have a greater effect than individual HRM practices. The findings from cross-industry analyses show similar results on the HRM–firm performance link. Ichniowski *et al.* conclude that the empirical evidence presents a consistent picture; HRM innovations can improve organizational productivity and the magnitude of performance effects is 'large'.

Betcherman *et al.*'s (1994) analysis, using data generated from Canadian companies, is consistent with the conclusion drawn by Casey Ichniowski and his colleagues. The Canadian study found a statistically significant association between the new HRM approach and unit costs, and the regression analysis confirmed that organizations that operated under more strategic and participation-based HRM models experienced outcome trends that were superior than those organizations that operated under a traditional employment model. The survey-based study of Canadian establishments provides evidence that new HRM practices operate best in certain organizational 'environments'. The more intangible corporate 'ideology' variables – 'progressive decision making' and 'social responsibility' – appear to have a more significant impact on performance outcomes than team-based programmes or incentive pay plans. These results suggests that 'innovative [HRM] practices and programmes on their own are not enough to substantially improve performance. What seems more important is that they be introduced into a supportive work environment' (Betcherman *et al.*, 1994, p. 72). This is consistent with Ichniowski *et al.*'s main conclusion that 'There are no one or two "magic bullets" that are *the* work practices that will stimulate worker and business performance. Work teams or quality circles alone are not enough. Rather, *whole systems* [our emphasis] need to be changed' (1996, p. 322). Looking ahead, longitudinal case studies can provide the data on the more 'intangible' aspects of workplace learning and change. The upshot is that the current body of empirical research finds that work organizations implementing a package of internally consistent and mutually reinforcing HRM practices, associated with the 'soft' HRM model, experience significant improvements in performance. This suggests an apparent paradox. If the pursuit of 'soft' HRM practices leads to improved organizational performance, from the perspective of 'economic rationality', one would expect such management practices to be more widely used. This apparent paradox may result from the long-term investment costs associated with the resource-based approach to strategic HRM and the pressure on individual managers to achieve short-term financial results.

Chapter summary

This chapter has examined different levels of strategic management. Strategic management was defined as a 'pattern of decisions and actions' undertaken by the upper echelon of the company. Strategic decisions were seen to be concerned with change and the achievement of superior performance and to involve strategic choices. In multidivisional companies, strategy formulation takes place at three levels – corporate, business, and functional – to form a hierarchy of strategic decision making. We discussed how the choices of HRM structures, policies and practices are dictated by corporate and business-level strategies, as well as environmental pressures. When reading the descriptive and pre-scriptive strategic management texts there is a great temptation to be smitten with what appears to be the linear and absolute rationality of the strategic management process. In this chapter, we draw attention to the more critical literature that recognizes that the strategic HRM option at any given time is partially constrained by the outcomes of corpo-rate and business decisions, the current distribution of power within the organization, and the ideological values of the key decision makers.

The problematic nature of strategic HRM and the two competing SHRM models – the matching model and the resource-based model – were identified. The matching model was seen to be a reactive model in the sense that HRM strategy is subservient to corporate strategy and to be more closely associated with the 'hard' version of the HRM model. We reviewed the literature that has critiqued the matching model of SHRM on both concep-tual and empirical grounds. It was noted that in the globalized economy with market tur-bulence the 'fit' metaphor might not be appropriate when flexibility and the need for organizations to learn *faster* than their competitors seems to be the key to sustainable competitiveness. We also emphasized how the goal of aligning a Porterian low-cost busi-ness strategy with a HRM strategy can contradict the core goal of employee commitment. The resource-based SHRM model which places emphasis on a company's human resource endowments as a strategy for sustained competitive advantage was outlined. Again, there seems little empirical evidence to suggest that many firms have adopted this 'soft' SHRM model, although there is much rhetoric and interest in academia and in many companies in the concept of workplace learning. We pointed out that senior managers are pragmatic and work organizations can adopt a 'hard' version of HRM for one category of workers or, in a multidivisional company, for one business while simultaneously pursuing a 'soft' ver-sion of HRM for another group of workers or establishment to provide a coherent under-standing of HRM policies and practices and why they vary. Whether senior managers adopt the 'matching' or the 'resource-based' model of SHRM will be contingent upon first the corporate and business strategies, as well as upon varying degrees of pressure and constraints from environmental forces. Case study work highlights the limitations of strate-gic choice model building. The growing literature on the HRM–organizational perform-ance link illustrates the methodological challenges, but also the value of such research. The stronger the linkages between HRM policies and practices and superior performance outcomes, the stronger the case that can be made to senior management for building sus-tainable competitive advantage around human endowments and synergies. The empiricial evidence on the HRM–organizational performance link is promising but, as Guest (1997) correctly argues, theories of competitive strategy, strategic integration, and expectancy theory of motivation need further development and testing to create hypotheses on HRM–performance linkages: 'the studies report a promising association between HRM and outcomes, but we are not in a position to assert cause and effect… we need to put a lot of flesh on the bones' (p. 274). The next chapter examines some of the environmental factors that underlie managerial decision-making processes in human resource management.

Key concepts

Strategic management   **Low-cost leader**
Hierarchy of strategy   **Differentiation strategy**
Strategic HRM   **Workplace learning**
Matching model   **Resource-based SHRM model**
Leadership   **Re-engineering**

Discussion questions

1. What is meant by strategy? Explain the meaning of 'first-order' and 'second-order' strategies?

2. Explain Purcell's statement that 'trends in corporate strategy have the potential to render the ideals of HRM unobtainable'.

3. 'Business-level strategies may be constrained by human resource issues but rarely seem designed to influence them.' Discuss.

4. What is meant by a 'resource-based' SHRM model of competitive advantage? What are the implications for HRM of this competitive strategy?

5. What are the linkages, if any, between strategic HRM, leadership and learning?

6. Why is it difficult to accurately quantify the HRM–organizational performance link?

7. Explain why recent research suggests that the HRM–organizational performance relationship is clearer and stronger when whole 'systems', rather than individual HRM practices are considered.

Further Reading

Boxall, P. (1992) 'Strategic human resource management: beginnings of a new theoretical sophistication?', *Human Resource Management Journal*, **2**(3): 60–79.

Boxall, P. (1996) 'The strategic HRM debate and the resource-based view of the firm', *Human Resource Management Journal*, **6**(3): 59–75.

Cappelli, P. and Singh, H. (1992) 'Integrating strategic human resources and strategic management', in Lewin, D., Mitchell, O. and Skerer, P. (eds) *Research Frontiers in Industrial Relations and Human Resources*. Madison, University of Wisconsin: Industrial Relations Association.

Champy, J. (1996) *Reengineering Management: The Mandate for New Leadership.* New York: Harper Business.

Ichniowski, C., Kochan, T., Levine, D., Olson, C. and Strauss, G. (1996) 'What works at work: overview and assessment', *Industrial Relations*, **35**(3): 299–333.

Kamoche, K. (1996) 'Strategic human resource management within a resource-capability view of the firm', *Journal of Management Studies*, **33**(2): 213–33.

Mintzberg, H., Ahlshand, B. and Lampel, J. (1998) *Strategy Safari: A Guided Tour Through the Wilds of Strategic Management.* New York: Free Press.

Chapter case study

Air National: Strategic Choice in the New Competitive Environment[3]

Air National's (AN) 1986 Annual Report glowed with optimism. Bradley Smith, CEO, stated in his letter to shareholders, 'As a newly privatized company we face the future with enthusiasm, confident that we can compete in a deregulated industry.' By April 1988, however, the tone had changed with a reported pre-tax loss of $93 million. The newly appointed CEO, Clive Warren, announced a major change in the company's business strategy that would lead to a transformation of business operations and HR practices in Europe's largest airline company.

Background

During the early 1980s, civil aviation was a highly regulated market and competition was managed through close, if not always harmonious, relationships between airlines, their competitors and governments. National flag carriers dominated the markets and market shares were determined, not by competition, but by the skill of their governments in negotiating bilateral 'air service agreement'. These agreements established the volume and distribution of air traffic and thereby revenue. Within these markets AN dominated other carriers. Despite the emergence of new entrants, in 1983 AN's share of the domestic market, for instance, increased by 60 per cent.

The competition

In the middle of the 1980s, Air National's (AN) external environment was subjected to two sets of significant changes. First, in 1986, AN was privatized by Britain's Conservative government. This potentially reduced the political influence of the old corporation and exposed the new company to competitive forces. Preparation for privatization required painful restructuring and 'downsizing' of assets and the workforce, driven largely by the need to make the company attractive to initially sceptical investors.

Paradoxically, however, privatization also offered significant political leverage which AN was able to deploy to secure further stability in its key product markets. It was this factor, rather than the stimulus of market competition, that gave senior management the degree of stability and security to plan and implement new business and HRM strategies. The second set of pressures, potentially more decisive, were generated by prolonged economic recession and the ongoing deregulation of civil aviation in Europe and North American.

With these environmental forces, AN attempted to grow out of the recession by adopting a low-cost competitive strategy and joining the industry-wide price war. Bradley Smith, CEO, when he displayed the following overhead transparency (Exhibit 2.1) to his senior management team (SMT) in April 1986 stated that 'this strategy requires us to be aggressive in the market place and to be diligent in our pursuit of cost reductions and cost minimization in areas like service, marketing and advertising'.

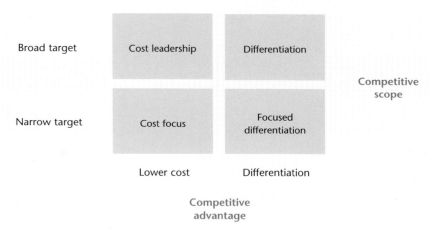

Exhibit 2.1 Air National's strategic choices

The low-cost competitive strategy failed. Passenger numbers slumped by 7 per cent during 1988 contributing to a pre-tax loss. Following the appointment of a new CEO, AN changed its competitive strategy and began to develop a differentiation business strategy (Porter, 1980) or what is also referred to as an 'added-value' strategy.

Air National's new competitive strategy
Under the guidance of the newly appointed CEO, Clive Warren, Air National prioritized high-quality customer service and 're-engineered' the company. Management structures were reorganized to give a tighter focus on operational issues beneath corporate level. Air National's operations were divided into route groups based on five major markets (see Exhibit 2.2).

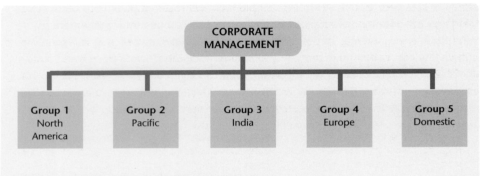

Exhibit 2.2 Air National's management structure

Each group was to be headed by a general manager who was given authority over the development of the business with particular emphasis on marketing. The company's advertising began also to emphasize the added-value elements of AN's services. New brand names were developed and new uniforms were introduced for the cabin crews and point-of-service staff.

AN's re-engineering also aimed at cutting the company's cost base. Aircraft and buildings were sold and persistently unprofitable routes either suspended or abandoned altogether. AN's overall route portfolio was cut by 4 per cent during 1989 alone. Labour costs offered the most significant potential savings and, with 35 000 employees AN's re-engineering included 'one of the biggest redundancy programmes in British history'. Once the redundancy programme was underway the company was able to focus on product development, marketing, customer service, and HR development. The company's sharpened focus on the new 'customer first' programme prompted a major review of the management of employees and their interface with customers.

Air National's HRM strategy

The competitive and HRM strategies pursued by AN in the wake of this re-engineering process are congruent with those SHRM models that emphasize empowerment and employee development. As the CEO, Clive Warren, stated in a TV interview:

> In an industry like ours, where there are no assembly lines or robots, people are our most important asset and our long-term survival depends upon how they work as part of a team. This means that, to get superior performance, managers have to care about how they live and develop, not just about how they work and produce.

The key features of leadership style associated with the adopted strategies were more formally illustrated by AN's Director of Human Resources, Elizabeth Hoffman, to the SMT (Exhibit 3). In the closing part of her presentation, Elizabeth Hoffman outlined the need for a new approach to managing AN's employees: 'We must emphasize to our managers that they must give up control if our employees are to improve their performance.'

As part of the 'new way of doing things', demarcations between craft groups, such as avionics and mechanical engineers, were removed and staff were organized into teams of multiskilled operatives led by team leaders. Even those middle managers who supported the new re-engineered workplace found this approach to managing their subordinates uncomfortable at times, as one maintenance manager acknowledged:

> The hard part is having to share power. No matter how you rationalize it, after a while you want to just make your own decisions and follow it through. I confess that my own thinking tends to be hierarchical in certain situations… I like to be able to say yes or no without having to confer all the time and seek consensus from the team. So there are some real disadvantages for me in this new regime we have, but I realize it's the right way to go.

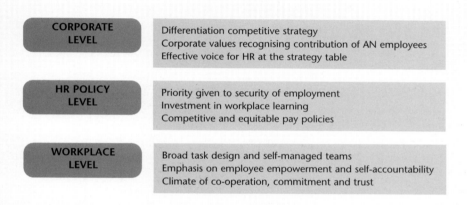

CORPORATE LEVEL	Differentiation competitive strategy Corporate values recognising contribution of AN employees Effective voice for HR at the strategy table
HR POLICY LEVEL	Priority given to security of employment Investment in workplace learning Competitive and equitable pay policies
WORKPLACE LEVEL	Broad task design and self-managed teams Emphasis on employee empowerment and self-accountability Climate of co-operation, commitment and trust

Exhibit 2.3   Key characteristics of Air National's strategic HRM and empowering–developmental approach

AN instituted a series of customer service training seminars and invested in training and development. The senior management also developed a 'strategic partnership' with the unions. At the onset of the re-engineering process Clive Warren and Elizabeth Hoffman undertook to 'open the books' to the unions and established team briefings and regular, formal consultation meetings with union representatives. A profit-related pay system was also launched with the full support of the unions. In addition, the senior management held major training programmes, designed and delivered by leading business school academics, on the importance of trust, motivation and 'visionary' leadership.

Running parallel to these developments was the company's concurrent objective of cost reductions. Between 1988 and 1992, AN shed 37 per cent of its workforce with nearly 25 per cent going in 1988. Job cuts were managed entirely through voluntary severance and redeployment. However, the requirement to sustain and improve performance in the face of such job losses produced a preoccupation with productivity levels and attempts to alter shift patterns at times provoked conflict. Disputes were resolved quickly and usually by the company reminding employees of AN's commitment to job security, training and development, and through senior management 'throwing money at the problem'.

Reviewing the last decade, Clive Warren considered that AN had been 'transformed by re-engineering'. Deep in debt in the late 1980s, Air National went into profit in the first quarter of 1997. The company's aircraft were flying to 164 destinations in 75 countries from 16 UK airports. AN accounted for 70 per cent of UK scheduled domestic and international passenger traffic and 'is now the largest international air passenger carrier in the world', said Warren.

Task

You are a HR consultant employed by a rival national airline to investigate Air National's competitive and HRM strategy. Prepare a written report on the following questions:

1. What factors enabled Air National's senior management to take a strategic approach to its business and to adopt an empowering–developmental approach to HRM?
2. How useful is the concept of 'strategic choice' in understanding the linkage between Air National's competitive and HR strategies?
3. To what extent do re-engineering principles affect management development and practices?

Notes

1. F.A. Jaljers, Chairman of the Board of Unilever.
2. Aktouf, O. (1996) *Traditional Management and Beyond*, Montreal: Morin, p. 91.
3. The case is based on Trevor Colling (1995) 'Experiencing turbulence: competition, strategic choice and the management of human resources in British Airways', *Human Resource Management Journal*, 5(5): 18–32.

The Context of Human Resource Management

chapter three

Global capitalism and competitive advantage

John Bratton

There are choices to be made over the kind of market economy we live in and the society we share.[1]

Re-envisioning work... requires that we rethink our notion of the body politic.[2]

A central issue now is whether Britain will continue to drift towards a system of individualized employment relations within a largely non-union environment, as in the United States, or will join the European mainstream in acknowledging a role for collective employee representation and statutory support for minimum employment standards.[3]

Chapter outline

Chapter objectives

After studying this chapter, you should be able to:

1. Identify the external contexts that affect human resource management policies and actions.
2. Understand the implications of these external contexts for the human resource management function.

● Introduction

Wider economic, technological, political, and social forces shape human resource management policies and activities. What happens in the global economy influences the local economy in terms of output and the demand for labour. The impact route is sometimes indirect and has a 'multiplier' effect: the electrical giant Siemens beats Philips Electronics, Philips lays off employees, belt-tightening employees press for cheaper services from local traders and are prepared to work for lower wage rates, thereby causing adjustments in the local labour market. Apart from the economic context, the wider technological, political, and social contexts influence and impinge upon HRM decisions. Williams (1993) is one of a number of theorists who have argued the importance of understanding the relationship between human resource management and economic and technological stability or instability. To understand the nature and scope of HRM it is necessary to understand the various external contexts that are presumed to be driving organizational change.

There is general agreement among academics and senior business executives that the structure as well as the fundamental dynamics of global business have dramatically changed in the past two decades. At the global level, in the advanced capitalist world, the previous dominance of the USA began to give way to a three-way rivalry between North America, the European Union and the Pacific Rim countries dominated by Japan and the four 'tigers' of Hong Kong, South Korea, Singapore and Taiwan. At European level, the year 1997 is widely viewed as a watershed in the process of European integration (Hyman, 1997). The EU has introduced a large number of measures to remove barriers to free trade, the transfer of capital and services, and the mobility of people. The EU's plan for monetary union, which compels member states to achieve the Maastricht Treaty's 3 per cent target for budget deficits, severely limits government regulation of the domestic economy. At national level, in Britain, contextual changes include high levels of unemployment, the wide diffusion and acceptance of microprocessor-based technologies, an entrenchment of a political ideology based on the pre-eminence of the individual and the free market, major pieces of government legislation affecting the employment relationship, and changes in demographics and values. Similar developments can be observed in North America. In the United States, the turbulent economic and political environment of the 1980s resulted in changes that led to what some writers called the 'transformation of American industrial relations'. Although the transformation thesis is not universally accepted, US employers have, with government indulgence, persuaded or compelled trade unions to accept significant changes in collective agreements (see, for example, Kochan *et al.*, 1986). In Canada, work organizations have been forced to re-examine virtually all of their operational practices because of intense competition, changes in technology, and the regulatory framework (Betcherman *et. al.*, 1994).

The key question that immediately arises is what has changed in the global economy and in the political, and social environments that impacts on HRM? Analysing the issues, the structural changes, the causes of the adjustments, and possible outcomes would fill several volumes. The aim of this chapter is not to provide a comprehensive analysis of the interrelated development of European and North American economies, but to attempt a much more modest review of the economic, political and social contexts and possible implications for human resource management. Analysing the external contexts of HRM is important, because in various ways the conditions external to the organization present particular opportunities and constraints in the management of human resources. In the 1960s, changing public policies covering productivity and employment law extended the personnel management function (Sisson, 1989). Farnham (1990) argues that personnel management practices arose as the result of changes in the political economy. He states: 'As British industrial capital-ism has developed, largely in response to changes in its market, technological and politico-economic contexts, so too have personnel management practices' (1990, p. 25). In the 1980s, the context of British human resource management has been profoundly influenced by the political environment: four consecutive Conservative governments and the emergence of the European Union as a political force on the employment front (Millward *et al.*, 1992). In the 1990s, the processes of 'globaliza-tion' have important consequences for 'high-value' businesses and strategic HRM (Williams, 1993). The term, 'globalization' describes recent changes in the world economy and reflects reduced trade barriers, more global capital flows, declining transportation costs, the portability of new technologies and more integrated finan-cial markets. Increasingly, multinational companies (MNC) can readily transfer pro-duction, in whole or part, to wherever the mix of materials, infrastructure, skilled workers, labour costs and regulatory requirements offers the greatest potential to compete in the international market. It would, however, be too simple to regard the influence of context as a one-way flow only. Senior management attempts to change the external context or environment. For example, a company might transfer its operations where there is little competition or few, if any, health and safety regula-tions. In addition, employers seek to influence government legislation and regulation by lobbying members of parliament. To understand fully the HRM function requires an appreciation of the external influences. The broad model for examining the exter-nal contexts of HRM is given in Figure 3.1. As you read this chapter, consider how economic, technological, political, and social forces affect HRM, and how the exter-nal pressures have impacted on your own workplace or on an organization you have studied. Also reflect on how employers and senior management have responded to such environmental pressures.

The economic context

Human resource management practices and the relative standing of HRM generally is strongly influenced by the prevailing economic climate. One feature of the global economy is economic integration. In the EU and in North America (NAFTA) tariff reductions on commodities pose economic challenges and opportunities for compa-nies. The collapse of the Communist regimes and their integration into the capitalist system opens new opportunities for investment and trade. Economic developments in Europe, North American and the Pacific Rim put pressure on British companies to gain competitive advantage. The challenge to increase productivity and improve quality means that European and North American organizations will have to devote more attention to managing their human assets.

The shape and changes in the global and national economy are usually described by opaque economic statistics. In broad terms, looking back over the 1980s, the UK economy started off with a severe recession, particularly in the manufacturing sector in the Midlands and the north of Britain; then, between 1985 and 1987, there was a short period of growth, until 1990 when another recession began which affected businesses and communities in the north and south of Britain. Real Gross Domestic

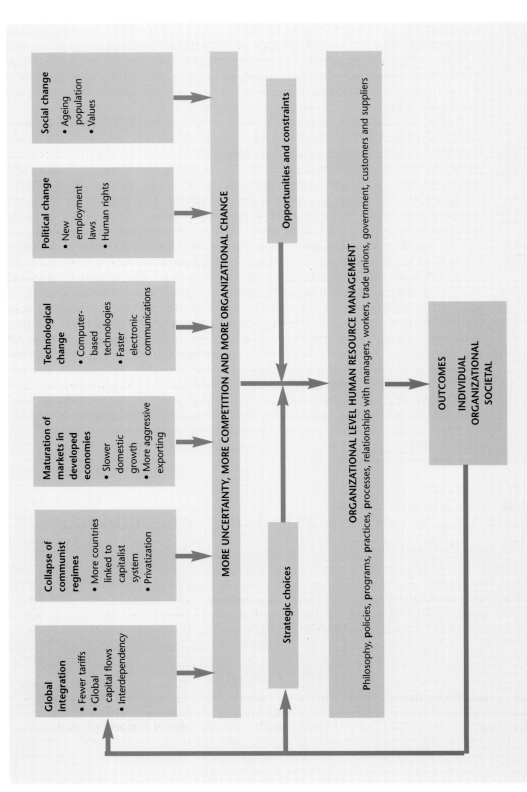

Figure 3.1 A model of the external contexts of human resource management

The figure contains the following text elements:

Global integration
- Fewer tariffs
- Global capital flows
- Interdependency

Collapse of communist regimes
- More countries linked to capitalist system
- Privatization

Maturation of markets in developed economies
- Slower domestic growth
- More aggressive exporting

Technological change
- Computer-based technologies
- Faster electronic communications

Political change
- New employment laws
- Human rights

Social change
- Ageing population
- Values

MORE UNCERTAINTY, MORE COMPETITION AND MORE ORGANIZATIONAL CHANGE

Strategic choices

Opportunities and constraints

ORGANIZATIONAL LEVEL HUMAN RESOURCE MANAGEMENT

Philosophy, policies, programs, practices, processes, relationships with managers, workers, trade unions, government, customers and suppliers

OUTCOMES

INDIVIDUAL
ORGANIZATIONAL
SOCIETAL

Product (GDP) increased by 5 per cent and real manufacturing output fell by 2 per cent between 1980 and 1984. The GDP upward path remained erratic and concealed the disappearance of large tracts of industrial landscape. Nonetheless, overall, real GDP increased by 23 per cent and manufacturing output rose by 25 per cent in the period 1984–90. High unemployment and, for millions of people, falling living standards marked the 1980s.

In 1984, unemployment was 13 per cent and real income per head of the UK population was lower in the mid-1980s than in eleven other advanced capitalist countries. Moreover, there were significant shifts between different parts of the UK economy. The percentage of output (GDP) accounted for by service industries had increased, while the proportion attributable to manufacturing had decreased. In 1950, manufacturing was 30 per cent of the UK's GDP, by 1984 it had fallen to 25 per cent. The UK's problems, as regards its competitiveness performance, is measured in terms of its overseas and domestic market shares. The UK's share of world exports of manufactures fell from approximately 17 per cent in 1960 to about 8 per cent in 1986. While the volume of international exports of manufactures increased by almost 42 per cent between 1978 and 1987, the volume of UK exports of manufactures increased by only 23 per cent (Griffiths and Wall, 1989). In manufacturing, UK output increased by 6 per cent in the period 1979 to 1991, compared with the OECD average (excluding the UK) of 35 per cent. The UK was 20th out of 21 OECD economies. The UK's share of total OECD manufacturing output declined from 6.5 per cent in 1979 to 5.2 per cent in 1991; for the period 1979–92, the UK was situated at the bottom of the league (Michie, 1992). The shift to service industries has been substantial in terms of jobs: 35 per cent of the total in civil employment were employed in manufacturing in 1950; this had fallen to 26 per cent in mid-1984 and to 23 per cent in 1990 (Millward *et al.*, 1992, p. 17). During the same period, 1950–90, employment in the service sector increased from 47 per cent to 60 per cent of total employment.

HRM in practice 3.1

Global mergers run ahead of competition rules
A maze of national laws frustrates companies and regulators
BY BRIAN COLEMAN The Wall Street Journal

BRUSSELS – Auto makers may be thinking globally, but their regulators remain mostly local.

Mergers like the one proposed by Daimler-Benz AG and Chrysler Corp. change the competitive situation in several national markets. But regulators are constrained by national laws that often clash with those of other countries, preventing companies from getting one-stop regulatory clearance.

The situation frustrates not just the companies that have to wade through a maze of regulations but also the antitrust officials. 'In the background, everyone is talking about the idea of international competi-tion rules,' says Andrzej Kmiecik, a partner specializing in antitrust law at the Brussels law firm of Van Bael & Bellis.

Last month, the European Union's competition commis-sioner, Karel Van Miert, called on the World Trade Organiza-tion to establish intern-ational competition guidelines.

Although he stopped short of calling for an international antitrust regulator – an idea he called 'infeasible' – he argued that the failure to improve cooperation on competition policy could wipe out the benefits of globalization.

The WTO already has a working group looking into ways that the Geneva-based trade body can take on some responsibility for cross-border competition concerns. The group is due to report its recommendations by year-end.

The United States and the EU signed an agreement in 1991 to work together on competition issues, and by most accounts they do so successfully. EU officials and their counterparts in the United States at the FTC and Justice Department work with one another on a regular basis.

Currently, they are looking into prominent merger cases with global implications, such as that of World-Com Inc. and MCI Communications Corp. The partnership between British Airways PLC and AMR Corp.'s American Airlines Inc. is also under joint review. A similar review of German media giant Bertelsmann AG's take-over of Random House Inc. appears certain. And regulators from either side of the Atlantic are closely co-operating on the antitrust investigation of Microsoft Corp.

'In the background, everyone is talking about the idea of international competition rules'

Any linkup between Daimler-Benz and Chrysler would be reviewed by the EU's executive commission. But antitrust lawyers and officials said yesterday they believe the marriage would face few, if any, regulatory hurdles in either the United States or Europe, largely because it wouldn't create a dominant player in the industry.

In this year's first quarter, Western Europe's biggest auto maker, Volkswagen AG, had a market share of just 16.6 per cent. Fiat SpA came in second with 12.2 per cent. The two protagonists in the current merger talk barely make a dent: Daimler-Benz's Mercedes-Benz unit had a market share of just 3.9 per cent while Chrysler's share was so small it didn't even register.

Moreover, the two companies have little overlap in their product lines.

But the EU and the United States can fall out with each other on cases that at first glance seem to pose no particular problem. Last year's merger of aerospace giants Boeing Co. and McDonnell Douglas Corp. easily cleared the antitrust hurdles in the United States, but nearly ran afoul of the EU's commission. Only some last-minute concessions by Boeing allowed the deal to go through.

Such differences make many antitrust lawyers wonder whether global competition rules are really possible. They note that in many countries, politics plays an important part in decisions on antitrust cases. 'Even if you had similarly written laws [in each country], you would have different politics,' said Mr. Arquit of Rogers & Wells. 'It's going to be hard to come to an agreement on issues of substance.'

Bruce Ingersoll in Washington contributed to this article.

Source: *Globe & Mail*, May 7, 1998.

HRM in practice 3.2

Halifax makes first move to all-weekend banking

A Sunday-opening trial at the former building society may trigger a jobs boom in the beleaguered banking sector

BY JILLY WELCH People Management, 19 March 1998

More than 1,000 Halifax staff will clock in to work this Sunday, as the bank's contentious pilot scheme begins in 200 branches across the country.

Britain's first large-scale pilot in the banking sector will run until the end of May and will include the Easter weekend. Although the scheme is likely to anger groups opposed to Sunday trading, the bank hopes that the service will appeal to the season's first mortgage-seekers. Saturday hours will also be extended beyond noon.

The Halifax is offering higher rates of pay of up to £22 an hour for staff who volunteer for the extra shifts. Flat-rate incentive payments of between £30 and £100 will also be awarded, based on the number of Sundays worked. Employees will be offered a separate contract for weekend working.

But if Sunday opening proves popular with customers, the bank anticipates that it will have to recruit thousands more staff specifically for that day.

'In setting this up, staffing levels have been a major concern of our employees', admitted David Fisher, head of retail sales and manager of the pilot. 'They don't want this to be really popular and then have us not recruit enough staff to cope.'

Fisher is anxious that the bank is not seen to be pressuris-

ing staff to volunteer for Sunday shifts and says he is keen to negotiate terms and conditions with the Independent Union of Halifax Staff

'One thing we need to look at is: do we recruit staff for Sundays only, or do we review our existing attendance patterns?' he said. 'It's dangerous to assume that weekday staff fit a stereotype and wouldn't want to work alternative shifts.'

> 'If it is successful, I think others would have to consider it very seriously,' he said. 'Let's put it this way: they can't afford to ignore it.'

But Ged Nichols, the union's general secretary, said he was 'deeply sceptical of the long-term benefits' of Sunday opening.

'We could open 24 hours a day, seven days a week if customers really wanted it and if staff working patterns were respected and protected, but I'm not confident that's going to be the case,' said Nichols, who believes that a disproportionate burden to work the unsociable hours will fall on 'key-holders' and supervisors.

'I'm more interested in seeing them tackle existing overtime and workload problems before

they stretch us further,' he added.

Despite its potential difficulties, the bold business move is being watched closely by Halifax's high-street competitors many of which are beginning, or are considering, smaller-scale trials of their own.

Barcalys Bank, which pioneered Saturday opening in 1982, will soon open six branches on Sundays after a trial in Milton Keynes. Abbey National intends to open 80 branches in key high street and estate agency locations on Good Friday and Easter Monday, and is set to launch a special 'mortgage line' service on subsequent Sundays.

Midland Bank, which is opening some branches within supermarkets, says it has not ruled out the possibility of extending the facility to other branches, while Lloyds TSB is also testing the market with branches based in shopping centres.

Barry Swanson, vice-chairman of the Building Societies Association, believes that if the Halifax's gamble pays off, it could create a recruitment boom in the previously moribund banking industry.

'If it is successful, I think others would have to consider it very seriously,' he said. 'Let's put it this way: they can't afford to ignore it.'

In Britain, the data collected by Millward *et al.* (1992) and, more recently, by Cully *et al.* (1998) provide an alternative source of information on important aspects of the changing nature of the economy and the workplace. The findings, covering the period 1984 to 1990, show some identifiable changes in the nature of product markets and the degree of competition, as seen by their management respondents (see Table 3.1). Overall, the markets served by the researcher's national sample of workplaces, both industrial and commercial, remained substantially unchanged. First, manufacturing plants continued to supply products mainly to national or international markets, with a small movement from the latter. Surprisingly, there was no noticeable shift towards international markets. A second finding that accords with mainstream economic analysis is the increased competition facing business organizations: 'more establishments faced highly competitive markets in 1990 than did so in 1984' (Millward *et al.*, 1992, p. 12). This was particularly the case in the service sector; the proportion whose sole or main product market had more than five competitors increased from 56 to 64 per cent. But in the manufacturing sector there was a smaller increase, from 49 to 54 per cent. Another indicator of competitive pressure, the sensitivity of demand to price increases, moved in the opposite direction according to the survey data.

Another major change in the British economy is the marked shift away from public ownership. Privatization has taken different forms. Most prominent has been the sale of public corporations, such as British Telecom. Findings from the 1990 survey show that employment in state-owned corporations fell by 38 per cent, from 1.3 million to 0.8 million, between 1984 and 1990 (Millward *et al.*, 1992, p. 17). The other form of privatization has been private contracting and competitive tendering in, for instance, the health care sector and city and central government. If events during the last years of public ownership are viewed as part of the preparation for privatization,

Table 3.1 The economic context of trading organizations, 1984 and 1990

	Manufacturing 1984	1990	Services 1984	1990
Market for main product			*Column percentages*	
Local	6	10	45	54
Regional	18	10	18	19
National	47	53	26	20
International	29	27	12	7
Number of competitors			*Column percentages*	
None	5	6	14	10
1–5	46	41	30	26
More than 5	49	54	56	64
Price sensitivity			*Column percentages*	
Insensitive	39	43	57	61
Moderate	12	5	9	6
Sensitive	49	53	34	34

Source: Millward *et al.*, 1992

then the evidence suggests that privatization has had a negative impact on employment levels (Pendleton, 1997).

It is argued that we cannot explain or understand the structural changes in the UK economy without understanding the global forces that have acted upon it and which UK capitalism has itself helped to shape. These broad changes in capitalism have been the subject of different interpretations. One influential school of thought links these broad economic changes to the concept of postmodernism: flexible specialization (Piore and Sabel, 1984), disorganized capitalism (Lash and Urry, 1987) and post-Fordism (Hall and Jacques, 1989). Lash and Urry (1987) argue that Britain and the USA, among other capitalist societies, are moving into an era of 'disorganized capitalism'. The increasing scale of industrial and financial corporations, combined with the growth of a global market, means that national markets have become less regulated by nationally based corporations, and individual nation states have less direct control and regulation over large transnational companies. The themes of post-Fordism, flexibility and disorganization are supportive of the broader themes of diversity of capital, political management, 'postbureaucratic' and 'postmodern' work organization (Thompson, 1993). Others have argued that the changes in the global economy are so profound as to constitute 'global industrial revolution' similar to the great industrial revolutions of the past. In the words of William Greider, 'The essence of this industrial revolution… is that commerce and finance have leapt inventively beyond the existing order and existing consciousness of peoples and societies… a new order based upon its own dynamics… People may wish to turn away from that fact, but there is essentially no place to hide, not if one lives in any of the industrialized nations' (1997, p. 15).

As we approach the next millennium, economists provide evidence that global economic conditions are improving (see Morgan *et al.*, 1998). Within the OECD, output growth in 1997 is estimated to have risen to 3 per cent, the best since the late 1980s. North America experienced particularly high growth, reflecting strong domestic demand. Economic prospects also improved in Europe (Figure 3.2). The dramatic

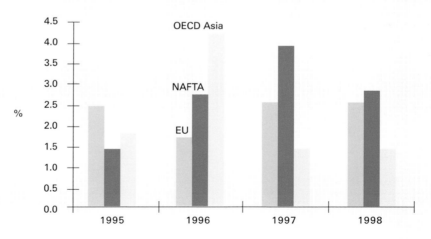

Figure 3.2 OECD GDP growth
Source: Morgan *et al.*, 1998

fall in GDP growth for the Asian economies is the result of the economic conditions in Japan and China and the knock-on effect of the currency crises in Korea, Indonesia, Malaysia, the Philippines and Thailand. For the UK, it is predicted that average growth in GDP between the years 2001 and 2005 will increase to 2.4 per cent compared to 1.0 per cent average for the period 1988–92 (see Table 3.2).

The aggregate data on economic growth, however, does not reveal the major shift in patterns of employment in Europe and North America that have resulted from the processes of globalization. As part of the transformation embodied in 'disorganized capitalism' there has been a divergence in the experience of manufacturing and service sectors. The manufacturing sector, in advanced industrialized economies, has experienced a reduction in the absolute and relative numbers employed and in the significance of this sector to modern capitalist society.

For those workers finding employment, they find that often the nature of the job has changed as work organizations globally have restructured their internal labour markets. Running parallel with globalization and the decline of full-time manufacturing jobs has been a growth of non-regular employment: part-time, short-term, and temporary agency work, and independent contractors. Some scholars refer to this phenomenon as labour market flexibility (LMF) defined as 'a variety of functional techniques that organisations deploy to maximise the increased efficiency of the labour contribution to the strategic purpose of the organisation' (Williams, 1993, p. 1). A whole new vocabulary sprang up around the notion of flexible labour markets in the 1980s. Atkinson's (1985) flexibility model identifies three types of flexibility; functional, numerical and financial; it also categorises the workforce into 'core' and 'peripheral' workers.

Those workers on ongoing full-time contracts constitute the core workforce; those on temporary or part-time contracts, subcontracted and self-employed workers constitute the numerical flexible or the 'peripheral' workforce. In 1993, 40 per cent of the

Table 3.2   Summary of gross domestic product, 1990–2005

	US	Japan	Germany	France	Italy	UK	Major 7 GDP
			GDP for selected countries				
1990	1.2	5.2	5.9	2.5	2.2	0.4	2.4
1991	−0.9	3.8	5.0	0.8	1.1	−2.0	1.4
1992	2.7	1.0	1.8	1.2	0.6	−0.5	1.7
1993	2.3	0.3	−1.2	−1.3	−1.2	2.1	1.0
1994	3.5	0.7	2.8	2.8	2.2	4.3	2.8
1995	2.0	1.4	1.9	2.1	2.9	2.7	2.0
1996	2.8	4.1	1.4	1.5	0.7	2.3	2.5
1997	3.7	1.1	2.3	2.5	1.5	3.6	2.9
1998	2.6	1.4	2.5	2.8	2.0	1.9	2.3
1999	2.2	2.4	2.6	2.9	3.0	2.2	2.4
2000	2.2	2.2	2.5	2.8	3.2	3.0	2.4
1988–92 av	2.0	4.2	4.0	2.6	2.1	1.0	2.7
2001–05 av	2.2	2.6	2.7	2.7	3.0	2.4	2.4

Source: Morgan *et al.*, 1998

Table 3.3   Non-regular forms of employment, selected countries, 1973–93

	Self-employed (per cent of non-agricultural employees)		Part-time (per cent of total employment)		Temporary (per cent of total employment)		Total non-regular (per cent of total employment)	
	1973	1993	1973	1993	1983	1993	1973	1993
USA	6.7	7.7	15.6	17.5	–	–	(22.3)	(25.2)
Canada	6.2	8.6	9.7	17.2	7.5	8.3	23.4	34.1
Australia	9.5	12.9	11.9	23.9	15.6	22.4	(37.0)	(49.2)
Japan	14.0	10.3	13.9	21.1	10.3	10.8	38.2	42.2
Austria	11.7	6.3	6.4	10.1	–	–	–	–
Belgium	11.2	13.3	3.8	12.8	5.4	4.7	20.4	30.8
Denmark	9.3	7.0	(22.7)	23.3	12.5	10.7	(42.5)	44.0
Finland	6.5	9.5	6.7	8.6	(11.3)	13.5	(24.5)	31.6
France	11.4	8.8	5.9	13.7	3.3	10.2	20.6	32.7
Germany	9.1	7.9	10.1	15.1	9.9	10.2	29.1	33.2
Ireland	10.1	13.0	(5.1)	10.8	6.1	9.0	(21.3)	32.8
Italy	23.1	24.2	6.4	5.4	6.6	5.8	36.1	35.4
Netherlands	9.2	8.7	(16.6)	33.4	5.8	10.0	(31.6)	52.1
Norway	7.8	6.2	23.0	27.1	–	–	(30.8)	(33.3)
Portugal	12.7	18.2	(7.8)	7.4	(13.1)	8.6	(33.6)	(34.2)
Spain	16.3	18.7	–	6.6	15.6	32.0	(31.9)	57.3
Sweden	4.8	8.7	(23.6)	24.9	(12.0)	11.9	(40.4)	45.5
UK	7.3	11.9	16.0	23.3	5.5	5.7	28.8	40.9

Source: Standing, 1997

UK workforce were employed in non-regular employment (see Table 3.3). The new 1998 Workplace Employee Relations Survey (WERS) also reports that 25 per cent of all jobs in workplaces with 25 or more workers are part time (working fewer than 30 hours per week) (Cully *et al.*, 1998). One theory is that many firms, largely in response to the globalization of markets and competition, have cut labour costs and achieved more flexible working practices by reducing their full-time 'core' workers by use of part-time workers, temporary workers or using 'outsourcing' (see Betcherman *et al.*, 1994; Standing, 1997). Non-regular employment contracts facilitate 'a looser contractual relationship between manager and worker' (Atkinson, 1985, p. 17) or, to put it more bluntly, employers can hire and fire workers as business circumstances change. Atkinson's 'flexible firm' model is a variant of the dual labour market approach with the distinction between 'core' (primary) and 'peripheral' (secondary) groups of workers. The flexible labour model has been challenged on both ideological and empirical grounds (Williams, 1993). Critics have argued that the notion of core and periphery is confused, circular, and value-laden (Hyman, 1988; Pollert, 1988).

At the centre of this debate on the restructuring of the global economy is the notion that the traditional view of mass markets, mass production, and division of labour is no longer an appropriate model to compete in the new economic order. As Piore and

Sabel (1984) succinctly put it, Fordism is 'dead'. The 'new' business model is 'customer-driven' (Champy, 1996), flexible and therefore requires a different approach to managing labour. A number of researchers have documented shifts in work reorganization from traditional job designs, based on Taylorist principles and rule-bound procedures, towards flexibility and commitment. The Massachusetts Institute of Technology (MIT) study by Womack *et al.* (1990), *The Machine That Changed the World,* identifies a work configuration labelled 'lean production' that incorporates Japanese-style manufacturing practices, including flexible work teams. The MIT study has been particularly influential among academics and practitioners but the MIT analysis has been criticized, not least because of its 'reliance upon an idealised mode of lean production' (Elger and Smith, 1994, p. 3). The logic of this line of argument also postulates a shift away from industrial-level collective bargaining to decentralized establishment-level bargaining in order to restructure the organization of work. At the micro level, flexible specialization requires a good 'fit' between technology and organization.

Whatever the academic merits of the academic debate, to the men and women who live in the industrialized economies, the terms 'deindustrialization' and 'employment flexibility' have real meaning. In concrete terms, they mean that people experience redundancy, long-term unemployment, immense upheaval and dislocation, poverty and despair, and employment insecurity. Making international comparisons on economic variables, such as the rate of unemployment, is problematic. One problem for researchers is how unemployment statistics are compiled. The number of

Figure 3.3   One view of the labour market in the 1990s
Source: *Vancouver Sun*, BC, Canada, June 25, 1995

times the method of compilation has altered since 1979 is a subject of political controversy. The Department of Employment states that there have been seven changes since 1979 which has reduced the number of 'unemployed' in the monthly count. Other commentators, more critical of Conservative government policies, argue that over the last 18 years there have been at least twenty changes in the way in which the unemployment series is calculated. As one observer said: 'The definition of unemployment is a question more of semantics than of economics' (Johnson, 1988, p. 82). However, there is agreement among academics of all persuasions and ideologies that, in the late 1990s, high levels of unemployment continue to remain an economic feature of all OECD countries.

Economic change and HRM

The economic changes taking place in the global economy have important consequences for HRM. As we discussed in Chapter 2, depending on which strategic option chosen – for example, cost minimization or 'differentiation' – economic changes will ultimately determine the HRM approach taken by management and the subsequent HRM outcomes (Figure 3.1). If the company selects to compete through product and service innovation and high quality, then HRM contribution flows from the need to create a highly skilled and committed workforce. According to Williams (1993) such a business strategy would involve the need for:

● flexible workers able to quickly cross over between job boundaries
● the creation and maintenance of the required knowledge base
● the creation of an appropriate corporate culture, which encourages commitment to organizational goals
● a strategy and planning function within HRM that aims to mesh strategic needs with operational requirements (see Chapter two summary).

The rationale for a new HRM model can be explained by the labour exigencies of a strategy of product differentiation based upon high value added and high quality. Such a strategic response to global price competition needs a workforce that is highly skilled, flexible, cooperative and committed (Betcherman *et al.*, 1994). The dialectic of flexibility and cooperation and conflict between employers and workers is a key to understanding the renaissance of interest in the 'human' element in production. Interest and support for the new HRM paradigm represents a conviction that HRM has a strategic role to play in gaining competitive advantage, and concomitantly that HRM innovations have an important role to play in creating an organizational culture that builds trust, flexibility, cooperation and commitment to organizational goals.

A cost minimization strategy, on the other hand, involves a different approach to labour management that would exploit employment insecurity. High levels of unemployment and structural changes shift the balance of power in individual or collective contract negotiations towards the employer; employees and union representatives become more tractable in order to preserve jobs, and managers find that they are more able to introduce unilateral changes in working practices. Taking the globalization of markets and competition together, what are the implications of these economic and technological changes for the recipients of HRM? Using the language of economists, it depends upon whether the recipient is a 'core' or 'peripheral' employee. As Legge (1998) argues, 'if you are a core knowledge worker with skills which are scarce and highly in demand, life may be good – empowerment, high rewards and some element of job security... For the bulk of the workforce, though, things are not so rosy' (p. 20). Williams (1993) estimates that in America, only approximately 20 per cent of the national population is engaged in creation of 'new value added production', so, for the other 80 per cent, employment insecurity will be a permanent feature of work.

⬤ The technological context

Technological change is another component of our model of the external contexts of HRM. Over the last two decades, **microprocessor-based technology** (MBT) has radically transformed the world of work for both blue-collar and white-collar employees. The terms 'new technology', 'high technology' 'microelectronic technology', and 'information technology' are all interrelated. Indeed, these terms are frequently used interchangeably in everyday speech. The importance of 'information technology' arises from the integration between developments in microelectronics and telecommunications. At the end of the 1970s, observers were predicting 'a new industrial revolution' based not on steam, but microelectronics (see, for example, Jenkins and Sherman, 1979). It was judgements of this kind, together with intense media coverage that prompted governments, industrialists and trade unions to wake up to the significance of microprocessor-based technology. In the 1990s, developments in information technology have led some social observers to predict that 'thinking machines' will perform 'conceptual, managerial, and administrative functions' thereby causing a further shift to 'a near-workerless, information society'; the final stage of the 'Third Industrial Revolution' (Rifkin, 1996). When it is reported that many workers in Britain and North America are actually working *longer* hours each week in 1998 than they were two decades ago, it might be premature to speak of the 'end of work'. What we are more confident about, however, is the reconfiguring of the relationship of technology and work.

Academics have identified at least three different forms of technical change that cause a reconfiguration of the relationship of technology and work (Millward and Stevens, 1986):

- advanced technical change: new plant, machinery or equipment that includes microelectronic technology (for example, computer aided design)
- conventional technical change: new plant, machinery or equipment not incorporating microelectronic technology (for example, containerization)
- organizational change: substantial changes in work organization or job design not involving new plant, machinery or equipment (for example, self-managed teams).

The data from the 1990 WIRS survey confirm just how far change has become a feature of British workplaces across all sectors of employment (Table 3.4). The technical changes involving MBT were considerably more prevalent in relation to non-manual than to manual employees in 1984 and this difference did not alter in 1990: 'Traditionally technical change was conceived of as a phenomenon that principally affected manual workers. Now it more frequently affects non-manual workers' (Millward *et al.*, 1992, p. 49). Taking all types of computing facilities together, 75 per cent of the sample had on-site computing facilities compared with only 47 per cent of

Table 3.4   Technical change, 1984 and 1990 (percentage)

	Manual employees		Non-manual employees	
	1984	1990	1984	1990
Proportion of workplaces experiencing in the previous three years:				
Technical change	37	40	57	55
Technical change involving micro-electronics	22	23	49	52
Organizational change	23	29	20	41
Technical or organizational change	47	53	63	67

Source: Millward *et al.*, 1992, p. 15

workplaces in 1984 (Millward *et al.*, 1992, p. 13). Recent research shows the continued diffusion of MBT in different sectors of the economy. For example, in financial services Wilson (1994) reports the adoption of computer-based technology, and in the UK clothing industry Lloyd (1997) describes the widespread diffusion of computer aided design (CAD).

Research efforts have also been undertaken at the 'micro' or organizational level. Much of this work has been concerned with describing and interpreting the complex interplay of technical innovation, job characteristics, skills, patterns of work organization and social relations, and the different levels of worker and trade union support for technical change (Batstone *et al.*, 1987; McLoughlin and Clark, 1988; Bratton, 1992; Clark, 1993; Hogarth, 1993). The analysis of technological change is not limited to Britain either. In Sweden (see, for example, Bansler, 1989; Lowstedt, 1988; Hammarstrom and Lansbury, 1991; Bengtsson, 1992), Finland (Penn *et al.*, 1992) and Denmark (Clausen and Lorentzen, 1993) there have been relatively recent European studies on work organization, the changing nature of employee skills, and the influence of trade unions in the process of technical change. In the early 1980s, much of this research was stimulated by Braverman's publication *Labor and Monopoly Capital* (1974), and the upsurge of interest in the labour process debate that followed in its wake (Thompson, 1989). In North America, the diffusion of MBT, and its effect on the nature of work and workplace social relations, has been studied by a number of academics taking different theoretical perspectives (see, for example, Womack *et al.*, 1990; Wells, 1993; Rinehart *et al.*, 1994; Drache, 1995).

Running parallel with the diffusion of MBT, however, is **organizational change**. Between 1984 and 1990, the proportion of workplaces experiencing substantial changes in work organization or working practices affecting manual employees increased from 23 per cent in 1984 to 29 per cent in 1990. For non-manual workers the increase was significantly greater, up from 20 per cent to 41 per cent (Millward *et al.*, 1992, p. 15). Of particular relevance here is the influence of Japanese management concepts and business process re-engineering (BPR). The Japanese manufacturing paradigm is noted for its 'lean production' and uses flexible cellular manufacturing, just-in-time (JIT) and total quality control (TQC) systems of production. BPR involves the radical redesign of business processes to create simultaneous changes in organizational design, culture, working practices, and performance improvements (see Chapter 4).

It is apparent from a review of the academic literature that technological change is widespread and the processes contain contradictions that present formidable challenges to the various participants: line managers, HRM professionals, workers, and trade union representatives. From a HRM perspective, the processes of technical and organizational change suggest profound changes in the organization, motivation and regulation of labour: flattened hierarchies, decentralized decision making, informal work team control, and flexible work structures. In turn, members of the post-industrial organization will undergo almost constant 'skill disruption', as workers switch from one obsolete skill set to enter another new set (Wallace, 1989). The post-industrial workplace would therefore logically give workplace learning a high priority. This transformation presents opportunities for cooperation between managers and workers (and their unions), but also such change has the potential for conflict between the parties. Where HRM professionals have played a prominent role in workplace technological change, their inclusion had a positive impact; 'their involvement was associated with a stronger level of workers' support for the change' (Daniel and Millward, 1993, p. 69).

● The political context

The political context in our model is most complex and the most difficult to analyse, both because of its power to shape the nature of the employment relationship and because of its effects on the other contexts. Moreover, the political environment is constantly changing, particularly in the area of regulatory requirements. Employment legislation, human rights, pay equity, occupational health and safety, industrial relations legislation, and pensions all impinge on most HRM activities, including selection, training, and rewards. Equally, the government can intervene in the economy to influence economic activity and thereby change labour market trends. During the last 18 years we have witnessed a fundamental shift in the role played by central governments in the Western hemisphere, via general economic management, labour law reform, and in its conception of 'good' human resource and industrial relations management.

Since the early 1980s, successive Conservative governments in Britain and North America have adopted 'supply-side economics' and rejected Keynesian post-war economic orthodoxy. Advocates of supply-side economics posited the theory that economic growth and employment creation is best achieved by governments withdrawing from economic intervention policies, by dismantling the administrative arrangements for regulating the labour market, and by adopting a policy of 'tough love' towards the business sector. The 'love' is for business as a creator of wealth and jobs. The 'toughness' is for business as regards non-protection and support. According to one management guru, 'Governments, with few exceptions, now realize that protecting business enterprises creates bloated companies unable to compete in global markets' (Champy, 1996, p. 18). Far better the 'New Right' argued, to limit government economic power and allow a 'free' market to enhance both the economic well-being of the individual and his or her individual liberty. Proponents of the 'new' economic orthodoxy argue that the market and zero deficits will remove impediments to investment, thereby creating jobs. Further, post-war welfare systems were depicted as a major source of non-wage costs and labour market rigidity (Standing, 1997). Another feature of the 'new' economic order is the dismantling of the public sector, with criticisms that the public sector 'crowds out' private investment and employment. Moreover, the ideology of supply-side economics has provided the impetus for reducing the role and size of government and the privatization of utilities.

Critics argue that Western society is increasingly 'corporatist' and only superficially based on the individual and democracy (Saul, 1995). They also posit that the 'contract culture' has induced 'fear' about job insecurity and caused a growing number of firms to relocate to low-wage developing countries (Hutton, 1996, 1997). Furthermore, they suggest that 'unfettered' markets have caused 'inequalities and insecurities' in global labour markets and, simultaneously, existing collective trade union rights have been eroded particularly in the United States, Britain, and New Zealand (Standing, 1997).

In Britain, the Conservative government led by Margaret Thatcher and her successor, John Major, using a 'step-by-step approach', systematically eroded the rights of both employees and the collective rights of trade unions. The individual employment legislation, or 'floor of rights', established in the 1970s was increasingly viewed by the government as a constraint on enterprise and an obstacle to efficiency and job creation. The Employment Acts of 1980, 1982, 1988, and 1989, the Trade Union Act of 1984, the Employment Act 1990, and the Trade Union Reform and Employment Rights Act 1993, aimed, on the one hand, to undermine individual employment protection and support for union organization and collective bargaining. On the other hand, their purpose was to increase the legal regulation of industrial action and trade union government. This body of legislation, affecting both individual and collective rights, was also considered by the Conservative government to be a central component of economic policy and a major contributor to improving the performance of the British economy ((Brown *et al*, 1997).

In terms of **individual employment rights**, amendments to the Employment Protection (Consolidation) Act 1978 reduced unfair dismissal provision. The numbers eligible to apply to the industrial tribunals were reduced by extending the service qualification needed to make an unfair dismissal claim from six months to two years. By the end of the 1980s the changes in legislative intervention were being reflected in legal statistics. The extension of the qualifying period for unfair dismissal was represented by a fall in tribunal applications; in 1987–88 there were only 34 233 applications compared with 41 244 in 1979 (McIlroy, 1991, p. 192). A critical study of the law of unfair dismissal indicates that of those unfair dismissal applications, few were successful at an industrial tribunal, that those who were successful were rarely offered reinstatement or re-engagement, and that the levels of compensation were low (Denham, 1990). In 1986–87, for example, 10 067 cases were heard at tribunals; of these there were only 103 cases of reinstatement or re-engagement, and the median compensation was £1805 (34.6 per cent of the awards did not exceed £999). Denham argues that unfair dismissal law as it stands has given employees a very limited degree of protection and employers can often obtain the dismissals they want. The purpose of the Employment Act 1989 was to further remove many regulatory restrictions, particularly for small businesses employing fewer than 20 employees. For example, Section 15 amended the 1978 EP (Consolidation) Act to increase from six months to two years the qualifying period of continuous employment after which employees were entitled to be given, on request, a written statement of the reasons for dismissal. Protection for low-paid employees was further limited by Section 35 of the Trade Union Reform and Employment Rights Act 1993 which in effect abolished Wages Councils by the repeal of Part II of the Wages Act 1986. For those workers who are in good health, not pregnant, and in a secure job, the changes in individual employment rights might seem to be of little consequence. However, for those workers in the enlarged peripheral labour market, primarily female, curtailment of employment protection is not inconsequential and has adverse implications for employment security. For many years Britain was one of a number of advanced capitalist countries most active in promoting the concept of international standards. During the last 18 years, it is argued that the UK largely played a negative role in relation to the improvement of international labour standards (O'Higgins, 1986).

The government's **industrial relations legislation** sought to regulate industrial action by, among other things, narrowing the definition of a trade dispute in which industrial action is lawful. The phrase *'in contemplation or furtherance of a trade dispute'* no longer fulfills the same function as it did prior to the 1982 Employment Act, and as argued, 'It now denies legitimacy to many disputes which are clearly about industrial relations issues' (Simpson, 1986, p. 192). The policy objective of the statutes was designed to deter strikes and to limit their scale, and to regulate the membership, discipline and recruitment policies of unions. According to one industrial relations academic, the legislation has marked 'a radical shift from the consensus underlying "public policy" on industrial relations during most of the past century' (Hyman, 1987, p. 93). According to the Secretary of State for Employment, the Employment Act 1988 seeks to give 'new rights to trade union members', notably protection from 'unjustified' discipline by union members and officials. The government justified the statute in the belief that in recent years some British trade unions have meted out harsh treatment to non-striking union members (Gennard *et al.*, 1989). The purpose of the Employment Act 1988 is further to discourage industrial action and reduce the likelihood of 'militant' union leadership (McKendrick, 1988).

The Employment Act 1990 deals with the rights to union membership, the closed shop, unofficial industrial action, dismissal of strikers, and limits of secondary action. The 1990 Act gives those refused employment on the grounds that they were not, or refused to become, a member of a union, a right to take the union to an industrial tribunal. Furthermore, the Act removes immunity from all forms of secondary industrial action. Thus, the complicated provisions of Section 17 of the Employment Act 1980, which made some form of secondary action lawful, were removed. The Trade Union Reform and Employment Rights Act 1993 had two main purposes: to further restrict trade union organization and activity and, second, to enact employment rights arising from EU directives and case law. Sections 1–7 of the 1993 Act relate to internal union governance such as the election of union officials. Sections 13–16 relate to union membership. For instance, Section 13 permits employers to provide inducements to employees to opt out of collective bargaining or leave the union. These provisions were included following the decision of the Court of Appeal in two cases – *Wilson* v. *Associated Newspapers Ltd* (1993) and *Palmer* v. *Associated British Ports* (1993). By the middle of the 1990s, it was unlawful for industrial action to involve secondary action, secondary picketing, action in defence of the closed shop, and action in support of union recognition by a third party. It was, however, lawful for an employer to dismiss on a selective basis individuals taking part in industrial action that the union had not authorized. These changes to industrial relations law were used to tilt the balance of power in an industrial dispute towards the employer (Brown *et al.*, 1997). In a scathing critique of the Conservative government's labour policies, Standing (1997) argues that: 'nobody should be misled into thinking that the rolling back of protective and pro-collective regulations constitutes 'deregulation'. What supply siders have promoted is pro-individualistic (anti-collective) regulations, coupled with some repressive regulations and greater use of promotional and fiscal regulations, intended to prevent people from making particular choices or to encourage, facilitate or promote other types of behaviour' (p. 14).

The Conservative government's employment legislation has not gone unchallenged, however. In the context of a strategically weakened trade union movement, the European Union emerged as a countervailing influence on matters affecting HRM. In 1989, the EU Social Charter (see Appendix I), adopted by all member states except the UK, introduced protection in such areas as improvement in the working environment to protect workers' health and safety, communications and employee involvement and employment equity. The UK's rejection of the Maastricht accord was, insists Towers (1992), the product of opportunism and belief that the Social Charter provisions would impose higher labour costs, leading to bankruptcies and job losses. During the last 18 years of Conservative governments, the influence of EU law increased steadily (Brown *et al.*, 1997). Although not a comprehensive body of employment legislation, EU employment law does draw on the Western European tradition in which the rights of employees are laid down in constitutional texts and legal codes. Part II of the Trade Union Reform and Employment Rights Act 1993 enacts certain individual employment rights as a result of EU directives and case law. For example, to comply with the EU Pregnant Workers' Directive, Sections 23–5 amended maternity rights. Sections 26–7 extended the right of employees to receive from their employer a written statement of principal employment details. Section 28 protects employees against being victimized by their employer for taking specified industrial action related to health and safety. How will EU law impact on HRM? Survey evidence among British employers suggests that the negative impact of EU legislation is 'relatively great' for large organizations that are 'skill intensive' and do a large amount of trade with other EU countries. Further, employers who pay relatively low wages are more likely to be adversely affected by EU law (Sapsford *et al.*, 1997).

With the election of 'New' Labour in 1997, UK employers will have to accept new labour law initiatives which will have ramifications for HRM. At the time of writing, precise details of the Labour government's reform have not been crafted, but three key policies are expected to impact on HRM: a national minimum wage, the Social Charter, and union representation. Shortly after being elected the Labour government announced that a minimum wage will be imposed in the UK. The UK's self-exclusion from the Social Charter in the Maastricht Treaty limited the development of 'social dialogue' or discussion between employers and employee representatives at transnational level. Despite the UK opt-out, 53 of the very largest UK-based companies and 151 overseas-based enterprises operating in Britain have negotiated 'Article 13' agreements that allow for voluntary European Works Councils (EWC) arrangements to be established (Brown *et al.*, 1997). The companies include ICI, GKN, British Steel, Pilkington Glass and NatWest. Cressey's (1998) case study of NatWest Group and NatWest Staff Association voluntary agreement found that the voluntary route gave benefits to both employers and employees. The Labour government's decision to sign up for the Social Charter will accelerate the diffusion of EWCs. Additionally, in 1997, the Labour government restored trade union rights to Government Communications Headquarters (GCHQ) workers, denied since 1984, and asked the TUC and the CBI to explore areas of agreement on union recognition. Not surprisingly perhaps, the parties failed to reach agreement on the key issues (Younson,

1998). A framework of employment law that could strengthen the scope for employee representation both directly and through the definition of individual rights has yet to be agreed.

● The social context

Changes in the age, the proportion of the population participating in the labour market, and the demographics of the labour force determine the size and composition of the workforce. The individuals who enter the organization bring with them different attitudes and values about work, parenthood, leisure, notions of 'fairness' and organizational loyalty. It is these external social forces which make up the social context of human resource management.

Demographic changes provide a starting point for analysing the social context. During the past two decades, the general pattern to emerge is that of an ageing population. Since 1951, the number of Britons of pensionable age has risen by over 40 per cent, from 5.5 million to over 9 million in 1998, or from just under 14 per cent to approximately 18 per cent of the population. However, the phrase 'population ageing' is often misunderstood. It does not mean that senior citizens are about to become the dominant group in society. Demographic data shows that the real era of 'grey power' will be 2018. Demographic projections are based on the most basic demographic fact; every year each person gets a year older. Analysing human behaviour according to age offers insights into socio-economic variables. For example, a 30-year-old is more likely to be married than a 20-year-old. A 55-year-old probably views work differently to a 25-year-old. The ability to forecast behaviour according to age has the advantage of allowing HRM professionals to know more about the composition of the workforce and their needs. A 55-year-old employee with a teenage family is less likely to be interested in child-care provision than a 25-year-old employee. Demographic data is an important source of information that can help HRM professionals in such areas as recruitment and selection, training and rewards management.[4]

Changes in the labour force – the number of people in the civilian working population – not only derive from changes in the size and age distribution of the population, but also from the variations in the labour force participation rates. The participation rate represents the labour force, expressed as a percentage of the working

Table 3.5 Changes in labour force and participation rates, 1960–93

	Labour force change		Participation rate: all adults			Participation rate: male		Participation rate: female	
	1960–73	1974–95	1960	1973	1995	1973	1993	1973	1993
USA	1.9	1.8	64.5	66.6	77.5	86.2	84.9	51.1	69.1
EC-12	0.3	0.7	67.5	65.5	65.7	88.8	77.6	44.9	55.5
Former EFTA	0.5	0.6	73.8	72.4	74.0	88.2	82.6	56.1	66.2

Source: Adapted from Standing, 1997

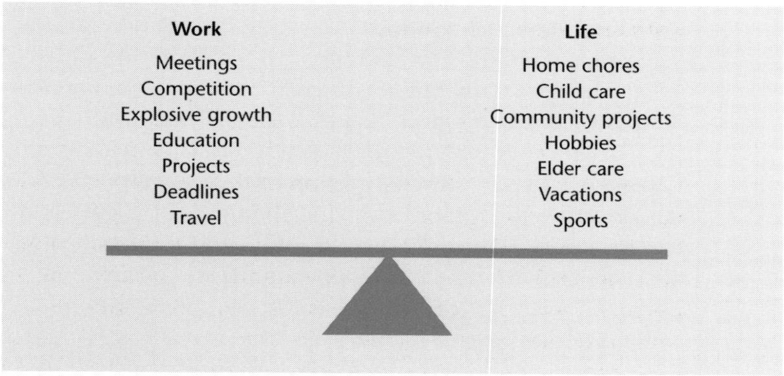

Work	**Life**
Meetings	Home chores
Competition	Child care
Explosive growth	Community projects
Education	Hobbies
Projects	Elder care
Deadlines	Vacations
Travel	Sports

Figure 3.4   The work–life balance goal
Source: Adapted from Platt, 1997

age population, that actually works. In the twelve EU countries, the participation rate for all adults fell from 67.5 per cent to 65.7 per cent. In contrast, the participation rate among women increased from 44.9 per cent to 55.5 per cent in the period 1973–93 (see Table 3.5). A falling participation rate among adults in the UK can be explained by the more restrictive definitions of 'unemployment' and the slow pace of job creation while the working-age population continued to rise (Standing, 1997).

Culture is a concept that can mean all things to all people. Abercrombie and Warde (1988) use the term 'culture' to delineate the symbolic aspects of human society which include beliefs, customs, conventions, and values. Europe and North America are culturally diverse. Within their borders are many cultures and subcultures formed out of divisions like social class, ethnicity, and gender. In turn, these cultures and subcultures are all locally differentiated. Changing cultural values have an impact on human resource management functions. For example, as the percentage of older workers increases, work values may change: work may not be as central to a 55-year-old as to a 30-year-old. Also, changes in traditional gender roles and new lifestyles change participation rates and the way employees are motivated and managed. Working women have the most difficult balancing act (Platt, 1997). A study of employees at the American company, Hewlett-Packard (HP), showed that professional men and women both spend about the same number of hours at work each week, about 50 hours. But HP's women spend an average of 33 hours a week on housework or child care, compared to about 19 hours for men. Thus, on average, women have about two hours a day less leisure than men (Platt, 1997). This dual role puts additional pressure on women workers and is a source of occupational stress (see Chapter 5). In America, the notion of 'work–life balance' for employees – the need to balance work and leisure/family activities – is said to impact on the way people are managed (Figure 3.4).

Although it is suggested that work–life balance is particularly relevant to women in the workforce, men are increasingly concerned as well. However, given the evidence of growing employment insecurity for many workers and the lack of provision for child care in the UK and North America, the probability of achieving the goal of a work–life balance seems remote for many people.

In the industrial relations arena, the 'consumer culture' promoting individualism may erode working-class customs and solidarity, which would undermine the collectivist culture of trade unions. In addition, it has been argued that while the 1980s saw the politicization of 'green' issues, one challenge facing organizations in this decade is the reassertion of underlying value systems. Chapman asserts, 'This implies that organizations will need to develop and communicate corporate cultures with which their staff can identify and to which they are willing to ally themselves' (1990, p. 29). Diversity in the workforce, changes in demographics and social values all, to varying degrees, make the management of people more complex and challenging for the HRM professional.

Chapter summary

We have attempted to cover a wide range of complex issues in this chapter. In essence, we have emphasized that the external contexts of HRM can have a significant impact on the organization and the way human resources are managed. The external domain influences the structure and functioning of a work organization, and in turn, organization decision makers influence the wider society. Guest (1987) argues that interest in HRM in Britain and North America arose as a result of the search for competitive advantage, the decline in trade union power, and changes in the workforce and the nature of work.

The global economy has become more integrated. For HR practitioners, the continuing restructuring of business operations will have a profound effect on competition, and thereby on such HR activities as HR planning, recruitment and selection. Technologically sophisticated processes and equipment, Japanese-style 'lean' production methods, and business process re-engineering (BPR) must not only be seen as a challenge, but also as an opportunity to harness new technology and enhance employee empowerment and job satisfaction. The linkage between the external contexts and the search for competitive advantage through employee performance and HRM activities is illustrated by the Fombrun *et al.* HRM model, Figure 1.2. As far as employment law is concerned, the Labour government's support for the EU Social Charter may encourage senior management to have more regard for HRM. The general indication is that the changing social context of HRM is placing more pressure on employers to pay more attention to the issues associated with a diverse workforce – in particular to be more sensitive to the issues and challenges related to women workers, ethnic minorities and the disabled.

Key concepts

Competitive advantage

Technological change

Demographics

Culture

Economic context

Political context

Employee work–life balance

Social Charter

Discussion questions

1. Describe the major economic challenges facing human resource managers.

2. How have the political developments since 1979 affected human resource management?

3. How will the Labour government's proposals for reforming employment law impact on human resource management?

4. How realistic is it to expect employees to achieve the goal of a work–life balance?

Further reading

Belanger, J., Edwards, P.K. and Haiven, L. (eds) (1994) *Workplace Industrial Relations and the Global Challenge*, New York: ILR Press.

Brown, W., Deakin, S. and Ryan, P. (1997) The effects of British industrial relations legislation, 1979–97, *National Institute Economic Review*, **161**: 69–83.

Grahl, J. and Teague, P. (1997) Is the European social model fragmenting?, *New Political Economy*, **2**(3):405–26.

Greider, W. (1997) *One World, Ready or Not: The Manic Logic of Global Capitalism*, New York: Simon & Schuster.

Hutton, W, (1997) *The State To Come*, London: Vintage.

Lash, S. and Urry, J. (1987) *The End of Organized Capitalism*, Cambridge: Polity Press.

McIlroy, J. (1991) *The Permanent Revolution? Conservative Law and the Trade Unions*, Nottingham: Spokesman.

Overbeck, H. (1990) *Global Capitalism and National Decline*, London: Unwin Hyman.

Saul, J.R. (1995) *The Unconscious Civilization*, Concord, Ontario, Canada: Anansi Press.

Chapter case study

Oil Tool Incorporated: Meeting the Challenges of Globalization

Oil Tool Incorporated was established in West Yorkshire in 1950, and four years later became part of Oil Tool International, an American multinational company engaged in the design, manufacture, and marketing of machinery used at the well-head in drilling for the production of oil and gas, both onshore and offshore. The company, whose corporate headquarters are in Houston, Texas, USA, has other manufacturing establishments in Scotland, Germany, France, and Mexico, and employs 4500 people throughout the world.

Oil Tool Incorporated dominated the oil extraction industry for nearly forty years. After growth and continual profits things started to go wrong in 1985. Low productivity, rising production costs, a decline in oilfield exploration, and new competitors entering the industry, culminated in a £76 million loss for the West Yorkshire plant. At this point the senior management decided to bring in an outside consultancy firm, Mercury Engineers Inc.

Bill Dorfman, the plant manager, called a meeting with his senior management team and the consultants. Dorfman started the discussion. 'We all know that we have considerable autonomy from the corporate management in Texas. That means we have the task of turning this plant around. If we fail the plant will close. This is the company's biggest manufacturing operation in the world. But, it would only be a question of months before another operation could be bigger. Headquarters have moth-balled several of our operations and the French and German plants could be 'geared up' to our size within twelve months. What has gone wrong and how do we turn this plant around?', he asked.

Yvonne Turner, the marketing manager, began. 'Our sales have fallen in the Middle East because our customers want equipment that is lighter and more mobile. The design and the materials of our block-tree valve haven't changed for ten years.' She went on, 'The Japanese are engineering equipment that is made with alloy metals and is lighter, stronger and has a microprocessor-based control system.'

Doug Meyer, the manufacturing manager, jumped in. 'Don't blame us. If the market is changing out there, it's marketing's job to tell us and keep us informed. It's not just our manufacturing practices, we all know our prices are higher because of sterling's high exchange rate. And besides,' he said angrily, 'we lost that last Middle East order because the government refused to give us an export licence. Whether there is a war or not, if we don't sell them the machinery, you can be damn sure, somebody else will. We ought to get the local MP to have a word with the bureaucrats in the Board of Trade.'

At this point, Wendy Seely, the human resource manager, intervened in the discussion. 'Well, I don't know whether we can blame everything on the government in London. I do know, however, that EU Directives on pay equity and recent court decisions on retirement and pensions will push our labour costs up. We must find ways to reduce labour costs and improve quality standards,' she said. 'We can't achieve high quality standards,' retorted Doug Miller, 'because your department stopped training apprentices and we can't find the quality we need using sub-contractors.'

Feeling defensive, Wendy Seely argued, 'We ended the training programme for apprentices because the local college closed the first year apprentice course, as part of its own cost-saving measures. You can't blame my department for that.' Bill Dorfman decided to bring the meeting to a close. 'Would each department address the issues discussed this morning? We shall meet in seven days and see whether there is a consensus on the way forward. Remember we have to be competitive to survive. We have to quit whining and save this plant,' he said.

(Source: Adapted from 'The drilling machine company: Japanization in small-batch production'. In Bratton, J. (1992) *Japanization at Work, Managerial Studies for the 1990s*, London: Macmillan.)

Task

1. Assume you are a member of the consultancy team. Prepare a report outlining the contextual changes affecting Oil Tool Engineering. What factors from the chapter can help explain what happened to this company? How can HRM help solve some of the problems?

Notes

1. Hutton, W. (1997) *The State To Come*, London: Vintage, p. 110.
2. Rifkin, J. (1996) *The End of Work*, New York: Tarcher/Putnam, p. 294
3. Brown, W., Deakin, S. and Ryan, P. (1979–97) *The Effects of British Industrial Relations Legislation, 1979–97*, pp. 78–9.
4. For a more in-depth examination of how demography impacts on business and society, see David Foot and Daniel Stoffman's book, *Boom, Bust and Echo*, Toronto, Canada: Macfarlane Walter & Ross.

chapter four

Restructuring work: Fordism and re-engineering

John Bratton

The one man [sic], one machine principle has gone completely out of the door.[1]

Workers in each cell see the manufacture of whatever they are making... from the assembly of components stage to completion. They are expected to be far more flexible, with some workers operating five or six machines rather than perhaps two under the old system. They are also expected to take on more responsibility.[2]

A handful of companies... Forced to choose between sure failure and radical change, opted for the latter. They began to reengineer. They ripped apart their old ways of doing things and started over with clean sheets of paper.[3]

Chapter outline

Chapter objectives

After studying this chapter, you should be able to:

1. Explain the meaning of the term 'work'.

2. Define job design and describe specific job design strategies.

3. Understand the theoretical arguments underpinning current organizational and job design practices.

● Introduction

In their model of HRM, Beer *et al.* (1984) see job design broadening employee responsibilities and resulting in 'substantial improvements in all four Cs', that is, commitment, competence, cost effectiveness, and congruence. Thus, the design of organizational structures and the way work is performed are critical features of the HRM model. As Guest (1990) points out, the HRM model is underpinned by the need to reconfigure organizational structures as the rhetoric is essentially 'anti-bureaucratic'. Guest further emphasizes the concomitant change in job design. 'HRM takes as its starting point the view that organizations should be designed on the basis of the assumptions inherent in McGregor's (1960) Theory Y.'[4] As we mentioned previously in Chapter 2, the new buzz word for the redesign of organizational structures and work processes is 're-engineering'. Much of the rationale for re-engineering has been developed initially in a USA context, then generalized across North America and European economies. Hammer and Champy (1993) inform us that re-engineering is necessary because the world is a different place. To respond more rapidly to global changes, to make organizations compete more aggressively in global markets, to have a workforce that is more flexible and attuned to the needs of customers, senior managers have fundamentally to restructure business processes. Re-engineering should be understood in the context of the debate on postmodernist thinking for organizations (Hassard and Parker, 1993). In terms of organizational design and analysis, postmodernism is linked to and underpinned by a portfolio of theories including flexible specialization, disorganized capitalism and post-Fordism (Thompson, 1993). To this family of theories we can add re-engineering.

Running parallel with debates on postmodernist organizational structures has been a renaissance of interest among academics in the field of technological change and job design. However, when academic observers refer to a 'degradation of work' or the 'enrichment of work', what theoretical perspectives are the authors employing? Work can be studied from two broad academic perspectives; psychological and sociological. A sociological perspective of work is concerned with the broader contextual and structural factors affecting peoples' experience of work. An important theme for sociologists is that of the division of labour, which refers to the way in which people in society can specialize in doing particular types of work. At the level of the organization, the internal division of labour is a basis of efficiency and control of workers. At society level, the division of labour has produced the occupational structure of professional, management, clerical, skilled and unskilled manual occupations. Another important topic in the sociology of work is that of work-based inequalities and, within this, the social division of labour, which shows that contemporary society allocates particular work to men and to women (Littler and Salaman, 1984; Thompson, 1989).

The psychological study of people at work attempts to understand individual behaviour, and there is a large body of literature covering the academic field of 'organizational behaviour', concerned with managerial problems of motivation, job satisfaction, work stress, job design, and any other factor relevant to working conditions that could impede efficient work performance. An early theory of individual work behaviour attempted to explain the nature of motivation in terms of the types of needs that people experience (Maslow, 1954). Subsequent theoretical contributions from behavioural scientists, such as McGregor's Theory X and Y (1960), Herzberg's motivation–hygiene theory (1966), and Vroom's expectancy motivation theory (1964), have practical implications for the way organization controllers design work structures and rewards. More recently, a model has been put forward that links core characteristics of work and the critical psychological processes acting on individuals and their immediate work groups (Hackman and Oldham, 1980).

This chapter is largely an explanation of job design strategies, as seen by sociologists and industrial psychologists researching the links between motivation, job satisfaction and work design. The chapter examines the meaning of work in contemporary Western society. The broader context of work should be seen as providing essential background knowledge for human resource practitioners concerned with current job design techniques. The chapter then proceeds to discuss the links between the design of work and the HRM cycle before critically evaluating alternative job design strategies including Taylorism, post-Fordism, flexible specialization, Japanese work designs and re-engineering.

The nature of work

When we refer to the term 'work', what do we mean? Filling in the forms for a student grant is not seen as work, but filling in forms is part of a clerical worker's job. Similarly, when a mature student looks after her or his own child that is not seen as work, but if she or he employs a child-minder to look after the child, that is paid work. We can begin to get a sense of what this question is about, and how society views work, by exploring the following definition:

> Work refers to physical and mental activity that is carried out at a particular place and time, according to instructions, in return for money.

This definition draws attention to some central features of work. First, the notion of 'physical and mental' obviously suggests that the activities of a construction worker or a computer systems analyst are deemed to be work. Second, the tendency for the activity to be away from our home and at set time periods of the day or night, 'place and time', locates work within a social context. Third, the social context also includes the social relations under which the activity is performed. When a mother or father cooks the dinner for the family, the actual content of the activity is similar to that performed by a cook employed by a hospital to prepare meals for patients. But the social relations in which the activity occurs are quite distinct. The hospital cook has more in common with factory or office workers because their activities are governed by rules and regulations – 'instructions' from the employer or the employer's agent. Clearly then, it is not the nature of the activity that determines whether it is considered 'work', but rather the social relations in which the activity is embedded (Pahl, 1988). Fourth, in return for physical effort or mental application, fatigue, and loss of personal autonomy, the worker receives a mix of rewards, including 'money', status, and intrinsic satisfaction. Watson (1986) refers to this mix of inputs (physical and mental activities and so on) and outputs (rewards) as the 'implicit contract' between the employer and the employee.

Although this definition helps us to identify key features of the employment relationship, it is too narrow and restrictive. First, there are all the activities, both physical and mental, that do not bring in money. Such activities can be exhilarating or exhausting; they may involve voluntary work for the Citizens Advice Bureau or may involve the most demanding work outside paid employment, child care. Again, the same activities – advising people on their legal rights and being paid for it or being employed in a nursery – would all count as 'work' because of the social relations and the monetary reward. Second, it is clear that the rewards, satisfaction and hazards of work are distributed highly unequally. Contemporary society rewards employees according to the kind of people they are and the kind of work they do. Historically, women receive less money than men in similar work. Work can also be dangerous and unhealthy, but the hazards are not distributed evenly. Despite the publicity surrounding managerial stress, the realities of the distribution of work-related hazards show that they are most prevalent among manual workers. Furthermore, it has been argued that this unequal distribution of work-related accidents represents the systematic outcome of values and economic pressures (Littler and Salaman, 1984).

There is no doubt that the nature and experience of work is changing. The 1998 WERS study, for example, reported that in around 25 per cent of workplaces surveyed, 'most employees in the largest occupational group are trained to be adaptable' (Culley et al., 1998, p. 9). As part of the wider process of globalization and the implementation of new managerial strategies, there is an ongoing shift of paid work into the service sector, an increase in information technology, and increasing numbers of women being drawn into the waged labour force. Contemporary forms of waged work, particularly in the less developed industrialized economies, are dependent on the integration between work and the family (Moore, 1995). The nature of work affects human resource management activities. For example, the pay an employee receives is related to social attitudes and traditions rather than the actual content of the activity; pay determination requires an understanding of the social division of labour, and gender divisions of labour in particular (Pahl, 1988). Management decides how the tasks are divided into various jobs, and how they relate to other tasks and other jobs, contingent upon different modes of production and technology. Decisions are also made about control systems, the ratio of supervisors to supervised, the training of workers, and the nature of the reward system. Thus HRM is both affected by and profoundly affects an individual's experience of work. Clearly, the way work is designed impacts both on the effectiveness of the organization and the experience and motivation of the individual and work group. It is this process of job design that we now consider.

⬤ Job design

The need to harness human resources in innovatory ways to give organizations a competitive advantage has focused attention on the question of job design. It is defined as:

> The process of combining tasks and responsibilities to form complete jobs and the relationships of jobs in the organization.

Job design and the HRM cycle

Job design is related very closely to key elements of the HRM cycle, selection, development, and rewards. Job design is basic to the selection function. Clearly, a company that produces small-batch, high value-added products using skilled manual labour will have different recruitment and selection priorities from an organization that specializes in large-batch production using dedicated machines operated by unskilled operators. Job design also affects the HR development. Specifically, any change to work patterns will require some form of systematic training. If an organization chooses either to fragment or combine tasks, alternative reward systems may have to be designed. For example, a pay-for-output system may be an obstacle to labour flexibility.

Early developments

Innovations in the way work is designed have interested academics and managers for centuries. For example, Adam Smith (1723–90), the founder of modern economics, studied the newly-emerging industrial division of labour in eighteenth-century England. For Smith, the separation of manual tasks was central to his theory of economic growth. Smith argued that the division of labour leads to an improvement of economic growth in three ways; output per worker increases because of enhanced dexterity; work preparation and changeover time is reduced; specialization stimulates the invention of new machinery. In his book, *The Wealth of Nations*, Smith describes the manufacture of pins and gives an early example of job design.

> One man draws out the wire; another straightens it; a third cuts it; a fourth points it; a fifth grinds it at the top for receiving the head… the important business of making a pin is, in this manner, divided into eighteen distinct operations (Smith, [1776] 1982, p. 109).

In the nineteenth century, Charles Babbage also pointed out that the division of labour gave the employer a further advantage. By simplifying tasks and allocating the fragmented tasks to unskilled workers, the employer may pay a lower wage; 'in a society based upon the purchase and sale of labour power, dividing the craft cheapens its individual parts' (Braverman, 1974, p. 80).

The emergence of industrial division of labour gave rise to more radical studies of job design. Karl Marx (1818–83) argued that the new work patterns constituted a form of systematic exploitation, and that workers are alienated from the product of their labour because of capitalist employment relations and the loss of autonomy at work: 'factory work does away with the many-sided play of the muscles, and confiscates every atom of freedom, both in bodily and intellectual activity' (quoted in Newton, 1980, p. 69).

Since the beginning of the twentieth century, interest in job design has intensified because of the writings of Frederick Taylor (1856–1915) on 'scientific management'. Between 1908 and 1929, Henry Ford developed the principles of Taylorism, but went further and developed new work structures based on the flow-line principle of assembly work. The human relations movement emerged in the 1920s and drew attention to the effect of work groups on output. In the late 1960s, concern about declining productivity and the disadvantages of scientific management techniques led to the job redesign movement. Current interest and discourse on job design centres around Japanese management. This deals with more than job design. It emphasizes management style, skill, and values and aims to incorporate job design into an organization's employment strategy.

● Scientific management

The scientific management movement was pioneered by the American, Frederick W. Taylor. This approach to job design, referred to as Taylorism, was also influenced by Henry L. Gantt (1861–1919) and Frank B. Gilbreth (1868–1924). Taylor developed his ideas on employee motivation and job design techniques at the Midvale Steel Company in Pennsylvania, where he rose to the position of shop superintendent. Littler has argued that 'Taylorism was both a system of ideological assertions and a set of management practices' (1982, p. 51). Taylor was appalled by what he regarded as inefficient working practices and the tendency of workers not to put in a full day's work – what Taylor called 'natural soldering'. He saw workers who do manual work to be motivated by money, the 'greedy robot', and to be too stupid to develop the 'one best way' of doing a task. The role of management was to analyse scientifically all the tasks to be done and then to design jobs to eliminate wasted time and motion.

Taylor's approach to job design was based on five main principles:

1. maximum job fragmentation
2. the divorce of planning and doing
3. the divorce of 'direct' and 'indirect' labour
4. minimization of skill requirements and job-learning time
5. the reduction of material handling to a minimum.

The centrepiece of scientific management was the separation of tasks into their simplest constituent elements (first principle). Most manual workers were sinful and stupid, and therefore all decision-making functions had to be removed from their hands (second principle). All preparation and servicing tasks should be taken away from the skilled worker, and performed by unskilled and cheaper labour (third principle). According to Littler this is the Taylorist equivalent of the Babbage Principle and is an essential element of more work intensification (1982, p. 51). Minimizing skill requirements to perform a task reduces labour's control over the labour process (fourth principle). Management should ensure that the configuration of machines minimizes the movement of people and materials to save time (fifth principle). Taylor's approach to job design, argues Littler, embodies 'a dynamic of deskilling' and offers to organizations 'new structures of control' (1982, p. 52).

Some writers argue that Taylorism was a relatively short-lived phenomenon that died in the economic depression in the 1930s. Rose argues that scientific management did not appeal to most employers: 'Some Taylorians invested a great effort to gain its acceptance among American employers but largely failed' (1988, p. 56). This view underestimates the diffusion and influence of Taylor's principles on job designers. In contrast to Rose, Braverman argues that: 'the popular notion that Taylorism has been "superseded" by later schools of "human relations", that it "failed"… represents a woeful misreading of the actual dynamics of the development of management' (1974, pp. 86–7). Similarly, Littler and Salaman have argued that 'In general the direct and indirect influence of Taylorism on factory jobs has been extensive, so that in Britain job design and technology design have become imbued with neo-Taylorism' (1984, p. 73).

Fordism

Henry Ford applied the major principles of Taylorism but also installed specialized machines and perfected the flow-line principle of assembly work. This kind of job design has come to be called, not surprisingly, Fordism. The classical assembly line principle should be examined as a technology of control of employees, and as a job design to increase labour productivity, both job fragmentation and short task-cycle times are accelerated. Fordism is also characterized by two other essential features, the introduction of an interlinking system of conveyor lines that feed components to different work stations to be worked on, and second, the standardization of commodities to gain economies of scale. Fordism established the long-term principle of mass production of standardized commodities at a reduced cost (Coriat, 1980).

The speed of work on the assembly line is determined through the technology itself, not through a series of instructions. Management control of the work process was enhanced also by detailed time and motion study inaugurated by Taylor. Work study engineers attempted to discover the shortest possible task-cycle time. Henry Ford's concept of people management was simple. 'The idea is that man... must have every second necessary but not a single unnecessary second' (Ford, 1922, quoted in Beynon, 1984, p. 33). Recording job times meant that managers could monitor more closely subordinate levels of effort and performance. Task measurement, therefore, acted as the basis of a new structure of control (Littler, 1982, p. 88).

Ford's production system was not without its problems however. Workers found the repetitive work boring and unchallenging. Job dissatisfaction was expressed in high rates of absenteeism and turnover. For example, in 1913 Ford required about 13 500 workers to operate his factories at any one time, and in that year alone the turnover was more than 50 000 workers (Beynon, 1984, p. 33). The management techniques developed by Ford in response to these human resource problems serve further to differentiate Fordism from Taylorism ((Littler and Salaman, 1984). Ford introduced the Five Dollar Day – double the pay and shorter hours for those who qualified. Benefits depended on a factory worker's lifestyle being deemed satisfactory and this included abstaining from alcohol. Ford's style of paternalism attempted to inculcate new social habits, as well as new labour habits, which would facilitate job performance. Taylorism and Fordism became the predominant approach to job design in vehicle and electrical engineering – the large-batch production industries – in the USA, Canada, and Britain.

As a job design and labour management strategy, scientific management and Fordist principles had limitations even when they were accepted by the workforce. First, work simplification led to boredom and dissatisfaction and tended to encourage an adversarial industrial relations climate. Second, Taylor-style job design techniques carry control and coordination costs. With extended specialization, indirect labour costs increase as the organization employs increasing numbers of production planners, controllers, supervisors and inspectors. The economies of extended division of labour tend to be offset by the increasing costs of management control structures. Third, there are what might be called cooperation costs. Taylorism increases management's control over the quantity and quality of workers' performance; however, as a result, there is increased frustration and dissatisfaction leading to a withdrawal of commitment on the part of the worker. Quality control can become a major problem for management. The relationship between controller and controlled can so deteriorate as to result in a further increase in organizational control. The principles of Taylorism and Fordism reveal a basic paradox 'that the tighter the control of labour power, the more control is needed' (Littler and Salaman, 1984, pp. 36–7; see also Huczynski and Buchanan, 1991, p. 307). The adverse reactions to extreme division of labour led to the development of new approaches to job design that attempted to address these problems. The human relations movement began to shift managers' attention to the perceived needs of workers.

●●● Human relations movement

The human relations movement emphasized the fact that job design had to consider the psychological and social aspects of work. The movement grew out of the Hawthorn experiments conducted by Elto Mayo in the 1920s. Mayo set up an experiment in the relay assembly room at the Hawthorn Works in Chicago, which was designed to test the effects on productivity of variations in working conditions (lighting, temperature, ventilation).

The Hawthorn research team found no clear relationship between any of these factors and productivity. The researchers then developed, *ex post facto*, concepts that might explain the factors affecting worker motivation. They concluded that workers are motivated by more than just economic incentives and the work environment; recognition and social cohesion are important too. The message for management was also quite clear. Rather than depending on management controls and financial incentives, it needed to influence the work group by cultivating a climate that met the social needs of workers. The human relations movement advocated various techniques, such as worker participation and non-authoritarian first-line supervisors, which, it was thought, would promote a climate of good human relations in which the quantity and quality needs of management could be met.

Criticisms of the human relations approach to job design were made by numerous writers. They charged managerial bias and that the human relations movement tended to play down the basic economic conflict of interest between the employer and employee. Critics also pointed out that when the techniques were tested, it became apparent that workers did not inevitably respond as predicted. Finally, the human relations approach is criticized because it neglects wider socio-economic factors (Thompson, 1989). Despite the criticisms, the human relations approach to job design began to have some impact on management practices in the post-Second World War environment of full employment. Running parallel with the human relations school of thought came newer ideas about work which led to the emergence of a job redesign movement.

●●● Job redesign movement

During the 1960s and early 1970s, job design was guided by what Rose (1985, p. 200) refers to as the neo-human relations school (Maslow, 1954; McGregor, 1960; Herzberg, 1966) and the wider-based quality of working life (QWL) movement. The neo-human relations approach to job design emphasized the fulfilment of social needs by recomposing fragmented jobs. The quality of working life movement can be traced back to the publication of two reports, the *Work in America* report (1973) and the British report *On the Quality of Working life* (Wilson, 1973).

Littler and Salaman (1984) put forward five principles of 'good' job design which typify the QWL movement's challenge to the principles of scientific management. First, there is the principle of closure, whereby the scope of the job is such that it includes all the tasks to complete a product or process, thus satisfying the social need of achievement. Second, there is the incorporation of control and monitoring tasks, whereby the individual or group assume responsibility for quality control. Third, there is task variety whereby the worker acquires a range of different skills so that job flexibility is possible. Fourth, there is self-regulation of the speed of work. Fifth, there is a job structure that permits some social interaction and a degree of cooperation among workers. In the late 1970s, competitive pressures compelled an increasing number of Western companies to reassess their job design strategies. Although several writers (for example, Kelly, 1985) have pointed out that the recent developments in job design cannot all be grouped together, it is possible to identify three broad types, job enrichment, reorganization of assembly lines, and Japanese-style job design. The following sections consider each of these in turn.

Job enrichment

The term 'job enrichment' refers to a number of different processes of rotating, enlarging, and aggregating tasks. An early example of this process was the use of job rotation. This involves the periodic shifting of a worker from one work-simplified task to another (Figure 4.1). The advantage of job rotation, it was argued, is that it reduces

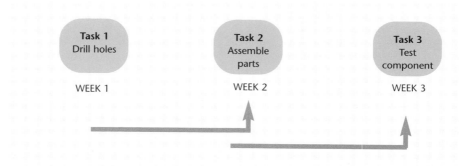

Figure 4.1   Example of job rotation

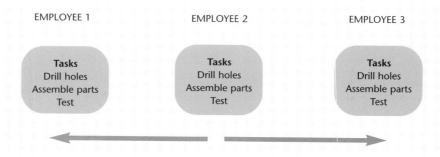

Figure 4.2   Example of job enlargement

the boredom and monotony of doing one simplified task, through diversifying the worker's activities (Robbins, 1989).

An alternative approach to job redesign was the horizontal expansion of tasks, referred to as job enlargement (Figure 4.2). For instance, instead of only grilling hamburgers, a griller's job could be enlarged to include mixing the meat for the burger or preparing a side salad to accompany the order. With a larger number of tasks per worker, the time cycle of work increases, thus reducing repetition and monotony.

A later and more sophisticated effort to address the limits of Taylorism and Fordism was the vertical expansion of jobs, often referred to in organizational behaviour textbooks as job enrichment. This approach takes some of the authority from supervisors and adds it to the job (Figure 4.3). Increased vertical scope gives the worker additional responsibilities, including planning and quality control. For instance, the fast-food worker from our previous example might be expected not only to grill the burgers and prepare the salad, but also to order the produce from the wholesaler and inspect the food on delivery for quality. The Hackman and Oldham (1980) model of job enrichment is an influential approach to job design. This model suggests that five core job characteristics result in the worker experiencing three favourable psychological states; these, in turn, lead to positive outcomes. The five core job characteristics are defined as:

1. *skill variety* – the degree to which the job demands a variety of different activities in carrying out the work, requiring the use of a number of the worker's skills and talents
2. *task identity* – the degree to which the job requires completion of a 'whole' and identifiable piece of work
3. *task significance* – the degree to which the job has a substantial impact on the lives or work of other people
4. *autonomy* – the degree to which the job provides substantial freedom, independence and discretion to the worker in scheduling the work and in determining the procedures to be used in carrying it out
5. *feedback* – the degree to which the worker possesses information of the actual results of her or his performance.

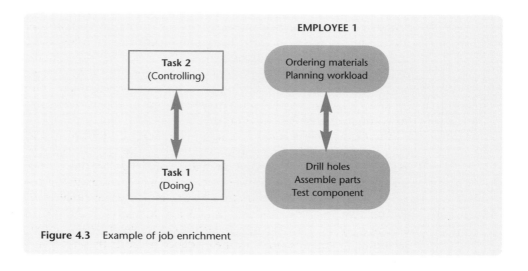

Figure 4.3 Example of job enrichment

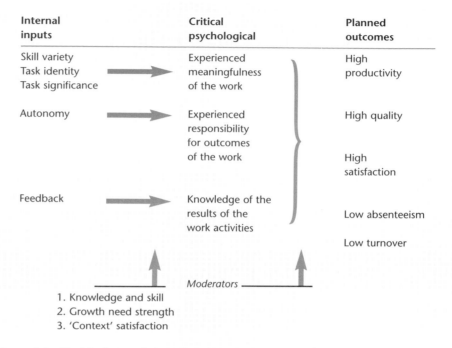

Internal inputs	Critical psychological	Planned outcomes
Skill variety Task identity Task significance	Experienced meaningfulness of the work	High productivity
Autonomy	Experienced responsibility for outcomes of the work	High quality
		High satisfaction
Feedback	Knowledge of the results of the work activities	Low absenteeism
		Low turnover

Moderators

1. Knowledge and skill
2. Growth need strength
3. 'Context' satisfaction

Figure 4.4 The job characteristic model
Source: Adapted from Hackman and Oldham, 1980

For example, a chef/manager of a small restaurant would have a job high on skill variety (requiring all the skills of cooking, plus business skills of keeping accounts, and so on), high on task identity (starting with raw ingredients and ending with appetizing meals), high on task significance (feeling that the meals brought pleasure to the customers), high on autonomy (decides the suppliers and the menus), and high on feedback (visits the customers after they have finished their meals). In contrast, a person working for a fast-food chain grilling hamburgers would probably have a job low on skill variety (doing nothing but grilling hamburgers throughout the shift), low on task identity (simply grilling burgers, seldom preparing other food), low on task significance (not feeling that the cooking makes much of a difference when the burger is to be covered in tomato ketchup), low on autonomy (grills the burgers according to a routine, highly specified procedure), and low on feedback (receives few comments from either co-workers or customers).

The model suggests the more that a job possesses the five core job characteristics, the greater the motivating potential of the job. The existence of 'moderators' – knowledge and skills, growth need strength, context satisfactions – explains why jobs theoretically high in motivating potential will not automatically generate high levels of motivation and satisfaction for all workers. This means that employees with a low growth need are less likely to experience a positive outcome when their job is enriched (Figure 4.4). The job characteristics model has been tested by theorists and, according to Robbins, 'most of the evidence supports the theory' (1989, p. 210).

A more critical and ideological evaluation of job enrichment has been offered by some theorists. Bosquet, for example, argues that modern management is being forced by labour problems to question the wisdom of extreme division of labour and factory 'despotism'. Job enrichment 'spells the end of authority and despotic power for bosses great and small'; in turn, this should lead workers liberated from boring jobs to demand total emancipation (Bosquet, 1980, p. 378). An influential study by Friedman (1977) argues that although job enrichment techniques may increase job satisfaction and commitment, the key focus remains managerial control. He maintains that job design strategies such as job enrichment result in individuals or groups of workers being given a wider measure of discretion over their work with a minimum of supervision, and this 'responsible autonomy' strategy is a means of maintaining and augmenting managerial authority over workers (Friedman, 1977, p. 265), or a 'tool of self-discipline' (Coriat, 1980, p. 40) over workers. One of the most penetrating critiques of job redesign techniques is offered by Thompson (1989). Drawing upon the contributions from various theorists and empirical evidence, he argues that many job enrichment schemes 'offer little or nothing that is new, and are often disguised forms of intensified [managerial] control' (1989, p. 141). By the early 1970s, over 200 factories in the USA and Europe had applied job enrichment schemes, reports Bosquet (1980).

The reorganization of assembly lines

This type of job design change has been associated with increased product differentiation in highly competitive consumer industries and unstable labour relations (Coriat, 1980). The Fordist model of production is product-specific, involving specialized machinery and labour which is not easily transferable. In contrast, new assembly line arrangements were introduced to increase labour productivity (Coriot, 1980) and to create more flexible work structures in order to accommodate more rapid product changes. These redesigned assembly lines consist of buffer inventories between distinct work stations and group all automatic operations together so that small groups of workers are decoupled from the machine pace by the buffer. Compared to the one worker, one job, one assembly line model, this procedure allows for increased capacity utilization because of greater flexibility, the elimination of some jobs and the reduction of indirect labour – the abolition of relief people and 'quality control' inspectors (Coriat, 1980; Littler and Salaman, 1984, p. 82).

Assembly lines were redesigned by the introduction of group technology. Typically, machines and workers are grouped to form a logical 'whole task' which can be performed with minimum interference. Machine tools on the factory floor or desks in an office are reorganized so that they are grouped not on the basis of their doing similar work (for example, drilling or purchase requisition), but on the basis of a contribution to a certain product or service. This approach to job design also explicitly recognizes the value of cooperative team work, group problem solving, and peer or 'clan' control. In the 1970s, group technology was tried in large-batch industries, such as automobile manufacturing.

More recently, cheaper information technology based on microprocessors, together with more flexible machine tools, has encouraged many companies to experiment with group or cellular technology in both large-batch and small-batch manufacturing and the introduction of work teams. Within the North American concept of 'lean' production, work teams are seen as a core element of modern automobile manufacturing (Womack et al., 1990). North American, British, German and Swedish car companies started to introduce work teams on the assembly lines in the last decade. For example, Volvo introduced group technology and self-managed work teams at a new plant in Uddevalla, Sweden, in 1987. It was reported (*Business Week*, August, 1989) that the new assembly line avoided the classic problems associated with work cycles of only one or two minutes by employing teams of seven to ten manual workers. Each team works in one area and assembles four cars per shift. The new work arrangements at Volvo were introduced to improve productivity and quality. Apparently, the improvement in productivity was not enough, in November 1992, Volvo announced the closure of its innovative plant at Uddevalla. For many organizational researchers, the Swedish plant had become an icon for a European, human-centred and productive organization and its closure suggested that Taylorist and neo-Taylorist solutions still dominate management thinking in the automobile industry (Cressey, 1993). The German automobile industry has also experimented with non-traditional job designs over several decades. Whereas, in the 1970s, the introduction of work teams in the German factories had failed – because of the resistance of management, trade unions and the works councils – in the 1990s, work teams were successfully reintroduced into assembly lines. The success was largely due to German management recognizing the superior performance of work teams (Murakami, 1995). In Canada, one study reported that over 20 per cent of electrical companies surveyed had implemented self-directed work teams (Betcherman *et al.*, 1994). HRM in practice 4.1 is an example of self-managed teams in a British automobile plant.

HRM in practice 4.1

Blue-collar steel deal has appeal

A shake-up of working practices at British Steel signals the end of the steelworker's traditional image

BY STEPHEN OVERELL People Management, 1997

British Steel is set to revolutionise working practices in heavy industry by offering the same employment conditions to blue-collar and white-collar staff.

Under proposals that are to be put out to local negotiations, blue-collar employees would be paid monthly salaries rather than weekly wages, and could be granted longer holidays and better sick-pay terms. In return, they will be asked to adopt flexible working practices.

'Steelworkers of today are miles away from the heat and the dust,' Allan Johnston, British Steel's personnel director, told *People Management*. 'There is not a significant job that isn't operated by a keyboard rather than a hammer, so we need an employment package that reflects this.'

The new deal, which would cost the company £175 million over five years, will also entail more redundancies. British Steel has been shedding jobs at a rate of 1000 every year. The unions fear this annual figure will increase eightfold, and they are to seek assurances that there will

be no compulsory redundancies.

In its heyday, British Steel had a workforce of 269 000 people, but the headcount fell to just 37 000 after privatisation. The company now has 54 000 employees, of whom two-thirds are blue-collar workers.

Johnston said there was an element of 'catch-up' about the employment conditions package, because the steel industry was following the broad thrust of changes that had occurred in other sectors. Last month, for example, 750 000 manual workers employed by local authorities secured a single-status agreement.

Improvements in flexibility mean that steelworkers will be responsible for the maintenance of the equipment they use. Teamworking is to be introduced, while promotion will be based on competence and capability criteria.

'Steel used to be a highly supervised, demarcated, labour-intensive industry, with promotion based on seniority, It is utterly different now,' Johnston said. 'We need highly skilled and highly motivated people, and we believe single status will be a catalyst for change, not an end in itself.'

Grades are likely to be eliminated under a broadbanding drive, and some management tiers will go, although Johnston stressed that none had yet been earmarked. 'We are decentralised, and it will be a matter for local negotiation,' he said.

> 'We need highly skilled and highly motivated people, and we believe single status will be a catalyst for change, not an end in itself.'

The programme will involve a 'substantial' increase in British Steel's spending on training from its current annual budget of £50 million, according to Johnston, who also confirmed that the unions' acceptance of the deal would bring opportunities for pay increases. 'As we make productivity gains, we are of course keen to move the pay of our people forward,' he said.

The main steelworkers' union, the Iron and Steel Trades Confederation (ISTC), said it was delighted with the move. 'The union has been pushing for single status for 20 years,' a spokesman said.

Keith Brookman, the ISTC's general secretary, added: 'It is essential that we help British Steel to stay one step ahead of the competion. But we cannot have – and will not have – compulsory redundancies'.

Various labels are used to describe these new developments in job design – 'flexible specialization', 'neo-Fordism', and 'post-Fordism'. All imply slightly different scenarios, but each identifies a transition away from traditional Taylorist and Fordist job design principles to a more flexible and less dehumanizing way of working. The ideal-typical characteristics of the two approaches to job design are listed in Figure 4.5. In the 1980s, there was a surge of interest in job design techniques developed by Japanese managers. In America, the principles underpinning Japanese job design strategies were later referred to as 'lean' production (Womack, 1990).

Japanese-style job design

The Japanese approach to production and people management, and the apparent diffusion of such practices outside Japan, has attracted considerable attention from academics, students and managers. This interest in Japanese management raises two important questions. The first question has to do with the concept. What are the major characteristics of the Japanese model of management and are these characteristics so unique as to constitute the basis for a new phase in job design? The second question has to do with the impacts of Japanese-style work organization. What are the implications of such management practices for HRM? This section presents answers to these questions and subsequently reviews some of the literature on Japanese management.

In 1986, a British industrial relations theorist, Peter Turnbull, described a new production system at Lucas Electrical (UK) that management had introduced to shift

HRM in practice 4.2

Council management forced to shed tiers

Hackney Council is ridding itself of its 'historical baggage' as part of a radical management overhaul

BY STEPHEN OVERELL People Management, 1997

London's Hackney Council will next week approve a radical organisational shake-up that will see tiers of management axed and top staff forced to reapply for their jobs.

Tony Elliston, Hackney's chief executive, has ambitious plans to see a total management overhaul completed by the beginning of 1998. This is intended to further his aim of pushing the troubled council to the top of Audit Commission league tables.

Under the new structure, units purchasing support services will be free to buy help from the private sector if in-house teams are not up to scratch. Personnel services and training, for example, will each operate as a trading unit, effectively as internal consultancies. There will also be a core central personnel function concerned with top-level recruitment and management and organisational development.

Elliston intends to scrap six director posts and replace them with four new exeuctive direc-

tors. These will have no budgets or staff, but will deal with corporate strategy.

The current tier of 15 assistant directors will be replaced with nine service directors responsible for targets and commissioning services. Delivery will be provided by units that will, in turn, buy support services such as legal, training or personnel from trading units operating in an internal market.

> 'the only thing
> that matters
> is the community
> getting their
> services promptly,
> efficiently and
> professionally.'

Asked about how top staff felt about reapplying for their jobs, Elliston replied: 'Huge changes are going to happen, not just a little here and a little there. If officers can't mirror that in their behaviours, they have got some life choices to

make. New staff will be those most able to do the job.'

Elliston said he was keen to avoid traditional titles such as director of education and director of housing. Instead, service directors will be responsible for areas such as learning and leisure, children and families and estate management and development.

'I do not want to see the creation of fiefdoms,' he said. 'It is only human to want to protect your patch, but they have got to be able to see that the only thing that matters is the community getting their services promptly, efficiently and professionally.'

The shake-up is expected to make initial savings of £5 million, which will be used to extend services or cut council tax bills. Hackney has already trimmed £58 off its bills this year, the largest cut in London. A parallel move towards devolution, with 'one-stop shops' for queries on, for example, housing and social services, is also under way.

labour productivity on to a higher growth path and improve product quality.[5] According to Turnbull, the introduction of a 'module' production system led to a new breed of 'super-craftsmen', who were proficient in a wide range of skills. Turnbull used the term 'Japanization' to describe the organizational changes at Lucas Electrical (UK), because they were based on production methods used by many large Japanese corporations.

	Fordist	Post-Fordist
1. Technology	● fixed, dedicated machines ● vertically integrated operation ● mass production	● micro-electronically controlled multi-purpose machines ● sub-contracting ● batch production
2. Products	● for a mass consumer market ● relatively cheap	● diverse production ● high quality
3. Labour process	● fragmented ● few tasks ● little discretion ● hierarchical authority and technical control	● many tasks for versatile workers ● some autonomy ● group control
4. Contracts	● collectively negotiated rate for the job ● relatively source	● payment by individual performance ● dual market: secure core, highly insecure periphery

Figure 4.5   Ideal types of Fordist and post-Fordist production systems
Source: Warde, 1990

The stereotyped model of Japanese production has three elements, flexibility, quality control, and minimum waste. Flexibility is attained using modular or cellular manufacturing. The system achieves flexibility in two ways, by arranging machinery in a group or 'cell' and by using a flexible multiskilled workforce. Machines are arranged into a 'U-shaped' configuration to enable the workers to complete a whole component, similar to the group technology principle. The job design underpinning a cellular work structure is the opposite to 'Taylorism'. The specialized machinist operating one machine in one particular work station is substituted by a generalized, skilled machinist with flexible job boundaries.

Quality control is the second component of the Japanese production system. The management philosophy of total quality control (TQC) attempts to build quality standards into the manufacturing process by making quality every operator's concern and responsibility. TQC results in job enlargement as cell members undertake new self-inspection tasks and participate in quality improvement activities. With TQC there are savings on labour and raw materials, fewer quality control inspectors, fewer rework hours and less material wasted (Schonberger, 1982, pp. 36–7).

Minimum waste is the third component of the Japanese production model. Waste is eliminated or at least minimized by just-in-time (JIT) production. As the name suggests, it is a hand-to-mouth mode of manufacture which aims to produce the necessary components, in the necessary quantities, of the necessary quality, at the necessary time. It is a system in which stocks of components and raw materials are kept to a minimum; ideally, they are delivered in a matter of days or even hours before use in the manufacturing process. A number of beneficial outcomes have been posited to stem from just-in-time production. At a lower or superficial level, JIT reduces inventory and scrap (Schonberger, 1982). Advocates of JIT argue that when components are produced in small quantities, just-in-time, any defects are discovered quickly and the production of large amounts of substandard work is avoided. At a higher level, JIT attempts to modify employee behaviour and to secure increased employee commitment. Total quality control management may stand alone or may operate in tandem with cellular and just-in-time production.

There is considerable debate among academics as to whether or not Japanese production methods constitute a discrete package of management techniques that can be lifted from their original social and economic context and universally applied. Do Japanese production techniques constitute a significant departure from existing job design principles, Taylorism and human relations (see, for example, Elger and Smith, 1994)? One of the authors, Bratton (1992), has argued elsewhere that the concept of Japanization is a helpful abbreviation for a range of Japanese management practices now being adopted by European and North American managers. The term describes a coherent and distinctive managerial strategy which seeks to enlist employees' ingenuity, initiative and cooperation at the point of production, in order to attain corporate goals (profitability and commitment).

To help you understand the diverse components of the Japanese model, we have developed a theoretical framework for examining the concept of Japanization. Our model is based principally on two recent contributions to the debate on Japanese-style management, Oliver and Wilkinson's (1988) theory of 'high dependency relationships', and Guest's (1987) HRM model. As Figure 4.6 shows, our model has six major components: a set of manufacturing techniques, a set of dependency relationships, a set of HRM policies, a set of supplier policies, a managerial ideology, and a series of outcomes. We shall examine the main dimensions of the model.

The set of manufacturing techniques are cellular technology (CT), just-in-time (JIT), and total quality control (TQC). The principles of these production methods have already been discussed. Japanese manufacturing processes, it is alleged, create a complex web of high-dependency relations which calls for adroit management. The cellular system implies a low level of substitutability and a heightened dependency on a multiskilled workforce. Also TQC heightens dependency when the safety net of the safety inspectors is removed. Further, just-in-time is vulnerable to delays and stoppages. If the company is operating on zero or minimum inventory, late delivery or stoppages due to strikes quickly affect the manufacturing process. As Oliver and Wilkinson point out, 'A mere work-to-rule or overtime ban could be as disastrous for a company operating a JIT system as could a strike for a company not doing so' (1988, p. 135).

Implicit in our model is the need for a set of 'moderators' to counterbalance the company's dependency on its workforce and suppliers. The organization needs to develop mechanisms that exert sufficient influence over employees and suppliers to prevent them exploiting the organization's dependency (Oliver and Wilkinson, 1988). A set of HRM policies is designed to promote a high degree of employee commitment and to minimize the likelihood of industrial stoppages. A unique set of supplier–buyer policies aims to generate a reciprocal obligation between the buyer and the supplier. Another dimension to our model is a managerial ideology which also acts as a moderator. Analyses of large Japanese companies have often conceptualized the corporation as a 'community', and theorists have focused on how workers are socialized into complying with the rules and norms of the 'corporate community'. Dore (1973) identified a multiplicity of ways that the employment relationship entailed obligations beyond the exchange of labour and cash both in the British and the Japanese factories he studied. Japanese workers in large corporations are constantly reminded by management of the 'competition' in the product market. The notion of corporate 'competitiveness' is an ideology that acts to regulate corporate members' behaviour independently from the actual market conditions outside the company. The Japanese approach to job design is characterized by cooperativeness, group problem solving, and attitude control (what may be described as the social organization of work), and the system is characterized by sophisticated production planning. But the social organization of work constitutes a sophisticated control system of employee behaviour. For example, Burawoy (1979) has given an account of how workers in self-organized teams created a work culture that reproduced the conditions of workers' own subordination.

A study of engineering companies in the north of England found evidence of the 'coercive culture system'. Operators working in the cells perceived a moral obligation to work hard, to 'put a full day in', because of peer-group pressure or clan control. The cell members had increased autonomy but the management had increased control through a computerized production system. Management control can therefore be conceptualized by the term 'computer-controlled-autonomy' (Bratton, 1991).

Finally, the outcomes or goals of the system are flexibility both in terms of workforce skills and tasks, minimum waste, and minimum quality defects as they arise in production. Some may question our model of Japanese management. Is it a descrip-

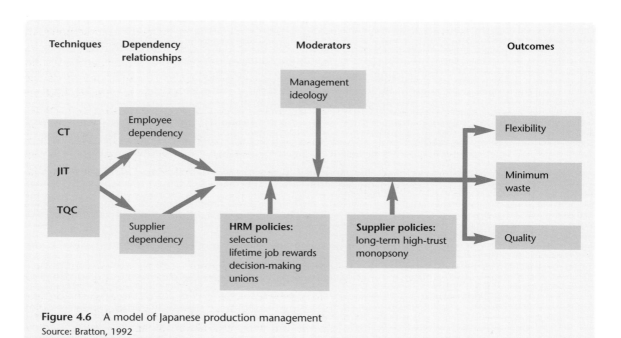

Figure 4.6 A model of Japanese production management
Source: Bratton, 1992

tion of what actually exists even in Japan, or is it a set of manufacturing and employment practices that organizations should implement? Is it a theory or a helpful way
to organize a complex social phenomenon, such as 'Japanese management'?

A number of observers have acknowledged that models of Japanese manufacturing
and employment practices may be based on myths. According to Whittaker (1990)
there are 'multiple' challenges to Japanese-style employment; for example, lifetime
employment and the 'nenko' payment system are undergoing reform in Japan. The
Japanese government has been prodding companies to reform their employment
policies in the light of an ageing population. For example, a Labour Ministry report
said that the practice of lifetime employment should be changed to mirror changing
attitudes about work and careers, and applauded the growing trend in which mainly
young Japanese opt to change jobs, often frequently, rather than sign up for lifetime
employment at a major corporation?[6]

The fact that Japanese employment practices are changing in Japan should not surprise us. A mature capitalist society is a highly complex and dynamic arrangement
and perhaps the only thing that is constant is change itself. Moreover, in the light of
empirical evidence, we should be careful not to dismiss Japanization as insignificant
(see, for example, Oliver and Wilkinson, 1988). Although current practice in job
design may be still some way behind the theoretical models examined in this chapter,
in our view the Japanese model is a perspective on job design worthy of serious study
because it is affecting the way managers approach job design and human resource
management in the workplace today. Jurgens' (1989) study of US, British and German
automobile industries and, more recently, case studies of kaizen and TQM techniques
by Malloch (1997) and Jones (1997) further serve to illustrate that the Japanese production model is more than a 'passing fad'.

The review of the research reported here testifies that, for avant-garde managers on
both sides of the Atlantic, the Japanese model represents the state of the art for job
design. In our view, the model (Figure 4.6) is a useful framework for organizing the
complexities of Japanese management practices and can be judged by its usefulness in
identifying key aspects of management innovations in job design and HRM practices.
It is best conceptualized as an 'ideal type' that can form the basis of experimentation
for Western organizations. It does not necessarily follow that all elements of the
model must, or can, be applied to every workplace. Indeed, there is evidence that the
transfer of Japanese industrial management into British and North American organizations has been highly selective (Jurgens, 1989), and many British companies that
have redesigned jobs do not fully appreciate the high dependency relationships
implicit in the Japanese model (Oliver and Wilkinson, 1988); further, Japanese job
design practices have been installed alongside traditional adversarial industrial relations systems (Bratton, 1992).

Re-engineering movement

The business process re-engineering (BPR) movement declares that organizational
structures and the way work is structured has to be 'radically' changed so that the re-
engineered company can become adaptable and orientated to continuous change and
renewal. According to the re-engineering guru, James Champy (1996), BPR is 'about
changing our managerial work, the way we think about, organize, inspire, deploy,
enable, measure, and reward the value-adding operational work. It is about changing

management itself' (p. 3). Structurally, the typical pyramid-shaped industrial model is stood on its head, management structures are leaner or 'delayered', and decision making pushed down to the 'front line' to meet the contemporary demands of quality, flexibility, low cost, and entrepreneurial autonomy (Hammer and Champy, 1993). Some writers have described these anti-hierarchical characteristics in organizational design as a shift from 'modernist' to 'postmodernist' organizational practices, Clegg outlines the main contrasting postmodern features:

> Where the modern organization was rigid, post-modern organization is flexible... Where modern organization was premised on technological determinism, postmodernism is premised on technological choices made possible through dedicated microelectronic equipment. Where modern organization and jobs were highly differentiated, demarcated and de-skilled, postmodernist organization and jobs are highly differentiated, demarcated and multi-skilled (Clegg, 1990 and quoted by Willmott, 1995, p. 90).

The re-engineered organization allegedly has a number of typical characteristics (see Figure 4.7). Central to these organizational forms, argues Willmott (1995), is the 'reconceptualization of core employees' from being considered a variable cost to being represented as a valuable asset; capable of serving the customer without the need for 'command and control' leadership style. With the ascendancy of 'customer democracy', employees are encouraged to exercise initiative in creating value for customers and thereby profits for the company. According to Hammer (1997):

> Obedience and diligence are now irrelevant. Following orders is no guarantee of success. Working hard at the wrong thing is no virtue. When customers are kings, mere hard work – work without understanding, flexibility, and enthusiasm – leads nowhere. Work must be smart, appropriately targeted, and adapted to the particular circumstances of the process and the customer... Loyalty and hard work are by themselves quaint relics... organizations must now urge employees to put loyalty to the customer over loyalty to the company – because that is the only way the company will survive (pp. 158–9).

Characteristic	Traditional model	Re-engineered model
Market	Domestic	Global
Competitive advantage	Cost	Speed and quality
Resources	Capital	Information
Quality	What is affordable	No compromise
Focal point	Profit	Customer
Structural design	Hierarchical	Flattened
Control	Centralized	De-centralized
Leadership	Autocratic	Shared
Labour	Homogeneous	Culturally diverse
Organization of work	Specialized and individual	Flexible and in teams
Communications	Vertical	Horizontal

Figure 4.7　The re-engineered organization

This passage is most revealing. First, it presents the debate on employee commitment, shared commitment and reciprocity in a different light. We shall return to this in some detail in Chapter 12. Second, in the re-engineered organization, responsibility for the fate of employees shifts from managers to customers. For as Hammer (1997) opines, 'The company does not close plants or lay off workers – customers do, by their actions or inactions' (p. 157). Unlike earlier movements and tendencies in work design, such as the quality of working life movement (QWL), re-engineering is *market driven*. It focuses on the relationship between buyer and seller of services or goods, rather than the relationship between employer and employee. Hammer and Champy emphasize that the 'three Cs ' – customers, competition, and change – and a shift in national government policy of 'tough love' towards business have created the need for re-engineering business processes. For Champy (1996), using a mixture of language discarded by the political 'old Left' and terminology of the 'new Right', 'a dictatorship of the customariat or... a market democracy... is the cause of a total revolution within the traditional, machine-like corporation' (p. 19).

Re-engineering has been criticized by practitioners and academics. One management consultant criticized the imprecise meaning of BPR and pointed out that senior managers were using the term 'to legitimize other objectives' (quoted in *Management Today*, February, 1995). A number of academics are critical of 'postmodern' or 're-engineered' formulations (see Craig and Yetton, 1993; Oliver, 1993; Reed, 1993; Thompson, 1993; Grint and Willcocks, 1995; Willmott, 1995). Thompson, for example, accuses postmodern organizational theorists of having fallen victim to technological determinism and of mistaking the surface of work organizations for their substance. Thompson argues that the 'leaner' organization actually gives more power to a few. 'Removing some of the middle layers of organizations is not the same as altering the basic power structure... By cutting out intermediary levels [of management]... the power resources of those at the top can be increased' (1993, p. 192). Grint and Willcocks (1995) offer a scathing review of BPR, arguing that BPR is not novel and point out that it is 'essentially political in its rhetorical and practical manifestations'. Willmott (1995) is similarly scathing about BPR, emphasizing that re-engineering is 'heavily top-down' and pointing out that the re-engineered organization, using information technology, while creating less hierarchical structures produces 'a fist-full of dynamic processes... notably, the primacy of hierarchical control and the continuing treatment of employees as cogs in the machine' (1995, p. 91). In his case-study analysis of BPR in a hospital, Buchanan (1997) observes that the lack of clarity in BPR terminology and methodology offers 'considerable scope for political maneuvering' by politically motivated actors. A case study of BPR in the public sector found that conflict arose from 'very human needs to justify one's role in the new organization, or individual managers' needs to maintain their power bases within the organization' (Harrington *et al.*, 1998, p. 50). Blair *et al.* (1998) also demonstrate, through case studies, the contradictory aspects of BPR. They emphasize that despite its stated departure from 'Taylorism', the outcomes of BPR are the same as many previous job design 'fads'; 'the development of organizational control systems to secure compliance' (p. 127). Moreover, within the context of the employment relationship, BPR does not obviate the inherent conflict of interest between the two parties: *employers* and *employees*. When examined in the context of employment relations, BPR can be interpreted 'as the latest wave in a series of initiatives... to increase the cooperation/productivity/adaptability of staff' (Willmott, 1995, p. 96).

● **Paradox in job design**

Paradox is evident in job design. The popular logic, for instance, that technological development leads to a more highly skilled workforce has been challenged by numerous observers. Much debate has centred upon the ambiguity involving alternative scenarios of 'upskilling' and 'deskilling' of workers. According to Piore and Sabel (1984), Japanese work arrangements exemplify 'the re-emergence of the craft paradigm'. This interpretation of the Japanese model has its critics. Observers of changes in work structures have asserted that new production regimes that give limited control do not reverse the general deskilling trend but have a tendency to increase the intensity of work (Sayer, 1986; Turnbull, 1986; Tomaney, 1990; Clarke, 1997) and offer management much 'tighter control' of the effort bargain (Malloch, 1997). Using Foucault's Panopticon metaphor a number of writers have produced pessimistic analyses of non-traditional job designs in which work teams function to 'reconstitute the individual as a productive subject' in order to enhance managerial control (Townley, 1994). Others offer a more optimistic analysis, in which the outcomes of new work regimes are less deterministic. Whether non-traditional job design results in 'upskilling' or 'deskilling' of workers depends, among other things, on factors such as batch size, managerial choice and negotiation (Bratton, 1992). Although managerial techniques for monitoring work teams remain primitive, work team autonomy has not eliminated worker resistance and managerial control continues to be contested (McKinlay and Taylor, 1998). Similarly, the debate on BPR has focused on whether the empowerment of employees has resulted in work structures that are necessarily less restrictive or repressive than those designed following Taylorist principles. Willmott (1995), for example, asserts that, with the assistance of micro-technology, re-engineering is an 'up-dating of Taylor's crusade against custom and practice in which the silicon chip plays an equivalent role in [re-engineering] to that performed by the stop watch in Scientific Management' (p. 96). The rewards for managers and non-managers of jettisoning the old ways of doing work and old values appear to be largely psychological and symbolic in terms of personal growth and empowerment.

Whether organizations adopt Japanese job design practices or BPR, advocated by Hammer and Champy (1993), Champy (1996) and Hammer (1997), will clearly impact on the nature of work and on managers and non-managers, and puts HRM centre stage. However, the precise nature of the impact of these job design strategies is subject to debate, as are the concepts of Japanization and BPR. For HRM practitioners, attention has focused on the implications of job redesign for employee's health and safety (see Chapter 5), the need for workplace learning (see Chapter 10), and the need to synchronize human resource management and labour relations to new work structures (see Chapter 12).

Chapter summary

The discussion of organizational and job design has been somewhat theoretical. This chapter first examined the meaning of work in contemporary Western society and proceeded to evaluate alternative job design strategies including scientific management, job enrichment, Japanese work structures, and organizational re-engineering. These job design movements are summarized in Figure 4.8. We must now conclude this discussion

Figure 4.8 Four approaches to job design

	Motivation assumptions	Critical techniques	Job classification	Issues
Scientific management	Motivation is based on the piecework incentive system of pay. The more pieces the worker produces the higher the pay	Division of tasks and responsibilities Task analysis 'one best way' Training Rewards	Division of tasks and of 'doing' and 'control' leads to many job classifications	Criteria of motivation may be questioned No role for unions Cooperation costs Product inflexibility
Job enrichment	Motivation is based on social needs and expectations of workers. To increase performance focus on achievement, recognition, responsibility	Combining tasks Increase accountability Create natural work units Greater responsibility	Some supervisory tasks are undertaken by workers as the 'control' is shifted downwards	Criteria of motivation may be questioned Undefined union role
Japanese management	Motivation is based on teamwork or 'clan-like' norms and the organization culture. Performance and motivation are social processes in which some workers try to influence others to work harder	Intensive socialization Lifetime employment Consensual decision making Non-specialized career paths Seniority-based pay	Requires fewer job classifications because of flexibility and a degree of autonomy	Criteria of motivation may be culture-bound Collaborative union role Work intensification
Re-engineering	Motivation is based on the need to serve the customer. Performance and motivation are social processes in which strong leaders enthuse workers to work smarter	Organizational norms and traditions abandoned Networking Strong top-down leadership Workplace learning IT enables change Processes have multiple versions	Multidimensional jobs Workers organized into process teams Workers are empowered to make decisions	Criteria of motivation may be questioned Market driven Undefined union role Work intensification

through the identification of some practical implications for HR professionals. It should be apparent to the reader that the way work is designed is critical for HRM. Job design affects both an organization's competitiveness and the experience and motivation of the individual and work group. Further, fundamental innovations in job design, implied in Japanese-style work structures or in the re-engineered organization, mean that recruitment and selection, performance appraisal, rewards, training and development must change. It also means that the HR professional has not only to develop new policies and competencies around these functional areas, but she or he has to cope with the contradictions, paradoxes, and tensions associated with any new work structure.

Key concepts

Work	**Job design**
Scientific management	**Job enrichment/Job enlargement**
Human relations movement	**Job characteristic model**
Fordism	**Postmodernism**
Japanization	**Business process re-engineering**

Discussion questions

1. What is meant by the term 'work'?

2. Explain the limits of Taylorism as a job design strategy.

3. 'Job rotation, job enlargement and job enrichment are simply attempts by managers to control individuals at work.' Do you agree or disagree? Discuss.

4. Students often complain about doing group projects. Why? Relate your answer to autonomous work teams. Would you want to be a member of such a work group? Discuss your reasons.

5. 'The notion of Japanization is a chaotic conception.' '"Japanization" is a useful framework for organizing the complexities of Japanese management practices.' Critically evaluate these two statements. Discuss your reasons.

6. Explain the stereotypical re-engineered work organization, as you would picture it, in terms of the job characteristic model. What main principles or practices can be identified as a source of efficiency? Can the re-engineered model be universal? Why?

Further reading

Bratton, J. (1992) *Japanization at Work: Managerial Studies for the 1990s*, London: Macmillan.

Elger, T. and Smith, C. (eds) (1994) *Global Japanization? The Transformation of the Labour Process*, London: Routledge.

Hammer, M. (1997) *Beyond Reengineering*, New York: HarperBusiness.

Malloch, H. (1997) Strategic and HRM aspects of kaizen: a case study, *New Technology, Work and Employment*, **12**(2): 108–22.

McKinlay, A. and Taylor, P. (1998) Through the looking glass: Foucault and the politics of production. In McKinlay, A. and Starkey, K. (eds) *Foucault, Management and Organizational Theory*, London: Sage.

Pahl, R.E. (ed.) (1988) *On Work: Historical, Comparative and Theroretical Approaches*, Oxford: Blackwell.

Piore M.J. and Sabel, C.F. (1984) *The Second Industrial Divide*, New York: Basic Books.

Whittaker, D.H. (1990) *Managing Innovation: A Study of British and Japanese Factories*, Cambridge: Cambridge University Press.

Willmott, H. (1995) The odd couple?: re-engineering business processes: managing human relations, *New Technology, Work and Employment*, **10**(2): 89–98.

Chapter case study

Wolds Insurance plc

Wolds Insurance plc is a large insurance company that employs 1850 people in its branches throughout the UK. The company's head office is in Manchester where it was established in 1928.

The underwriting department at the Newcastle branch consists of thirteen clerks, of whom one is a section head and one a head of department. The nature of the work in the department has fundamentally changed over the last twenty years, from book-keeping and an accounting process to clerical processing. There are various types of policy, the main difference being between 'commercial' and 'personal'. The vast majority of policies taken out are personal. Until late 1991, the underwriting department was divided into personal and commercial sections, but in January 1992 these were combined. Although clerks vary in the mix of commercial and personal policies they deal with, the variety in the work of each clerk is small.

Before 1988, the process of policy issue at branch level was manual with the premium being calculated by the use of manuals and charts. Details of the policy would be sent to head office and issued from there. Head office introduced a mainframe computer for this process in 1983, but the procedure at branch level remained much the same until mid-1988, when the VDTs were installed in the underwriting department.

At first the department was not 'on-line' and premiums still had to be calculated manually. Policy details, however, were to be keyed in directly and the VDT was used to check the details of any given policy. In 1989 the system went 'on-line', details of the policy being keyed in direct at branch level. In 1991, the computer was programmed to calculate premiums automatically. Management's aim was to computerize as many policies as possible through complex programming and standardization of product. This reduced the processing time. For the majority of policies it was necessary only to transfer details from form to screen and to use the right classification as specified in the manual. Before on-line computerization a clerk could do 35 policies a week and after computerization 80 policies a week could be processed.

Clerical staff numbers were reduced to a third inside three years and the previously separate departments of commercial and personal were combined into one. The division of work in the branch was divided into four functions, underwriting, claims, cash, and accounts. In addition, the clerks were divided into two types of employee, those knowledgeable on insurance, capable of answering enquiries and dealing with non-standard cases, and those who processed routine policies. In terms of knowledge required, standardization had reduced the differences between the policies and for some had reduced the knowledge required. Many of the policies are now offered on a 'take it or leave it' basis and the processing of the policy is routine and repetitive, requiring little knowledge of insurance. Details of the customer and cover required are keyed into the computer in the specified order and the premium is calculated automatically. Some knowledge of insurance is still required nonetheless for dealing with the enquiries.

The underwriting clerks are beginning to show signs of frustration, as much of their working day is spent on routine processing. There is also tension between the clerks doing the routine processing and those clerks working on the non-standard and more interesting cases. These factors are resulting in serious morale problems, high absenteeism and increasing mistakes in the processing. The manager of the department and the HR manager realize that changes are needed, but it is not clear to them how to improve the situation.

(The case is based on 'Skill, deskilling and new technology in the non-manual labour process' by Heather Rolfe (1986) *New Technology, Work and Employment*, **1**(1): 37–49.)

Task

You have recently been appointed HR assistant at Wold Insurance. You have been asked by June Cole, the HR manager, to consider ways of 'enriching' the work of the underwriting clerks. Prepare a written report focusing on the following questions:

1. What symptoms suggest there is something wrong in the underwriting department?
2. Using the job design concepts discussed in this chapter, suggest how to improve the clerical jobs in the underwriting department.

You may make any assumptions you feel are necessary in your response, providing they are realistic and you make them explicit.

Notes

1. A shop steward discussing the changes in job design (quoted in Bratton, 1992, p. 165).
2. Smith, M. (1989) Team spirit makes workers happier at Lucas, *Financial Times*, 31 January.
3. Hammer, M. (1997) *Beyond Reengineering*, New York: HarperCollins, p. xi.
4. According to David McGregor (1960) *The Human Side of Enterprise*, New York: McGraw-Hill, 'people work because they want to work', not because they have to work. Thus, the Theory Y view of people assumed that when workers are given challenging assignments and autonomy over work assignments, they will respond with high motivation, high commitment, and high performance.
5. Turnbull, P. (1986) The Japanisation of British industrial relations at Lucas, *Industrial Relations Journal*, **17**(3): 193–206.
6. Annual labor report applauds job hopping and predicts fewer services for consumers, *Asahi Evening News*, Japan, 1 July, 1992, p. 4.

chapter five

Employee health and safety

John Bratton

In Britain today more people die from occupational disease than from accidents at work but nearly half the working population has no access to an occupational health service.[1]

There is a fair amount of air contamination on the [factory] floor. Ventilation is poor. It's far too hot. There is a build up of fumes. We get people complaining of headaches. Dermatitis is a problem, that's been linked to the coolant we use... We are supposed to have safety representatives, but it's become so lax.[2]

Chapter outline

Chapter objectives

After studying this chapter, you should be able to:

1. Explain the benefits of a healthy and safe workplace.
2. Discuss some key developments in occupational health and safety.
3. Describe the major health and safety legislation in Britain.
4. Identify some contemporary health and safety hazards in the workplace.
5. Summarize the health and safety responsibilities of management and employees.

● Introduction

The need to provide a safe work environment for employees has had a long history in personnel management. In Beer *et al.*'s (1984) model of HRM, it is acknowledged that work systems can not only affect commitment, competence, cost effectiveness, and congruence – the 'four Cs' – but also have long-term consequences for individual well-being, 'there is some evidence to indicate that work system design may have effects on physical health, mental health, and longevity of life itself' (1984, p. 153). This certainly understates the importance of safe and healthy work systems to the health of employees. Compared to other elements of the HRM model, workplace health and safety is under-researched by HRM scholars and has been largely neglected in the HRM discourse. This is one reason – together with the rising cost of health, new laws and the 'deregulatory' proposals – why more research should be devoted to workplace health and safety by HRM specialists, and why we have included the topic in *Part one* of this book, as part of the context of HRM. However, there is another important reason why HRM scholars and practitioners need to pay more attention to health and safety. It is this. If strategic HRM means anything, it must encompass the development and promotion of a set of health and safety policies to protect the organization's most valued asset, its employees.

Health and safety legislation and regulations provide part of the legal context of HRM. But health and safety is not simply a technical issue such as, for instance, supplying hard hats and goggles or ensuring adequate ventilation. Above all, workplace health and safety raises the question of economic costs and power relations. As Sass (1982, p. 52) emphasized:

> In all technical questions pertaining to workplace health and safety there is the social element. That is, for example, the power relations in production: who tells whom to do what and how fast. After all, the machine does not go faster by itself; someone designed the machinery, organized the work, designed the job.[3]

The management of health and safety is influenced by a variety of factors, internal and external to organizations, including economic costs, government, trade unions, and public opinion. The economic cost of occupational health and safety to the organization is double-edged. On the one hand, health and safety measures which protect employees from the hazards of the workplace can conflict with management's objective of containing production costs. On the other, effective health and safety policies can improve the performance of employees and the organization, by reducing costs associated with accidents, disabilities, absenteeism, or illness.

As in other aspects of the employment relationship, government legislation and the health and safety inspectorate influence managements' approach to health and safety. The Health and Safety at Work etc. Act. (HASAWA) 1974, for instance, requires employers to ensure the health, safety and welfare at work of all employees. Furthermore, since the passing of the Single European Act in 1987, an organization's health and safety policies are also influenced by EU directives and the Social Chapter. In Britain, the Health and Safety Commission (HSC) has the overall responsibility for workplace health and safety. Growing public awareness and concern about 'green' and environmental issues has had an effect on occupational health and safety. Organizations have had to become more sensitive to workers' health and general environmental concerns. Manufacturing, for example, 'environment friendly' products and services and using ecologically sustainable processes present a continuing challenge to all managers in the 1990s. Survey data also appear to confirm that managers in British workplaces are having to deal with health and safety issues unilaterally (Millward *et al*, 1992, pp. 162–3). Running parallel with these social developments is the growing demand from powerful business lobbies to 'deregulate' business operations, including dismantling health and safety legislation (Bain, 1997)

Health and safety and the HRM cycle

The employer has a duty to maintain a healthy and safe workplace. The health and safety function is directly related to the elements of the HRM cycle – selection, appraisal, rewards and training. Health and safety considerations and policy can affect the selection process in two ways. It is safe to assume that in the recruitment process potential applicants will be more likely to be attracted to an organization that has a reputation for offering a healthy and safe work environment for employees. The maintenance of a healthy and safe workplace can be facilitated in the selection process by selecting applicants with personality traits that decrease the likelihood of an accident. The appraisal of a manager's performance that incorporates the safety record of a department or section can also facilitate health and safety. Research suggests that safety management programmes are more effective when the accident rates of their sections are an important criterion of managerial performance. Safe work behaviour can be encouraged by a reward system that ties bonus payments to the safety record of a work group or section. Some organizations also provide prizes to their employees for safe work behaviour, a good safety record or suggestions to improve health and safety. Training and HR development play a critical role in promoting health and safety awareness among employees. The HASAWA (1974) requires employers to provide instruction and training to ensure the health and safety of their employees. Studies indicate that safety training for new employees is particularly beneficial because accidents are highest during the early months on a new job.

On the question of the importance of occupational health and safety, while economic cost and HRM considerations will always be predominant for the organization, the costs of ill-health and work-related accidents are not only borne by the victims, families, and their employers. Clearly, the costs of occupational ill-health and accidents are also borne by the taxpayer and public sector services. The health care sector, for example, bears the costs of workplace ill-health and accidents. Reliable estimates of the total costs of occupational ill-health and accidents are incomplete, which is perhaps symptomatic of the low priority given to this area of work in the UK. A Health and Safety Executive (HSE) document admitted that: 'Although occupational diseases kill more people in the UK each year than industrial accidents, there is only limited information about them'. A recent official survey put the costs to society for deaths and accidents (excluding occupational disease) in British workplaces at £10–15 billion or 1.75–2.75 per cent of the Gross Domestic Product.[4]

This chapter explains why a working knowledge of occupational health and safety is important for every manager in general, and its importance to HRM functions in particular. After giving a brief history of occupational health and safety, we review health and safety legislation in Britain, and draw some comparisons with the legislation elsewhere. The chapter also discusses several contemporary health and safety problems including sick building syndrome (SBS), occupational stress, smoking, alcoholism and drug use, and AIDS. The chapter then proceeds to examine what managers can do to develop, promote and maintain a healthy and safe workplace.

The World Health Organization defines health as 'a state of complete physical, mental and social well-being, not merely an absence of disease and infirmity'.[5] According to this definition, managers are immersed in one of society's greatest challenges: the design and maintenance of a work organization that is both effective in meeting business objectives and healthy and safe to its employees. It is unfortunately true that, until relatively recently, the attitude of managers and employees towards accident and safety did not promote a healthy or safe workplace.

The changing approach to workplace health and safety

The traditional approach to safety in the workplace used the 'careless worker' model. It was assumed by most employers, the courts and accident prevention bodies that most of the accidents were due to an employee's failure to take safety seriously or to protect herself or himself. The implication of this is that work can be made safe simply by changing the behaviour of employees by poster campaigns and accident prevention training. In the past, the attitudes of trade unions often paralleled those of the employers and managers. Early trade union activity tended to focus on basic wage and job security issues rather than safety. Trade union representatives used their negotiating skill to 'win' wage increases, and health and safety often came rather low down in their bargaining priorities. If union representatives did include health and safety as part of their activities, it was often to negotiate the payment of 'danger' or 'dirt' money, over and above the regular wage rate. According to Eva and Oswald (1981, p. 33), the tendency for union officials was 'to put the onus on to inspectors and government rather than to see health and safety as part of the everyday activity of local union representatives'. Among employees dangerous and hazardous work systems were accepted as part of the risk of working. Lost fingers and deafness, for instance, were viewed as a matter of 'luck' or the 'inevitable' outcome of work. In the early 1970s, a major investigation into occupational health and safety concluded that 'the most important single reason for accidents of work is apathy' (Robens, 1972, p. 1). There is a paradox here. When there are major disasters on land, air and sea involving fatalities, society as a whole takes a keen interest. Yet, although every year hundreds of employees die and thousands receive serious injuries in the workplace, society's reaction tends to be muted.

In the 1960s, something like a thousand employees were killed at their work in the UK. Every year of that decade about 500 000 employees suffered injuries in varying degrees of severity, and 23 million working days were lost annually on account of industrial injury and disease. Such statistics led investigators to argue that 'for both humanitarian and economic reasons, no society can accept with complacency that such levels of death, injury, disease and waste must be regarded as the inevitable price of meeting its needs for goods and services' (Robens, 1972, p. 1). Since the Robens report, there has been a growing interest in occupational health and safety. Moreover, it has been recognized that the 'careless worker' model does not explain occupational ill-health caused by toxic substances, noise, and badly designed and unsafe systems of work. Nor does this perspective highlight the importance of job stress, fatigue and poor working environments in contributing to the causes of accidents. A new approach to occupational health and safety, the 'shared responsibility' model, assumes that the best way to reduce levels of occupational accidents and disease relies on the cooperation of

Figure 5.1   A trade union view on workplace health and safety
Source: Eva and Oswald, 1981

both employers and employees; a 'self-generating effort' between 'those who create the risks and those who work with them' (Robens, 1972, p. 7).

In the late 1970s, the British TUC articulated a 'trade union approach' to health and safety, which emphasized that the basic problem of accidents stems from the hazards and risks that are built into the workplace. The trade union approach argued that the way to improve occupational health and safety was through redesigning organizations and work systems so as to 'remove hazards and risks at source'.[6] A Health and Safety Executive (HSE) document would seem to support this approach by stating 'Most accidents involve an element of failure in control – in other words failure in managerial skill... A guiding principle when drawing up arrangements for securing health and safety should be that so far as possible work should be adapted to people and not vice versa.'[7] Trade unions can have a different approach to health and safety as Figure 5.1 depicts. Statistics show that in Britain, during 1993–94, for instance, 403 employees were killed and 29 531 suffered major injuries (fractures, loss of limbs and so on) at work, and 137 459 employees suffered injuries necessitating at least three days off work.[8]

The importance of health and safety

Apart from the humanitarian reasons, there are strong economic reasons why managers should take health and safety seriously. In considering the economics of an unhealthy and unsafe workplace it is necessary to distinguish between costs falling upon the organization and costs falling upon government funded bodies, such as hospitals.

According to the Central Statistical Office's annual *Social Trends* survey, UK employees take more days off sick than any other country in the European Union apart from the Netherlands. In 1991, on average about 2.7 per cent of the working week is lost through illness or injury in the UK, compared to under 1 per cent in Greece. It is not difficult for an organization to calculate the economic costs of a work-related accident. An accident is an unforeseen or unplanned event that results in an injury and material damage or loss. The list of cost headings, shown in Figure 5.2, demonstrates that designing and maintaining a safe work environment can improve productivity by reducing time lost due to work-related accidents, as well as avoiding the costs present in every work-related accident and illness.

HRM in practice 5.1

Death renews charge of 'SAS-style' training

Employer and peer pressure on trainees to succeed on outdoor courses may be as dangerous as poor safety procedures

BY JILLY WELCH People Management, March 1997

Questions are again being raised about the safety of outdoor training programmes after the death of a participant on a management development event in Scotland.

It is believed that Stewart Barr, a 39-year-old ambulance man, suffered a fatal heart attack while on a hike. Other participants claim that his request to be excused from carrying a 13kg rucksack 600m up a steep incline was refused by instructors.

Another man had to be taken to hospital, and several others on the course complained of exhaustion.

Unison, the public services union, has called for a ban on 'SAS style' commercial training courses. It has also asked the Health and Safety Executive to conduct a full inquiry into the incident.

Outdoor activity courses, which are used by many organisations (including Barr's employer, the Scottish Ambulance Service), are still not covered by the safety legislation

enacted last year in response to the Lyme Bay canoeing tragedy. Courses open to adults are a low priority for safety inspectors – a situation that must change, according to David Taylor, an outdoor training safety advisor to the executive.

'I could not stand up in a coroner's court and justify some of the practices that go on in the name of training around the UK,' said Taylor, who is also development advisor at the Dove Nest training

> **'I could not stand up in a coroner's court and justify some of the practices that go on in the name of training around the UK'**

centre in Cumbria. 'After Lyme Bay, we thought we had got rid of these sorts of operators, but a minority are not carrying out adequate risk assessments on trainees.'

But Taylor believes there is an underlying problem rooted in

companies' attitudes to outdoor training and pressure. The practice of putting participants under both mental and physical strain in order to assess their aptitude may be causing individuals to push themselves too hard.

'There is minimal justification for putting men and women under physiological stress,' he said. 'You have to separate mental agility from physical strength.'

The Royal Navy is about to offer employers just such a mix of physical and mental rigour. Its new School of Leadership and Management is planning to apply a technique it uses to train officers, the 'deep-water challenge' simulation, to civilian participants.

But the course leader, Lieutenant Commander Andrew Griffiths, does not feel that the challenge, involving a small cabin rapidly filling with water, would prove dangerous for unfit trainees. 'The exercise does become more and more demanding and we get a lot of energy going in there, but people can drop out if they want,' he said. 'It's absolutely voluntary.'

Mars, which has used fire services' training facilities, also says that there is an unwritten agreement whereby its employees can choose not to complete a course. But these assurances are challenged by Alan Bickerstaff, Unison's branch secretary at the Scottish Ambulance Service.

'Whether it is through peer pressure or direct management pressure to succeed on these courses, accidents are happening,' he said. 'Staff on Barr's course certainly felt that their performance would have a bearing on their future at work – and that has a bearing on this tragedy.'

There are also indirect costs associated with work-related accidents. In the example cited in the Robens Report, the costs arising from an accident involving a fork-lift truck which was driven too fast round a factory gangway corner is calculated (Figure 5.2). The indirect costs include overtime payments necessary to make up for lost production, cost of retaining a replacement employee, a wage cost for the time spent by HRM personnel recruiting, selecting and training the new employee and, in less typical cases, the cost associated with loss of revenue on orders cancelled or lost if the accident causes a net long-term reduction on sales, and attendance at court hearings in contested cases. The economic costs of work-related accidents, and the techniques for assessing them, require further research. A Canadian study, however, suggests that indirect costs of work-related accidents could range from 2 to 10 times the direct costs (Stone and Meltz, 1988, p. 502). Recent case studies conducted by the Health and Safety Executive indicate that the cost of industrial accidents can be as high as 37 per cent of associated profits and 5 per cent of operating costs (quoted in *Personnel Management Plus*, February 1993). A healthy and safe work environment helps to reduce costs and improve organizational effectiveness. If work-related illnesses and accidents can be transposed on to the balance sheet the organization can apply the same management effort and creativity to designing and maintaining a healthy and safe workplace as managers customarily apply to other facets of the business. As Robens stated 'accident prevention can be integrated into the overall economic activity of the firm' (1972, p. 140).

In addition to improving productivity and reducing costs, maintaining a healthy and safe work environment helps to facilitate employee commitment to quality and to improve industrial relations. One of the side effects of a proactive health and safety policy is that it leads to improved productivity and quality. Collard (1989) reports that in two foreign companies studied, a CAP (cost and productivity) programme was continually emphasized by top management and 'one major aspect of this was the highest standards of housekeeping' (1989, p. 4). Further, it is argued that employee and union–management relations can be improved when employers satisfy their employees' health and safety needs. Increasingly, trade unions have been focusing their attention on health and safety concerns.

In some cases, new provisions covering health and safety have been negotiated into collective agreements. When employers take a greater responsibility for occupational health and safety it can change employee behaviour and employees might take a less militant stance during wage bargaining if management pay attention to housekeeping. Implied in Beer *et al.*'s (1984) HRM model, attention to workplace health and

Figure 5.2 The estimated cost of a workplace accident

1. Cost of wages paid for the time spent by injured workpeople: £
    (a) assisting the injured person, or out of curiosity, sympathy and
    so on, or
    (b) who were unable to continue work because they relied on his
    aid or output
    In category (a) 6 employees lost on average 20 minutes 13.46
    In category (b) 3 workers lost on average 60 minutes 20.19

2. Cost of material or equipment damage:
    In this instance the casing of a 5 hp electric motor was cracked
    beyond repair and replaced by a new motor 400.00
    Installation cost 100.00

3. Cost of injured worker's time lost:
    Treatment for abrasion on leg. 2 hours lost at £6.73 per hour 13.46

4. Supervisor's time spent assisting, investigating, reporting, assigning
    work, training or instructing a replacement and making other
    necessary adjustments:
    One and a half hours at £8.00 12.00

5. Wage cost of decreased output by injured worker after return to work:
    4 days at 2 hours/day light work 56.00

6. Medical cost to the company:
    (A reduction in accidents does not necessarily mean lower expenses
    for running the works medical centre) 35.00

7. Cost of time spent by administration staff and specialists on
    investigations or in the processing of compensation questions.
    HM Factory Inspector reports, insurance company and Department of
    Health and Social Security correspondence and so on:
    Low in this case 50.00

    TOTAL: **700.11**

Additional Charges
Other cost elements not applicable to this accident but which must be considered in
others include:
Overtime necessary to make up for lost production.
Cost of learning period of a replacement worker.
A wage cost for the time spent by supervisors or others in training the new worker.
Miscellaneous costs (includes the less typical costs, the validity of which will need to be
clearly shown with respect to each accident):
– renting equipment
– loss of profit on orders cancelled or loss if the accident causes a net long-term
   reduction in sales
– cost of engaging new employees (if this is significant)
– cost of excess spoilage of work by new employees (if above normal)
– attendance at court hearings in contested cases.
Costs such as these are present in nearly every accident.

Source: Robens, 1972, p. 189. The original figures have been adjusted for inflation.

safety can have a strong, positive effect on employee commitment. When employees work in a healthy and safe workplace, higher levels of motivation, performance and loyalty will result.

A major challenge to HRM professionals is to provide a healthy and safe work environment for employees. Humanitarian and economic reasons dictate such a policy but, as we have already stated, there is also a pervasive portfolio of legislation, regulations, codes of practice, and guidance notes dealing with occupational health and safety and, as with other employment law, the human resource practitioner has taken on the role of advising managers on the content and legal obligations of this.

Health and safety legislation

The history of occupational safety legislation can be traced back to the Industrial Revolution and the early factory system in the eighteenth century. The conditions of employment in the new factories were appalling. Dangerous machinery, long hours of work, and poor diet caused physical deformity, as indicated by this 1833 testimony:

> I can bear witness that the factory system in Bradford has engendered a multitude of cripples, and that the effect of long continued labour upon the physique is apparent not only in actual deformity, but also, and much more generally, in stunted growth, relaxation of the muscles, and delicacy of the whole frame.[9]

The early conditions of employment have to be related to their context before they can be evaluated historically. It must be remembered that employment standards were low before the process of industrialization began. Comparisons of conditions of employment and health and safety provisions must begin from here, not from late twentieth-century standards. Many employment practices in the early factories were inherited from the pre-industrial era. An example of this is child labour. In the new factories children worked for their parents, collecting wastes and tying threads, as they had done at home. These children were necessarily involved in the same hours of work as the adults for whom they worked. Family labour was a bridge between the conditions of employment in the pre-factory world and the new factory system. Family labour was not automatically abolished by the early Factory Acts. Early legislation attempted to regulate the hours of work and employment conditions of women and children.

Up to the 1820s, the main pressure for imposing a minimum age and for limiting the hours of factory work came from humanitarians, and some enlightened employers, such as 'the philanthropic Mr Owen of New Lanark' (Mathias, 1969). The 1802 Health and Morals of Apprentices Act was designed to curb some of the abuses of child labour. This Act applied only to pauper apprentices in the factories; it restricted hours of work to twelve, prohibited night work, and provided for instruction in the 'three Rs'. Inspection was to be by a magistrate appointed by the local justices of the peace.

Enforcement of the 1802 Factory Act was ineffective since the inspectors were 'generally well disposed to the mill-owner' (Gregg, 1973, p. 55). The 1833 Factory Act outlawed the employment of children under 9, limited the hours of work of children between 9 and 13 to eight hours per day, and appointed four government factory inspectors to enforce the legal requirements. An Act of 1844 imposed limited requirements for guarding dangerous machinery in textile mills where women and children were employed. The early safety legislation was confined to textile factories and affected the conditions of employment for women and children only. No limitations were imposed on adult men in the textile factories, and it was not until the 1870s that safety regulations extended to cover non-textile factories, such as pottery, match making, iron and steel making, railways and shipping. During the period 1850 to 1900, Factory Acts were amended, tightened and extended to new industries due to a combination of factors, including social reformers, the inspectorate and, more significantly, campaigning by a growing and more militant trade union movement. Eva and Oswald (1981) assert that many of the work stoppages and campaigns, and the occasional 'mob riot', were over a variety of issues in which safety at work played a part. The introduction of safety regulations was painfully slow. Progress was hindered by consistent opposition from the majority of employers who claimed the Factory Acts would make British industry uncompetitive. In 1856, for instance, employers succeeded in lowering the standards for guarding machinery where women and children worked. The 1867 Factory Act extended safety laws beyond the textile mills, and even began to abandon the myth that safety law's only purpose was to protect women and children; adult male employees were considered, theoretically at least, capable of protecting themselves (Hobsbawm, 1968). The 1901 Factories and Workshops (Consolidation) Act introduced a more comprehensive health and safety code for industrial workplaces. The 1901 Act drew together five other statutes passed since 1878, and was followed in its turn by a large number of detailed regulations. It remained the governing Act until the Factories Act of 1937. The subsequent Acts of 1948 and 1959 added some new provisions but produced no fundamental changes in the scope and pattern of the legislation. Industrial safety legislation was consolidated by the Factories Act of 1961.

The 1961 Factories Act defined a 'factory' as any premises in which two or more persons are employed in manual labour in any process for the purpose of economic gain. One aspect of the definition – a place cannot be a factory unless it is one in which manual labour is performed – caused some litigation. Part I of the Act is concerned with general provisions affecting the health of the factory employee. Thus, the Act establishes minimum standards in factories on cleanliness, space for employees to work in, temperature, ventilation, and lighting. The Act laid down very specific standards: for example, a factory will be deemed to be overcrowded if the amount of cubic space is less than 400 cubic feet for every employee in the workroom. The basic rule for temperature is that after the first 30 minutes the temperature should not be less than 60°F (15.5°C) in rooms where much of the work is done sitting and does not involve serious physical effort.

Part II of the Act lays down general requirements aimed at promoting the safety of factory employees. The Act governs the fencing of machinery in factories. Section 14(1) provides that 'Every dangerous part of any machinery... shall be securely fenced'. There are further requirements relating to lifting equipment, floors and gangways, access to the workplace, ventilation and inflammable gas. The Act also contains general welfare provisions such as the adequate supply and maintenance of washroom facilities, and a statutory reporting system for accidents and industrial diseases.

The Mines and Quarries Act 1954 provides a comprehensive and detailed code governing safety underground and in quarries. The rise in employment in the service sector and the growth of white-collar trade unionism help explain the extension of legal protection to office and retail employees. The Offices, Shops and Railway Premises Act

1963 extended to these premises protection similar to that provided for factories. The general provisions follow that of the Factories Act 1961 and deal with cleanliness, lighting and temperatures, and so on. The Factories Act 1961 and the Offices, Shops and Railway Premises Act 1963 were the principal provisions on health and safety before the subsequent Health and Safety at Work etc. Act 1974.

The Robens Report

Occupational health and safety came under detailed scrutiny in the early 1970s by a government appointed committee chaired by Lord Robens. In the 1960s, white-collar trade unions pressed for health and safety legislation to be extended to cover employees in laboratories, education, hospitals and local government who were not covered by any of the earlier statutes. In 1968, the Labour government set up the Robens Committee on Safety and Health at Work to review the whole field and to make recommendations. The Robens Committee's wide-ranging report criticized attitudes and the existing state of health and safety law. To summarize the findings of the Committee:

- Despite a wide range of legal regulation, work continued to kill, maim, and sicken tens of thousands of employees each year. The Committee considered that the most important reason for this unacceptable state of affairs was *apathy*.
- There was *too much law*. The Committee identified eleven major statutes which were supported by nearly 500 supplementary statutory instruments. The Committee believed that the sheer volume of law had become counterproductive.
- Much of the law was often *obscure*, *haphazard*, and *out of date*. Many laws regulated obsolete production processes. Further, the law focused on physical safeguards rather than preventive measures such as training and joint consultation.
- The provision for *enforcement* of the existing legislation was fragmented and ineffective. The Committee felt that the pattern of control was one of 'bewildering complexity'.
- Existing health and safety law *ignored large numbers of employees*. Over 8 million workers in communication, education, hospitals and local government were not covered by any statutes prior to 1974.

The Committee made four main proposals to improve occupational health and safety:

1. The law should be rationalized. A unified framework of legislation should be based upon the employment relationship (not on a factory or mine). All employers involved with work or affected by work activities (except domestic servants in private homes) were to be covered by the new legislation.
2. A self-regulating system involving employers, employees and union representatives should be created to encourage organizational decision makers to design and maintain safe work systems and help employees to take more responsibility for health and safety. The basic concept should be that of the employer's duty to his or her employees; employers should design and maintain safe and healthy systems of work, and the concomitant duty of the employee is to behave in a manner that safeguards her or his own health and that of her or his co-workers.

3. A new unified statutory framework setting out general principles should be enacted.
4. A new unified enforcement agency headed by a national body with overall responsibility should be established, and should be provided with new, stronger powers of sanction.

The Labour government lost the 1970 general election before the Committee completed its research. In 1972, the Robens Committee published its report and the Conservative government introduced a new Bill in Parliament. Two years later, the Conservatives lost the general election. In 1974, the Labour government re-introduced a similar Bill which became the Health and Safety at Work etc. Act 1974, which the next section examines.

The Health and Safety at Work etc. Act (HASWA) 1974

HASWA vested trade unions with significant powers in regard to workplace health and safety matters and as Nichols (1990) points out, compared to the 1980s and 90s, the Act was 'a product of a different politics and philosophy' (p. 336). The complete coverage of this complex Act is outside the scope of this chapter. The approach we have adopted is to highlight the salient features of the Act so that the student of HRM can become familiar with some important principles and terminology. The main duties on employers are contained within Section 2 of the Act (Figure 5.3).

EU legislation

In the 1990s, EU directives under Article 189 of the Treaty of Rome are an important source of health and safety legislation. Directives are binding, although member states can decide upon the means of giving them legal and administrative effect. In the UK this is usually in the form of regulations. The Noise at Work Regulations 1989 is an example of a European directive, which was enacted in 1990. Regulations are normally published with associated approved codes of practice and guidance notes. EU directives have covered a wide range of health and safety issues such as asbestos and the control of major industrial accident hazards, and the HR specialist needs to be appraised of EC health and safety legislation. As a result of EU legislation, as of 1 January 1993, all British workplaces became legally and financially responsible for ensuring that health and safety regulations were implemented. However, as Legge (1995) points out, the track record of the EU in the area of health and safety has been 'modest' and, particularly in economic recession, employers, unions and governments tend to 'water-down' directives and fail to comply with health and safety regulations.

The Social Charter (see Appendix), adopted by all member states, except the UK, in 1989, prompted an action programme which included ten directives related to workplace health and safety. Teague and Grahl (1992, p. 136) optimistically argue that the new EU health and safety legislation will 'not be of the "lowest common denominator" type but "maximalist" in nature'. The government of 'New' Labour is committed to embracing the Social Charter. If the research findings by Reilly *et al.* (1995) that show the benefits of union safety committees can be reproduced, the existing health and safety legislation in France and Germany, which obliges companies above a certain size to have joint consultative health and safety committees, may become the norm or 'maximalist' model. The implications for HRM and health and safety special-

Figure 5.3 The Health and Safety at Work etc. Act 1974, Section 2: the duties on employers

General duties

2. (1) It shall be the duty of every employer to ensure, so far as is reasonably practicable, the health, safety and welfare at work of all his employees.

   (2) Without prejudice to the generality of an employer's duty under the preceding subsection, the matters to which that duty extends include in particular:

   (a) the provision and maintenance of plant and systems of work that are, so far as is reasonably practicable, safe and without risks to health;

   (b) arrangements for ensuring, so far as is reasonably practicable, safety and absence of risks to health in connection with the use, handling, storage and transport of articles and substances;

   (c) the provision of such information, instruction, training and supervision as is necessary to ensure, so far as is reasonably practicable, the health and safety at work of his employees;

   (d) so far as is reasonably practicable as regards any place of work under the employer's control, the maintenance of it in a condition that is safe and without risks to health and the provision and maintenance of means of access to and egress from it that are safe and without such risks;

   (e) the provision and maintenance of a working environment for his employees that is, so far as is reasonably practicable, safe, without risks to health, and adequate as regards facilities and arrangements for their welfare at work.

ists are formidable. The Health and Safety Commission stated 'Accidents and ill-health are never inevitable; they often arise from failures in control and organization. A central requirement in the regulations is for a risk assessment in order to help the employer decide what health and safety measures are needed.' If the ensuing debate on the Social Charter results in the EU adopting the 'maximalist' model, joint consultative health and safety committees will play a key role in determining strategic approaches to workplace health and safety. Bain (1997), however, provides a more pessimistic analysis of trends in workplace health and safety. He persuasively argues that, in Europe and the USA, powerful business lobbies and governments have mounted an offensive against health and safety legislation. The source of the current campaign for 'deregulation' of health and safety safeguards is market driven and can be located in growing competitive pressures (Bain, 1997).

Occupational health problems and issues

Many employees would probably say they were not healthy if the WHO definition of health quoted above was used as a benchmark. This section examines several health problems that are of special concern to today's HRM practitioners: sick building syndrome, job stress, alcohol abuse, smoking and AIDS.

Sick building syndrome

Interest in the physical aspects of the work building, as a factor affecting employee performance, goes back to at least the 1930s with the Hawthorne experiments in the USA. The construction of 'tight' office buildings with no openable windows in Europe and North America and building-related ill-health problems focused attention on the working conditions of office workers in the 1980s. In 1982, 'sick building syndrome' (SBS) was recognized by WHO as occurring where a cluster of work-related symptoms of unknown cause are significantly more prevalent among the occupants of certain buildings, in comparison to others. Typical symptoms of SBS listed by WHO include eye, nose and throat irritation, sensation of dry mucous membranes and skin, skin rash, mental fatigue, headaches, high frequency of airway infections and cough, nausea, dizziness, hoarseness, and wheezing (Bain and Baldry, 1995). In 1992, the HSC calculated that 30–50 per cent of newly 'remodelled' buildings in Britain suffered a high incidence of illness among the staff. In Canada, it is estimated that there are 1800 'sick' buildings affecting 250 000 workers. Based on such data, Bain and Baldry (1995) argue that the problem of SBS has been 'severely underestimated' (p. 21).

The causes of SBS have concentrated on possible structural or technical factors, such as inadequate ventilation. The UK Health and Safety Executive suggest that SBS may be caused by lack of fresh air supply, inadequate ventilation, unsuitable lighting, airborne pollutants and, more generally, low levels of morale. Bain and Baldry suggest, in the context of global price competition, recession and high energy costs, that SBS is related also to an emphasis on cost reductions and the intensification of office work. They conclude that 'Changes in the balance of power in the office environment have undoubtedly made it easier for management to gain employee acceptance of much more demanding practices and patterns of work' (1995, p. 30). The growing incidence of SBS is a major challenge for the HR professional. SBS increases labour costs via absenteeism which, in turn, may undermine the empowerment approach associated with the 'soft' HRM model, as managers resort to disciplinary measures to reduce absenteeism.

Job stress

The term 'stress' is now part of the regular vocabulary of managers and employees. While some stress is normal to life, if stress is repeated or prolonged individuals experience physical and psychological discomfort. The experience of work can lead to a variety of symptoms of stress that can harm employees' health and job performance. Figure 5.4 illustrates some common symptoms of stress.

Much research into job stress has tended to focus on 'executive burnout' and on individuals in the higher echelons of the organizational hierarchy. However, stress can affect employees at lower levels. A US study found that the two most stressful jobs were a manual labourer and a secretary. In another US study researchers found that the incidence of first heart attack was 2.5 times greater among skilled manual employees than among senior management grades. In fact, the incidence increased in inverse relation to the occupational grades.[10] A US health organization also found that women in clerical occupations suffer twice the incidence of heart disease as all other female employees.[11] In addition to the physical and psychological disabilities, occupational stress costs individuals and business considerable sums of money. For example, in 1994 it was estimated that depression, a common symptom of occupational stress, cost Canadian business more than $300 000 million in terms of lost productivity.[12]

Causes of stress

Occupational stress occurs when some element of work has a negative impact on an employee's physical and mental well-being. For example, work overload and unrealistic time deadlines will put an employee under pressure and stress may occur. Job stress cannot be separated from personal life. For example, illness in the family or divorce put an employee under pressure and lead to stress. Factors that cause stress are numerous and their relationships complex. However, researchers identify two major types of stressors, work-related factors and individual factors.

Work-related factors

A variety of work-related factors can lead to stress including role ambiguity, frustration, conflict, job design and harassment.

1. *Role ambiguity* exists when the job is poorly defined, uncertainty surrounds job expectations and where supervisory staff and their subordinates have different expectations of an employee's responsibilities. Individuals experiencing role ambiguity will be uncertain how their performance will be evaluated and will experience stress.

Figure 5.4 Typical symptoms of stress

Tension and anxiety	Sleep problems
Anger and aggression	Digestive problems
High blood pressure	Chronic worry
Inability to relax	Irritability and boredom
Excessive alcohol and/or tobacco use	Uncooperative attitudes
Forgetfulness	Increased accidents
Increased absenteeism	Reduced job satisfaction

2. *Frustration*, a result of a motivation being blocked to prevent an individual from achieving a desired goal, is a major stressor. A clerical employee, trying to finish a major report before finishing time, is likely to become frustrated by repeated PC breakdowns that prevent attainment of the goal. Huczynski and Buchanan (1991) draw on Swedish research to illustrate the frustration of information technology.

    > Office workers who used to wait happily for hours while folders were retrieved from filing cabinets now complain when their computer terminals do not give them instant information on request... Stress arose mainly from computer breakdowns and telephone calls which interrupted their work. The employees never know how long these interruptions would last, and had to watch helplessly while their work piled up. So they worked rapidly in the mornings in case something stopped them later (1991, p. 352).

3. *Conflicts,* both interpersonal and inter-team, are another source of occupational stress. When employees with different social experiences, personalities, needs and points of view interact with co-workers, disagreements may cause stress.

4. *Job design* is a further cause of stress in the workplace. Jobs that have a limited variety of tasks, low discretion, and do not activate employees' upper level needs may cause stress. Huczynski and Buchanan (1991) report research showing that the most stressful jobs are those that combine high workload and low discretion. Craig also identifies job design as a stressor for office workers.

    > Countless office staff work in high bureaucracies which have been described as 'honeycombs of depression'. The work you're doing can make you sick: work under pressure of time, to keep up the production quotas or deadlines, work that 'drives you crazy' because it's so boring... Office workers frequently keep tablets in their desks to get through the days, or take frequent days off. They then go to their doctor, where the problem is treated as a personal one, in isolation (1981, p. 10).

5. *Harassment* (sexual and racial) at work is another source of stress. Sexual harassment can take two forms. First is a hostile environment that involves behaviour that is unwelcome and undesirable or offensive. This kind of sexual harassment would include, for example, unwanted propositions and sexual innuendo. It can be difficult for an HR manager to convince employees and other managers to take this kind of sexual harassment seriously. It is often viewed as a joke, something to do with 'chatting-up' attractive female co-workers or bottom pinching. However, evidence of behaviour that is sufficiently severe or pervasive as to cause changes in the conditions of employment can lead to a legal case. The second form of sexual harassment is *quid pro quo* harassment, which is essentially a kind of sex-for-promotion blackmail. The alleged perpetrator is normally a superior, and the blackmail is either 'give in to my sexual desires and I'll give you promotion' or 'give in or your job prospects will suffer'. Both forms of sexual harassment are about power relationships. It is about harassment aimed at women by men who occupy positions of power. It is, as one writer put it: 'a new, formal title for an age-old predicament, the boss-man with anything from a lascivious line of chat, to wandering hands, to explicit demands for sex as a reward for giving you, the women, work'.[13] Sexual harassment is extremely stressful; it is also unlawful. The

Figure 5.5 The EU code on sexual harassment

This defines sexual harassment as 'unwanted conduct of a sexual nature' affecting 'the dignity of women and men at work'. It defines harassment as largely subjective, in that it is for the individual to decide on whether conduct is acceptable or offensive.

The code says that member states should take action in the public sector and that employers should be encouraged to:

- issue a policy statement
- communicate it effectively to all employees
- designate someone to provide advice to employees subjected to harassment
- adopt a formal complaints procedure
- treat sexual harassment as a disciplinary offence.

The code obliges member states to make a report on the measures taken to implement it, by 1994.

legal concept of 'detriment' is important here. Sexual harassment is a 'detriment' *per se*. It can lead to an employment-related detriment to the female employee and, as such, it has serious implications for management. In 1986, the European Parliament passed a resolution on violence against women. As a consequence it commissioned a report on *The Dignity of Women at Work*. This report led to the adoption of the EU code of practice (Figure 5.5).

In 1998, the allegations of sexual impropriety against the US President, Bill Clinton, highlight some difficult issues that arise during sexual harassment cases in the workplace. The first is credibility, because there is seldom a witness to support whether the conduct being complained about actually happened. For example, there are no witnesses to the alleged conduct of Mr Clinton and the White House employee, Monica Lewinsky. The issue is credibility and circumstantial evidence. Who has more credibility? Is there indirect evidence that might support or dismiss the allegations? The Clinton case raises another issue, which often applies to workplace investigations, the question of containment. In the presidential investigation, the public prosecutor apparently had no interest in limiting the scope of the investigation. But for many HR professionals, in addition to what is legitimate and necessary in terms of conducting a sexual harassment complaint, containment will also be an issue. The aim will be to contain the allegation and limit the knowledge about the complaint to those who need to know. HR professionals have to take appropriate action to prevent sexual harassment and to inform employees of the consequences of sexual harassment.[14]

Racial harassment in the workplace can also cause stress. It can range from racist jokes or verbal abuse to racist graffiti in the workplace and physical attacks on black employees. No matter how subtle it is, racial harassment is extremely stressful. It can damage black employees' health and presents a major challenge for managers.

Individual factors

Individual factors causing stress are equally varied and complex. Individual factors that can produce stress include financial worries, marital problems, pregnancy, problems with children, and death of spouse. In 1992, a record number of mortgages were foreclosed in Britain, doubtless causing considerable stress. A major personal factor that can cause stress among working women is the 'dual-role' syndrome, the additional burden of coping with two jobs, the paid job and the unwaged 'job' at home (cooking, housework and shopping, and so on). As Craig (1981) puts it:

> The pressures on working mothers are enormous. Feeling guilty because you're not an ideal stay-at-home mum... get the breakfasts, get the shopping done, go to the launderette, fetch the kids from school, do the ironing, clean the house. A carefully worked out timetable can be upset and life thrown into chaos when your lunch hour is switched or you're required to do overtime without notice (p. 18).

Research appears to support the dual-role syndrome as an explanation of work-related stress. A Canadian study among bank employees reported that 22 per cent of the respondents said their stress is triggered by balancing family and work.[15]

Figure 5.6 Stress caused by the 'dual-role' syndrome
Source: *Personnel Management Plus*, April 1992

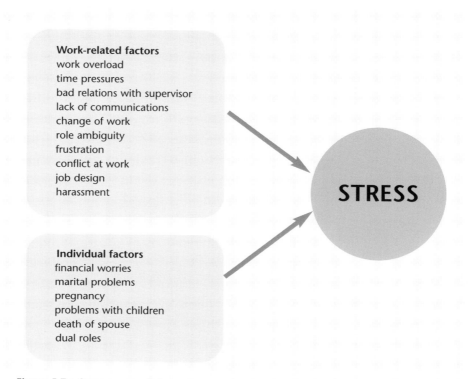

Figure 5.7 Some causes of stress

A general and widely recognized cause of stress is a person's personality. For example, 'Type A' personalities, that is, those individuals who are highly competitive, set high standards, place considerable emphasis on meeting deadlines and are 'workaholics', tend to have a higher propensity to exhibit symptoms of stress (McShane, 1995). Figure 5.7 illustrates work-related and individual causes of stress.

Until recently, job stress has been considered to be a personal problem. Today, it is recognized that stress is a major health problem at work, and it is a general management responsibility to provide the initiative to eliminate or reduce the causes of stress. At organizational level, attention to basic job design principles can alleviate the conditions that may cause stress. At the individual level, HR professionals have conducted workshops on stress management to help the individual employee to cope with stress and avoid overexposure to stress-causing situations. Workshops designed to change 'lifestyles' by promoting healthy eating and fitness, while helping employees relieve the strains caused by job stress, cannot eliminate the source of stress. Like other occupational hazards, stress needs to be controlled at source. As discussed, stress arises from a variety of sources and it is important for HR managers to identify priorities and investigate ways of dealing with the problem. Management should look at the design of jobs (see Chapter 4) and organization structure, and conduct detailed surveys to identify priorities for action. Figure 5.8 shows some of the specific actions individuals and HR practitioners can take to alleviate occupational stress.

Figure 5.8 Action to reduce workplace stress

Individual strategies	Organizational strategies
Physical exercise	Meeting with employees to discuss extent of stress
Hobby	
	Conduct a survey and inspect workplace for stress-causing factors
Meditation	
Group discussions	Improve job and organizational design Improve communication
Assertiveness training	
	Develop a stress policy and monitor its effectiveness
	Train managers to be sensitive to the causes and early symptoms of stress

Alcohol and drug abuse

A recent estimate indicates that in England and Wales there are approximately 3 million excessive drinkers and 850 000 problem and dependent drinkers. About one in 25 of the population in England and Wales, and possibly as high as one in ten in Scotland, may be personally affected by severe alcohol-related problems.[16]

Excessive consumption of alcohol is both a health problem and a job performance problem in every occupational category, manual, white collar, and managerial. In alcohol abuse, behavioural problems range from tardiness in the early stages to prolonged absenteeism in the later stages. A US study estimated that problem drinkers are absent from work, on average, 22 days per year and are at least twice as likely as non-alcohol drinkers to have accidents.[17] The direct and indirect costs of alcohol abuse to employers include the costs of accidents, lower productivity, poor quality work, bad decisions, absenteeism, and loss of managers' time in dealing with employees with an alcohol problem.

Employers have been advised to have a written statement of policy regarding alcohol abuse, which can be discussed and agreed with employees and, where applicable, union representatives. The policy should recognize that alcohol abuse is an illness and it should be supportive, rather than punitive, otherwise employees will hide their drink problem as long as possible. The Health and Safety Executive (HSE) advocates that a policy should encourage an employee who believes he or she has a drink problem to seek help voluntarily, and, subject to certain provisions, that the employee should have the same protection of employment and pension rights as those granted to an employee with problems that are related to other forms of ill-health. Research in Scotland estimated that 20 per cent of employers had a policy to deal with the problem drinker. In addition to preparing a policy, management can devise a procedure for dealing with alcohol abuse. To encourage employees to seek advice, it is suggested that

HRM in practice 5.2

Workplace stress more prevalent than illness, injury

National survey finds Canadians more likely to suffer emotional, mental woes from jobs

BY JANE COUTTS Globe and Mail, 8 April 1998

Toronto Workers are almost three times more likely to complain of health problems arising from workplace stress than from work-related illness or injuries, a Canadian survey shows.

The survey, conducted by Canada Health Monitor, found that 25 per cent of workers reported stress, mental or emotional health problems arising from work, compared with 9 per cent reporting workplace injury and another 9 per cent who said they suffered from work-related physical illness (such as headaches from bad air or noise).

'People aren't acknowledging workplace ill health as a major health issue, when it's a really big drag on healthcare budgets and productivity,' said Earl Berger, managing director of the Health Monitor, which is a national, semi-annual survey on health issues.

The tendency has been to focus on more tangible health problems than stress, an emphasis that is costing employers and employees a lot in the long run, Dr Berger said.

'People are staying away from work and they are staying away for long periods of time and somebody is paying for it,' Dr Berger said. While employees suffer from the stress they are feeling, employers lose productivity, insurance companies pay

in disability claims and drug expenses, and the health system pays for care.

The research released to The *Globe and Mail*, based on random national telephone interviews of 1515 people done in 1996, was prepared for the Homewood Centre for Organizational Health, a new organization based in Guelph, Ontario, studying non-medical pressures on health.

'It's not necessarily change people have difficulty with, it's the uncertainty and loss associated with change'

The research shows that while 20 per cent of white-collar workers report health problems because of workplace stress, compared with 25 per cent of blue-collar workers, it is blue-collar workers who are more likely to report being absent from work because of stress and who, when they are sick, stay off longer.

More than one-third of blue-collar workers said they stayed off work because of stress: 59 per cent of those who missed work were absent 13 days or more. In comparison, 24 per cent of white-collar workers with stress-related health problems stayed home from work:

35 per cent of them were absent more than 13 days.

Rick Lash, a consultant at the Hay Group in Toronto, which specializes in human resources issues, said in an interview that there are multiple messages for employers in the Health Monitor study.

'They have to deal with the culture they've created that's causing such a level of stress and anxiety for people on the job, right back to reassessing their strategy and looking at the impact of that strategy on workers,' he said.

Companies should also look at their managers' skills and their ability to help people handle change and manage their emotions on the job, he said. Employers also need to look for ways to support workers in times of change.

'It's not necessarily change people have difficulty with, it's the uncertainty and loss associated with change,' he said.

Today's unstable work environments are demanding from workers a flexibility many have not developed, coupled with incresing job expectations, Dr Lash said.

That was certainly the experience of Bradley Young, a music teacher who was interviewed at a stress management and relaxation class at the Dorothy Madgett Clinic in Toronto.

Mr Young's problems with stress started when government cutbacks doubled his teaching load in September, 1996. He found he was teaching 30 children in a class for 30 minutes at a time, eight times a day, working in two and sometimes three schools a day.

'Keeping that schedule, keeping control, keeping them interested in the content and trying to get from one school to another or one class to another and keeping them engaged was just too much,' he said.

Mr Young said he was too stressed to capture the interest of one Grade 6 class; he came in for escalating hazing that culminated in what he said was a false charge of assault against a student in January, 1997. He has been on paid leave since, await-ing trial. He believes none of it would have happened if he hadn't been so pressured that he couldn't keep the Grade 6 pupils interested.

The Health Monitor survey found that equal numbers of men and women stayed off work because of stress

---

Christine, who didn't want her last name used, is also following the program at the Madgett Clinic. She's now on welfare since losing her job after a five-year battle with stress that came from constant pressure to enter information more quickly into the inventory computer she ran. Her weight ballooned by nearly 100 pounds; her doctor put her on tranquilizers, but they compounded the problem by making her slower on the job.

'I probably called in sick less than I should have done because I knew if I wasn't there someone else would do my work and I'd come back and find my job in such a mess it would be worse than ever. I had to be really, really ill before I'd take a day off.'

Her doctor believes her health problems arise from the stress of that time.

The Health Monitor survey found that equal numbers of men and women stayed off work because of stress and that the overwhelming majority (79 per cent of men and 91 per cent of women) returned to the same job that caused the stress in the first place.

the procedure should be separate from the disciplinary procedure. Finally, the HRM department is advised to establish links with an external voluntary organization to obtain help and develop an employee assistance programme.

Smoking

It has been estimated that of the 600 000 deaths in the UK each year, 100 000 are caused by tobacco.[18] Smokers comprise around 90 per cent of all deaths from lung cancer and chronic bronchitis. Some 40 per cent of heavy smokers (over 20 cigarettes a day) die before retirement age compared with only 15 per cent of non-smokers.[19] One North American manager calculated the cost of smoking to his company at about US$71.5 million per year, or US$71 500 per smoker. This figure was estimated by putting a money value to such items as the time each employee spends smoking (estimated at 30 minutes each day), absenteeism due to smoking-related illness, property damage and additional maintenance.[20] Smoking increases employers' costs as Figure 5.9 (money that 'goes up in smoke') shows. Recent research has highlighted the health risk of 'second-hand smoking' (inhaling other people's smoke). In 1997, the first second-hand smoking case against the USA tobacco industry resulted in a US$300 million settlement. The lawsuit was filed on behalf of thousands of US-based flight attendants in 1991.[21]

In the past, employers have restricted employees' smoking in order to reduce fire risks or to comply with hygiene standards. To reduce the risks and costs associated with smoking, to appease non-smokers, and to deter possible legal action from employees suffering from polluted air caused by smoking, many organizations now have established policies on smoking at the workplace. The Civil Service, for example, has recently restricted smoking in Inland Revenue offices. Management and union representatives at British Telecom agreed to ballot employees on their views on a smoking ban. The result was a 3 to 1 majority in favour of a smoking ban in common work stations. The company set up a union–management working party to examine the details of implementation. Many employers believe that they would face hostility from employees if they implemented a non-smoking policy. Companies that have implemented non-smoking policies report increased awareness of the health risks of smoking and little employee or union resistance. A government report found that '79 per cent of smokers interviewed acknowledged the right of non-smokers to work in air that is free of tobacco smoke (and not surprisingly, 84 per cent of non-smokers and 78 per cent of ex-smokers also thought so)'.[22] HRM professionals agree that successful non-smoking policies require consultation with employees. In a unionized workplace it requires a joint approach by management and union.

Acquired immune deficiency syndrome (AIDS)

I was not trained to manage fear, discrimination, and dying in the workplace.[23]

A textbook on human resource management for the next millennium would be incomplete if no reference were made to society's most recent menace, AIDS (acquired immune deficiency syndrome). AIDS is caused by the human immuno-deficiency

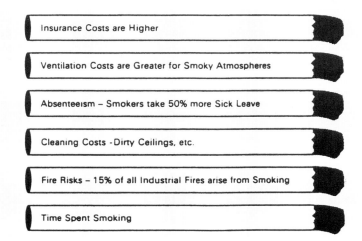

Figure 5.9 Smoking-related costs

virus (HIV), which attacks the body's immune system. In 1994, almost 14 million people were infected with AIDS in the three continents of Africa, Europe and the Americas. One adult in six in Botswana, Zimbabwe, and Zambia is infected.[24] Data from studies in Tanzania and Uganda show that between the ages of 25 and 35, four deaths in five are HIV-related[25] and in India, WHO estimated the number of people affected with AIDS is between 3–5 million.[26] In the USA between 1992 and 1996, AIDS was the leading cause of death among 25- to 44-year-olds and to date 343 000 Americans have died of AIDS and another 900 000 are HIV-infected, about 1 in 250 people.[27]

In Canada, mandatory testing for AIDS is regarded as a serious intrusion on individual rights and employers are prohibited from subjecting job applicants to any type of medical testing for the presence of the HIV virus. Further, the employer is obligated to accommodate the needs of an employee with a disability such as AIDS by, for example, redefining work assignments. The fear of catching HIV can create problems for human resource managers. Employees might refuse to work with a person with AIDS. As one North American human resource manager explained 'No matter how sophisticated or educated you are, AIDS can trigger irrational things in people… There's a big potential for disruption. It could close a plant down.'[28] A North American chain store manager had to call in the Red Cross to explain to distraught employees that AIDS cannot be transmitted through normal contact in the workplace. This happened when an employee developed AIDS and died. Six months later employees were still refusing to use the drinking fountain or the toilet (see chapter case study).

Greene (1998) reported that few US firms surveyed had a policy regarding AIDS and larger firms were more likely to have HIV-specific policies. More than 50 per cent of companies with more than 100 employees had a specific AIDS policy. More worrying perhaps, is the finding that among employers there is a 'declining interest' in AIDS education in the workplace. In 1997, 18 per cent of surveyed US companies provided HIV education for their employees compared with 28 per cent in 1992 (Greene, 1998). Companies that have encountered the problem of managing AIDS in the workplace have found that it is better to expect a problem and be proactive in educating employees about the issues AIDS raises. As with any HRM policy, it requires a clear endorsement from top management down. The chairman of Levi Strauss, Robert Hass, confirms the need for senior management support. 'This [AIDS] is frequently viewed as something that the personnel department should take care of, but there has to be support from the top. You can't do it with one flyer.'[29] As attitudes and legal considerations change, AIDS has important implications for HRM policy and practices.

●● Role of management

Perhaps, more than any other HR activity, health and safety offers the HR manager an opportunity to be more proactive than reactive. This, if effective action followed, would increase the HRM department's contribution to improving the health and safety of the organization's employees. There are a number of strategies that can be used by organizations to ensure a healthy and safe workplace and ensure compliance with legal requirements. This section does not aim to be prescriptive, offering advice on what HRM managers should be doing. The strategies summarized in Figure 5.10 are

Figure 5.10   Strategies to improve workplace health and safety

1.	Design	safe and healthy systems of work
2.	Exhibit	strong management commitment
3.	Inspect	workplace for health and safety problems
4.	Establish	procedures and controls for dealing with health and safety issues
5.	Develop	training programmes
6.	Set up	health and safety committees
7.	Monitor	safety policies
8.	Draw up	action plan and checklist

intended primarily to generate discussion on the implications of health and safety on management practices, and how health and safety measures can be reconciled with broader management objectives.

Design safer systems of work

The most direct approach to ensuring a safe and healthy workplace is to design systems of work that are safe and without risk to health. This can often only be done satisfactorily at the design, planning or purchasing stage. It may be far more difficult to modify existing machinery or systems of work to eliminate or reduce hazards, than at the investment stage. Thus, management must take cognizance of long-term organizational changes to control hazards. Simply trying to persuade employees, for instance by poster campaigns, to adapt their behaviour to unsafe systems of work is unacceptable. The Health and Safety Executive (HSE) maintains that the basic problem of accidents stems from hazards inherent in the workplace. 'Most accidents involve an element of failure in control – in other words *failure in managerial skill* [our emphasis]. A guiding principle when drawing up arrangements for securing health and safety should be that so far as possible work would be adapted to people and not vice versa.' As managers identify processes, machines and substances that are hazardous to the health and well-being of employees, they must modify the process to eliminate or reduce the hazard and risk 'at source'. In some cases, robots can perform hazardous tasks, such as paint spraying and welding. The provision of protective equipment is the typical means used by organizations to reduce physical hazards, and it is also an employer responsibility.

Exhibit commitment

Senior management carries the prime responsibility under the 1974 Act for ensuring a safe and healthy workplace. The Robens Committee believed that 'apathy' was a major cause of workplace accidents. No matter how much activity on health and safety is initiated by HR professionals, health and safety should be an integral part of every manager's responsibility, from the chief executive officer down to the lowest level supervisor. Anything less than total support from top management raises questions about the sincerity of the organization's commitment in the eyes of employees, government agencies and the public at large. To exhibit commitment, managers' salaries and promotion might be tied to a satisfactory safety record and compliance. Larger organizations have also appointed specialists in the area, including health and safety officers, safety engineer and medical technicians. If the safety officer is to be effective she or he must be given adequate authority in the management hierarchy to implement changes.

Inspect the workplace

Another proactive approach to the management of health and safety is regular formal inspections of the workplace, regular monitoring of the work environment and regular physical examination of employees. For example, construction sites and manufacturing plants require regular inspections to check the application of safety standards and relevant laws. In some manufacturing processes frequent monitoring of air quality, levels of dust and noise is needed. Organizations may monitor a wide range of matters relating to employees' health, from routine eye tests and chest X-rays to screening for breast and cervical cancer and incidents of infertility and abnormal childbirths. A 'health' survey of employees can also help identify hazardous and unhealthy processes.

We can identify three main types of formal inspection, accident, special and general. *Accident inspections* will follow an accident or dangerous incident ('near miss') in the workplace. *Special inspections* might concentrate on a particular work station, system of work or hazard. The safety committee might decide that it is necessary to examine the training of fork-lift truck operators or dust problems; this would be the first step in a plan of action. A comprehensive survey of the entire workplace is the purpose of *general inspections*. In a unionized workplace these inspections are frequently conducted jointly with the union safety representative. The SRSC (Safety Representatives and Safety Committees) *Guidance Notes* recognize the advantages in formal general inspections being jointly conducted by the employer or manager and union safety representative.

> The safety representatives should coordinate their work to avoid unnecessary duplication. It will often be appropriate for the safety officer or specialist advisers to be available to give technical advice on health and safety matters which may arise during the course of the inspection.[30]

Thorough preparation, including designing a comprehensive set of checklists covering all aspects of the workplace, is essential if managers are to discover physical health hazards.

Establish procedures and controls

A health and safety policy is likely to fail unless there are effective procedures and controls established. The procedures for handling health and safety problems need to meet some basic requirements:

1. allow employees and union representatives to talk *directly* to the managers who can make decisions
2. operate without undue delay
3. be able to handle emergency problems and
4. permit discussion about long-term decisions affecting health and safety.

Clearly, these recommendations have important implications for HRM policy and action. Let us briefly examine these considerations. Problems might occur if line managers are expected by senior management to be responsible for safe working practices, but at the same time are denied the authority to make decisions and implement changes. In principle, organizational procedures should ensure that the responsibility of each level of management for health and safety is matched by the authority at that level of management to make decisions. The appointment of a safety officer may be a necessary prerequisite to establishing effective procedures and controls, but it is not sufficient. The position must be placed into the management hierarchy with clear lines of reporting and accountability, which will enable procedures for raising problems to operate without undue delay and avoid other managers absolving themselves from responsibilities.

It is recommended that the committee on health and safety include key departmental managers, employees and union representatives. At best, committees can be a vehicle for discussion and the strategic planning of health and safety. At worst, they can degenerate into a 'talking shop' which will draw scepticism from the rest of the workforce. HR specialists and line managers must perceive their rewards, or a significant proportion of them, as contingent upon the success of a health and safety programme. To evaluate that success, monthly, quarterly, and annual statistics need to be reported directly to the senior management team.

Develop training programmes

One way to obtain compliance with health and safety regulations is through enhancing employees' knowledge, understanding and commitment, which can be achieved through health and safety programmes. The purpose of safety training is generally the same as that of any other training programme: to improve job knowledge and skills and to ensure optimum employee performance at the specified level. In health and safety training, specified performance standards include attention to safety rules and regulations regarding safe work behaviour. Like any other training, health and safety training should be developed systematically. First, problems or training needs are identified by inspection, by accident reports, and through discussion at the health and safety committee. Next, the planning, execution and evaluation of the training take place (Chapter 10).

The HASAWA 1974 imposes a duty on employers to provide training to ensure a healthy and safe workplace. Research suggests that safety awareness training programmes only have a short-term effect on employees' behaviour. This would suggest that after employees complete their safety training at the orientation stage, the HR department should organize regular refresher courses. Experience suggests that line managers, supervisors, and safety representatives need to be exposed to regular training. Top management support is a key ingredient in the availability and success of health and safety training. Evidence suggests, however, that the number of representatives attending TUC health and safety courses has fallen along with a large fall in the incidence of health and safety representatives (Millward *et al.*, 1992).

Set up health and safety committees

As already noted under the EU Social Charter, joint health and safety committees may represent the future shape of European health and safety legislation (Reilly *et al.*, 1995). The HASAWA requires employers to establish safety committees where this is requested by a safety representative. Where these committees are not initiated by the union, organizations often have safety committees which have employee members and are chaired by the safety or HRM specialist. Making the committee effective is mainly in the realm of senior management. A safety committee may develop into a 'talking shop' with no effective decision-making authority. To avoid this, a senior member of the management team, with executive authority, should be a member of the committee.

The functions of the committees, their terms of reference, depends on individual company policy, relevant safety legislation and the employee–union relations situation. The SRSC *Guidance Notes* suggest the following terms of reference.

1. The study of accidents and notifiable diseases statistics and trends, so that reports can be made to management on unsafe and unhealthy conditions and practices, together with recommendations for corrective action.
2. Examination of safety audit reports on a similar basis.
3. Consideration of reports and factual information provided by inspectors of the enforcing authority appointed under the Health and Safety at Work Act.
4. Consideration of reports which safety representatives may wish to submit.
5. Assistance in the development of works safety rules and safe systems of work.
6. A watch on the effectiveness of the safety content of employee training.
7. A watch on the adequacy of safety and health communication and publicity in the workplace.
8. The provision of a link with the appropriate inspectorates of the enforcing authority.

(Reg 9, pp. 37–8)

Employers or their representatives are primarily responsible for compliance with health and safety laws. The existence of these committees does not diminish the employer's duty to ensure a healthy and safe workplace. The work of the safety committees should supplement management's arrangements for regular and effective monitoring for health and safety precautions; it cannot be a substitute for management action. All forms of safety arrangements that encourage employee participation in workplace health and safety matters reduce the incidence of accidents. The study by Reilly *et al.* (1995), however, shows strong support for union–management health and safety committees as an important variable for promoting a safer workplace. Reilly *et al.*'s study found that establishments with joint health and safety commit-

Table 5.1   Arrangements for dealing with health and safety, 1984 and 1990

	All establishments		Private manufacturing		Private services		Public sector	
	1984	1990	1984	1990	1984	1990	1984	1990
Joint committee for health and safety	22	23	33	32	15	18	23	25
Joint committee for health, safety and other matters	9	9	15	10	7	8	9	11
Workforce representatives, no committee	41	24	25	20	39	16	52	40
Management deals, consultation with employees	–	5	–	3	–	5	–	5
Management deals, without consultation with employees	–	37	–	34	–	51	–	14
Management only, consultation	22	–	22	–	34	–	10	–
Other answer	6	2	5	1	5	1	7	4
Don't know/not answered	*	*	*	*	–	–	*	*

Source: Adapted from Millward *et al.*, 1992, p. 161

tees – and with all employee representatives chosen by the union – have 'on average, 5.7 fewer injuries per 1000 employees compared with establishments where management deals with health and safety matters without any form of worker consultation' (1995, p. 283).

A critical study of the implementation of the Safety Representatives and Safety Committees Regulations (SRSC) has been undertaken by Walters (1987). The findings from his small sample of cases in the print industry suggest that the joint regulation of health and safety is based on the assumption of trade union organization and power in the workplace. With an inimical economic and political environment in the 1980s and much of the 1990s, this power diminished and the SRSC Regulations have had a very limited direct effect on the joint regulation of health and safety in the workplace. 'It is only in the large workplaces that any significant application of the SRSC Regulations with regard to joint inspections, provision of information and time off for training seems to have been made' (Walters, 1987, p. 48).

The authoritative study by Millward *et al.*, however, indicates that in spite of the hostile industrial relations climate of the 1980s, joint health and safety committees were just as likely to exist in 1990 as in 1984. In 1990, 23 per cent of managers reported having joint committees specifically for health and safety issues, in 1984 it was 22 per cent (Millward *et al.*, 1992, p. 162). Another finding, which is relevant to the point that increasingly managers seem to be assuming responsibility for health and safety issues unilaterally, is that health and safety committees were much less commonly found in non-unionized workplaces in 1984 than in 1990, and the decline in health and safety representatives was particularly marked in the service sector. Table 5.1 shows the arrangements for dealing with health and safety in Britain for each broad sector in the economy.

Monitor policy

Safety specialists argue that the safety policy should reflect the employer's commitment to develop safe systems of work, and to pursue a healthy work environment.

Apart from giving details of the specialist safety services provided by the organization, the safety policy also outlines the safety responsibilities of all levels of management within the hierarchy. This part of the safety policy is particularly important for identifying which member of the management hierarchy should be involved when a health and safety problem arises in the workplace.

There is a growing awareness that, in practice, many employers are 'turning a blind eye' to new health and safety requirements. Furthermore, many safety policies are not that helpful in practice because of failure to monitor their relevance to workplace arrangements, inadequate training, and supervisors and safety officers lacking authority to make decisions. The TUC is critical of safety policies, arguing that 'many safety policies are just pious blue-prints which look good but are either ignored or unworkable'.[31] A proactive approach would involve HRM professionals regularly checking to ensure that safety policy, management procedures and arrangements work, and are changed to suit new developments or work structures in the workplace.

Draw up action plan

HRM professionals can be more proactive in the area of health and safety by developing an action plan and checklist (Figure 5.11)

Chapter summary

Employee health and safety should be an important aspect of HRM. To follow the logic of the HRM model, organizations need to protect their investment in their human 'assets'. This chapter has examined the role of health and safety in organizations and the development of legislation. Sick building syndrome, occupational stress, alcoholism, smoking and AIDS are health problems discussed in this chapter. Trade unions have attempted to secure improvements in health and safety at work through collective bargaining and, at times, through direct action by work stoppages; unions have also pressed for some stringent health and safety legislation. Deregulation (Bain, 1997) and growth of outsourcing (Mayhew and Quinlan, 1997) operate to reduce protection for the organization's 'human assets'. If organizations adopt an HRM model that is 'union free', it might, given the research evidence (see, for example Reilly *et al.*, 1995), expose employees to greater workplace hazards, thereby offering a further paradox in the HRM paradigm. European Union directives and the Social Charter will be an important source of health and safety regulations and counterbalance to market-driven policies in the years ahead. With such developments in the law, and a growing awareness of health and safety hazards, it is likely that HRM professionals will face challenges and greater responsibilities in this area during the foreseeable future.

HSE OHS checklist for employers
Preventing occupational ill health

Yes/No/Uncertain

● Do I know whether any of my operations involve a health risk?
For example exposure to skin irritants such as solvents, poor working practices when using harmful materials, exposure to excessive noise, exposure to harmful dusts, fumes or gases, frequent heaving lifting or carrying

● Do I take account of any specific regulations or recommendations applying to these risks?
For example specific regulations covering work with lead and asbestos

● Are all the risks that have been identified adequatley controlled?
For example through improved workplace design engineering controls or by using personal protection

● Is the effectiveness of controls being assessed and monitored?
For example by regular environmental monitoring, possibly backed up with health checks

Placement and rehabilitation

Yes/No/Uncertain

● Do I know whether any of my operations carry specific health requirements?
For example good eyesight or colour vision

● Do I know whether any of my operations present a hazard to people with a particular problem?
For example dusty conditions may be unsuitable for some workers with chest problems

● Do I take these factors into consideration in a clear and fair way at recruitment and subsequently?
For example by ensuring that the specific health requirements for a job are assessed and people are not turned down because of irrelevant health conditions

● Am I prepared to modify working arrangements where practicable to accommodate employees with health problems?
For example by rearranging working hours, adjusting the height of work surfaces.

First aid and treatment

Yes/No/Uncertain

● Do my first aid procedures comply with the First Aid at Work Regulations?
See HSE guidance booklet HS (R)11

● Have I considered my first aid needs for coping with illness at work, and made appropriate arrangements?
For example emergency on call arrangements with a local doctor or nurse

● Have I considered whether any additional treatment services would be cost-effective in my operation and if so, made suitable arrangements?
For example regular visits to the workplace by physiotherapists or dentists to avoid workers having to take time off for appointments

Health promotion

Yes/No/Uncertain

● Have I considered whether the benefits of health education, employee assistance or counselling programmes would justify their introduction, and have I introduced such programmes?
For example programmes aimed at improving diet and reducing smoking and problem drinking. The workplace can be an ideal location in which to encourage employees towards healthier living

● Do I know whether screening tests are available that could improve the health of my staff by detecting treatable illness at an earlier stage, and if so, have I arranged for them to be carried out?
For example arrangements with local health authorities or others for cervical smears to be carried out at the workplace

Information, instruction and training

Yes/No/Uncertain

● Do my employees understand any health risks involved in their work and how to minimise them?

● Have my employees received sufficient instruction and training in how to avoid ill health?
For example hygiene procedures and correct use of personal protective equipment

If you answered NO or UNCERTAIN to any of these questions you need help.

Figure 5.11 Checklist for health and safety
Source: Health and Safety Executive

Key concepts

'Careless worker' model   Safety committee
Self-regulatory   Safety policy
Robens Report   Health and Safety at Work etc. Act 1974
'As far as reasonably practicable'   'As far as practicable'

Discussion questions

1. Explain the 'careless worker' model.

2. 'Spending money on health and safety measures is a luxury most small organizations cannot afford.' Build an argument to support this statement. Build an argument to negate it.

3. Explain the role of an HRM specialist in providing a safe and healthy environment for employees.

4. Explain the symptoms and causes of job stress, and what the organization can do to alleviate it.

5. 'Employers with poor safety records often have poor written safety policies.' Do you agree or disagree? Discuss.

6. Explain how training can improve occupational health and safety.

7. 'Stress on women both inside and outside the work organization is a huge challenge.' Discuss.

Further reading

Bain, P. (1997) Human resource malpractice: the deregulation of health and safety at work in the USA and Britain, *Industrial Relations Journal*, **28**(3): 176–91.

Codrington, C. and Henley, J.S. (1981) The industrial relations of injury and death, *British Journal of Industrial Relations*, **XIX**(3).

Cooper, C.G.L. and Smith M.G.J. (eds) (1985) *Job Stress and Blue Collar Work*, Chichester: Wiley.

Green, J. (1998) Employers learn to live with AIDS, *HR Magazine*, **43**(2): 62–7.

Health and Safety Commission (1976) *Safety Representatives and Safety Committees*, London: HMSO.

Robens, Lord (1972) Report of the Committee on Safety and Health, London: HMSO.

Reilly, B., Paci, P. and Holt, P. (1995) Unions, safety committees and workplace injuries, *British Journal of Industrial Relations*, **33**(2): 275–87.

Managing AIDS at Johnson Stores plc

Gwen Fine is the HRM manager at Johnson Stores plc, a large department store located in SE England. One Monday morning in January, Norman Smith, a trainee manager in the hardware and electrical goods department, walked into Gwen's office, sat down and broke the news that he was terminally ill. But that was not all he said. He rambled on about a friend who had died of AIDS. Both of them knew what he was trying to say, but neither knew how to express it. Finally, Norman stopped and asked: 'You know what it is, don't you?' 'Yes, I do,' replied Gwen. 'It's a terrible thing in our society.' Norman went on to tell her that he could expect to live two more years, at best. Later that morning, Gwen reflected on the meeting with Norman and felt ashamed of her insensitive comment. She confided in a close co-worker her feelings. 'What a stupid, impersonal thing to say,' she chided herself. 'The man is dying.'

Norman was on sick leave for six weeks following the meeting in early January with Gwen Fine; a doctor's note described his illness as shingles. The staff in Norman's department were an understanding group and carried the extra work. In February, Norman phoned Gwen Fine with good news. He was feeling better and the store could expect to see him back at work the following Monday.

When Norman walked into the store his co-workers were overwhelmed by the stark change in his appearance. 'My God, he looks terrible,' Gwen thought when she met him later in the day. At 43, Norman was a handsome man. Yet he had lost 30 pounds since Gwen had last seen him. Dark rings circled his eyes, and his cheeks were sunken. His tall frame seemed unsteady as he leaned on a walking stick he was now carrying. The illness had also caused unsightly skin eruptions and irritation on his legs.

Norman was confident, until returning to work, that he could keep his condition private. He had offered himself as a 'guinea pig' to a group of specialist doctors searching for an AIDS cure at the regional hospital. The treatment demanded Norman leave the store once a week. 'Why are you always going to the hospital?' his co-workers began asking. Rumours began to circulate in the store about Norman's illness, focusing on his sexuality and the possibility he had AIDS. Co-workers began behaving differently to him. Staff in his department avoided Norman and attempted to ostracize him. Employees in the store also refused to use the water fountain, cups in the canteen, or the toilet. As another department manager stated, 'The linking of Norman's illness to AIDS triggered irrational things in people and Johnson's entire employees simply panicked. People are totally misinformed about AIDS.'

The reaction from Norman's co-workers began to affect morale and cause disruption. In April, three long-serving employees in the hardware and electrical department requested a transfer. The sales in the department fell sharply in the first quarter. Shortly after the release of the quarterly sales figures, Gwen Jones received an e-mail message from her boss, Stan Beale, the store's general manager, requesting an urgent meeting to discuss Mr Norman Smith.

(*Note*: the names of the characters and the company are fictitious, but the case is based on a true story taken from 'Managing AIDS: How one boss struggled to cope', in *Business Week*, February 1993.)

Questions

1. If you were in Gwen Fines' position would you have handled the case differently? Explain.

2. Drawing on the concepts in this chapter, and your own research, what policy or procedural changes could be instituted at Johnson Stores plc to prevent such disruption in the future?

Notes

1. Dr J. Cullen, Chair of the Health and Safety Commission (1986) and quoted in *Workplace Health: A Trade Unionist Guide*, London: Labour Research Department, 1989, p. 2.
2. Andrew, a machine operator at Servo Engineering, quoted in Bratton, *Japanization at Work*, 1992, p. 124.
3. Quoted in Giles A. and Iain, H. (1989) The collective agreement. In Anderson, J., Gunderson, M., Ponak, A. (eds) *Union-Management Relations in Canada*, 2nd edn, Ontario: Addison-Wesley.
4. Institute of Professional and Managerial Staffs, *Health and Safety: Keep it Together*, 1993, pp. 5–6 and quoted by Bain (1997), p. 177.
5. Quoted in Kinnersley, P. (1987) *The Hazards of Work*, London: Pluto Press, p. 1.
6. TUC (1979) *The Safety Rep and Union Organization*, London: TUC Education, p. 10.
7. TUC (1989) *Workplace Health: A Trade Unionists' Guide*, London: Labour Research Department, p. 2.
8. *IRS Employment Review 600*: Health and Safety Bulletin 241, January 1996 and quoted in Bain (1997) p. 177.
9. Witness to the Factories' Inquiry Commission, 1833, and quoted in Engels, F. (English edn, 1973), *The Conditions of the Working Class in England*, London: Progress Publishers, p. 194.
10. See Fletcher, B. *et al.* (1979) Exploring the myth of executive stress. In *Personnel Management*, May, and quoted in Craig, M. *Office Survival Handbook*, London: BSSRS, p. 10.
11. Haynes, S.G. and Feinleils, M. (1980), Women, work and coronary heart disease, prospective findings from the Framingham Heart Study, *American Journal of Public Health*, **70**, February, and quoted in BSSRS, p. 10.
12. Costs of depression, *Human Resources Professional*, Canada, **12**(3): 15.
13. Anna Raeburn (1980) *Cosmopolitan*, August, and quoted in Craig (1981) p. 19.
14. Malcolm MacKillop (1998) How the Clinton case connects to work, *Globe and Mail*, 29 January, p. B12.
15. Ijeoma Ross and Gayle MacDonald (1997) Scars from stress cut deep in workplace, *Globe and Mail*, Canada, 9 October, p. B16.
16. Quoted in *Bargaining Report*, London: Labour Research Department, 1983.
17. Filipowicz, C.A. (1979) The Troubled Employee: Whose Responsibility?, *The Personnel Administrator*, June and quoted in Stone, T.H. and Meltz, N.M. (1988) *Human Resource Management in Canada*, 2nd edn, Toronto: Holt, Rinehart and Winston, p. 529.
18. *Workplace Health*: A Trade Unionist Guide, 1989 London: Labour Research Department, p. 29.
19. From *Smoking – the Facts*, Health Education Council.
20. Falconer, T. (1987) No butts about it, *Canadian Business*, February.

21. Tobacco firms agree to pay in secondhand-smoke case, *Globe and Mail*, Canada, 11 October, 1997, p. A12.

22. From *Smoking – Attitudes and Behaviour*, HMSO, quoted in *Smoking at Work*, 1984, London: TUC, p. 62.

23. Lee Smith, a former executive of Levi Strauss & Co., quoted in Managing AIDS: how one boss struggled to cope, *Business Week*, 1 February, 1993, p. 48.

24. Stein, Z. and Susser, M. (1997) Editorial: AIDS –an update on the global dynamics, *American Journal of Public Health*, Washington, **87**(6).

25. Anonymous, International: serial killer at large, *The Economist*, London, 7 February, 1998.

26. Anonymous, India wakes up to AIDS, *The Economist*, London, 20 Dec–2 Jan, 1998.

27. Jay Greene, Employers learn to live with AIDS, *HR Magazine*, February, 1998.

28. *Business Week*, 1 February, 1993, pp. 53–4.

29. *Business Week*, 1 February, 1993, pp. 53-4.

30. SRSC Guidance Notes, paragraph 18. HMSO. 1979.

31. TUC (1986) *Health and Safety at Work: TUC Course Book for Union Reps*, 4th edn, London: TUC, p. 163.

part three

Planning and Selection

chapter six

Human resource planning

Jeffrey Gold

Strategic personnel planning must be far sighted, but action based; imaginative and flexible but conceptually bound; authoritative but not authoritarian; and meet business needs but not ignore the needs of its employees.[1]

...there has been little or no learning of the importance of the contribution that an integrated set of personnel policies can make.[2]

Can we even talk of organisational careers, when the essence of the careers of the 1970s – security and promotion prospects – have all but disappeared? Is it feasible to manage careers today when the organisational and business environments are so unpredictable as to make any sort of planning next to impossible?[3]

Chapter outline

Chapter objectives

After studying this chapter, you should be able to:

1. Understand the place of planning in HRM.
2. Understand the different approaches to manpower planning.
3. Explain the difference between manpower planning and human resource planning.
4. Explain the growing importance of career management in organizations.
5. Understand the use of competency-based approaches to planning individual development.

● Introduction

In Chapter 3, we argued that external conditions and pressures for change are having a considerable and continuing impact on the way that an organization manages its human resources. The nature of the changes has led to the recognition of people as the source of competitive advantage. If identical non-people resources, in the form of raw materials, plant, technology, hardware and software are available to competing organizations, then differences in economic performance between organizations must be attributed to differences in the performance of people.

For senior managers in an organization, whose task it is to plan a response to such pressures, the attraction, recruitment, utilization, development and retention of people of the required quantity and quality for the present and the future ought now to rival finance, marketing and production in the construction of strategic plans. Either explicitly or implicitly, all organization strategies will contain HR aspects. However it has been a long-running issue as to whether HR managers have an input into the process of strategy making, and the nature of the influence of such inputs.

Becoming more strategic represents something of a dilemma for the HR function. On the one hand, HR inputs might emphasize the importance of integrating policies and procedures with business strategy, where people are seen as a factor of production who are required to make sure the business plan is implemented. The more that business plans were based on figures and mathematical models, the greater the need for information about people to be expressed in a similar fashion; the plan for people should 'fit' the plan for the business. The growth of manpower planning techniques through the 1960s, which provided such information, and their incorporation into comprehensive computer models, was a key factor in the personnel function's development.

This 'hard' version of HRM (Legge, 1995, p. 66) was part of a push in the 1980s to address the traditional weakness of personnel managers in making themselves more strategic. It can be contrasted with a 'soft' version which emphasizes people as assets who can be developed and through whose commitment and learning an organization might achieve competitive advantage. It is interesting that the two different orientations, while representing a contrast, are not always incompatible. Indeed, living with ambiguities and conflicting pressures is a common experience for many HR practitioners (Gold, 1997, p. 138). Tamkin *et al.* (1997, p. 26) in a study of UK organizations showed that while there were many challenges to HR in becoming strategic, HR functions were adopting a variety of approaches to find a strategic role, both 'soft' and 'hard'. In some cases, this involves supporting business strategy by developing appropriate policies and procedures. However, not all organizations are so effective in developing strategy and the HR function could develop policy to move the organization in an appropriate direction. In some cases, the HR function is able to be proactive and play a leading role in driving strategy. There are a number of organizations where the future of the business has been based on the learning and development of its people with the HR a function playing a key role in facilitation.

The uncertainty and complexity of organization and business conditions in the 1990s has resulted in the employment of both 'hard' and 'soft' versions of HRM with concomitant approaches and methods relating to planning. Over the years, theoretical developments increased the number and sophistication of manpower planning techniques but the activity slid in and out of favour at strategic levels. This was partly because the data and the computer models failed to live up to expectations, possibly, that personnel departments were unable to make use of the theoretical advances.

It was also because the people issue fluctuated in importance. Thus in times of relatively full employment, people and their skills were important because of their scarcity. During the years of recession in the 1980s the manpower plan was used to slim down the workforce, while the demographic issues of the late 1980s appeared to make people important again. The recession in the first half of the 1990s, with the accompanying trends for 'downsizing' and 'delayering', paradoxically has made the idea of detailed long-term planning less attractive (Tyson, 1995a, p. 75) while at the same time it has increased the need for more complex and organization-specific approaches to planning the employment of human resources (Parker and Caine, 1996, p. 31).

HRP and the HRM cycle

In terms of the HRM cycle (Figure 1.2), human resource planning (HRP), in theory, serves as the integrating link between strategic business planning and strategic HRM. HRP specifies recruiting and selection goals, including the number and type of individuals to be employed. Appraisal affects HRP by giving information on individual performance and productivity, which can determine the number and type of employees needed to achieve strategic goals. Additionally, HRP specifies future job requirements, which form the basis for workplace training and development. HRP affects rewards through the type and quality of employees required. This chapter will look at the transition from manpower planning driven by techniques towards human resource planning as an aspect of HRM. The emphasis on quantities, flows and mathematical modelling, which appeared to be the main concern of manpower planning in the 1960s and 70s, is at least complemented by, and integrated with, a qualitative view of people whose performance lies at the core of business strategy. We have also shown that performance lies at the core of the HRM cycle. HRP therefore will be concerned with the development and provision of a framework that allows an organization to integrate key HR activities so that it may meet the needs of employees and enhance their potential and meet the performance needs of business strategy.

⬤ Manpower planning

Manpower planning owed its significance to the importance of business strategy and planning in many organizations. It is worth, just for a moment, paying attention to the process of planning at this level. A plan represents one of the outcomes from a process that seeks to find a solution to a defined problem. There have been many attempts to rationalize this process to provide a set of easy-to-follow linear steps, so that efficient decisions can be made to formulate a plan from a choice of alternatives prior to implementation. Plans therefore represent the precise articulation of an organization's strategy, produced as a result of a rational consideration of the various issues which affect an organization's future performance before making a choice of the action required. In this process senior managers will conduct an appraisal of both internal and external situations using a range of techniques to assess the organization's strengths and weaknesses and the threats and opportunities – the so-called SWOT analysis. Formally the emphasis will be on data that can be quantified. This is not surprising, since the planning process itself is an organization's attempt to pre-empt and deal with identified problems and uncertainty, and numbers are certain, precise and simple to comprehend. This image of certainty and control is one that gives comfort to many senior managers, despite the doubts expressed by some about the reality of the process (Mintzberg, 1990).

If business strategy and plans find their expression in measurable financial, marketing and production targets, the manpower plan represents a response of the personnel function to ensure that the necessary supply of people is forthcoming to allow the targets to be met. The rationalized approach to manpower planning and the key stages are shown in Figure 6.1. The manpower plan could therefore be expressed in a way that matches the overall business strategy and plan. In theory at least, a manpower plan could show how the demand for people and their skills within an organization can be balanced by supply.

The rationalized approach leading to a balance of demand and supply can be found in some of the definitions and explanations of manpower planning over the last 25 years. According to Smith (1980, p. 7), manpower planning means:

1. Demand work – analysing, reviewing and attempting to predict the numbers, by kind, of the manpower needed by the organization to achieve its objectives.
2. Supply work – attempting to predict what action is and will be necessary to ensure that the manpower needed is available when required.
3. Designing the interaction between demand and supply, so that skills are utilized to the best possible advantage and the legitimate aspirations of the individual are taken into account.

In 1974 the Department of Employment had defined manpower planning as:

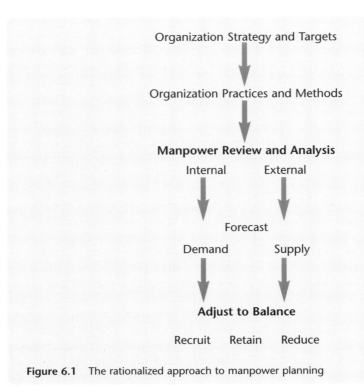

Figure 6.1 The rationalized approach to manpower planning

strategy for the acquisition, utilisation, improvement and preservation of an organisation's human resources.

This definition was broad and general enough to cover most aspects of personnel management work. Four stages of the planning process were outlined:

1. An evaluation or appreciation of existing manpower resources.
2. An estimation of the proportion of currently employed manpower resources which are likely to be within the firm by the forecast date.
3. An assessment or forecast of labour requirements if the organization's overall objectives are to be achieved by the forecast date.
4. The measures to ensure that the necessary resources are available as and when required, that is, the manpower plan.

Stages 1 and 2 were linked in the 'supply aspect of manpower' with stage 1, being part of the 'normal personnel practice'. Stage 3 represents the 'demand aspect of manpower'. There were two main reasons for companies to use manpower planning, first, to develop their business objectives and manning levels and second, to reduce the 'unknown factor'.

While equilibrium can serve as an ideal, organizations will be composed of a variety of supply and demand problems throughout their structure, which planning will need to bring into overall balance at optimum levels. The movement towards equilibrium involves a variety of personnel activities such as recruitment, promotion, succession planning, training, reward management, retirement and redundancy. The complexity of the interaction of these factors in the context of the aims of optimization and overall equilibrium made manpower planning a suitable area of interest for operational research and the application of statistical techniques (Bartholomew, 1971). In this process, organizations could be envisaged as a series of stocks and flows as part of an overall system of resource allocation. Models of behaviour could be formulated in relation to labour turnover, length of service, promotion flows and age distributions. These variables could be expressed as mathematical and statistical formulae and equations allowing solutions for manpower decisions to be calculated. With the growing use of computers, the techniques and models became more ambitious and probably beyond the comprehension of most managers (Parker and Caine, 1996, p. 30). In large organizations there was a growth in the number of specialist manpower analysts who were capable of dealing with the complex processes involved.

In the UK, the Institute of Empoyment Studies (IES), previously the Institute of Manpower Studies based at Sussex University, has been a principal advocate of manpower modelling. According to the Institute (Bennison, 1980, p. 2), the manpower planning process involves:

1. determining the manpower requirements; how many people
2. establishing the supply of manpower
3. developing policies to fill the gap between supply and demand.

The Institute favours a flexible approach where plans are developed based on an understanding of the whole manpower system. The first step in manpower analysis is to describe the present manpower system and set its expected objectives. The system can be drawn as a 'collection of boxes and flows representing the way that manpower behaves in the organisation' (Bennison, 1980, p. 5). Planners can assess the critical 'decision points' for manpower policy. For example, decisions for the recruitment and promotion of managers can occur in a meaningful way using statistical planning techniques where the 'practical limits of variation' (Bennison, 1980, p. 17) can be defined for factors such as levels of labour turnover at particular points, technology development impact and forecasts for growth. If possible, the relationship of the factors to the decisions will be quantified, allowing the generation of promotion paths under different assumptions of demand and supply.

The IES, and others involved in the development of models and techniques, would be the first to accept that manpower planning is more than 'building a statistical model of the supply of manpower' (Bennison, 1980, p. 2). An emphasis on the models, at the expense of the reality of managing and interacting with people, was bound to be greeted with suspicion, certainly by employees and their representatives, but also by managers 'forced' to act on the results of the calculations. It may be argued that the manpower analysis is there to serve as an aid to decision making, but the presentation of data and an inability to deal with the ever-increasing complexity of models was always likely to result in the manpower analysis being 'seen' as the plan. The domination of equations, which mechanistically provide solutions for problems based on the behaviour of people, may actually become divorced from the real world and have a good chance of missing the real problems. Hence the poor reputation of manpower planning. Cowling and Walters (1990, p. 6), reporting on an IPM survey of human resource planning, found that few respondents attributed benefits of planning to increasing job satisfaction or motivation (33.5 per cent), reducing skills shortages (30.2 per cent) and reducing labour turnover (22.4 per cent). Of the respondents who used computers, 3.3 per cent reported a use for job design and 9 per cent for job analysis. These were all, and still are, vital areas of concern for any organization – areas which are at the heart of HRM approaches.

There were also a number of doubts about the connection between the business plan and the manpower plan. In a survey of US firms by Nkomo (1988), while 54 per cent of organizations reported the preparation of manpower plans, few reported a strong link between this activity and strategic business planning. Pearson (1991, p. 20) reports the problem for manpower planners where business objectives may be absent or where they may not be communicated. Cowling and Walters (1990, p. 6) found that 58.4 per cent of respondents faced a low priority given to planning compared with immediate management concerns. They concluded, 'Of comprehensive and systematic manpower planning fully integrated into strategic planning there exist few examples at the present time'.

There have been a number of attempts to make manpower planning techniques 'user-friendly' to non-specialists. Thus the fall-out from theoretical progress in manpower analysis has been the application of techniques to help with particular problems in the workplace. Bell (1989, p. 42) argued that personnel managers understood the concept of manpower planning, even if line managers and corporate planners did not, and that they were able to use basic techniques.

Many personnel managers have been able to use manpower planning techniques to help them understand and deal with 'real' manpower problems, for example, why one department in an organization seems to suffer from a dramatically higher labour turnover than others, or why graduate trainees are not retained in sufficient numbers. At times when most people employed in most organizations were employed on permanent contracts with defined tasks to perform, based on stable skills-sets, personnel managers were able to build up a 'toolbag' of key manpower measures such as turnover, retention and stability and absenteeism. All could be relatively easily calculated either monthly or quarterly and expressed graphically to reveal trends and future paths. In recent years, such techniques have been incorporated into PC-based computerised personnel information systems (CPIS). As the software became more user-friendly, personnel departments were able to take advantage and make themselves more responsive to business needs.

This could seen as part of a continuing search by the personnel function to find areas of expertise that would legitimize its position and prove its value by 'adding to the bottom line'. In this approach, manpower plans and policies serve as initiators of operations, and techniques are used to monitor the progress of operations and to raise an awareness of problems as they arise. There is an attempt to use manpower information as a way of understanding problems so that action can be taken as appropriate. The disproportionate influence of the plan as a solution is replaced by an attention to planning as a continuous process. In this way personnel managers have been practising what Fyfe (1986, p. 66) referred to as 'the diagnostic approach to manpower planning'. This approach built on and broadened the rationalized approach to identify problem areas, and to understand why they were occurring. The theoretical idea of a balance of demand and supply and equilibrium can only occur on paper or on the computer screen. The more likely real-life situation is one of continuous imbalance as a result of the dynamic conditions facing any organization, the behaviour of people and the imperfections of manpower models. The diagnostic approach is based on the following thesis:

> before any manager seeks to bring about change, or reduce the degree of imbalance, he or she must be fully aware of the reasons behind the imbalance (or the manpower problem) in the first place. Unless managers understand more about the nature of manpower problems, their attempts to control events will suffer from the hit-and-miss syndrome (Fyfe, 1986, p. 66).

By comparison with the rationalized approach, manpower problems using a diagnostic approach are identified and explored so that they can be understood, with the data used to help in this process and the speed of the computer providing support at an early stage (Figure 6.2). The rationalized approach seeks to minimize the time spent on such matters, preferring instead to focus on problems that can be easily defined or that most closely match ready-prepared solutions which may be difficult to challenge. For example, in the rationalized approach, organization practices and methods – which include the division of labour, the design of work, the technology used, the relationships between departments and groups and the degree of management supervision – will precede the manpower review and be taken as a set of 'givens' in the ensuing calculations. Yet these may be the very factors which lie at the heart of manpower problems. Thus a telephone sales organization that faces a problem of retaining staff may respond to this imbalance by stepping up recruitment or increasing pay. A diagnostic approach however would mean becoming aware of this problem by monitoring manpower statistics such as wastage and stability, and obtaining qualitative data by interviewing staff. The interviews may reveal concerns with job satisfaction and career paths open to staff, reflecting their aspirations which are not being met by current practices. Rather than express these aspirations openly for fear

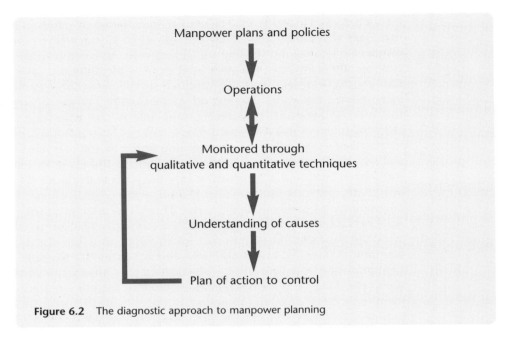

Figure 6.2 The diagnostic approach to manpower planning

of conflict with management, many staff prefer to seek employment elsewhere. The loss of skilled labour has important cost implications and, in the face of continuing shortages of skilled workers, a diagnostic approach to retention can provide a significant pay-off. Bevan (1991) provides a guide to some of the reasons for high staff turnover. Significantly, but not unexpectedly, pay was not the only issue. Among the main factors identified were:

● job not matching expectation for new employees
● lack of attention from line managers and lack of training
● lack of autonomy, responsibility, challenge and variety in the work
● disappointment with promotion and development opportunities
● standards of management including unapproachable, uncaring and distant behaviour and a failure to consult.

These are all complex factors reflecting general areas of concern, but which require solutions that are specific to the context of each organisation. In the case of the telephone sales example, the organization could respond to the diagnosis in various ways. For example, management could accept the problem and do nothing except lower the quality of recruitment so that, hopefully, those staff would be less likely to have career aspirations. Hardly very progressive and not very complex, but certainly an option. However, the organization could also attempt to improve the work environment and work practices so as to provide avenues for greater job satisfaction and personal growth. This may have implications for job design, department structure and management style, creating a tension that will have to be resolved. In this way, manpower planning becomes integrated into the whole process of management of the employment relationship, which itself plays a proactive part in affecting organization, strategy, structure and practices. Importantly, manpower planning has a part to play in bridging the gap between the needs of the organization (as defined by senior management) and the needs of individual employees. This theme will be explored later in the chapter.

While the diagnostic approach to manpower planning will have an incremental impact, the changes that it will bring about will accumulate in the organization's value system and mould its response to significant human resource issues. A good example was provided by responses to the decline in the number of young people entering the UK workforce in the late 1980s. It had been predicted that such a decline would cause labour markets to tighten all over the UK, particularly in those areas and sectors where organizations had already faced constraints on production posed by shortages of skilled workers. Atkinson (1989, p. 22) outlined a range of responses to this problem based on three characteristics:

1. *Sequential* – 'introduced only slowly as the full seriousness of the shortage problem becomes apparent to firms'.
2. *Hierarchical* – 'with more difficult/expensive responses deployed only when easier/cheaper ones have proved inadequate'.
3. *Cumulative* – 'they will build on each other'.

Starting with tactical responses, such as doing nothing or competing for the diminishing supply, an organization could progress to more strategic options such as identifying new and substitute supplies of labour and improving the use and performance of existing workers, the latter responses having important implications for the nature of the employment relationship and the approach to manpower planning.[4]

Human resource planning

In the 1990s the term human resource planning (HRP) gradually replaced manpower planning but its meaning and practice have been subjected to much discussion and variation. These can be seen as features of soft–hard dichotomy in HRM. The 'soft' version where, to use David Guest's phrasing, HRM 'is carefully defined to reflect a particular approach to the management of people in organisations' (1989, p. 48). This will occur as a consequence of senior management's belief that people represent the key source of competitive advantage and that the continuing development of those people will be a vital feature of strategy both in its formation and implementation. In this version, HRP builds on and develops the rationalized and diagnostic approaches to manpower planning that we have already identified in this chapter. It certainly may involve the use of manpower modelling, simulations and statistical techniques. However, these will be set within an overall approach to planning that will underpin the package of interdependent policies and activities, which form the HRM cycle that we identified in Chapter 1, with the emphasis on *human resource* management (Legge, 1995, p. 67).

The external factors that we identified in Chapter 3, combined with recession in the 1990s, resulted for many organizations in approaches to HRP that have more in common with the 'hard' version of HRM, where HR activities are designed to respond to strategy, with people viewed as a resource whose cost must be controlled. The emphasis is on human *resource management* (Legge, 1995, p. 66). Taking the lead from strategy, in this version HRP is concerned more with the right quantity of people in the right place at the right time who can be utilized in the most cost-effective manner.

The two versions of HRM and HRP are not necessarily incompatible but they have posed something of a dilemma to organisations over the past few years, which has resulted in a number of tensions in the way that HRP works out in practice. As with all dilemmas, there is a danger of overemphasis of one factor at the expense of others. For example, what are the implications of emphasizing 'hard' HRM in a recession?

Reconciling the soft–hard dilemma

In the diagnostic approach to manpower planning, quantitative planning techniques are used in combination with qualitative techniques to identify and understand the causes of manpower problems. The information can then be used to generate solutions equal to the complexity of the problems. We also saw that such an approach had the potential to affect organization structure, job design and work practices. Organizations could also work out short-term tactics to deal with external manpower issues like skills shortages and a decline in the number of young people in the labour market. In both the diagnostic approach and the rationalized approach, manpower plans are established with reference to a predetermined strategy for the long term. HRM seeks to make the links between strategy, structure and HRP more explicit although the interplay of such links might be quite varied. For example, consider the case of clearing banks in the UK. While for much of their history these banks could take a generally reactive approach to a relatively stable environment, by the end of the 1980s and through the 1990s, they faced an environment of continuous flux and change in the form of growing competition, deregulation in the markets for products and services and the introduction of new technology. In the past, clearing banks were considered to be places of employment where loyalty and commitment were rewarded with job security and continuous but slow career progression through a multi-tiered grading structure. These would make traditional banks ripe to adopt many 'soft' version HRM activities but, at the same time, the banks have been forced to adopt the 'hard' version resulting in branch closures and the loss of many jobs (Storey *et al.*, 1997, p. 26).

This is a pattern that has been repeated across many organizations. HRP has been used to provide a framework to accommodate 'multifarious practices' of 'pragmatic and opportunistic' organizations (Storey, 1995, p. 14). Thus at the same time as HRP can respond to the direction given by changes in organization structure and strategy to cut costs and staff numbers, a trend referred to as 'downsizing', it can also provide the means to achieve desirable HR outcomes such as commitment and high performance. You might be forgiven for thinking that HRP is no different to the use and reputation of manpower planning in this respect. Indeed those involved in the formation and delivery of HR plans may sometimes feel the conflicts and pressures referred to earlier require some inventive word play to maintain any appearance of sense. Consider, for example, the decision in an organization to implement business process re-engineering (BPR) (Hammer and Champy, 1993). BPR is based on the view of radical change of business processes by applying information technology to integrate tasks to produce an output of value to the customer. As the change unfolds, unnecessary processes and layers of bureaucracy are identified and removed and staff become more empowered to deliver high-quality service and products. HRP might focus on the need for skills and learning and other 'soft' HRM practices. However, despite the efforts of advocates to disassociate BPR from 'downsizing' (Hammer and Stanton, 1995), BPR has almost always been accompanied by unemployment (Grey and Mitev, 1995, p. 11), a fact that HRP planners may attempt, with difficulty, to disguise.

BPR and other initiatives to restructure organizations have all posed similar difficulties for HRP and a number of organizations began to realise that losing staff could have negative consequences for the organization and society at large as well as for those made unemployed. First of all, there is the loss of skill, knowledge and wisdom which employees accumulate over years of practice at work. Second, there is the effect on those employees who remain at work after a period of downsizing, who may experience such effects of guilt, lower motivation and commitment, mistrust and insecurity where they respond sympathetically towards those made redundant (Thornhill *et al.*, 1997, p. 81).

It is also possible to take a less deterministic view of strategy, which can provide a vital interdependent link between HRP, organization structure and strategy. Mintzberg (1978, p. 935) has criticized definitions of strategy as an explicit, rationally predetermined plan as incomplete. For Mintzberg, strategy is a 'pattern in a stream of decisions'. The source of such patterns may be formulations of conscious and rational processes expressed by senior managers as intended strategy but also emergent, probably unintentional, learning and discoveries as a result of decisions made gradually over time. Included in this latter process of strategy formation will be the learning of and from employees through their interaction with the organization's structure, work processes and suppliers, clients and customers. Realized strategy will be a result of both intended and emergent processes. Diagnostic techniques of planning will tap some of this learning and, in the context of an HRM value system, learning will feed through into strategic decisions. As we will see in later chapters, this view of awareness and understanding emerging from the HRP process is fundamental to generating the energy to keep the HR cycle moving and to the achievement of desirable HR outcomes such as commitment and high performance. It is also a requisite of such approaches as total quality management and the learning organization.

HRP may have to oscillate between 'soft' and 'hard' versions of HRM and this can be shown in the way that information technology is adopted to support HRP activities via human resource information systems (HRIS). Advances in software and hardware have meant improved HRIS availability and accessibility. Increasingly, software matches an organization's HR information needs on a customized basis. In addition, the installation of HRIS software on company Intranets allows the possibility of access to employees and managers. For example, training programmes could be notified and booked via the Intranet removing routine administration from HR departments. What role does an HRIS have in the management of the hard–soft dilemma? According to Broderick and Boudreau (1992, p. 11) there are three types of IT application in HRM.

1. Transaction processing, reporting and tracking applications covering operational activities, for example payroll, record keeping, performance monitoring.
2. Expert systems to improve decisions based on an analysis of information concerning such issues as sources of new recruits, salaries and training needs.
3. Decision support systems to improve decisions through the use of scenario modelling in areas where there are no clear answers, for example team formation and management development programmes.

Research by Kinnie and Arthurs (1996) found widespread use of HRIS for transaction applications in operational areas such as employee records, payroll and absence control. There was however less use in expert systems and decision support applications which represent more advanced uses of HRIS. Part of the explanation for the relatively unambiguous use of HRIS lies with the way HR departments prove their worth in organizations. Concentrating on transaction applications provides vital flows of data for others to make decisions. However, the use of HRIS for expert systems and decision support applications, which reduce people to numbers, might be resisted by many HR practitioners as representing too much of a clash with people-orientated values (Kinnie and Arthurs, 1996, p. 13). Therefore, it is argued, a 'half-way position' has been adopted which emphasizes the value of a limited use of HRIS but which adds cost effectiveness combined with the professional performance of HR tasks which cannot be performed by IT.

External and internal labour

The rationalized approach to manpower planning is based on a neutral view of the sources of supply for forecasted demands for labour. Based on an assumption of the interchangeability of workers, the main consideration relates to costs. Thus it may be cheaper on balance to recruit workers from outside the organization and save on the costs of training those workers already employed. Similarly, the aim of minimizing costs was a key factor for many years in the process of deskilling work so that workers who left, 'wastage', could be easily substituted by new recruits. In traditional manufacturing organizations, the restrictive practices of craft-based trades unions based on time-served apprenticeships and demarcation was seen by management as justification to seek opportunities over the years to deskill the work where possible. A deskilling strategy was not always possible or desirable (see Chapter 3) and in the face of 'tight' labour markets for workers with appropriate skills, managers began to pay more attention to keeping scarce workers, using a diagnostic approach to manpower planning.

The HRP approach takes this process several stages further. Accepting that vital skills may not be available in the required quantities in the external labour market, the focus shifts to workers already employed and their potential for further development allied to the need for flexibility. Previous attention to the right number of people is superseded by attention to the right kind of people. This of course requires further explanation.

Academics working in the fields of sociology and labour economics have developed a theoretical framework, referred to as *labour market segmentation*, to classify and explain the ways in which organizations seek to employ different kinds of labour. Loveridge (1983, p. 155) developed a classification based on the following factors:

1. the degree to which workers have flexible skills which are specific to an organization
2. the degree to which work contains discretionary elements which provide stable earnings.

The classification, shown as Figure 6.3, helps to explain how and why some organizations will adopt different approaches to the management and planning of the employment relationship for different groups of employees. Thus workers in the primary internal market would include those with important and scarce skills that are specific to a particular organization; an organization would be anxious to retain such workers and develop their potential. It would be such employees who would form the focus for the application of the full range of HRM activities. On the other hand, some workers operating in the secondary internal market will be deemed by management to be of less importance, except in their availability at the times required by an organization. This could include part-time, seasonal and temporary employees. Employers might wish to recruit and retain those employees deemed by management to be the kind of workers who could be trained to the organization's requirements, but there would be less interest in applying the whole package of HRM policies to them. Workers operating in the external markets would be considered to be someone else's concern.

While the idea of labour market segmentation has been recognized for many years, recent times have seen the acceptance of a range of terms and practices, which come under the umbrella of the idea of *flexibility*. It is a term that is widely used although it often lacks specific meaning. Its ambiguity has allowed a number of interpretations to justify a variety of organization activities (see Chapter 4). Among these is the model of a *flexible firm* which

> draws into a simple framework the new elements in employers' manpower practices, bringing out the relationships between the various practices and their appropriateness for different companies and groups of workers (Atkinson and Meager, 1985, p. 2).

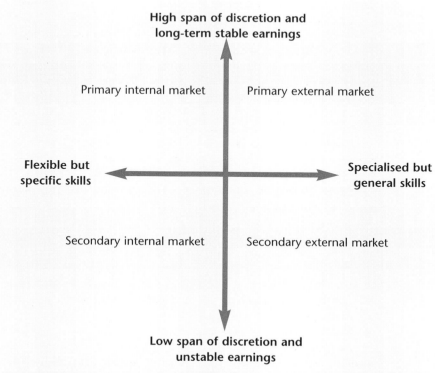

Figure 6.3 A framework of labour market segmentation
Source: Edwards *et al.*, 1983

The model identifies four types of flexibility:

1. *Functional* – a firm's ability to adjust and deploy the skills of its employees to match the tasks required by its changing workload, production methods or technology.
2. *Numerical* – a firm's ability to adjust the level of labour inputs to meet fluctuations in output.
3. *Distancing strategies* – the replacement of internal workers with external subcontractors; that is, putting some work, such as running the firm's canteen, out to contract.
4. *Financial* – support for the achievement of flexibility through the pay and reward structure.

The flexible firm will achieve these flexibilities through a division of its workforce into a 'core' group surrounded by 'peripheral' groups. The core group would be composed of those workers expected to deliver functional flexibility and would include those workers with firm-specific skills and high discretionary elements in their work. The peripheral group would be composed of a number of different workers. One category might be directly employed by a firm to perform work with a low discretionary element. Another category would be employed as required on a variety of contracts, for example, part-time, temporary and casual workers. This category might also include highly specialized workers such as consultants. The final category would be composed of trainees on government-financed schemes, some of whom may be prepared for eventual transfer to the core group.

The concept of the flexible firm has been subject to much debate during the 1980s and 90s. The model has been criticized (Pollert, 1988, p. 281) as being unsupported by the evidence and as presenting a self-fulfilling prediction of how such a firm should be created. The evidence, however, showed a confused picture. At the time of the 1987 *Employers' Labour Use Strategies* survey (Hakim, 1990, p. 162), only a small minority of employers had a conscious core–periphery manpower strategy. However an ACAS survey (1988), in the same year, found a growing range of flexible working practices. This would suggest that in the late 1980s there were many organizations adopting flexible working practices in an *ad hoc*, unplanned and, occasionally, opportunistic manner. Hakim praised the model of a flexible firm as a 'simplified synthesis' of key ideas whose achievement was to 'reveal the inner logic of existing labour strategies, to disclose the implicit structure of segmented labour markets' (1990, p. 180).

During the 1990s it has been difficult to discern whether the flexible firm has remained as an ideal type providing managers with a new set of labels. During the difficult times of recession, when downsizing was adopted by many organizations to reduce costs and intensify the use of labour, flexibility could be presented more positively as way of dealing with change and responding more rapidly to customer requirements thus securing future survival of organizations and employment. In the UK flexibility has become something of a national virtue with successive governments making use of the notion.

There are indications that flexible working methods have been adopted and are part of the expectations of many workers. For example, more people are taking temporary jobs on both a full and part-time basis, often to allow organizations to deal with seasonal fluctuations or to carry out specific projects (Department for Education and Employment, 1997, p. 16). There has also been a growth in subcontracting or outsourcing non-core activities.

An important variation in working patterns has been the growth in telework or homeworking. Recent research has identified five main types of teleworking (Huws, 1997).

1. *Multi-site* – alternation between working on an employer's premises and working elsewhere, usually at home but also in a telecottage or telecentre.
2. *Tele-homeworking* – work based at home, usually for a single employer and involving low-skilled work, performed by people who are tied to their homes.
3. *Freelance* – work for a variety of different clients.
4. *Mobile* – work carried out using communication technologies such as mobile phones, fax machines, PC connections via the Internet, often by professional, commercial, technical and managerial staff who work 'on the road'.
5. *Relocated back-functions* – specialist centres carrying out activities such as data entry, airline bookings, telephone banking, telephone sales and helpline services.

There can be little doubt that these forms of flexibility will continue to develop, particularly where they are based round the growth of information technologies, especially the Internet. What are the HR implications of the emerging 'virtual' organization? For example you might examine how staff might be recruited and selected for teleworking. What special attributes or competencies are required? How might performance be monitored or managed and what special features of reward and development need to be considered? These are the same issues that would feature in any HRP process; however, the introduction and management of telecommuting demonstrates even more starkly some of the tensions that we have already mentioned. See HRM in practice 6.1 for an example of the way one organization is managing teleworking.

The concept of flexibility has been referred to as a 'panacea of restructuring' (Pollert, 1991, p. xx), as a way of conflating different changes in the organization of work such as multiskilling, job enlargement, labour intensification, cost control (Pollert, 1991, p. 3) and, more recently, self-managed teams (Wageman, 1997). However, many organizations have adopted the language of flexibility and attempted to apply the practices, and HR planners have to respond accordingly. The level of success is not yet entirely convincing. For example, research for the Institute of Personnel and Development into the implications of 'lean systems of production' found that multiskilling and more involvement in decision making was offset by greater stress, more workloads and feelings of blame and isolation (IPD, 1996). Managers have been too easily convinced by the hype of flexibility and failed, once again, to consider the impact of changes to working practices and arrangements on the employment relationship.

Career management

One area of HRP that needs to be examined in the light of changes in the workplace is the ways careers are managed and developed. Mayo (1991, p. 69) has defined career management as follows:

> The design and implementation of organizational processes which enable the careers of individuals to be planned and managed in a way that optimizes both the needs of the organization and the preferences and capabilities of individuals.

HRM in practice 6.1

Nationwide moves over to telework

Nationwide Building Society has joined the growing
number of firms examining new ways of working

BY DAVID LITTLEFIELD People Management, 12 September 1996

One hundred and fifty employees in the Nationwide's estates department are championing a teleworking project that, if successful, may be rolled out to more of the company's 2400 head office staff.

Tim Plummer, head of estates, said change programmes can be introduced in one of two ways: piecemeal or all at once. Plummer has opted for the latter. Over the past two years his department has delayered, introduced self-managed teams, expanded the role of secretaries and reduced the number of job descriptions from 58 to five. Now it is experimenting with teleworking.

The company joins a growing number of employers, including NatWest, Lloyds Bank, Oxfordshire County Council and Hewlett-Packard, which have offered teleworking opportunities to staff. Teleworking (regularly working from home using computer technology) has been seized upon as a sort of management panacea that promises huge savings as a result of reduced office space

and the greater efficiency of participating staff.

> **Teleworking (regularly working from home using computer technology) has been seized upon as a sort of management panacea that promises huge savings as a result of reduced office space and the greater efficiency of participating staff.**

Nationwide's project is still in its infancy, but the hope is that the changes will be largely self-financing and will not require any compulsory redundancies. At present just one person has opted for full-time teleworking, with another half a dozen choosing to do so on a part-time basis. Plummer, whose department runs the company's buildings, guesses that 10 per cent of his department will eventually move to teleworking, although he hopes that other departments will

keep the ball rolling.

'We're trying to recognise the full potential of technology, but we can't destroy the psychology of work,' said Plummer, who is keen to proceed slowly and assess the impact of the practice in six to eight months' time.

One of the problems is spotting the people who would benefit from working at home, and making sure that they could return to full-time office working should their circumstances change. 'We've got to be very careful to show a revolving door,' said Plummer, who has been working with consultants Advanced Workplace Associates (AWA) for the past six months with the aim of putting together a 'toolkit' to help implement a working policy.

The priority is to make teleworking voluntary. 'Don't impose it – simply make it available,' said Andrew Mawson, managing director of AWA. 'Quite a large number of people will come forward if it suits their lifestyle.'

In the past, the term 'career' is one that has usually been applied to managerial and professional workers. Many organizations responded to the career aspirations of such employees through HRP policies and processes such as succession planning, secondment, 'fast-track' development for identified 'high-flyers' and a vast array of personal and management development activities. While organizations were structured into a number of hierarchical levels and grades, such employees could look forward to a path of promotion that signified the development of their careers. Of course, along the way, many employees might encounter blocks to their careers such as lack of opportunities and support, and for women, cultural and structural prejudices to career progress referred to as the 'glass ceiling' (Davidson and Cooper, 1992). Graduates too might find their aspirations unsatisfied as they experienced a gap between what they expected and what their organizations provided (Pickard, 1997, p. 27).

During the 1980s, with the growing influence of ideas relating to a people-orientated HRM, reflecting a *unitarist perspective* on the employment relationship of a common interest between the organization and employees, many organizations began to extend career development activities to a wider range of employees. You might question whether the idea of a career can be extended to a larger number of employees. After all, not everyone can be 'promoted' through the organization hierarchy even if they had the potential to be so. This is a view that is often presented to justify the *status quo* and to limit the resources devoted to employee development. However, it is a view based on a traditional concept of career. As many organizations have discovered, continuous personal development is possible among large groups of employees if limiting factors that prevent the exposure of employees to new opportunities and experiences for development can be removed. Limiting factors may include organization structure and climate, and the design of work. In this sense, the term 'career' is extended to apply not only to movement through pre-defined stages such as those found in professions or organization hierarchies, but also to personal growth and development through the employees' interaction with their work environment. This view matches Hirsh's (1990, p. 18) 'developing potential' emergent model of succession planning where 'in a person-based approach, posts can be considered as ephemeral and may be designed around people'.

Hirsh and Jackson (1997, p. 9) refer to a 'pendulum of ownership of career development' between the organization and individual responsibility. Their research in case studies of UK organizations, found that this had swung towards emphasizing individuals in driving career and development processes with the provision of career workshops, learning centres and personal development plans (PDPs) (Tamkin *et al.*, 1995). At the same time, as many organizations began to engage in restructuring activities that led to the removal of layers of grades, referred to as 'delayering', the spread of career development initiatives could be seen as way of empowering and motivating staff who remained in place as part of a core workforce. Through HRP, an organization could aim to provide a framework for the integration of career management activities and processes. Within this framework, the HRM cycle shows the links between the key HR activities that are required for integration. However, the dynamics of career management will depend on the process for bridging the multiple and possibly conflicting demands of the organization and the needs and aspirations of employees. Verlander (1985, p. 20) proposed a model of career management based on career counselling between employees and their line manager. The main elements of this model are shown in Figure 6.4. The model highlights the importance of the role of line managers in HRM processes. The nature of this role, and the skills required, will be explored further in Chapters 8 (Performance Appraisal) and 10 (Human Resource Development).

HRM in practice 6.2 shows how some companies are responding to the issue of career management.

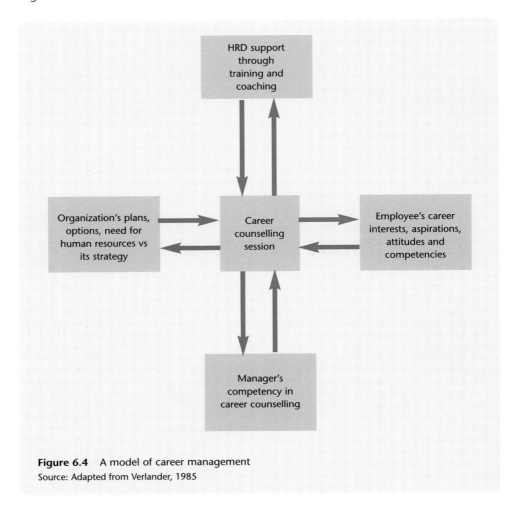

Figure 6.4 A model of career management
Source: Adapted from Verlander, 1985

Simultaneously with the positive emphasis on careers, in some organizations delayering, downsizing and the closure of traditional paths of promotion create both job insecurity and confusion. Employees may find their expected progress blocked and their careers plateaued (Appelbaum and Santiago, 1997, p. 13). Hirsh and Jackson (1997) reported that various tensions such as competition, recession and short-term financial pressures, a breakdown in functional structures in favour of process structures and even the loss of bureaucratic personnel systems which planned career moves, have all combined, for some companies, to 'dump the basic idea of the corporate career.' However, more optimistically, the research also found evidence of organizations recognizing the negative impact of such pressures and attempting to swing the pendulum of responsibility towards a position of 'partnership', where there is more emphasis on sharing responsibility. Once again, however, there seems to be emerging a rhetoric of career development for everyone at work but with different patterns for different work groups:

HRM in practice 6.2

Staff value a career path above salary

Companies are learning that they will hold on to staff
only if they give them the chance to develop

BY RUTH PRICKETT People Management, 16 April 1998

Staff retention is once again a key concern for almost two-thirds of UK companies, while turnover in the retail sector is twice as high as the national average. But firms wishing to buy their employees' loyalty would be well advised to offer career opportunities rather than money, according to a survey by Reed Personnel Services.

With staff turnover at 26 per cent, it is not surprising that three out of four retailers have introduced, or are considering introducing, measures to retain people. Less predictably, however, respondents put a higher salary second to the chance of career progression in a list of the top five reasons why people change jobs.

Employers' responses to the problem vary widely, from staff recognition programmes to multi-skilling and team-building exercises, but 70 per cent of those surveyed listed training as their primary solution. 'This research emphasises how effective it can be to concentrate on increasing staff morale rather than pay,' said James Reed, chief executive of Reed.

Tesco, one of the retailers featured in the survey, began a staff retention programme some years ago. Although turnover was 33 per cent last year, the company is confident that morale is rising and long-term loyalty has increased.

Employees in every store have recently gone through a management programme focusing on improving core skills and process development. Managers scrutinised jobs and attempted to eliminate unnecessary or bureaucratic processes so that staff were able to concentrate on the main business.

> 'This research
> emphasises how effective
> it can be to concentrate
> on increasing staff
> morale rather than
> pay...'

'Gone are the days when a member of staff on the customer service desk had to ask permission from a senior manager to give a refund,' said Andrea Cartwright, corporate HR policy manager at Tesco. 'This was a waste of time that annoyed customers and demotivated staff.'

The company has been running a programme called Project Future since early 1997 and, according to Cartwright, it is now an ongoing process. Managers attend short core skill workshops in their stores, together with shopfloor staff who are earmarked for promotion.

This training fits in with managers' individual career development plans, and the company is also keen to encourage employees to apply for jobs in different functions. 'I've been here for 12 years, but never in the same job for more than two,' Cartwright said. 'It's almost like working for a different company each time you move.'

Tesco's expansion into central Europe has opened up new possibilities for long-term posts abroad. More than 100 of its British managers are working in Poland, Hungary and the Czech and Slovak republics, and 31 more central European hypermarkets are planned for the next few years.

Back at home, the company has introduced more flexibility to encourage the store's predominantly female workforce to return to work after maternity leave. More people are taking career breaks and returning to part-time management positions.

'We are operating a 24-hour, seven-days-a-week business,' Cartwright said. 'If a mother wants to fit her work around her kids or her husband's shifts, then we can accommodate that.'

1. senior managers and 'high potential' staff – careers managed by the organization, not always for life, but succession planning to fill senior positions
2. highly skilled workers – attempts to attract and keep key workers by offering career development
3. the wider workforce – more limited development opportunities often caused by, and resulting in, uncertainty over career paths.

This segmented pattern is in line with the earlier discussion. What seems to be emerging is a varied pattern of careers for the next century and it is probable that many people will not be able to rely on a linear career path through their working lives. HRP will be increasingly concerned with lifetime learning, continuous professional development and employability through the acquisition and development of key competencies.

In embracing an idea of development and careers for all employees, many organizations have sought a language that could enable discussions about the performance, capabilities and aspirations of individuals to take place on the basis of a common understanding of terms. In recent years, such understanding has been achieved by the development of competency-based approaches, developed to create a taxonomy of either criterion-related behaviours or standards of performance. According to research evidence (Coverdale, 1995), competency frameworks have a wide range of applications, including a more structured approach to training and development (see Chapter 10), managing performance (see Chapter 8) and provision of a benchmark for rewards and promotion. It is claimed that competency frameworks 'lie at the heart of all' approaches to HRM (Boam and Sparrow, 1992, p. 13)

The difference between an emphasis on behaviours and standards of performance may seem trivial but is interesting since it reflects differences in approaches and terms employed. The standards approach employs the term 'competence' and, in the UK, has mainly been used in the development of National Vocational Qualifications (NVQs). The key definition of competence is

> the ability to perform particular activities within an occupation to a prescribed standard (Fletcher, 1991).

NVQs are now available for most occupations in the UK including the work of managers where the Management Charter Initiative (MCI) has had the responsibility for developing a set of management qualifications. NVQs, including the management qualifications, differ from academic qualifications by focusing on performance at work and outcomes that can be assessed against standards defined as performance criteria. NVQs are provided at different levels, starting at Level 1 for work which is composed of routine and predictable activities, through to Level 5 for work involving application of complex techniques in unpredictable contexts. This allows people to build up qualifications from the time they complete formal education to the end of their career. NVQs have become a key part of government initiatives to improve the skill base of the UK economy and an important means for many people to progressively achieve higher qualifications.

The behaviour approach has formed the focus for definitions of 'competency':

> the set of behaviour patterns that the incumbent needs to bring to a position in order to perform its tasks and functions with competence (Woodruffe, 1992, p. 17).

Competency frameworks are concerned with behaviour that is relevant to the job, and the effective or competent performance of that job. Usually such frameworks are developed within organizations and are based on understandings and meanings of behaviour that exist within an organization. The analysis should be able to identify and isolate dimensions of behaviour that are distinct and are associated with competent or effective performance. Once identified, competencies can provide a user-friendly starting point for the assessment and development of people in an organization and a link of such processes to organization strategy.

The following is a list of competencies developed for managers at a software company in Yorkshire:

- Managing own performance
- Planning, decision making and controlling
- Dealing with administration
- Financial awareness
- Organizational awareness
- Recruiting
- Appraising
- Educating, training and developing
- Managing staff performance
- Managing meetings
- Customer appreciation
- Responding to customers.

It is now recognized that competency or NVQ competence-based frameworks can be an important means of integrating HRM processes for all employees.

Chapter summary

HRP is more than just the sophisticated application of quantitative manpower planning techniques for the forecast of demand and supply flows into, through, and from organizations. It is an inseparable part of an organization's overall approach to the management of its human resources. This chapter has outlined the way early approaches to manpower planning had limited and fluctuating popularity. However, through problem-solving diagnostic approaches, planning techniques could be used to learn about employee problems and explore possible solutions that have the potential ultimately to affect organization strategy. HRP can be a continuation and extension of this process, which fully recognizes the potential of people and their needs in the development of strategies and plans. However we have also shown that HRP has become part of a rhetoric in the 1990s where organizations reconciled the dilemma of soft and hard versions of HRM. In many organizations, HRP used sophisticated software packages to reduce the size of the workforce, or 'downsize', and develop policies to provide a 'flexible' workforce. At the same time, for those that remained in employment, there has been an increase in job insecurity and frustrated career expectations. Some organizations have recognized that losing staff also means a loss of key skills and knowledge and have sought to ameliorate the difficulties with career management policies and competency frameworks. However, there will continue to be significant changes in the structure and location of work. How organizations deal with such changes will lie at the heart of HRP in the future.

Key concepts

Manpower planning
Planning techniques and modelling
The diagnostic approach
Human resource planning
Telecommuting

The flexible firm
Core and periphery workforce
Career management
Labour market segmentation
Competencies and competences

Discussion questions

1. 'When an organization is mapping out its future needs it is a serious mistake to think primarily in terms of number, flows and economic models.' Discuss.

2. How is HRP linked to corporate planning?

3. What would be your response to the publication of figures which showed an above-average turnover of students in a university or college department?

4. Should organizations faced with shortages of skilled labour 'poach' these workers from other organizations by bidding up wages?

5. What is meant by the 'flexible firm'? Explain the implications of the flexible firm for the management of human resources.

6. How can competencies help organizations improve the management of careers?

Further reading

Bramham, J. (1989) *Human Resource Planning*, London: IPM.

Fyfe, J. (1986) Putting people back into the manpower planning equations, *Personnel Management*, October, pp. 64–9.

Hirsh, W. and Jackson, C. (1997) *Strategies for Career Development: Promise, Practice and Pretence*, Report No. 305, Brighton: IES.

Pollert, A. (ed.) (1991) *Farewell to Flexibility?*, Oxford: Blackwell.

Rothwell, S. (1995) Human resource planning. In Storey, J. (ed.) *Human Resource Management: A Critical Text*, London: Routledge.

Career management at JJJ Bank plc

Read the following case study and prepare responses to the questions that follow. Please attempt to illustrate your responses with examples.

JJJ Bank is one of the UK's major clearing banks. Over the last decade, the bank has faced an environment that is increasingly competitive and fast moving. The bank has been undergoing a major strategic review of its structure and activities. A key belief has been that greater responsibility for the development and delivery of activities should be passed to front-line employees. Successive voluntary redundancy programmes had made for a relatively young workforce.

Hitherto, career development had equated to promotion through a 17-grade structure. Hence, prior to the redundancies, such promotion could be expected through the grades every 2 to 3 years. Fairly simple manpower planning techniques now reveal a slowing-down in the number of future promotions. A formal integrated career management framework does not currently exist.

Recently, a series of one-day workshops concerning career management at the bank was held by the HR manager for a random selection of managers and employees. One of the key issues highlighted was that career progression was seen as a 'gradist' concept due to the number of grades. This was seen to reduce emphasis on career management issues – such as developmental job moves, sideways job moves, rewards for on-the-job and self-directed development – promoting an entrepreneurial job culture based on knowledge, experience, skill and opportunity and the evolution of a flatter, more flexible organization structure. It soon became clear that there was little congruence between the fast-moving environment which the bank now faced and career management. Perhaps most important of all, line managers often did not promote development, seeing it as the role of the HR function to develop people and manage careers.

In a follow-up survey of all staff, some of the key findings were as follows:

- when looking at career issues in the organization, it is suggested that line managers are not willing to develop staff, particularly 'on the job'
- the organization does not readily promote development or on-the-job development
- the organization does not help people manage their own careers
- the organization does not often explain the career options open to people
- the organization needs to devote more resources to helping people to manage their development and career planning.

There is an overall belief that it is important to work for an organization that allows people to build their own careers, since this:

- encourages personal development
- allows people to develop by experiencing different fields of work
- allows people to develop their existing competencies and skills

- provides information on career development
- regards career development as important.

Further research about the criteria used for promotions revealed that while individuals wanted promotion decisions to take into account their career development, they believed that they were promoted on the simple basis of suitable vacancies being available. Furthermore, with regard to whom the system promoted, women felt that expediency was favoured over and above career development.

Task

Please illustrate your responses to the following questions with examples.

1. What are the key issues in the management of careers in this organization?

2. What suggestions would you make for improving career management in this organization? What are the key roles and responsibilities?

3. How could a competency framework help this organization plan and manage careers?

Notes

1. Cowling, A. and Walters, M. (1990) Manpower Planning – where are we today?, *Personnel Review*, **19**(3).
2. Sisson, K. and Temperley, S. (1994) From manpower planning to strategic human resource management. In Sisson, K. (ed.) *Personnel Management*, Oxford: Blackwell.
3. Herriot, P. (1995) The management of careers. In Tyson, S. (ed.) (1995b) *Strategic Prospects for HRM*, London: IPD.
4. It is interesting to note that fears concerning the 'demographic time bomb' proved to be largely unfounded in the UK as a consequence of the recession in the first half of the 1990s. Some organizations clearly did make efforts to respond. For example, some of the supermarket chains adopted a policy of recruiting older workers. However, for many organizations, there were a number of new issues which had manpower implications that required a strategic response.

chapter seven

Recruitment and selection

Jeffrey Gold

We get people with degrees and God knows what applying for bog standard jobs.[1]

We don't interview people, we audition them.[2]

We didn't want the traditional 20-minute interview, and the you-go-to-the-same-football-match-as-me-so-you-must-be-okay line.[3]

Chapter outline

Chapter objectives

After studying this chapter, you should be able to:

1. Understand the place of recruitment and selection in HRM.

2. Explain the nature of attraction in recruitment.

3. Explain the effectiveness of various selection techniques.

4. Understand the place of recruitment and selection as a stage in the formation of the employment relationship.

⬤ Introduction

Towards the end of the 1980s recruitment and selection were seen as two of the key issues facing organizations as they prepared for the 1990s. Continuing skills shortages and the prospect of a significant decline in the number of young people (the so-called 'demographic time bomb') would, according to Curnow (1989, p. 40), mean that 'recruitment is moving to the top of the personnel professional's agenda' and that the 1990s would be 'the era of the recruiter' (see also Table 1.1, Chapter 1). Such would be the difficulties in recruiting and retaining staff, with a shift in power to those with skills to sell, that many organizations would require a 'radical response' (Herriot, 1989, p. 35). Thus employers would also be compelled to see the attraction and retention of workers as part of the evolving employment relationship, based on a mutual and reciprocal understanding of expectations. Recruitment followed by selection would be vital stages in the formation of such expectations, with an emphasis on a two-way flow of communication. Employees would be selecting an organization and the work on offer as much as employers would be selecting employees. Traditional approaches, that attempt to attract a wide choice of candidates for vacancies before screening out those who do not match the criteria set in job descriptions and personnel specifications, would be too one-sided.

For a short time at least, a number of organizations did react to the impending shortages along the lines suggested. Some organizations began to adjust and widen their recruitment criteria in order to increase the numbers of recruits (Hendry *et al.*, 1988, p. 38). However, many of the changes adopted could be seen as tactical adjustments only. By the end of the 1980s, recession had already begun and power in the labour market swung back to employers, except in continuing cases of skills shortages.

In the 1990s there have been wide variations in recruitment and selection practices reflecting an organization's strategy and its philosophy towards the management of people. Employees may be seen as part of the *primary internal market* (See Chapter 6) and become the focus for measures intended to bring about increased motivation, increased acceptance of responsibility, deepened skills and greater commitment, providing the organization with a competitive edge. Such employees become part of an organization's core workforce, and recruitment and selection represent the entry point activities. Seen in this way, emphasis may be placed on admitting only those applicants who are likely to behave, acquire skills and show 'attitudinal commitment' (Guest, 1989, p. 49) in line with the requirements of an organization's strategy. In many organizations, competency frameworks have been developed and utilized to specify the skills and qualities required from potential employees (Roberts 1997). Such frameworks have allowed organizations to adopt a range of sophisticated recruitment and selection techniques in order to identify and admit the 'right' people. In this way, as 'organizationally defined critical qualities' (Iles and Salaman 1995, p. 204), a competency framework augments an organization's power. Once selected, employees may be able to move on to the HRM cycle as part of a progression and development of a career within that organization. In theory, through the use of competencies, employees could be moving round the cycle several times during their working lives and thus subject to recruitment and selection processes on more than one occasion in the same organization. More advanced approaches to recruitment and selection are part of a package of HRM activities. As a contrast, approaches to the recruitment and selection of employees forming the *secondary internal market* would include less screening at the point of entry, with attention paid mainly to possession of the skills required. Such employees might be recruited and selected by cheaper methods but still, perhaps, with a connection to organization strategy via the specification of competencies.

Variations in practice, however, are bound by the law of the land. Recruitment and selection have been notorious areas for prejudice and subjective influence and these could well result in infringements under legislation dealing with discrimination. In the UK the key legal provisions are contained in the Sex Discrimination Act 1975 (amended 1986), and the Race Relations Act 1976. Both acts disallow discrimination and in general there are two forms of discrimination which are against the law:

1. Direct – where workers of a particular sex, race or ethnic group are treated less favourably than other workers, for example, a policy to recruit only men to management posts.
2. Indirect – where a particular requirement apparently treats everyone equally but has a disproportionate effect on a particular group and the requirement cannot be shown to be justified. For example, a job advert which specified that applicants should be 1.85 metres tall might unjustifiably result in a low proportion of female applicants.

Under certain circumstances, however, both acts allow for discrimination on grounds of genuine occupational qualifications. For example, under Section 7(2) of the Sex Discrimination Act it is possible to recruit a man only when 'the essential nature of the job calls for a man for reasons of physiology (excluding physical strength or stamina) or, in dramatic performances or other entertainment, for reasons of authenticity, so that the essential nature of the job would be materially different if carried out by a woman'. HRM in practice 7.1 shows an attempt by the police force, in collaboration with the Comission for Racial Equality, to increase the number of ethnic minority applicants. This practice is allowed under the Race Relations Act.

In general, personnel departments have played a key role in bringing organization practices relating to recruitment and selection in line with the provisions of the law. Certainly, there are few examples of direct discrimination, although indirect discrimination is more difficult to uncover and eliminate.

In addition to the above Acts, the Disability Discrimination Act 1996 makes it illegal to discriminate against disabled persons unless discrimination can be justified by the 'circumstances of the particular case'. The Act requires organizations employing more than 20 people to remove or adjust any working conditions and procedures that might disadvantage disabled persons, for example working hours, physical features of premises, special equipment. The Act also widens the definition of disabled persons to include those registered as disabled and those discriminated against because of 'severe' disfigurements such as scars and skin disease and progressive conditions such as HIV and multiple sclerosis.

Recruitment, selection and the HRM cycle

If HRM is concerned with the development of an integrated package of policies towards the management of people, then recruitment and selection represent vital stages in the determination of which employees will be able to benefit from such policies. Watson (1994, p. 185) refers to recruitment and selection as:

the processes by which organizations solicit, contact and interest potential appointees, and then establish whether it would be appropriate to appoint any of them.

Watson goes on to note that it is the task of management to influence this process to the advantage of the organization but other parties involved may have different interests. We have already mentioned that, under different labour market conditions, power in this process will swing towards the buyers or sellers of labour, employers and employees respectively. It is therefore important to understand that the dimension of power will always be present in recruitment and selection, even in organizations that purport to have a 'soft' HRM orientation. Thus, in the 1990s there have been more graduates entering the labour market but the number of 'graduate' jobs has not kept pace with a consequent reduction in the power of many new graduates to find employment on terms to their advantage (IPD, 1997, p. 3). It is also reported that many employers have reservations about employing graduates for 'non-graduate' jobs. Why do you think this might be happening?

 HRM in practice 7.1

Ethnic minorities aim for high-flying squad

A scheme offering police officers fast-track promotion is attracting increasing interest from black and Asian people

BY NEIL MERRICK People Management, 20 February 1997

Police recruitment officers have been encouraged by a 50 per cent increase in the number of ethnic minority applicants attempting to join the accelerated promotion scheme for graduates (APSG).

Of the 2 237 applications for the APSG received this year, 137 were from ethnic minority candidates – their biggest representation in the history of the scheme. It follows a slump in applications from ethnic minorities during 1995–96, when the total number of candidates was also down.

This year's increase coincides with a campaign run in conjunction with the Commission for Racial Equality (CRE) to foster careers in the police. 'Ethnic minorities are definitely show-

ing more interest in the scheme,' said Superintendent John Crosse, graduate liaison officer.

> **Police recruitment officers have been encouraged by a 50 per cent increase in the number of ethnic minority applicants attempting to join the accelerated promotion scheme for graduates (APSG).**

The APSG gives graduates the chance to become sergeants within 36 months and to attain the rank of inspector after around five years. Applicants for the programme attend a

similar three-day selection event to those hoping to enter through the non-accelerated route. Individuals who pass this stage move on to an extended interview, based around an assessment centre, which lasts a further four days.

There is no quota for the APSG intake, although the total of successful candidates is usually small. Last year, for example, there were 26. The number offered APSG status this year will not be known until April, when extended interviews are held.

Just one ethnic minority candidate was selected in 1994–95, but officers managing the scheme hope that they will soon start to make a greater impression in the same way as women have done since the early 1990s.

'We are getting a steady stream of excellent women,' Crosse said. 'Once they apply, they are normally more successful at completing each stage than male candidates. We hope the increase in applications from ethnic minorities will be reflected in the numbers chosen in April.'

In the West Midlands, where about ten per cent of the total annual intake of new officers comes from the ethnic minority population, applications to join the APSG from ethnic minorities rose from 13 to 20.

Inspector Steve Whitehead, recruiting officer for the region, attributed the increase to advertisements placed in *Kaleidoscope* and *Hobson's Ethnic Minority Casebook*, national journals with a substantial ethnic minority readership.

One of the officers featured in these adverts was Jawad Akhtar, a chief inspector with West Yorkshire constabulary. He was selected for the scheme in 1982, became an inspector in 1989 and gained promotion to his present rank two years ago.

Akhtar said that some members of the Asian community might see his progress in the police as 'tokenism', but added: 'Once they see it's actually possible for an Asian officer to gain the rank of chief constable, they may decide to go for it themselves.'

Officers also visited universities, where the number of ethnic minority students is rising. 'They have a lot of doubts and queries that need answering, and they want to see a profile of someone who is already working in the police,' Whitehead said.

Pam Smith, a senior officer with the CRE, said that forces were making more effort to ensure that they reflected the composition of local communities. But she added that the scheme was the only way that large numbers of ethnic minority officers would reach senior ranks in the near future.

Just over one-third of APSG applications have come from women during each of the past four years. IN 1994–95, half of the 24 applicants offered APSG status were female. This figure fell to eight out of 28 last year, but Crosse believes that assessment centres seem to favour women in the police in the same way that they do in other professions by drawing out the competences required of future leaders.

Much will depend on the extent to which the overall management philosophy supports and reinforces an approach to HRM that focuses on the utilization and the development of new employees once they have gained entry to an organization. Throughout this book we have referred to the HRM cycle as a representation of HRM activities. While the policies will be designed to achieve particular organization targets and goals, those policies will also provide an opportunity for individual needs to emerge and to be satisfied. This view assumes that organization targets and goals and individual needs can coincide, with mutual benefits to both sides of the employment relationship. While many commentators would doubt that such mutuality could ever occur on the basis of equality, and that organization needs, as determined by senior management, would always take precedence, we have already argued that through HRM activities individual needs may influence the perception of organization needs. Recruitment and selection processes will therefore aim to attract and admit those whom management view as the 'right' people for such an approach. Who are the 'right' people and what do organizations expect of them? At a general level, we can use some of the literature to point to the outcomes an HRM approach is intended to achieve, and work backwards to gain some understanding of the kind of employees organizations with an HRM strategy may be seeking to attract.

In Guest's (1989, p. 49) model of HRM (see Figure 1.5, Chapter 1) the HRM outcomes may provide some guidance.

Strategic integration

This is concerned with:

1. the integration of HRM into strategic planning
2. the coherence of HRM policies across policy areas and across hierarchies
3. the acceptance and use of HRM practices by line managers.

We have already mentioned in Chapter 6 on HRP that deterministic views on strategy and strategic planning are somewhat problematic. During the 1990s, very few organizations have been able to follow a plan with any certainty; change and uncertainty became the norm. Mintzberg's (1978, p. 935) view of strategy as a 'pattern in a stream of decisions' could allow HRM to be placed in an interdependent position in relation to decision making on objectives, structure, job design and work processes. Research by Tyson (1995a, p. 82) found that while there were many differences between organizations, HRM could help shape the direction of change, influence culture and 'help bring about the mind set which decides which strategic issues are considered'. Such decisions will clearly affect the quantity and quality of recruits. The acceptance of HRM as a major aspect of strategy will generate systems, such as *performance management* (see Chapter 8) based on competency frameworks, to ensure coherence throughout an organization, and appropriate actions by line managers. Both coherence and actions will be a function of the set of values that permeate an organization, often referred to as culture, that serve to reward and reinforce management actions.

Commitment

In recent years there has been a great deal of attention paid to the concept of commitment, particularly organizational commitment. Mottaz (1988, p. 468) views organizational commitment as

> an affective response (attitude) resulting from an evaluation of the work situation which links or attaches the individual to the organization.

In his review of the literature on commitment, Mottaz groups the factors which determine this attitude into two categories – individual characteristics and organizational characteristics. Individual characteristics might consist of demographic or status variables such as age, tenure, education and gender, and personality factors such as work values and expectations. Organizational characteristics include factors such as task characteristics, pay, promotion opportunities and social involvement. However there seemed to be little overall agreement on the relative impact of the factors on commitment. Mottaz goes on to establish and test a model of organizational commitment based on the notion of exchange, where individuals attach themselves to an organization on the basis of their work values composed of specific skills, desires and goals in return for work rewards – the extent to which individuals can use their skills, satisfy desires and achieve goals. The model therefore focuses attention on the indi-

vidual characteristics (values) and organizational characteristics (rewards) where organizational commitment is determined by the degree of fit between values and
rewards. Among Mottaz's conclusions, and of significance for recruiting and selecting
for commitment, is the finding that workers with high work values and high work
standards will require levels of work rewards to match these standards. Focusing on
individual characteristics alone in recruitment and selection will not ensure commitment as an outcome. In order to attract potential employees for an HRM approach
requires management to examine work rewards on offer in the form of interesting
and meaningful work and a supportive environment as well as good pay and promotion and development prospects.

Flexibility

In the 1990s, flexibility is the key outcome which highlights the contribution of HRM
to organization performance. The ability to respond to and deal with rapid change is
essential in an environment of uncertainty and even chaos. In particular, the term
'functional flexibility' implies the recruitment of employees to form a core group that
possesses flexibility or is willing to learn and adapt.

Flexible employees have the potential to learn new skills continuously, that is, to
broaden the range of skills possessed and deepen understanding and performance in
existing areas of work. The latter would include taking increasing authority and
responsibility for work performance. This multiskilled workforce, often working in
teams, gives rise to the new forms of organization structure and job design implied in
HRM organizations (see Chapter 3).

Quality

Total Quality Management (TQM) has been one of the key sets of ideas and practices
associated with HRM and, particularly, the Japanese influence on HRM. Many organizations have espoused quality as a key objective along with associated ideas relating to
customer service and continuous improvement. For several years, organizations in the
UK and the US were unable to reap the same benefits of TQM as Japanese organizations.
In particular, many managers saw TQM as the application of a range of statistical techniques in order to understand and measure physical processes, while neglecting their
responsibility in the management and development of people. Wilkinson *et al.* (1991,
p. 31) found that while there were many similarities between TQM and HRM, short-
term considerations such as costs interfered with implementation. Management
became preoccupied with the achievement of 'hard' results and neglected aspects such
as employee development, motivation and commitment. More recent evidence suggests
that TQM becomes less of a fad or fashion when it is combined with employee involvement. Ed Lawler and his research team examined the practices of US organizations from
1987 and found that there was a positive link between involvement and TQM that produced financial performance (Lawler 1996, p. 39).

The desirable HR outcomes that enable an organization to create competitive
advantage will enable organizations to form a loose model of the kind of employees
it would wish to attract through recruitment. While it may be possible, through competencies and other techniques, to state the model more clearly, the image of the
model itself will be projected from the organization into the labour markets, as will
knowledge about the system of selection for potential candidates. For example, the

selection process for production teams at Toyota's UK plant in Burnaston, Derbyshire in 1992 included:

● a five-page application form with questions on personal values
● tests of numeracy, attitude and ability to learn
● a video-interactive test of learning
● a targeted behavioural interview lasting 75 minutes
● a simulated production line test
● references and medical
● a final interview.

The image and selection system did not seem to worry 20 000 applicants for 400 jobs.

Attraction

Whatever the image projected, an organization's commitment to its HR processes will form part of its evolving value system and make it even more attractive to those seeking employment. For example, research into the success of Hewlett-Packard since 1992 (Gratton 1997, p. 23) found the following features that formed 'the HP way':

● values that place concern and respect for the individual at the centre
● a performance management process that links strategic and individual objectives
● embedded people-processes treated as important
● measurement of people's needs, aspirations and commitment
● management sensitivity to feelings of employees about their work.

The HP way is clearly designed to bring about increased motivation, increased acceptance of responsibility, deepened skills and greater commitment from workers already employed within the organization. The research reported that 80 per cent of staff believed that they put in a great deal of effort and that the company had integrity. While the main beneficiaries of the evolving philosophy will be those already employed, the enhanced focus on people will also increase the attraction of the organization among those external to the organization and form part of the image projected.

Images projected, values and information on espoused goals will interact with workers in the external labour markets, including both employed and unemployed. This interaction will determine the degree of attraction to an organization on the part of potential recruits. Think about an organization you would like to work for. What images, values and information about that organization came into your mind?

Schneider (1987, p. 437), using a theory of interactional psychology, has proposed an attraction–selection–attrition framework to explain differences between organizations that are due to the attraction of people to organization goals, their interaction with goals, and 'if they don't fit, they leave'. The proposed framework is shown as Figure 7.1. Schneider uses the findings from vocational psychology to argue that people are attracted to an organization on the basis of their own interests and personality. Thus people of similar types will be attracted to the same place. Furthermore, the attraction of similar types will begin to determine the place. Following selection, people who do not fit, due to error or misunderstandings about the reality of an organization, will result in an attrition from that organization. At the

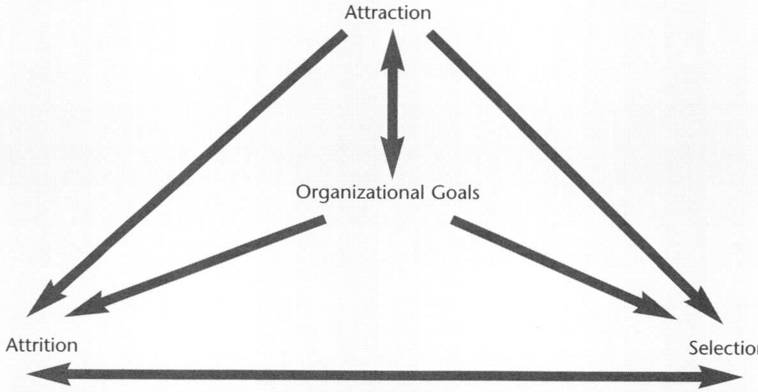

Figure 7.1 An attraction–selection–attrition framework
Source: Schneider, 1987

heart of the framework are organizational goals, originally stated by the founder or articulated by top managers, out of which the structures and processes will emerge that will form the basis for attraction decisions. The framework has been supported by research conducted by Judge and Cable (1997, p. 359) who found that job seekers attempt to match their values with the reputation of an organization's culture. HRM in practice 7.2 shows how the motor industry attempted to make car trading attractive to graduates.

In recruitment the manifestation of values, ethos and desired image will usually take the form of advertising and other recruitment literature, including glossy brochures that are often aimed at graduates. In recent years, the undoubted expertise that exists within the UK advertising industry has been utilized in company recruitment. The utilitarian approach that focused on specifying job details, terms and conditions is being increasingly superseded by advertising that attempts to communicate a message about the company image. There has been a marked shift towards recruitment adverts that are creative and reflect the skills normally used in product marketing. Recruitment advertising is now fully established within the advertising mainstream. In recent years, there has been a growing trend to use the Internet in support of recruitment. For example, an organization can invite potential applicants through their newspaper advertisement to view their website, which might contain further details of the advertised post but also details about the company including history, products, personnel, events and news. Various newspapers such as the *Guardian* put all their job advertisements on the World Wide Web (http://www.recruitment.guardian.co.uk) as do many recruitment consultants.

Images presented in recruitment adverts and brochures will only form part of the attraction. There is not a great deal of evidence that it is entirely effective, often informal 'word-of-mouth information about jobs may be more accurate and effective' (Iles

HRM in practice 7.2

Car traders rally to find graduates

An unlikely alliance has formed to banish the industry's
'Arthur Daley' image and attract high-quality talent

BY JILLY WELCH People Management, 9 October 1997

Arch rivals in the motor industry are calling a truce in their battle for sales in order to tackle their recruitment difficulties.

A task force of major manufacturers and dealerships, including Mercedes, Rover, Inchcape and Evans Halshaw, are joining forces to change graduates' unfavourable perceptions of car traders and raise the calibre of managers in dealerships.

More than 60 per cent of companies in the industry have agreed to pool their knowledge and recruitment resources to convince top business-studies graduates that a career as a dealership manager rivals those offered by other retail positions.

The partnership approach, which has been described by its architects as unique for the motor industry, may be returning as a viable solution to recruitment and training difficulties in other sectors, many of which lost their training bodies during the 1980s and early 1990s.

'It makes an awful lot of sense for us to pitch in and help dealerships to attract and select the best people,' said Robert Browett, Peugeot's sales, development and training director. 'We as manufacturers receive thousands of applications, but motor retail has never been an obvious field for graduates before.'

Participants admit, however, that the motor sales sector has some work to do to convince female applicants that it no longer judges women's sales skills on their more personal attributes.

> A task force of major manufacturers and dealerships, including Mercedes, Rover, Inchcape and Evans Halshaw, are joining forces to change graduates' unfavourable perceptions of car traders and raise the calibre of managers in dealerships.

The initiative, named Autoroute, is to be launched at this year's London motor show. A hotline will be set up in readiness for recruitment campaigns planned at 34 universities in 1998. Manufacturers will then take responsibility for shortlisting candidates for their dealerships, but have agreed to refer 'overflow' applicants to other participating organisations.

'There are a lot of small players in this field who are not necessarily well versed in the latest recruitment skills,' said Steve Parker, manager of quality and business strategy at Ford. 'We have considered the issue of [aiding] competitors, but if we take the longer-term view, we will all benefit.'

A two- to three-year management development qualification, built on Vauxhall's successful 'Red' programme, is being prepared with the help of industry bodies. A motor retail NVQ is also in the pipeline.

Most dealerships – which are either independent or franchised to individual manufacturers – appear eager to sign up to the initiative, as they are anxious to prove that managing a complex business with a turnover of £100 000 a year is a far cry from the image of 'Arthur Daley' characters flogging dodgy motors.

'That image is born out of a simple lack of knowledge,' Parker said. 'We're slowly wearing it down.'

and Salaman 1995, p. 211). In any case, formal advertising can be expensive and an organization will take account of a number of other factors in forming its recruitment plans and choice of media. These might include the following:

1. costs
2. time to recruit and select
3. labour market focus, for example, skills, profession, occupation
4. mobility of labour – geographic and occupational
5. legislation on sex discrimination, race discrimination and disability.

A further manifestation of the image to which recruits will be attracted is a description of the actual work that potential employees will be required to do. The traditional way of providing such information is through the form of a *job description*. Job descriptions are usually derived from job analysis and describe tasks and responsibilities that make up a job. Against each description, there would normally be the specification of standards of performance. A typical format for a job description is given in Figure 7.2.

In addition to a description of a job, there would be some attempt to profile the 'ideal' person to fill the job in the form of a *personnel specification*. It is accepted that the ideal person created may not exist in reality and that the specification would only be used as a framework within which a number of candidates could be assessed. A common format for a personnel specification is the seven-point plan based on the work of Alec Rodger (1970), shown as Figure 7.3. An alternative to the seven-point plan is Munro-Fraser's five-fold grading system (1971) shown as Figure 7.4. In both forms of personnel specification, it is usual to indicate the importance of different requirements. Thus certain requirements might be expressed as essential and some as desirable. Both job descriptions and personnel specifications have been key elements in the traditional repertoire of personnel managers. Over the years, various attempts

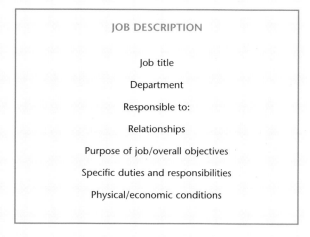

Figure 7.2 Job description format

```
┌─────────────────────────────────────────────┐
│                                               │
│           PERSONNEL SPECIFICATION             │
│                                               │
│           Physical characteristics            │
│                                               │
│                 Attainments                   │
│                                               │
│             General intelligence              │
│                                               │
│              Specific aptitudes               │
│                                               │
│                  Interests                    │
│                                               │
│                 Disposition                   │
│                                               │
│                Circumstances                  │
│                                               │
└─────────────────────────────────────────────┘
```

Figure 7.3 Seven-point plan

have been made to develop and fine-tune techniques and practices. One such development has been the shift of emphasis in job descriptions away from specifying tasks and responsibilities and towards results to be achieved (Plachy, 1987, p. 56). However, there has been a growing awareness of the limitations and problems with such approaches. Watson (1994, p. 189) noted that job analysis, used to produce job descriptions and personnel specifications, relied too much on judgement to identify key aspects of a job and to identify the important qualities that determine success. In addition, the use of frameworks such as the seven-point-plan may provide a 'cloak for improper discrimination'.

```
┌─────────────────────────────────────────────┐
│                                               │
│           PERSONNEL SPECIFICATION             │
│                                               │
│            Impact on other people             │
│                                               │
│          Qualification and experience         │
│                                               │
│                Innate abilities               │
│                                               │
│                  Motivation                   │
│                                               │
│                  Adjustment                   │
│                                               │
└─────────────────────────────────────────────┘
```

Figure 7.4 Five-fold grading system

The drive towards flexibility and changing work practices has seen the appearance of new forms of work descriptions. For example, some organizations have begun to replace or complement job descriptions with *performance contracts*. These contain details of what a job holder agrees to accomplish over a period of time. It summarizes the purpose of a job, how the purpose will be met over the time specified and how the achievement of objectives will be assessed. This approach allows job requirements to be adjusted by agreement between the job holder and his or her manager. It also allows a clear link to be established with other HR processes. Performance contracts signal to new recruits the expectation that their jobs will change and that they cannot rely on a job description as the definitive definition of their work.

Competencies are increasingly used to create a specification for the characteristics of the persons sought for a position (Roberts, 1997). It has been argued (Feltham, 1992, p. 92) that using competencies allows organizations to free themselves from traditional stereotypes in order to attract applicants from a variety of sources. Stereotypes of the 'ideal' person may be contained within personnel specifications. Despite warnings, organizations may be reinforcing the stereotype in their recruitment practices. Competencies appear to be more objective, have a variety of uses in attracting applicants, and will allow an organization to use more reliable and valid selection techniques.

Selection

As we have seen, it is usual for an organization that wishes to recruit new employees to define criteria against which it can measure and assess applicants. Increasingly, however, such criteria are set in the form of competencies composed of behavioural characteristics and attitudes which cannot easily be measured. Rather than trust to luck, organizations are using more 'sophisticated' selection techniques. Organizations have become increasingly aware of making good selection decisions. Selection involves a number of costs; the cost of the selection process itself including the use of various instruments, the future costs of inducting and training new staff and the cost of labour turnover if selected staff are not retained. It is also crucial to remember that decisions are being made by both employers and potential employees and that the establishment of mutually agreed expectations during selection forms part of a *psychological contract*, which will strongly influence an employee's attitudes and feelings about the organization (Herriot *et al.*, 1997, p. 152).

Underlying the process of selection and the choice of techniques are two key principles.

1. *Individual differences* – Attracting a wide choice of applicants will be of little use unless there is a way of measuring how people differ. People can differ in many ways such as intelligence, attitudes, social skills, physical characteristics, experience and so on.
2. *Prediction* – Recognition of the way people differ must be extended to a prediction of performance in the workplace.

Selection techniques will meet these principles of measuring differences and predicting performance to varying degrees. Increasingly, organizations may use a variety of techniques, and statistical theory is used to give credibility to techniques that attempt to measure people.

Some commentators would suggest that this credibility is 'pseudoscientific' and that many limitations remain with selection techniques. Iles and Salaman (1995, p. 219), for example, claim that this psychometric model appears to value:

1. *individualism* – where individual characteristics are claimed to predict future performance
2. *managerialism* – where top managers define the criteria for performance
3. *utility* – where the costs and benefits in money terms of using different selection techniques are assessed.

What do you think the implications of and difficulties with such values might be? We are reminded once again that power is an important consideration in making decisions about the employment of people. Selection instruments have an image of neutrality and objectivity but the criteria built into such instruments which allow the selection and rejection of applicants make up a knowledge base which provides power to the organization and its agents.

Two statistical concepts have been of particular importance in selection, reliability and validity.

Reliability. This refers to the extent to which a selection technique achieves consistency in what it is measuring over repeated use. For example, if you were being interviewed by two managers for a job in two separate interviews, you would hope that the interview technique would provide data so that the interviewers agreed with each other about you as an individual. Alternatively, if a number of candidates are given the same selection test, you would want to have some confidence in the test providing consistent results concerning individual differences between candidates. The statistical analysis of selection techniques normally provides a reliability coefficient, and the higher the coefficient (the closer to 1.0), the more dependable the technique.

Validity. This refers to the extent to which a technique of selection actually measures what it sets out to measure. There are different forms of validity but in selection the most important is criterion validity, which measures the results of a technique against criteria; this may be the present success of existing employees (concurrent validity) or future performance of new employees (predictive validity).

In practice, validation is a complex process and would require an organization to conduct studies with large numbers of candidates. By the time such studies were completed, it is highly likely that the work from which some of the criteria were derived would have changed. Validity is also related to the particular environment in which performance is carried out and may have different values for different sexes and different ethnic groups. Such problems have not stopped many organizations using tests and other selection techniques which have been validated elsewhere.

Of all the techniques used in selection, the interview is the oldest and most widely used along with application forms and letters of reference, referred to as 'the classic trio' by Cook (1994, p. 15). Various attempts have been made to classify interviews, and it may be useful to point out some of the categories that have been developed.

Information elicited. Interviews have a specific focus and require information at different levels.

⬤ An interview may focus on facts. The style of the interview will be direct, based on a question and answer session.

- An interview may focus on subjective information, once factual information has been obtained.
- There may also be a focus on underlying attitudes, requiring intensive probing techniques and usually involving qualified psychologists.

Structure. Interviews may vary from the completely structured, based on planned questions and responses, to the unstructured, allowing complete spontaneity by an applicant and little control by the interviewer. A compromise between the two extremes is most likely where an interviewer maintains control by the use of guide questions but allows free expression on relevant topics.

Order and involvement. The need to obtain different kinds of information may mean an involvement from more than one interviewer. Applicants may be interviewed serially or by a panel.

The selection interview has been the subject of much review and research over the last 50 years. During much of that time, the overall results on the validity and reliability of interviews has been disappointing. In 1949 Wagner (1949, p. 17) carried out the first comprehensive review of research associated with the employment interview. Wagner noted that from 174 sets of ratings that were reported, reliabilities ranged from a correlation coefficient of $r = 0.23$ to 0.97, with a median of $r = 0.57$. Validity, from 222 results, ranged from $r = 0.09$ to $r = 0.94$, with a median of $r = 0.27$. Wagner considered such results to be not particularly high. This pattern continued for the next four decades. In their 1965 review, Ulrich and Trumbo (1965, p. 100) agreed that the interview seemed deficient in terms of reliability and validity and were forced to conclude that judgements about overall suitability for employment should be made by other techniques.

There have been two lines of research to examine the reasons behind such poor results for the selection interview. The first focuses on the processing of information by interviewers leading to a decision on acceptance or rejection. The second focuses on the skills of effective interviewing. Table 7.1 gives a summary of this research.

By 1982 Arvey and Campion (1982, p. 281) were able to report less pessimism about reliability and validity when interviews were conducted by boards (panels) and based on job analysis and job information. In particular, reference was made to the success of situational interviews (Latham *et al.*, 1980, p. 422) where interview questions are derived from systematic job analysis based on a critical incident technique. Questions focus on descriptions of what an applicant would do in a series of situations. Responses are judged against benchmark answers that identify poor, average or excellent employees. In addition to situational interviews, Harris (1989, p. 696) reported on other new developments in interview format which relied on job analysis. These include behaviour description interviews, which assess past behaviour in various situations, and comprehensive structured interviews, which contain different types of question, for example, situational, job knowledge, job simulation and work requirements. Such developments have resulted in an enhanced effectiveness for the selection interview and improved scores for reliability and validity.

The use of questions about past behaviour combined with competencies in selection interviews have enhanced effectiveness even further. Pulakos and Schmitt (1995, p. 289) compared the validity results in selection of experience-based questions against situational questions. The former are past-orientated questions and are based

Table 7.1 Summary of research on selection interviews

A. Processing of Information

Pre-interview	Use of application forms and photographs to reject on grounds of sex, scholastic standing and physical attractiveness.
First impressions	Decisions made quickly leading to a search for the rest of the interview to support the decision. Negative information will be heavily weighted if the decision is rejection but a positive early decision may lead to warm interviewer behaviour.
Stereotypes	Interviewers may hold stereotyped images of a 'good' worker against which applicants are judged. Such images may be personal to each interviewer and potentially based on prejudice.
Contrast	Interviewers are influenced by the order in which applicants are interviewed. An average applicant who follows below-average applicants may be rated above average. Interviewers may compare applicants against each other rather than against objective criteria.
Attraction	Interviewers may be biased towards applicants they 'like'. This attraction may develop where interviewers hold similar opinions and attitudes to applicants.

B. Skills of Interviewing

Structure	Variation in interview structure affected reliability, with low scores for unstructured interviews.
Questions	Interviewers may use multiple, leading, embarrassing and provocative questions.
Listening	Interviewers may talk more than listen, especially if they view the applicant favourably. Interviewers may not be 'trained' to listen effectively.
Retention and interpretation	Interviewers may have poor recall of information unless guides are used and notes are made. Interviewers have difficulty in interpreting information.

on the view that the best predictor of future performance is actual past performance in similar situations. Applicants are asked job-related questions about what they did in other situations rather than what they would do, as in situational questions. Responses to both types of question can be scored on behaviour scales but experience-based questions showed better results with respect to predictions of job performance, that is, predictive validity. These results can be used by organizations with competency frameworks. For example, a IT company has a competency relation to managing meetings. Interviewers could base questions around an applicant's past behaviour in managing meetings by asking the applicant to explain what he or she did in managing a specific meeting. Follow-up questions can be used to reveal further features of the applicant's performance which can then be assessed against the competency indicators. Research by Campion *et al.* (1997, p. 655) included such topics as 'better questions' which enhance the effectiveness of interviews.

It is interesting at this point to note that much of the progress in interviews as a selection technique has occurred where organizations have sought to identify behaviour and attitudes that match their models of employees to be selected. This has required an investment in more sophisticated techniques of analysis. Traditional job analysis techniques allow models of jobs in terms of task and responsibilities to be produced. Organizations faced with change and seeking to employ workers whose potential can be utilized and developed will increasingly turn to techniques of analysis that will produce inventories of characteristics and behaviour, such as competencies, associated with effective performance in the present and the future.

Lists of competencies that provide organization-specific characteristics and behaviour are developed through the use of sophisticated analytical techniques, and can provide the raw material for selection techniques that have a good record of reliability and validity such as *psychometric tests*. Most people have some fears about any test and this has caused some confusion over the meaning, use and value of psychometric tests, which we take to be a generic term for the range of techniques that attempt to measure a sample of a person's behaviour. The 1990s have seen a rapid growth in the number of organizations using such tests. McHenry (1997a, p. 32) claims that the growth is the result of a larger number of people who were trained to administer tests, especially HR practitioners. McHenry argues that the market for tests has come to be seen as 'commercial' with a number of adverse implications for the reputation of the process of testing. What would your reaction be if you were told that you were going to be 'tested' for a job?

We can make the following distinctions between different kinds of tests:

1. *Ability tests* – focusing on mental abilities such as verbal reasoning and numerical power but also including physical skills testing such as typing speeds. In such tests there may be right or wrong answers or measurements, which allows applicants for a position to be ranked.
2. *Inventories* – usually self-report questionnaires that indicate traits, values, interests, attitudes and preferences. There are no right or wrong answers, but a range of choices between possible answers.

Both forms of tests would provide a set of norms as standardization. These are developed from the scores of a representative group of people, the 'norm group', of a larger population, for example, UK adult males or females in a sales role. Figures are then expressed in percentiles, which provides the standardization. Thus a raw score of 120 on a test or a section of a test might be placed in the 60th percentile, indicating that the applicant's result was higher than 60 per cent of the norm group but less than 40 per cent. This would be a valuable indicator if the test had good predictive validity to allow comparisons between different applicants to be made. Inventories would also include some allowance for 'distortions' and 'fake' responses, although such tests are generally thought to be less reliable than ability tests. An important issue here is the exent to which a test might discriminate against particular groups of people. C. Jackson (1996, p. 2) reports that there have been a number of challenges in the US courts relating to unfairness in testing and McHenry (1997a, p. 34) argues that work needs to be done to eliminate and correct tests that contain unfair items. He quotes the example of a questionnaire on personality that contained the item, 'I think I would make a good leader'. This was answered 'true' by twice as many men as women implying that men are twice as likely to become good leaders. What do you think of such an item and the implication? In the UK, organizations that make selection decisions based on tests that discriminate may find themselves taken to an Industrial Tribunal.

Increasingly an organization may use competencies to draw up a range of selection techniques by which to assess the competencies identified. Techniques may be combined and applied together at events referred to as *assessment centres*. Such events may last one to three days during which a group of applicants for a post will undertake a variety of techniques. We can make a distinction here between *development centres* (see Chapter 8), which yield information to help identify development needs, and assessment centres, which are designed to yield information that can be used to make decisions concerning suitability for a job. It is argued that it is the combination of techniques, providing a fuller picture of an applicant's strengths and weaknesses, that makes an assessment centre so valuable. While there may be no such thing as a 'typical' assessment centre (Spychalski *et al.*, 1997, p. 71), the general methods used would be group discussions, role plays and simulations, interviews and tests. For example, the following activities were used in the assessment centre to select customer service assistants for European Passengers Services Ltd (Mannion and Whittaker 1996, p. 14):

- perception exercise
- communication exercise
- structured interview
- personality inventory
- customer service questionnaire
- tests for clear thinking and numerical estimation.

The objectives for using these methods were to generate information about:

- ability to work under pressure
- characteristic behaviour when interacting with others
- preferred work styles
- ability to think quickly
- ability to make quick and accurate numerical estimates
- experience and aptitude for a customer service role.

The EPS assessment centre process was judged to be a success, underpinned by the objective and standardized decision making of the assessors. Candidates attending an assessment centre will be observed by assessors, who should be trained to judge the performance of candidates against criteria contained within the competency framework used.

Have any of your colleagues applying for graduate training programmes been 'through' an assessment centre? What was their reaction to this process? How a selection technique appears to those subjected to it, its *face validity*, is not important in a technical sense, but could be important in attracting good applicants to an organization. If your colleagues relayed negative reactions to you about their experience of selection techniques with one organization, this may affect your image of it. Techniques that may be effective from an organization's perspective may be seen as negative and unfair by applicants. In work carried out by Mabey and Iles (1991, p. 50) on the reactions of MBA students to selection and assessment techniques, interviews were rated fair and useful while tests left many feeling negative. However the combination of techniques in an assessment centre was seen as fair and useful in that the event allowed for the use of objective techniques and the opportunity for a dialogue between the applicant and the employer. The findings remind us of the dilemma facing organizations in the 1990s. That is, while it is increasingly important to select the 'right' kind of employees using a suitable range of techniques, there is also a danger that, in using such techniques, the organization may simultaneously manage to alienate the very candidates it wants to attract.

The view of recruitment and selection practices as features of a dialogue goes some way towards Herriot's (1989, p. 34) idea of 'front-end' loading processes as a development of the social relationship between applicants and an organization. Both parties in the relationship are making decisions during recruitment and selection and it would be important for an organization to recognize that high-quality applicants, attracted by their image of an organization, could be lost at an early stage unless applicants are supplied with realistic organization and work information. Applicants have a picture of expectations about how the organization will treat them, and recruitment and selection represents an opportunity to clarify the picture. One method of developing the picture, suggested by Herriot (1989, p. 48), are realistic job previews (RJPs) which can take the form of case studies of employees and their work, the chance to 'shadow' someone at work, job sampling and videos. The aim of RJPs is to enable the expectations of applicants to become more realistic. Work by Premack and Wanous (1985, p. 706) found that RJPs lower initial expectations about work and an organization, causing some applicants to deselect themselves but RJPs also increase levels of organization commitment, job satisfaction, performance and job survival among applicants who continue into employment.

Chapter summary

This chapter has examined the nature of recruitment and selection for organizations that are pursuing an HRM approach to the management of people. It is essential that such organizations see that whatever the state of the labour market and their power within it, contact with potential recruits is made through the projection of an image that will impact on and reinforce their expectations. Such images are used by recruits to self-select in the initial stages. Organizations now have the ability to construct models of the kind of employees they wish to recruit, and to identify how far applicants match their models using reliable and valid techniques of selection. However, we have also seen that such models, increasingly based on competency frameworks, provide organizations with further power by generating the knowledge against which applicants are assessed. But recruitment and selection are also the first stages of a dialogue, between applicants and the organization, which forms the employment relationship. Failure to appreciate the importance of forming expectations during recruitment and selection may result in the loss of high-quality applicants and set the initial level of the employment relationship so low as to make the achievement of desirable HRM outcomes most difficult.

Key concepts

Recruitment	Reliability
Attraction	Validity
Selection	Job descriptions
Psychometric tests	Personnel specification
Assessment centres	Performance contracts

Discussion questions

1. How is organization strategy linked to recruitment and selection?

2. Decision making in selection has become a two-way process. How can the decisions of applicants be improved?

3. How can the predictive validity of the employment interview be improved?

4. Should job descriptions be abandoned?

5. '…appeal to their guts instead of just their brains'. How far do you agree with this view of graduate recruitment?

6. Are assessment centres a fair and valid way of selecting employees?

Further reading

Cook, M. (1994) *Personnel Selection and Productivity*, London: Wiley.

Roberts, G. (1997) *Recuitment and Selection*, London: Institute of Personnel and Development.

Schneider, B. and Goldstein, H.W. (1995) The ASA framework: an update, *Personnel Psychology*, **48**: 747–73.

Smith, J.M. and Robertson, I.T. (eds) (1991) *Advances in Selection and Assessment*, Chichester: Wiley.

Watson, T. (1994) Recruitment and selection. In Sisson, K. (ed.) *Personnel Management*, Oxford: Blackwell.

Chapter case study

Meister Software UK

Meister Software UK is the British subsidiary of a German-owned world-wide network of software companies. Meister Software is the generic name for a range of software modules that provide a total information solution for manufacturing companies with turnovers of at least £50m. The British branch is growing rapidly and during the past year the number of employees has increased from 78 to 108. Most of the employees are graduates with either sales, computer or finance backgrounds. The work is highly pressured and results-focused, in return for which large reward packages are available.

Salesmen and women in particular need strong presentation and negotiation skills since the market is very competitive and contracts can be worth in excess of £0.5m. Recently, however, the company has had enormous difficulty in selecting the right calibre of staff for the sales role even though they are able to attract candidates in sufficient numbers.

They recently commissioned an analysis of the role to help provide a more successful model for the selection of salesmen and women at Meister. The model should allow the selection process to:

1. identify differences between recruits that are important to the role
2. carry out the identification of differences in a reliable and consistent manner
3. make valid predictions about the future performance of recruits with confidence.

The findings revealed some interesting features relating to the basic skills and attitudes needed for such a role but they also indicated how the role was expected to be performed at Meister. The first of these Meister factors concerned what was seen as 'professionalism', suggested as 'an ability to deal sensitively with prospective customers, being "human"' rather than clinical. References were made to a style of behaviour which was 'non-threatening' and 'non-arrogant' but also 'challenging' when required.

Complementing 'professionalism' was the need to 'make decisions in a complex manner'. This meant that salesmen and women were expected to be able to use large and differing amounts of information, often simultaneously, to identify patterns and develop several possible alternative actions. Such skills were accompanied by a 'tolerance for ambiguity and a capacity to empathise' with prospective customers. In particular, reference was made to the need to be able 'to understand people and political issues as well as "facts"'.

It was expected that salesmen and women would 'show pride' in working for Meister and in the Meister product. However, it was not expected that a salesman or woman would sell at all costs. Prospective customers had to be 'right' for Meister. In part this depended on how far sales staff could 'present information in a confident manner' but also how far they could 'adapt their behaviour as they formed relationships with prospective customers'. The establishment of mutual expectations were seen as a core value at Meister and a salesman or woman would need to be able quickly to identify if these could not be formed with a prospective customer. The salesman's or woman's understanding of this would partly be formed by his or her interactions with others at Meister and this highlighted the need for 'peer respect and being a team player' rather than an individualist. However, it would still be expected that sales staff would be 'self-motivating and be able to work alone'.

Task

Using the information about the sales role, you are required to investigate an appropriate selection strategy. You should consider:

1. Preparation of appropriate documentation.
2. Which selection techniques could measure the attributes identified.
3. How an assessment centre would operate for the selection of sales staff.

Include a justification for your results.

Notes

1. Quoted in IPD (1997) *Overqualified and Underemployed?*, London: Institute of Personnel and Development.
2. UK Managing Director, *TGI Friday*, BBC Radio 4, 13 November, 1997.
3. Bryan Jackson, Director of Human Resources at Toyota's Derby plant. Quoted in *Guardian*, 17 December, 1992, p. 18.

part four

Rewards and Development

chapter eight

Performance appraisal

Jeffrey Gold

A great deal depends on the extent to which you have a good relationship with your boss, as a team. I, now, have a super boss and we work very well together. The comments on my appraisal depend not on an hour's discussion, but on a whole year's interaction. But if you get off badly with your first two managers, you may as well just forget it.[1]

Appraisal as we know it has outlived its usefulness. It is time to get rid of it.[2]

Muddle and confusion still surrounds the theory and practice of appraisal.[3]

Chapter outline

Chapter objectives

After studying this chapter, you should be able to:

1. Explain the purpose and uses of assessment and appraisal.
2. Understand contrasting approaches to assessment and appraisal.
3. Explain the use of assessment and appraisal in performance management and employee development.
4. Understand the use of different assessment and appraisal techniques.

⬤ Introduction

Of all the activities in HRM, performance appraisal is arguably the most contentious and least popular among those who are involved. Managers do not seem to like doing it, employees see no point in it, and personnel and human resource managers, as guardians of an organization's appraisal policy and procedures, have to stand by and watch their work fall into disrepute. Remarkably, despite the poor record of appraisal within organizations, it is an accepted part of management orthodoxy that there should be some means by which performance can be measured, monitored and controlled (Barlow, 1989, p. 499). Indeed a failure to show that management is in control would be regarded as highly ineffective by those with an interest in the affairs of an organization. As a result, appraisal systems for some time have served to prove that the performance of employees is under control or to give the appearance of control. As Barlow (1989, p. 500) has stated:

> Institutionally elaborated systems of management appraisal and development are significant rhetorics in the apparatus of bureaucratic control.

It might be that the idea of control is at the heart of the problem of appraisal in organizations.

In recent years, appraisal has become a key feature of an organization's drive towards competitive advantage through continuous performance improvement. In many organizations, this has resulted in the development of integrated *performance management systems* (PMS), usually based on a competency framework. Indeed, survey evidence has found that discussing and appraising performance is one of the main uses of competencies (Strebler *et al.*, 1997, p. 25). Appraisal therefore acts as an information-processing system providing vital data for rational, objective and efficient decision making regarding improving performance, identifying training needs, managing careers and setting levels of reward.

⬤ Performance appraisal and the HRM cycle

At the prescriptive level, the relation of performance appraisal to other key dimensions of the HRM cycle is shown in Figure 1.2. The information relative to an employee's behaviour and performance can lead to HRD activities. Performance appraisal data can determine employee rewards and are also used as predictors in the human resource planning, recruitment and selection processes. This chapter will seek to explain why, in the past, appraisal systems have continuously failed to find respect among employers and employees alike. However, it will also explore how, through performance management, appraisal has the potential to reverse past trends so that it is viewed less as a threat and a waste of time and more as the source of continuous dialogue between organizational members.

⬤ Assessment, appraisal and control

Assessment is the process by which data are collected and reviewed about an individual employee's past and current work behaviour and performance. This allows appraisal, which can be seen as an analysis of overall capabilities and potential, allowing a decision to be made in line with a purpose. In reality both assessment and appraisal are likely to be combined and this can mean that the two terms may be synonymous in many organizations.

There are a variety of declared purposes for appraisal and the most usual rationalization and justification for appraisal is to improve individual performance. However under such a broad heading come a number of more focused reasons. The reasons for performance review, given in a survey by Phil Long (1986), are to:

- assess training and development needs
- help improve current performance
- review past performance
- assess future potential and promotability
- assist career planning decisions
- set performance objectives
- assess increases or new levels in salary.

In many organizations appraisal will take place formally at predetermined intervals and will involve a discussion or interview between a manager and an individual employee. The purposes of such discussions can be broadly categorised into:

1. the making of administrative decisions concerning pay, promotions and careers, work responsibilities
2. the improvement of performance through the discussion of development needs, identifying training opportunities and the planning of action.

Both categories of purpose require judgements to be made. In the first category, a manager may be required to make a decision about the value of an employee both in the present and the future, and this may cause some discomfort. Several decades ago, McGregor (1957, p. 89) reported that a key reason why appraisal failed was that managers disliked 'playing God', which involved making judgements about the worth of employees. Levinson (1970, p. 127) thought that managers experienced the appraisal of others as a hostile and aggressive act against employees which resulted in feelings of guilt about being critical of employees. The tension between appraisal as a judgemental process and a supportive development process has never been resolved and is likely to continue for some time to come.

Making judgements about an employee's contribution, value, worth, capability and potential has to be considered as a vital dimension of a manager's relationship with employees. Although the occasion may be formally separated from the ongoing relationship, appraisal activities and decisions will be interpreted by an employee as feedback and will have a potentially strong impact on an employee's view of 'self', for example, self-belief and self-esteem. What is particularly interesting is the way individuals respond to feedback, because there is no simple formula for how feedback can be used to motivate people, even though managers may be quite convinced, in their own minds, that there is. We do know however that feedback has a definite influence in demotivation! Try a test on yourself. Make a list of what motivates you to work and make another that indicates what demotivates you. It is likely that the latter will be longer, covering a wide range of factors. Thus there is always a danger in any situation when a manager has to provide feedback to employees that the outcome will be

Table 8.1   Performance appraisals – findings from the General Electric Company study

- Criticism often has a negative effect on motivation and performance

- Praise has little effect – one way or another

- Performance improves with specific goals

- Participation by the employee in goal-setting helps produce favourable results

- Interviews designed primarily to improve performance should not at the same time weigh salary or promotion in the balance

- Coaching by managers should be day-to-day and not just once a year

Source: Adapted from Meyer *et al.*, 1965

demotivated employees. The seminal study that highlighted this possibility was carried out by Meyer *et al.* (1965, p. 123) at the General Electric Company. Although this work was carried out in the mid-1960s, it is remarkable how the lessons have been forgotten and the mistakes uncovered at that time have been repeated many times over in many organizations. The study looked at the appraisal process at a large plant where appraisal was judged to be good. There were 92 appraisees in the study who were appraised by their managers on two occasions over two weeks. The first interview discussed performance and salary, the second discussed performance improvement. The reactions of the appraisees was gathered by interviews, questionnaires and observation. It was discovered that while interviews allowed for general praise, criticism was more specific and prompted defensive reactions. Defensiveness by appraisees involved denial of shortcomings and blaming others. On average 13 criticisms per interview were recorded and the more criticism received, the more defensive the reaction of the appraisee. The study revealed that the defensive behaviour was partly due to most appraisees rating themselves above average before the interviews – 90 out of 92 appraisees rated themselves as average or above. It was also found that, subsequent to the interviews, criticism had a negative effect on performance. A summary of some of the conclusions from this study is set out in Table 8.1.

In many respects, since this study, there has been a long search to find a way of appraising employees that mitigates the negative outcomes. In recent years, for example, there has been a growth in *multi-source feedback* (Kettley, 1997, p. 1) where individuals receive feedback from different sources including peers, subordinate staff, customers and self. Where feedback is received from 'all round' a job, this is referred to as *360° appraisal or feedback*. The growth in such approaches is based on the view that feedback from different sources allows for more balance and objectivity than the single view of a line manager. We will examine multi-source feedback and 360° appraisal in more detail later in this chapter. Competencies have also been seen as a way of facilitating the review process, linking personal development plans to strategy and increasingly, despite many warnings, to pay (Sparrow, 1996, p. 26).

The last conclusion in Table 8.1 gives emphasis to the role of managers as developers of their employees on a continuous basis. It is a role which will be explored in more detail in Chapter 10, Human resource development. However, it is worth stating at this point that assessing and appraising are likely to occur on both formal and informal occasions, and the latter will occur far more often than the former. Employees are able to accept criticism if it is useful and relevant to them and the work they are doing. Feedback provided in this way has a strong chance of improving performance and, crucially, provides an opportunity for a continuing dialogue between managers and employees out of which will emerge joint understanding of individual development needs and aspirations. As many managers and employees have found, where the informal and continuous processes are operating effectively, this will make the formal appraisal less isolated and less prone to negativity. The extent to which employees are able to accept feedback will vary to a considerable extent among employees, and managers will need to be able to cope with such variations. That is, they will need to 'know' their people as individuals and this itself will be a reflection of the development of managers. Recent work in understanding what makes people exert effort has shown that a variety of factors contribute to this process, such as clarity of role, recognition, challenge, self-expression and contribution. However, how these factors are combined cannot be generalized and each person will have their own perception of what is important. To understand this, managers are advised to 'get inside the head' of the employee (McHenry, 1997b, p. 29).

As has already been mentioned, it is an accepted part of management orthodoxy that there should be some means by which performance can be measured, monitored and controlled (Barlow, 1989, p. 499), and that appraisal systems provide evidence that management is in control. Randell (1994, p. 235) points out that most appraisal schemes in the UK are underpinned by a 'performance control approach' to appraisal. Figure 8.1 provides the key stages of this approach.

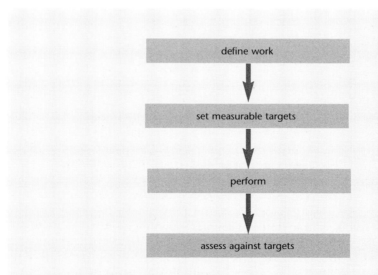

Figure 8.1 A performance control approach to appraisal
Source: Adapted from Randall, 1994

It is argued that the control approach is an outcome of the drive towards rationality and efficiency in our organizations. Certainly such beliefs may become part of a set of taken-for-granted assumptions that dominate life in organizations, and may also be difficult to challenge. Organization leaders, managers and employees may often be unaware of the ways in which such beliefs lie behind their actions. Thus, even though the experience of appraisal in organizations is very mixed, to say the least, it would be tantamount to heresy radically to alter its orientation towards the control of performance. There are, however, other approaches which may carry greater potential in bringing the best out of employees but this requires a risk to be taken and an awareness by managers of their taken-for-granted beliefs.

Gareth Morgan's *Images of Organization* (1997) provides an examination of the way metaphors lie at the foundation of our ideas and explanations about organizations. In this book Morgan draws on the literature that highlights the role of metaphor in explaining complex phenomena, like organizations, by the crossing of images and language. Thus an organization may be crossed with the image of a machine and this may be very useful in understanding what happens and what should happen in organizations. However, metaphor only provides a partial view of a phenomenon and not a whole view, For example, an organization may be compared with a machine or said to have machine-like qualities, but it is not, and will never be, a machine. A danger occurs however when the metaphor, in this case a machine, becomes a taken-for-granted assumption. In such cases the partial explanatory power of the metaphor may be taken as a whole and the organization may be seen literally as a machine! This is not as ridiculous as it sounds because much of the language of organizations, and many of the processes developed, can be related back to an assumption of an organization as a machine. Henry Mintzberg (1989, p. 339) has argued that the form of structure called 'machine bureaucracy' has dominated thinking about how organizations should be constructed and that terms like 'getting organized', 'being rational', and 'achieving efficiency' represent evidence of this domination. As Mintzberg has written, 'I believe that to most people what I am calling machine bureaucracy is not just a way to organize, it is the way to organize; it is not one form or structure, it is structure' (Mintzberg, 1990, p. 340).

We should not be surprised therefore to find an attachment by many managers to the idea of control in appraisal (Townley, 1994, p. 67), and the perception by employees that they are being controlled by appraisal systems. Barlow (1989, p. 500) takes the argument further. He points out that appraisal serves to make rational, simple and static a relationship between managers and employees which is ambiguous, complex and dynamic. Ambiguity, complexity and dynamism cannot be eliminated in reality, and therein lies the falseness of the experience of appraisal. For many employees, appraisal is just not seen as relevant. The following reflect the opinions of managers about appraisal, gathered in a field study in a sector of the petrochemicals industry.

Successful types are spotted early on. You usually find that it would seem those people are going to start moving fast. I think we're talking about a fairly small percentage in the fast-moving track, because one always has to consider the constraints of availability of positions for people to move to: you actually have to have slots available for them. There is a strong element of being in the right place at the right time. Or being known by your managers so that they can earmark slots for you.

I think success is having the ear of higher management. To be noticed by higher management, and having opinions asked for, often. It's being able to influence the decision-maker in a department. And I think an awful lot depends on being in the right place at the right time.

If we were asked for a good man, we certainly wouldn't go hunting through appraisal forms. We'd do it by personal knowledge and I suppose, to some extent, by rule of thumb. Appraisal forms are no use. It's what's left out rather than what's put in that's important (Barlow, 1989, pp. 505–7).

In this section, we have discussed the espoused purposes of appraisal and how some of the research evidence has indicated that, in reality, appraisal may be less than effective in the achievement of these. The problem may be due to the way appraisal processes are formulated, based on an explicit or implicit performance control orientation. If we refer back to some of the HRM approaches and the outcomes of flexibility, quality and commitment, we can see that organization leaders and managers will need to ask themselves some fundamental questions on the purpose of appraisal and the nature of organization control mechanisms.

From control to development?

It is highly unlikely that the pressure for rationality, efficiency and control in organizations will ease. In the 1990s the threats of competition and uncertainty have, if anything, increased that pressure. The questioning of underlying principles that is required for the development of a culture that supports and reinforces the ideas and practices of a 'soft' HRM model can be a painful process. For example, it may be difficult to resist the requirements of financial controllers to show conformity to standardised budgets, and so on. However, there are other views of reality that challenge the mechanistic view of organizations and its privileged status. Such views need to show an accommodation of the values of control combined with values which argue for the development of people and the gaining of employee commitment and trust.

Walton (1985, p. 79) has written about the disillusionment with the apparatus of control which assumes low employee commitment and mere obedience. He reports on a number of organizations that have attempted to move towards a workforce strategy based on commitment. In recent years the drive towards leaner and flatter organization structures has meant the removal of layers of supervision and an investment, both psychologically and physically, in harnessing the potential of employees. However, the crucial contribution towards creating commitment, pride and trust is management's devotion to nurturing a culture that supports the long-term development of people (Gratton, 1997, p. 24). Assessment and appraisal serve as the fulcrum of such a process. The contrast between control approaches and commitment could not be greater for managers; the former involves a concentration on techniques, the latter a shift towards attitudes, values and beliefs. The skill for HRM practitioners is to acknowledge the importance of the former while arguing for a greater place for the latter.

A developmental approach to appraisal that attempts to harness potential for many organizations would mean a spread in the coverage of appraisal systems to all employees who form the primary internal labour market. For many years, discussions of potential and prospects for development have been confined to managers only. This provided a strong signal to the rest of the organization that only managers were worthy of such attention, with the implicit assumption that non-managers cannot

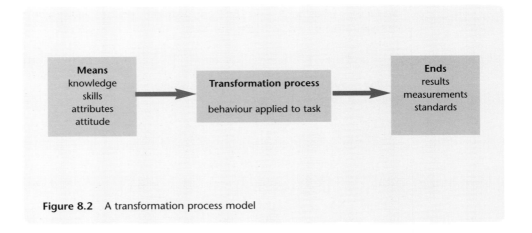

Figure 8.2 A transformation process model

develop. In the 1990s more organizations have attempted to harmonize conditions between different grades of employees and adopt HRM ideas and practices such as appraisal and performance management.

In shifting towards a more developmental approach, the suspicion that surrounded control approaches may remain. Harper (1983, p. 69) suggested dropping the word 'appraisal' because it put employees on the defensive. Instead, he recommended a shift towards future-orientated review and development which actively involved employees in continuously developing ways of improving performance in line with needs. The outcome could be a set of objectives to be achieved by individual employees. Such objectives may be concerned with immediate performance against current tasks and standards, but they might also be concerned with a variety of work and personal changes, for example, change of standards, task, job and career. Once employees are encouraged to pay attention to their progress at work, the organization must be able to respond to their medium- and long-term career aspirations (see Chapter 6). The manager's role will be to resolve the inevitable tension that will result between individual goals and the manager's interpretation of organization goals. How can data about employees be gathered for such purposes?

The performance of a work task can be presented as a relationship between means and ends (Ouchi, 1979, p. 843). The means take the form of the attributes, skills, knowledge and attitudes (competencies) of individual employees which are applied to a task in a specific situation. The ends are the outcomes, taking the form of results achieved, which may be measurable quantitatively or qualitatively against an explicit or implicit standard or target. Between means and ends is the behaviour of the individual in a 'transformation process', as shown in Figure 8.2.

While all phases of this process can be the focus of appraisal, particular attention to behaviour in the transformation process will reveal how an individual has applied knowledge, skills and attitudes to a task, taking account of all aspects including time and place, machinery and equipment, other employees and other circumstances – for example, the presence of a manager or a customer. The attention to how an employee performs will provide rich data on current effectiveness and potential for further development. For example, if we assume that an employee has been trained to complete a basic task, attention to the transformation process will provide data on a number of issues. The first time she completes the task, assessment of behaviour reveals nervousness until completion, when the results achieved can be compared against a standard. The nervousness can be corrected by adjustment to her skills and practice until confidence is gained. Further attention reveals that once confidence is gained, she performs with some sense of rhythm and flow that achieves perfect results. Given static conditions and standards, this is as far as she can go in this task. She can continue to perform with confidence but after some time this becomes too easy. This feeling prompts the employee to ask for some adjustment; at first this may be to the work targets and then to an extension of tasks within the job. The important point is that ease within the transformation process, assessed by the employee and others, leads to developmental adjustments. Continued attention to process may eventually result in a further range of adjustments, such as increased responsibility through job enlargement and job enrichment, and a reconsideration of future direction within the organization. On the way, the organization may benefit from rising efficiency and effectiveness, including better standards. Through attention to the behaviour of an employee in the transformation process, data can be provided for a whole gamut of developmental decisions over time, starting with adjustments to reach minimum standards, to career changes and progression. Figure 8.3 shows a representation of this

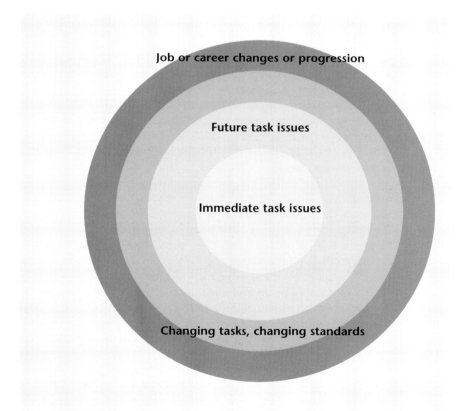

Figure 8.3 Developmental decisions

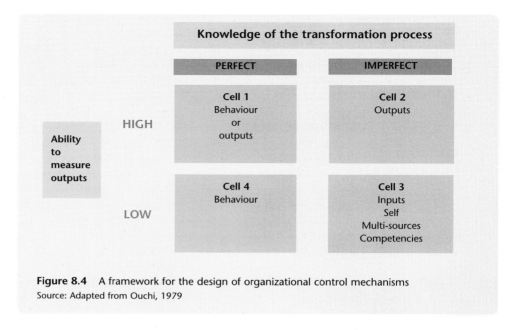

Figure 8.4 A framework for the design of organizational control mechanisms
Source: Adapted from Ouchi, 1979

development, starting at the centre with attention to immediate performance and extending outwards to career changes and progression. Individual employees are able to set targets, objectives and goals for each stage through appraisal.

A number of techniques have been developed that allow for the assessment and appraisal of the various stages of the transformation process. The ability to employ various techniques in appraisal will depend on a number of contingencies. William Ouchi (1979, p. 843) has provided a model which specifies these and allows a choice of techniques to be made. Figure 8.4 has been adapted from Ouchi's work.

This model can be used to reconcile the dilemma that organizations may face in appraisal; that is, between the desire to maintain control and the desire to foster a developmental emphasis. Bureaucratic forms of control depend on the feasibility of measuring desired performance:

> the ability to measure either output or behaviour which is relevant to the desired per-formance is critical to the 'rational' application of ...bureaucratic forms of control (Ouchi, 1979, p. 843).

In Ouchi's model, if an organization has either the ability to measure outputs of behaviour or a high understanding of the transformation process involved in produc-tion, the organization could opt for bureaucratic control and base appraisal on either behaviour or output measurements or both. Thus in Cell 1, typical of traditional man-ufacturing and service organizations where work process steps can be clearly stated, both behaviour and output techniques can be used. In Cell 2 only outputs can be appraised successfully, perhaps because work processes cannot be observed, for exam-ple, sales workers. In Cell 4 employees' behaviour can be observed but outputs are more difficult. This may be due to groups of employees producing group outputs or measurable outputs produced over a long period of time, for example, research workers. In all the above cases, the logic of control may be extended to tie appraisal to some form of performance or merit-related pay system (see Chapter 9). However in Cell 3 there is imperfect knowledge of transformation and low ability to measure outputs, making bureaucratic control virtually impossible. Ouchi refers to this cell as a 'clan', based on a ritualised, ceremonial or 'cultural' form of control arising from shared attitudes, values and beliefs. Most professional workers would fit most of the time into this category as would most managers and, increasingly, workers in forms of work organization where higher levels of discretion and autonomy are granted to individual employees or teams. Behaviour, while difficult to observe formally, can be observed by those present at the point of production. For example, those able to observe the performance of a university lecturer are the students being taught and the lecturer him or herself. A university can bureaucratically control who becomes a lecturer through its selection processes, hence it is possible to assess 'inputs', for example, qualifications and other attributes. However, once installed, the performance of a lecturer is much more difficult to assess rationally. It can however be assessed and appraised by the lecturer through self-appraisal and by others, for example, students and peers. Such forms of appraisal are not without their problems, especially if organizations wish to exert bureaucratic control. For example, recent efforts to appraise teachers through classroom observation and interviews against performance criteria, while ostensibly aimed at professional development, have also been used to identify 'incompetent' teachers and potentially provide a link to pay. It should not be surprising that such an approach has had 'little impact' (Ofsted, 1996). However such techniques could be highly productive in allowing the development focus of appraisal to emerge and fostering a culture which supports this. Increasingly, as we have shown, control based on shared values and beliefs which attempts to engender commitment, high trust and continuous development among all employees lies at the heart of 'soft' HRM strategies. Therefore, the appraisal techniques suggested in Cell 3 may form part of a repertoire of techniques even where it is possible to employ the performance control techniques of Cells 1, 2 and 4. How organizations can manage the process and the conflicting demands will now be examined.

⬤ Appraisal and performance management

We have shown that there is considerable pressure on organizations to adopt performance control approaches to appraisal, and that even in organizations that espouse an HRM orientation, beliefs that emphasize rationality and efficiency may become part of a set of taken-for-granted assumptions. Clearly an organization which desires to develop appraisal with a development focus will need to challenge such assumptions but also accommodate them. The result is likely to be the emergence of sophisticated models that make use of multiple techniques that satisfy the demands of multiple users. In Chapter 9, Reward management, we will examine how appraisal can have a key impact on decisions on remuneration within organizations. However, in the interests of equity, such decisions will need to be taken on the basis of data that are both reliable and valid (see Chapter 7).

Referring back to our earlier analysis, we saw that evidence had been accumulated showing the problems of appraisal. These stemmed mainly from the way systems were established as a way of evaluating employees by their superiors for a variety of purposes, for example, improving performance, pay, promotion, and so on. Over the years, a large battery of techniques has been made available to organizations. Some of these techniques carry validity and reliability scores suggesting greater 'objectivity', for example, psychometric tests and, more recently, assessments based on competency frameworks. However what cannot be escaped is that all employees will have an opinion on how well they are performing, the rewards they desire and deserve, and the training they require. That is, whatever techniques of appraisal are employed, self-appraisal and self-rating will always be there too. Where the emphasis of appraisal is on evaluation and performance control it is only to be expected that differences will exist between an individual's self-appraisal and the appraisal by his or her superior. Campbell and Lee (1988, p. 303) suggest a number of discrepancies between self and supervisory appraisal.

1. *Informational* – disagreement about work to be done, how it is done, and the standards to be used in judging results.
2. *Cognitive* – behaviour and performance are complex and appraisers attempt to simplify this complexity. Different perceptions will result in disagreement between appraisers and appraisees.
3. *Affective* – the evaluative nature of performance control appraisal is threatening to appraisees and triggers defence mechanisms, leading to bias and distortions in interpreting information. Appraisers also may find appraisal threatening.

All of the above would suggest that self-appraisal in an environment of evaluation and control is not effective and this is not surprising. However Campbell and Lee suggest that:

> such pessimistic conclusions do not rule out the possibility that self appraisals can be used as important developmental and motivational tools for individuals (1988, p. 307).

We have already shown that employees are able to observe their own performance and obtain data for appraising strengths and weaknesses and identifying future goals from the processes of working. We have also shown that such observations may allow the organization to benefit from rising efficiency and effectiveness including better standards. Allowing employees to appraise themselves for development purposes is an acceptance of the values of such a process for individuals and the organization. The extent to which employees are able to appraise themselves objectively becomes a question of how willing they are to seek and accept feedback from their work behaviour and the environment that they are in. Employees can learn to appraise themselves and will treat it as part of their own development, if they can see the value of it for themselves rather than as a manipulative management tool. HRM in practice 8.1 provides a discussion relating to the appraisal of clergy in the Church of England.

Self-appraisal for development will not occur unless it is set in an environment that facilitates and encourages such a process. Where a positive experience from self-appraisal is gained, employees may then be willing to share their thoughts on the process with others. In recent years, many organizations have sought to increase the amount of feedback received and the number of sources of feedback. Kettley (1997, p. 2) claims that the growing popularity of multi-source feedback (MSF) is due to a number of factors which offer a way to:

1. empower employees and promote teamwork, by allowing them to appraise their managers
2. increase reliability of appraisals and balance, in flatter organizations
3. reinforce good management behaviour, by allowing people to see themselves as others see them.

Most schemes would appear to involve feedback to managers although there are likely to be increased attempts to extend the process to all employees in the future. The various sources of feedback might include the immediate manager, subordinates (upward appraisal), peers, other parts of the organization (internal customers), external clients and customers and self-rating. Where a scheme provides feedback from all or most of these sources, this is referred to as 360° appraisal or feedback.

As the number and range of MSF schemes has grown, interest in their impact has also developed. The crucial factor will be the extent to which self-ratings are supported by the ratings of others. What do you think the outcome would be if a manager had a positive perception of his or her performance but was rated less well by others such as subordinate employees and internal customers? Yammarino and Atwater (1997, p. 40) have provided a model of possible HRM outcomes based on the range of agreements between self–other ratings, shown as Table 8.2.

There has been only limited evidence of the impact of MSF. A study by Reilly *et al.* (1996) of the effect of upward appraisal on management performance shows improvement where managers started from a low or moderate rating and the feedback process was sustained over time. There was less impact on managers who already had high performance ratings. The study found that the process created an awareness of the behaviours measured, leading to efforts by managers to improve these, especially in the early phases of the scheme. In addition, the scheme itself provided a powerful message to managers that performance would be assessed and improvement was expected. Other studies have shown that there are still dangers in feedback schemes that are used to judge employees and provide information for their development and performance improvement. Handy *et al.* (1996, p. 14), in a survey of organizations using 360° feedback, found that while most were positive about its use and were confident that it was a stimulus for personal growth, there were also some problems. Individuals could be hurt by too much negative feedback and there might be confusion

Table 8.2 Self–other rating agreement and HRM

Type	Ratings	HRM outcomes
Over-estimator	Self-ratings greater than other ratings	Very negative
In agreement/good	High self-ratings similar to other high ratings	Very positive
In agreement/poor	Low self-ratings similar to other ratings	Negative
Under estimator	Self-ratings less than other ratings	Mixed

Source: Yammarino and Atwater, 1997, p. 40

HRM in practice 8.1

Judgment day looms for church ministers

The Church of England is developing national guidance on how the performance of clergy should be assessed

BY STEPHEN OVERELL People Management, 8 August 1996

Britain's clergy will undergo a system of peer appraisal reviews if new best-practice guidelines being developed by Church of England leaders are taken up by diocese.

In the clearest sign yet that secular managerialism has permeated the second estate, the 13 500 clergy in Britain's 43 diocese are being encouraged to 'take responsibility for their own professional development' through the first national guidance on performance reviews. The word 'review' is preferred to 'appraisal', which is seen as having connotations of reward and punishment.

A national conference next month will discuss the basis of best-practice guidelines, which will be recommended for adoption by diocese. Currently, different diocese have a hotchpotch of arrangements by which clergy are monitored; most rely on 'hierarchical reviews' by bishops and bishops' nominees.

The Rev Margaret Jackson, secretary for continuing ministerial education with the Advisory Board of Ministry, said diocese were being strongly encouraged to move towards peer group reviews. 'The message that is coming through loud and clear is that ministerial review works best when it is done in a peer appraisal scheme or by suitably trained lay

people,' she said.

'It is ridiculous to try to ape commerce, because there are fewer clear lines of responsibility in the church. But most clergy are keen to set their own agenda and be encouraged to work towards reaching its targets. It is about individuals sorting out where they are in a supportive environment, adapting the best of secular practice to the church,' she added.

> **Many fear that bishops are responding to falling numbers on pews and moral relativism by tightening their grip on their church in an attempt to offer an improved service to churchgoers.**

Hierarchical reviews have been dogged by suspicion from the clergy, because of the complex employment relationship between the church and its representatives. Clergy are not 'employees' – this much was established in an infamous case in the diocese of Southwark last April over whether a curate could claim employment protection rights and bring an unfair dismissal action – but neither are they self-employed.

'We are answerable to God,' said the Rev Tony Bell, an industrial chaplain on Teesside

who is leading an appraisal task group for the MSF union's clergy section. 'We are theologians, pastoral leaders, not managers. Appraisal is a good idea, but one of the reasons it is frowned on is that it is seen as a means of diocesan control. Bishops are not trained in how to offer positive support.

'It is right to put aims and objectives to some sort of examination, but it must be done by people who understand our work,' he added.

MSF is likely to recommend a system of trained clerical appraisers training other clergy on appraisal techniques. In September 1994 a survey by the union found that 62 per cent of clergy had experience of appraisal systems. Of these, 67 per cent found them helpful.

The debate over appraisal strikes at the heart of the old question of what the established clergy's role should be in a cynical age. Many fear that bishops are responding to falling numbers on pews and moral relativism by tightening their grip on their church in an attempt to offer an improved service to churchgoers.

It is such fears of compromising a priest's prerogative to carry out their calling in the way they see fit that prompted the birth of MSF's clergy section, now growing steadily with about 600 members.

Some have looked in admiration at the Methodist Church's system, introduced several years ago on the advice of a personnel consultant. Its approach of 'accompanied self-appraisal' involves 500 trained accompanists sitting down with ministers to agree a confidential outline of responsibilities and identify areas of improvement.

'The accompanist is there to enable self-management – standing alongside a minister so he can be responsible to his vocation,' said Dr John Simmonds, the Methodist Church's continuing development in ministry team leader.

Where bishops do assess their clergy, a peer appraisal system will be needed as well, said the Rev Margaret Jackson, who was a personnel manager at BP before being ordained two years ago.

The system developed by some diocese, where a continuing ministerial education officer trains clergy in how to review each other, is likely to be a popular model at next month's conference on guidelines.

'The days of sitting in the same job for 30 years have gone, just as they have elsewhere,' Jackson said. 'There is more uncertainty now. Different skills are needed to do different jobs. A rural parish in Norfolk requires different training to an urban parish in London. Reviews are about equipping clergy to be better clergy.'

There are some important implications for how MSF is positioned in an organization and how support processes are established. In particular, organizations need to consider the preparation of employees to give and receive feedback and to use the various ratings techniques. Training programmes for such skills before the implementation of MSF schemes would be crucial. It would also seem that such schemes have more value as development and performance improvement processes than as a judgement mechanism for pay and promotion (Garavan *et al.*, 1997, p. 145).

The various approaches to MSF are usually incorporated into and seen as an integral part of an overall approach to the management of performance in organizations as an aspect of performance management systems (PMS). During the 1990s PMS have become an important response by many organizations to link the needs of business strategy to all employees. Walters (1995, p. x) sees PMS as concerned with

directing and supporting employees to work as effectively and efficiently as possible *in line with the needs of the organization* [original emphasis].

A key feature of a PMS is the attempt to provide a link between all levels of an organization through goals, critical success factors and performance measures. Thus an organization's goals will be derived from business strategy and translated respectively into sector goals, departmental goals, manager goals and employee and team goals. At each stage, there will be an attempt to provide measurable performance indicators of the achievement of goals. In addition to goals, which provide the direction for performance, a PMS will also provide a means of supporting performance through diagnosing development needs, providing ongoing feedback and review and coaching where required. The integrated nature of PMS is shown in the performance management cycle shown as Figure 8.5.

A PMS might incorporate, especially for managers, a development centre. Development centres are the same as assessment centres in that assessment tests and exer-

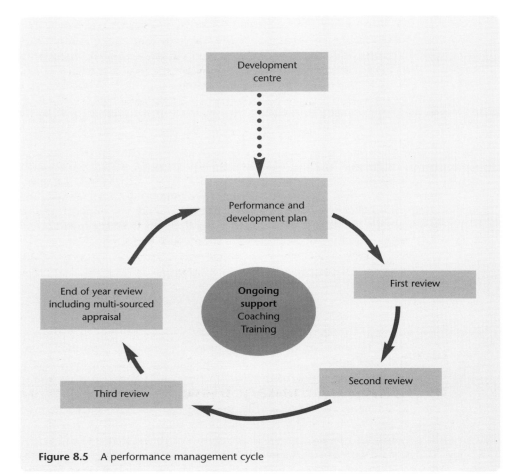

Figure 8.5   A performance management cycle

Table 8.3   The inputs of a development centre held for managers at Yorkshire Water plc

1. Participant and boss inputs	a SWOT analysis for the participant and a discussion of hopes for the future.
2. Psychometric measures	– SHL OPQ, a personality questionnaire
	– FIRO-B, an interpersonal behaviour measure
	– Myers-Briggs type indicator, a measure of psychological types
	– GMAA spatial relationships, a measure of ability to make sense of complex data
3. Colleague survey	feedback from 15 colleagues
4. Interview	to discuss results of tests and feedback
5. Self-assessment and PDP	

Source: Adapted from Davies, 1996

cises are used to provide a report on individual strengths and limitations, but they differ by their emphasis on suggested development activities and a performance and development plan (PDP). While there may be a range of activities used, a development centre would usually involve psychometrics and feedback from a qualified occupational psychologist, multi-source feedback and a self-diagnosis against the organization's competency framework. A PDP would also include an attempt to link the overall business aim with key areas of responsibility and measurable objectives. Table 8.3 shows the inputs of a development centre held for managers at Yorkshire Water plc.

Once a PDP has been established, according to the performance management cycle, work is carried out to meet objectives set. There should also be ongoing coaching from the immediate manager and support for any training and development needs identified. Objectives and performance are reviewed, perhaps every quarter, to monitor progress. During the course of the year, feedback might be obtained from different sources which can be used to improve performance but will also feed into the end of year review where an overall assessment and appraisal might also be carried out. HRM in practice 8.2 provides an example of PMS at Barclays Mortgages.

HRM in practice 8.2

Performance management in Barclays mortgages

BY TREVOR BRUNTON Learning and Development Adviser

Barclays Mortgages, part of Barclays Bank plc, employs around 800 people on a single site in Leeds. In formulating our business strategy, we recognised that in the fiercely competitive market place in which we work, merely having top quality products and a cost efficient operation was not going to give us sufficient competitive advantage to survive and thrive – we need to be able to fully harness the talents and commitment of our people. Aligning every individual's performance plan more directly to business strategy was considered key to achieving this and consequently an effective Performance Management (PM) process was to be core and fundamental to achieving our strategic intent.

How it works
Everybody in the business, from Managing Director down, uses the same system. An important principle in the business is that the way we interact and work with our colleagues is fundamental to the way we do business and effective teamwork is essential for us to succeed. Performance is therefore assessed 50 per cent on what people do, and 50 per cent on the way they do it.

Objectives – what you do
Departments' aims are determined by team members, linking to our Strategic Intent and Business Objectives. As part of rolling out PM to everybody in the business therefore, our strategy, the way it was formed, and the way it translates into action through the performance plans of everyone in the business has been explained to everyone by one of the senior management team, who 'set the scene' for each of the training courses. Having defined the purpose of their department, individuals and teams then determine their own Key Responsibility Areas, objectives and measures, facilitated and assisted (but not directed) by their team leaders. This sets out the expectations of the role as far as the measurable deliverables are concerned, and wherever possible, specifying

what exception performance would look like.

The plan is a living document. Performance is reviewed quarterly against planned objectives which are expected to change during the year to reflect changing circumstances and business priorities. Each individual has an Achievement log as part of the form-set. This is intended to record achievements over and above what's been planned for an effective quarter's performance, recognising that all too often significant deliverables are missed when it comes to reviewing the individual's performance. The Achievement Log can also be used to record exceptional circumstances which may have impacted the achievement of planned objectives. The onus is on the individual to keep the Achievement log up to date, in the knowledge that entries on this log could well influence the quarterly assessment, particularly if it demonstrates that they have delivered significantly more than expected. There is a degree of trust involved. However it is intended to make for a better informed decision. Taking into account all objectives and circumstances documented in the plan, an assessment of Exceed, Met, Fall Short or Fail is agreed each quarter, relating to the individual's delivery of their objectives against expected standards.

Attributes – the way you do it

The Attributes Library (competencies) describe the sorts of behaviours and qualities we expect people to be demonstrating when performing effectively and what these behaviours and qualities look like in practice. The Library consists of 18 Attributes such as Delivering Results, Attention to Detail and Developing People, each structured into Dimensions, to reflect differing levels in the organisation, and Performance Bands to describe what the behaviours or qualities would look like in someone performing to an acceptable standard. Some Attributes are single dimension – for example the qualities someone demonstrates when exercising self-control are much the same at whatever level they are working at, it's just the circumstances under which they need to exercise that self-control that differ. With other attributes, the behaviours people would be required to exhibit are different at different levels.

An important principle in the business is that the way we interact and work with our colleagues is fundamental to the way we do business

---

Appropriate Attributes and Dimensions are identified for each role in the business by agreement between a representation of jobholders and their team leaders, the process facilitated by someone from the HR project team. Most roles have ended up with between 14 and 17 Attributes. Up to eight of these Attributes are then selected as being core to the role; each individual role-holder will then have these eight Attributes assessed at each quarterly review, with the remaining ones assessed at least once during the year. Assessment of Attributes is by agreement between the jobholder's self assessment and the reviewer's assessment, with a requirement for each individual to seek feedback from at least six people during the year against around eight of the Attributes in the profile. The people to be asked for feedback are agreed between jobholder and reviewer and the information received feeds in to the quarterly discussions between jobholder and reviewer.

Feedback is delivered in writing using the statements in the Attributes Library as the benchmark, giving a rating of Less than Effective, Fully Effective or Outstanding and people are encouraged to give specific examples of occasions they have observed to support their assessments as appropriate, particularly for Less than Effective or Outstanding assessments.

Similar to Objectives, an overall assessment of Exceed, Met, Fall Short or Fail against Attributes is agreed each quarter as outlined above, the benchmark being that someone established in a role should be demonstrating Fully Effective qualities in all the relevant Dimensions of each Attribute relevant to the role. Someone developing into the role will be able to agree with their reviewer an appropriate timescale in which they would expect to be demonstrating Fully Effective qualities and they will be measured on progress against this development plan.

We can see that throughout the performance management cycle, there are a number of opportunities for rating of performance and performers to occur. The different approaches to rating can be classified as follows.

Inputs

This is a broad and potentially vague category which has been concerned traditionally with listing traits or personality attributes. Typical attributes might be dependability, loyalty, decisiveness, resourcefulness, stability, and so on. Because such attributes may be difficult to define, there will be little agreement among different users of lists of measures of their presence in employees. In Chapter 7, Recruitment and selection, we referred to the issue of reliability. The use of personality attributes in assessing and appraising can lack reliability, giving rise to charges of bias, subjectivity and unfairness. This is normally the case when managers attempt to measure their employees in appraisal interviews. As indicated above, many organizations now prefer to use reliable and valid psychometric instruments as a way of helping employees diagnose strengths and weaknesses for a development plan.

Results and outcomes

The results and outcomes from work performance provide the most objective techniques of providing data for appraisal. When available, measurements can be taken at different points in time and comparisons made with objectives. Typical measurements might relate to production, sales, numbers of satisfied customers or customer complaints. We can also include in this section the achievement of standards of competence as contained within National Vocational Qualifications (NVQs). A growing number of organizations are attempting to include NVQs as targets for their workforce.

It is not surprising that most measurements are quantifiable although many organizations will attempt to modify quantification with qualitative measurements or comments. The attractiveness of results and outcomes as objective sources of data makes them a feature of many appraisal systems in the UK. Long's (1986) survey found them to be a feature in 63 per cent of organizations. Will such approaches reflect performance control or development approaches? Key questions will relate to how objectives, targets and goals are set, how managers and employees will interact in work towards their achievement, and the use made by employees of measurements as feedback in order to develop further.

During the 1960s, there was a growth in schemes of management by objectives (MBO), designed to control the performance of managers and stimulate them as regards their development. If this could be achieved, the needs of managers and the organization could be integrated. However, such schemes soon came under attack and many fell into disrepute. Levinson (1970, p. 134) attacked the practice of MBO as self-defeating because it was based on 'reward–punishment psychology' which put pressure on individuals without there being any real choice of objectives. Modern approaches to objective setting, especially where they feature as part of a performance management system, will face similar charges unless managers pay as much attention to the process by which objectives are set as to the content and quantification of objectives and the environment in which employees work towards their achievement.

Behaviour in performance

We have already examined how attention to the behaviour of employees in the transformation process will reveal how an individual has applied aptitudes, attitudes and competencies to the performance of work and will provide rich data on current effectiveness and potential for further development. Such attention can occur on a continuous basis taking into account both subjective and objective data. Such an approach forms the foundation of performance management systems concerned with the direction of performance and support for continuing development of employees. Once established, employees may be more willing to accept more codified approaches to rating their behaviour. For example, we have referred to frameworks of competencies associated with effective performance which can provide a user-friendly starting point for the assessment, appraisal and development of people in an organization. In addition to competencies, but closely related, are the use of behaviour anchored rating scales (BARS) which provide descriptions of important job behaviour 'anchored' alongside a rating scale. The scales are developed (Rarick and Baxter, 1986, p. 36) by generating descriptions of effective and ineffective performance from people who know the job and these are then used to develop clusters of performance and scales. Each scale produced describes a dimension of performance which can be used in appraisal. An example from a scale developed for a planning role is shown as Figure 8.5.

Between excellent and unacceptable would come the whole range of possible behaviours of varying degrees of effectiveness. Since BARS are based on specific performance and on the descriptions of employees involved in a particular job, it is claimed that they provide better feedback and a consistent means of improving performance and setting targets. What is particularly interesting is the potential of such instruments as BARS for enhancing self-appraisal and allowing a dialogue between employees and 'others', based on more objective criteria.

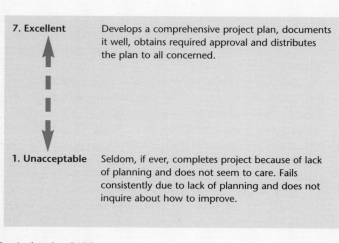

Figure 8.6 A planning BARS
Source: Schneier and Beatty in Rarick and Baxter, 1986

The recent trend towards performance management systems has gone some way to reconcile the competing uses of assesssment and appraisal in organizations. The development of competency frameworks along with other measurement devices has improved the reliability and validity of feedback about employees' attitudes, aptitudes and performance. This still does not remove the underlying control emphasis. Indeed some would claim (Townley, 1994, p. 50) that the use of the various techniques of appraisal serve to enhance the 'manageability' of employees. PMS also puts a great deal of faith in management support as appraisers and facilitators of other people's development. There is no guarantee of either and our understanding of what really happens in appraisals and in organizations generally is still limited. Importantly, so much of the literature concerning appraisal and performance management works from the neo-human relations assumption that all employees have an interest in achieving the objectives set or responding to measurements even where they have participated in the process (Newton and Findlay, 1996, p. 43). Of course, employees do have an interest in what they do at work but they also have many other interests that have only a tangential connection to workplace performance

Chapter summary

For organizations that claim to have an HRM approach to the management of people, appraisal has a central place. In the HRM cycle, it is the vital link between performance and the processes of rewards and development that are key features in the evolution of a primary internal labour market discussed in previous chapters. Appraisal, and especially performance management systems, can be viewed as processes to bridge the gap between an organization and individuals, which allows a flow of information between managers, employees and, increasingly, other sources that provide the context for the performance of work. If HRM outcomes are sought, information that is generated through assessment and appraisal processes has to serve the interests of the organization and employess. Thus an organization may fail to use appraisal to identify the aspirations and potential of employees, who may in turn prefer to seek fulfilment elsewhere. In addition, appraisal provides an opportunity for feedback from employees to managers on work issues and processes. However, the release of potential and the free flow of information within appraisal systems will require a shift in values and attitudes and a reform of our view of appraisal as a fragmented and separable part of the employment relationship. Performance management systems may be going some way towards such a shift, although we await evidence of their effects. In this chapter, we have sought to establish that organizations will need to concentrate on creating a learning and developing culture if appraisal is to be accepted by employees as a means of tying the satisfaction of their needs and their development to the objectives of the organization.

Key concepts

Assessment	Transformation process
Appraisal	Bureaucratic control
Performance management systems	Upward appraisal
Development centres	Developmental approaches
Multi-source feedback	360° appraisal or feedback

Discussion questions

1. What should be the purpose of appraisal?

2. Is performance management, management by objectives by another name? Will it suffer a similar fate?

3. Should pay and performance appraisal be linked?

4. How can employees learn to appraise themselves?

5. Do you think students should have more say in appraising and assessing themselves and each other?

6. Do you think appraisal and assessment techniques enhance the 'manageability' of employees?

Further reading

Barlow, G. (1989) Deficiencies and the perpetuation of power: latent functions in management appraisal, *Journal of Management Studies*, **26**(5): 499–517.

Hartle, F. (1997) *Transforming the Performance Management Process*, London: Kogan Page.

Newton, T. and Findlay, P. (1996) Playing God? The performance of appraisal, *Human Resource Management Journal*, **6**(3): 42–58.

Randell, G. (1994) Employee appraisal. In Sisson, K. (ed.) *Personnel Management*, Oxford: Blackwell.

Walters, M. (ed.) (1995) *The Performance Management Handbook*, London: Institute of Personnel and Development.

Chapter case study

Hamilton Foods Ltd

Hamilton Foods Ltd (HFL) is a medium-sized food manufacturer in the West Midlands. The company produces a range of quick-cook fresh foods, sold mainly via two supermarket chains. There are over 150 employees, organized into production teams, many of whom have been with the company since it was started ten years ago by the Hamilton brothers, Tony and Alan. During the last year, HFL has faced an environment that is increasingly competitive and fast-moving. On at least two occasions during last year, the company has had to explain failures to meet orders to their key customers. The brothers have become aware that they can no longer rely on traditional approaches to managing the business. They accept that they must put more faith in managers and team supervisors while they take strategic and customer management responsibilities.

Following a major strategic review of its structure and activities, a number of constraints have been identified which inhibit the effectiveness of HFL's organization structure and its human resources. These include:

- Lack of empowerment and expertise among managers and team supervisors.
- A lack of performance management orientation as evidenced by the recent failure to effectively cascade the business plan into team objectives and individuals' key results areas. Staff do not know where HFL is going and how they contribute.
- Weak relationship of reward to management and team supervisor results.
- Deficiencies in manager and team supervisor skills.

The brothers now believe that a new performance management system is needed to put the business on a growth path for the future. Hitherto, a performance management system at HFL has equated to an annual appraisal process and this has not adequately served the company. HFL needs a performance management system which sets challenging standards for managers and team supervisors. HFL now need PMS which is an extension of the business planning process – what needs to be done and when will we know if we have done it – to individual objectives for every manager and team supervisor.

Task

You have been asked to prepare a report for HFL on:

1. The requirements for an effective performance management system for managers and team supervisors.
2. The roles and responsibilities in performance management of:
   a. managers
   b. the manager's manager
   c. others.
3. The training and development implications of performance management.

You should research some of the evidence on the operation of performance management systems.

Notes

1. Barlow, G. (1989) Deficiencies and the perpetuation of power: latent functions in management appraisal, *Journal of Management Studies*, **26**(5): 499–517.
2. Hartle, F. (1997) *Transforming the Performance Management Process*, London: Kogan Page.
3. Randell, G. (1994) Employee appraisal. In Sisson, K. (ed.) *Personnel Management*, Oxford: Blackwell.

chapter nine

Reward management

John Bratton

There is no such thing as a good pay system; there is only a series of bad ones. The trick is to choose the least bad one.[1]

Chapter outline

Chapter objectives

After studying this chapter, you should be able to:

1. Explain the key functions of reward management.
2. Explain the importance of job analysis information.
3. Describe the job evaluation process.
4. Describe the key determinants of pay.
5. Evaluate the merits of alternative reward systems.
6. Explain how governments intervene in the pay-determination process.
7. Explain the paradoxes and tensions in reward systems in relation to the HRM model.

⬤ **Introduction**

Reward systems are one of the four human resource management policy areas incorporated into Beer *et al.*'s (1984) and Fombrun *et al.*'s (1984) HRM models (see Chapter 1). In most theoretical models of HRM, pay[2] is central to the regulation of the employment relationship. At the level of prescription, academics, policy makers, and corporate leaders recognize the difficulty of evaluating the use of reward systems as a key lever in the pursuit of substantive HRM goals of commitment, flexibility and quality. Beer *et al.* affirm that 'The design and management of reward systems constitute one of the most difficult HRM tasks for the general manager' (1984, p. 113). Practitioner accounts, as our opening quote suggests, also reaffirm the challenge.

Economic and social factors present further challenges with managing reward systems. Global forces at work today compel managers to improve labour productivity and the quality of their organization's products and services, while controlling wage costs. Social factors impinge on reward management, such as employee expectations and notions of 'fairness' regarding their pay. Given these pressures, human resource managers seek to design reward systems that facilitate achieving the organization's strategic goals and meet the goals of individual employees.

In most organizations, both private and public sector, an array of pay levels exists. The pay levels in an engineering company differ for different jobs; a skilled machinist might be paid £2 per hour more than an unskilled labourer. Similarly, a supermarket pays different rates to checkout operators, department managers and cleaners. An employer's pay structure is the cluster of pay levels associated with jobs in the organization. The pay structure defines the relationships between jobs in terms of pay. Why do some employers pay more (or less) than other employers? Why are different jobs within the same organization paid differently? And why do different employees doing an identical job for the same employer receive different pay? How are these decisions made? How does the government influence reward management? Decisions about paying employees for the work they perform are increasingly complex. Decisions must be consistent with the organization's goals, with society's values about notions of fairness, and with government legislation.

This chapter discusses some of the important changes that are taking place in reward management. At the prescriptive level, it examines the functions of pay systems, describes different forms of remuneration, and outlines a pay model. Job analysis and job evaluation as techniques for determining different pay rates are explained. The chapter proceeds to examine the determinants of pay, alternative reward systems, and the role of government in reward management. At the more theoretical level, the chapter concludes with a critical analysis of the position of rewards in the normative HRM model, which reveals tensions, conflicts and contradictions with the rhetoric and practice of HRM.

⬤ **Reward in organizations**

Reward management is one of the central pillars of human resource management. While the term 'reward management' is problematic, we consider that the term best captures the current changes in management assumptions and practice about pay. Reward is defined in the following terms:

Reward refers to all forms of financial returns and tangible services and benefits employees receive as part of an employment relationship.

Reward is the centre-piece of the employment relationship, but before we can fully
understand the conceptual analysis of the place of rewards within any HRM model, it
is first necessary to recall the nature of the employment relationship discussed in
Chapter 1. We noted there that the way in which workers are rewarded for their work,
as part of the wage–effort bargain, is central to the capitalist employment relationship. All reward systems contain two elements that are in contradiction with each
other. First, *cooperation* between worker and employer or manager is an essential
ingredient of the employment relationship if anything is to be produced, and is fostered through the logic of financial gain for the worker. Second, *tensions* and *conflict*
are engendered through the logic that makes the 'buying' of labour power the reward
to one group the cost to the other. This fundamental tension underlying the employment relationship makes for an unstable contract between the two parties which, in
the context of global price competition and technological change, is constantly being
adjusted. For example, to increase market 'viability' employers attempt to increase
performance through pay incentives or pay cuts to reduce labour costs. Further,
'effort' or individual performance itself is 'a highly unstable phenomenon ' and payment systems form part of an array of managerial strategies designed as 'effort controllers' (Baldamus, 1961).
   The nature of the employment contract means that the employee and those
responsible for reward management have different objectives when it comes to
rewards. For the individual employee the pay cheque at the end of the month is typically the major source of personal income and hence a critical determinant of an
individual's purchasing power. The absolute level of earnings determines the standard
of living and social well-being of the recipient, and will therefore be the most important consideration for most employees. Employees constantly seek to maximize their
reward because of inflation and rising expectations. Further, the axiom of 'a fair day's
pay for a fair day's work' raises the question of relative income. In most cases what is
seen to be 'fair' will be a very rough, personalized evaluation.
   The organization, on the other hand, is interested in reward management for two
important reasons. First, it is concerned about the absolute cost of the payment
because of its bearing on profitability or cost effectiveness. The importance of this
varies with the type of organization and the relative cost of employees. Thus in a
refinery labour costs are minimal, in education or health they are substantial. Second,
the organization views pay as a determinant of employee work attitudes and behaviour. Pay may affect an individual's decision to join a company, to work effectively, to
undertake training, to accept additional responsibilities, or to join a trade union.
   The three principal objectives of reward management are to:

● attract and retain suitable employees
● maintain or improve levels of employee performance
● comply with employment legislation and regulations.

These objectives have to be achieved within an agreed budget for rewards. First, the
reward must be competitive to encourage membership of the organization. In other
words, it must attract and retain qualified and competent people to the organization.
Rewards that are perceived by prospective members to be inadequate or inequitable

will make it difficult for the organization to attract the types of people necessary for success. Second, reward systems are designed and managed to improve productivity and control labour costs. The question of what motivates employees to perform effectively is difficult to answer. Among practising managers there is a widespread conviction that pay alone motivates workers. This over-simplistic assumption underpins individual wage incentives. Psychological theory and research suggest that the link between individual behaviour and performance is a more complex process.

One of the most widely accepted explanations of motivation is Vroom's (1964) expectancy theory. This approach to worker motivation argues that managers must have an understanding of their subordinates' goals and the linkage between effort and performance, between performance and rewards, and between the rewards and individual goal satisfaction. The theory recognizes that there is no universal principle for explaining everyone's motivation, which means that to link performance and reward successfully is difficult to accomplish in practice. Changing the pay system can modify employees' behaviour, which in turn can impact on performance. The reward system is a major element in determining the psychological contract within an organization, particularly in circumstances of change. By specifying the new performance requirements of employees as a result of strategic change, and the rewards employees will receive upon their fulfillment, management define new expectations and so alter the employment relationship (Stiles *et al.*, 1997). The third objective, compliance, means that a reward system should comply with pay legislation. As UK and European Union employment laws change, reward systems may need to be adjusted to ensure continued compliance.

Types of reward

The types of reward used will result from decisions made concerning the nature of the effort in relation to the reward. Managers are particularly interested in effort-related behaviours, those behaviours that directly or indirectly influence the achievement of the organization's objectives.

Figure 9.1 classifies some of these behaviours into four groups: time, energy, competence, and cooperation. To be efficient, managers must ensure that employees turn up for work at the scheduled times; absenteeism and lateness must be minimized. Also, employees must put sufficient energy into the job to complete their allotted tasks within set time limits. In addition, job incumbents must be competent so that the tasks are completed without errors and above performance standards. (Performance standard is a minimum acceptable level of performance.) Changes in job design (see Chapter 4) require employees to work cooperatively with co-workers to improve the organization's effectiveness.

Different types of rewards, individual, team, and organizational are shown in Figure 9.1. *Individual rewards* are paid directly to the individual employee and are based upon either time or energy commitment, or a combination of both. The *basic wage* is the irreducible minimum rate of pay. In many organizations it is a basis on which earnings are built by the addition of one or more of the other types of reward. The basic wage is usually based on a predetermined rate per hour, which tends to reflect the value of the work itself, and generally excludes differences in individual performance. For example, the basic wage for a skilled machine operator may be £4 an hour, for a thirty-five hour week, but operators may receive more because of additional incentive and overtime payments. A distinction is often made between *salary* and *wage*. A salary is a fixed

Figure 9.1 Types of reward system

Type of Reward		Type of Effort
Individual rewards	Basic wage Overtime	Time: maintaining work attendance
	Piece rate Commissions Bonuses	Energy: performing tasks
	Merit Paid leave Benefits	Competence: completing tasks without errors
Team rewards	Team bonuses Gainsharing	Cooperation: cooperation with co-workers
Organizational rewards	Profit sharing Share ownership Gainsharing	

periodical payment to a non-manual employee. It is usually expressed in annual terms, and salaried staff typically do not receive overtime pay. A wage is the payment made to manual workers. It is nearly always calculated at an hourly rate. In North America and Britain, an increasing number of employers have lessened the divide between salaries and wages by introducing single status payment schemes. This type of payment system is designed to harmonize the terms and conditions of employment between manual and white-collar employees. Common terms and conditions of employment (for example, manual and non-manual employees receiving the same number of holidays, sickness benefit, and pensions) were included in the so-called 'strike-free' agreements negotiated in the 1980s in Britain. If employees work beyond the contracted hours they are generally paid an enhanced rate for the additional hours or *overtime*. For example, an employee may work from 8am to 5pm for £4 per hour. If the individual works overtime from 5pm to 8pm, the extra three hours may be paid at 'time and a quarter', that is, £5.00 per hour. Overtime working on Saturdays or Sundays may be paid at 'time and a half' or 'double time'.

An *incentive* scheme ties pay directly to performance. It can be tied to the performance of an individual or a team of employees. This scheme includes most of the *payment-by-results* (PBR) systems, as well as *commission* payments to sales people. Merit pay rewards past behaviours and accomplishments. It is often given as lump-sum payments or as increments to the base pay. Incentive and merit payments differ. While both may influence performance, incentives influence behaviour by offering pay as an inducement. *Merit* pay, on the other hand, does so by recognizing outstanding past performance. The distinction is a matter of timing. Incentive systems are offered prior to the actual performance. Merit pay, on the other hand, typically is not communicated beforehand. Other forms of individual rewards include *benefits* (pensions, private health and dental insurance), and *paid leave* from work (for example, paid leave for full-time education, civic duties).

Reward systems can be designed in an unlimited number of ways, and a single employer typically will use more than one programme. Current thinking is based on the opinion that pay should be seen as part of the wider relationship between management and employee, and that the reward system adopted should act as a medium for the expression of management style and their attempt to create commitment among the workforce. Current trends reveal attempts to break links with external pressures on the pay system, for example, norms, averages, the 'going rate'. In preference, many organizations are shifting the focus towards internally designed factors, team and organizational rewards. *Team reward* systems have become more prevalent in Europe and North America as organizations have reconfigured work systems to emphasize self-managed teams. *Organizational rewards*, such as profit sharing, have also grown in popularity as a way of motivating employees and to gain employee commitment to customer-driven work cultures (Pryce and Nicholson, 1988). The next section takes a more detailed look at these developments in reward systems.

● Developments in reward management

The way managers have managed remuneration has undergone significant change in the last decade. A growing number of companies appear to be rewarding their employees, within the same organization and doing an identical job, at different levels of pay. Some writers have described these changes in pay practices as revolutionary because they overthrow the old assumption that employees should be paid the same even though their contribution differs, and because this philosophy is being transmitted down through the organization (Curnow, 1986). Other writers have been more critical and have interpreted these developments as an attempt to construct a more individually orientated (as opposed to union or collectively orientated) organizational culture (Bacon and Storey, 1993). In Canada, the US and the UK, top management pay is increasingly linked to the achievement of business objectives. And for their subordinates too, pay is being geared to individual potential and performance.

The contingency approach has been used as an analytical tool for explaining the factors influencing the choice of reward systems, and for outlining developments in compensation management over time. The selection of payment systems has been explained in terms of managerial goals and internal and external organizational exigencies. Thus in the post-World War II consumer boom, a payment system based upon high individual output, for example piecework, met the needs of a high volume production model. Similarly, with the alleged shift to skills-based competition, payment systems, such as pay-for-knowledge, productivity gainsharing, and profit sharing seek to encourage flexibility and behavioural traits that promote both speed and quality and meet the perceived needs of 'post-Fordist' production models.

Performance-related pay arrangements have assumed a high profile in UK and North America. A recent survey, for instance, found that in a poll of 316 Canadian companies, 74 per cent of employers offered performance-related pay arrangements, up 8 per cent from 1996 (*Globe and Mail*, August 26, 1997, p. B12). The present debate is whether the current managerial drive to establish a close relationship between individual pay and individual performance constitutes a qualitative change from past management strategies. In other words, is the shift an *ad hoc*, reactive response to contextual changes or do the reported changes in reward systems represent a more proactive and strategic HRM approach (Kessler, 1995)?

Management literature on the perennial managerial concern of motivation suggests that payment systems directly linking pay to individual or group performance are certainly not new. Evidence of reward systems linking pay to individual performance can be found well before the Industrial Revolution in eighteenth-century Britain. In the 1960s, it was advocated that an individual performance-based payment system – regulated through productivity bargaining – be adopted to increase labour productivity. As most prescriptive texts on organizational behaviour affirm, understanding the nature of the relationship between pay, commitment and motivation is complex and requires, at the very least, knowledge of both the individual and the context. From this perspective, it is not surprising therefore to find disagreement about the strength or effectiveness of the reward–commitment link. In addition to the problems associated with the nebulous notion of 'commitment', the causal links between two variables, such as pay and commitment–performance are difficult to isolate. In the debate on the rewards–motivation link there is the tendency for writers to view workers through a management lens, at the expense of failing to analyse management *per se*; what managers do, and how well they do it. Blinder's (1990) insightful conclusion is particularly helpful in understanding the complexity of the reward–commitment link. 'Changing the way workers are treated may boost productivity more than changing the way they are paid' (quoted by Kessler, 1995, p. 261).

Management interest in the reward–flexibility link is associated with the goal of improving labour productivity or what detractors refer to as the 'intensification of work' whereby workers are utilized to produce more in a given period of time. More of the potential that is labour power is squeezed out into actual production or service. Company time, the time that is spent actually 'doing' physical or mental labour, drives out what is left of 'free time' in each moment of the working day (Nichols, 1980). The management techniques that can be used to achieve this include increasing the speed of machinery (for example, an assembly line); a machinist operates two or more machines instead of one; one worker performs a task previously undertaken by two (for example a carpenter does the work of a painter); coffee breaks are eliminated and so on. Advocates of new work structures, such as work teams, just-in-time and TQM, on the other hand, argue that these management innovations do not result in an intensification of labour, rather output is increased because people learn to work 'smarter'.

The pursuit of quantity and quality is a traditional managerial concern. However, recent contextual changes have focused more attention on quality. External pressures have increasingly forced North American companies to seek competitive advantage through quality, rather than price. Internal restructuring of work (for example just-in-time, work teams, TQM) has placed 'a premium upon combining speed with the maintenance of quality' (Kessler, 1995, p. 267). The difficulty of establishing viable quality measures and the costs of administration has meant that few companies have attempted to establish a direct pay–quality link (ibid.).

The current trend towards variable pay arrangements and HRM goals can best be understood in terms of the political context that existed in the 1980s and for much of the 1990s in Britain and North America. In the 1980s, a concerted ideological campaign against automatic annual pay increases and 'artificially inflated' public sector pay by the Thatcher government encouraged a movement towards linking pay to individual performance and to local labour markets (Curnow, 1986; Pendleton, 1997). Researchers have chronicled these new developments, such as decentralized collective bargaining (for example, Millward *et al.*, 1992). Two trends have been identified, a significant decline in the influence of multi-employer, national agreements, and a shift towards single-employer bargaining at establishment level and the decentralization of pay negotiations to the level of the business unit, profit centre or plant. It was reported by ACAS that 'it seems, increasingly, companies are organized into separate budget and profit centres, in which unit managers have responsibility for all operations' (1988, p. 12). Millward *et al.* (1992) also reported that between 1984 and 1990, over 50 per cent of the establishments in the trading sector of the economy had some form of broadly-based financial participation such as profit sharing or employee share ownership. Since then the number of establishments with financial participation has increased. By 1995, over 10 per cent of the employed labour force participated in profit-related pay (PRP) schemes alone.[3] Recent studies suggest that privatization in the UK has not had a depressing impact on pay. Rather the pressure to reduce labour costs in newly privatized companies has focused instead on increasing productivity and reducing employment levels (Pendleton, 1997b). Poole and Jenkins' (1998) study of reward practices within British companies adds to the rhetoric-versus-reality debate. The authors conclude that, at 'a policy level', HRM approaches – the rewards that link pay with performance – are endorsed as policies, but there is little evidence of 'the widespread adoption of many of the "new pay" practices' (p. 242).

Whether current pay practices conform to the historical pattern and can be judged reactive, or more proactive and strategic, is debatable. Recognizing the difficulty in identifying the strategic intent of managers, it is posited by Kessler that there is insufficient evidence to support the hypothesis that the selection of payment systems is based upon the theoretical principle of 'fit' commonly cited in the HRM literature. Further, to depict recent developments in pay systems as evidence that pay is a 'key lever' in pursuit of HRM goals of commitment, flexibility and quality is to ignore historical data. The alternative pay systems, currently gaining popularity with managers, indicate that pay options are being selected to deal with new versions of traditional managerial problems. What may be qualitatively different and would indicate attempts to use pay in a strategic way, argues Kessler, is the use of variable pay systems to facilitate cultural change.

Smith (1992) suggests that contingent reward systems are linked to the rhetoric of the 'enterprise culture' and the enterprise culture in turn is the context for substituting performance-related pay for more traditional pay systems. Performance-related pay is said to underpin a more purposeful and 'objective achieving' strategy for managing workers. As Smith (1992, p. 178) states, the apparent change to performance-related pay represents 'a move away from the traditional view of rewards as incentives aimed at generating short-term improvements in employee performance, and towards rewards or total pay systems aimed at improving organizational performance'. Individual performance-related pay and the growing use of performance appraisal is symbolic of the desire by firms to move towards an organizational culture, 'a system of *shared meaning*' (Robbins, 1990, p. 438), that is individually orientated (Bacon and Storey, 1993). Contingency pay when linked to an appraisal system produces knowledge of the manager and non-manager, operates to 'individualize and standardize', provides a 'disciplinary matrix', a mechanism to communicate and reinforce organizational values, and to 'inculcate employee loyalty, commitment and dependency' (Townley, 1989, 1994; Legge, 1995). The appraisal process is designed to elicit information from the individual, to make them 'known', to shape individual behaviour, and to assist in the process of managerial control. As such, 'appraisal remains inextricably linked to the contested terrain of control and thus lies at the heart of the management of the employment relationship' (Newton and Findlay, 1996, p. 56).

Evidence that variable pay systems are being used as an engine for cultural change is supported by case studies. Performance-related pay arrangements were perceived as being central to changing workers' attitudes and values in the financial services sector, government departments and public utilities (Kessler, 1995). Examples are not restricted to these sectors. Bratton (1992) draws attention to the careful consideration given to the selection of a payment system that would change behaviour patterns at Flowpak Engineering. In this instance, to encourage cooperation and to tap the synergy from team working, the company substituted the individual performance-related pay system for a straightforward payment by time arrangement. The HR Director described the cultural change on the factory floor like this:

> As soon as people realized that there was no personal, peculiar advantage in hiding bits of knowledge, being flexible, hogging the good jobs, and all that... it was like suddenly turning the key (quoted in Bratton, 1992, p. 171).

In assessing and explaining the notion of 'new' rewards, we should be careful not to generalize too much from a relatively small sample of cases, and investigate any divergence between reward policies and practices. Beer *et al.* recognize the problem: 'Of the four major policy areas in HRM, this [rewards] is where we find the greatest contradiction between the 'promise' of the theory and the reality of implementation' (1984, p. 113).

⬤ Rewards and the HRM cycle

By now, it should be clear that reward management is vital to effective HR management. Brown (1989, p. 25) has stated that 'The satisfactory management of employment requires the satisfactory management of remuneration as a necessary, if not a sufficient, precondition'. Reward management is directly related to the other elements of the HRM cycle. In the selection process, pay can be a major factor in attracting highly qualified and competent people to the organization. It can also facilitate a lowering of the turnover ratio. Pay influences an employee's development and career plan. Performance-related pay can motivate an employee to undertake a course or a training programme. A reward system that directly links pay to performance will require an appraisal system that is both reliable and valid.

⬤ A model of reward management

To help us examine the complexities of pay, we have developed a framework of reward management. Figure 9.2 contains three basic elements, internal equity, external competitiveness, and the objectives.

Our model shows two broad areas that any organization must consider in reward management, internal equity and external competitiveness. *Internal equity* refers to the pay relationships among jobs within a single organization. This is translated into practice by the basic techniques of reward management, job analysis, job evaluation, and performance appraisal. The focus is on comparing jobs and individuals in terms

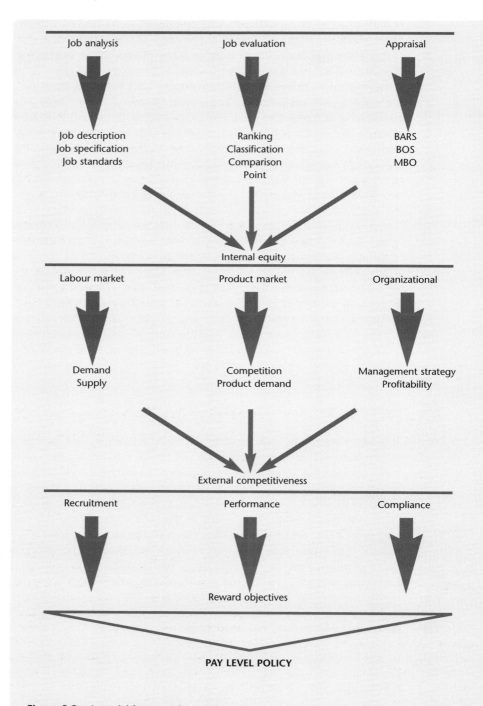

Figure 9.2 A model for reward management

of their relative contributions to the organization's objectives. How, for example, does the work of the chef compare with the work of the receptionist and the waiter? Job evaluation is the most common method used to compare the relative values of different jobs inside the organization.

External competitiveness refers to comparisons of the organization's pay relative to the pay of competitive organizations. The organization has three options, to be a pay leader, to match the market rate, or to lag behind what competitive organizations are paying. The determination of the policy on external competitiveness depends on, *inter alia*, labour conditions and the state of the job market and affordability stemming from product market conditions. Our model also shows that reward packages have explicit or implicit objectives. The balance or relative emphasis between the two basic policies is a key decision to be made in any organization's reward strategy. For example, some organizations emphasize external competitiveness of pay to attract a competent workforce. Other organizations tend to emphasize internal equity of pay, and to place less emphasis on external competitiveness. The policy on external competitiveness is important if the organization is going to attract, retain, and motivate its employees while achieving the other objectives of controlling labour costs and complying with pay legislation. Thus, the two policies, internal equity and external competitiveness, are important components of the concept of human resource management.

 HRM in practice 9.1

United Distillers deal has millennium spirit

The drinks manufacturer looks likely to extend its employment security agreement to the year 2000

BY DAVID LITTLEFIELD People Management, 6 March 1996

By the time this magazine arrives through your door, 3500 employees at Scotland's United Distillers should be toasting a deal guaranteeing them inflation-beating pay rises for three years.

As *People Management* went to press, the AEEU and MSF unions had already signed the agreement for their members, while the GMB and T&G were expected to put pen to paper earlier this week.

Both the management and the unions are also hopeful that the firm's employment security deal will be extended a further 12 months to the year 2000.

United Distillers, part of the Guinness group, is building a reputation for good industrial relations. Its employment guarantee has been seized upon by the Labour Party, which is eager to find models of successful workplace partnerships.

The deal, originally struck in 1994 to last for three years, has already been extended twice. A further extension is likely to be announced this autumn, when managers review the company's strategic objectives.

'If the workforce continues to improve efficiency and flexibility, then employment security falls out of that. It is a natural result,' said Ishbel Morrison, United Distillers' employee relations manager.

The company stresses that the agreement guarantees employment, not job security – that is, if staff are prepared to retrain and move from post to post, they have a future with United Distillers.

The deal is now separated from pay negotiations, but the unions assume that it will be renewed annually. 'Employment security has become a way of life,' said Harry Donaldson, regional industrial officer for the GMB in Scotland. 'We do not see a need to negotiate that now.'

Donaldson has recommended that his members accept the proposals. The first year of the settlement provides for a 3.5 per cent increase plus a £250 one-off bonus; and years two and three will see pay rise by another 3.5 per cent or the retail price index plus 1 per cent, whichever is greater.

Taking the bonus into account, this year's pay increase comes close to 5 per cent – way above the average for the manufacturing sector.

'We have achieved our objectives, in terms of the negotiations, as far as you can ever achieve them'

'We have achieved our objectives, in terms of the negotiations, as far as you can ever achieve them,' Donaldson said.

The CBI has reported that pay settlements averaged 3.1 per cent in the three months to December last year, which is the same figure as for the previous quarter.

The Engineering Employers' Federation has announced that pay deals in the industry averaged 3.11 per cent in the three months to January. More than half were for 3 per cent or less.

Internal equity is typically established through a series of pay techniques commencing with job analysis. *Job analysis* is the process of determining the content of a job by collecting and evaluating information. *Job evaluation* uses selected criteria to compare jobs within an organization so that the jobs can be ranked for the purpose of building a rational and consistent pay structure. *Performance appraisal* is the process of evaluating individuals in terms of their job performance.

External competitiveness is established by reference to job advertisements in the press, or by more systematic labour market surveys. This information is then used to construct a pay structure within the organization. The factors that affect the determination of external competitiveness and pay level include the demand and supply pressures in the labour market, competition for the organization's products or services, and organizational considerations, such as the ability to pay.

While external competitiveness is important, it is internal equity that will often be a priority for HR managers. We have already discussed the notion of fairness in reward, and for employees internal relatives, rather than external comparisons, can be a major source of negative perceptions about reward. To illustrate the importance for managers of achieving internal equity take the following scenario. If three children in the Doe household each receive the same weekly allowance, but their allowance is less than their neighbour's children of similar age, they might grumble but the external differences are generally accepted by the Doe children. However, if on their birthdays only one child in the Doe family receives an increase in his or her allowance, the internal differences in payment will typically cause an outcry. The point is that, generally, there is less scope for error in internal imbalance than external, because any inequities as a result of internal anomalies are more likely to be perceived among co-workers.

So far this chapter has discussed the nature of pay, highlighted some important developments in reward management, and outlined a framework for examining the essential components of remuneration in organizations. The following sections take a more prescriptive view and examine the basic components of the model, first focus-

HRM in practice 9.2

Global share plan is not to be sneezed at

Kimberly-Clark is giving 3.4 million share options to 51 000 staff worldwide in an ambitious loyalty scheme

BY JENNIE WALSH People Management, 6 November 1997

Kimberly-Clark, the maker of Andrex and Kleenex tissue products, has launched one of the biggest employee share-option schemes ever undertaken.

In a co-ordinated announcement, 51 000 employees in 58 countries were called to meetings to hear the news that they could buy a total of 3.4 million share options in an ambitious one-off programme to celebrate the organisation's 125th birthday.

Up to 2500 full- and part-time staff on permanent contracts at Kimberley-Clark's offices and mills in this country will be among those offered a number of share options, in proportion to their income, at a cost of £32 each – the company's closing share price on the day the scheme was announced. They will be able to take up the options in three years' time.

The fact that the share price plummeted as a result of the recent turmoil in the international stock markets, only days after the announcement of the scheme, may have discouraged a number of Kimberly-Clark's potential shareholders from participating. And, although the company estimates that individual employees could

eventually net £4,000 apiece, the average employee will receive only around 60 share options. The highest earners – those making more than £3,000 a month – will get the maximum allocation of 125. The lowest-paid staff will be granted 25 options, but this will still represent a welcome windfall for many workers in East Asia.

> **Kimberly-Clark, the maker of Andrex and Kleenex tissue products, has launched one of the biggest employee share-option schemes ever undertaken.**

The company says that a scheme giving equal numbers of shares to all employees, regardless of income, would have been impractical, given its large scale.

Global employee share-option schemes are still rare as a consequence of strict tax rules in many nations. A further 5000 Kimberly-Clark staff in countries including China and Norway, where legal restrictions rule out giving share options, will receive alternative awards of a similar value.

Kimberly-Clark has been selling Kleenex tissues in this country since 1924. It has mills in Cumbria, East Yorkshire, North Wales and Kent, and its European head office is based in Reigate, Surrey. The directors believe that its expansion and acquisition have resulted in many employees having greater loyalty to their factory than to the company, so the scheme is an important 'bonding' exercise.

Wayne Sanders, the company's chairman and chief executive, said the programme was designed to help unify the 'growing global organisation'.

'This grant is another incentive for employees to achieve Kimberley-Clark's business objectives,' he said. 'It provides employees at all levels with another means of sharing in the company's prosperity.'

Keith McNeish of Hewitt Associates, which helped to design, communicate and administer the plan worldwide, told *People Management* that the announcement had come as a shock to most employees.

'The scheme had to be kept a secret,' he said. 'Most employees were expecting a pen or an extra day of holiday as part of the birthday celebrations.'

ing on internal equity and the traditional reward techniques of job analysis and job evaluation (appraisal is examined separately in Chapter 8), and proceeding to discuss external competitiveness and the establishment of pay rates.

● Job analysis

Information technology has made it possible for a keyboard operator, a university lecturer, and an insurance broker to perform different jobs using the same equipment, the computer terminal. If reward is to be based on work performed, a technique is needed to identify the differences and similarities among different jobs in the organization. Observing employees is necessary but not sufficient. Knowledge about jobs and their requirements is collected through job analysis. Job analysis can be defined as:

> The systematic process of collecting and evaluating information about the tasks, responsibilities and the context of a specific job.

Job analysis information informs the HR practitioner about the nature of a specific job, in particular, the major tasks undertaken by the incumbent, the outcomes that are expected, the job's relationships with other jobs in the organizational hierarchy, and job holder characteristics. The basic premise underlying job analysis is that jobs are more likely to be described, differentiated, and evaluated consistently if accurate information is available to reward managers (Milkovich and Newman, 1990).

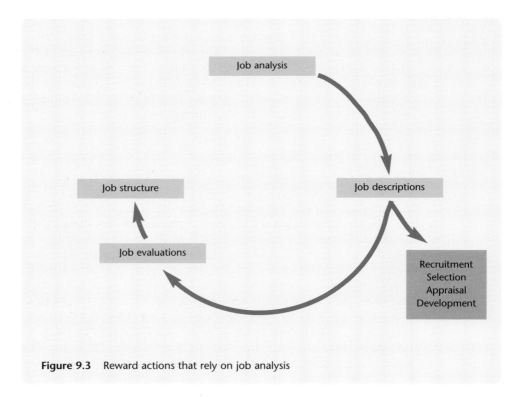

Figure 9.3   Reward actions that rely on job analysis

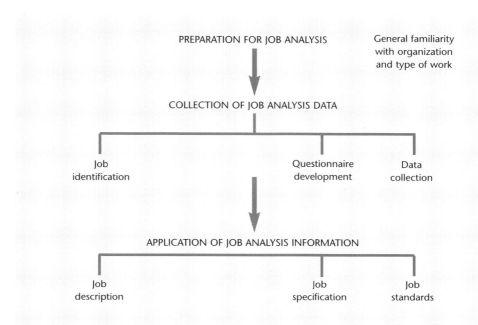

Figure 9.4 The process of job analysis

Figure 9.3 shows that job analysis information is a prerequisite for preparing job descriptions and for comparing jobs within an organization, job evaluation. Job analysis is also critical for decisions affecting recruitment and selection, appraisal, and employee development. In terms of reward management, unless there is a clear definition of the job and job performance standards, it would be difficult to imagine how pay could be linked to individual performance.

The process of job analysis

The process of job analysis consists of two main stages: data collection, and the preparation of job descriptions, job specifications and job standards. The process is shown in Figure 9.4. Job analysts collect information about jobs and job holder characteristics. The job information is then used to prepare job descriptions, specifications, and standards.

Data collection

Collecting the information involves three tasks: identifying the jobs to be analysed, developing a job analysis questionnaire, and collecting the data. *Job identification*: to collect information about the firm's jobs, analysts must first identify the jobs within the organization. In stable organizations this can be done from past job analysis reports. The analyst might also have to rely on discussions with workers, the organ-

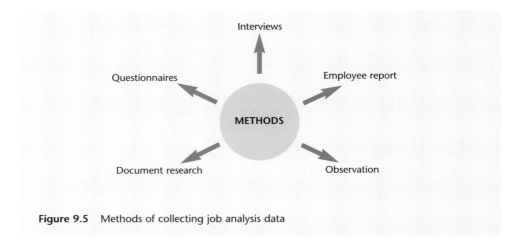

Figure 9.5 Methods of collecting job analysis data

izational charts, or the analyst's knowledge of the organization. To collect data in a systematic way analysts usually develop a *questionnaire* that gathers information about the duties, responsibilities, human abilities, and performance standards of the jobs investigated. Questionnaire design is not easy. There is no one best way to collect the data. Analysts make trade-offs between accuracy, time, and cost. Figure 9.5 illustrates five different methods of gathering job analysis data.

Let us briefly examine these job analysis methods. A face-to-face interview with the job incumbent is an effective way to gather job information. A major disadvantage with this method is that it is time consuming. Employee report involves the job incumbent collating the information about his or her job. Employees summarize their tasks and activities in the report over a given period of time. Direct observation is a method derived from work study techniques, and is usually applied to manual occupations. It involves making notes of job-related information. Observation is often regarded as the best method of collecting information, and is particularly useful because the trained observer might identify 'unofficial' duties. The method is time-consuming, however. An invaluable source of job information will be existing documents, including organizational charts, letters of appointment, and statements of objectives for departments.

Finally, questionnaires can be completed by employees individually or by the job analysts. The advantage with this approach is that it permits a larger sample to be collected quickly, and at a lower cost.

Application of job analysis information

The object of collecting job information is to develop job descriptions, job specifications, and job standards. A job description is a written statement that explains the purpose, scope, duties, and responsibilities of a specified job. A job specification is a detailed statement of the human characteristics involved in the job, including aptitudes, skills, knowledge, physical demands, mental demands, and experience required to perform the job. A job performance standard is a minimum acceptable level of performance. This completes our discussion of job analysis. The next section examines how job analysis information is used to evaluate jobs in organizations.

⬤ Job evaluation

British Telecom employs a chief executive officer, departmental managers, technicians, keyboard operators, janitors, and so on. How is pay determined for these different jobs? This question and the techniques employed to answer it lie at the heart of reward management. Our framework for analysing pay shows that the results of job analysis serve as an input for evaluating jobs. Job evaluation is a generic label for a variety of procedures used to establish pay structures inside an organization. Job evaluation can be defined as:

> A systematic process designed to determine the relative worth of jobs within a single work organization.

The technique of job evaluation is concerned with achieving internal equity of pay among different jobs in the organization. The importance of job evaluation to HR managers has increased as a result of equal pay legislation. European and Canadian equal pay legislation requires, either implicitly or explicitly, that gender-neutral job evaluation schemes be adopted and used to determine and compare the value of jobs within the organization. Thus, it has been argued that job evaluation constitutes the foundation of pay equity (Conway, 1987).

Job evaluation is often misunderstood, so the following three characteristics of all job evaluation schemes are noteworthy with respect to their adequacy for measuring job worth. First, the technique is *systematic* rather than scientific. The job evaluation process depends upon a series of subjective judgements. Job evaluation ratings may be gender biased through the gender linkage of job titles. In one study, for example, subjects assigned significantly lower job evaluation ratings to jobs with a female-stereotyped title – for example senior *secretary*–accounting – than to the same job with a more gender-neutral title – for example special assistant–accounting (McShane, 1995). Second, selection of the compensable factors is inherently subjective. Criteria for determining job worth often vary between employers, and even between job families within the organization. Thus, 'objective' measurement of job worth is impossible. Third, job evaluation methods differ in their capability to measure differences among jobs. For example, the simple ranking method is less sensitive to changes in job characteristics than the point system.

In addition, it is worth noting that job evaluation is concerned with the job and not the performance of the individual job holder. Individual merit is not assessed. Neither does job evaluation eliminate collective bargaining. It determines the differential gaps between pay; it does not determine pay level. Further, job evaluation produces only a structure of pay rates. Other elements of earnings, such as incentives, are not determined by the method.

Job evaluation process

The job evaluation process has the following four steps: gather the data, select compensable factors, evaluate job, and assign pay to the job. Let us look at each of these in turn.

Gather job analysis data

Information must be collected through a method of job analysis. In this first step validity should be a guiding principle; that is, the job analyser must accurately capture all of the job content. It is also important for the purpose of job evaluation that similarities and differences among jobs are captured. Ambiguous, incomplete, or inaccurate job descriptions can result in some jobs being incorrectly evaluated.

Select compensable factors

Compensable factors are the factors the organization chooses to reward through differential pay. The most typical compensable factors are skill, effort, knowledge, responsibility, and working conditions.

Evaluate job using evaluation methods

There are four fundamental methods of job evaluation, ranking, job grading, factor comparison, and point method. The following sub-sections offer some specifics on each of the four methods.

Ranking. Jobs are ordered from least to most valued in the organization. This rank order or hierarchy of jobs is based on subjective evaluation of relative value. In a typical factory we might finish up with the following rank order (Figure 9.6). In this example, the evaluators have agreed that the job of inspector is the most valued of the six jobs listed. Rates of pay will reflect this simple hierarchy. This method has a number of advantages. It is simple, fast and inexpensive. The ranking method will be attractive for small organizations and for those with a limited number of jobs. Obvious disadvantages are that it is crude and entirely subjective, and therefore the results are difficult to defend and legal challenges might make it costly.

Job Grading. Also referred to as job classification. As the name suggests, it places jobs in a hierarchy or series of job grades. It is decided in advance how many grades of pay shall be created, and the jobs fall into each grade based on the degree to which the jobs possess a set of compensable factors. The lowest grade will be defined as containing those jobs which require little skill and are closely supervised. With each successive grade, skills, knowledge and responsibilities increase. To illustrate, Grade A

Figure 9.6 Typical job ranking

Job Title	Rank
	Most valued
1. Forklift driver	1. Inspector
2. Machinist	2. Machinist
3. Inspector	3. Secretary
4. Secretary	4. Forklift driver
5. File Clerk	5. Labourer
6. Labourer	6. File clerk
	Least valued

Figure 9.7 Typical ranking of jobs by compensable factors

Job Title	Skill	(£)	Mental effort	(£)	Responsibility	(£)	Physical effort	(£)	Working condition	(£)	Current Wage Rate (£)
Forklift driver	4	(3.00)	5	(2.40)	4	(.90)	2	(.50)	2	(.60)	(7.40)
Machinist	1		2		3		3		3		
Inspector	2		3		1		4		4		
Secretary	3		1		2		6		6		
File Clerk	5		4		5		5		5		
Labourer	6		6		6		1		1		

Note: Rank of 1 is high.

includes jobs that require no previous experience, under immediate supervision, with no independent judgement. Grade F contains jobs that require an apprenticeship training, under general supervision, with some independent judgement. In our example in Figure 9.6, the file clerk and the machinist might be slotted into grades A and F respectively. The advantage of this method is that it is relatively simple, quick and inexpensive. A disadvantage is that complex jobs are difficult to fit into the system; a job may seem to have the characteristics of two or more grades.

Factor Comparison. This is a quantitative method that evaluates jobs on the basis of a set of compensable factors. It is a more sophisticated method of ranking in which jobs in the organization are compared to each other across several factors, such as skill, mental effort, responsibility, physical effort and working conditions. For each job, the compensable factors are ranked according to their relative importance in each job. In our example, under the compensable factor heading of 'skill' our six factory jobs are ranked showing the machinist at the top and the labourer at the bottom (Figure 9.7).

Once each benchmark job is ranked on each factor, the job evaluator allocates a monetary value to each factor. Essentially this is done by deciding how much of the wage rate for each benchmark job is associated with skill requirement, how much with mental effort, and so on across all compensable factors. For example, in Figure 9.7, of the £7.40 per hour paid to the forklift driver, the evaluator has decided that the job's skill requirements equal £3.00, mental effort is worth £2.40, responsibility equals 90p, physical effort is worth 50p and working conditions are worth 60p. The total £7.40 is therefore allocated among the five compensable factors. This exercise is repeated for each of the benchmark jobs. The advantage with this method is that the criteria for evaluating jobs are made explicit. The main disadvantage is that it is a complex and difficult method to explain to dissatisfied employees. Translating factor comparison into actual pay rates is a somewhat cumbersome exercise, and can be overcome by using a quantitative technique based on points.

Point Method. This is also a quantitative method and is the most frequently used of the four techniques. Like the factor comparison method, the point method develops separate scales for each compensable factor to establish a hierarchy of jobs. But instead of using monetary values, as the factor comparison method does, points are used. Each job's relative value, and hence its location in the pay structure, is determined by adding up the points assigned to each compensable factor.

The exercise starts with the allocation of a point score, from a range of points, to each compensable factor. Any number between 1 and 100 points might be assigned to each factor. Next, each of the factors is given a weighting; this is an assessment of how important one factor is in relation to the other. For example, in the case of the machinist, if skill is twice as important as working conditions, it is assigned twice as many points (20) as working conditions (10). The results of the evaluation might look like Figure 9.8.

The point values allocated to each compensable factor are totalled across factors, allowing jobs to be placed in a hierarchy according to their total point value. In our example, it would mean that the machinist's wage rate is twice that of the labourer. Such a differential might be unacceptable, but this difficulty can be overcome by tailoring the job evaluation scheme to the organization's pay policy and practical objectives. The point system has the advantage that it is relatively stable over time, and, because of its comprehensiveness, is more acceptable to the interested parties. The shortcomings include the administrative costs, which might be too high to justify its use in small organizations. A variation of the point system is the widely used Hay Plan. This method employs a standard points matrix, which is applicable across organizational and national boundaries. However, the HR manager should be aware that as far as job evaluation is concerned, there is no perfect system; the process involves subjective judgement.

Moreover, where women are employed care needs to be taken to ensure that gender bias in job evaluation ratings does not exist, for example, by giving higher weighting to physical demands and continuous service in the organization, which tend to favour men. Aspects of the Equal Pay Act are discussed later in this chapter. The focus in this section has been on job evaluation as a technique to achieve internal equity in pay within the organization.

Figure 9.8 Point system matrix

Job Title	Skill	Mental effort	Responsibility	Physical effort	Working conditions	Total
Forklift driver	10	10	10	10	5	45
Machinist	20	15	17	8	10	70
Inspector	20	20	40	5	5	90
Secretary	20	20	35	5	5	85
File clerk	10	5	5	5	5	30
Labourer	5	2	2	17	9	35

Assign pay to the job

The end product of a job evaluation exercise is a hierarchy of jobs in terms of their relative value to the organization. Assigning pay to this hierarchy of jobs is referred to as pricing the pay structure. This practice requires a policy decision on how the organization's pay levels relate to their competitors.

Performance appraisal

Performance appraisal is the process of evaluating individuals in terms of their job performance and is examined in detail in Chapter 8. The next section is concerned with how employers position their pay relative to what their competitors are paying: the external competitiveness.

External competitiveness

While employees' negative feelings concerning internal pay equity might be removed by an effective job evaluation scheme, employees will still compare their pay with those in other organizations and industries. How an organization's pay rates compare to other relevant organizations is known as external competitiveness. Figure 9.2 shows how an organization's policy on external competitiveness fits into the framework for reward management. The policy expresses the management's intentions regarding their pay levels relative to the pay levels of other organizations competing in the same labour and product markets.

What is the 'going rate'? Can the organization match its competitors? To answer these questions most organizations rely on wage and salary surveys. Informal or formal pay surveys collect data on what other comparable organizations are paying for comparable jobs. Survey data are used to price benchmark jobs, jobs that are used to anchor the organization's pay scale and around which other jobs are then slotted based on their relative worth to the employer. Evidence suggests that 55 per cent of British employers review newspaper job advertisements, and 71 per cent rely to some extent on informal communications with other organizations, as a means of obtaining comparative pay information.

Once a survey has been conducted, management has three choices, to lead the competition, to match what other firms are paying, or to follow what competitors are paying their employees. Generally high-wage employers are able to recruit and retain a workforce better than low-wage competitors; so decisions regarding external competitiveness and pay level are important because they affect the quality of the workforce as well as operating expenses.

The policy on external competitiveness is determined by a number of economic and organizational factors; first, labour conditions, stemming from competition in the labour market or union bargaining; second, affordability, stemming from product market conditions and the organization's financial state; and third, organizational factors such as the strategic and operating objectives that the organization has established (see Figure 9.2).

Labour markets

Throughout the 1980s and 90s, managers typically may be heard saying 'Our pay levels are based upon the market'. Understanding markets requires analysis of the demand for and supply of labour. The demand for human resources focuses on organizations' hiring behaviour and how much organizations are able and willing to pay their employees. The demand for human resources is a derived demand in that employers require people not for their own sake but because they can help to provide goods and services, the sale of which provides revenue. The supply of human resources focuses on many factors, including the wage rate for that particular occupation, its status, the qualifications of employees and the preferences of people regarding paid work and leisure. Economists inform us that in a perfectly 'free market', the pay level of a particular occupation in a certain geographic area is determined by the interaction of demand and supply. However, most markets, including labour, are not free and have what economists call 'imperfections' on both the demand (for example, discrimination) and the supply (for example, membership of professional body) side. The labour market provides a context for reward management and can set limits within which it operates.

Product market

Competitive pressures, both national and global, are major factors affecting pay levels. An employer's ability to pay is constrained by her or his ability to compete, so the nature of the product market affects external competitiveness and the pay level the organization sets. The degree of competition among producers and the level of the demand for products are the two key product market factors. Both affect the ability of the firm to change the prices of its products and services. If prices cannot be changed without suffering loss of revenues due to decreased sales, then the ability of the organization to pay higher rates is constrained. The product market factors set the limits within which the pay level can be established.

Organization

Conditions in the labour market and product market set the upper limits within which the pay level can be established. Within the European Union and in Canada, the floor, or minimum, is set by minimum-wage legislation. The conditions in both the labour and product markets offer managers a choice; the pay level can be set within a range of possibilities. The concept of strategic choice emphasizes the role of managerial choice in determining the pay level to be established within an organization. Faced with a range of options, managers might choose to set the pay level relatively high in the range to 'lead' the competition in order to recruit and retain highly qualified people. Further, the organization's profit levels can directly affect its pay levels. For instance, executive salaries are tied to their companies' profits. This general model of the factors influencing the determination of external competitiveness and pay level is presented in Figure 9.9.

Figure 9.9 A model of factors influencing pay level

Establishing pay rates

Our pay model emphasizes two basic policy issues, internal equity and external competitiveness. The object of this is to design pay levels and structures that organizational members feel are 'fair', and that will help accomplish management's goals. The appropriate pay level for a job reflects its relative and absolute worth. The job's relative value to the organization is determined by its ranking by the job analysis and job evaluation processes. The absolute value of a job is determined by what the labour market pays similar jobs. To establish the pay level the two components of the pay model are merged, the job evaluation rankings and the pay survey going rates.

The results of the job evaluation process and the pay survey are combined through the use of a graph as depicted in Figure 9.10. The horizontal axis depicts an internally consistent job structure based on job evaluation. Each grade is made up of a number of jobs within the organization. The jobs in each category are considered equal for pay purposes; they have about the same number of points. Each grade will have its own pay range, and all the jobs within the grade have the same range. Jobs in grade 1 (that is, jobs A, B and C), for example, have lower points and pay range than jobs in grade 2 (D, E and F). The pay range defines the lower and upper limits of pay for jobs in a grade. The actual minimum and maximum wage rate paid by the organization's competitors is usually established by survey data. Individual levels of pay within the range may reflect differences in performance or seniority. As depicted in Figure 9.10, organizations can structure their rate ranges to overlap with adjacent ranges a little so that an employee with experience or seniority might earn more than an entry-level person in the next higher pay grade. The job evaluation process helps translate internal equity into practice through job structure.

The midpoint can be determined by pay survey data from similar jobs. In Figure 9.10, on the vertical axis the pay level policy line has been set to equal the average paid by the organization's competitors for each of the jobs: a matching-competition policy. Management could establish a lag or lead policy by shifting the pay level policy line down or up. Market survey information helps to translate the concept of external competitiveness into pay-setting practice. The pay policy line represents an organization's pay level in the market and serves as a reference point around which

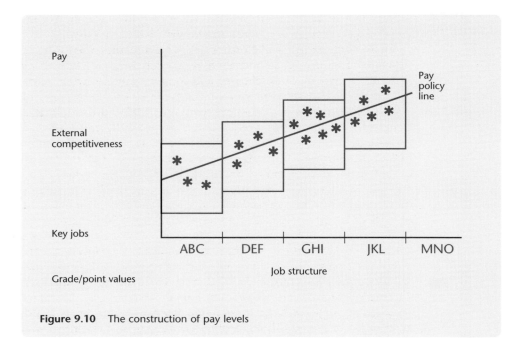

Figure 9.10 The construction of pay levels

pay structures are established. The pay policy line can be raised in response to competitors' pay awards or the cost of living. Thus, pay structures are combinations of external competitiveness considerations and internal equity, and depict pay rates for different jobs within an organization.

Adopting a competitive pay policy is akin to establishing a niche in a product market; there are conventional and new directions in external pay policies. However, there is little empirical evidence of the consequences of these different options (Milkovich and Newman, 1990, p. 198). In the absence of data, the least-risk approach is to set the pay level to match the competition, although some organizations set different policies for different occupations or skill levels, for example adopting a lead policy for critical skills, such as computer design engineers, a matching policy for less critical skills, and a lag policy for jobs that can be easily filled in the local labour market. Thus organizations may establish a variety of pay level policies.

● Pay and performance

Can reward systems be designed to affect performance? Many of the answers to this question come from theories of motivation and empirical research evaluating strategies to motivate employees. The 'need' theories of motivation emphasize what motivates people, rather than how people are motivated. The two most well-known need theories include Maslow (1954) and Herzberg (1966). Maslow argued that higher-order needs become progressively more important as lower-order needs are satisfied. Herzberg demonstrated that pay takes on significance as a source of satisfaction when it is perceived as a form of recognition or reward. Monetary variables are a key component in the more recent 'process' theories of motivation. For example, Vroom's (1964) expectancy theory grants a prominent role to rewards.

Increasingly British and North American companies attempt to relate pay to performance. The precise methods used vary widely from one firm to another; examples include piecework, bonus schemes, and commission. Piecework (payment-by-results – PBR) is a reward system in which rewards are related to the pace of work or effort; simply put, the faster an employee works, the higher the output and the greater her or his reward. With the proportional scheme, pay increases in direct proportion to the increase in output. With the regressive scheme, pay increases proportionally less than output. In contrast, the progressive scheme increases pay proportionally more than output. In some forms of PBR the reward is based on the performance of a team rather than an individual. A commission is a reward paid on the performance of an individual, typically salaried staff in sales functions. The commission earned is a proportion of total sales and may be added to basic salary. In 1990 just over a third (34 per cent) of all workplaces in Britain had some form of merit pay, that is, pay dependent on the subjective judgement of a superior (see Chapter 8 and Millward *et al.*, 1992, p. 258).

So far we have discussed how jobs are evaluated according to some criteria of internal worth to the organization, and how, based on some combination of internal equity and external competitiveness, jobs are assigned pay grades. Movement within those grades might be based on individual performance appraisal. Although this characterization of reward still dominates many organizational practices, the changed economic climate in which European and North American employers must operate has generated alternative reward systems. Parallel with a growth in alternative reward systems has been a relative decline in some of the more traditional reward practices. It is to some of these alternative pay systems that we now turn.

Alternative reward systems

All-salaried workforce

Both manual and non-manual employees receive a prescribed amount of money each pay period that is not primarily dependent on the number of hours worked. For example, as early as 1987, it was reported that at Optical Fibres, the UK's leading cable manufacturer, there are no differences between clerical and manufacturing workers in holiday entitlements, pensions, and medical insurance. Every employee – including the plant's general manager – signs on daily in a reception register on arrival and departure; there is no clocking on and off.

Pay-for-knowledge system

These systems vary pay as a function of the number of different jobs or skills that employees are able to perform competently. Pay increases are tied to learning multiple jobs at ever-higher levels of proficiency. From a management perspective, it is argued that pay-for-knowledge systems (PFKS) reverse the trend towards increased specialization. They encourage functional flexibility and diversification in workers. In turn, it is alleged that increased functional flexibility gives core workers greater job security. From a union perspective, pay-for-knowledge arrangements individualize the employment relationship because they sever the link between increased pay and collective bargaining (Bacon and Storey, 1993). Critics of pay-for-knowledge systems also point out the higher training costs, and are sceptical about claims for increased productivity; PFKS flouts a major tenet of Taylorism, that specialization improves efficiency.

Group incentive (gainsharing) plans

Gainsharing plans tie pay to performance by giving employees an additional payment when there has been an increase in profits or a decrease in costs to the firm. Incentives are based on a comparison of present profits or costs against historical cost accounting data. Increases in productivity do not necessarily result because employees individually or collectively work harder (work intensification). Typically improvements arise because employees work more smartly, identifying means to perform tasks efficiently without increasing physical effort. The beneficial outcomes arise from what is termed 'group synergy'. Survey data indicate that gainsharing is increasingly common in North American corporations, even though in many firms it does not cover a majority of employees. Between 1987 and 1990, the number of Fortune 1000 firms using gainsharing increased from 26 per cent to 39 per cent.[4] Recent studies show that gainsharing is more or, at least, equally common in unionized US companies (Kim and Voos, 1997).

Profit sharing

In profit sharing the employer pays current or deferred sums based on company profits, in addition to established wages. Payment can be in the form of current distribution (paid quarterly or annually), deferred plans (paid at retirement or upon disability) or combination plans. Advocates of profit sharing contend that it can increase performance, result in greater employment stability and be a 'win-win' for employees and employers (Tyson, 1996). Profit sharing is seen by senior management as either a way to increase organizational performance, through improving employee motivation, promoting greater cooperation among employees, and 'helping employees understand the business' (Long, 1997). Profit sharing is also associated with the growth of employee participation schemes (Pendleton, 1997)

Cost savings (Scanlon plan)

Scanlon plans are designed to lower labour costs and distribute the benefits of increased productivity using a financial formula based on labour costs and the sales value of production (SVOP). Payments are typically fairly frequent (for example, monthly). The best-known plan was devised by Joseph Scanlon in the 1930s. The rationale for the Scanlon plan is that psychological growth needs are fulfilled if the employee participates in organizational decision making while being equitably compensated for participation. The Scanlon plan creates shop-floor production committees in which employees generate suggestions to improve productivity and reduce waste. Screening committees that have both union and management representation act on employee suggestions. Bonuses in the Scanlon plan are paid monthly or quarterly on a plant-wide basis. While many formulas can be used, a common one gives 25 per cent of the benefit of increased productivity to the company and 75 per cent to the employees.

Cafeteria-style benefits

Employee benefits refer to that part of the total reward package, other than pay for time worked, provided to employees in whole or in part by organization payments (for example, medical and dental care, pension). There is some debate regarding employee benefits. For example, do employee benefits facilitate organization performance? Do benefits impact on an organization's ability to attract, retain, and motivate employees? Conventional wisdom says employee benefits can affect recruitment and retention, but there is little research to support this conclusion (Milkovich and Newman, 1990). Following the experience of the 'yuppie' phenomenon, 'designer' compensation arrangements are a vogue. Reward packages in the UK include employee benefits ranging from membership of health clubs to the use of the company box at Ascot races. Given the absence of empirical evidence on the relationship between employee benefits and performance, and their escalating cost, benefits are under constant scrutiny by HR managers.

One innovation is 'cafeteria' benefit programmes (CBP). These programmes allow employees to select benefits that match their individual needs. Employees are provided with a benefit account with a specified payment in the account. The types and prices of benefits are provided to each employee in the form of a printout. This programme creates additional administrative costs, but through participation, employees come to understand what benefits the organization is offering. For example, young employees might select dental and medical insurance while older employees might select pension contributions.

All these alternative reward systems represent experiments by employers to better link rewards to individual performance, to encourage functional flexibility and team synergy, and to foster individually orientated organizational cultures (Bacon and Storey, 1993). Flexibility and common terms and conditions (for all-salaried workforces) are important features of new work regimes in many post-industrial work organizations. Additional empirical data, however, is needed before HR practitioners and scholars can demonstrate positive linkages between motivation and alternative reward systems.

⬤ Government and pay

This chapter has dealt with two policy decisions shown in the pay model, internal equity and external competitiveness. In this section the focus shifts to the political and legal context and examines the role government and legislation play in the management of pay. In European countries and in North America governments have a profound impact, both directly and indirectly, on employees' rewards. In the UK, the direct effect on pay is through legislation, such as the Equal Pay Act 1970 and the Equal Pay (Amendment) Regulations 1983, which requires equal pay for equal work (*Garland* v. *British Rail Engineering Ltd*, 1983). In this regard, 'pay' includes any other benefit, whether in cash or in kind, which an employee receives directly or indirectly in respect of employment. When considering pay, organizations within the European Union must take account of Article 119 of the Treaty of Rome, which requires equal pay for equal work. Through such laws, governments in Europe and in Canada and the US intervene directly in the pay-setting process.

Government can also affect reward management by introducing pay control programmes. These typically aim at maintaining low inflation by limiting the size of pay increases. Pay controls can vary in the broadness of the application and in the stringency of the standard. The broadness of the application can include all employees, public and private, or focus on one particular group, for instance civil servants. The standard for allowable pay increases can range from zero to increases equal to some price change or productivity measure. Over the past two decades, in Britain and North America, Conservative governments used tight control of public sector pay to try to influence pay trends in their wider economies. In Britain, the Conservative government's approach to public sector pay was summarized in 1990 by Norman Lamont, then Chief Secretary to the Treasury, when he said that the government had used a 'combination of pressures' to 'reproduce the discipline which markets exert in the private sector'.[5]

In addition, government has an indirect influence on the pay-setting process as depicted in Figure 9.11. Government actions often affect both the demand and supply of labour; consequently, wages are also affected. Legislation can restrict the supply of labour in an occupation. For instance, a statute that sets minimum age limits would restrict the supply of young people. Government also affects the demand for labour. The government is a dominant employer; consequently it is a major force in determining pay levels in and beyond the public sector. Government fiscal and monetary policies that affect the economy indirectly affect market forces which, in turn, influence pay. The reward techniques (performance appraisal, job evaluation) and the outcomes of those techniques (pay levels, pay structures) must be designed to be in compliance with the laws passed by parliament and the European Union. This responsibility falls on the HR specialist. Given the importance of equal pay legislation for reward management, the next section examines important issues of pay equity.

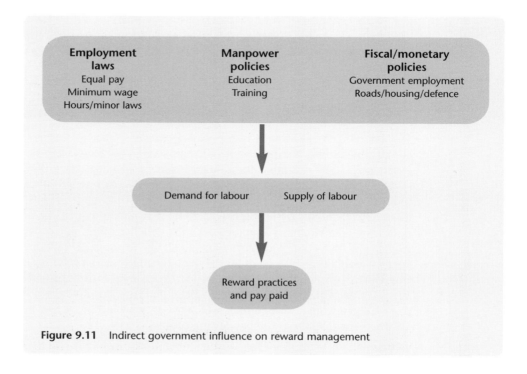

Figure 9.11　Indirect government influence on reward management

Equal pay legislation

> Discriminatory employment practices are a manifestation of prejudicial patterns of behaviour in society generally.[6]

The concept of equal pay for women is in conflict with the view that employees' pay should be dictated by the supply and demand of labour. Equal pay legislation, therefore, curtails market forces. Equal pay legislation has existed in the UK for over two decades. Let us look briefly at the development of the UK legislation.

In 1919, the International Labour Organization (ILO) made the concept of equal pay for work of equal value one of its founding principles. In 1951, the ILO passed Convention 100: 'Each member shall... ensure the application to all workers of the principle of equal remuneration for men and women workers for work of equal value'. In 1972, the UK became bound to EEC Article 119 of the Treaty of Rome: 'Each Member State shall... maintain the application of the principle that men and women should receive equal pay for equal work'. The Equal Pay Act 1970 inserted into contracts of employment an implied term, the 'equality clause'. The equality clause enforced equal terms in the contract of employment for women in the same employment; it required the elimination of less favourable terms where men and women are employed on like work, and where the work has been rated as equivalent by a job evaluation assessor in the same employment.

Despite the existence of equal pay legislation in the UK since 1975 aimed at eradicating pay discrimination, the existence of income disparity between men and women is widely acknowledged. Women in the UK are still in receipt of only 79.5 per cent of the hourly earnings received by men (Gilbert and Secker, 1995). The gender pay gap is particularly significant in retail distribution, and banking and finance. In these sectors, Britain had the widest earnings gap in Europe at 53 per cent and 61 per cent respectively (EOC, 1992). Equal pay legislation has failed to address the problem of occupational segregation, that is, the gap between the kinds of jobs performed by men and those performed by women, which is acknowledged to be an important source of lower earnings of women relative to men. Research suggests that the proportion of women employed in an occupation is negatively associated with earnings. 'In sum, being a women has a negative effect on income', conclude Gattiker and Cohen (1997).

Pay equity

In 1982, the European Court held that the UK's Equal Pay Act did not comply with Article 119 of the Treaty of Rome, because equal pay was available for work of equal value only where the employer had chosen to conduct a job evaluation study. There was no way a woman could compel her employer to carry out such a study. Consequently, the Equal Pay Act was amended by the 1983 Equal Pay (Amendment) Regulations, which meant that even where there is no 'like work' or non-discriminatory job evaluation, if the women's work is of 'equal value' to that of a man, the equality clause entitles her to corresponding conditions to the man. The new Regulations were first tested in the case of *Hayward* v. *Cammell Laird Shipbuilders Ltd* (1987), where a cook – supported by her trade union and the EOC – established her work as of equal value to that of men working in the shipyard as insulation engineers, painters, and joiners. Conway (1987) argues that 'The equal value concept recognizes that occupational segregation persists and that the concomitant undervaluation of "women's" work is responsible for a large part of the earning's gap'. The European Commission further expanded the provision for equal opportunities within the European Union with the Fourth Medium-Term Action Programme on Equal Opportunites which came into operation on 1 January 1996 (see Singh, 1997).

The time, legal expenses and the bad publicity for the company might provoke the proactive-thinking HR practitioner to avoid such legal judgements and seek pay equity through enlightened decisions or collective bargaining. Equal pay for women

---

 HRM in practice 9.3

Merit pay schemes discriminate against women, says report

BY S. BEVAN Personnel Management Plus, November 1992

Appraisal schemes and merit pay systems, which are used by around 50 per cent of British companies are often biased against women.

This is the conclusion of an Institute of Manpower Studies report, funded by the Equal Opportunities Commission, which examines merit schemes in a finance company, a local authority, a manufacturer and a catering organisation.

Sexual stereotypes still prevail, according to the report, with managers often valuing different attributes for men and women.

Managers in the finance company were found to rate intelligence, dynamism, energy and assertiveness as important for males, while thoroughness, organisation, dependability and honesty were valued more highly for females.

Discrimination is most obvious, it says, where staff are set qualitative objectives which can be subjectively assessed.

Widening of line management responsibility to cover reward systems has also increased management discretion.

> **'There may be very strong business reasons to devolve responsibility to line managers but unless companies realise the implications they could be building discrimination into the system'**

'There may be very strong business reasons to devolve responsibility to line managers but unless companies realise the implications they could be building discrimination into the system,' says Stephen Bevan, one of the authors of the report.

Merit schemes are common in the private sector and are spreading in the public sector, particularly as the Citizen's Charter involves the introduc-

tion of performance pay for civil servants, teachers and other state employees, IMS points out.

Bevan warns employers that many merit pay schemes may be illegal and may breach the European Court's ruling in the Danfoss case. Where merit rises are unequally distributed between the sexes, this ruling states that the burden of proof is on the employer to show that discrimination has not occurred.

'Companies are poor at monitoring performance pay against any criteria, but particularly in terms of equal opportunities,' says Bevan. He advises employers to monitor gender bias in appraisal schemes and to check access to training and promotion.

'Merit pay, performance appraisal and attitudes to women's work' is published by the IMS, Mantell Building, University of Sussex, Falmer, Brighton BN1 9RF.

will not be guaranteed by collective bargaining and legislation alone however, for, as Wedderburn observes, pay equity will be secure 'only when its justice is adequately understood and practised by men' (1986, p. 503).

Pay equity and job evaluation

All legislation requires, either implicitly or explicitly, that gender-neutral job evaluation schemes be adopted or developed, and used to determine and compare the value of female-dominated and male-dominated jobs. Thus, job evaluation constitutes the foundation of pay equity. It is critical that job evaluation schemes are designed and applied with the least possible amount of bias, particularly gender bias.

Paradoxical perspectives on rewards and HRM

Let us finish our discussion of reward management by examining some of the fallacies and inconsistencies in payment systems in relation to the HRM paradigm. First, attempts to foster worker commitment through variable pay arrangements might be undermined if reward to superior performers cannot be paid due to poor financial performance of the company. Disappointment due to unfulfilled expectations might be a source of dissatisfaction with the company, rather than increased commitment. Betcherman *et al.*, for example, note that most variable reward systems fail to 'stick' for economic reasons; there were no profits or productivity gains to share (1994, p. 42). We should note Beer *et al.*'s (1984) argument that performance-related pay (PRP) creates tensions that can undermine workers' 'motivation'. Tying pay to performance, warn the authors, might reduce the 'intrinsic motivation' that comes when workers are given greater job autonomy. 'By making pay contingent upon performance (as judged by management), management is signaling that it is they – not the individual – who are in control, thus lowering the individual's feelings of competence and self-determination' (1984, p. 114). The fact that this type of pay system is administered by management raises other limitations, the 'twin vices of subjectivity and inconsistency' (Kessler, 1994). A PRP system might become discredited in the eyes of subordinates and, consequently, worker commitment weakened, because of perceived 'procedural injustices' caused by subjective and inconsistent appraisals by managers without the requisite skills. Further, the judgemental process associated with many variable pay arrangements raises another management problem, the cost of administering the reward system and the indirect costs associated with disputes over implementation. Writing of the piecework reward system in the 1960s, a Ford executive, for example, noted that:

> [A] day-rate plant probably requires 25 per cent more supervision than one on pay by results... this is a small price to pay for freedom from disputes and control over costs and methods (quoted in Nichols, 1980, p. 266).

In addition, the goal of flexibility through reward (for example pay-for-knowledge) might not 'stick' due to economic reasons, especially if the high cost of paying for additional skills that are not directly relevant to increasing productivity leads to the 'capping' of skill and knowledge acquisition. Again, in the context of raised expectations, disappointment is likely to impact negatively on the commitment goal. Also, as a model of social organization, the team concept has impressed its image upon an increasing number of companies. But a payment system based on individual performance can encourage a myopic and inflexible approach to work thereby contradicting the multiskilling philosophy behind work teams (Kessler, 1995, p. 266).

Another point worth noting is that the focus on quantifying individual performance and pay appears to epitomize the 'hard' version of HRM (treating workers as a variable cost). It can be perceived to be at odds with the 'soft' developmental model (treating workers as an asset) which seeks worker commitment, flexibility and quality through, among other things, investing in workplace learning. A further contradiction in the use of performance appraisal is pointed out by Legge (1995). She posits that, in theory, performance appraisal is more likely to operate on manual 'peripheral' workers (workers on non-standard employment contracts) because this category of the workforce is more associated with treating workers as a variable cost. In reality, it is the core workers, the highly skilled, the professional and technical staff, who are more often subjected to systematic performance appraisal. Finally, we should appreciate the relationship between the type of reward system and managerial power. The selection of pay options does not operate in a vacuum and, as we have already discussed elsewhere, managerial choice is contingent upon perceived reconfigured traditional external and internal circumstances. Reward practices are dictated by perceptions of the balance of power between labour and management. The implication is that we can predict that pay systems will change according to their effectiveness, *vis-à-vis* the relation of effort to wages (Baldamus, 1961), and balance of power (Nichols, 1980). In the context of a neutered, politically weak labour movement (for example Britain and the US) it is likely to awaken employers' interest in reward systems that focus on ways to increase effort levels. Thus, the relation of effort to reward and the balance of power between labour and management are strategic factors that help explain the selection of pay arrangements within any HRM model. In this section, much of the literature has suggested that the reward system is part of a diverse range of interlocking control techniques, that contain internal tensions and inconsistencies, and form part of the rhetorical vision of the post-industrial work organization.

Chapter summary

This chapter has stressed that reward management is central to the activities of HR managers. An effective compensation system is designed to satisfy employee needs and reinforce job behaviour consistent with organizational objectives. No single best compensation system exists. The design of reward systems is contingent on the organizational and environmental context in which they must operate. The pay model we have developed in this chapter emphasizes two fundamental policy issues, internal equity and external competitiveness. The model provides a useful framework for examining the techniques and issues surrounding reward management. Job evaluation, which seeks to ensure that the job structure is based on the content and relative contribution of the work, ideally should be seen as a technique to achieve internal fairness or equity in pay. Empirical evidence testifies that job evaluation contains subjective elements, however. Organizations can use pay survey data to position their rewards, to lead, to match, or to lag behind their competitors, depending upon external and internal pressures. This chapter has also documented the interest in alternative pay systems and the relative decline in some of the more traditional compensation practices. We have examined how government intervenes both directly and indirectly in the pay determination process. Keeping up to date and complying with pay legislation is the prime responsibility of HRM specialists. Finally, we have explored some of the ambiguities and inconsistencies in reward systems in relation to the HRM model. Under the logic of political economy HRM, pay systems – whether associated with the 'hard' or 'soft' HRM models – cannot obviate the contradictory tensions that bedevil employment relations.

Key concepts

Job analysis	Job evaluation
Point method	Pay model
Internal equity	External competitiveness
Government	Pay equity

Discussion questions

1. What can a pay system do for:
   a. an organization, and
   b. an employee?

2. What is job analysis? Why is it desirable and what problems are associated with its use?

3. What does job evaluation have to do with internal equity and efficiency?

4. You are a manager, and the annual wage negotiations are being concluded. Management has acceded to the trade union's demand for a 9 per cent wage increase, and is now considering whether prices should be increased by 9 per cent to cover this increase. You are asked to comment. Without considering changes in other possible variables, what would your comments be in the following circumstances?

   a. Your firm's only product is one popular make of car.

   b. Your firm has a world patent on a new computer game which has made all previous designs redundant, and this is your only product.

5. 'Equal pay for women will be secure only when its justice is adequately understood and practised by men' (Wedderburn, 1986). Do you agree or disagree? Discuss.

Further reading

Beer, M., Spector, B., Lawrence, P.R. *et al.* (1984) *Managing Human Assets*, Chapter 5, Reward systems. New York: Free Press.

Curnow, B. (1986) The creative approach to pay, *Personnel Management*, October: 32–6.

Kessler, I., (1995) Reward systems. In Storey, J. (ed.) *Human Resource Management: A Critical Text*, London: Routledge.

Kruse, D. (1996) Why do firms adopt profit-sharing and employee ownership plans? *British Journal of Industrial Relations*, **34**(4): 515–38.

McShane, S. (1990) Two tests of direct gender bias in job evaluation ratings, *Journal of Occupational Psychology*, **63**: 129–40.

Pendleton, A. (1979b) What impact has privatization had on pay and employment? *Relations Industrielles/Industrial Relations*, **52**(1): 554–82.

Rollins, T. (1988) Pay for performance: is it really worth the trouble? *Personnel Administrator*, **33**(5).

Saxby, M. (1987) Integrated job evaluation, *Management Services*, December.

Schwab, D. and Grams, R. (1985) Sex-related errors in job evaluation; a real-world test, *Journal of Applied Psychology*, **70**(3): 218–37.

Singh, R. (1997) Equal opprtunities for men and women in the EU: a commentary, *Industrial Relations Journal*, **28**(1): 68–71.

Spencer, S. (1990) Devolving job evaluation, *Personnel Management*, January: 15–19.

Veres, J. (1990) Job analysis in practice: a brief review of the role of job analysis in human resource management. In Ferris, G. *et al.* (eds) *Human Resource Management: Perspectives and Issues*, 2nd edn. London: Allyn & Bacon.

Woodley, C. (1990) The cafeteria route to compensation, *Personnel Management*, May: 26–31.

Chapter case study

City Bank

The 1990s were a watershed for the UK banking industry, and particularly for City Bank, a medium-size clearing bank. Following the deregulation of the financial sector in 1986, City Bank has faced increased competition from other financial institutions such as building societies, an intense squeeze on profit margins, and the need to make considerable provisions for bad debts. Under such pressure, City Bank introduced new technology, new financial products and a new reward system for bank managers and staff. Information and communication technologies (ICTs) enabled the bank to process much larger volumes of business and, just as importantly, the new ICTs themselves facilitated the development of new, technically based products and services (such as home banking, smart cards and debt cards and so on) which City Bank started to market to its customers.

Running parallel with these technical changes was the dismantling of the paternalistic personnel management system. In essence, City Bank's bureaucratic culture and its associated belief system for managers and staff of appropriate behaviour being rewarded by steady promotion through the ranks was swept aside. The new culture, in the fast-changing environment, emphasized customer service and the importance of measuring and rewarding staff according to their performance. Other features of the new culture are the widening gulf between career and non-career staff, the segmentation of recruitment and training, growing occupational specialization, and declining employment levels.

The new performance-related reward system was introduced at a senior management meeting in January, 1996. Addressing the meeting, Elizabeth Mulberry, Director of Human Resources, said that the proposed reward system would be a key strategy to 'maintain our share of the high street business'. She went on to outline that in future the salary of bank managers would be tied to their 'leadership skills and the quality of customer service'. The CEO of City Bank explained the new direction thus:

> City Bank's culture has entered a new phase and the climate is favourable for a shift in emphasis from management by paternalism to management by leadership. It is essential that bank managers make sure that the broad picture is known, understood and reflected in measurable personal objectives for those in their management team. They must provide individual members of those teams with personal job satisfaction through feedback on performance against objectives. Branch leadership also requires the ability to discriminate in the reward given to the exceptional, compared with the standard, performance.

Under the new reward system, the pay of each branch manager would be linked to his or her leadership skills and the quality of customer service. The reward system would link managers' pay to behaviour traits that relate to leadership and customer service. Central to the drive for quality customer service, explained Elizabeth Mulberry, is the way bank managers and their staff treat their customers. A questionnaire would be sent out periodically to a sample of the branch's customers and branch manager and staff would be evaluated for base salary on such variables as:

1. length of time customers wait in line for service
2. customer focus
3. ability to communicate bank products and services.

In turn, each bank manager will be rated on:

1. bank revenue variables (for example number of new mortgages)
2. employee development
3. leadership.

According to the inter-office memorandum that was to be sent out to the 400 branch managers, variable pay for both managers and staff would be based on what is accomplished 'because customer service is central to City Bank's strategic plan, a three category rating system that involves 'not meeting' customer expectations, 'meeting' them or 'far exceeding' them is the essence of the new reward system.

Task

As a research assistant for Right Consulting Services, a large consulting firm that specializes in management development in the finance and banking sector, you have been given the task of drafting a report to one of the firm's associates, Dr D. Perry. Your report to Dr D. Perry should:

1. Outline the merits and limitations of City Bank's proposed reward system for the managers and staff.

2. Identify an alternative reward system for City Banks' employees congruent with their strategic plan.

Notes

1. Richard Johnston, Human Resources Director of Flowpak Engineering, quoted by Bratton (1992), p. 171.
2. While there has been some discussion in the literature on the precise meaning and appropriate use of the words 'reward', 'pay', 'compensation' and 'remuneration', they are used interchangeably in this chapter.
3. Inland Revenue, *Inland Revenue Statistics 1994–95*, HMSO, 1996 and quoted by Pendleton (1997b), pp. 554–79.
4. Lawler, E.E., Mohrman, A. and Ledford, G. (1992) *EI and Total Quality* and quoted by Kim and Voos (1997), p. 304.
5. Quoted in Future uncertain for public sector pay, in *Bargaining Report*, Labour Research Department, May, 1991.
6. Smith, A., Craver, C. and Clark, L. (1982) *Employment Discrimination Law*, 2nd edn, p. 1, and quoted in Wedderburn (1986), p. 447.

chapter ten

Human resource development

Jeffrey Gold

The available evidence... suggests that HRM policies and practices associated with training have taken root in only a few British companies – falling far short of that which would be required in order to fuel an HRM revolution.[1]

Training? It's a joke... as a setter operator you can be asked to do a job that you have never done before. And, the only training you get is maybe fifteen minutes with a setter.[2]

My contribution can only be limited by the responsiveness of my organisation to the themes of the Learning Organisation.[3]

Chapter outline

Chapter objectives

After studying this chapter, you should be able to:

1. Discuss the place of human resource development (HRD) within HRM.
2. Understand the connections between strategy, HRM and HRD.
3. Discuss the requirements of a national infrastructure for HRD.
4. Explain how an HRD policy may be implemented.
5. Explain the principles of learning and their role in HRD and organization learning.

⬤ Introduction

In most formulations of HRM, training and employee development represent significant if not the pivotal components. Ashton and Felstead (1995, p. 235) regard the investment by an organization in the skills of employees as a 'litmus test' for a change in the way they are managed. Usually retitled to human resource development (HRD), an organization's investment in the learning of its people acts as a powerful signal of its intentions. First, the replacement of the words 'training cost' with 'investment' should allow everyone involved in HRD to take a longer-term view, particularly with respect to the outcomes of HRD where the continuation of viewing training as a short-term cost has persistently acted as a powerful break on many training strategies. HRD implies that learning will be a strategic consideration in an organization. Second, HRD acts as a triggering mechanism for the progression of other HRM policies that are aimed at recruiting, retaining and rewarding employees who are recognized as the qualitative difference between organizations. The investment in employee learning is a way of creating a primary internal market and policies aimed at progressively upgrading skills reduce an organization's dependency on external sources of skill. Third, if it is an HRM strategy to engender the conditions whereby loyalty and commitment towards an organization's aims can be encouraged, HRD carries the prospect of unleashing the potential that lies within all people, allowing employees to contribute to and indeed transform strategy.

In recent years, ideas and practices relating to HRD have moved beyond a narrow conception of training and development. Many organizations now attempt to take a holistic view that embraces the idea of learning at individual and organizational levels as a crucial source of competitive advantage. Technology, global markets, customer expectations and competition have all contributed to the view that learning is the only strategy to cope with change. HRD has moved out of training departments into every aspect of organizational life as many have attempted to become *learning organizations* with increasing moves towards finding ways to integrate work and learning. There has been a growing emphasis on viewing an organization as a total learning system and finding its 'core competencies' which reveal its 'collective learning' (Prahalad and Hamel, 1990, p. 82). In addition, continuing advances in networked information technology and accelerating change have stimulated a growing interest in *organization learning and knowledge management*, the development of an organization's intellectual capital (Edvinsson and Malone, 1997) and the potential for learning between organizations.

⬤ Human resource development and the HRM cycle

The relationship of HRD to organizational performance and other HRM activities is shown in Figure 1.2. Selection information can be used to identify and place new employees in appropriate training and development programmes. HRD, as we discussed in Chapter 9, is indirectly and sometimes directly related to rewards. Generally, higher levels of education and qualifications are associated with higher levels of pay. Performance appraisal often precedes HRD activities, identifying individuals with performance deficiences or career development needs who can benefit from learning.

The role of HRD in strategic HRM

The HRM cycle prescribes the integration of HRM activities to create an internal labour market with links to organization structure and strategy. While the cycle highlights the pivotal place of development, context will limit and constrain the design of policies, their implementation and the extent to which the HRD elements of the cycle can be integrated in reality. Guest (1989, p. 50) refers to the 'cement' that binds the system to ensure successful outcomes to HRM policies. Included in the 'cement' are both the support of leaders and senior managers and a culture that reinforces HRM. There are two important implications of this view.

First, employees are recruited for a skilled working role that will require learning and change, rather than for a job which may soon become obsolete. Employees are expected to retrain and indeed many employees undertake courses of self-study in order to continue their learning. Employees are therefore carefully selected as much for their ability to learn as for their current repertoire of skills. Once recruited, employees become worth investing in although the form of this investment may be more subtle than simply having a large training budget. That is, learning becomes embedded into workplace practice as an ongoing process. Second, line managers are fully involved in the development of their subordinates to such an extent that the differentiation between learning and working becomes virtually impossible to discern (and included in a budget). There is an emphasis on informal learning, and an appreciation of its value, which line managers regard as part of their job and a responsibility on which they will be assessed. It is the acceptance of this responsibility by line managers, more than any other within the HRM cycle, that carries the potential to produce the HRM outcomes of loyalty, flexibility, quality and commitment. Not least of these outcomes is that more formal HRD activities, such as training courses, are likely to prove their value, but also the transfer of learning into the workplace can alter the nature of work itself and the relationships between managers and employees. Thus the processes linking performance, appraisal and development would be carried out effectively by line managers as part of normal work, resulting in the assessment of needs for job improvement and career development. Do you recognize this image of line managers? What factors might prevent its realization?

McGoldrick and Stewart (1996, p. 14) have identified leadership as a key variable in linking strategy, culture and the commitment of employees. The view of leadership employed draws upon Bass' (1985) transformational leadership made up of four components, charisma, inspiration, individualized consideration, and intellectual stimulation. Such views of leadership are particularly important when strategy is considered. Over the years, particularly in the West, managers in organizations and writers have viewed the process of planning strategy as deliberate and purposeful. Leaders and senior managers scan the environment, develop alternative goals aligned with mission, and formulate business plans and policies. Thus it would seem that the extent to which HRD becomes a feature of strategy depends on the ability of senior managers to sense important environmental trends and signals in HRD terms, that is, learning for employees. Pettigrew *et al.* (1988, p. 29), in a model of factors that trigger and drive training activity, identified the external forces that may begin the process. Technological and market changes may signal a skills gap, government requirements on health and safety may force training to be considered, or financial support from external agencies such as Training and Enterprise Councils (TECs) or Local Enterprise Companies (LECs). Crucially, their model recognizes the importance of a positive culture for training and the existence of training 'champions' among leaders and senior managers who contribute to a company philosophy that supports training in espoused terms at least. While crucial, this view of strategy places great reliance on the ability of senior managers to deliberate on the factors, which include HRD action through plans and policy.

This is however a top-down view of the process. Mintzberg (1987, p. 66) provides a view of strategy making which can foster learning within an organization if senior managers allow it. Strategies can emerge from the actions of employees.

> A salesman visits a customer. The product isn't quite right, and together they work out some modifications. The salesman returns to the company and puts the changes through; after two or three more rounds, they finally get it right. A new product emerges, which eventually opens up a new market. The company has changed strategic course (Mintzberg, 1987, p. 68).

Through the employees' interaction with production processes, customers, suppliers and clients, both internal and external to their organization, employees can monitor, respond to and learn from evolving situations. If the information can flow to create knowledge, strategies can be formed by such interactions as well as deliberately formulated. The whole process requires the reconciliation of emergent learning with deliberate control. Leaders and senior managers must be able to use the tension between the two processes of deliberate and emerging strategy making, and resolve the dilemma, to craft a strategy for the real world. If they can only see strategies in deliberate planning terms they not only run the risk of such strategies becoming unrealized, but also waste the learning that can emerge from their employees. Integrating HRD into strategy therefore requires the development of the senior management team so that the dilemma to be resolved between control through planning and emergent learning becomes an acceptable form of their thinking. Recent years have seen increased attention to the view of managers as strategic learners who are able to appreciate the complexity of the issues that impact on organizations and the groups and individuals within them. Managers are encouraged to debate and discuss the key issues that emerge, set them in a wider context and utilize the learning gained to bring competitive advantage (Grundy, 1994, p. 5).

Establishing HRD

If employees are worth investing in, some consideration is required of why this may be the case, including some understanding of the potential that may lie within all employees and a consideration of the work that they do. Discussion of an employee's potential, and his or her prospects for development, was usually confined to an organization's managerial cadre. The various models that have been produced in the literature focused almost solely on the development of managers, with the implicit assumption that non-managers' potential is limited. For example, Hall (1986, p. 235) provided a progressive model of career growth and effectiveness through an integration of task and personal learning shown as Figure 10.1.

Managers, as well as mastering the knowledge and skills required to improve their work performance in the short term and their adaptability in the long term, should also have the chance to assess themselves through an exploration of attitudes towards career and personal life. Such an assessment will determine suitability for higher posi-

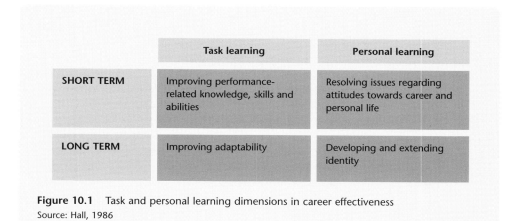

Figure 10.1 Task and personal learning dimensions in career effectiveness
Source: Hall, 1986

tions within organizations. Progression continues towards 'being truly one's own person to being a self-directed, self-aware organizational leader' (Hall, 1986, p. 252).

If models of development and fulfilment of potential were reserved for the élite ranks of managers, the rest of the workforce faced a more limited and restricted framework. Nowhere in the industrialised West is the restriction on development more in evidence than in the UK, where Taylorist–Fordist approaches to control, through job design and the deskilling of jobs in order to reduce training costs, continue to hold sway in many organizations. In Chapter 7 we referred to the role of metaphor in understanding organizations and how the machine may come to be seen as the ideal way of organizing. Marsick (1987) has written of a paradigm of workplace training and development represented by an organizational ideal of a machine. A paradigm can be thought of as a framework of thinking that provides an explicit or implicit view of reality (Morgan, 1980, p. 606) based on fundamental assumptions about the nature of reality. Marsick argues that the machine ideal causes jobs to be seen as parts coordinated by a rational control system, where performance can be measured as observable behaviour, and which is quantifiable and criterion referenced. Attitudes are important only insofar as they can be manipulated to reinforce desired performance. Each individual has a responsibility for his or her part, but no more, and has to work against a set standard. Learning is based on a deficit model which assesses the gap between the behaviour of employees and the set standard. Training attempts to close the gap by bringing employees up to the desired standard or competence but not beyond. There is little place for the consideration of attitudes, feelings and personal development.

A further implication of the above ideal may be a subservience of learning and training to accounting procedures that measure the cause and effect relationships between training programmes and output and profit in the short term. If a relationship cannot be shown, there will be pressure to provide the proof or cut the cost of the training. Even where organizations espouse an HRD approach, all too often sufficient amounts of the machine ideal remain in place, and hidden from view, to present an effective and powerful barrier to organization learning.

The accumulation of deskilling combined with standardized products for mass markets resulted in what Finegold and Soskice (1988, p. 22) presented as a self-reinforcing cycle of low quality products and low skills in the UK. They argued that as a nation the UK's failure to educate and train its workforce to the same levels as its competitors was both a cause and a consequence of a relatively poor economic performance – a cause because the absence of a well-educated and trained workforce restrained the response of UK organizations to changing world economic conditions, and a consequence because the mass production techniques of UK organizations for many years signalled a demand for a low-skilled workforce. It is not difficult to see how such signals fed into attitudes towards learning outside organizations. For example, there had been in the UK, until the recession of the 1990s, a comparatively low staying-on rate in full-time education compared to other countries, and the examination system protected A-levels as an academic gold standard, despite efforts to raise the status of vocational education.

It is against this background that efforts have been made in recent years to equip the UK with a flexible and skilled workforce whose talents are seen by organizations as crucial to their ability to compete in world markets on the basis of quality and speed. Successive governments in the UK have based their policies on the idea of a training and development market where demand and supply determine the amount of training provided. The overall aim is to improve the UK's training infrastructure. Important foundations in the infrastructure have been the establishment of a framework of vocational qualifications based on national standards, that is, National Vocational Qualifications (NVQs) and Scottish Vocational Qualifications (SVQs), and a national network of locally based TECs in England and Wales and LECs in Scotland to coordinate national training initiatives aimed at improving the functioning training markets at a local level. In addition, there have been various reforms of schools in attempts to increase the number of young people achieving qualifications before they enter the labour market. There has been an increase in the number of young people gaining five or more GCSEs at grades A–C from 34.5 per cent in 1990 to 44.5 per cent in 1996 (DfEE, 1997, p. 53) although there is some concern at the growing differences in performance between boys (40 per cent in 1996) and girls (48 per cent). Why do you think this is occurring? There has also been an increase in participation in full-time education including the numbers staying at school or attending college beyond the age of 16.

NVQs and SVQs have been developed to provide a national framework of vocational qualifications in the UK. The framework, covering most occupations, provides qualifications based on the required outcomes expected from the performance of a task in a work role, usually referred to as competences. It is claimed that NVQs and SVQs are directly relevant to employers needs since they are based on standards set by employers. There may be up to five levels of a qualification, each level defined by the national framework. For example Level 1 is defined as 'competence in the performance of a range of varied work activities, most of which may be routine and predictable'. Level 5 is defined as 'competence which involves the application of a significant range of fundamental principles and complex techniques across a wide and often unpredictable variety of contexts. Very substantial personal autonomy and often significant responsibility for the work of others and for the allocation of substantial resources feature strongly, as do personal accountabilities for analysis and diagnosis, design, planning, execution and evaluation.' What do you think the value of NVQs and SVQs has been in the UK? While there has undoubtedly been an increase in the number people gaining qualifications in the UK, competence-based NVQs and SVQs have not been without their critics. There have been concerns over the meaning of competence, with its emphasis on the achievement of outcomes and assessment against standards in preference to an attention to knowledge and understanding, and whether NVQs and SVQs provide a more effective framework for training compared to other approaches (Hillier, 1997, p. 39). However, despite the criticisms, NVQs and SVQs have become an important feature of the training infrastructure. They are used by governments to set national targets and by some organizations to build training plans.

TECs and LECs have been established to ensure that the operation of the training market meets local needs. They undertake a wide variety of activities including the finance and administration of the various programmes designed to improve the position of young people in the training market and enhance their employability. Such programmes include Youth Training (now called National Traineeships) and Modern Apprenticeships, which aim to improve the numbers qualified in technical, craft and junior management skills. Importantly, NVQs and SVQs are a required component of such schemes and are used by TECs and LECs to measure the success of programmes and to meet targets set by government. However it is unlikely that the TECs and LECs alone will have an impact on the forces that maintain the low quality–low skills equilibrium in the UK. Action is required from within organizations.

Fonda and Hayes (1986, p. 47) have shown how some organizations can actually ask 'Is more training really necessary?' in their outline of a range of training and development models that are suited to organizations' intentions in relation to their environment. The models they termed '*ad hoc*' (meeting HRD needs as they arise) and 'planned maintenance' (HRD carried out to keep the organization in shape but not seen as making a central contribution) assume stable and predictable product markets and unchanging skill requirements. In both cases training is not central and may not exist. It is also not clear whether training and development has a direct causal impact on improvements in organization measurements such as profitability. Green (1997) reports that the benefit to employers of training is established through 'intermediate' variables such as labour turnover and organizational commitment, although the evidence is not robust. Probably of most importance is the interpretation given to the place of skill in production. If tasks are designed as requiring high levels of skill, then this will trigger a requirement for a highly trained workforce and for investment in that workforce if skilled labour is not available in the external market. Further, the presence of skilled employees is likely to contribute to the interpretation by managers that any changes, particularly in technology, can be dealt with by their employees and thus they are able to take advantage of the benefits the changes may bring (Green and Ashton, 1992, p. 294). It is possible to foresee two scenarios as the reaction to technology. First, on the basis of pressures to meet short-term targets and a poor training infrastructure, investment in skills is considered too risky. The consequence is the use of new technology to deskill employees and reduce costs. Alternatively, on the basis of an established skill base and belief and trust in the ability of employees to learn, new technology is used to take advantage of human talents and upskill employees. It is important to understand that the second scenario may be part of an overall pattern where the organization seeks to satisfy the expectations of a number of stakeholders including those of employees, the community at large as well as those of finance.

The second scenario is also one that has been supported by government policy through the Investors In People (IIP) initiative. Established in October 1991, IIP provides a set of standards for training and development requiring organizations to develop business plans that include plans to develop all employees and evaluate the results. The initiative has been managed by the TECs and is a feature of their targets both in terms of the number of organizations that commit to IIP and the number that achieve the standard. While for some organizations, even those committed to IIP, the processes involved proved to be too difficult or circumstances such as restructuring caused delays in reaching the standard, the main result appears to be an improvement in training practice (Hillage and Moralee, 1996, p. 33). Furthermore, a study that examined organizations that had already gained IIP found that the main benefits from IIP came if it was used as a way to assess performance and implement continuous improvement (Alberga, 1997, p. 31). What is beginning to emerge, after a very slow start, is an initiative that is bringing about the kind of changes to ideas and practices that embrace the whole organization in a dynamic and systemic manner. It is helping to create the conditions for HRD. HRM in practice 10.1 shows an example of how IIP was introduced in a medium-sized food company.

The implications are clear. Breaking out of the low quality product–low skill equilibrium requires a challenge to the very mindset that transformed the UK economy once in the past. A policy of HRD has to reflect the strategy of senior managers who are able to view their organizations in a variety of ways. Seeing people as being worth investing in means being able to ward off the competing pressures that might challenge this view, while at the same time providing the support for a value system that we might call a learning environment. In such an environment, key participants are able to respond to calls for the spread of HRD activities throughout the workforce and ensure their success. Of particular importance are the actions of managers at all levels in supporting learning and turning an aversion to risk taking towards opportunity spotting. The HRD approach identifies and utilizes what the Japanese have called the 'gold in workers' heads'. Thus managers learn to recognize the value of front line employees who have the closest contact with customers and are thus first to learn about new needs and desires.

Implementing HRD

It would seem that a crucial feature of any attempt to successfully implement HRD would be links between an organization's business plan, its HR plan and HRD plan and policies. Recent initiatives in the UK such as IIP would see links as the foundation and the growing number of organizations that are now achieving the IIP standard would seem to suggest that, on paper at least, there is a growing commitment towards HRD. A survey of 4005 establishments in the UK in 1997 (IFF, 1997) found that 65 per cent had a training plan and 63 per cent had a training budget. Overall, 41 per cent of employees had received off-the-job training for an average of 7.9 days in a period of 12 months, although, as the survey's authors remind us, such estimates are subject to inaccuracy caused by sampling error. These figures have remained relatively stable since 1995. The survey found that employers were more likely to train those in high-skilled occupations, which would suggest an important positive connection between resources devoted to HRD and the definition of skill in the workplace. One group of particular interest is managers. Following a number of adverse reports in the 1980s about Britain's provision of management development (Handy, 1987), more recent evidence suggests significant improvements (Thomson et al., 1997, p. 73) with almost no larger companies and only a few smaller companies failing to report provision for management training. It appears that there has been an accumulation of understand-

Investors in people at Lenders Foods Ltd

BY PETER LENDERS, VICKY YATES AND STEVE FRANCIS

Lenders Foods Ltd is a family-owned business that produces stir-fry and quick cook chilled foods. Customers include major multiples. More recently, the company has invested in sauce-making equipment and intends to become a key producer. There are 130 employees and the company operates on two sites in Worsley, near Manchester.

The company first identified IIP in June 1994 and registered in October 1994. However, it was not until a restructuring exercise in summer 1995 that IIP was seen as a crucial vehicle for organizational change. Peter Lenders, a family member of the management team, undertook 'ownership' of the project and by September 1995 began to accumulate evidence against a plan and targets set with a consultant. Rapid progress was made and accreditation was achieved at the first attempt in June 1996.

A crucial role of IIP was its impact on management's view of the business plan. The company had paid little attention to its planning however IIP made the management more disciplined in its approach to planning and served to bind the team towards its achievement – 'We all pushed it,' reported Peter.

A vital feature of IIP's role in improving performance has been its effect on company culture. A staff survey in 1995 revealed negative staff attitudes towards management. Senior management responded by drawing up plans to create a more open culture by making management more approachable and seeking more ideas from staff. There has been a clear link between the change in management behaviour on the factory floor and organisation performance measures such as absenteeism, sickness and staff turnover. Such improvements are attributed to improved understanding between management and staff. Productivity, turnover and profit have all increased over the period but it would be difficult to directly attribute such improvements to IIP.

> ## At the level of the individual, the main effect has been on first level management and their relationships with staff.

At the level of the individual, the main effect has been on first level management and their relationships with staff. The improvements were the result of pressure from senior management, by the establishment of targets through the appraisal system. Senior management conducted their own interviews of 80 per cent of staff to monitor the changes and a follow-up survey in March 1996 revealed significantly improved reactions from staff.

IIP diagnosis revealed some gaps in the company's training provision and prompted the company to seek to improve its training in relation to health and safety, IT and quality. Since registration the company has increased spending on training by 10 per cent. The principal mechanism for identifying training needs and the formation of a training plan is a new appraisal system, developed as a direct consequence of IIP registration. The process ensures that all needs are developed against the requirements of the business plan. Appraisal discussions are 'two-way', that is appraisees have the opportunity to provide upward feedback to their appraisers.

Organisation communications have been improved by the introduction of a company newsletter which ensures that staff are informed of what is happening in the business and key events in advance. In addition, relationships between management and staff have also improved with management now seen as more 'approachable' and staff feeling more 'belonging'.

Initially the company wasted their consultant funding. The company was not ready for the process of accreditation until commitment was gained from the senior management team.

It was necessary to establish a vital link between IIP and the business plan. In the case of Lenders Foods, this link was provided by the negative staff survey and need to improve relationships between management and shop floor staff. Once the link was made, a momentum and commitment was established and the company was far more able to make plans and gather evidence to achieve IIP accreditation. The company also began to deal directly with Manchester TEC and visits from the TEC assured the company that they were meeting requirements on evidence and management felt more confident about reaching their targets.

A crucial advantage was gained from IIP in the company's relationship with its major customer. Of particular importance has been the growth in knowledge of shop floor staff of the production process. Buyers and food technologists from customers pay frequent visits to the factory and management now feel confident that any member of staff would be able to respond to questions posed on such visits.

IIP accreditation has 'enabled Lenders to focus on business strategies and to develop people to achieve such strategies'.

ing about the value of management development, with senior managers more prepared to support the process once they had been through it themselves.

While there are many recommendations to adopt a more strategic approach to HRD and to make it more business driven, there remains the crucial factor of how HRD is implemented. There are a number of uncertainties and tensions that make a close examination difficult and problematic. For example, who should take responsibility for HRD? Should it be training specialists with their sophisticated repertoire of interventions and techniques or line managers who are close to work performance and are able to influence the way people learn and develop and the environment in which this occurs. How should learning needs be identified and whose interest should they serve; the employee seeking opportunity and reward for the sacrifice of their effort or the organization in the pursuit of goals and targets? How does HRD relate to business goals and do activities add value? Overall, there is little evidence about what is happening inside organizations when HRD is considered and this is compounded when we consider both formal and informal approaches to HRD. It is becoming clearer that while formal aspects of HRD such as plans, policies and activities can have a crucial impact, informal features may be of even greater importance. In particular, we might consider the impact of work groups on learning or how line managers really inhibit or support HRD processes. These aspects of HRD are certainly significant although they are also more difficult to examine and measure.

Formal models of training and development have shown a remarkable tendency to match the conventional wisdom of how organizations should be run. Depending on the resources committed to their activities, trainers have had to justify the commitment by adherence to prescriptive approaches. Traditionally, employees learnt their jobs by exposure to experienced workers who would show them what to do ('sitting by Nellie'). Undoubtedly much learning did occur in this way, but as a learning system it was haphazard, lengthy and bad habits could be passed on as well as good ones. In some cases, reinforced by employers' tendencies to deskill work, employees were unwilling to give away their 'secrets' for fear of losing their jobs. Most importantly, line managers did not

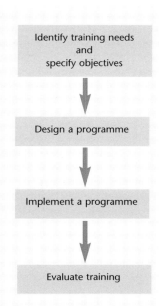

Figure 10.2   A four-stage training model

see it as their responsibility to become involved in training, thus adding to forces that served to prohibit any consideration of valuing employee potential.

In the 1960s, following their establishment by the Industrial Training Act 1964, the Industrial Training Boards encouraged a *systematic training model*. The approach was widely adopted and became ingrained in the thinking of most training practitioners. The approach was based on a four-stage process shown as Figure 10.2.

The approach neatly matches the conception of what most organizations would regard as rationality and efficiency. There is an emphasis on cost effectiveness throughout; training needs are identified so that wasteful expenditure can be avoided, objectives involving standards are set, programmes are designed and implemented, outcomes are evaluated, or more precisely validated, to ensure that the programme meets objectives originally specified and organization criteria. There is a preference for off-the-job learning, partly because of the weaknesses identified by the 'sitting by Nellie' approach, and partly to formalize training so that it is standardized, measurable and undertaken by specialist trainers. The trainer can focus on the provision of separate training activities that avoid the complexity of day-to-day work activities and make evaluation all the easier.

In this systematic model, training needs assessment and analysis is concerned with identifying gaps between work performance and standards of work or performance criteria that have a training solution. Once these have been identified, clear and specific objectives can be established that can be used to design learning events and evaluate the outcomes. Training needs can exist and be identified throughout an organization. Boydell (1976) has identified three possible levels, organization, job or occupation, and individual. In theory, needs are identified at corporate or organization levels and feed through to individual levels. The approach reflects a mechanistic view of organizations and people within it. In particular, there is an emphasis on the flow of information down the hierarchy to individuals, whose training needs are assessed against standards defined by others. Each person has a responsibility to perform against the standard and to receive appropriate training if they are unable to do so.

Emerging from a consideration of needs will be plans for development activities. These may take the form of on-the-job or work-based opportunities supported by line managers and others, or off-the-job courses run by specialists, which may or may not lead to qualifications, and, increasingly, open and distance learning activities. Whatever the form of development activities undertaken, the key questions concern whether and how learning will actually occur, and whether learning can be integrated into workplace behaviour and sustained.

The systematic model of training places evaluation as the last stage of a four-stage model. Although a number of writers have pointed out the value of evaluation at each stage of the model (Donnelly, 1987), the image of evaluation encompassed by many trainers is that of a final stage added on at the end of a training course. In such cases, evaluation serves to provide feedback to trainers, so that small adjustments and improvements may be made to activities, or to provide data to prove training meets objectives set, so that expenditure on training may be justified. Given the precarious standing of HRD in many organizations, the collection of data by evaluating activities is a vital process in establishing the credibility and value of training.

Over the years the basic elements of this systematic training model have remained and most organizations that claim to have a systematic and planned approach to training would have some representation of it. There have also been a number of refinements by advocates of a more realistic and more sophisticated model. Donnelly (1987, p. 4) argued that in reality senior management may abdicate responsibility for training policy to training departments, with a consequent potential for widening the gap between training and organization requirements. Essential prerequisites for any effort to implement a training model are a consideration of budgets, attitudes, abilities and culture or climate. A key requirement of training activity is that it should be relevant and 'reflect the real world'.

Bramley (1989, p. 6) also argues that the training sub-system may become independent of the organization context. He advocates a cycle that is open to the context by involving managers in analysing work situations to identify desirable changes, and designing and delivering the training to bring the changes about. Evaluation occurs throughout the process with an emphasis on managers taking responsibility for encouraging the transfer of learning, that occurs during training, into workplace performance. Bramley's effectiveness model is shown as Figure 10.3.

Refinements to the basic form of the systematic model imply that a more sophisticated view of training is taken. Essentially this involves taking account of reality and organization context. Implicit in the models are the inherent limitations of organization reality that may prevent the models from operating or maintain training activity at a low level. Thus the reality may be little consideration for training in relation to organization strategy and a culture which emphasizes short-term results against set standards. Managers may refuse to accept responsibility for identifying staff training needs and supporting the transfer of learning where training is undertaken. These are all features of an organization's learning climate and are essential conditions for implementing an HRD approach.

Taylor (1991, p. 264) argued that it is possible to present two views of why system-

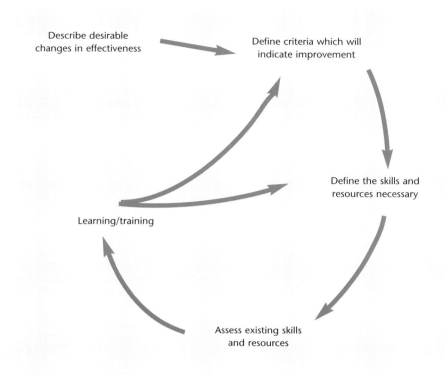

Figure 10.3 Bramley's effectiveness model
Source: Bramley, 1989

atic training models may not match organizational reality. In the first, the rehabilita-
tive critique, it is argued that the systematic model's concepts are sound and can be
used as a heuristic device and an approximation to reality. The models serve to highlight the problems to be overcome at each stage by refining techniques. For example,
in identifying training needs, trainers may not have access to the 'real' learning needs
of the organization because of a lack of access to information and low credibility with
senior managers. The refinement would be for trainers to raise the profile of training.
The radical critique, however, argues that the systematic model is based on flawed
assumptions and is merely a 'legitimising myth' (1991, p. 270) to establish to role of
the trainer and to allow management's right to define skill within the employment
relationship. For example, it is often assumed that training is in everyone's best interest. However, in times of rapid change, the definition of skill and the redesign of
work, which determines and is determined by employee learning, may lead to a divergence of interest between employees and management and unbalance the employment relationship between them. Taylor (1991, p. 273) concluded that while
systematic models may have helped to professionalize the training activity and to
provide a simple and easily understood explanation of training procedures, such
models were incomplete and really only suitable for organizations operating in stable
environments where goals can be clearly set, outcomes measured and mere compli-

ance obtained from employees. However, according to Taylor, 'Continued adherence towards what is still essentially a mechanistic procedure may well prevent trainers tapping into the more nebulous but powerful organizational forces such as mission, creativity, culture and values' (Taylor, 1991, p. 273).

Recent years have seen many organizations, especially those facing uncertain environments and the expectation of rapid and continuous change, develop competency frameworks (see Chapter 6) in a bid to link employee performance and business objectives. As we explained in Chapter 8, Performance appraisal, competencies can be utilized within a *performance management system* to provide a *performance and development plan* which would include an identification of training needs and a plan to meet such needs. Research into the use of competencies has found that discussion and rating of job performance and identifying training needs are the main uses (Strebler *et al.*, 1997, p. 25). It is interesting to note that overall satisfaction with competencies depended on the way they were introduced and the provision of training for those who would be required to use them. However, it was also found that, where competencies were used in performance review, to identify training and development needs may actually be detrimental to confidence in using competencies. It seems that some respondents were sceptical that actions agreed in performance reviews would actually be carried out. As one manager observed:

> I am convinced that unless the system is undertaken professionally, it has negative value and becomes a cynics' charter. It is therefore all or nothing (quoted in Strebler *et al.*, 1997, p. 76).

The difficulty highlights the importance of the line manager's role in the assessment and development of others. HRM in practice 10.2 shows how an NHS Trust attempted to combine training, development and assessment through a competency programme.

A policy of HRD has to be translated into the structures, systems and processes that might be called a learning climate. Paul Temporal (1978, p. 93) has identified the learning climate in an organization as being composed of subjectively perceived physical and psycho-social variables that will fashion an employee's effectiveness in realizing learning potential. Such variables may also act as a block to learning. Physical variables cover the jobs and tasks an employee is asked to do, the structure within which they are set, and factors such as noise and the amount of working space. Of particular significance is the extent to which the work contains learning and the extent to which work can be adjusted in line with employee learning. Psycho-social variables may be more powerful. These include norms, attitudes, processes, systems and procedures. They appear within the relationships in which an employee is involved, for example, with superiors, peers, subordinates, customers and suppliers. Few organizations have paid any attention to their learning climate and yet any attempt to implement strategies and policies of HRD and HRM are inevitably doomed unless the learning climate can be influenced to provide support.

At the heart of the learning climate lies the line manager–employee relationship. HRD requires integration of the various activities, and the key to achieving this lies in the thoughts, feelings and actions of line managers. A number of roles have been associated with managers to support the fusion, including coach, counsellor and mentor. A brief examination of the activities will highlight the key features of these roles.

In Chapter 8, Performance appraisal, a distinction was made between performance

HRM in practice 10.2

Innovative grading system lifts morale at NHS trust

A pilot scheme linking nurses' pay and promotion with individual development has cut staff turnover in Ealing

BY RUTH PRICKETT People Management, 22 January 1998

A London health trust claims that a pilot competency programme for nurses has reduced staff turnover, cut absence rates and increased patient satisfaction.

Ealing Hospital NHS Trust has pioneered a grading scheme linking pay and competencies with staff development, managers told a conference at the Royal College of Nursing (RCN). They hope their experience will help to inform current discussions about national pay structures for the profession.

The pilot, which has been running for a year, is loosely based on the concept of clinical ladders: a system under which nurses are promoted according to their level of competence in defined areas. It encourages nurses to gather and present evidence of their competencies to move up a series of levels within the overall grades of house-keeper, healthcare worker, general nurse and nurse clinician.

Each level has its own standards. For example, an interim nurse clinician is expected to be 'proficient' in both the category of clinical practice and of professional education, and to be 'competent' in management; whereas, further down the scale, the senior general nurse has to be 'competent' in clinical

practice and 'intermediate' in the other two classes.

Managers, trade unions and staff worked together to identify the necessary competencies for each level and every nurse on the scheme has an individual training plan. Staff representatives have welcomed the emphasis on individual training and development and the opportunity to identify the core elements of their jobs.

'We said: "We will decide what we will do – we're not doctors' assistants, we're professional nurses",' explained Carole Heaton, director of nursing at the trust.

> **A London health trust claims that a pilot competency programme for nurses has reduced staff turnover, cut absence rates and increased patient satisfaction.**

Steve Godercharle, RCN lead officer for the North Thames region, admitted he was initially sceptical when he was asked to join the scheme's Clinical Review Group in 1995. But, like the trust managers, he was concerned about high staff turnover and backed the con-

tinuing development aspect of the scheme. 'I was impressed by the idea of finding roles that helped individual progression as well as the hospital,' he said.

'The Ealing model is not just a pay system,' according to Deborah O'Dea, the trust's HR director, 'It's a training, development and assessment tool.'

But she stressed that the trust is too small to introduce a true clinical ladders system. The pilot has been based on two wards only, so although nurses move up internal levels according to their competencies, they still have to apply for a job vacancy when they wish to advance an overall grade.

The results, however, have been encouraging. Sickness absence dropped from 5 per cent to 4.2 per cent between 1994 and 1997 and staff retention has improved – no nurses on the scheme have left in the past year. This makes a big difference to a trust that is within eight miles of seven other hospitals and has regularly had to recruit staff from as far afield as Norway and Finland at a cost of about £4500 per person. Customer satisfaction surveys and patients' letters have been complimentary and regular staff meetings have shown a dramatic improvement in nurses' morale and confidence.

Managers are now keen to extend the system to the rest of the trust, but they argue that Ealing is too small and too short of funds to do this without sponsorship from the NHS Executive. They claim that the initial costs of implementing the scheme are offset by improved staff retention, increased trust, co-operation and enthusiasm.

'Costs balance out because you attract people who stay,' Heaton said. 'For me, the greatest success is the fact that people aren't afraid to speak out now.'

'We would probably have closed the project down at Christmas 1996, but the staff really wanted it to work,' O'Dea added. 'It's been something of a workers' revolution.'

control approaches to assessment (Randell, 1994, p. 235), and appraisal and developmental approaches. The latter may use sophisticated techniques such as behaviour anchored ratings scales (BARS), behavioural expectations scales (BES) (Leat and Lovell, 1997, p. 150) or competencies combined with multi-source feedback (MSF) in order to foster development and learning. Line managers will be involved in the review of employee performance on a continuous basis. Where this occurs in a climate of mutual trust and support and an absence of fear, it is likely to release a flow of information about all aspects of workplace performance. Employees who are closest to their work are able to identify their own problems, the problems of their work, and the opportunities for development for themselves and their work.

Line managers play the crucial role in facilitating the positive transfer of learning from development activity to workplace behaviour and performance. Baldwin and Ford (1988, p. 65) have provided a model of the transfer process shown as Figure 10.4. The model specifies six crucial linkages in the transfer of training. For example, we can see that new skills can be learnt and retained but support and opportunity to use the learning must be provided in the work environment. Baldwin and Ford (1988, p. 93) draw on research to identify support activities by line managers to include goal setting, reinforcement activities, encouragement to attend, and modelling of behaviours.

The responsibility of the line manager for the development of his or her employees has come to be seen as essential in HRD and HRM and the route towards continuous employee development. However, while many organizations might espouse such a policy, there has so far been insufficient evidence of widespread practice and acceptance of these responsibilities by managers. Leicester (1989, p. 53) found an absence of implemented continuous development policies, but in organizations where managers had been trained in interpersonal skills and had an explicit responsibility for managing people, employees were more likely to be fully trained 'not just for the job... but continuously prepared for a work performance that is a regular contribution to corporate success. In this sense, training begets training: only a fully trained management will create and continue to maintain a properly trained workforce' (Leicester, 1989, p. 57).

Workplace learning

If there is a single theme that has widened and transformed the idea of HRD in recent years, from a subset of HRM into a matter of strategic concern, that is central to organ-

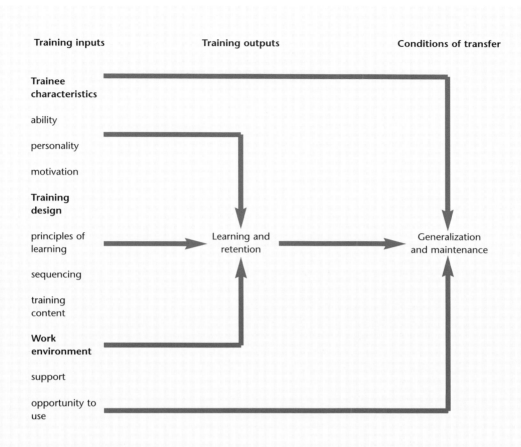

Figure 10.4 A model of the transfer of learning
Source: Baldwin and Ford, 1988

ization progress and survival, it is the theme of learning. Learning in the workplace is seen as the crucial contributor to dealing with change, coping with uncertainty and complexity in the environment and creating the opportunities for sustainable competitive advantage.

Many organizations have been attracted by the idea of becoming a learning organization or learning company. It is an idea that has had a significant impact in recent years with a growing number of conferences, books and journals devoted to it. While there is significant ambiguity about the meaning of the term, there is little doubt about its impact. It has become the vision of many organization leaders and managers. A survey in 1996 of chief executives (KPMG, 1996) found that respondents believed that:

● learning and adaptation must be accelerated through innovative and creative means
● learning must at least keep pace with the change in their organization's environment
● learning and innovation is the key to their organization's survival and success

● building a learning organization is a way of challenging and moving away from their current culture.

In the UK, the idea of the learning organization was developed by Pedler *et al.*'s (1988) *Learning Company Project Report* which provided the following definition:

an organization which facilitates the learning of all its members and continuously transforms itself.

They went on to provide a list of dimensions of a learning company that could be used to differentiate it from a non-learning company. Among the dimensions were a learning approach to strategy, participative policy making, 'informating' (that is, the use of information technology to inform and empower people), reward flexibility and self-development opportunities for all (Pedler *et al.*, 1991, p. 18).

Another source of encouragement for learning organizations has been Peter Senge's (1990) idea of five disciplines that are required as a foundation. These are:

● personal mastery
● shared vision
● team learning
● mental models
● systems thinking.

What has become clear is that such models represent an ideal of a learning organization, which may become difficult to implement. The KPMG survey (1996) found that even where managers were in favour of learning organizations, they often faced difficulties in finding support for the idea:

I have been trying to foster the learning concept for some time but with little success as the resistance to change is too great (KPMG, 1996).

Why do you think the learning organization idea is difficult to implement?

Part of the reason, as explained by Garavan (1997, p. 26), is that the idea of a learning organization is an ideal rather than a reality that can be achieved. In recent years, the idea has been compared to a journey and possibly one that is never completed. Of course, this has not prevented many organizations from trying but it may be the case that the various models of learning organizations rest too far away from organization realities.

A further difficulty may be to do with the way we understand and explain learning in organizations. Throughout the twentieth century there have been many ideas concerning learning. A distinction is usually made between 'associative learning or behavourism' and 'cognitive learning'. The main differences between the two traditions are summarized in Figure 10.5.

We can see how the nature of the work that employees are required to perform will lead to the acceptance of a particular view of learning. It will also underpin much of a manager's understanding of human behaviour and motivation. Thus the reduction of work into low-skilled and repetitive tasks will favour associative and behaviourist views of learning even where, in the initial phases of learning, knowledge and understanding is required. The main thrust of the learning is to produce behaviour that can

Associative learning	Cognitive learning
Learning in terms of responses to stimuli; 'automatic' learning	Insightful learning
Classical conditioning (Pavlov's dogs)	Thinking, discovering, understanding, seeing relationships and meaning
Operant or instrumental conditioning	New arrangements of previously learned concepts and principles

Figure 10.5 Traditions of learning

be repeated time after time in relatively unchanging conditions. This matches very closely the form of learning required for task learning identified in Figure 10.1 above by Hall (1986, p. 235). More complex work favours the need for knowledge, understanding and higher-order cognitive skills, underpinned by cognitive learning theories. However, the acquisition of knowledge and understanding also requires an outlet for action through behaviour in the workplace.

Modern theories of learning contain elements of both associative and cognitive learning but most importantly emphasize the process of learning and its continuity. This has resulted in a great deal of attraction to such theories in organizations pursuing HRD policies. Kolb (1984, p. 42) provided an integrated theory of experiential learning where learning is prompted through the interaction of a learner and his or her environment. The theory stresses the central role of individual needs and goals in determining the type of experience sought and the extent to which all stages of learning are completed. For learning to occur, all stages of a learning cycle should be completed. However, individual learners will have an established pattern of assumptions, attitudes and aptitudes that will determine effectiveness in learning. Kolb's learning cycle is shown as Figure 10.6.

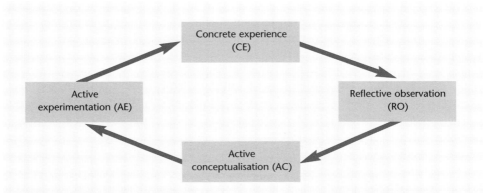

Figure 10.6 Kolb's learning cycle
Source: Kolb, 1984

According to Kolb, learning occurs through the grasping of experience and the transformation of it. The transformation of the impact of experience on the senses (CE), through internal reflection (RO), allows the emergence of ideas (AC) that can be extended into the external world through new actions (AE). Unless the process can be completed in full, learning does not occur and individuals may not begin the journey to qualitatively finer and higher forms of awareness, which may be called development.

In some respects, Kolb's model has become the new orthodoxy for many trainers particularly in the field of management development. While there has been a growing critique and reassessment of the model (Holman *et al.*, 1997), it heightens our awareness of the factors that contribute to learning and prevent learning at work. Learning activities at work could be designed on the basis of individual and group learning preferences. Learners might also attempt to overcome their intrinsic or internal blocks to learning. Temporal's (1978, p. 93) classification of these blocks is:

Perceptual	where the learner is unable to see what the problem is.
Cultural	where the learner cuts him or herself off from a range of activities through the acceptance of norms regarding what is 'done' or 'not done', as right or wrong.
Emotional/Motivational	where the learner feels insecure in certain situations, which causes reluctance to take action based on the learner's ideas and beliefs.
Intellectual	where the learner has not developed the right learning skills, the mental competence to resolve problems and approach situations correctly.
Expressive	where the learner has poor skills of communication.

Kolb's model links to other models of learning which examine personal meanings, feelings and emotions towards learning. For example, neurolinguistic programming (NLP) examines the way learners represent the world in their brains and order their thoughts by language to produce largely automatic actions (Dowlen, 1996, p. 27). Learners can examine how such processes occur and how they can model themselves on the processes of others whom they see as more effective. Harri-Augstein and Webb (1995) present an approach to learning based on the uncovering of personal meanings and myths which produce 'robot-like' performance and appear very difficult to change. Through critical awareness, learners can begin to experiment and change. Such views of learning link to a growing interest in adult learning and development and the importance of reflection to examine behaviour, and assumptions and premises about learning (Mezirow, 1991).

Concurrent with the interest in individual learners, we have also been concerned with ideas related to learning in groups and the way learning can become organizational. An immediate set of difficulties arises when considering such learning. First, apart from formal group and team development programmes, most learning with others takes place within relationships that are to be found in the 'dark side' of organizations (Pedler and Aspinall, 1996, p. 29), and this is territory that is often unknown to organization researchers. Second, ideas about organization learning, particularly when referred to by managers in the context of seeking competitive advantage, frequently take the view of an organization as a single unified entity with a common culture.

Some of the research that has been carried out indicates that learning in organizations is mostly informal and improvisational. It is 'situated' in a particular context and is a function of the activity that occurs at a local level (Lave and Wenger, 1991). Furthermore, such learning is likely to be at variance from what is supposed to happen, at least in the eyes of managers, who will have formed and espoused abstract versions of what should be learnt but miss vital details in the process. Brown and Duguid (1991, p. 41) use the idea of situated learning to make a distinction between canonical practice and non-canonical practice where the former refers to what is supposed to be learnt and the latter refers to what is actually learnt and practised in the working context. Learning is strongly related to becoming a practitioner within a group or a community with its own norms, stories and views about what is effective. Any place that we call an organization is likely to be composed of many such communities of practice. This makes the task of achieving the benefits of organization learning even more complex. It also explains how so much insight and understanding remains hidden in organizations and how the downsizing trends of the early 1990s often resulted in the break up of such communities and the loss of core knowledge. Brown and Duguid (1991, p. 53) argue that an organization needs to be conceived as a 'community-of-communities' and 'see beyond its canonical abstractions of practice to the rich, full-bloodied activities themselves'.

The capture of knowledge that is generated by learning is one of the key factors that is driving the interest in *knowledge management* which Mayo (1998, p. 36) defines as:

> the management of the information, knowledge and experience available to an organization – its creation, capture, storage, availability and utilisation – in order that organizational activities build on what is already known and extend it further.

A number of organizations are appointing managers as learning officers or knowledge officers and installing networked software to accentuate the process.

Chapter summary

The growing interest in learning as crucial to an organization's survival and a source of competitive advantage has resulted in a reinterpretation of HRD in recent years. Significant attention has been given to HRD by government, organizations and individuals and some progress has been made. In the UK, there is now a national framework of vocational qualifications which, while criticised by some as too basic and too bureaucratic, is resulting in many more people gaining accreditation for their learning. The expansion of higher education in the 1990s has also created a set of expectations among graduates that they will find challenging work where their skills and intelligence will be utililzed and developed. This, in turn, focuses attention on the opportunities for workplace learning. Much depends on the extent to which the key features of an HRD policy are seen as part of an integrated HRM strategy. There has been clear progress in many organizations and a great deal of energy devoted to the development of a learning workforce. We noted in Chapter 7,

Recruitment and selection, how the assessment of ability to learn may be a feature of an organization's selection activities. We also noted that this may influence the expectations of employees. In such organizations, learning and development become key features of the employment relationship, and the provision of resources and support for HRD activities an accepted part of working life. In such circumstances, it is not difficult to imagine the creation of a virtuous cycle of continuous development and enhanced performance, and how the visions of the learning organization and knowledge management may play a crucial role in constructing the future in an uncertain and chaotic world. However, in many other organizations in the UK, there remain significant barriers to HRD, most notably the attitudes of managers and employees. Low expectations, lack of confidence and self-belief and negative memories of learning from school can all play a role in preventing individuals from taking opportunities for further development. Employees may also be adversely influenced by the attitudes of fellow workers. Negative attitudes to HRD still remains a key issue to be addressed in the years to come.

Key concepts

Human resource development　　　　　**Learning climate**
Organization learning　　　　　　　　　**The learning company or organization**
Knowledge management　　　　　　　　**Systematic training model**
Workplace learning　　　　　　　　　　**Transfer of learning**
Learning

Discussion questions

1. What is the relationship between strategy and HRD?

2. What have been the main benefits of a systematic approach to training? What are the criticisms of the systematic model for an organization pursuing an HRD policy?

3. How will your learning at school or college be transferred to work?

4. What is meant by the ideas of a learning organization and knowledge management?

5. How can employees be motivated to learn? Who should be responsible? Do we all learn in the same way?

6. What kind of learning skills will organizations require in the future?

Further reading

Ashton, D. and Felstead, A. (1995) Training and development. In Storey, J. (ed.) *Human Resource Management*, London: Routledge, pp. 234–53.

Baldwin, T.T. and Ford, J.K. (1988) Transfer of training: a review and directions for future research, *Personnel Psychology*, **41**: 63–105.

Burgoyne, J., Pedler, M. and Boydell, T. (1994) *Towards the Learning Company*, Maidenhead: McGraw-Hill.

McGoldrick, J. and Stewart, J. (eds) (1996) *Human Resource Development*, London: Pitman Publishing.

Chapter case study

David Johnson and Co., Solicitors

David Johnson and Co. is a law firm operating from two locations in Cardiff. There are 19 partners and 90 staff (including 32 fee-earners). The Managing Partner, David Johnson, following his attendance at a presentation on the benefits of the learning company, is now seeking to find a way of making such ideas relevant to his firm. He sees HRD as a way of providing a boost to staff morale, following the departure of three founding partners. Staff also felt that they were low paid. In addition, many staff were women 'returners' with little recent experience of learning and rather resistant to change. Solicitors were also likely to have problems of adapting to new requirements in a very competitive environment for law firms. The ideas of learning are attractive because they provide the key ingredient to managing change. In particular, David Johnson wants to take advantage of the pools of knowledge that must exist within the firm but remain relatively untapped.

Task

You have been asked to prepare a report for the firm on:

1. How ideas about the learning company can be applied in practice.

2. How this firm could manage knowledge more effectively.

You should research some of the evidence on the application of the ideas of the learning company and knowledge management. Present your findings in a form appropriate to the partners of a law firm.

Notes

1. Ashton, D. and Felstead, A. (1995) Training and development. In Storey, J. (ed.) *Human Resource Management*, London: Routledge, pp. 234–53.
2. Quoted in Bratton, J. (1992) *Japanization at Work: Managerial Studies for the 1990s*, London: Macmillan, p. 109.
3. Quoted in KPMG (1996) *Learning Organisation Benchmarking Survey*, KPMG: London.

part five

Employee and Industrial Relations

chapter eleven

Communications and employee involvement

John Bratton

People actually know who the managing director is now... He is actually trying to communicate.[1]

Previously we had very formal joint consultations. We have stopped that too. The only thing that's at all formal is when occasionally we have to negotiate something like an annual wage deal... What we do now is, we get them [shop stewards] in and have a chat. We don't keep minutes.[2]

Chapter outline

Chapter objectives

After studying this chapter, you should be able to:

1. Explain why managers might want to increase employee involvement and participation.
2. Describe the different dimensions of employee involvement and participation.
3. Appreciate the importance of organizational communications in the HRM paradigm.
4. Explain different approaches to organizational communications.
5. Understand the effects of employee involvement on organizational outcomes.
6. Summarize the structure and operation of joint consultation committees and some obstacles to employee involvement initiatives.

● Introduction

Organizational communication, employee involvement (EI) and participation concepts are associated with the 'soft' HRM model. In the last decade, in tandem with the growth of interest in the HRM phenomenon, interest in communications and EI has grown considerably in Britain and North America (Marchington, 1995). In January 1993, it was reported that Lloyds Bank had given a promise to its 40 000 employees that it would be honest and open with them whether the news was good or bad. Lloyds Bank introduced an employee communication 'charter'. Another large business, ICL (UK), used its team briefing system to communicate to its workforce the rationale behind the company's announcement of a pay freeze in late 1992. The two cases of Lloyds Bank and ICL (UK) are part of the evidence confirming the substantial increase in methods to improve communications between managers and workers and other senior management initiatives to raise employee involvement and commitment (Millward et al., 1992). Evidence has been produced from a number of case studies about the nature of employee involvement (for example, Marchington 1987, 1995; Marchington et al., 1992, 1993). The majority of studies of employee involvement have focused on the private business sector. With a few notable exceptions, the public sector, and particularly local government, employee participation policies have gone largely undocumented (Perkins, 1986). The call for improving organizational communication and for greater worker involvement in work itself is not new; it has a long history (Brannen et al., 1976). Four key features that influence workers' involvement have been identified; the pattern of industrial relations, the views of the main interested parties, the importance of personnel policy, and the legislative context (Guest, 1986).

British industrial relations are based on the traditions of voluntarism, centring on collective bargaining. Voluntarism means a preference by managers, trade unions and the government for the voluntary regulation of the employment relationship, and a preference for a non-legalistic form of joint regulation or collective bargaining. However, the tradition of voluntarism has been increasingly circumscribed since the 1960s by government legislation and the decline of traditional industrial sectors, formerly the bastions of British trade unionism. These trends reduce the capacity of trade unions to take radical initiatives to extend workers' involvement in workplace decision making through collective bargaining. The views of the principal actors in the industrial relations system are also determinants of EI. In the 1990s, the consensus among employer groups and the Conservative government can be summarized as follows; employee involvement is desirable, the aim of employee involvement is to promote workers' interest in the success of the organization, and policies for involvement should be directed at the workforce as a whole. The legislative context further affects organizational communications and the nature and extent of worker involvement. The 1975 Employment Protection Act gives limited rights to union representatives to obtain certain information from their employers. The 1974 Health and Safety at Work etc. Act encourages employee participation. The 1982 Employment Act requires certain companies to include a statement in the annual report describing the action taken during the year to introduce, maintain or develop employee involvement. However, in terms of changing actual practice and encouraging participation, the law is likely to be marginal (Marchington and Wilding, 1983).

The renewed interest and policy initiatives supported by the government and many employers adopting, either implicitly or explicitly, a HRM paradigm tend to centre on the voluntary development of EI. The extent and nature of EI would appear to depend upon which version of HRM is adopted. If senior management adopt the 'hard' HRM variant, communication is critical to a 'transformational' leadership style, but EI is far from assured. More open and direct communication between senior management and line managers and workers and involvement initiatives at the point of production is likely, although not guaranteed, where 'soft' HRM is espoused (Marchington, 1995, pp. 280–1). EI does not extend to involvement in corporate policies such as product or service strategy, pay, or employment security (Beer *et al.*, 1984). In practice, to date, participation is limited to immediate work goals and operations.

There are two interrelated aspects of the contemporary debate on the HRM approach to organizational communication and employee involvement and participation. From a managerial perspective, there is the argument that communication plays a critical role in constructing and maintaining a 'strong' organizational culture (Trethewey, 1997), and in the leadership process 'leadership is to a great extent a communication process', Witherspoon (1997, p. x). Further, there is the argument that EI fundamentally transforms the climate of the employment relations because it leads, not only to changes in worker behaviour, but more significantly to long-term changes in worker attitudes and commitment, and that these in turn will result in gains in labour productivity and quality. From a critical perspective, there is the argument that EI techniques, by promoting the individual employee rather than employees' collective bodies, deliberately undermine the role of the trade union representative.

This chapter examines these themes. The chapter defines and seeks to clarify the terms which have been used in the debate on employee involvement and participation. It therefore begins by defining 'employee involvement' and 'employee participation'; the meaning of the term is quite elastic. It goes on to explain the growth of interest in HRM directed at employee involvement and participation. The defining characteristics of organizational communications are explained, as are the different perspectives on the role of communications. The nature of worker involvement in organizational decision making, the EI–organizational performance link, and some impediments to EI are also discussed.

Communications, involvement and the HRM cycle

A central concept of strategic HRM is the individual employee-orientated approach to involvement and participation. The techniques developed in the 1990s span a number of different spheres of the employment relationship and the HRM cycle; job design, for example, self-managed work teams, quality circles; rewards, for example, profit-related pay; employee communication programmes; and decision making. One consequence of introducing EI in an organization is an increase in HR development, training and learning. Another important consequence of introducing EI is an increased demand for information that tests management communication. These HRM innovations are designed to enhance both the commitment and performance of the workforce.

⬤ The nature of employee involvement

A review of the literature reveals that the terms 'employee participation' and 'employee involvement' have different meanings. In essence, *employee participation* involves workers exerting a countervailing and upward pressure on management control, which need not imply unity of purpose. *Employee involvement*, in contrast, is perceived to be a 'softer' form of participation, to imply a commonality of interest between employees and management, and stresses that involvement should be directed at the workforce as a whole and not restricted to trade union channels. As Guest states, 'involvement is considered to be more flexible and better geared to the goal of securing commitment and shared interest' (1986, p. 687).

When people talk about participation or involvement, they are reflecting their own attitudes and work experiences, and their own hopes for the future. Managers tend to talk about participation when in fact they mean consultation. For example, the CBI believes that 'Employees at all levels must understand and appreciate the economic and commercial realities of operating in today's highly competitive trading climate' (ACAS, 1987). Consultation in practice usually means a structure for improving organizational communications, usually 'top-down' or 'upward problem-solving' communications. Employees and union representatives, when offered consultation, believe they are about to be given participation. For example, 'in order to play their full part they [employees] need to be provided with *full* information and *real* opportunities [our emphasis] to influence decisions which affect their working lives' states the TUC.[3] Differing expectations among employees will affect their attitude, their propensity to participate, and ultimately the success of participation techniques in the organization. Therefore, a vital first step, if there is to be any meeting of minds, is to create a common language and conceptual model.

Definitions of employee participation or involvement do not always reflect the range of possibilities, from some small degree of influence to 'total control'. For instance, Salamon defines participation as:

> a philosophy or style of organizational management which recognizes both the need and the right of employees, individually or collectively, to be involved with management in areas of the organization's decision making beyond that normally covered by collective bargaining (1987, p. 296).

The process of employee involvement should provide employees with the opportunity to influence and, wherever possible, take part in decision making on matters which affect their working lives. Charlton (1983) has suggested that the most prevalent classification is that which differentiates direct from indirect participation. The term 'direct' is used to refer to those forms of participation where individual employees, albeit often in a very limited way, are involved in the decision-making processes that affect their everyday work routines. Direct participation, such as briefing groups or the creation of new work organization arrangements (self-managed teams), is viewed as a device to increase labour productivity and implicitly to improve job satisfaction. On the other hand, indirect participation is used to refer to those forms of participation where representatives or delegates of the main body of employees participate in a variety of ways in the decision-making processes within the organization. Indirect forms, such as joint consultation, widening the content of collective bargaining and 'worker directors', are associated with the broader notion of 'industrial democracy' (Brannen *et al.*, 1976; Bullock, 1977).

Conceptual models have been provided by Salamon (1987) and, more recently, by the American management theorist Richard Daft (1998). Figure 11.1 depicts an adaptation of such models and shows the relationship between three constituent elements, the forms of involvement, direct and indirect; the level of involvement in the organi-

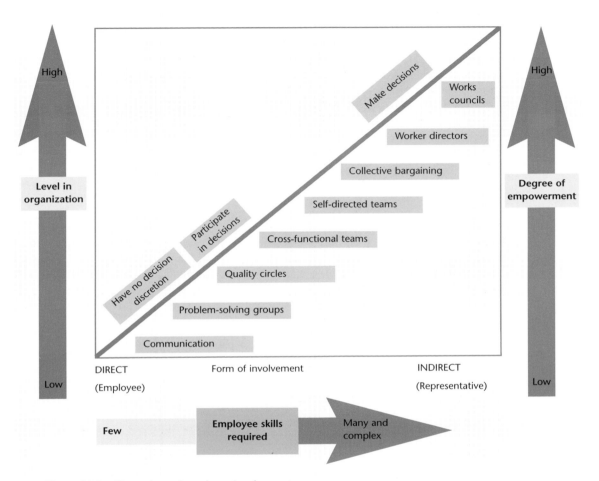

Figure 11.1 Dimensions of employee involvement

zational hierarchy; and the degree of involvement. Figure 11.1 shows a continuum of employee involvement, from a situation where employees have no autonomy (for example, a traditionally designed assembly line) to full involvement, where workers participate in strategic decision making. Current methods of EI fall along this continuum. Those methods are involvement through the *communication* of information, *upward problem solving*, *quality circles*, extended *consultation*, *cross-functional teams*, *self-directed teams*, *collective bargaining*, *worker directors* and *works councils*.

In North America many companies have introduced self-directed teams and have empowered team members to hire, discipline and dismiss employees and to make decisions over how they do their jobs, set targets, and set pay rates. In a number of EU countries works councils involving worker representatives deal with issues such as investment decisions and can use various forms of pressure to achieve outcomes favourable to employees. It is outside the scope of this chapter to examine the wider

HRM in practice 11.1

Report finds partnership equals profit

Partnership with employees, individually and collectively, is being shown to pay dividends

BY JENNIE WALSH People Management, 19 March 1998

Companies that continue to resist any form of employee participation risk losing business advantage, according to a report due to be published by the Involvement and Participation Association.

More than 65 per cent of organisations that allow their workforce full involvement in all business activities, including long-range planning and product development, believe they are gaining a competitive edge.

The study, Benchmarking the Partnership Company, is based on a survey to benchmark key principles at work in firms committed to partnership, and includes case studies from Rover, Remploy, Scottish Power, The John Lewis Partnership and HP Bulmer.

The report concludes that successful partnership operates within a set of mutual commitments and obligations between an organisation and its people. These include commitment to business goals, job security and direct employee participation in training, development and job design.

Although 70 per cent of companies in the survey were unionised, partnership operated in the same organisations on both a representative level (using formal bargaining structures) and through individual participation (such as self-managed teams).

The report's authors, David Guest, professor of occupational psychology at Birkbeck College, and Riccardo Peccei, lecturer in industrial relations at the London School of Economics, admitted to being surprised by the survey results.

> **'By opening the books and involving everyone in the business it is now possible for everyone to see how business decisions impact on us all.'**

'The most striking thing is that partnership pays off,' Guest said. 'Organizations have a better psychological contract, there is greater trust between employees and employers and performance is higher.'

To ensure that these positive results were not simply employer propaganda, the survey cross-matched managers' responses with those of employee representatives – and achieved the same results.

But although employee involvement is clearly beneficial to 'partnership' companies, the practice is not widespread.

'Some organizations still have relatively low trust in their employees and in employee bodies such as trade unions,' Guest said. 'But, according to the evidence, this view is misplaced. Organisations that are prepared to take risks are reaping the benefits.'

According to Guest, the principles of shared obligations that underpin the benchmarks are important in making them an accepted part of the overall culture of the organisation. The most successful examples are companies, such as Rover, where the partnership culture continues to exist despite changes in the leadership of the company and the unions.

Stephen Dunn, head of group HR at Scottish Power, admitted that partnership is not an easy option for companies facing shrinking profits and increased competition. But he believes that partnership arrangements between Scottish Power and its three trade unions has forced all parties to think in new ways and to work for business advantage.

'It is about looking for solutions to things that, in the past, may have led to conflict,' he said. 'By opening the books and involving everyone in the business it is now possible for everyone to see how business decisions impact on us all.'

debate on works councils and worker directors and European-style industrial democracy. Employee involvement, through organizational communication and consultation, is directly pertinent to HRM techniques and has replaced earlier variants, such as worker participation and industrial democracy (Marchington, 1995). Employee involvement through the process of collective bargaining is examined in Chapter 12. Before examining participation techniques in detail, the following section addresses the question, why the enthusiasm for EI?

● A general theory of employee involvement

Management has continually to address two interlinked problems with regard to human resources, control and commitment. Fox (1985) argues that faced with the management problem of securing employee compliance, identification and commitment, management have adopted a range of employment strategies including organizational communication and worker involvement and participation. The current enthusiasm for improved management communication and EI needs to be viewed within the context of a management HRM strategy, the purpose of which is to secure employee support, involvement and commitment to facilitate change, and so ensure the most effective operation of the organization. Organizational cultures are important during times of significant organizational change, as when a firm attempts to introduce business process re-engineering (BPR) and in maintaining an empowered work structure. Management communication shapes and determines the communication experiences employees have and it also plays a part in structuring the official organizational culture. EI is associated with high levels of worker commitment and superior performance. The commitment–performance link is predicated on questionable assumptions; that giving workers more autonomy over work goals, resources, and processes will have a positive effect on worker attitudes, behaviour commitment to the organization's goals, and that the change in behaviour increases motivation and satisfaction and results in enhanced individual and organizational performance. The involvement–commitment cycle is depicted in Figure 11.2, and is the reverse of the vicious circle of control discussed by Clegg and Dunkerley (1980) (see also Huczynski and Buchanan, 1991, pp. 306–9).

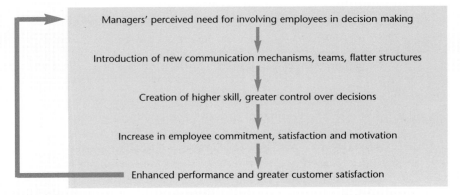

Figure 11.2 The involvement–commitment cycle

The management view of employee involvement is based on a perception of consensus. The British Institute of Management (BIM) assumes, for example, that there is a 'community of interest between employer and employee in furthering the long term prospects of the enterprise'. Consequently the main purpose of employee involvement is to 'achieve a greater commitment of all employees to the definition and attainment of the objectives of the enterprise' (BIM, 1977, p. 1). The CBI puts forward a similar view; 'a company with good relations is more likely to succeed than one where the workforce remains uninformed and uncommitted... [employees] need to be fully informed about their company's opportunities and problems in order to achieve the united effort needed to beat the competition' (ACAS, 1987). The Advisory, Conciliation and Arbitration Service (ACAS) sees employee involvement as a key to improved efficiency; 'if you do involve people and get some sort of identification with the aims of the organization, people feel committed and involved. They will work more effectively and the organization will become more successful and that's in everybody's interests.'

HRM theorists have put forward three main reasons why senior management introduce employee involvement schemes. The first reason is derived from a ethical, political and moral base (Verma, 1995). In a democratic society, workers should be involved in the decision-making process when the outcomes of those decisions impact on their lives. Employee involvement therefore presents a socially acceptable management style. Development of employee communications and involvement will be encouraged because generally companies desire to project 'a socially responsible stance on such issues' (Marchington and Wilding 1983, p. 32). The second reason, championed by Japanese management and the 'model of excellence' school in North America, derives from the utilitarian principle that EI improves quality and productivity. Thus, according to Verma (1995), 'employee participation leads to better outcomes for all parties because it improves productivity and creates more satisfied and energized workers' (p. 288). Employee involvement and participation can improve the quality of a decision and its chances of successful implementation on the factory floor (Marchington, 1982, p. 157).The third justification for introducing employee involvement derives from the perennial managerial problems associated with conflict in an organization (Beer et al., 1984; Guest, 1986). These problems may be inflexibility to change, strikes or absenteeism, and management sees a solution in the introduction of employee involvement (Charlton, 1983, p. 76). According to Beer et al., by introducing worker participation:

> Employers hope that participative mechanisms will create a greater coincidence of interests between employers and employees, thereby increasing trust, reducing the potential for conflict, and increasing the potential for an effective mutual influence process on matters such as pay, employment security, and other working conditions (1984, p. 53).

This view is also captured by Bassett's statement that the 'new' industrial relations has seen a development in trade union leaders' attitudes that rejects the 'idea of the employer as an enemy, the replacement of the class struggle with the struggle for markets' (Bassett, 1987, p. 174). Surveys of British employers have shown that the reasons most frequently cited for the introduction of financial involvement (for example profit-sharing schemes) are to promote worker identification and commitment to the organization (Marchington, 1995). In addition, employee involvement arrangements might be introduced in order to avert union organization. As Beer et al. posit, 'Some companies introduce participative methods at the shopfloor in the hope that a greater congruence of interest will make it less likely that workers will organize' (1984, p. 53). Critics of EI have pointed out that organizational communication and EI might go hand-in-hand to change an organization's culture aimed at undermining existing workplace trade union representatives by promoting 'a direct relationship between the worker and management' (Batstone *et al.*, 1986, p. 117; Legge, 1995), and used as a 'tool' in educating employees 'to reconstitute the individual as a more productive subject' with a view of making workers' behaviour and performance more manageable (Townley, 1994).

Organizational communication

The exchange of information and the transmission of meaning is the very essence of work organizations. Information about the organization – its production, its products and services, its external environment and its people – is essential to management and employees. Communication can be viewed simply as the process by which information is exchanged between a sender and a receiver. However, the organizational communication process is more complicated; complicated by organizational characteristics such as hierarchy, complicated by power relations, and complicated by the fact that individual managers and non-managers have idiosyncrasies, abilities and biases. Organizational communication is central for the other processes of power, leadership, and decision making.

We need to begin with a notion of what is meant by organizational communication. The UK employee and labour relations agency, ACAS, defined organizational communication as 'The systematic provision of information to employees concerning all aspects of their employment and the wider issues relating to the organization in which they work' (1987, p. 3). Organizational communication is a more complex process. Communication has traditionally been defined as 'behaviour'. It has been argued that we 'cannot not communicate' (Watzlawick *et al.*, 1967, p. 49 and quoted by Yuhas Byers, 1997), just as we cannot not behave. According to this perspective, every human act, both conscious and unconscious, contains information that is then interpreted by a receiver. Yuhas Byers (1997), in her book, *Organizational Communication*, brings together three notions associated with communications, behaviour, meaning and context, and defines organizational communications as 'both behaviours and symbols, generated either intentionally or unintentionally, occurring between and among people who assign meaning to them, within an organizational setting' (p. 4).

The role of organizational communication can be seen in studies of managers and their work. American writers have found that managers spend an overwhelming amount of their time in communications. Some writers estimate that 80 per cent of the time of managers is spent on interpersonal communications. In other words, the business of managers is communications. The internal characteristics of an organization affect the centrality of communications. For example, the more the company's manufacturing and human resource management strategies empower people and are ideas-orientated, the more important communications become. Information is transmitted through an organization so that appropriate decisions can be made by the communications system. This section discusses the human resource department's role in managing the communication system. Generally, the size of the organization will affect how sophisticated the communication system is. In small organizations, the system might be informal and subject to frequent management intervention; in large organizations, on the other hand, specialists may serve as employee communications managers. Most organizations use a mixture of formal and informal, *ad hoc* arrangements to communicate to their employees.

Communication scholars have emphasized that to be effective, organizational communication must take place regularly, it must be a two-way process to give employees the opportunity to participate, and it should involve all members of the management team including first line supervisors. Writers on communication have also stressed that:

- communicating is the fundamental process of organizing
- understanding organizational communication provides insights into management strategies
- there should be commitment from senior management to communication
- communication skills are the basis for effective leadership
- management should take the initiative in devising and maintaining the comunication system
- a combination of written and face-to-face channels of communication is best
- messages should be in a form which can be readily understood
- information should be perceived to be relevant to employees
- messages should be consistent with actions
- training in communication skills increases the effectiveness of the system
- the communication system should be monitored and evaluated.

Approaches to organizational communications

When reading organizational communication literature it is important to be alert to the different perspectives that authors and researchers select when dealing with the subject. This section briefly discusses three major perspectives for understanding organizational communication – functionalist, interpretivist, and critical.

Functionalist approach

This approach is the dominant perspective and studies communication as intended or unintended action. The work organization is viewed as an entity, and different communication acts are variables that shape and determine the operations of that entity (Neher, 1997). The functionalist approach views communication as a metaphorical pipeline through which information is transmitted between a sender and receiver. Organizational members thus have three basic methods of transmitting information, as depicted in Figure 11.3. Verbal communication ranges from a casual conversation between two employees to a formal speech by the managing director. In face-to-face meetings the meaning of the information being conveyed by the sender can be expressed through gesture or facial expressions, what is referred to as non-verbal communication. Written communication ranges from a casual note to a co-worker to an annual report. Electronic mail systems and video machines have revolutionized written and verbal communication in organizations. Functionalists categorize behaviours or messages in terms of accomplishing goals and objectives (Neher, 1997).

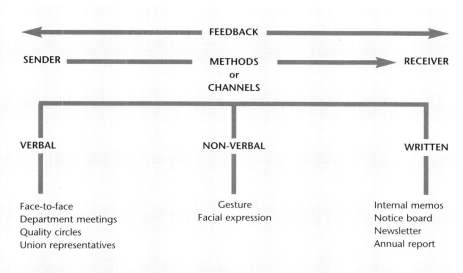

Figure 11.3 Organizational communication as action

Interpretivist approach

The interpretivist approach is a reaction against the functionalist perspective (Neher, 1997). It attempts to understand human communication within the work organization rather than managing the organization. Interpretivists argue that human beings do not behave as predictably as suggested by the functionalist school. Thus, we may be able to predict that most organizational members or some members will react to a certain message in a certain way, but we cannot make the prediction for all members. Some members will do one thing and some another when presented with identical information. Interpretivist scholars argue that because people are so complex in their behaviours and exhibit choice in responding to stimuli, functionalist explanations of organizational behaviour are inappropriate.

Critical approach

The critical approach derives from the critical theory school which seeks to expose the often hidden but pervasive power that post-industrial organizations have over individuals, while also challenging the assumed superiority of unfettered market capitalism. While the functionalist approach is concerned with making the organization more efficient, the critical theorist is more concerned with examining organizational communication, such as myths, metaphors and stories, as a source of power and, moreover, understanding why organizational practices that maintain strong controls over workers are considered legitimate and, hence, not resisted (Eisenberg and Goodall, 1997, p. 156). Organizational communication is thus studied in terms of hidden exercises of power and managerial hegemony. The object of the framework depicted in Figure 11.4 is to help you envision the range of topics and levels of analysis developed in the field of organizational communication.

⬤ Developing a communication system

Communication theorists, adopting a functionalist perspective, have identified a number of challenges which must be taken into account when HR managers try to

---

Figure 11.4 A model of organizational communication

Context

Organizations exist in a context provided by:

- Environment – History (Time) – Ecology
- Culture
- Technology
- Material and economic conditions
- Purposes and goals
- People or members

Shape and Form

These factors largely influence:

- Organizational culture
- Patterns of interaction
- Relationships within the organization
- Networks for organizational communication

Communication within organizations is studied in terms of:

Messages

- Content
- Symbols
- Codes (verbal and nonverbal)

Methods and Modalities of Communication

- Channels
- Media and technologies of communication

Communication Activities

- Organizing, coordinating, or controlling
- Leading or motivating
- Problem solving and decision making
- Conflict managing, negotiating and bargaining
- Influencing organizational change and development

Source: Neher, *Organizational Communication*, 1997

HRM in practice 11.2

Broadmoor primed for its 'domestic works council'

An innovative consultation body may be formed at the top-security hospital – if union resistance can be overcome

BY MIKE THATCHER People Management, 5 February 1994

Broadmoor Special Hospital is set to introduce a consultative committee modelled on European works councils and incorporating non-union representatives.

The high-security psychiatric hospital, which houses around 450 inmates with mental illnesses or personality disorders, intends to invite non-unionised delegates to sit on its joint consultation and negotiating committee (JCNC).

'The idea is to move away from what I consider to be a 1970s industrial relations model to one that is fit for the year 2000,' said Kelvin Cheatle, Broadmoor's director of human resources. 'It is more about working groups, policy development and wider staff consultation.'

More than 300 of the hospital's 1100 employees are not in a union, and they are currently considered to have 'no voice'.

Discussions on the issue are to take place this week when the institution, based in Crowthorne, Berkshire, hosts a conference on industral relations featuring speakers from both sides of the social partnership. Cheatle told *People Management* that he intends to introduce the new structure by the middle of this year. But

trade union resistance seems likely.

At present, representation on the staff side of the committee is divided equally among Broadmoor's six trade unions. The Prison Officers' Association (POA), the strongest union at the hospital, has never been comfortable with this arrangement. It prefers the previous system in which JCNC representation was in proportion to membership levels.

> **More than 300 of the hospital's 1100 employees are not in a union, and they are currently considered to have 'no voice'.**

One option now under consideration is to give the non-unionised staff equal representation on the committee to that of the individual unions. But this proposal is certain to face even stronger opposition from the POA, which represents more than 600 Broadmoor staff.

Brian Caton, the union's assistant general secretary, warned that such an outcome would cause the management to get a 'rocket like they have never had before'.

Caton was scathing about the 'undemocratic' nature of consultation bodies with non-union representatives. 'I would suggest that these people start paying some money and join the POA or another union, rather than taking a free ride on the back of my surf board,' he said.

The other unions are cautious about the move, although they are not as vociferous as the POA. David Cook, regional officer for Unison, said he had 'great reservations', but admitted that the existing model had not worked well over the past year. 'We are concerned that the representative structures have broken down,' he said. 'There has been a lack of unity on the staff side.'

This lack of unity was illustrated last year when managers tried to consult the unions on plans to introduce random searches for employees. According to Cheatle, the staff side could not work together to undertake collective consultation. 'At that time, we had representations from individual employees, who said this was such a fundamental issue that they should be consulted more widely, and that the current consultation arrangement bypassed them.'

devise a communication system that will enable the organization to run more efficiently and productively.

● *Disparate geographical locations*
In large organizations, for example a hospital, university, or an electricity company, there might be multi-sites or plants which create a problem of contact and
consistency in the communication system.

● *Large variety of skill groups*
A large public organization such as a local authority is responsible for different
types of employees – refuse collectors, social workers, environmental officers.
This might mean that there is no commonality of interest and no common corporate objective, which normally binds employees together. Considerable time
and effort may have to be spent on identifying relevant information for each of
the skill groups and in disseminating it to them. This also indicates that there are
challenges in centralizing and coordinating the communication system in such
organizations.

● *Employment arrangements*
The growing tendency to employ part-time workers creates challenges in ensuring
that face-to-face communication takes place with all employees. Added to this is
the fact that certain groups of employees, for example sales representatives, might
spend a large proportion of their time away from their office.

● *Financial constraints*
In a highly cost-conscious business environment, HR managers may face a challenge justifying the cost of practising effective communication, for example an
employee news bulletin. In a study conducted by one of the authors, a respondent
said that 'communications is unfunded and undervalued'.[4]

● Two-way communication

The functionalist literature on organizational communication provides guidance on
what constitutes good practice. It is therefore emphasized that communication can
flow in three directions: downwards, upwards, or horizontally, as depicted in Figure
11.5. Communication that flows from one level of the organization to a lower level is
a downward communication. When we think of managers communicating with subordinates, the downward pattern is the one we usually think of. Upward communication flows to a higher level in the organization. Upward communication keeps
managers aware of how employees feel about their jobs and the organization in general. Communication that flows between employees at the same level in the organization is horizontal communication. This type of communication includes
communication between co-workers in different departments or divisions of the
organization, or between co-workers in the same team. Formal communication follows the organization's chain of command or hierarchy. The organization's informal
communication network, the grapevine, is not based on hierarchy but on social relationships. The grapevine is an important means through which employees fulfill their
need to know about the organization. For example, new employees generally digest
more information about the company informally from their co-workers than from
formal orientation programmes (McShane, 1995).

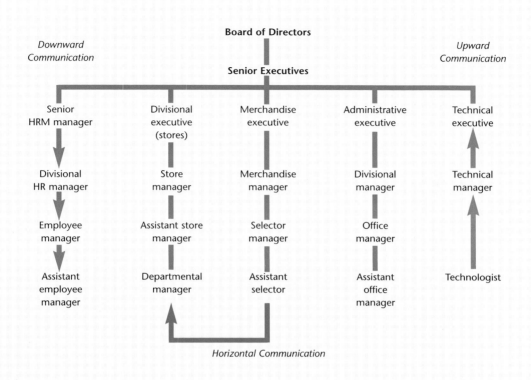

Figure 11.5 Downward, upward and horizontal communication in a retail store

In prescriptive organizational communication texts it is also emphasized that communication is a two-way process, upward and downward communication flows. The most common forms of two-way communication are suggestion schemes, attitude surveys, and employee appraisals. However, the popularity of the two-way concept should not blind us to the fact that the dominant orientation is still downward communication. In addition, two-way communication should not be confused with consultation. The aim of the two-way process is often only to ensure that employees have understood the message and does not necessarily imply that employees' reactions, feelings, and criticisms will have any effect upon the decision-making process. This might be true even where briefing groups, which we discuss below, have been installed. In organizations where there is a commitment to participation there will be other structures and processes whereby employees are involved more directly in decision making. Thus, in reality, communication systems are viewed as an essential prerequisite to genuine employee participation, but often fall short of being a form of it.

The systematic use of the management chain, regular meetings between junior managers and their subordinates, suggestion schemes, newsletters, and opinion surveys were all cited as the channels managers use to communicate with their subordinates (Millward *et al.*, 1992). The most observable change between the 1984 and 1990 large-scale surveys was regular meetings between junior managers and their immediate subordinates, a rough substitute for team briefings, up from 36 per cent to 48 per cent. Other changes included regular newsletters, up from 34 per cent to 41 per cent; surveys or ballots, up from 12 per cent to 17 per cent; and suggestion schemes, up from 25 per cent to 28 per cent. The findings also show great variation in the use of these methods between sectors of the British economy (Table 11.1). Overall in 1990, 90 per cent of workplaces surveyed used one or more of these methods (Millward *et al.*, 1992, p. 166). There was also variation with size of the organization, small organizations being least likely to use any of the specified methods. The CBI's 1986 review of fifteen audits they had conducted shows that 65 per cent of employees responded that they did not agree that 'There is a good two-way communication here and that management talks and listens'. The CBI also reports that 'often excessive reliance is placed on the written word. If this is not reinforced by face-to-face briefing it can be ineffective' (CBI, 1986, p. 425). However, it could be argued that the CBI's report presents a more despondent picture than that prevailing in a majority of organizations, because the organizations on whom they are reporting have probably called in the CBI because a communication problem exists. The lessons to be learnt are clear. There should be a combination of written and face-to-face methods of communication used in an organization and a genuine effort on the part of managers to make the communication two way.

In our 1987 survey of local authorities we asked about the methods they employed to communicate to their workforce. The majority completing the questionnaire used a combination of departmental meetings (86 per cent), union representatives

Table 11.1 Some methods used by managers to communicate with their employees, 1984–90 (percentages)

	All establishments		Private manufacturing		Private services		Public sector	
	1984	1990	1984	1990	1984	1990	1984	1990
1 Regular meetings of workgroups	–	35	–	23	–	33	–	45
2 Regular meetings of junior management	36	48	24	31	34	47	46	62
3 Regular meetings of senior management	34	41	37	38	33	40	33	46
4 Management chain	62	60	58	57	58	58	69	65
5 Suggestion scheme	25	28	15	14	25	31	31	31
6 Regular newsletters	34	41	24	22	33	44	41	52
7 Surveys or ballots	12	17	10	7	11	17	14	24
Other methods	8	13	8	11	8	13	8	16
None of these	12	9	17	14	15	11	7	4

Source: Adapted from Millward *et al.*, 1992, p. 167

(86 per cent), and written methods – internal memos/circulars (100 per cent), and notice boards (95 per cent). Two authorities reported that they had 'no regular planned method' of communication. Again, the channels by which information was communicated to employees tended to vary according to the size of the authority. The use of departmental meetings and briefing groups tended to be more prevalent in authorities employing fewer than 2000 employees. Authorities with 30 000 plus employees tended to use trade union representatives, internal memos and notice boards.

Briefing groups

Briefing groups are considered an effective way of passing information downward and upward through the hierarchy – that is, of increasing the two-way communication flow. A briefing group is a group of employees who are called together regularly and consistently in order that decisions and policies, and the reasons for them, may be explained to other employees. Those briefed communicate in turn to their own briefing group so that information is systematically passed down the management line. Briefing groups are designed to convey understanding of the information to organizational members through face-to-face communication.

Another important aspect of briefing groups is that the system supports and develops the leadership role of management. As Perkins states 'Briefing groups reduce the oft-stated problem of union representatives becoming the source of information because the system relies on regular briefing of supervisory staff and them taking on the role of work-group communicators' (1986, p. 32). Opposition from trade unions to team briefing stems from the perceived threat to the shop stewards' traditional leadership role within the organization. A team briefing is seen by the unions as an attempt to bypass established consultative and negotiating procedures. In North America team briefing has been used as part of a union-avoidance strategy (see Chapter 12). If an organization does decide to adopt team briefing, support from top management is essential. Further, to be effective, team leaders need to be trained; they need to be aware of the objectives of the system and learn how to run briefing sessions. Survey findings seem to indicate that team briefings are the most popular EI activity in Britain in the early 1990s (Marchington, 1995).

Monitoring the communication system

Monitoring is essential for maintaining and improving the effectiveness of the communication system. However, the monitoring of communication effectiveness is not well developed in most organizations. A survey of local government authorities found that the overwhelming majority, 95 per cent, of the respondents did not monitor. And, the one authority that did employ monitoring methods employed fewer than 400 people.[6] The joint ACAS, CBI and TUC survey of communication also found that 50 per cent of their respondents did not monitor the effectiveness of their communication system. They further added that 'the availability of management resources and associated costs appeared to be the critical factor in determining whether or not any evaluation of the communication process between management and the workforce was carried out'.[7]

It is recommended that clear objectives must be established and reasonable measures of them developed. Measures of communication effectiveness might include:

- the extent of employee cooperation
- information on employee perceptions of the employee–management climate, collected by an organizational survey
- absence and labour turnover levels.

This information is valuable only if there is some basis of comparison. Therefore, the data must be broken down by employee constituency, by factory or site, or by a time period. Comparing information enables the HR manager to identify where objectives have been achieved and where they have not. It also indicates where to look for the causes of problems in the achievement of communication objectives.

Information disclosed by management

Through the various communication activities, what type of information is communicated? The two issues that are the subject of most communication are terms and conditions of employment and major changes in working methods or work organization, while investment plans were the least commonly reported. In 1984, managers in organizations with recognized unions reported giving more information on all topics than the managers in organizations without recognized trade unions (Millward and Stevens, 1986, p. 155). In this author's survey of local authorities, respondents reported that information disclosed to the workforce is largely limited to health and safety and internal vacancies. With the exception of internal vacancies and promotions, manual employees tended to receive more information than their colleagues in the non-manual areas (Bratton and Sinclair, 1987).

The sort of information disseminated by management is shown in Table 11.2. Overall, the findings reveal that information relating to wage costs and training are most frequently disclosed by management. Another interesting finding is that UK-owned establishments are less likely than their foreign-owned counterparts to disclose information to their employees; around 50 per cent of UK-owned establishments gave their workforce information on at least one of the items listed in Table 11.2, compared with 60 per cent of foreign-owned establishments.

The extent of organizational communication

As previously mentioned, the evidence from UK national survey investigations suggests an increase in the extent of organizational or workplace communication during the 1980s (Daniel and Millward, 1983; Batstone, 1984; Millward and Stevens, 1986; Millward et al., 1992). In 1980, Daniel and Millward asked both management and union representatives to assess the amount of information given on three broad areas, pay and conditions of service, human resource requirements, and the financial position of the organization. Trade union representatives were also asked how useful they found the information received from management in negotiations. Managers assessed rather differently the amount of information they gave on the three broad areas. Pay and conditions of employment were the subject of more communication, while the financial position of the company was the subject of least communication. Managers tended to assess the information they gave more highly than the union representatives assessed the information they received (Daniel and Millward, 1983, p. 148).

Table 11.2 Information given to employees or their representatives, by ownership in the private sector, 1990 (percentages)

	All establishments	UK-owned establishments	Foreign-owned establishments
Wage costs	25	27	36
Training received	25	23	28
Accidents	25	21	31
Employee sickness/absenteeism	24	23	29
Labour productivity	20	21	32
Occupational health	18	17	21
Skills/qualifications	15	15	8
Number of resignations	14	11	7
Gender mix	11	7	2
Ethnic mix	10	5	2
None of the above	44	48	36

Source: Adapted from Millward *et al.*, 1992, p. 174

However, for both managers and union representatives there was a general tendency for the information given to be assessed more highly in larger establishments.

Since the early 1980s, Batstone argues, as part of a 'logical development' many companies facing intense competitive pressures not only have attempted to draw upon their employees' skills and knowledge more fully, but also have disclosed more information to employees to highlight the organization's problems and to enlist their cooperation in overcoming them (Batstone, 1984, p. 261). In a study of communication in local authorities in the north of England, it was reported that communication tended to be 'good' in the smaller authorities, employing fewer than 2000 employees. About 29 per cent of the local authorities falling in the 'below 500' category reported communication was 'good'. In contrast, only one authority with over 20 000 employees reported communication was 'good' (Bratton and Sinclair, 1987, p. 12). The implication is that size is a factor affecting the success of communication between management and their subordinates. The 1982 Employment Act which required certain companies to include a statement in the annual report describing the action taken during the year to introduce, maintain or develop employee involvement has had no impact on communication in the local authorities surveyed.

In 1990, Millward and his research team probed for evidence of mechanisms managers had introduced for involving employees or their representatives in the activities of their workplaces. Overall, the findings show that more methods of communication were being used simultaneously in 1990 than in 1984. Over the period 1984 to 1990, the average number of methods used by management to communicate with or consult employees was up from 2.0 to 2.4 (1992, p. 168). In the case of employee involvement, the findings show a substantial increase in initiatives to raise employee involvement, up from 35 per cent to 45 per cent (1992, p. 176).

● Joint consultation

Let us turn to another dimension of EI, consultation. In its simplest form consultation in the workplace may take the form of an informal exchange of views between a group of employees and their manager on an incoming piece of machinery or a reorganization of the office. However, where the size of the organization makes access for employees to management problematic, then more formal structures need to be created. Joint consultation has been defined as:

> Involving employees through their representatives in discussion and consideration of relevant matters which affect or concern those they represent, thereby allowing employees to influence the proposals *before* [our emphasis] the final management decision is made (IPM, 1981).

Joint consultation, on the other hand, differs from collective bargaining, or joint regulation, because the latter utilizes the processes of negotiation and agreement between representatives of management and employees. We can develop the difference between joint consultation and joint regulation further. The difference between joint consultation and collective bargaining appears to rest on the notion that both conflict and a common interest are inherent elements of the employment relationship that need to be handled in different ways. Consultation may be viewed as a means of promoting action when there are no obvious conflicts of interest, whereas joint regulation or collective bargaining is a means of reconciling divergent interests. However, Salamon believes that every aspect of the employment relationship has the potential for conflict. The distinction between the two approaches to participation is concerned with the 'formal identification of those aspects of the employment relationship in which this conflict should be legitimized and subject to joint agreement by inclusion within the process of collective bargaining' (Salamon, 1987, p. 259). The balance between joint consultation and joint regulation will depend upon the extent and power of workplace trade organization. Daniel and Millward (1983) found that the existence of Joint Consultative Committees (JCCs) is closely allied to workplace trade unionism; 'consultative committees may tend to become an adjunct to the institutes of collective bargaining where workplace trade union organization is well established, but provide an alternative channel of representation where it is weak' (Daniel and Millward, 1983, p. 135). In 1990, management appeared to be less enthusiastic about joint consultation (Millward *et al.*, 1992).

Models of consultation

Researchers have put forward two different models of consultation. A 'revitalization' model suggests that recent support for consultation has coincided with the increased use of direct employee involvement approaches by employers. This, a number of writers have argued, has the effect, whether planned or not, of undermining collective bargaining and consequently weakening workplace trade unionism (Batstone, 1984; Edwards, 1985). In contrast, the 'marginality' model put forward by some authors suggests that the early 1980s witnessed an increased trivialization and marginalization of joint consultation, particularly in organizations confronted by deteriorating economic conditions (MacInnes, 1987; Cressey *et al.*, 1985).

These two models, revitalization and marginality, have been critically evaluated by Marchington (1987). The models of consultation, argues Marchington, do not describe the full range of processes that may take place in the consultative arena. A third model, the 'complementary' model, is proposed, in which joint consultation complements rather than competes with joint regulation or collective bargaining. According to Marchington 'consultation acts as an adjunct to the bargaining machinery' (1987, p. 340). With this model, collective bargaining is used to determine pay and conditions of employment, whereas joint consultation focuses on issues of an integrative nature and helps to lubricate employment relationships; both processes can provide benefits for employees and the organization.

Evidence has been collected from a number of surveys about the extent of joint consultation since the early 1970s (Brown, 1981; Millward and Stevens, 1986; ACAS, 1987; Millward et al., 1992). The majority of the writers are agreed that there has been an increase in the extent of consultation since the early 1970s. Brown (1981), in a survey of manufacturing industry, found that 25 per cent of managers said that their establishments had taken initiatives, between 1975 and 1978, to increase employee involvement. This trend seems to have continued until the mid-1980s. In 1983, Daniel and Millward reported a substantial growth in consultative committees. Establishment size and ownership appeared to be the main characteristics associated with the presence of consultative committees, suggested the researchers. In establishments employing more than 1000 employees, 71 per cent of the managers reported the existence of a consultative committee. In establishments employing fewer than 100 employees the figure was 25 per cent. Further, committees were more likely to occur in the public sector; almost 46 per cent of public sector establishments had them, compared with 33 per cent of private sector establishments (Daniel and Millward, 1983, pp. 130–1). Batstone's survey found that 47 per cent of manufacturing companies reported a policy of increasing employee involvement (1984, p. 263). More specifically, managers in 45 per cent of the establishments said that the shop stewards had become more involved in consultative committees. There was a marked increase in the number of organizations using 'direct' EI strategies: quality circles, autonomous work groups and briefing groups. Such techniques were used in an attempt to secure cooperation for difficult changes (Batstone, 1984, p. 271).

It was also found that overall, between 1980 and 1984, the proportion of workplaces with a joint consultative committee remained constant at 34 per cent (Millward and Stevens, 1986, p. 138). In private manufacturing, the proportion of establishments with a JCC decreased from 36 per cent to 30 per cent. Significantly, there appeared to be a relationship between the existence of JCCs and the financial performance of private sector establishments. 'Establishments that were doing better than their competitors were more likely to have joint consultative committees' (Millward and Stevens, 1986, p. 141). The authorities suggest that such a change could indicate a propensity on the part of management to 'experiment with the appropriate forms of employee involvement for their circumstance' (p. 141). Support for Marchington's complementary model, that is, joint consultation operating alongside collective bargaining machinery, was provided by Daniel and Millward (1983) and Millward and Stevens (1986). The 1984 survey found that 'complex consultative structures co-exist with complex collective bargaining arrangements in the public sector in particular' (Millward and Stevens, 1986, p. 143).

By 1990, the situation had changed. The number of establishments reporting the existence of joint consultative committees was down, from 34 per cent in 1984 to 29 per cent in 1990. The picture in the late 1980s across broad sectors of the economy is given in Table 11.3. The reduction in the incidence of JCCs is explained by the changing composition of the establishments, the number of larger, more unionized workplaces, rather than management abandoning the JCC model. The finding is significant, argues Sisson, because, given the antipathy towards trade unions throughout the 1980s, British management might have been expected to substitute joint consultation for joint regulation (1993, pp. 203–4).

As regards the types of activity and the issues dealt with, all three surveys by the Millward team have highlighted that where consultative machinery and collective bargaining machinery exist together there is overlap between consultation and bargaining or joint regulation arrangements (1992, p. 157). The separation of joint consultation from collective bargaining is often attempted by simply excluding from the latter's agenda any item that is normally the subject of joint regulation. Inevitably this means that if the scope of collective bargaining expands, then the scope of joint consultation will reduce. The result can be the creation of the 'canteen, car park, toilet paper syndrome'. This has prompted some observers to characterize the subject matter of JCCs as a 'diet of anodyne trivia and old hat' (MacInnes, 1987, pp. 103–4). However, Millward *et al.* found that in 1990 in manufacturing, production matters were most frequently mentioned, by 18 per cent of respondents, as the most important item to discuss. This was followed by employment issues (12 per cent) and government legislation or regulations (9 per cent) as the third most important issue (1992, pp. 157–8).

Since 1985, a European Commission directive has required large companies, those with 1000 or more employees, to create European works councils. The 1998 WERA study reported on this development. The authors found that 19 per cent of multinational companies surveyed operated a European works council and that some 67 per cent of employees surveyed are in workplaces where some joint consultative arrangement exists. Details of how these joint consultative committees are related to workplace and organization size are shown in Table 11.4.

A study of the extent of EI activities in Canadian private sector establishments reported that 43 per cent of the 714 Canadian establishments surveyed had some

Table 11.3 Extent of JCCs by sector, 1984–90 (percentages)

	All establishments		Private manufacturing		Private services		Public sector	
	1984	1990	1984	1990	1984	1990	1984	1990
Consultative committee currently exists	34	29	30	23	24	19	48	49
Workplace consultative committee or higher-level committee with local representatives	41	35	33	25	28	25	62	59

Source: Adapted from Millward *et al.*, 1992, p. 152

Table 11.4 Extent of JCCs by workplace and organization size, 1998

	No committees	Workplace committee only	Workplace and higher level	Higher level committee only
	% of workplaces	% of workplaces	% of workplaces	% of workplaces
Workplace size				
25 to 49 employees	52	11	8	29
50 to 99 employees	47	20	10	23
100 to 199 employees	38	27	14	21
200 to 499 employees	28	28	28	16
500 or more employees	22	43	23	11
Organization size				
Less than 100 employees	80	16	0	4
100 to 999 employees	57	31	4	8
1000 to 9999 employees	31	17	14	38
10 000 or more employees	20	11	23	45
All workplaces	46	17	11	25

Base: all workplaces with 25 or more employees
Figures are weighted and based on responses from 1890 managers

Source: Adapted from Cully et al., 1998, p. 12

form of employee involvement. The 1993 Human Resource Practices Survey (HRPS) was limited to four industrial sectors – wood products, fabricated metal products, electrical and electronic products, and business services – and although EI was only found in a minority of Canadian workplaces, 'its practice has established a foothold in many organizations' (Verma, 1995, p. 286).

In UK local government it has been recognized that since the participants involved in the consultative and negotiating machinery could well be the same individuals, JCCs may sometimes discuss substantive issues that would normally be negotiable (Perkins, 1986, p. 41). In the survey conducted by Bratton and Sinclair, almost all (95 per cent) of the local authorities responding to the questionnaire confirmed that it was their practice to consult with trade union representatives and provide JCCs.

The 1990 survey shows that the proportion of workplaces in the public sector reporting JCCs increased slightly, up from 48 per cent in 1984 to 49 per cent in 1990 (Millward et al., 1992).

The structure and operation of joint consultative committees

When choosing a joint consultative structure, or developing an existing one, it is necessary for an organization to make a number of decisions guided by its aims, philosophy and strategy. Joint consultation is based on a high-trust relationship and requires sound and regular information to be communicated to all participating parties (see above). An organization has to decide how much information will be disclosed, by whom and how. Generally, management's role in a consultative structure is to communicate information and be fully involved in the process, otherwise, decisions may be made or agreed upon without their knowledge or support. However, Perkins points out that managements must also be 'involved in their role as employees in the sense that management employees, if they have a duty to consult, also have a right to be consulted with' (1986, p. 48). Finally, the organization will have to have regard to its size and the nature of collective bargaining. Management may adopt either of two broad approaches. It can combine the two processes of consultation and negotiation within the collective bargaining machinery. Alternatively, it can maintain a separate machinery of joint consultation and regulation and simultaneously expand the scope of employee involvement through the joint consultative machinery, without the need formally to concede that these issues are subject to joint determination (Salamon, 1987).

Three main reasons have been identified for the integration of consultative and negotiating machinery within the organization. First, communicating, consulting and negotiating are integrally linked together in the handling of employee relations. Second, trade union representatives need to be fully involved in the consultative process, if only as a prelude to negotiations. Third, as the scope of collective bargaining expands the issues left are otherwise allocated to what may be viewed as an irrelevant process. Substantive reasons have also been cited for establishing formal joint consultative machinery alongside established collective bargaining structures. First, it may help to overcome organizational complexity which tends to hinder the operation of informed means of consultation. Second, the concept of collective bargaining as dealing with substantive or procedural matters, while consultation is concerned with joint discussion of matters of common interest, forces the two structures apart. Third, regular JCC meetings and the publication of minutes ensure that joint consultation is accorded a proper place in the organizational system and confirms management's commitment and responsibility to consultation with its employees. When there are two sets of arrangements, the terms of reference of the JCC need to be specified by defining both its subject matter and the nature of its authority. An example of joint consultation and collective bargaining structure in the public sector is shown in Figure 11.6.

The subject matter may be defined:

1. by excluding from its deliberation anything which is subject to joint regulation, that is, substantive and procedural matters; or
2. by enumerating the items that are to be regarded as matters for joint consultation (for example, a corporate plan, human resource trends, education and training); or
3. on an *ad hoc* basis, whether or not an issue should be dealt with in the joint regulation machinery.

This method can be used only when union representatives are formally included in the JCC and are able to ensure that there is no management abuse of this privilege (Salamon, 1987).

In the public sector, while joint consultation and regulation machinery usually function separately, it is recognized that at lower levels of the consultative machinery substantive issues may be discussed. The main problem is that unless a consultative procedure allows for an element of negotiation, it may become irrelevant and wither (Perkins, 1986). To ensure the JCC's relevance and survival, management may need to be flexible when interpreting the terms of reference. Finally, when formulating a consultative structure, senior management have to decide the level of authority to be vested in the JCC. In this respect, the JCC may be either purely advisory to manage-

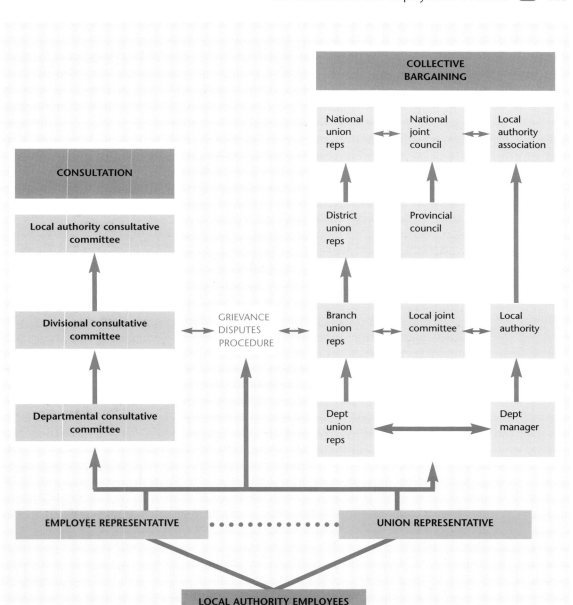

Figure 11.6 Example of joint consultation and collective bargaining in local government

ments' decision making or it may have, in effect, a delegated decision. Evidence reveals that the work of the JCCs is usually conducted on a fairly formal basis, with an elected or rotating chair and published minutes. Generally, employee representation on the JCCs in the public sector is union appointed, but it would appear that 'the closer the procedure is to the grass roots the more realistic is individual (employee) representation' (Perkins, 1986, p. 46).

On the question of dealing with multi-unionism, the approach varies from one organization to another. Some organizations aim to bring together all the unions for consultation although they are treated separately for collective bargaining purposes. In local government the division of the consultative machinery for staff, manual, and craft employees is prevalent. This may be appropriate in a highly diffuse organization like local government, where the work of the various departments can be quite distinct, but it does not avoid the possible problems of multi-unionism.

The effects of employment involvement on performance

Since the 1940s, numerous studies have been conducted to quantify the effects of EI techniques on individual and organizational performance. Although a majority of studies do show a positive effect, the effects tend to be modest and some writers remain sceptical. Kelly and Kelly (1991), for example, question whether the techniques associated with the 'new industrial relations' have made much impact on 'them and us' attitudes in industry. Guest *et al.* (1993) also support this view, arguing that the meaning of worker commitment is open to question. Marchington *et al.*'s (1992) survey took a more sanguine view and suggested that EI has 'a mildly favourable' impact on worker attitudes. The majority of EI schemes in British organizations tend to be 'passive', and constitute little more than 'listening to information' and not surprisingly, perhaps, the impact of EI upon workers has been 'marginal' (Marchington, 1995). Research on employee participation in local government in the north of England (Bratton and Sinclair, 1987) attempted to assess the value management placed on employee involvement. The large majority of local authorities responding to our questionnaire acknowledged that employee participation and consultation had an important contribution to make in improving the quality of the services and on performance and industrial relations. Verma (1995) summarized the results of over fifty research studies on EI and found that 'While a majority of studies do show a positive impact, the effects frequently vary, and a number of studies have found no effects' (p. 291). As we discussed in Chapter 2, there are major methodological challenges in measuring the precise EI–organizational performance link.

Obstacles to employee involvement

A number of impediments to the introduction of EI have been identified in the literature. One we have already discussed, divorcing consultation from collective bargaining. Two other major obstacles have been recognized; the attitude of trade unions, and the attitude of management to the consultative procedure.

Trade union attitudes

Traditionally, trade unions have distrusted consultation procedures as a management strategy for incorporating union representatives into management forms of control or undermining collective bargaining and hence trade union power (Clarke, 1977). As two trade union researchers state 'Joint consultation came to be seen as at best an inadequate expedient, at worst a positive menace, preventing unions from defending their members as resolutely as they might' (Coates and Topham 1980, p. 238).

HRM in practice 11.3

The key to staff commitment

Personnel Management Plus, June 1993

Swamping staff with videos, posters and brochures may seem like an efficient way to get management messages across, but according to new research, it is not slick graphics but a sense of involvement and influence that creates commitment.

The 'Employment in Britain' study, which surveyed 5000 people last year, points to relatively inexpensive means employers can use to make jobs more attractive and engender greater loyalty without altering pay.

The survey is the most comprehensive national study of employee attitudes undertaken in the last decade.

The study aimed to provide a portrait of workers' priorities, motivations and their attachment to work in general.

The report found that money and job security were important but that real influence over the way work was done and over the organisation as a whole was highly valued by employees – and, conversely, was a source of frustration when absent.

IMP director of professional policy John Stevens sees the report as highlighting the importance of participation. 'At one time we tended to treat many people in the workforce as semi-detached from the organisation. Competitive pressure, decentralisation and awareness of the need to develop skills, have merged

what people want out of work and what employees want out of people. Some industries have been quicker.'

The study concludes: 'The most powerful influence over a worker's perception of the general quality of management/employee relations was the degree of participation allowed to employees over decisions involving changes in work organisation.'

> **Swamping staff with videos, posters and brochures may seem like an efficient way to get management messages across, but according to new research, it is not slick graphics but a sense of involvement and influence that creates commitment.**

Where people felt their influence was high, 47 per cent said relations with management was very good, but where it was seen to be low, only 17 per cent felt that things were going so well.

Very few employers were adopting a participative approach to gaining commitment. Quality circles were shown to have a significant effect. Around 78 per cent of those who took part in such activities thought that these had a great deal or a fair amount of influence on deci-

sions about work practices. 'The most striking feature of our data is just how rare it is for employees to be involved in this kind of decision.' Only 20 per cent of respondents took part in such initiatives.

The research confirmed the view that pay is not the sole component of motivation and that involvement and a sense of personal development play a vital role.

Good training

Respondents viewed promotion as less important than training: only 11 per cent rated good promotion prospects as 'essential', compared with 27 per cent who felt that good training provision was imperative. The value placed on training was exceeded only by factors such as job security, 'work you like doing' and good relations with a manager.

Meeting aspirations

Examining motivation in its most basic form, the research investigated employees' reasons for working and their commitment to full-time jobs.

Although many claim to cherish a fantasy of winning the pools and giving up work, the study found that most people would work even if there were no financial imperative to do so. Almost 70 per cent said they would prefer to have a job even if there were no financial necessity.

Quality standards

The study examined what influenced their quality standards. Pay incentives were thought to be an important influence on quality standards by fewer than one in 10.

The study says these findings confirm many current personnel practices. 'This analysis reinforces the importance... of developing "responsible workers"', especially where raising quality standards is a central aim.

Highest-rated jobs

The most satisfying jobs were those involving people, and least satisfying were assembly-line positions. Jobs involving caring for people scored highest. The report says: 'The higher the level of social skills required by the job, the greater people's satisfaction with their work.'

The other key factor in job satisfaction was age. The least satisfied employees were those between 25 and 34, but after 35 satisfaction was greater with each age group. Women were slightly more satisfied than men at all ages until the 55-plus age group, where women were far more satisfied than their male counterparts.

The workforce of Britain does not want an easy working life, but it does want more control over that life.

One industrial relations theorist has asserted that 'increasing the involvement only of employees... appears to be part of a strategy aimed at reducing the role and influence of stewards' (Batstone, 1984, pp. 264–5). This perception of joint consultation is revealed in case study investigations. In one case, objections to the joint consultative structure from shop stewards were based on the investment and significance that management at the company attributed to the JCC. This support, the union representatives argued, 'undermined the position of the union' (Bate and Murphy, 1981, p. 395). In the case of a participative management experiment in the DHSS, the principal reason given by the union representing the junior grades for boycotting the new machinery was that it resulted in non-management grades becoming implicated in management decision making and it 'blurred' the union's traditional role in representing staff interests (Charlton, 1983, p. 74).

In another study, union representatives forcefully expressed concern that joint consultative procedures might be used by management to circumvent traditional collective bargaining machinery. Some of their comments on this point are interesting:

> A system which would undermine trade unions is one where, say, a section of staff actually nominated a member of staff to make comments on their behalf. That would clearly be parallel with the steward's role... Some sort of Works Council where a sweetheart system was set up in parallel and which would address people's concerns.[8]

The union representatives, however, believed that 'participative management is good management' and supported greater workforce involvement, but with the caveat that the traditional role of the steward should not be marginalized. Consultative procedures are more likely to succeed if managers are aware of the fears and potential problems that may confront union representatives sitting on participative bodies. It would be counterproductive for an organization committed to greater employee participation if workplace union representatives were resentful of a perceived managerial intention to alienate them (Marchington, 1982).

The potential problems confronting workplace union representatives include role conflict, loss of contact with membership, and lack of knowledge and expertise, for instance, on interpreting company accounts. When the shop steward is confronted by divergent role expectations, the result is role conflict. It may happen when a steward finds that compliance with one role requirement (for example, representing members at a grievance hearing) may make more difficult the compliance with another (for example, participation in a team examining changes in the organization). Human resource managers can help the union representatives overcome these problems by ensuring that they are given the necessary facilities to keep the channels open between the union and its constituents. For example, in one organization it was found that the stewards were consistently keener on more involvement in the organization of the company than were their constituents and, providing the union representatives did not neglect the 'protective' aspects of their responsibilities, the stewards were free to become more involved in the decision-making process (Marchington, 1980, p. 34).

Management attitudes

The other major obstacle to consultation is managerial beliefs and ways of thinking. Managers seek to construct an organizational culture that reflects their ideologies and styles of management and which will reinforce their strategies and control (Gospel and Palmer, 1993). Therefore, it is perhaps not surprising to find evidence that the major obstacle to EI is resistance to change by middle and junior management (see, for example, Marchington, 1980; West, 1980). EI, by its very nature, might be expected to pose a threat to the more autocratic manager. It is, argues Rendall, 'the unspoken refusal of a hard core of managers and supervisors to implement change that prevents companies from evolving from authoritarian to participative' (1986, p. 42).

What is clearly apparent in the debate is that EI activities are a critical component of the 'soft' HRM philosophy. Employee involvement is characterized by a high-trust employment relationship and a more open style of management, one of operating by consent rather than coercion. However, evidence suggests that many managers tend to resist participation because 'it's contrary to their habit-formed ways of thinking and behaving' (Rendall, 1986, p. 42). Further, to re-engineer the organization involves EI, as we discussed in Chapter 4, and requires managers to 'let go' (Champy, 1996). As is the case with all human resource management policies, the effective implementation of EI necessitates management commitment from top to junior level. If key decision makers in the organization are not fully committed to participation there is a tendency for joint meetings to be 'squeezed out' because of pressure of work. As one industrial relations commentator put it:

> Time is probably a big problem, time and pressure of work... making time to do it... that's why most things go by the board because everybody is busy... Also, it's not just a question of going into meetings... need to prepare the brief, think about what you are going to say... it's as much time again.[9]

What is apparent from a survey of the empirical evidence is that the attitudinal aspects of EI are much more crucial than the mechanics of the various structural configurations of the employee involvement schemes. Provided organizations are aware of these attitudinal problems among managers, they may be ameliorated through training, not just in conventional communication skills, but in the process and dynamics of living with employee involvement.

Chapter summary

Communicating is the fundamental process of organizing and leading in the workplace. Organizational communication channels include written, verbal, and non-verbal, each of which has several methods of transmitting information. Communication flows downwards, upwards, and horizontally in organizations. From a functionalist perspective, the role of the human resource management department is to ensure that there are no deviations or blockages in that flow that can cause communication problems. The fewer obstacles that occur in communication, the more that goals, feedback, and other management messages to employees will be received as they were intended. Organizational communications can also be interpreted as a strategy to build a strong corporate culture in order to exert more control over the workforce.

Employee involvement occurs when employees take an active role in the decision-making process in the organization. EI may be formal or informal, direct or indirect, and voluntary or legislated; it may range from a manager exchanging information with an employee or an employee representative on a specific issue, to complete participation in a major investment decision. Greater participation has been identified with the 'soft' HRM model, business process re-engineering, and changes in job design, such as self-managed teams. The terms 'employee participation', 'employee involvement' and 'employee empowerment' have different meanings. Therefore, differing expectations among employees and union representatives tend to affect the attitudes of the key players in the industrial relations system, the propensity to participate, and ultimately the success of any experiments in EI. Hence, a vital first step, if there is to be any meeting of minds, is to create a common language and conceptual framework. Recent studies indicate that British managements, to secure employee support and commitment, are adopting HRM-type techniques. Other studies, however, also provide evidence of deep scepticism and concern among commentators and practitioners that EI and joint consultative procedures might be used by managers to circumvent established collective bargaining machinery, marginalize the role of the workplace union representative and strengthen 'individualism' in the management of the employment relationship. Organizational communication and EI innovations are more likely to succeed if management is aware of the concerns and potential problems confronting union representatives.

Key concepts

Organizational communication	Non-verbal communication
Grapevine	Empowerment
Functionalist approach	Interpretivist approach
Participation	Involvement
Briefing groups	Joint consultation

Discussion questions

1. Describe the communication process, identifying its key components. Give an example of how this process operates with written, verbal and non-verbal messages.

2. Discuss a situation in which you learned some new information from the grapevine and took action on the basis of that information.

3. Identify and discuss different schemes that the HR department manages in order to improve organizational communications.

4. 'EI is a central component of human resource management philosophy.' Do you agree or disagree? Discuss.

5. Explain the difference between joint consultation and collective bargaining.

6. In what ways might employee participation improve decision making in organizations?

Further reading

Marchington, M. (1995) Involvement and participation. In Storey, J. (ed.) *Human Resource Management: A Critical Text*, Routledge: London.

Neher, W. (1997) *Organizational Communication*, Boston: Allyn & Bacon.

Perkins, G. (1986) *Employee Communications in the Public Sector*, London: IPM.

Townley, B. (1989) Employee communication programmes. In Sisson, K. (ed.) *Personnel Management in Britain*, Oxford: Blackwell.

Verma, A. (1995) Employee involvement in the workplace. In Gunderson M. and Ponak A. (eds) *Union-Management Relations in Canada*, 3rd edn, Ontario: Addison-Wesley.

Chapter case study

Communications at Forrest Computer Services

In this age of flatter management structures, Forrest Computer Services (FCS) must have one of the flattest. Last year it reduced its management hierarchy almost to pancake proportions when it introduced self-managed teams and abolished all but the most senior management jobs.

Forrest Computer Services has a business team of fourteen senior managers reporting to the three people who make up the board. Below that are a host of manager-less client teams with about fifteen members each and operating as separate commercial units.

Teams have to be able to provide a full client support service and draw on all the technical, financial and administrative skills which that requires. Within this framework employees can decide who they want to team up with and teams can elect whether or not they want a leader. Those that have opted for a team leader have not necessarily chosen the person most senior under the older organization. It was a radical reorganization brought about by necessity. The decision followed a massive deficit of £2 million on a turnover of £26.5 million in 1989. It shocked the company which had been growing steadily. Initially it meant slashing costs and therefore staff, so the workforce shrank from 750 to fewer than 500 employees.

But FCS senior management knew they had to do more than cut costs; they had to improve productivity and competitiveness if the company was to stay in an ever-tightening market. 'We introduced self-managed teams to build up our client service because that is where we must have the edge', said Forrest's human resource director, Carolyn Oliver. 'Every software house can provide the software and systems the clients want: it is the efficiency with which the client is handled that makes the difference and that comes down to the way we are organized,' she said.

Reorganization put a tremendous burden on the human resource department, the way it had to work and the communication system. On top of the reorganization, working practices were completed reassessed – recruitment processes, reward strategies, training and development, and employee participation. On the one hand, it created a free-flowing organization with the flexibility and motivation to react to changes in the market. On the other hand, it bolstered the need for watertight human resource systems to keep this motivated mass from running out of control. Oliver said that the implementation of the plan proved a massive employee participation exercise. In the early weeks there was much misleading and irrelevant information being communicated through the grapevine.

'Top management wanted the ideas to come from the shop floor. So we brought together twenty people from all levels of the organization bar the most senior, put them into two teams and sent them away for the weekend to thrash out their own ideas of how the company should be organized,' explained Carolyn Oliver. However, this was only the beginning of the consultation process. The next step involved the setting up of employee task forces to look at the different issues which a reorganization implied. FCS's senior managers disseminated information from the two working parties around the company and asked people to apply for one of the seventy places available on the ten task forces. About two hundred people applied from the spectrum of jobs and locations in the company.

Six weeks later the task forces presented their findings to the board. 'They ranged from one extremity to the other. Some liked the way things were and simply wanted to stay put. Others wanted to do away with all senior managers right to the top,' remarked Oliver. Forrest opted for something in the middle – a senior business team with many client teams reporting in. The human resource department had to make the system work. Carolyn Oliver admits frankly that she underestimated the reaction of managers to their sudden loss of power. 'They felt threatened and that their services would no longer be required by the company,' she said. 'It was a "hard slog" convincing them that the new-style FCS was for them too,' Oliver said. 'You cannot reassure managers by writing to them or making promises in a company newsletter,' she went on to explain.

As all the teams are essentially operating in the same computer services market there was a danger that they would all end up competing against each other, instead of against company competitors. Oliver admitted there has to be a tight coordination of client service teams, close control of the standards they work to, and effective organizational communication. Introducing multiskilled, self-managed teams also threw up demands from employees for a more permanent system of employee participation in the company.

(Source: Adapted from an article by L. Carrington, 'Working as a team member', in *Personnel Today*, January 1991.)

Questions

1. What methods could the company have adopted to convince the managers that they had a future at Forrest Computer Services?

2. Should managers try to eliminate the organizational grapevine?

3. Discuss the alternative channels of communication that FCS could have used to disseminate information from the first two working parties to employees.

4. What recommendations would you make for establishing a permanent system of employee participation at FCS? Justify your case.

Notes

1. Cell leader, Flowpak Engineering, and quoted by Bratton, J. (1992) *Japanization at Work: Managerial Studies for the 1990s*, London: Macmillan, p. 188.
2. Richard Johnston, personnel manager of Flowpak Engineering, and quoted in Bratton (1992) op. cit., p. 188.
3. Quoted in ACAS (1987) *Working Together: The Way Forward*, Leeds: ACAS.
4. Comment made by a respondent and quoted in Bratton and Sinclair (1987) *New Patterns of Management: Communications and Employee Involvement in Local Government In Yorkshire and Humberside*. Report for Leeds City Council, p. 10.
5. Ibid., p. 12.
6. Ibid., p. 24.
7. ACAS, CBI, TUC (1987) *Working Together: The Way Forward*, Leeds: ACAS, p. 8.
8. Interview between author and union representatives.
9. ACAS spokesperson, Leeds, October 1987 and quoted in Bratton and Sinclair (1987) op. cit., p. 39.

chapter twelve

Human resource management and industrial relations

John Bratton

The workforce went down to 250. People began to think; 'I'm on my bike here if I'm not careful.' So the strength of the union went away.[1]

The management is definitely more aggressive... they got rid of a lot of the older workforce which was the old stalwart union men.[2]

Chapter outline

Chapter objectives

After studying this chapter, you should be able to:

1. Describe contemporary trends in industrial relations.
2. Explain and critically evaluate different types of managerial policies and practices.
3. Explain the pattern of trade union membership and union structure.
4. Understand the nature and importance of collective bargaining.
5. Critically evaluate the implications of the HRM model for union–management relations.

⬤ **Introduction**

Much of the critical literature presents the new HRM model as inconsistent with traditional industrial relations and collective bargaining, albeit for very different reasons
(Godard, 1991; Wells, 1993). Critics argue that HRM policies and practices are designed
to provide workers with a false sense of job security and obscure underlying sources of
conflict inherent in employment relations. According to Godard, historically a major
reason for managers adopting 'progressive' HRM practices has been to avoid or
weaken unions. However, he does concede that 'it would also be a mistake to view
progressive practices as motivated solely or even primarily by this objective' (1994,
p. 155). Yet other industrial relations scholars, taking a more traditional 'orthodox
pluralist' perspective, have argued that independent trade unions and variants of the
HRM model cannot merely coexist but are actually necessary to its successful implementation and development. They argue that trade unions should become proactive
or 'champions' of change, actively promoting the more positive elements of the 'soft'
HRM model. Such a union strategy would create a partnership between management
and organized labour which would result in a 'high-performance' workplace with
mutual gains for both the organization and workers (Betcherman *et al.*, 1994; Guest,
1995; Verma, 1995).

What is clearly apparent from a review of the literature is that this aspect of the
HRM discourse has been strongly influenced by political-legal developments and the
demise of trade union membership and power in the UK and USA over the past two
decades. Analysis of empirical evidence gathered over that period reveals that British
industrial relations has been substantially modified by a combination of economic,
political and social factors. Indeed, 30 years after the Donovan Report was published,
the change is so substantial that the Donovanist industrial relations model, and the
very label 'industrial relations', might be an anachronism in the late 1990s (Dunn,
1993). The changed economic and legal climate has altered the contours of workplace
union–management relations so much as to cause one eminent industrial relations
scholar to state 'It is difficult to believe that such a world existed less than twenty
years ago' (Hyman, 1997b, p. 317). In Chapter 3, we provided a glimpse of some of
these economic and political developments and discussed the beginnings of a process
of change and adaptation by management and labour. Since the election of the Conservative government in 1979, many observers consider the period 1983–87 as a
watershed in British industrial relations. And, although the history of British industrial relations can cite a number of watersheds, what is not in doubt is that the past
two decades have witnessed major contextual changes in industrial relations, including the introduction of trade union legislation to curtail union activities (marking the
end of the so-called 'voluntarist' tradition that dates back to 1871), mass unemployment and a diminution of trade union membership, institutional protection, and bargaining power.

The experience of fundamental changes in the context, institutions and processes
in the industrial relations system was not unique to the United Kingdom. In the rest
of the European Union, the traditional pattern of industrial relations underwent profound modifications. In some respects, the pattern of European industrial relations
systems remains sharply diversified, as it was in the 1970s. But in other respects, comparative analysis identifies similarities between European member states, pointing to
what writers refer to as a 'transnational convergence' (Baglioni and Crouch, 1991;
Streeck and Visser, 1997). Throughout Europe the drive for competitive advantage has

been pursued consistently and universally, and employers and managers have demonstrated initiative and determination in remodelling their national industrial relations system. For example, European employers have increasingly exercised their prerogative over key business decisions and enhanced management legitimacy, with government help, by popularizing the ideological argument for the veneration of the marketplace. European trade unions have been weakened numerically and politically and have been forced, in general, to retreat. The trade unions' participation in the collective bargaining process has similarly been marked by retreat and action to defend living standards, working conditions and rules governing the use of human resources (Baglioni and Crouch, 1991, pp. 14–19).

In North America the global competition of the 1980s has resulted in changes in the USA that have prompted some writers to describe them as the 'transformation of American industrial relations' (Kochan *et al.*, 1986). Although the transformation thesis might be an exaggeration of the perceived changes in that country and the thesis is not universally accepted in the USA, US companies have, with government indulgence, persuaded or compelled a weakened trade union movement to accept significant changes in collective agreements and working practices. Further, US companies have increasingly turned to a union-free environment, what is referred to as a 'union replacement' strategy. This management response to trade unions includes either relocating the business to a rural region where unionization is less well developed (for example, southern states such as Kentucky), and using consultants to run employee programmes to induce the workforce to consider withdrawing from their union. Industrial relations in North America have not followed identical routes. As numerous Canadian scholars have pointed out, in terms of legal support for unions, membership trends and bargaining strength, trade unions are in a more favourable and stronger position in Canada than in the USA and Britain. Overall there appears to be evidence that in the United Kingdom and the USA the pressures for change, accelerated by successive Conservative governments, have significantly modified both the behaviour of the two key actors in the industrial relations system, management and unions, and that these changes seem more than transitory and will in some degree become the accepted terrain for HR managers to operate in for the foreseeable future.

The HRM–industrial relations discourse poses some interesting questions for academics and practitioners alike, and is not normally covered by the prescriptive HRM textbooks. For example, can a worker be committed both to the organization's goals and the trade union's goals simultaneously? How does the HRM concept of 'high worker commitment' present a threat to unions? Is 'dual commitment' possible? Can the new HRM initiatives, such as work teams and flexible working, coexist with seniority and 'job-control' unionism? In terms of the individualization of the employment relationship can the progressive HRM model function alongside traditional collective bargaining? Some industrial relations scholars suggest that trade unions face strategic choices; they can either simply oppose the changes or opt for a proactive interventionist strategy that will embrace the more positive elements of the HRM model. Others, on the other hand, cogently argue that HRM and strong unions are incompatible. This chapter examines these interrelated questions by providing an analysis of management strategies. Then, drawing on the latest data, it discusses trends in union membership and structure. Finally, the chapter turns to the issue of worker commitment and an assessment of the unions' response to the HRM model.

● Industrial relations

At the core of industrial relations is work and the employment relationship. The academic study of industrial relations focuses on the social institutions, legislative controls and social mechanisms which regulate and control the employment relationship. Gospel and Palmer define the subject as concerned with:

> The processes of control over the employment relationship, the organization of work, and relations between employers and their employees (1993, p. 3).

The employment relationship is a social, economic and political relationship in which an employee provides manual and mental labour in exchange for rewards allocated by the employer (Watson, 1986). In organizations where employees are represented by a trade union, the price of the exchange – the pay level – is determined through the collective bargaining process. Thus, at the core of industrial relations is work, and managing the interactions between the representatives of trade unions and management is the most significant area of HRM.

● Industrial relations and the HRM cycle

Trade unions organize employees in the organization with a common interest and seek to regulate terms and conditions of employment through negotiation and agreements. Trade unions seek to exert influence on each of the four key constituent elements of the HRM cycle. Traditionally, trade unions influence *rewards*; union representatives attempt to maximize the reward side of the wage–effort contract. In the area of *recruitment* and *selection*, in some industries, most notably printing and construction, trade unions traditionally had considerable control over external recruiting. Trade unions also take an active interest in *human resource development*. They try to ensure that training opportunities are distributed equitably and that the employer adheres to the principle of maintained or improved earnings during training. Perhaps most controversially, the whole area of *appraisal* poses challenges to unions. The central tenet of traditional trade unionism has been the collectivist culture, namely the insistence on rewards according to the same definite standard and its application in the organization. Such collectivist goals have resulted in trade unions strongly resisting all forms of performance appraisal based on individual merit. Thus, most HRM literature presents the HRM model as inconsistent with traditional industrial relations systems in Britain and North America. To judge this assumption it is necessary to examine the principal actors in the industrial relations system and ask, 'In what ways have the relations between the key actors – management and unions – changed?'

● Management practices

Management plays a predominant role in constructing industrial relations in the workplace; management choices shape the options and largely determine the outcomes (Hyman, 1997a). Employees and their unions react to management initiatives. Over the past two decades, British scholars have shown a much greater interest in the study of management. There is a large body of literature that examines the effects of

Taylorism, technological change, and Japanese management practices (see Chapter 4). A number of studies have also examined how British managers have responded to the challenge of trade unions and how, since the Donovan Report, management has reorganized the conduct of workplace industrial relations (see, for example, Millward and Stevens, 1986; Millward *et al.*, 1992; Guest 1995; Cully *et al.*, 1998).

The management of an organization involves choices and constraints. On the one hand, management may seek to maintain unilateral control of the organization by retaining or extending its managerial prerogative or the right to management. Alternatively, management may accept the legitimacy of trade unions in the decision-making process – management by agreement. In the 1970s, public policy and managers were strongly influenced by the recommendations of the Donovan Commission. In the 1980s, and for most of the 1990s, employers shifted more towards individualistic approaches to managing human resources. This trend finds expression in the changing terminology, for example, employee relations, rather than the traditional concept of industrial relations (see Marchington and Parker, 1990). In essence, the debate on HRM–industrial relations centres on the belief that management has introduced new initiatives, found new confidence, and changed the emphasis in its industrial relations policies. For example, an analysis of the developments in HRM practice by Sisson (1994, p. 15) pessimistically concludes that 'The rhetoric may be the people-centred approach to the "soft" [HRM] version: the reality is the cost reduction approach of the "hard" [HRM] version.' To examine management's decisions and actions in industrial relations we need to focus on the concept of strategic choice, industrial relations strategies, and managerial styles.

Constraints and choices

The variations in organizational design and relations between managers and employees will be shaped by the strategic choices facing top management. John Child (1972) first used the concept of strategic choice to emphasize the role of managerial choice, rather than technology, in shaping organizations and work. As we discussed in Chapter 2, the importance of the concept of strategic choice is that it highlights the question of who makes decisions in business organizations and why they are made. The constraints which affect organizational decision makers include the government, technology, culture and domestic and global economic conditions. These environmental constraints affect all organizations eventually and 'tend to direct choices along particular channels while curtailing other modes of initiative' (Poole, 1980, p. 40). However, although strategic choices on such issues as organizational design and the management of human resources are taken by top management, they can be modified by other key players, particularly by trade unions (Child, 1972, pp. 13–14).

Management strategies

A modern corporate strategy is a plan for interacting with the competitive environment to achieve organizational goals (Daft, 1998). Organizations also develop functional strategies, which are the plans and procedures developed by the various functional areas within the organization: manufacturing, finance, marketing, industrial relations and human resource management. All these functional strategies are developed to facilitate the implementation of the corporate strategy. It is important to stress that the human resource management and the industrial relations strategies –

or to use the more generic term, the employment strategy – are formulated and developed as part of the corporate planning process (see Chapter 2). According to Gospel and Littler an employment strategy refers to 'The plans and policies used by management to direct work tasks; to evaluate, discipline, and reward workers; and to deal with their trade unions' (1983, p. 10). The concept of managerial strategy has given rise to fierce debate among academics (see Child, 1985; Hyman, 1987). The assumptions of rationality, the levels of formulation and the relation between strategy and outcomes are some of the questions addressed by scholars.

Global price competition has caused companies on all continents to search for alternative industrial relations strategies. Within the context of industrial relations in Europe in the 1990s, the outcomes of the collective bargaining process will have a direct impact on senior management's ability to implement the business strategy. For instance, under the EU monetary system, British managers will need to ensure that local pay and productivity movements correspond with those of other EU competitors. Therefore, it is much less likely after the year 2000 than in the 1970s that the industrial relations manager will enter the negotiations with a 'do your best' mandate from senior management. Taken from a case study, the following quote illustrates the likely pressures in the area of pay negotiations:

> Previously we would have a management meeting. I would then do the negotiating. If at the end of the day I had to go two or three per cent more than we intended, that would be it... Now, if I want to go outside the budget I have to get permission from head office.[3]

In North America and Britain three broad industrial relations strategies can be identified, union recognition, union exclusion and union opposition. The *union recognition* strategy is defined here as a decision by top managers to accept the legitimacy of the union role and, in turn, of collective bargaining as a process for regulating the employment relationship to support their corporate strategy. The reform and restructuring of workplace bargaining arrangements during the 1960s and 70s have been characterized as an industrial relations strategy designed to engender 'a degree of order, regulation and control' (Nichols and Beynon, 1977, p. 129; Purcell, 1979; Purcell and Sisson, 1983). Recent research suggests that even in the inimical environment of the 1980s, a number of important Japanese companies chose a union recognition strategy to achieve employment objectives, albeit in a modified form (Bassett, 1987; Wickens, 1987). In Britain, between 1984 and 1990, there was apparently a significant decline in the adoption of a union recognition strategy. The proportion of workplaces adopting a union recognition strategy was down, from 66 per cent to 53 per cent (Milward *et al.*, 1992, p. 70; Waddington and Whitston, 1994, p. 798).

The *union exclusion* strategy means that top management have decided to achieve their strategic goals by curtailing the role of trade unions. The strategy involves business decisions by top management to, for example, introduce new technology, to relocate to another part of the UK or European Union, to subcontract out work, or to adopt the more aggressive tactic of derecognition of a union (Anderson, 1989). Derecognition refers to a decision by top management to withdraw from collective bargaining in favour of unilateral arrangements for the governance of employment relations. Douglas Smith, chair of ACAS, said in October 1987 in his address to the IPM conference that 'across the spectrum there were now managements whose intention was increasingly to marginalise trade unions'. One study identified 50 cases of derecognition and four unsuccessful attempts at derecognition in Britain (Claydon, 1989) and, in the provincial newspaper sector, Smith and Morton (1993) provide evidence of employers eliminating unions from the decision-making process. In the USA there is evidence that a relatively large proportion of companies have adopted a union exclusion strategy and an increasing number of top management have decided to decertify (derecognize) the existing union (Cappelli and Chalykoff, 1985). Opposition to unions is so intense in US business organizations that 'American employers are willing to engage in almost any form of legal or *illegal* action [our emphasis] to create and maintain a union-free environment' (Deery, 1995, p. 538). It should be noted, however, that the employment relationship is dynamic and therefore, when management creates a non-union environment, it is not necessarily permanent. Moreover, the successful implementation of a union exclusion strategy must always be followed by a union opposition strategy (Anderson *et al.*, 1989).

 HRM in practice 12.1

Vauxhall deal on pay and flexibility gets green light

The car manufacturer has put flexible working at the heart of its unique pay and conditions agreement

BY JENNIE WALSH People Management, 30 April 1998

Vauxhall workers at the car giant's Luton and Ellesmere Port plants have voted overwhelmingly for a ground-breaking wages, conditions and productivity deal that links pay to the strength of the pound and secures long-term job security.

The linking of pay to the exchange rate is a novel move that could herald the start of pan-European pay deals based on the single currency and the euro (see News & Analysis, page 10). But the deal is equally significant for the flexible working arrangements accepted by the 9000 shopfloor employes, along with white-collar staff. It includes 'corridor agreements', voluntary part-time working and greater holiday flexibility.

Despite all parties to the agreement acknowledging that employees will be worse off under the three-year pay deal – which is linked to inflation but includes extra money in the third year if the pound falls below DM2.70 for two months running – they believe the

> **The worst elements of the initial demands have been removed, but it is still not without pain.**

negotiations have given a massive boost to industrial relations. General Motors had threatened to close the Luton plant because of the pound's strength and the crisis in the Far East, but now Luton has been promised production of the Vectra car, while Ellesmere Port will produce the new Astra.

'This deal had to be done in an incredibly short space of time, because of decisions being made by General Motors in Zurich,' Bruce Warman, director of personnel at Vauxhall, told *PM*. 'There were intense discussions about the seriousness of the situation and we really were making policy on the hoof. There were no glossy presentations, but the workforce understood why [it was needed] and, at the end of it all, the atmosphere is the best I have ever known it.'

'If the plant closed, it would never reopen,' said Tony Woodley, lead negotiator for the Transport and General Workers' Union. 'Vauxhall originally wanted us to accept wage cuts, but we were not prepared to. The worst elements of the initial demands have been removed, but it is still not without pain. It comes on top of the previous three-year deal and is in contrast to the 4.5 per cent rises secured elsewhere in the industry. But I never believed the closure threat was a plot to get us to accept this. It was genuine and deadly serious.'

New employees will be the biggest losers in the agreement, being taken on at 82 per cent of the full pay rate and receiving five days' less holiday a year, which can then be earned back over time.

The corridor agreement is similar to one operating at Opel in Germany and was provisionally agreed at Vauxhall last October. It allows employees to work more hours in busy times and fewer in slack periods without it affecting pay.

Elements of the package include less rigidity in the timing of holiday closure periods to better respond to production demands, and part-time working in the after-sales warehouses. Volunteers will be sought from employees. Warman hopes that the arrangement can be flexible to individual needs.

The pay talks hit the headlines when Nick Reilly, the company's chairman, gave up his £160,000 basic pay for a year. The lower-paid Warman gave up 5 per cent. Their controversial move was received with great cynicism in the press.

'I think the gesture was genuine,' Woodley said. 'But it was seen as cynical by the workforce and had no influence on the outome of the negotiations.'

'We thought hard about doing it,' Warman said. 'But if we are expecting people to accept less to save jobs, we have to acknowledge that it is saving our jobs too. But we didn't use the decision in negotiations – and Nick Reilly is no Cedric Brown.'

The *union opposition* strategy is defined here as a decision to maintain the status of a non-union company by pursuing a number of tactics such as employee participation, job redesign and paternalistic human resource management policies. Given that the majority of business organizations are not unionized, we can assume that union opposition is the most prevalent industrial relations strategy in North America and Britain. Researchers argue that employee involvement schemes increase employees' motivation and commitment to organizational goals and, therefore, reduce the need for a trade union (see Chapter 11). Management also uses key elements of the HRM cycle and paternalistic HRM policies to avoid trade unions. The selection process can be used to screen out applicants likely to be prone to joining a union, and training can be used to build commitment to the organization. The retail giant Marks & Spencer exemplifies the union opposition strategy. The company's chairman and chief executive put it like this: 'Human relations in industry should cover the problems of the individual at work, his or her health, well-being and progress, the working environment and profit-sharing. Full and frank two-way communication and respect for the contribution people can make, given encouragement – these are the foundations of an effective policy and a major contribution to a successful operation.'[4]

The choice of an appropriate industrial relations strategy for a particular organization will depend upon the interrelationship between constraints and strategic choices and between managerial objectives – as delineated by the corporate strategy and alternative management styles. Whatever industrial relations strategy is selected, it must also be evaluated in order to identify where objectives have been achieved and where they have not. For example, comparative measures of industrial conflict, cooperation and grievance rates can be used to evaluate an industrial relations strategy. Finally, it is also important to recognize that there is no single strategy adopted by employers and managers. Management can choose from a variety of strategies. As Gospel and Littler state: 'The combination of strategies has been highly complex, and employers have searched in a zig-zag backwards and forwards movement between them' (1983, p. 12).

Managerial styles

The approach to or style of managing the employment relationship influences strategies and HRM practice. Managerial style is related to the managerial variables between managerial prerogative at one end and management by agreement at the other. Fox (1966) first proposed two contrasting styles of management, the pluralist and the unitary, according to the degree of legitimacy afforded by management to the trade unions. In 1974, Fox developed four different styles of industrial relations management, traditionalist, sophisticated paternalist, 'sophisticated moderns' and 'standard moderns'. The *traditionalist* approach is associated closely with authoritarian management which is hostile and refuses to recognize trade unions. The *sophisticated paternalistic* approach is also associated with a refusal to recognize trade unions, but it differs from the traditionalist style because management develops key elements of the HRM cycle to ensure that individual employees are committed to organizational goals and their needs are mostly satisfied without trade union representation. Among large British businesses, this style might be found in such companies as Marks & Spencer and in American companies such as IBM. The *sophisticated moderns* approach accepts the role of trade unions and the inevitability of collective bargaining as a social mechanism for establishing the terms and conditions of the employment relationship. Finally, the *standard moderns* style is essentially pragmatic, with managers changing their approach to trade unions in response to internal and external changes and pressures. The typologies of managerial styles were further developed by Purcell (1987), with an elaboration of two dimensions of style, individualism and collectivism. Individualism referred to 'the extent to which the firm gives credence to the feelings and sentiments of each employee and seeks to develop and encourage each employee's capacity and role at work' (1987, p. 536). Collectivism, on the other hand, referred to 'the extent to which the organization recognizes the right of employees to have a say in those aspects of management decision-making which concern them' (1987, p. 537).

In their study of four organizations, Marchington and Parker (1990) had difficulty applying Purcell's model of styles. They developed an alternative set of dimensions of managerial style: the investment–orientation approach depicts the extent to which managers are concerned with controlling labour costs or developing employees and the partnership orientation dimension, is 'management attitudes and behaviour towards the trade unions in the workplace' (1990, pp. 235–7).

The study by McLoughlin and Gourlay (1992) emphasizes the importance of allowing for the coexistence of individual and collective approaches in the management of the employment relationship. McLoughlin and Gourlay identify two dimensions of managerial style (Figure 12.1). The individualism–collectivism dimension refers 'to variations in the "mix" of individual and collective approaches to regulating different substantive and procedural aspects of the employment relationship' (1992, p. 674). Here there is a spectrum which runs from high individualism to high collectivism. 'High levels of individualism or collectivism do not denote the exclusion of the other approach to job regulation, merely that the one is more predominant in the "mix" than the other', state the authors. The strategic integration dimension represents the

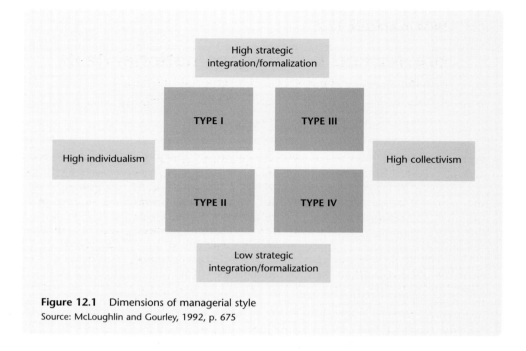

Figure 12.1 Dimensions of managerial style
Source: McLoughlin and Gourley, 1992, p. 675

extent to which there is 'a tight coupling of strategic intention with workplace prac-tice' (1992, p. 674). Again there is a spectrum from low, little formalization of policies or procedures, to high strategic integration.

Drawing upon the work of Streeck (1987) and Sisson (1993), Hyman (1997) offers an alternative typology of management style with two fundamental dimensions: exclusion and inclusion and status and contract (Figure 12.2).

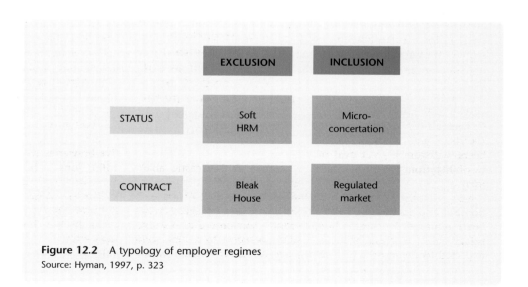

Figure 12.2 A typology of employer regimes
Source: Hyman, 1997, p. 323

HRM in practice 12.2

Brewer and union agree national deal

Carlsberg-Tetley has conceded a national bargaining agreement in return for improvements in flexibility

BY MIKE THATCHER People Management, 30 April 1998

Carlsberg-Tetley has reached an agreement with the Transport and General Workers' Union that will introduce national collective bargaining to front-line distribution staff for the first time.

The new deal, due to be signed on 30 April, will cover around 900 workers in 25 distribution depots and supersedes a number of local agreements with the T&G and the GMB. In contrast, local recognition arrangements remain in place for production workers at the company's main breweries in Leeds and Northampton.

Colin Povey, Carlsberg-Tetley's HR ditrector, told *People Management* that the pace of change in the troubled Danish-owned company required a partnership approach. 'We think we have got a mature enough relationship with our trade unions for us not to be scared off by national bargaining for that [employee] population.'

In return, Carlsberg-Tetley, which is famous for its Skol, Castlemaine XXXX, Calder's, Carlsberg and Tetley range of beers, will gain a great deal of flexibility from the new agreement.

All overtime payments, bonuses and supplements have been replaced by a standard salary, and workers will be expected to stay until a job has

been completed. More than 25 job titles have been reduced to four: driver, driver's mate, team leader and warehouse operative. According to Povey, a large number of 'Spanish practices' have also been abolished.

But he accepted that national bargaining had its critics. 'Five years ago we wouldn't even have contemplated national negotiations, because if you hit a snag, you could have a real problem delivering beer across the whole of the country.'

Brian Revell, the T&G's national secretary for food, drink and tobacco, described the deal as 'historic' in the brewing industry. 'It is the first national negotiations for distribution within any of the major brewers,' he said.

> 'We think we have got a mature enough relationship with our trade unions for us not to be scared off by national bargaining for that [employee] population.'

Scottish & Newcastle abandoned national negotiations when it took over Courage to form Scottish Courage. Bass has recently outsourced its distribution operation to a new company called Tradeteam which

has retained local bargaining. Whitbread has always had local bargaining.

Revell accepted that the deal would weaken terms and conditions, but described it as a 'defensive' agreement. The T&G's main concern was that Carlsberg-Tetley would follow the outsourcing approach taken by Bass. 'At least we have ended up with better terms and conditions than we would have done under a Tradeteam situation,' he said.

There is no clause in the agreement barring the outsourcing route, but it would clearly go against the spirit of negotiations. Povey recognised that any move in that direction by the firm would be seen as 'at best inconsistent and at worst ungentlemanly.'

He said the increased flexibility would produce 'substantial and essential' cost savings, necessary because of the company's difficult trading position.

An agreed takeover by Bass was blocked last year by the government. Carlsberg-Tetley subsequently announced the closure or sale of three of its five breweries with the loss of 1500 jobs. The Burton-on-Trent brewery was sold to Bass in January, Alloa finishes production this week and the plant in Wrexham will close next year.

The close relationship

between Carlsberg-Tetley and the T&G, however, does not extend to some other unions. At the end of last year the company announced that it was derecognising the MSF, which negotiated on behalf of around 400 middle managers.

Povey admitted that the firm could be seen as adopting a contradictory approach, but suggested that union members were in a minority and that there had been no outcry from the majority of those affected.

'We are not the type of employer that is into union bashing,' he added

The first dimension addresses the fundamental issue as to whether to attempt to operate the business without trade unions, 'exclusion', or to seek to integrate unions 'inclusion'. The second dimension to the model depicts a choice between the 'extension of status' (integrating employees as members of the organization) and 'return to contract' (seeking flexibility through downsizing). These two fundamental managerial choices combine to give four 'ideal-typical' options. According to Hyman, the 'regulated market' typifies the traditional adversarial industrial relations model found in Britain and North America. The ideal-type 'soft' HRM approach to managing the employment relationship is found in the opposite quadrant. In reality, Hyman argues that the more prevalent style is the 'union-free' workplace, the 'Bleak House' approach (Sisson, 1993), where management seeks flexibility and compliance through 'fear'. The 'micro-concertation' variant, for Hyman, is the most interesting because this style does not emerge through deliberate strategy, but rather as an 'outcome of a lengthy interactive process' in which management and unions move towards 'joint management'. This approach can emerge as both parties realize that global price competition requires a reassessment of traditionally adversarial activities. In post-apartheid South Africa, the trade unions have shifted from confrontation with employers to participation in a newly created 'tripartite forum' in order to encourage private investment and further the economic interests of working people (Barrett, 1996). The 'micro-concertation' style closely resembles Kochan and Osterman's argument (1994) in respect of a partnership among American management, labour and government to attain sustainable competitive advantage. In Canada, Betcherman et al. have posited that tripartite collaboration among management, labour and government is needed to create 'high-performance' workplaces. The development of collaborative workplace union–management relations as a strategy to meet the demands of global competition has also been suggested for Britain (Terry, 1995) and for Germany (Streeck, 1996).

The significance of this debate is this; the 'soft' HRM variant is not restricted to the 'exclusion' quadrant but could exist alongside a 'micro-concertation' style. Guest (1995) summarizes a body of research that analyses four strategic industrial relations options available to management, new realism, traditional collectivism, individualized HRM, and the 'black hole'. The new realism option, through a joint approach, endeavours to shape a new relationship between union and management and appears to illustrate the case of HRM and industrial relations operating in tandem (Kochan et al., 1986; Storey, 1992; Betcherman et al., 1994). The evidence that HRM and industrial relations can be integrated might mean, however, that in the context of weak unions industrial relations issues receive low priority from management, the 'empty shell' hypothesis (Guest, 1995). As far as UK and US trends are concerned, current evidence suggests that managers are withdrawing support from the traditional collectivism of representative industrial relations systems towards the 'black hole of no industrial relations and *no* HRM' (our emphasis). The 'black hole' policy choice is market-driven and views workers as a variable cost, the 'hard' HRM model. Alternatively, with cooperation from the New Labour government, British trade unions could take a more proactive approach towards the more positive developmental elements of the 'soft' HRM model. We shall look at these suggestions later in this chapter after examining the changes in the trade unions.

To summarize this section. These different managerial strategies and styles can provide insights into the nature of management and the diffusion of HRM practices. For example, in a sub-sample of 30 workplaces, both unionized and non-unionized, McLoughlin and Gourlay identified distinctive managerial styles corresponding to their model, '"Type I" (high strategic integration/high individualism) were found at a third of the workplaces' (1992, p. 678). McLoughlin and Gourlay's findings also provide evidence for 'the existence of HRM type approaches defined in terms of high degrees of strategic integration and a stress on individualized modes of job regulation' (1992, p. 685). It is, however, important to understand that management styles can and do change depending on the economic and political climate, and that different styles can be applied to different categories of employees. With this caveat, the implications of monetary policy in the EU and growing globalization of corporate structures will compel top management to make strategic choices about their business processes and how they will arrange related aspects of human resource and industrial relations management.

Trade unions

In the 1970s, British trade unions were considered powerful social institutions which merited close study. One scholar referred to trade unions as 'one of the most powerful forces shaping our society' (Clegg, 1976, p. 1). Between 1968 and 1979 trade union membership increased by 3.2 million to 13.2 million, with union density exceeding 55 per cent. The sheer scale of union increase represented a 'decade of exceptional union growth' (Bain and Price, 1983, p. 6). In contrast, since 1979, the membership of British trade unions has fallen by over 5 million, standing at around 8 million and union density around 32 per cent in 1998. The 1980s was referred to as the 'decade of non-unionism' (Bassett, 1987), and, more recently, observers have declared that UK union membership decline has reached 'critical proportions' (Waddington and Whitson, 1997). This section examines trends in union membership over the past two decades and goes on to examine trade union structure and bargaining power, in the belief that an understanding of these developments is an important backdrop to the HRM–trade union discourse.

Trade union membership

The significant decline in aggregate membership of British trade unions is shown in Table 12.1. In the period 1976–80 trade union membership reached a peak of 12 916 000. Since then membership has fallen by over 4 million, or 32 per cent. From the peak years of 1976–80, union density – that is, actual union membership as a proportion of potential union membership – fell from 55.1 per cent to 36.7 per cent in 1995.

Table 12.1 Trade union membership in the UK, 1971–96

	Certification Officer Data	
	Members (000s)	% of employed
5-year annual average		
1971–75	11,548 (+1.5)	50.0
1976–80	12,916 (+1.5)	55.1
1981–85	11,350 (–3.5)	53.2
1986–90	10,299 (–1.7)	46.1
1991–95	8,740 (–4.0)	40.2
annual		
1989	10,158 (–2.1)	44.2
1990	9,947 (–2.1)	43.9
1991	9.585 (–3.6)	43.8
1992	9,048 (–5.6)	42.3
1993	8,700 (–3.8)	40.2
1994	8,278 (–4.9)	38.1
1995	8,089 (–2.3)	36.7
1996	n.a.	n.a.

Source: Brown *et al.*, 1997

In the 1980s, the proportion of workplaces with union members was 66 per cent; by 1990 this proportion had fallen to 53 per cent (Millward *et al.*, 1992). The same survey also seems to indicate that union density had fallen substantially, from 58 to 48 per cent, between 1984 and 1990. The decline was more marked for manual employees, down from 66 to 53 per cent. The fall in union density was also substantial in private manufacturing and the public sector. A survey of 115 high-technology workplaces in south-east England also found that 80 per cent of workplaces did not recognize trade unions (McLoughlin and Gourlay, 1992, p. 675). The 1998 WERS survey found that there were no union members present in 47 per cent of the workplaces surveyed, a substantial change from 36 per cent of workplaces in 1990 (Cully *et al.*, 1998, pp. 14–15). The WERS study also provides data that shows a 'strong association between the type of union presence and workplace employment size, and union presence and management attitudes towards union membership, as shown in Table 12.2. According to Cully *et al.*, 'Nearly two-thirds of employees are union members in the 29 per cent of workplaces where management are in favour of union membership' (1998, p. 15).

It is helpful to situate Britain's trade union experience in an international perspective (Table 12.3). In the EU and North America trade union density in the 1990s is highly variable. In four of the EU member states, Spain, Netherlands, Germany, and France, trade union density is less than 30 thirty per cent of the workforce. In three EU member states, Sweden, Finland, and Denmark, union density exceeds 80 per cent

Table 12.2 Indicators of union presence, by workplace size and management attitudes, 1998

	Union density	Any union members	Union recognition
	% of employees who are members	% of workplaces	% of workplaces
Workplace size			
25 to 49 employees	23	46	39
50 to 99 employees	27	52	41
100 to 199 employees	32	66	57
200 to 499 employees	38	77	67
500 or more employees	48	86	78
Management views on union membership			
In favour	62	98	94
Neutral/not an issue	23	40	29
Not in favour	7	16	9
All workplaces	36	53	45

Base: all workplaces with 25 or more employees
Figures are weighted and based on responses from 1889 managers

Source: Cully *et al.*, 1998, p. 15

Table 12.3 Trade union membership by country as a percentage of all employees, 1970–95

Country	1970	1980	1990	1995
United Kingdom	45 (9th)	50 (10th)	39 (10th)	32 (11th)
Australia	50	48	40	33
Austria	62	56	46	43
Belgium	45	56	51	53
Canada	31	36	36	34
Denmark	60	76	71	82
Finland	51	70	72	81
France	22	17	10	9
Germany (West)	33	36	33	29
Greece	36	37	34	n.a.
Ireland	53	57	50	38
Italy	36	49	39	38
Japan	35	31	25	24
Netherlands	38	35	25	26
New Zealand	41	56	45	22
Norway	51	57	56	56
Portugal	61	61	32	32
Spain	27	25	11	15
Sweden	68	80	82	83
Switzerland	30	31	27	26
United States	23	22	16	15

Source: Brown *et al.*, 1997

of the workforce. In North America, trade union density in Canada stands at 34 per cent, exceeding the UK, whereas in the United States it is 15 per cent. There are difficulties in interpreting absolute differences in union membership between countries, but the trend is clear. Many have experienced substantial declines in union membership over the past two decades (Brown *et al.*, 1997).

Interpreting trade union decline

Although the general pattern clearly indicates that membership and density have declined significantly and continually since 1979, there is debate about the precise scale of the trend, its cause and likely duration. Part of the problem is measurement. Estimates of the decline in union density between 1979 and 1986, for example, range from as little as 8.3 percentage points to as much as 12.1 percentage points. These strikingly different estimates occur because the key statistic of union density can be measured in nine different ways, depending on which of three different data series for potential membership, and trade union membership, are used (see Kelly and Bailey, 1989).

One influential explanation of variations in rates of unionization over time, and differences at any one time between industries and occupation groups, categorizes the determinants under six headings (Bain and Price, 1983):

- composition of potential union membership
- business cycle
- employer policies and government action
- personal and job-related characteristic
- industrial structure
- union leadership.

Although the Bain and Price approach is comprehensive, it is difficult to 'disentangle' the relative importance of each of the six determinants in interpreting aggregate union decline in the UK since 1979. Within the business cycle framework, Disney (1990) suggests the downturn in union density in the 1980s was caused by macroeconomic factors. Trade unions' traditional difficulties in recruiting and gaining recognition in the private services sector, smaller establishments, foreign-owned plants, and newly established greenfield sites have intensified. As a TUC document acknowledged: 'Unions are finding it generally difficult to recruit and bargain in the fastest growing parts of the economy'.[5] Proponents of the business cycle explanation also assume that high levels of unemployment have eroded the constituencies of manual workers from which unions have traditionally recruited (Waddington, 1992).

Following the election of a Conservative government in 1979, public policy towards trade unions shifted away from positive encouragement of trade union recognition. The suggested determinant, government action, clearly can affect unionization. Public policies that create a favourable environment for union recognition will initiate a virtuous circle of recognition and membership increase. The circle can be put into reverse by adverse policies and government 'example-setting' or role model (Towers, 1989). Freeman and Pelletier (1990), using a quantitative analysis of changes in union density, estimate that the Thatcher government's industrial relations laws reduced British trade union density by 1 to 1.7 percentage points per year from 1980 to 1986. This type of analysis, however, is fraught with problems. It is very difficult to disentangle cause and effect in dealing with trade union law (Disney, 1990).

Others argue that employers have used the fear of unemployment, hostile trade union legislation, and the concomitant shifts in power towards employers to change radically the structure of workplace industrial relations. The studies by Batstone (1984), Edwards (1985) and Batstone *et al.* (1986) into workplace trade unionism broadly concluded that shop steward organization had held up well. The study by Millward *et al.* (1992) comments on the main determinants of union membership changes between 1984 and 1990. The variation in union density was explained by structural characteristics, such as changes in establishment size and the age of the workplace; 'older workplaces have higher densities', argue Millward *et al.* (1992, p. 63). Workforce characteristics such as the proportion of employees on part-time contracts were also important in explaining union membership. One of the most significant findings in 1990 has been the overall decline in the proportion of workplaces with recognized unions where at least one shop steward was reported. In the period between 1984 and 1990, the number fell from 82 per cent to 71 per cent, and the fall was particularly concentrated in smaller establishments. In the highest density establishments, with 90 per cent or more membership, Millward *et al.* found 'little or no change' in the incidence of union representatives (1992, pp. 110–12). The pattern of representation across broad sectors is given in Table 12.2. Another significant development is collapse of compulsory unionism – the 'closed shop' – among non-manual workers in highly unionized British companies. Wright's (1996) study of British unionized workplaces found that among white-collar workers, mandatory unionism has been all but eliminated. However, among manual workers, post-entry mandatory union membership continues in the form of 'verbal agreement' or 'unofficial' arrangement between the local management and union. Waddington and Whitston (1994, 1997) support the 'shift in power' explanation of membership decline. After reviewing the competing explanations, they conclude that 'the capacity of employers to resist recognition, or even an effective union presence, has made unions unavailable to vast numbers of potential members' (1997, p. 537).

In Britain, Bassett (1988) has suggested that derecognition of unions is a small but growing trend. Of 21 known examples of derecognition, two – the government's intelligence centre (GCHQ) and British Rail's senior managers – were in the public sector; the others ranged from chemicals to book publishing. A survey of British-based companies in the UK found 39 cases of either derecognition, threat of derecognition or an attempt to move to a single-union arrangement.[6] The spate of examples of de-unionization has been associated with the growing adoption of the HRM model. Addressing the IPM conference in 1987, John Monks, deputy general secretary of the TUC, said that while most companies used to be at least neutral, and often favourable, towards unions, recent labour relations practice and theory, originating from the US or Japan, in the main attempted to persuade workers that trade unions now no longer served any useful purpose (*Financial Times*, 23 October 1987). More recently, there is growing evidence of a shift towards more 'strategic derecognition' among European firms in many industries where once trade unions were strong (Brown *et al.*, 1997). The analysis of trade union decline over the last two decades emphasizes the interplay between long-term economic developments, the shift towards the service sector, the increasing numbers of peripheral workers, the adverse political and legal environments and the growing number of firms adopting a union exclusion strategy.

Trade union structure

The word 'structure' in relation to trade unions denotes the 'external shape' of trade unions (Hyman, 1975) or job territories; an area of the labour market where the union aims to recruit. A union's internal structure, the relationship between its parts, is referred to as trade union government. There are many variants of union structure within countries, traditionally expressed in terms of the classic differentiation between craft, industrial, general and white-collar unions. Historically, the craft union came first and typically based itself on the principle of recruiting skilled employees in distinct trades or occupations. A craft union, such as the Amalgamated Society of Engineers (ASE), restricted membership to those workers who had served a recognized apprenticeship. The advantages of this form of unionism were obvious; the union could regulate the supply of its type of labour and therefore influence the exchange for the labour. In contrast, industrial unions aimed to recruit all the workers within a given industry regardless of their occupation or level of skill. On this principle, all employees of the steel industry, whatever their actual job, should belong to a single inclusive union for steel workers. This structure has the advantage of eliminating the problem of multi-unionism and demarcation disputes; it also simplifies the collective bargaining between employee groups and management representatives. The general unions date from the 1880s with the growth of 'new unionism'. By definition, they recruit across both occupational and industrial boundaries, and in theory general unions recognize no restrictions on their potential membership. An example of such a union would be the Transport and General Workers Union (TGWU). The advantages claimed for this type of union structure are numerous. Such unions can provide extensive services – for example legal, welfare, research, education – to their membership. The fourth category, the white-collar unions, describes an identifiable and significant sector of the labour market which is organized into unions. An example of such a union would be the National Union of Journalists (NUJ).

The British union movement is associated with multi-unionism, as craft and general unions cross the boundaries of workplaces and industries (Visser and Waddington, 1996). Technological change has both undermined the traditional craft unions and created new occupations thus blurring the once clear distinction between manual and non-manual. The classic differentiation between craft, industry, general and white-collar unions is no longer applicable. In essence, the traditional classification confuses rather than clarifies; one distinguished observer of British industrial relations described the old classification of unions as 'slogans of dead ideological debate'.

In Britain, a traditional response of the unions to falling membership and revenue has been mergers and amalgamation. Since 1979, the number of trades unions affiliated to the TUC has fallen from 109 to 74, almost entirely from mergers (see Table 12.4). In the period 1986-95, there were 99 mergers and the overall number of British unions fell by 142 (Willman, 1996). A philosophy of 'big is best' seems to be emerging in the trade union movement. The process of merger and absorption is sometimes seen as a prelude to further 'natural growth', to mitigate the effects of membership decline. Mergers allow for extensions of existing recruitment bases as the post-merger union is in practice regarded as organizing from the recruitment bases of the pre-merger unions (Waddington, 1988). Explanations for union merger activity have included the prevalence of an 'industrial logic' and the avoidance of duplicate administrative costs. For example, in 1992 the formation of the Graphical Paper and Media Union (GPMU) united the craft tradition in printing represented by National Graphical Association

(NGA) with the primarily non-craft Society of Graphical and Allied Trades (SOGAT82). In explaining merger activity, a 'political logic' was also influential. For example, the merger of ASTMS and TASS to form the MSF reflected the political similarities of each union's 'left-led Executive' (see Waddington and Whitston, 1994).

The structure of British trade unions is recognized to be complex, diverse and 'chaotic' (Hyman, 1997). The competitive scramble to seek membership anywhere has created trade union structures which are even more bewildering and incomprehensible. The membership distribution among individual trade unions is skewed. At one extreme there is a relatively small number of trade unions with a disproportionate share of total union membership, while at the other extreme there is a large number of unions with very small memberships. As the data in Table 12.4 shows, the ten largest TUC affiliated unions have a total membership of over 5 million, 78 per cent of all TUC membership. The major structural characteristic of British trade unions in the 1990s is the predominance of horizontal or 'conglomerate' unions, that is, large individual unions having members distributed over a wide range of different industries.

In the past decade, parallel trends of organizational restructuring have become manifest among trade unions in advanced industrial economies (Visser and Wadding-

Table 12.4 Change in membership of the 10 largest TUC affiliated unions, 1979–98 (thousands and percentage)

Union	1979	1998	Affiliated membership per cent change 1979–98
1. UNISON [1]	1 697	1 374	(–)19.0
2. TGWU	2 862	890	(–)68.9
3. AEEU [2]	1 505	725	(–)51.8
4. GMB	967	718	(–)25.7
5. MSF [3]	691	425	(–)38.5
6. USDAW	470	290	(–)38.3
7. CWU [4]	197	274	(+)39.1
8. PCS	n.a.	265	
9. GPMU [5]	313	209	(–)33.2
10. NUT	291	188	(–)35.0
Total TUC membership	12 175	6 778	(–)44.3
Number TUC unions	109	74	(–)32.1

1. Merger in 1992 of NALGO, NUPE, and COHSE
2. Merger in 1992 of AEU and EETPU
3. Merger in 1987 of Technical, Administrative & Supervisory Staff (TASS) and Association of Scientific, Technical & Managerial Staff (ASTMS).
4. Growth is due to merger activity within communications industry
5. Merger in 1992 of SOGAT and NGA

Source: Kessler and Bayliss, 1995 and TUC Web page, 1998

ton, 1996; Streeck and Visser, 1997). The study by Visser and Waddington (1996) of union structures in Sweden, the Netherlands and Britain show similar trends; in each country the number of unions has declined. A similar finding is documented by Streeck and Visser (1997, p. 305): 'In many countries, from the USA to Britain and Australia, and from Scandinavia to mainland Europe, unions are now in a process of regrouping, through bargaining cartels, mergers and take-overs. As a result sectoral and occupational boundaries are becoming increasingly unimportant for union organization.' Conglomerate unions, like conglomerate companies, straddle and disregard sectoral boundaries.

Union bargaining power

There has been considerable debate on the effects of the decline in union membership and density on unions' bargaining power. The contraction of employment in the unionized manufacturing sector is widely assumed to undermine union bargaining strength. One indicator of union bargaining power is the propensity of strike activity. The most noticeable feature of Table 12.5 is the fall in the number of stoppages during the 1980s and 90s. In the 1970s, with both Conservative and Labour governments, the number of stoppages each year never fell below 2000. Throughout the 1980s the figure has never gone above 2000. The figures for 1990–94 give the number of working days lost through industrial action to be 37 per 1000 employees, the lowest figure since records began 100 years ago. Although comparisons involving the number of strikes must be made with caution because of the exclusion of some of the smallest stoppages from the statistics, nonetheless the trend is unequivocally downward, and secondary industrial action has virtually disappeared as a union tactic. The reasons may be numerous; draconian fines meted out to the print unions (Kelly,

Table 12.5 Strikes and working days lost due to stoppages, 1990–96

	Stoppages reported	Working days lost per 1000 employees	Per cent of stoppages lasting not more than 3 days
1960–64	2 512	139	74
1965–69	2 380	168	65
1970–74	2 917	629	49
1975–79	2 345	509	43
1980–84	1 363	484	54
1985–89	895	180	58
1990–94	334	37	65
1995–96	240	39	67

Source: Adapted from Brown *et al.*, 1997

1988), the failure of the miners' strike leading many workers to doubt whether going on strike would be successful, and the pre-strike ballot provisions of the Trade Union Act 1984 (Bassett, 1987). The introduction of balloting legislation has also contributed to the decline of strikes because they signalled to employers 'resolve without recourse to action' and they were used as 'a cheap substitute for action, with an element of bluff' (Brown *et al.*, 1997).

All earlier evidence suggests that the strike pattern is strongly cyclical; propensity to strike rises during economic booms and falls during a recession. Further, the decline in strike activity over the past two decades occurred in all OECD countries (see Kessler

HRM in practice 12.3

NHS Trust gets close to 'no strike' deal

BY PHIL HILTON Personnel Management Plus, April 1992.

A deal which makes it 'pretty well impossible' for strike action to occur has been reached at a National Health Service Trust for the first time.

The Homewood Trust in Chertsey has signed an agreement which amounts to a virtual no-strike deal through the use of conciliation and binding pendulum attraction.

The trust has established single-table bargaining and a 'partnership' deal which, says director of human resources Chris Wilson, makes it 'pretty well impossible for the unions to take industrial action'.

Tim Carter, staff side secretary, was adamant the agreement was not a no-strike deal. 'If we reach a failure to agree, we retain the right to ballot members if members want a ballot. Hopefully the need for strike action will be minimised.'

The arrangement allows one side to opt for conciliation if there is no agreement in the course of conventional negotiations. During conciliation all

industrial action is suspended.

If conciliation fails to bring the two sides together, then binding pendulum arbitration is an option. But both sides have to agree before it can be triggered.

The only opportunity for strike action within the agreement is if one side refuses to accept a failure of conciliation in order tó move to arbitration. Wilson said that in that case 'the deal wouldn't be worth the paper it's written on.'

The only opportunity for strike action within the agreement is if one side refuses to accept a failure of conciliation in order to move to arbitration.

Pendulum arbitration has previously been restricted to the private sector where, according to recent research, it can be established without an explicit no-strike clause.

The aim of the partnership is

to reduce the possibility of disrupting service to patients and clients. The trust includes two mental health centres, a substance misuse team and a resource centre for people with learning disabilities.

The agreement was the product of 18 hours of negotiation over a number of weeks and includes single-table bargaining for all groups, including professional organizations such as the British Medical Association and the Royal College of Nursing.

Members of the eight bodies will have four representatives at the single table, elected to represent all staff. Carter said that they would have an equal say in negotiations and that no members-to-seats ratio would operate. 'We are not into numbers games. All the staff side members will get equal representation.'

Both sides have committed to work towards a single pay spine, to establish a minimum wage and local performance management and pay.

and Bayliss, 1995). The strike pattern cannot be used as an unambiguous index of trade union power, nor does it mean that strikes are a thing of the past (Kelly, 1988).

● Collective bargaining

We have mentioned the term 'collective bargaining' on several occasions in this chapter. We define collective bargaining as:

> An institutional system of negotiation in which the making, interpretation and administration of rules, and the application of statutory controls affecting the employment relationship, are decided within union–management negotiating committees.

Several important points arise from this definition. First, collective bargaining is a process through which representatives of the union and management jointly determine some of the employment rules. Second, there are two types of rules, substantive and procedural. Substantive rules establish terms and conditions of employment, pay, hours and holidays. Procedural rules regulate the way in which substantive rules are made and interpreted, and indicate how conflicts are to be resolved. Third, the parties which negotiate the collective agreement also enforce agreement. The British system of collective bargaining is perhaps most noted for its lack of legal regulation. Collective agreements, with a few exceptions, are not regarded as contracts of legal enforcement between the parties.[7]

Collective bargaining structure

The structure of collective bargaining is the framework within which negotiations take place and defines the scope of employers and employees covered by the collective agreement. In Britain, there is no single uniform structure of collective bargaining, and the major structural characteristic of the system is wide variety. Thus, collective bargaining is conducted at several levels. Collective bargaining may be multi-employer bargaining. This arrangement involves a number of employers reaching a central collective agreement on pay and conditions with recognized trade union(s); the collective agreement covers all those companies that are signatories to it. Collective bargaining can also be single-employer bargaining. This form of collective bargaining, particularly in large multi-plant organizations, can either be centralized or decentralized. Where a holding company covers a group of companies, one single collective agreement for the whole group may be negotiated between the parent company and the recognized unions. However, the level of single-employer bargaining can be conducted at the level of the subsidiary companies or below, at the divisional level or at the level of the individual plant. Some multi-plant companies have a single-company agreement applying to all their plants, while other similar companies have separate agreements at each plant. In practice, survey evidence shows that collective bargaining structures are closely linked with business structures. In firms which operate in a single industry, decision making is more centralized and the pattern of union recognition and collective bargaining is more uniform than is the case in more conglomerate companies, where there is much more diversity. Table 12.6 shows the level at which pay is determined in Britain.

Between 1984 and 1990, fewer employees had their basic rates of pay primarily

Table 12.6 Basis for most recent pay increase in private manufacturing, 1984–90 (%)

	Manual employees 1984	1990	Non-manual employees 1984	1990
Result of collective bargaining	79	70	59	50
Most important level:				
Multi-employer	24	19	8	6
Single-employer, multi-plant	19	15	19	17
Plant/establishment	35	34	31	24
Other answer	2	2	*	3
Not result of collective bargaining	21	30	41	50

Source: Millward *et al.*, 1992, p. 223

determined by industry or multi-employer agreements with trade unions (Millward *et al.*, 1992, p. 223). According to Millward *et al.*, the shift away from multi-employer negotiations was accompanied by an increase in bargaining structures at enterprise or company level (1992, p. 355). It should be noted that the reduction in the proportion of workers covered by collective bargaining between 1980–94 also occurred in Australia, Japan, and the United States (see Table 12.7). Several of these countries have experienced substantial reductions in union membership and density. This is important if seeking to attribute the causes of these developments solely to post-1979 Con-

Table 12.7 The proportion of the workforce covered by collective bargaining and statutory sectoral wage arrangements by country, 1980–94

Country	1980	1985	1990	1994
United Kingdom	83	76	65	48
Australia	88	85	80	80
Canada	n.a.	37	38	36
Finland	95	n.a.	95	95
France	85	92	95	95
Germany	91	91	90	92
Japan	28	n.a.	23	22
Netherlands	76	76	71	81
Spain	n.a.	67	68	66
United States	26	20	18	18

Source: Brown *et al.*, 1997

servative industrial relations legislation. What is evident, however, is that Britain, within the past two decades, has become exceptional within the EU in its coverage of collective agreements (see Brown *et al.*, 1997).

Collective agreement

The outcome of collective bargaining is a collective agreement. In Britain, the collective agreement is not legally enforceable and therefore there is no legal remedy if either party reneges on the deal, but both sides have an interest in keeping industrial peace. The absence of legal enforceability in the UK is one of the principal differences in the output of the UK, US and Canadian industrial relations. The content of collective agreements varies widely. Generally, the greater the level of aggregation (national or industry-wide agreements), the fewer the subjects that can be covered in detail. The following are some of the typical provisions found in collective agreements in Britain: wage rates and benefits; hours of work and overtime; working arrangements; technological change; disciplinary procedures; grievance procedures; arbitration clause; status quo clause; and redundancy.

Strategic choice and collective bargaining

In terms of the structure of collective bargaining management might have to exercise strategic choice in at least two key areas, bargaining levels and bargaining units. In large multi-establishment companies management has to make a choice of level of collective bargaining – whether the bargaining is multi-employer (membership of employers' association), corporate bargaining or single-establishment bargaining. Purcell and Sisson (1983) highlight the fact that managements in similar circumstances can have different approaches to levels of bargaining. After the 1979 national engineering strike, GEC and Philips withdrew from membership of the EEF. However, in choice of bargaining levels they moved in diametrically opposite directions. GEC decentralized bargaining around constituent profit centres, whereas Philips centralized bargaining at national level. Decentralized single-employer bargaining often allows trade union negotiators to 'leapfrog' over wage settlements reached by other negotiating committees in the industry or geographic region. However, there are several advantages associated with single-establishment collective bargaining. The collective agreement can be tailored to the specific needs of a company or plant rather than to the more general needs of an industry (for example, multi-employer agreements would be inappropriate when pay is largely determined by job evaluation work study). The company or plant collective agreement can also reflect more accurately the product market circumstances and the company's ability to pay. Thus, collective bargaining is at the level of the profit centre and this arrangement can exert more control over union representatives. For example, when BL and Ford shifted from plant- to company-level bargaining in the early 1980s, this undermined union solidarity. The militant plants such as Cowley (BL) and Halewood (Ford) were isolated and neutralized by being outvoted in pay and strike ballots (Purcell and Sisson, 1983). As the authors argue 'The levels at which collective bargaining takes place both reflect the balance of power between management and trade unions and are a major influence on it' (1983, p. 109). Recent developments provide evidence of strategic choice in collective bargaining. Parallel with the decline in the proportion of workers covered by collective bargaining has been the decentralization of collective bargaining. It has been argued that decentralized collective bargaining is linked to globalization. That is, 'the development of company-specific industrial relations regimes can be seen as a response to intensified global product-market competition' (Hyman, 1997, p. 312). In North America and Europe, unions are bargaining with 'increasingly centralized corporations at increasingly decentralized level' (ibid.).

What is the significance of all the data on trade union membership, density, the proportion of workers covered by collective bargaining, and strike activity to HRM? In a nutshell, the dramatic reduction in union membership, the significant decline in strikes, and the trajectory of decentralized bargaining has led to a shift in power towards management. Where the preferences of management and unions differ, as they often do, the party with the perceived power will dictate the outcome closer to their preferences. The argument here is that this shift in bargaining power makes it more likely that employers will be tempted to take a short-term view and choose the 'black hole' or 'Bleak House' policy option. Such a strategy would pose a traditional challenge to trade unions and would be an impediment to more collaborative workplace relations discussed in this chapter. It would also be a major impediment to unions adopting a more proactive approach towards the more progressive elements of HRM, as suggested by Guest (1995). The next section addresses the question of whether HRM is compatible with traditional trade unionism. It begins by examining the notion of 'worker commitment' and concludes with an analysis of union strategic responses to the HRM paradigm.

● Trade unions and HRM

To understand the unions' strategic responses to HRM we need to examine the centre-piece of the new HRM model, high worker commitment to the organization.

Worker commitment

Organizational commitment implies a social psychological state of deep identification with a work organization and acceptance of its goals and values. Guest's (1995) HRM model explicitly contrasts the relative advantages of two approaches to workplace control systems, compliance and commitment. Compliance to management demands is a control system based upon formally established rules and procedures. In other words it is 'bureaucratic control' (Edwards, 1979). This control system, it is argued, generates 'reactive' behaviour patterns such as working to contract.

In contrast, the new HRM model seeks to elicit high commitment from workers and thereby cultivate 'proactive' behaviour with committed workers expending effort levels 'beyond contract' for the enterprise (Guest, 1995). The notion of worker commitment as a powerful, cost-effective mechanism of control is a common theme in critical industrial relations literature (for example, Friedman, 1977; Burawoy, 1979; Edwards, 1979). The rationale behind the goal of worker commitment is explained by the tensions inherent in the capitalist employment relationship; the need to achieve both control *and* consent of workers, in order to maximize profits. Lincoln and Kalleberg put it like this:

> The problem of control in organizations is in large measure solved when the commitment of its members is high. Committed workers are self-directed and motivated actors

whose inducement to participation and compliance is their moral bond to the organization (1992, pp. 23–4).

The case for eliciting the commitment of workers seems plausible but the literature on the topic suggest that the commitment concept is problematic. As Guest (1987) argues, the first issue is 'commitment to what?' Writers taking a managerial perspective are interested in commitment to values that drive business strategy, but Guest (1987, 1995) points out that workers can have multiple and perhaps competing commitments to a profession, career, craft, union and family. Arguably, the higher the level of commitment to a particular set of skills or professional standards, the greater the likelihood of resistance to multiskilling and flexible job designs. Thus the goal of commitment might contradict the goal of flexibility.

The second issue concerns the form of commitment. The orthodox approach is to see commitment as referring to 'attitudinal commitment' which Mowday *et al.* (1982) define as the 'relative strength of an individual's identification with and involvement in a particular organization' (quoted in Guest, 1987, p. 513). In contrast, Salancik (1977) views commitment in terms of 'behavioural commitment' which involves the binding of the individual to behavioural acts through, for instance, personal acceptance of responsibility. Mowday *et al.* (1982) suggest that a reciprocal relationship might exist between attitudinal and behavioural commitment whereby attitudes affect behaviour and vice versa. Assuming organizational controllers can secure commitment, 'what is the employee committed to?' There is a body of opinion that argues that employee complacency engendered by a common, unchallenged commitment to the organization's goals might be a barrier to innovation and change. Ultimately, workplace learning and the concomitant change to new technologies and new ways of working arise from the various exigencies of the free market and the tensions and conflicts stemming from *multiple* commitments within the organization, not through denial of reality (Legge, 1995).

The third issue is 'dual commitment'. If we assume a pluralistic model of the work organization, with workers represented by independent trade unions, observers have posed the question whether workers can be committed to the goals and values of the work organization and their trade union simultaneously. If HRM models place 'individualism' and organizational commitment at their core, then, in theory at least, the new approach must be incompatible with the core ideologies of workplace trade unionism – 'collectivism' and representation. Using a simple matrix model, Guest (1995) argues that, logically, if commitment to company and union are caused by the same variable, they operate from competing ends of the same continuum, and dual commitment is not possible. On the other hand, if they are caused by different variables, then dual commitment is possible, because a change in a variable affecting company commitment need not influence union commitment.

The majority of research on this topic has been undertaken in the US. The work, reported by Murphy and Olthuis (1995), found support for the notion of dual commitment. Two groups of unionized workers at a Canadian company were studied, one organized in Japanese-style work teams and one organized in traditional work structures. The authors found no significant differences in attitudes toward the company and union between workers in non-traditional and traditionally designed jobs. The findings suggest that 'many workers are attached to *both* the union and the company and have a type of "dual commitment" [and] attachment to the company does not necessarily lessen attachment to the union, and vice versa' (1995, p. 77). This, and the body of research that Guest reviews appears to support the hypothesis that dual commitment is possible where the industrial relations climate is characterized as cooperative and non-adversarial. The evidence of dual commitment still presents challenges for trade unions. There is some contradictory evidence which suggests that work teams might undermine support for the union in the long term. Unions must strengthen their internal communication and participation structures to counter any erosion of union support (Murphy and Olthuis, 1995). How does the research on organizational commitment help us to understand the new HRM–industrial relations discourse? The theoretical proposition is that the commitment-maximizing logic is a central plank in management strategies of control in the post-industrial workplace and, as such, will influence labour's strategic response to HRM.

Trade union's strategic responses

The literature presents the new HRM model as inconsistent with traditional stereotype industrial relations systems in North America and Britain. As Adams (1995) points out, the adversarial traditions of both the American and Canadian industrial relations systems elicit 'low trust' and non-cooperation between labour and management rather than a propensity of 'high trust' and cooperation. Guest (1987, 1990) suggests there is a *prime facie* case that, in theory at least, the 'collectivist' traditions of trade unions must be at odds with the 'individualistic' goal in the 'soft' normative HRM model; 'there is no recognition of any broader concept of pluralism within society giving rise to solidaristic collective orientation' (1987, p. 519). The TUC's study of HRM in 1994 provided evidence that some employers had used the rhetoric of HRM to conceal a deliberate anti-union policy by replacing collective machinery with an individualized employee relations regime. The HRM model poses a threat to trade unions in four ways; the individualization of the employment contract, the demise of union representation, the intensification of work and the undermining of union solidarity through organizational commitment.

The 'webs of rules' that regulate the modern employment relationship are being increasingly established unilaterally by employers, argue management critics, rather than through bilateral processes – union–management negotiations. Although appraisal has been characterized as an explicit HRM technique to 'control' workers' activity (Townley, 1994), when used to determine reward for individual performance it also undermines the *raison d'être* of unions, bargaining the effort–wage contract. As Bacon and Storey (1993, pp. 9–10) correctly argue 'Performance-related pay individualizes the employment relationship because it isolates employees and personalizes issues such as design and evaluation of work'. Moreover, by reducing the role of unions in pay determination, performance appraisal severs the link between increased rewards and collective action. In effect, the HRM reward system offers the formal and psychological contracts for hourly workers that have been the norm for many managers (Guest, 1989). Individual performance-related pay and pay-for-knowledge are the paradigm individualistic HRM techniques that symbolize attempts by management to move towards an 'individually orientated', rather than union-orientated organizational culture (Bacon and Storey, 1993).

The collective logic of trade union representation is further challenged by other HRM high-commitment practices. Training programmes that strengthen support for corporate culture and 'socialize' the workers to accept the hegemony of managerial authority can undermine workplace unionism (Bratton, 1992). At Xerox, for example,

Wells argues that training attempted 'to shape the workers' attitudes to management as well as to provide job skills' (Wells, 1993, p. 67). Promotion based on individual performance and competencies, rather than seniority, inevitably removes an area of the internal labour market from union influence. The HRM practice of circumventing workplace union representatives by communicating directly to the workforce information on quality and business operations can weaken the position and authority of union stewards. Unions represent their members in the disciplinary and grievance handling process. Logically, if, as HRM protagonists prescribe, workers *are* treated as the organization's most valued assets, the need for union representation as protection against arbitrary and exploitative action is diminished. Bramham, for example, adopts a managerial perspective and argues that the 'human resource company holds its employees in such high regard that exploitation would be *inconceivable'* (our emphasis) (1989, p. 114). This is certainly going too far. Nonetheless, the logic of the new HRM model (at least in theory) is that workplace unionism will eventually 'wither and die' (Guest, 1995).

Second, the new work regimes associated with the new HRM model (work teams, quality circles and employee involvement) can undermine collective union consciousness. These practices have required work organizations to try to engender a new corporate culture where workers identify with the symbols and values which managers communicate directly to them (Bacon and Storey, 1993), where deviant behaviour is managed by the workers themselves and where, in some instances, union stewards act as an agent of control over the bargaining unit members (Bratton, 1992). Burawoy (1979) has given an account of how workers in self-managed work teams created a culture that reproduced the conditions of workers' own subordination. Among other functions, work teams handle team deviants and peer pressure or 'clan' control is a means of maintaining performance standards. Case studies provide evidence into this form of self-organized control:

> I think it's a matter of conscience. A person who under the old system might go away for an hour, now he will think twice: Are they [co-workers] going to think they are carrying me because I've been away? ...Because you are a close-knit community in the cell system. You get little niggly remarks: 'Where have you been all morning?' That sort of thing, and it gradually works its way in psychologically (Bratton, 1992, p. 186).

> There was tension by workers against workers who were not pulling their own weight. Peer pressure in the groups was very important. [Team members] are tougher on [fellow workers] than management is (Wells, 1993, p. 75).

Third, critical writers on the labour process have plausibly argued that new HRM work structures are a sophisticated form of labour intensification and therefore have largely negative implications for workers (Sayer, 1986; Turnbull, 1988; Tomaney, 1990; Bratton, 1992; Wells, 1993). If we accept the tenor of this research and we adopt the same earlier logic, the new HRM model will fulfill a historic role of creating working conditions that *encourage*, rather than weaken, workplace unionism. The ability of HRM flexibility and quality practices to mortally weaken workplace unionism is contingent upon the context in which they are utilized and union strategies adopted. The HRM goal of flexibility and adaptability is akin to management demands for the removal of 'restrictive working practices' in the 1960s. On this issue, the unions demonstrate a willingness and have the capacity to bargain.

Fourth, the HRM goal of employee commitment is potentially the 'main challenge to the union', writes Guest (1989, p. 43). Selection testing is an important means of recruiting people who closely identify with the company and will be less prone to engage in union activities. HRM advocates call for the 'socialization of the workforce' (Champy, 1996, p. 155). Wells (1993, p. 70) cites a union official supporting Xerox's policy of recruiting people 'who are okay attitude-wise'. John Monks (1998b), the General Secretary of the TUC, explained the threat to unions from HRM like this: 'In the wrong hands HRM becomes both a sharp weapon to prise workers apart from their union, and a blunt instrument to bully employees'.[8] Certainly, the new collective corporate culture is unitarist and aims to encourage workers to identify with their work team and the company ideals, rather than the union collective. However, despite these challenges to organized labour from HRM, the research suggests that the theory that unions and HRM cannot coexist is not consistent with the empirical evidence on dual commitment and the 'lack of association found between unionization and high commitment management' (Wood, 1995, p. 57).

As the literature suggests, the trade unions have adopted different responses to these challenges (Betcherman et al., 1994; Guest, 1995). Several reasons can explain this diversity of responses to HRM. First, trade unions are complex organizations that have developed with different ideologies and associated strategies. For example, business unionism – dealing with bread and butter issues – is the dominant ideology in the US and has also played a large part in union development in Britain, Canada, and Japan (Adams, 1995). A popular view of business unionism would imply that US workers' attitudes are more accommodating to HRM practices than those of British workers belonging to more politically orientated British unions. However, this theory is not supported by Saporta and Lincoln's (1995) study. Second, the unions' response will be partly conditioned by their experience of management-initiated HRM policies. Further, the response will be different depending on whether the union perceives management adopting 'hard' or 'soft' versions of the HRM model (Legge, 1995).

Several industrial relations theorists have sought to clarify the types of responses made by European, Canadian and US unions (Beaumont, 1991; Martinez Lucio and Weston, 1992). Four different union responses to HRM initiatives can be identified; simple opposition, passive cooperation, bargaining approach and partnership. A study of the trade union response to HRM, however, has to be cognizant of the possible difference between trade union rhetoric and labour's actual response at the workplace. In the 1980s, observers suggested that the Canadian unions were relatively more opposed to HRM initiatives than US unions (Beaumont, 1991). More recently, industrial relations observers have argued that unions need to develop 'strategic partnerships' that build high-performance organizations and can keep 'win–win' rewards coming to labour (Kochan et al., 1986; Betcherman, et al., 1994; Guest, 1995; Verma, 1995). Rather than viewing the 'soft' HRM model as a threat, 'unions should champion it, becoming more enthusiastic than management', writes Guest (1995, p. 134). He goes on to suggest that unions should turn the HRM rhetoric back on management and 'transform it into reality'. The premise is that the policies inherent in the 'soft' HRM model include many to which unions could subscribe. Betcherman et al. (1994) correctly argue that the adoption of a new HRM model can only be sustained successfully if it holds the promise of real benefits for both the employer and employees. Marks et al. (1998) emphasize the complex and contradictory aspects of the 'mutual gains and partnership' approach for trade unions. In this study, moves to 'mutual gains and partnership' strengthened the influence and involvement of full-time union officers, but significantly reduced the influence of shop stewards, and left workers with limited representation. The interests of employers and labour are not identical and therefore an effective approach to HRM must involve acceptable trade-offs. The trade-offs associated with the HRM high-performance model are shown in Figure 12.3.

Despite the risks to unions of a partnership-type response to HRM, Wells (1993), a strong critic of the new HRM model, appears to come to a similar conclusion to that proposed by Guest (1995). Wells argues that the challenge for unions is to transcend the polarized extremes of militant opposition or 'collaborationist' cooperation, and focus on a strategy 'to fulfill the *promises* [our emphasis] of the HRM reforms' (p. 82). In theory, at least, the new HRM model embodies principles that offer management

Figure 12.3   The benefits and costs of a HRM high-performance model

	Benefits	Costs
For firms	Efficiency gains	Greater investment in training and other HR programs
	Lower turnover	Have to share information
	Better employee–employer relations	Have to share decision-making
	Potential for a better bottom line	
For workers	Access to information	No guarantee of job security
	Participation in decision-making	Need for greater commitment to the organization
	Discretion over work process	Some compensation based on performance
	Enhanced employability	
	Support for family responsibilities	
For unions	Affirmation of an independent voice for workers	Can take positions on work organization
	Access to information	Move away from job-control unionism
	Input into range of workplace issues	

Source: Adapted from Betcherman *et al.*, 1994, p. 97

the opportunity to maximize their side of the effort–wage exchange. Current evidence suggests, however, there are no inevitable impacts stemming from HRM-type practices. The outcome is indeterminant. It will depend upon the way the workforce perceives the changes and the ongoing interaction between union and management. This perspective recognizes the role of power in HRM decision making and as such brings a certain realism to the study of HRM and trade union relations that is frequently lost in the rhetoric and in the prescriptive texts (Kochan, 1996).

The fashionable perception that EU labour markets are 'inflexible' and US labour markets are 'flexible' fuels public policy on industrial relations and this explains the differences in the unemployment rates and labour productivity performance. The assumption is that the US companies achieve superior performance and are in a much better position to compete in the global marketplace. This is a simple characterization of reality. Europe is a large and diverse continent and cannot be treated as having a single market. This is also true for North America. Canada, for example, has not experienced the substantial decline in the coverage of collective bargaining and unionization and the Canadian labour market is more closely aligned to the EU than its southern neighbour. In Britain, the industrial relations policies of 'New' Labour focus on three areas, union recognition, low pay, and training. One question that arises is how the 'New' Labour government proposes to deal with employer resistance. On consideration of four fundamental factors influencing industrial relations, the state of the labour market, management's strategic capacity, labour's strategic capacity and the legal and political context of union–management relations, the weight of academic analysis suggests no reversal of industrial relations trends in the foreseeable future (Hyman, 1997).

Within this politico-economic context, management's strategic capacity, and its ability to manage employees effectively at the workplace to ensure managerial control and to achieve corporate objectives, is predicted to continue into the next century. There is evidence that management is playing a much more proactive role than ever before in determining the regulation of the employment relationship. It would appear that the traditional trade union strategy of bargaining for improvements in pay and employment conditions is threatened by the new HRM paradigm. The 'hard' HRM variant which promises the further marginalization of workplace unionism and collective bargaining poses a more obvious threat to trade unions and collective bargaining. Perhaps, the greater challenge is posed by the 'soft' HRM variant which, in theory at least, could involve the unions in an alliance to restructure workplace relations in a fashion that promotes mutual gains. Much of this reasoning is of course speculative, but if a closer alliance does develop between management and labour it will be interesting to observe how the parties manage the contradictions that lie in wait.

Some North American and British unions have moved from a position of simple opposition to a more 'proactive' approach (Betcherman *et al.*, 1994; McKenna, 1995). John Monks, the General Secretary of the British TUC, articulates the 'new realism' that seeks to establish a more cooperative relationship with employers like this: 'there are positive experiences of HRM… employees and their trade union representatives working together to create more positive arrangements which recognize each other's interests and which acknowledge a shared commitment to quality work, the importance of skills, and the need for change to be achieved by agreement'.[9] If, however, this partnership strategy has not been adopted extensively, there are at least three possible explanations. Employers might be too preoccupied with downsizing, rather than introducing the relatively costly 'soft' HRM alternative. The investment costs associated with the 'soft' HRM model are high and so are the risks, given that any social partnership arrangement will experience the underlying conflicts inherent in employment relations. Finally, employers might also be reluctant to invest in 'soft' HRM practices because the effect on the bottom line is unclear.

Chapter summary

Management strategies are the result of constrained strategic choices and have the object of maintaining managerial control and achieving corporate objectives. There is no single strategy adopted by management, and employers and managers can choose a variety of human resource and industrial relations strategies. There is evidence that management is playing a much more proactive role than ever before in determining the regulation of the employment relationship. British trade unions have lost 37 per cent of their membership since 1979, which has led to union amalgamation and mergers and created an even more complex and diverse union structure. All aspects of collective bargaining are in flux; pressures for change have come and will come from the growing globalization of corporate structures, global price competition, monetary policies in the EU, and the shifting balance of power between management and unions. From this analysis it would appear that the traditional trade union strategy of bargaining for improvements in pay and employment conditions is threatened by the new HRM paradigm. The 'hard' HRM variant, which promises the further marginalization of workplace unionism and collective bargaining, poses a traditional threat to unions. Perhaps, the greater challenge is posed by the 'soft' HRM variant which, in theory at least, could involve the unions in an alliance to restructure workplace relations in a fashion that promotes mutual gains.

Key concepts

Management style	Management strategy
Collective bargaining	Collective agreement
Industrial relations	Union density
Union structure	Worker commitment

Discussion questions

1. What is meant by the term 'industrial relations'?

2. 'Management industrial relations strategies are the result of strategic choices.' Discuss.

3. To what extent, and why, can Japanese management techniques be viewed as a union exclusion strategy?

4. 'The growth and structure of British trade unions cannot be understood without reference to contextual factors.' Explain this statement.

5. Define collective bargaining structure and assess whether collective bargaining in Britain is too fragmented or too centralized to function effectively in enlarged European product and labour markets.

6. What contradictions might be found in the twin goals of individualism and commitment on the one hand and team working and flexibility on the other?

7. How does the concept of 'high worker commitment' present a challenge to trade unions?

8. What strategies towards HRM innovations could the trade union movement adopt?

Further reading

Brown, W., Deakin, S. and Ryan, P. (1997) The effects of British industrial relations legislation, 1979–97, *National Institute Economic Review*, **161**: 69–83.

Hyman, R. (1997) The future of employee representation, *British Journal of Industrial Relations*, **35**(3): 309–36.

Kessler, S. and Bayliss, F. (1995) *Contemporary British Industrial Relations*, 2nd edn, London: Macmillan.

Monks, J. (1998a) Government and trade unions, *British Journal of Industrial Relations*, **36**(1): 125–35.

Waddington, J. and Whitston, C. (1995) Trade unions: growth, structure and policy. In Edwards, P., (ed.) *Industrial Relations*, Oxford: Blackwell.

Chapter case study

East City Council

Rose Peller, the newly appointed Chief Executive of East City Council, had a mandate to restructure the city's local government. One of her first tasks was to set up a quality committee of senior managers to transform the Council's culture, employee attitudes and performance. Her objective was to introduce total quality management (TQM) throughout the Council's administration. Workshops on TQM started with the senior management team and department managers. Some of the workshops on leadership aimed to turn old-fashioned local government managers into 'active leaders', trying to enthuse instead of dictate.

The proposed changes are physical and cultural. Part of the restructuring is to introduce open-plan working throughout the Council's buildings, in terms both of dismantling counters between staff and customers and of getting managers out of their offices. It is envisaged that the manager's role will become one of facilitator, and employees, after they become organized into quality teams, will have greater autonomy and no longer hand the problem solving automatically to managers. In addition, Rose Peller, with support from the Conservative-controlled council, is planning to introduce performance-related pay (PRP). PRP will be linked to personal goals rather than office targets. Together with TQM it is expected that PRP will contribute to the new culture in local government. At a planning meeting, Rose Peller expressed her views in a forceful manner, 'Since the department managers will be working in teams, they should know more about the people they are working with, which should make the appraisal system fairer. The more people work together and get rid of these hierarchical barriers the better,' she said.

East City Council employs 620 manual and non-manual employees; 85 per cent of the Council's workforce are in UNISON, the recently created public sector union.

(Source: Devised by J. Bratton.)

Task

As an assistant HR officer at East City Council, you have been asked to produce a report for the planning committee on the industrial relations and negotiating issues associated with the introduction of TQM and PRP. Your report should include the anticipated reaction of the trade union, UNISON, and its likely objectives in future negotiations with senior management.

Notes

1. George Wyke, personnel manager, Servo Engineering, and quoted in Bratton, J. (1992) *Japanization at Work: Managerial Studies for the 1990s*, London: Macmillan, p. 128.
2. Andrew, machine operator, Servo Engineering, and quoted in Bratton (1992) op. cit., p. 109.
3. Richard Johnston, personnel officer, Flowpak Engineering, quoted in Bratton (1992) op. cit., p. 162.
4. Lord Sieff (1981) chairman and chief executive of Marks & Spencer, and quoted by Purcell, J. and Sisson, K. (1983) Strategies and practice in the management of industrial relations. In Bain, G. (ed.) *Industrial Relations in Britain*, Oxford: Blackwell, p. 114.
5. Trades Union Congress (1988) *Meeting the Challenge: First Report of the Special Review Body*, London: TUC, p. 5.
6. Labour Research Department (1988) New wave of union busting, *Labour Research*, **77**(4): 28–9. *Ford Motor Co. v. Amalgamated Union of Engineering and Foundry Workers* (1969). For a discussion of this important judgment see Davies, P. and Freedland, M. (1984) *Labour Law: Text and Materials*, London: Weidenfeld & Nicolson, p. 779.
8. From the Foreword by John Monks in Mabey, C., Skinner, D. and Clark, J. (eds) (1998) *Experiencing Human Resource Management*, London: Sage, p. xiii.
9. Ibid.

chapter thirteen

Back to the future

John Bratton

Chapter outline

Chapter objectives

After studying this chapter, you should be able to:

1. Explain the evolving role of HRM in the next millennium.

2. Outline the key aspects of international and comparative HRM and understand the limitations of current HRM research in this field.

● Introduction

This book started by examining the evolution of human resource management and described and evaluated some of the theoretical models used to study human resource management. It was acknowledged that all personnel or human resource management activity involves ambiguity. It was also emphasized that a range of situational or contextual factors impacts on HRM activities within an organizational setting. The purpose of this chapter is to examine the future of HRM against the background trends in British and global capitalism and to review some aspects of the international scene to complete our learning journey of HRM. The complexities, interdependencies and particularities of national experiences and organizational needs make the task of predicting the future an heroic, some may say foolhardy, challenge. The evidence presented in the preceding chapters, however, points to a number of developments during the 1990s that have affected the way managers manage the employment relationship and which, in all likelihood, will continue to influence management practices in the next decade.

● HRM: continuity or transformation?

In Chapter 1, we discussed the change from personnel to HRM and the meaning and theoretical significance of the HRM model. From a managerialist perspective, the HRM phenomenon represents a transformation of human resource management. This perspective has emphasized the differences between the stereotype personnel and HR models. Whereas personnel management evokes images of 'welfare' professionals interfering and hindering the line manager, of reactive 'fire-fighting' management, and of submitting to militant shop stewards, HRM emphasized strategic integration and the HRM professional as a member of the senior corporate team and 'strong' proactive leadership within a new corporate culture. From a critical perspective, the HRM phenomenon is viewed less positively, as largely rhetoric and containing inherent contradictions. Sisson (1993, 1994) and Legge (1995, 1998) strongly argue that the rhetoric associated with HRM hides the reality of managerial prerogative and power to minimize labour costs. According to Sisson (1993) HRM may be an 'ideological project masquerading for greater individualization and work intensification' (Sisson, 1993, p. 202). The differences between the rhetoric identified with the 'soft' HRM and the reality for recipients in the workplace is summarized in Figure 13.1. Karen Legge's (1995) in-depth study of HRM models similarly draws attention to the way HRM as a rhetoric 'has been "hyped" as something new and consistent with the demands of the enterprise culture' (1995, p. 325)

In 1991, Guest argued that HRM represented a new management orthodoxy which had partly replaced the pluralist Donovan model. By new orthodoxy, Guest meant what constitutes good practice and what the appropriate role model for employee relations should be. Guest warned of the danger of rhetoric being well ahead of reality, of 'talking up' HRM; the evidence from the USA and UK in the early 1990s revealed no general trend, and much of the innovation in HRM was 'piecemeal and lacking in the crucial ingredient of strategic integration' (Guest, 1990, p. 387). Similarly, Brewster and Smith's (1990) survey reported that only 50 per cent of respondents claimed that the person responsible for human resources was involved in the formulation of corporate strategy. Hendry and Pettigrew (1990) also emphasize that there was no straightforward link from business strategy to HRM. By the middle of the 1990s, Storey (1995) was able to assert that there were 'many signs that HRM has carved a secure foothold' (p. 383). However, Storey also emphasized that there were conflicting trends. On the one hand, the notion that workers are the key to sustainable competitive advantage has gained centre stage in the management lexicon. But, on the other hand, argued Storey, there is increasing evidence of firms following traditional approaches to HRM. Under growing competition, these organizations are making low investments in employee training and development, offering low pay, maintaining Taylorist job designs and offer low job security. The reality is akin to the 'Bleak House' or 'black hole' employment strategy. Storey (1995) also notes other developments that undermine the progressive 'soft' HRM model, most notably the competing management philosophy of business process re-engineering (see Chapter 4).

A problem we face, when trying to assess the validity of the rhetoric versus reality debate, is the lack of empirical data on workplace accounts of HRM interventions. After almost a decade of HRM innovations, has HRM delivered on its promises? The Mabey et al. (1998) collection of case studies takes a refreshing approach to address this issue. The authors cogently argue that although following HRM innovations in the workplace, the burden of adjustment is greatest at the individual level, the voice of the recipients – in some cases the victims – of the HRM phenomenon has been under-represented in the HRM literature. Using qualitative case study research methodology, these workplace accounts of HRM interventions provide compelling insights into employment relations and help move the somewhat moribund academic debate on 'soft' versus 'hard' HRM models a step forward. The case studies affirm the view that significant changes are taking place under the guise of HRM. On

Figure 13.1   The rhetoric and reality model of HRM

Rhetoric	Reality
Customer first	Market forces supreme
Total quality management	Doing more with less
Lean production	Mean production
Flexibility	Management 'can do' what it wants
Core and periphery	Reducing the organization's commitments
Devolution/delayering	Reducing the number of middle managers
Downsizing/rightsizing	Redundancy
New working patterns	Part-time instead of full-time jobs
Empowerment	Making someone else take the risk and responsibility
Training and development	Manipulation
Employability	No employment security
Recognizing contributions of the individual	Undermining the trade union and collective bargaining
Teamworking	Reducing the individual's discretion

Source: Sisson, 1994

the question concerning the delivery of HRM goals (more empowered workers, greater commitment, more unified culture), Mabey *et al.* (1998) conclude that, 'many of [HRM's] prized goals... remain unproven at best, and unfulfilled at worst' (p. 237). In terms of the benefits from HRM innovations, the evidence suggests that it 'is not all gloom and doom', with case study data providing evidence that 'the majority of participants in a given HR change [benefit] in a way which outweighs the costs to the minority' (1998, p. 240). One challenge we face when trying to evaluate the successes of the HRM model, one we have alluded to in this textbook, is the longevity of the project. The progressive HRM strategy is not a panacea for all management HR problems, neither can the predicted synergy from HRM innovations be attained in a short time-scale to suit short-term financial performance goals.

Thus, we are left with a number of problems that must be addressed before predicting the future of HRM. First, the evidence suggests that perhaps the greatest challenge facing HRM professionals is an internal issue: convincing senior and middle management that human resource activities do contribute significantly to organizational goals. The most recent evidence suggests that the HRM 'thumb print' will prove to be far less of a euphemism than a predecessor such as 'human relations' (Ulman, 1992). Survey data accords with this thinking that some of the concepts and practices associated with the HRM model appear to be implanted in a growing number of British workplaces (Storey, 1995). As we enter the new millennium, the increasing influence of the EU Social Charter is likely to compel UK managers to reappraise their social ideals and focus less on US values and more upon European models (Brewster, 1995). In other words, the gap between the rhetoric and the reality of the HRM paradigm may be closed. This leads us to conclude that more systematic case study research is needed that examines both the practice of HRM and its effects on recipients in the workplace.

Second, capitalist societies are characterized by constant innovation and change. As noted in the introduction to this chapter, future human resource management activities and their role within the organization will be affected by external pressures. The major external pressures affecting British business include the globalization of markets, international competition, technological progress, national macroeconomic conditions, national public policy changes such as employment legislation, and cultural changes. Each of these external pressures affects companies differently. As a result, the evolutionary process of change in the management of human resources will be different across sectors, and therefore give rise to different outcomes over the next decade.

● HRM practices: the future

Predicting the possible directions in which organizations will manage their workforce in the next decade requires us to make assumptions about environmental factors that can exert a significant influence on management's choices. Each of the pressures for change will not be equally strong in organizations. Every work organization faces different external and internal pressures and each HR strategy is likely to be unique to that company. Additionally, predicting future HRM interventions and practices assumes that the HRM model will continue to be considered the best strategic option to achieve sustainable competitive advantage. Extrapolating trends from the 1990s, we can assume that management in both the UK and North America will have the strategic capacity to manage human resources on their terms into the next century

(Voos, 1997). With this in mind, what lies ahead for HRM? How are work organizations likely to respond to the external pressures in terms of managing people? Let us examine each of the four key constituent elements of the HRM cycle.

Selection

During the next five years there will be a growing number of people attempting to enter employment with high expectations that their skills will be used and their talents developed. Increasingly they will be attracted to many organizations by information obtained from company websites on the Internet. In some cases, organizations will be able to use Internet-based technology to help them screen out applicants before they make contact with a company. In the language of the flexible firm, more people will aspire to become part of a core workforce, show their commitment and receive appropriate rewards in return. Not everyone can qualify and organizations will continue to seek the means by which they can admit the right people. For the present, this is being provided by competency frameworks which specify the skills and qualities required from potential employees (Roberts, 1997) and more organizations are likely to develop such frameworks in the future. While we have argued that competencies augment an organization's power in selection, it does not mean that they will have things all their own way. In some areas and some types of employment, labour markets will remain tight and recruitment of the 'right' people will remain problematic. However, the apparent precision provided by competencies will allow organizations to utilize a growing range of sophisticated selection techniques. How applicants will respond to all this remains to be seen.

Appraisal

Productivity improvements will continue to be of vital importance to HRM in the next five years and, increasingly, many organizations will be turning to the development of integrated performance management systems based on a competency framework to help bring this about. Such systems seem to offer the hope of reconciling competing demands for judging performance to control it and providing feedback data for development purposes. More employees will be required to generate and receive multi-source feedback. Therefore more resources will be devoted to helping employees learn how to provide feedback for others and to use feedback to form personal development plans. There will still remain the problem of how any appraisal process can serve the often competing interests of the organization and its employees. There will be increasing efforts to find out what employees see as their interests so their energies can be harnessed.

Human resource development

It seems that many UK organizations are beginning to accept the importance of utilizing and developing the potential of their employees as a means of enhancing competitive capability. Government policies in education and training will attempt to provide a supply of qualified, skilled and employable labour. However, the key issue will be the extent to which organization policies and practices facilitate the use of skills and the development of employee potential. One emerging trend is the importance of employee talent in the way organizations are judged by external stakeholders (Edvinsson and Malone, 1997). Employee talent will only be retained if organizations are able to provide work which is sufficiently challenging and opportunities for development which meet their aspirations. Of particular importance in the future will be the capture of knowledge that is generated by learning and the management of such knowledge (Mayo, 1998). This will be accompanied by recognition in the way learning takes place at work. The learning organization may be a difficult idea to grasp and implement, however, there will be greater effort and growing sensibility to how and where learning takes place in organizations and how knowledge can be generated collectively. Technology will be used to facilitate this including the use of group-based software for joint problem solving. More organizations will be interested in work-based qualifications for their workforce.

⬤ Reward management

The reward function will continue to present major challenges to HRM professionals. The Social Charter is a framework for EU action on issues directly pertinent to the HRM department, including reward management. It is likely that the EU's intervention in the employment laws of member states will affect pay and benefits – for example, equal pay for work of equal value. However, in the area of benefits, there have also been significant European Court decisions allowing women to stay at work after the state retirement age (the Marshall case), and men to benefit earlier from company pension schemes (the Barber case). In the future, HRM departments face the challenge of seeking ways to control benefits costs, and simultaneously comply with the provisions of the Social Charter of the Maastricht Treaty and New Labour's support for a national minimum wage.

The past two decades have witnessed a dramatic reduction in collective bargaining at industry and national level. The decentralization of collective bargaining is expected to continue in the future (Hyman, 1997a). During the 1980s and 90s, it has become fashionable for writers to dismiss trade unions as either an anachronism or irrelevant in an organization following an HRM style (for example, Bramham, 1989). Although 'high-commitment' HR policies and alternative forms of employee representation, such as works councils, might reduce the demand for union representation, we do not share this view. European unions are likely to orientate towards 'business unionism with a European social conscience' and become more highly heterogeneous and 'conglomerate' in structure (Streeck and Visser, 1997), but they will not wither and die. The propensity for HRM professionals to convene informal meetings with union representatives and foster 'individualized' mechanisms of communication is likely to continue given that the union's strategic capacity is not strong. We predict that most employers will continue to behave pragmatically and opportunistically as far as union organization and collective bargaining are concerned (Kelly, 1990). Chapter 12 discussed the need for companies to ensure that, given the emerging European monetary regime, domestic pay and productivity movements are synchronized with those in other EU states (Gospel, 1992). HR specialists will continue to offer expertise in the negotiating process.

⬤ International and comparative HRM

In this final section we address aspects of the international scene to help us put the discourse on the new HRM model into a wider global context. In doing so, we make a distinction between international HRM and comparative HRM. The subject matter of the former revolves around the issues and problems associated with the globalization of capitalism. Comparative HRM, on the other hand, focuses on providing insights into the nature of, and reasons for, differences in HRM practices across national boundaries. This section addresses a number of questions which will further develop our knowledge and understanding of HRM. Can the Anglo-American HRM model be transplanted to other national systems? To what extent are HRM practices culturally determined? In terms of national models, is it feasible to speak of a distinctively 'European HRM model'?

The growing interest in international and comparative HRM should not be a surprise to the perceptive reader, given the globalization of capitalism in general, and the increased mobility of technology and labour across national boundaries in particular. The evidence to support the notion of globalization abounds. For instance, it is reported that, in early 1992, US companies employed more than 6.5 million people in other countries, 3 million in Western Europe, 1.5 million in Asia and almost 1.5 million in South America. Foreign direct investment continues to grow at a faster pace. In China, more foreign joint ventures were registered in 1992 than in all previous years combined (Shenkar, 1995, p. 1). As one management guru, Peter Drucker, points out, 'Increasingly, companies, even quite small ones, have to be run as "transnational" businesses. Their market may still be local or regional, but their competition is global. Their strategy also has to be global, in respect to technology and finance, products and markets, information and people' (1997, p. 3).

So far, the majority of *international HRM* research has focused on issues associated with the cross-national transfer of people, such as how to select and manage expatriate managers in international job assignments (for example, Tung, 1988; Shenkar, 1995). It has been argued elsewhere that much of this work is descriptive, managerialist and lacks analytical rigour (for example, Kochan *et al.*, 1992). This emerging field of study has been defined as 'HRM issues, functions and policies and practices that result from the strategic activities of multinational enterprises and that impact the international concerns and goals of those enterprises' (Scullion, 1995, p. 356). International HRM tends to emphasize the subordination of national culture and national employment practices to corporate culture and HRM practices (Boxall, 1995). The issue of transplanting Western HRM practices and values into culturally diverse environments needs to be critically researched. Late twentieth-century capitalism, when developing international business strategy, faces the perennial difficulty of organizing the employment relationship to reduce the indeterminacy resulting from the unspecified nature of the employment contract (Townley, 1994). If we adopt Townley's approach to international HRM, the role of knowledge to render men and women in the workplace 'governable' is further complicated in culturally diverse environments. For example, it behoves researchers to examine whether managers and workers in Mexico, Chile, India, Pakistan, South Africa and elsewhere will accept the underlying ideology and embrace the HRM paradigm.

In terms of critical research the field of study referred to as *comparative HRM* is also relatively underdeveloped. As with international HRM, the growth of interest in comparative HRM is linked to the globalization of business. Of considerable interest to academics and practitioners is the question of the extent to which HRM practices that work effectively in one country and culture can be transplanted to others. Drawing upon Bean's (1985) work on comparative industrial relations, comparative HRM is defined here as a systematic method of investigation relating to two or more countries, which has analytic rather than descriptive implications. On this basis, comparative HRM should involve activities that seek to explain patterns and variations encountered in cross-national HRM rather than simply descriptions of HRM institutions and practices in selected countries. Simple description, what can be called a 'tourist approach' where 'the reader is presented with a diverse selection of exotic ports of call and left to draw his own conclusion about their relevance to each other and to the traveller himself [sic]' (Shalev, 1981 and quoted by Bean, 1985, p. ii), lacks academic rigour. The case for the study of comparative HRM is made by a number of HRM scholars (for example, Bean, 1985; Boxall, 1995; Moore and Devereaux Jennings, 1995). There is, of course, an intellectual challenge and intrinsic interest in comparative studies. However, current research and interest is associated with the rise of foreign direct investment and international joint business ventures. Comparative studies can lead to a greater understanding of the factors and processes that determine HRM phenomena. The common assumption found in many undergraduate North American textbooks on HRM is that 'best' practice has universal application. Such an assumption, argues Boxall (1995), is untenable since HRM phenomena reflect different cultural milieux.

Comparative HRM studies can provide the basis for reforms in a country's domestic public policy by offering 'lessons' from off-shore experience. Comparative HRM studies can also challenge the rhetoric of the more prescriptive international HRM literature. It can promote wider understanding of, and foster new insights into, human resource management, either by reducing what might appear to be specific and distinctive national characteristics by providing evidence of their occurrence elsewhere or, equally well, demonstrating what is unique about any set of national HR arrangements. Using comparative analysis, Brewster (1993, 1995) examines the HRM paradigm from a European perspective. Drawing upon the data from a three-year survey of fourteen European countries, Brewster puts forward the notion of a new 'European HRM model' that recognizes state and trade union involvement in the regulation of the employment relationship. According to Brewster, the European HRM model has a greater potential for 'partnership' between labour and management:

One of the main reasons that the trade unions continue to exert such an influence in Europe is that in most countries the unions are not seen, and do not see themselves, as 'adversaries'. Rather, they are seen as partners (Brewster, 1995, p. 323).

Inherent in controversies around the notion of a European model or an American model are questions of the limitations and value of cross-national generalizations in human resource management (Hyman, 1994). Building on Tyson and Brewster's (1991) hypothesis, we might have to acknowledge the existence of discrete 'HRM models' both between and within nations, contingent on distinct contextual factors. It is easier to formulate questions than answers, and this section has taken the easier route rather than the more difficult. Yet there is value in asking questions. Questions can stimulate reflection and increase our understanding of the new HRM paradigm. Our object has been to do both.

Chapter summary

The resurgence of management and the changing fortunes of employees and trade unions were scrutinized in Chapters 1, 3 and 12. The evidence gathered in the preceding chapters points to both continuity and change. Moreover, the HRM debate illustrates the need for critical thinking to interpret complex data that employment practices represent and to evaluate the HRM model. In the foreseeable future it is likely that British management will remain in the ascendancy. Yet a look to the 1960s and early 1970s should provide a constant reminder that the employment relationship is dynamic and ever-changing. There is a school of thought that sees union membership and collective bargaining changes as representative of a paradigm shift away from the traditional industrial relations model. However, despite growing pressures on unions, technological change and the need for employers to achieve sustainable competitive advantage, in our view the next decade could herald a period of collectivist optimism. There are at least three reasons for this. First, only trade unions provide a countervailing power to management, and as survey evidence seems to demonstrate, workers who do enjoy the protection of collective bargaining are, on average, more favoured than non-unionized workers ; second, union representatives are committed to technological change and the 'soft' HRM variant that recognizes the importance of skills and learning and a shared commitment to quality work; and third, workplace union organization can provide an important basis for cooperation and help promote greater employee participation and involvement (Marchington, 1995). Looking forward to the future, then, it is reasonable to conclude that the progressive elements of the HRM model will play a key role in meeting the challenges posed by external and internal pressures and enhancing organizational effectiveness.

Key concepts

Globalization

International HRM

Convergence

Social Charter

Comparative HRM

European model of HRM

Discussion questions

1. Discuss the major external changes which will have the most impact on HRM practices in the future. Explain the impact.

2. To what extent will there be both convergence and divergence in the way European companies manage their human resources in the year 2000?

3. How realistic is it to envision an international HRM strategy?

4. To what extent, if at all, can we refer to a distinctive 'European' HRM model?

Further reading

Mabey, C., Skinner, D. and Clark, T. (eds) (1998) *Experiencing Human Resource Management*, London: Sage.

British Journal of Industrial Relations (1997) Industrial relations: Looking to the future, **35**(3): 307–447.

Industrial Relations Journal (1997) Jobs and justice in European and American workplaces, **28**(4): 257–352.

● Final comment

Your study of *Human Resource Management: Theory and Practice* is now drawing to a close. The time has come to reflect on what you have learned from your studies. Adult education scholars advocate that reflection plays a critical part in effective learning. Reflection is like using a mirror to help us to look back on our actions and thought processes. Reflective learning occurs where we have experiences and then step back from them to evaluate the learning we have experienced. There are several ways of carrying out reflection. One approach is to go back systematically through all that you have learned so far. Another approach, however, is to look at the additional reading listed at the end of each chapter. Other sources of information, particularly material that tends to differ from the approach in this textbook, provide mirrors for us and allow us to look at topics from another perspective. Further, other people – friends, relatives and co-workers – provide mirrors for us, allowing us to understand human resource management from another perspective. Talk to other people about the topics covered in *Human Resource Management: Theory and Practice*. Finally, your own experience of work is excellent material for reflection and can provide insightful information and understanding on HRM theory and practice. To help you start the reflection process go back to the beginning of each chapter and consider whether you have personally achieved the major learning objectives.

Appendix
The European Union Social Charter

The Social Charter was adopted by all member states, except the UK, in December 1989. The Social Charter is not a legal text. It is a statement of principles by which governments agree to abide. They will be required each year to present a report on how they are implementing the Charter. Its aim is to highlight the importance of the social dimension of the single market in achieving social as well as economic cohesion in the EC.

The preamble of the Social Charter gives added weight to other international obligations such as ILO conventions. The preamble also includes a commitment to combat every form of discrimination, including discrimination on grounds of sex, colour, race, opinions and belief.

Summary of the rights set out in the Social Charter:

1. Freedom of movement throughout the Community with equal treatment in access to employment, working conditions and social protection.

2. Freedom to choose and engage in an occupation, which shall be fairly remunerated.

3. Improvement of living and working conditions, especially for part-time and temporary workers, and rights to weekly rest periods and annual paid leave.

4. Right to adequate social protection.

5. Right to freedom of association and collective bargaining.

6. Right to access to lifelong vocational training, without discrimination on grounds of nationality.

7. Right of equal treatment of men and women, especially in access to employment, pay, working conditions, education and training and career development.

8. Right to information, consultation and participation for employees, particularly in conditions of technological change, restructuring, redundancies, land for transfrontier workers.

9. Right to health protection and safety at the workplace including training, information, consultation and participation for employees.

10. Rights of children and adolescents, including a minimum working age.

11. Right for the elderly to have a decent standard of living on retirement.

12. Right of people with disabilities to programmes to help them in social and professional life.

Glossary

Assessment centre The combination of assessment techniques at a single event to make judgements about people for selection or promotion.

Attraction Favourable interaction between potential applicants and images and values of and information about an organization.

Autonomy The extent to which a job allows employees freedom and discretion to schedule their work and decide the procedures used to complete it.

Bargaining scope The range of issues covered by the subject matter of collective agreements.

Behaviourally anchored rating scale (BARS) A performance appraisal technique with performance levels anchored by job-related behaviours.

Briefing groups Groups called together on a regular and consistent basis so that organization decisions and the reasons for them may be communicated. Group members may in turn meet with another briefing group so that information is systematically communicated down the management line.

Bureaucracy An organizational structure marked by rules and procedures, hierarchy of authority and division of labour.

Business process re-engineering (BPR) A radical change of business processes by applying IT to integrate tasks.

Career management Activities and processes to match individual needs and aspirations with organization needs, set within an integrative framework.

'Careless worker' model Assumption that most accidents at work are due to an employee's failure to take safety seriously (or to protect him or herself).

Collective agreement The outcome of collective bargaining, an agreement between employers and trade unions respecting terms and conditions of employment. Unlike in Canada and the USA, in the UK the agreement is not legally enforceable.

Collective bargaining An institutional system of negotiation in which the making, interpretation and administration of rules, and the application of the statutory controls affecting the employment relationship, are decided within union–management negotiating committees.

Communication The process by which information is exchanged between a sender and a receiver.

Competences The outcomes of work performance in an occupational area with specified performance criteria.

Competencies Underlying characteristics of a person which result in competent or effective performance taking into consideration the nature of the tasks and the organization context.

Computerised personnel information systems (CPIS) The use of software to record manpower data and calculate measures such as turnover, absenteeism and staff profiles.

Core workforce Workers with organization-specific skills and high discretionary elements in their work.

Culture The set of values, understandings, and ways of thinking that is shared by the majority members of a work organization and is taught to new employees as correct.

Delayering Restructuring an organization by reducing the number of grades and levels of work.

Development centres The use of assessment techniques to provide feedback for development.

Developmental approach (to appraisal) An attempt to harness the potential of employees through the discussion of the development needs of employees.

Downsizing The laying-off of employees to restructure the business.

Emergent learning Learning derived by interaction with evolving situations such as dealing with customers; used in the formation and formulation of strategy.

Employee involvement (EI) Processes providing employees with the opportunity to influence decision making on matters which affect them.

Empowering Limited power sharing; the delegation of power or authority to subordinates.

Ethics The code of moral principles and values that governs the behaviour of an individual or group with respect to what is right or wrong.

Expectancy theory A process theory of motivation stating that employees will direct their work effort towards behaviours that they believe will lead to desired outcomes.

Experience-based interview The use of questions in selection interviews that examine past performance in real situations.

Face validity How selection and assessment techniques appear to those subjected to them.

Fordism The application of Taylorist principles of job design to work performed on specialized machines, usually based on flow-line production assembly work. First applied by Henry Ford.

Foucauldian analysis This refers to the application of Michel Foucault's concepts of taxinomia, mathesis, examination and confession to HRM. The hypothesis is that HRM practices play a key role in constituting the self, in defining the nature of work, and in organizing and controlling employees.

Group technology The grouping of machines and workers to form a logical 'whole task' which can be performed with minimum interference.

Groupthink The tendency of members of a highly cohesive group to adhere to shared views so strongly that they totally ignore external information inconsistent with these views.

Human relations movement A movement, which grew out of the Hawthorn experiments conducted by Elton Mayo in the 1920s, which emphasizes the psychological and social aspects of job design.

Human resource development (HRD) A term used to indicate training and development as an organization's investment in the learning of its people as part of an HRM approach.

Human resource management (HRM) That part of the management process that specializes in the management of people in work organizations.

Human resource planning (HRP) An HRM approach to planning set in the context of organization views of people as the source of competitive advantage.

Image projection A loose model of the values, personality and attitudes of potential employees directed at appropriate labour markets.

Industrial relations The processes of regulation and control over the employment relationship.

Japanization A term used to encapsulate the adoption of Japanese-style management techniques such as team or cellular production, just-in-time and total quality control systems in Western organizations.

Job analysis The systematic process of collecting and evaluating information about the tasks, responsibilities and context of a specific job.

Job characteristic model A job design model developed by Hackman and Oldham (1976) suggesting that five core job characteristics – skill variety, task identity, task significance, autonomy and feedback – result in positive work experience.

Job description Descriptions of tasks and responsibilities that make up a job, usually derived from job analysis.

Job design The process of combining task and responsibilities to form complete jobs, and the relationships of jobs in the organization.

Job enlargement The horizontal expansion of tasks in a job.

Job enrichment Processes that assign greater responsibility for scheduling, coordinating and planning work to the employees who actually produce the product.

Job evaluation A systematic process designed to determine the relative worth of jobs within a single work organization.

Job rotation The periodic shifting of a worker from one task to another to reduce monotony or increase skill variety.

Joint consultation The involvement of employee representatives in discussion and consideration of matters which affect employees.

Knowledge management Management of information and knowledge to enhance organisation activities.

Labour market segmentation A method of classifying the ways in which organizations seek to employ different kinds of worker.

Learning climate Physical and psycho-social variables in an organization which affect the efficiency of employees in realizing learning potential.

Learning cycle A modern view of learning emphasizing learning as a continuous process. Usually linked to the work of Kolb (1984).

Learning organization A concept representing an ideal of whole organization learning by all employees and the use of learning to transform the organization.

Learning transfer Learning from HRD activities transferred to workplace behaviour and performance.

Line manager responsibility The acceptance by line managers of responsibility for the development of subordinates.

Low-cost leadership A business strategy that attempts to increase market share by emphasizing low cost compared to competitors.

Low quality product–low skill equilibrium Finegold and Soskice's (1988) explanation of the UK's failure to educate and train its workforce to the same levels as its competitors.

Managerial prerogative A belief that management should have unilateral control within an organization.

Managerialist perspective An ideology concerned primarily with the maximization of employee commitment and motivation through the adoption of appropriate HRM practices.

Manpower planning Processes, techniques and activities to ensure the necessary supply of people is forthcoming to allow organization targets to be met.

Manpower planning techniques and modelling Application of statisitical techniques to models of manpower stocks and flow, allowing calculation of manpower decisions.

Multi-source feedback (MSF) Feedback from a variety of sources for appraisal and development.

Normative model A theoretical model that describes how managers should make choices and decisions and provides guidelines for reaching an ideal outcome for the organization.

Organizational communication The systematic provision of information to employees concerning all aspects of their employment and the wider issues relating to the organization in which they work.

Organizational politics Those activities that are not required as part of a manager's formal role, but that influence the distribution of resources for the purpose of promoting personal objectives.

Paradigm A framework of thinking based on fundamental assumptions providing explicit and implicit views about the nature of reality.

Pay equity Pay relationships among jobs both within an organization (internal equity) and between comparative or competing organizations (external competitiveness).

Pendulum arbitration Form of arbitration which prohibits the arbitrator from recommending a compromise solution. The arbitrator must find in favour of either the employer or the union.

Performance appraisal Analysis of an employee's capabilities and potential drawn from assessment data of past and current work, behaviour, and performance, allowing decisions to be made in relation to purpose – for example HRD needs.

Performance contracts Details of what a jobholder agrees to accomplish over time.

Performance control approach (to appraisal) Means by which employee performance can be measured, monitored and controlled.

Performance management system A way of linking business strategy and objectives via goals and measures for employee performance.

Peripheral workforce Workers outside the core workforce (for example temporary or casual workers).

Personal development plan The result of a review process that links company or department objectives with employee objectives (or development).

Personnel specification Profile of the requirements of a person to fill a job used as a framework to assess applicants. Requirements may be expressed as essential and desirable.

Pluralist perspective A view of workplace relations which assumes that management and employees have different goals but seeks a reconcilation of such differences.

Post-industrial society or organization The thesis that posits that modern Western industrial society is moving into a 'post-industrial' era, where traditional manual work will disappear and large bureaucratic work organizations will be replaced by smaller organizations, 'adhocracies', charactized by high levels of flexibility and participation in decision making.

Power A term denoting the ability to influence others' behaviour.

Psychological contract The set of mutually agreed expectations by employers and employees relating to rewards and effort at work.

Psychometric tests Techniques to measure a sample of a person's behaviour.

Realistic job previews An opportunity for applicants to obtain a realistic picture of a job through job sampling, video, shadowing and case studies.

Recruitment Processes to attract applicants within appropriate labour markets for vacant positions within an organization.

Re-engineering A cross-functional initiative by senior management involving fundamental redesign of business processes to bring about changes in organizational structure, culture, information technology, job design and the management of people.

Reliability A statistical measure of the extent to which a selection or assessment technique achieves consistency in what it is measuring over repeated use.

Reward All forms of financial returns and tangible services and benefits employees receive as part of the employment relationship.

Scientific management A process of determining the division of work into its smallest possible skill elements and how the process of completing each task can be standardized to achieve maximum efficiency. Also referred to as Taylorism.

Selection Processes to establish the most suitable applicants for vacant positions within an organization from a number of applicants.

Self-managed team (SMT) A group of employees with different skills who rotate jobs and assume managerial responsibilities as they produce an entire product or service.

Shared responsibility model A view that the best way to reduce levels of occupational accidents and disease and improve health and safety at work lies with cooperation between employers and employees.

Sophisticated moderns A style of industrial relations management that encourages union membership, membership participation in trade unions, workplace union organization, and joint union–management involvement in areas of common interest in order to gain acceptance for change, to maximize cooperation, and to minimize conflict.

Sophisticated paternalists A style of industrial relations management that does not take for granted that employees accept the organization's goal (unitary perspective) and therefore management devote considerable resources in ensuring that their employees have the 'right' attitude and approach.

Standard moderns A style of industrial relations management that is pragmatic or opportunist. Trade unions and workplace union organization are recognized but union–management relations tend to be viewed primarily as a 'reactive' activity; it is assumed to be non-problematic until events prove otherwise.

Synergy The concept that the whole is greater than the sum of its parts. The condition that exists when a group interacts and learns and produces a group outcome that is greater than the sum of the individuals acting alone.

Systematic training model An approach to training encouraged by Industrial Training Boards in the 1960s, based on a four-stage process of identifying training needs and specifying objectives, designing a programme, implementing training and evaluation.

Taylorism A management control strategy named after F.G.W. Taylor. A systematic theory of management, its defining characteristic has been the identification and measurement of work tasks so that the completion of tasks can be standardized to achieve maximum efficiency (*see also* Scientific management).

Teleworking Working at a distance from an employer's premises but maintaining contact via telecommunications.

Time and motion study The systematic observation, measurement and timing of movements in the completion of tasks to identify more efficient work behaviour.

360° appraisal Feedback regarding performance from all round the job.

Training champions Senior managers who contribute to an organization's philosphy of support for training and development.

Transformation process Behaviour by which an employee converts attributes, skills, knowledge and attitudes into work outcomes and results.

Transformational leadership The ability of leaders to motivate followers to believe in the vision of organizational transformation or re-engineering.

Union density A measurement of current union membership expressed as a percentage of potential union membership.

Union recognition strategy A management strategy to accept the legitimacy of a trade union role and of collective bargaining as a process for regulating the employment relationship. This contrasts with union exclusion, a strategy to curtail the role of trade unions, and union opposition, a strategy to maintain a non-union company.

Unitarist perspective A view of workplace relations which assumes that management and employees share common goals.

Validity A statistical measure of the extent to which a selection or assessment technique actually measures what it sets out to measure. Criterion validity measures the results of technique against criteria such as present success of existing employees (concurrent validity) and future performance of recruits (predictive validity).

Welfare management The acceptance by employers of responsibility for the general welfare of their employees.

Whistle-blowing Employee disclosure of illegal, immoral, or illegitimate practices on the part of the organization.

Work Physical and mental activity that is carried out at a particular place and time, according to instructions, in return for money.

Working arrangements Activities associated with the work–effort exchange, allocation of work, work-teams, functional flexibility.

Bibliography

Abercrombie, N. and Warde, A. (1988) *Contemporary British Society*, Cambridge: Polity Press.

ACAS (1987) *Working Together: The Way Forward*, Leeds: ACAS.

ACAS (1988) *Labour Flexibility in Britain: The 1987 ACAS survey*, London: ACAS.

Adams, R. (1995) Canadian industrial relations in comparative perspective. In Anderson, J., Gunderson, M. and Ponak, A. (eds) *Union–Management Relations in Canada*, 3rd edn, Don Mills, Ontario: Addison-Wesley, pp. 495–526.

Adams, R. and Meltz, N. (1993) *Industrial Relations Theory: Its Nature, Scope & Pedagogy*, Metuchen, NJ: Scarecrow.

Aktouf, O. (1996) *Traditional Management and Beyond*, Montreal: Morin.

Alberga, T. (1997) Time for a check-up, *People Management*, 6 February, pp. 30–2.

Alvesson, M. and Billing Y. (1992) Gender and organization: towards a differential understanding, *Organization Studies*, **13**(1): 73–103.

Alvesson, M. and Willmott, H. (1996) *Making Sense of Management: A Critical Introduction*. London: Sage.

Amit, R. and Shoemaker, P.J.H. (1993) Strategic assets and organizational rent. *Strategic Management Journal*, **14**: 33–46.

Anderson, J., Gunderson, M. and Ponak, A. (1989) *Union–Management Relations in Canada*, Ont: Addison-Wesley.

Anthony, P. and Norton, L.A. (1991) Link HR to corporate strategy, *Personnel Journal*, April: 75–86.

Appelbaum, S.H. and Santiago, V. (1997) Career development in the plateaued organization, *Career Development International*, **2**(1): 11–20.

Arthur, J. (1992) The link between business strategy and industrial relations systems in American steel mini-mills, *Industrial and Labor Relations Review*, **45**(3): 488–506.

Arthur, J. (1994) Effects of human resources systems on manufacturing performance and turnover, *Academy of Management Journal*, **37**: 670–87.

Arvey, R.D. and Campion, J.E. (1982) The employment interview: a summary and review of recent research, *Personnel Psychology*, **35**: 281–322.

Ashton, D. and Felstead, A. (1995) Training and development. In Storey, J. (ed.) *Human Resource Management*, London: Routledge, pp. 234–53.

Atkinson, J.S. (1985) The changing corporation. In Clutterbuck, D., *New Patterns of Work*, Aldershot: Gower.

Atkinson, J.S. (1989) Four stages of adjustment to the demographic downturn, *Personnel Management*, August pp. 20–4.

Atkinson, J.S. and Meager, N. (1985) Introduction and summary of main findings. In Atkinson, J.S. and Meager, N. (eds) *Changing Work Patterns*, London: National Economic Development Office, pp. 2–11.

Bacon, N. and Storey, J. (1993) Individualization of the employment relationship and the implications for trade unions, *Employee Relations*, **15**(1): 5–17.

Baglioni, G. and Crouch, C. (1991) *European Industrial Relations: The Challenge of Flexibility*, London: Sage.

Bain, G. (ed.) (1983) *Industrial Relations in Britain*, Oxford: Blackwell.

Bain, G.S. and Price, R. (1983) Union growth: determinants and density. In Bain, G.S. (ed.) *Industrial Relations in Britain*, Oxford: Blackwell.

Bain, P. (1997) Human resource malpractice: the deregulation of health and safety at work in the USA and Britain, *Industrial Relations Journal*, **28**(3): 176–91.

Bain, P. and Baldry, C. (1995) Sickness and control in the office – the sick building syndrome, *New Technology, Work and Employment*, **10**(1): 19–31.

Baldamus, W. (1961) *Efficiency & Effort: an Analysis of Industrial Administration*, London: Tavistock.

Baldwin, T.T. and Ford, J.K. (1988) Transfer of training: a review and directions for future research, *Personnel Psychology*, **41**: 63–105.

Bamberger, P. and Phillips, B. (1991) Organizational environment and business strategy: parallel versus conflicting influences on human resource strategy in the pharmaceutical industry, *Human Resource Management*, **30**: 153–82.

Bansler, J. (1989) Trade unions and alternative technology in Scandinavia, *New Technology, Work and Employment*, **4**(2): 92–9.

Barlow, G. (1989) Deficiencies and the perpetuation of power: latent functions in management appraisal, *Journal of Management Studies*, **26**(5): 499–517.

Barney, J.B. (1991) Firm resources and sustained competitive advantage, *Journal of Management*, **17**(1): 99–120.

Barrett, J.T. (1996) Trade unions in South Africa: Dramatic change after apartheid ends, *Monthly Labor Review*, **119**(5): 37–46.

Bartholomew, D.J. (1971) The statistical approach to manpower planning, *The Statistician*, **20**: 3–26.

Bass, B.M. (1985) *Leadership and Performance beyond Expectations*, New York: Free Press.

Bassett, P. (1987) *Strike Free: New Industrial Relations in Britain*, London: Papermac.

Bassett, P. (1988) Non-unionism's growing ranks, *Personnel Management*, March.

Bate, S.P. and Murphy, A.J. (1981) Can joint consultation become employee participation?, *Journal of Management Studies*, **18**(4): 389–409.

Batstone, E. (1984) *Working Order*, Oxford: Blackwell.

Batstone, E. and Gourlay, S. (1986) *Unions, Unemployment and Innovation*, Oxford: Blackwell.

Batstone, E., Levie, H. and Moore, R. (1987) *New Technology and the Process of Labour Regulation*, Oxford: Oxford University Press.

Bean, R. (1985) *Comparative Industrial Relations*, London: Croom Helm.

Beaumont, P. (1991) Trade Unions and HRM, *Industrial Relations Journal*, **22**(4): 300–8.

Beaumont, P. (1992) *Public Sector Industrial Relations*, London: Routledge.

Beer, M. and Eisenstat, R. (1996) Developing an organization capable of implementing strategy and learning, *Human Relations*, **49**(5): 597–619.

Beer, M., Spector, B., Lawrence, P.R. *et al.* (1984) *Managing Human Assets*, New York: Fress Press.

Belanger, J., Edwards, P.K., Haiven, L. (eds) (1994) *Workplace Industrial Relations and the Global Challenge*, New York: ILR Press.

Bell, D. (1989) Why manpower planning is back in vogue, *Personnel Management*, July pp. 40–3.

Bengtsson, L. (1992) Work organization and occupational qualification in CIM: the case of Swedish NC machine shops, *New Technology, Work and Employment*, **7**(1): 29–43.

Bennis, W. and Nanus, B. (1985) *Leaders*, New York: Harper Business.

Bennision, M. (1980) *The IMS Approach to Manpower Planning*, Brighton: IMS.

Benyon, H. (1984) *Working for Ford*, London: Pelican.

Bessant, J. (1993) Towards Factory 2000: designing organizations for computer-integrated technologies. In Clark J. (ed.) *Human Resource Management and Technical Change*, London: Sage.

Betcherman, G., McMullen, K., Leckie, N. and Caron, C. (1994) *The Canadian Workplace in Transition*, Ontario: IRC Press.

Bevan, S. (1991) *Staff Retention – A Manager's Guide*, Report 203, Brighton: IMS.

Blair, H., Grey Taylor, S. and Randle, K. (1998) A pernicious panacea: a critical evaluation of business re-engineering, *New Technology, Work and Employment*, **13**(2): 116–28.

Blinder, A. (ed.) (1990) *Paying for Productivity*, Washington, DC: Brooking Institute.

Blyton, P. and Turnbull, P. (eds) (1992) HRM: debates, dilemmas and contradictions. In *Reassessing Human Resource Management*, London: Sage.

Boam, S. and Sparrow, P. (1992) *Designing and Achieving Competency*, Maidenhead: McGraw-Hill.

Bosquet, M. (1980) The meaning of job enrichment. In Nichols, T. (ed.) *Capital and Labour*, Glasgow: Fontana.

Boxall, P. (1992) Strategic human resource management: beginnings of a new theoretical sophistication?, *Human Resource Management Journal*, **2**(3): 60–79.

Boxall, P. (1995) Building the theory of comparative HRM, *Human Resource Management Journal*, **5**(5): 5–17.

Boxall, P. (1996) The strategic HRM debate and the resource-based view of the firm, *Human Resource Management Journal*, **6**(3): 59–75.

Boydell, T.H. (1976) *Guide to the Identification of Training Needs*, 2nd edn, London: BACIE.

Bramham, J. (1988) *Practical Manpower Planning*, London: IPM.

Bramham, J. (1989) *Human Resource Planning*, London: IPM.

Bramley, P. (1989) Effective training, *Journal of European Industrial Training*, **13**(7).

Brannen, P. *et al.* (1976) *The Worker Directors*, London: Hutchinson.

Bratton, J. (1991) Japanization at work: the case of engineering plants in Leeds, *Work, Employment and Society*, **5**(3): 377–95.

Bratton, J. (1992) *Japanization at Work: Managerial Studies for the 1990s*, London: Macmillan.

Bratton, J. and Sinclair, L. (1987) *New Patterns of Management: Communications and Employee Involvement in Local Government in Yorkshire and Humberside*. A report for Leeds City Council.

Braverman, H. (1974) *Labor and Monopoly Capital*, New York: Monthly Review Press.

Brewster, C. (1993) Developing a 'European' model of human resource management, *International Journal of Human Resource Management*, **4**(4): 765–84.

Brewster, C. (1995) Towards a 'European' model of human resource management, *Journal of International Business Studies*, **6**(1): 1–21.

Brewster, C. and Smith, C. (1990) Corporate strategy: a no-go area for personnel?, *Personnel Management*, July: 57–61.

British Institute of Management (1977) Employee participation: the way ahead. In Salamon M. (1987) *Industrial Relations: Theory and Practice*, London: Prentice-Hall.

Broderick, R. and Boudreau, J.W. (1992) HRM, IT and the competitive edge, *Academy of Management Executive*, **6**(2): 7–17.

Brown, J.S. and Duguid, P. (1991) Organizational learning and communities-of-practice: toward a unified view of working, learning and innovation', *Organization Science*, **2**(1): 40–7.

Brown, W. (ed.) (1981) *The Changing Contours of British Industrial Relations*, Oxford: Blackwell.

Brown, W. (1989) Managing remuneration. In Sisson, K. (ed.) *Personnel Management in Britain*, Oxford: Blackwell.

Brown, W. (1993) The contraction of collective bargaining in Britain, *British Journal of Industrial Relations*, **31**(2).

Brown, W., Deakin, S. and Ryan, P. (1997) The effects of British industrial relations legislation, 1979–97, *National Institute Economic Review*, **161**: pp. 69–83.

Buchanan, D.A. (1997) The limitations and opportunities of business process re-engineering in a politicized organizational climate, *Human Relations*, **50**(1): 51–72.

Bullock, Lord (1977) *Report of the Committee of Inquiry on Industrial Democracy* (Cmnd 6706) London: HMSO.

Burack, E. (1986) Corporate business and human resource planning practices: strategic issues and concerns, *Organizational Dynamics*, **15**.

Burawoy, M. (1979) *Manufacturing Consent: Changes in the Labour Process under Monopoly Capitalism*, Chicago: Chicago University Press.

Burgoyne, J., Pedler, M. and Boydell, T. (1994) *Towards the Learning Company*, Maidenhead:McGraw-Hill.

Burgoyne, J. and Reynolds, M. (eds) (1997) *Management Learning*, London: Sage.

Byers, P.Y. (ed.) (1997) *Organizational Communication: Theory and Behavior*, Boston: Allyn & Bacon.

Campbell, D.J. and Lee, C. (1988) Self-appraisal in performance evaluation, *Academy of Management Review*, **13**(2): 3–8.

Campion, M.A., Palmer, D.K. and Campion, J.E. (1997) A review of structure in the selection interview, *Personnel Psychology*, **50**: 655–702.

Cappelli, P. and Chalykoff (1985) The effects of management industrial relations strategy: results of a survey, quoted in Anderson, J., Gunder, M. and Ponak, A. (1989).

Cappelli, P. and Singh, H. (1992) Integrating strategic human resources and strategic management. In Lewin, D., Mitchell, O. and Skerer, P. (eds) *Research Frontiers in Industrial Relations & Human Resources*, Madison, University of Wisconsin: Industrial Relations Association, pp. 165–192.

Carsten De Dreu and Evert Van De Vliert (1997) (eds) *Using Conflict in Organizations*, Thousand Oaks, CA: Sage.

CBI (1986) Checking on employee involvement: the CBI Communication Audit, *Employment Gazette*, October.

Champy, J. (1996) *Reengineering Management: The Mandate for New Leadership*, New York: Harper Business.

Chandler, A. (1962) *Strategy and Structure*, Cambridge, MA: MIT Press.

Chapman, R. (1990) Personnel management in the 1990s, *Personnel Management*, **22**: 28–32.

Charlton, J.H. (1983) Employee participation in the public sector: a review, *Journal of General Management*, **8**(3): 129–48.

Child, J. (1972) Organizational structure, environment and performance: the role of strategic choice, *Sociology*, **6**(1): 331–50.

Child, J. (1985) Managerial strategies, new technology, the labour process. In Knights, D. *et al.* (eds) *Job Design: Critical Perspectives on the Labour Process*, Aldershot: Gower.

Clark, J. (ed.) (1993) *Human Resource Management and Technical Change*, London: Sage.

Clarke, L. (1997) Changing work systems, changing social relations, *Relations Industrielles/Industrial Relations*, **52**(4): 839–61.

Clarke, T, (1977) Industrial democracy: the institutional suppression of industrial conflict. In Clarke, T. and Clements, L. *Trade Unions under Capitalism*, London: Fontana.

Clausen, C. and Lorentzen, B. (1993) Workplace implications of FMS and CIM in Denmark and Sweden, *New Technology, Work and Employment*, **8**(1): 21–30.

Claydon, T. (1989) Union de-recognition in Britain in the 1980s, *British Journal of Industrial Relations*, **XXVII**(2).

Clegg, H. (1976) *Trade Unionism under Collective Bargaining*, Oxford: Blackwell.

Clegg, H. (1979) *The Changing System of Industrial Relations in Great Britain*, Oxford: Blackwell.

Clegg, S. (1990) *Modern Organizations: Organization Studies in the Postmodern World*, London: Sage.

Clegg, S. and Dunkerley, D. (1980) *Organization, Class and Control*, London: RKP.

Coates, D. (1975) *The Labour Party and the Struggle for Socialism*, Cambridge: Polity.

Coates, K. and Topham, T. (1980) *Trade Unions in Britain*, Nottingham: Spokesman.

Codrington, C. and Henley, J.S. (1981) The industrial relations of injury and death: safety representatives in the construction industry, *British Journal of Industrial Relations*, **XIX**(3): 297–315.

Cohen, M.D. and Sproull, L.S. (eds) (1996) *Organizational Learning*, Thousand Oaks: Sage.

Collard, R. (1989) *Total Quality: Success Through People*, London: IMP.

Colling, T. (1995) Experiencing turbulence: competition, strategic choice and the management of human resources in British airways, *Human Resource Management*, **5**(5): 18–32.

Conger, J. and Kanungo, R. (eds) (1988) *Charismatic Leadership*, San Francisco: Jossey-Bass.

Conway, H.E. (1987) *Equal Pay for Work of Equal Value Legislation in Canada: An Analysis*, Ottawa: Studies in Social Policy.

Cook, M. (1994) *Personnel Selection and Productivity*, Chichester: Wiley.

Cooper, C.G.L. and Smith M.G.J. (eds) (1985) *Job Stress and Blue Collar Work*, Chichester: Wiley.

Coopey, J. (1996) Crucial gaps in the 'Learning Organization'. In Starkey, K. (ed.) *How Organizations Learn*, London: International Thomson Business Press.

Coriat, B. (1980) The restructuring of the assembly line: a new economy of time and control, *Capital and Class*, **11**: 34–43.

Coverdale Ltd (1995) *Competencies: The Current State of Play*, London: Coverdale Organisation.

Covey, S. (1989) *The Seven Habits of Highly Effective People*, New York: Fireside.

Covey, S. (1990) *Principle-Centered Leadership*, New York: Fireside.

Cowling, A. and Walters, M. (1990) Manpower planning – where are we today?, *Personnel Review*, **19**(3): 3–8.

Craig, J. and Yetton, P. (1993) Business process redesign: A critique of process innovation by Thomas Davenport as a case study in the literature, *Australian Journal of Management*, **17**(2): 285–306.

Craig, M. (1981) *Office Workers' Survival Handbook*, London: BSSR.

Cressey, P. (1993) Kalmar and Uddevalla: the demise of Volvo as a European icon, *New Technology, Work and Employment*, **8**(2): 88–90.

Cressey, P. (1998) European works councils in practice, *Human Resource Management Journal*, **8**(1): 67–81.

Cressey, P., Eldridge, J. and MacInnes, J. (1985) *Just Managing*, Milton Keynes: Open University Press.

Crouch, C. (1982) *The Politics of Industrial Relations*, 2nd edn, London: Fontana.

Cully, M., O'Reilly, A., Woodland, S. and Dix, G. (1998) The 1998 Workplace Employee Relations Survey, First Findings, www.dti.gov.uk/emar

Curnow, B. (1986) The creative approach to pay, *Personnel Management*, October: 32–6.

Curnow, B. (1989) Recruit, retrain, retain: personnel management and the three Rs, *Personnel Management*, November, pp. 40–7.

Daft, R. (1998) *Organization Theory and Design*, 6th edn, South-Western: Cincinnati, Ohio.

Daniel, W.W. and Millward, N. (1983) *Workplace Industrial Relations in Britain*, London: Heinemann.

Daniel, W.W. and Millward, N. (1993) Findings from the workplace industrial relations surveys. In Clark, J. (ed.) *Human Resource Management and Technical Change*, London: Sage.

Davidson, M.J. and Cooper, C.L. (1992) *Shattering the Glass Ceiling*, London: Paul Chapman Publishing.

Davies, L. (1996) Development centres for senior managers in Yorkshire Water, *Career Development International*, **1**(6): 17–24.

Davies, P. and Freedland, M. (1984) *Labour Law: Text and Materials*, London: Weidenfeld & Nicholson.

Deery, S. (1995) The demise of the trade union as a representative body?, *British Journal of Industrial Relations*, **33**(4): 537–43.

Denham, D. (1990) Unfair dismissal law and the legitimation of managerial control, *Capital and Class*, **41**: 32–41.

Department of Employment (1974) Company manpower planning, *Manpower Papers*, **1**.

Dermer, J. (ed.) (1992) *The New World Economic Order: Opportunities and Threats*, North York, Ont.: Captus Press.

Devanna, M.A., Fombrun, C.J. and Tichy, N.M. (1984) A framework for strategic human resource management. In Fombrun, C.J. *et al.*, *Strategic Human Resource Management*, Chichester: John Wiley.

Dex, S. (1988) Gender and the labour market. In Gallie, D. (ed.) *Employment in Britain*, Oxford: Blackwell.

DfEE (1997) *Labour Market and Skill Trends 1997/98*, Sheffield: Department for Education and Employment.

Dickens, L. (1994) Wasted resources? Equal opportunities in employment. In Sisson, K. (ed.) *Personnel Management: A Comprehensive Guide to Theory and Practice in Britain*, Oxford: Blackwell.

Dickens, L. (1998) What HRM means for gender equality, *Human Resource Management Journal*, **8**(1): 23–45.

Disney, R. (1990) Explanations of the decline in trade union density in Britain: an appraisal, *British Journal of Industrial Relations*, **28**(2): 165–77.

Dixon, N. (1992) Organizational learning: a review of the literature with implications for HRD professionals, *Human Resource Development Quarterly*, **3**(1): 29–49.

Donnelly, E. (1987) The training model: time for a change, *Industrial and Commercial Training*, May/June, pp. 3–6.

Donovan, Lord (1968) *Royal Commission on Trade Unions Employers' Association*, Report, Cmnd 3623, London: HMSO.

Dore, R. (1973) *British Factory, Japanese Factory*, London: Allen & Unwin.

Dowlen, A. (1996) NLP – help or hype? Investigating the uses of neurolinguistic programming in management learning, *Career Development International*, **1**(1): 27–34.

Downie, B. and Coates, M. (1994) *Traditional and New Approaches to Human Resource Management*, Kingston, Ont.: IRC Press.

Drache, D. (1995) The decline of collective bargaining: is it irreversible?, *Proceedings of the XXXIst ACRI/CIRA*, pp. 101–22.

Drucker, P.F. (1997) Toward the new organization. In Hesselbein, F., Goldsmith, M. and Beckhard, R., *The Organization of the Future*, San Francisco: Jossey-Bass

Dunn, S. (1993) From Donovan to wherever, *British Journal of Industrial Relations*, **31**(2): 169–87.

Dyer, P. (1984) Studying human resource strategy: an approach and an agenda, *Industrial Relations*, **23**(2):, 156–69.

Edvinsson, L. and Malone, M.S. (1997) *Intellectual Capital*, London: Piatkus.

Edwards, P.K. (1985) *Managing Labour Relations Through the Recession*, University of Warwick, IRRU.

Edwards, P. (ed.) (1995) *Industrial Relations*, Oxford: Blackwell.

Edwards, R. (1979) *Contested Terrain: The Transformation of the Workplace in the Twentieth Century*, London: Heinemann.

Eisenberg, E.M. and Goodall, H.L. (1997) *Organizational Communication*, 2nd edn, New York: St. Martin's Press.

Elger, T. and Smith, C. (1994) *Global Japanization? The Transformation of the Labour Process*, London: Routledge.

EOC (1992) *Women's Pay in EC Countries*, Equal Opportunities Commission, Manchester.

Eva, D. and Oswald, R. (1981) *Health and Safety at Work*, London: Pan Original.

Evans, A.L. and Lorange, P. (1989) The two logics behind human resource management. In Evans, P., Doz, Y. and Laurent, A., *Human Resource Management in International Firms*, London: Macmillan.

Farnham, D. (1990) *Personnel in Context*, London: IPM.

Feltham, R. (1992) Using competencies in selection and recruitment. In Boam, R. and Sparrow, P. (eds) *Designing and Achieving Competency*, Maidenhead: McGraw-Hill.

Finegold, D. and Soskice, D. (1988) The failure of training in Britain: analysis and prescription, *Oxford Review of Economic Policy*, **4**(3): 21–53.

Fletcher, S. (1991) *NVQs, Standards and Competence: A Practical Guide for Employers, Managers and Trainers*, London: Kogan Page.

Fombrun, C., Tichy, N.M. and Devanna, M.A. (eds) (1984) *Strategic Human Resource Management*, New York: Wiley.

Fonda, N. and Hayes, C. (1986) Is more training really necessary?, *Personnel Management*, May, pp. 64–9.

Fox, A. (1985) *Man Mismanagement*, 2nd edn, London: Hutchinson.

Fox, A. (1966) *Industrial Sociology and Industrial Relations*, London: HMSO (Donovan Commission Research Paper 3).

Freeman, R. and Pelletier, J. (1990) The impact of industrial relations legislation on British union density, *British Journal of Industrial Relations*, **28**(2): 141–64.

Friedman, A. (1977) *Industry and Labour: Class Struggle at Work and Monopoly Capitalism*, London: Macmillan.

Fyfe, J. (1986) Putting people back into the manpower planning equations, *Personnel Management*, October, 64–9.

Garavan, T. (1997) The learning organization: a review and an evaluation, *The Learning Organization*, **4**(1): 18–29.

Garavan, T.N., Morley, M. and Flynn, M. (1997) 360 degree feedback: its role in employee development, *Journal of Management Development*, **16**(2): 134–47.

Gattiker, U.E. and Cohen, A. (1997) Gender-based wage differences, *Relations Industrielles/Industrial Relations*, **52**(3): 507–29.

Gennard, J., Steele, M. and Miller , K. (1989) Trends and developments in industrial relations law: Trade union discipline and non-strikers, *Industrial Relations Journal*, **20**(1): 5–15.

Georgiades, N. (1990) A strategic future for personnel?, *Personnel Management*, February: 47–53.

Gilbert, K. and Secker, J. (1995) Generating equality? Equal pay, decentralization and the electricity supply industry, *British Journal of Industrial Relations*, **33**(2): 191–207.

Godard, J. (1991) The progressive HRM paradigm: a theoretical and empirical re-examination, *Relations Industrielles/Industrial Relations*, **46**(2): 378–99.

Godard, J. (1994) *Industrial Relations: The Economy and Society*, Toronto: McGraw-Hill Ryerson.

Gold, J. (1997) Learning from story telling, *Journal of Workplace Learning*, **9**(4): 133–41.

Gospel, H.F. (1992) The single European market and industrial relations: an introduction, *British Journal of Industrial Relations*, **30**(4): 483–94.

Gospel, H. and Littler, C.R. (eds) (1983) *Managerial Strategies and Industrial Relations*, London: Heinemann.

Gospel, H.F. and Palmer, G. (1993) *British Industrial Relations*, 2nd edn, London: Routledge.

Grahl, J. and Teague, P. (1997) Is the European social model fragmenting?, *New Political Economy*, **2**(3): 405–26.

Grant, D. and Oswick, C. (1998) Of believers, atheists and agnostics: practitioner views on HRM, *Industrial Relations Journal*, **29**(3): 178–93.

Gratton, L. (1997) Tomorrow people, *People Management*, 24 July, pp. 22–7.

Green, F. (1997) *Review of Information on the Benefits of Training for Employees*, Research Report No.7, Sheffield: Department for Education and Employment.

Green, F. and Ashton, D. (1992) Skill shortage and skill deficiency, *Work, Employment and Society*, **6**(2): 287–301.

Green, J. (1998) Employers learn to live with AIDS, *HR Magazine*, **43**(2): 62–7.

Gregg, P. (1973) *A Social and Economic History of Britain, 1760–1972*, 7th edn, London: Harrap.

Greider, W. (1997) *One World, Ready or Not*, New York: Simon & Schuster.

Grey, C. and Mitev, N. (1995) Reengineering organizations: a critical appraisal, *Personnel Review*, **24**(1): 6–18.

Griffiths, A. and Wall, S. (1989) *Applied Economics*, 3rd edn, London: Longman.

Grint, K. and Willcocks, L. (1995) Business process re-engineering in theory and practice: business paradise regained?, *New Technology, Work and Employment*, **10**(2): 99–108.

Grundy, T. (1994) *Strategic Learning in Action*, Maidenhead: McGraw-Hill.

Guest, D.E. (1986) Worker participation and personnel policy in the UK: some case studies, *International Labour Review*, **125**(6): 406–27.

Guest, D.E. (1987) Human resource management and industrial relations, *Journal of Management Studies*, **24**(5): 503–21.

Guest, D. (1989) HRM: implications for industrial relations. In Storey, J., *New Perspectives on Human Resource Management*, London: Routledge.

Guest, D. (1990) Human resource management and the American Dream, *Journal of Management Studies*, **27**(4): 377–97.

Guest, D. (1991) Personnel management: the end of orthodoxy?, *British Journal of Industrial Relations*, **29**(2): 149–75.

Guest, D. (1995) Human resource management, trade unions and industrial relations. In Storey, J. (ed.) *Human Resource Management: A Critical Text*, London: Routledge.

Guest, D. (1997) Human resource management and performance: a review and research agenda, *The International Journal of Human Resource Management*, **8**(3): 263–76.

Guest, D., Peccei, R. and Thomas, A. (1993) The impact of employee involvement on organizational commitment and 'them and us' attitudes, *Industrial Relations Journal*, **24**(3): 191–200.

Hackman, J.R. and Oldham, G.R. (1980) *Work Redesign*, New York: Addison-Wesley.

Hakim, C. (1990) Core and periphery in employers' workforce strategies. Evidence from the 1987 ELUS survey, *Work, Employment and Society*, **4**(2): 157–88.

Hall, D.T. (1986) Dilemmas in linking succession planning to individual executive learning, *Human Resource Management*, **25**(2): 235–65.

Hall, S. and Jacques, M. (1989) *New Times*, London: Lawrence & Wishart.

Hamel, G and Prahalad, C.K. (1993) Strategy as stretch & leverage, *Harvard Business Review*, March–April: pp. 75–84.

Hammarström, O. and Lansbury, R. (1991) The art of building a car: the Swedish experience re-examined, *New Technology, Work and Employment*, **6**(2): 85–90.

Hammer, M. (1997) *Beyond Reengineering*, New York: Harper Business.

Hammer, M. and Champy, J. (1993) *Reengineering the Corporation*, Nicholas Bealey: London.

Hammer, M. and Stanton, S. (1995) *The Reengineering Revolution: A Handbook*, Harper Business Press: New York.

Handy, C. (1987) *The Making of Managers*, London: MSC/NEDC/BIM.

Handy, L., Devine, M. and Heath, L. (1996) *360° Feedback: Unguided Missile or Powerful Weapon?*, Ashridge Management Research Group: Berkhamsted.

Harper, S.C. (1983) A developmental approach to performance appraisal, *Business Horizons*, September/October, pp. 68–74.

Harri-Augstein, S. and Webb, I.M. (1995) *Learning To Change*, McGraw-Hill: Maidenhead.

Harrington, B., McLoughlin, K. and Riddell, D. (1998) Business process re-engineering in the public sector: a case study of the Contributions Agency, *New Technology, Work and Employment*, **13**(11): 43–50.

Harris, M.M. (1989) Reconsidering the employment interview: a review of recent literature and suggestions for future research, *Personnel Psychology*, **42**: 691–726.

Hartle, F. (1997) *Transforming the Performance Management Process*, London: Kogan Page.

Hassard, J and Parker, M. (1993) *Postmodernism & Organizations*, London: Sage.

Hendry, C., Pettigrew, A. and Sparrow, P. (1988) Changing patterns of human resource management, *Personnel Management*, November, 31–41.

Hendry, C., Pettigrew, A. (1990) Human resource management: an agenda for the 1990s, *International Journal of Human Resource Management*, **1**(1): 17–44.

Herriot, P. (1989) *Recruitment in the 1990s*, London: IPM.

Herriot, P. (1995) The management of careers. In Tyson, S. (ed.) *Strategic Prospects for HRM*, London: IPD.

Herriot, P. and Fletcher, C. (1990) Candidate-friendly, selection for the 1990s, *Personnel Management*, February: 32–5.

Herriot, P., Manning, W.E.G. and Kidd, J.M. (1997) The content of the psychological contract, *British Journal of Management*, **8**(2): 151–62.

Herzberg, F. (1966) *Work and the Nature of Man*, Chicago, Ill.: World Publishing Co.

Herzberg, F., Mausner, B. and Snyderman, B. (1959) *The Motivation to Work*, New York: John Wiley.

Hillage, J. and Moralee, J. (1996) *The Return on Investors*, Report 314, Brighton: Institute of Employment Studies.

Hill, C. and Jones, G. (1998) *Strategic Management Theory*, Toronto: Houghton-Mifflin.

Hillier, Y. (1997) Competence-based qualifications in training, development and management, *Journal of Further and Higher Education*, **21**(1): 33–41.

Hirsh, W. (1990) *Succession Planning: Current Practice and Future Issues*, IMS Report No. 184, Brighton: IMS.

Hirsh, W. and Jackson, C. (1997) *Strategies for Career Development: Promise, Practice and Pretence*, Report No. 305, Brighton: IES.

Hobsbawm, E.J. (1968) *Industry and Empire*, London: Weidenfeld & Nicolson.

Hogarth, T. (1993) Worker support for organizational change and technical change, *Work, Employment and Society*, **7**(2).

Holman, D., Pavlica, K. and Thorpe, R. (1997) Rethinking Kolb's theory of experiential learning in management education: the contribution of social constructionism and activity theory, *Management Learning*, **28**(2): 135–48.

Huczynski, A. (1996) *Management Gurus*, London: Routledge.

Huczynski, A. and Buchanan, D. (1991) *Organizational Behaviour*, 2nd edn, London: Prentice-Hall.

Hutton, W. (1996) *The State We're In*, London: Vintage.

Hutton, W. (1997) *The State To Come*, London: Vintage.

Huws, U. (1997) *Teleworking: Guidelines for Good Practice*, Report 329, Brighton: Institute for Employment Studies.

Hyman, R. (1975) *Industrial Relations: A Marxist Introduction*, London: Macmillan.

Hyman, R. (1987) Trade unions and the law: papering over the cracks?, *Capital and Class*, **31**: 43–63.

Hyman, R. (1988) Flexible specialization: miracle or myth? In Hyman, R. and Streeck, W. (eds) *New Technology and Industrial Relations*, Oxford: Blackwell.

Hyman, R. (1989) *Strikes*, 4th edn, London: Macmillan.

Hyman, R. (1991) European unions: towards 2000, *Work, Employment and Society*, **5**(4): 621–39.

Hyman, R. (1994) Industrial relations in Western Europe: an era of ambiguity? *Industrial Relations Journal*, **33**(1): 1–24.

Hyman, R. (1997a) Editorial, *European Journal of Industrial Relations*, **3**(1): 5–6.

Hyman, R. (1997b) The future of employee representation, *British Journal of Industrial Relations*, **35**(3): 309–36.

Ichniowski, C., Kochan, T., Levine, D, Olson, C. and Strauss, G. (1996) What works at work: overview and assessment, *Industrial Relations*, **35**(3): 299–333.

IFF (1997) *Skills Needs in Britain 1997*, London: IFF Research.

Iles, P. and Salaman, G. (1995) Recruitment, selection and assessment. In Storey, J. (ed.) *Human Resource Management*, London: Routledge.

IPD (1996) *The Lean Organisation: Managing the People Dimension*, London: Institute of Personnel and Development.

IPD (1997) *Overqualified and Underemployed?*, London: Institute of Personnel and Development.

IPM (1981) *Representative Structures*, Institute of Personnel Management, London: IPM.

Jackson, B. (1996) Re-engineering the sense of self: The manager and the management guru, *Journal of Management Studies*, **33**(5), September, pp. 571–90.

Jackson, C. (1996) *Understanding Psychological Testing*, Leicester: BPS Books.

Jackson, S., Schuler, R., and Rivero, J. (1989) Organisational characteristics as predictors of personnel policies, *Personnel Psychology*, **42**(4): 418–36.

Jenkins, C. and Sherman, B. (1979) *The Collapse of Work*, London: Eyre Methuen.

Johnson, C. (1988) *Measuring the Economy*, London: Penguin.

Johnson, G. (1987) *Strategic Change and the Management Process*, Oxford: Blackwell.

Jones, O. (1997) Changing the balance? Taylorism, TQM and the work organization, *New Technology, Work and Employment*, **12**(1): 13–23.

Judge, T.A. and Cable, D.M. (1997) Applicant personality, organizational culture and organization attraction, *Personnel Psychology*, **50**: 359–94.

Jurgens, U. (1989) The transfer of Japanese management concepts in the international automobile industry. In Wood, S. (ed.) (1989) *The Transformation of Work?*, London: Unwin Hyman.

Kamoche, K. (1996) Strategic human resource management within resource-capability view of the firm, *Journal of Management Studies*, **33**(2): 213–33.

Keenoy, T. (1990) Human resource management: rhetoric, reality and contradiction, *International Journal of Human Resource Management*, **1**(3): 363–84.

Keenoy, T. and Anthony, P. (1992) HRM: metaphor, meaning and morality. In Blyton, P. and Turnbull, P. (eds) *Reassessing Human Resource Management*, London: Sage.

Keep, E. (1989) Corporate training policies: the vital component. In Storey, J. (ed.) *New Perspectives in Human Resource Management*, Routledge: London.

Kelly, J. (1985) Management's redesign of work: labour process, labour markets and product markets. In Knights, D., Willmott, H. and Collinson, D. (eds) *Job Design: Critical Perspectives on the Labour Process*, Aldershot: Gower.

Kelly, J. (1988) *Trade Unions and Socialist Politics*, London: Verso.

Kelly, J. (1990) British trade unionism 1979–1989: change, continuity and contradiction, *Work, Employment and Society*, Special Issue, May: 29–65.

Kelly, J. and Bailey, R. (1989) Research note: British trade union membership, density and decline in the 1980s, *Industrial Relations Journal*, **20**(1): 54–61.

Kelly, J. and Kelly, C. (1991) 'Them and us': social psychology and the 'the new industrial relations', *British Journal of Industrial Relations*, **29**(1): 192–200.

Kessler, I. (1994) Performance pay. In Sisson, K. (ed.) *Personnel Management*, 2nd edn, Oxford: Blackwell.

Kessler, I. (1995) Reward systems. In Storey, J. (ed.) *Human Resource Management: A Critical Text*, London: Routledge.

Kessler, S. and Bayliss, F. (1995) *Contemporary British Industrial Relations*, 2nd edn, London: Macmillan.

Kettley, P. (1997) *Personal Feedback:Cases in Point*, Report 326, IES: Brighton.

Kim, D.O. and Voos, P.B. (1997) Unionization, union involvement, and the performance of gainsharing programs, *Relations Industrielles/Industrial Relations*, **52**(2): 304–29.

Kinnie, N.J. and Arthurs, A.J. (1996) Personnel specialists: advanced use of information technology, *Personnel Review*, **25**(3): 3–19.

Knights, D., and Willmott, H. (eds) (1986)*Gender and the Labour Process*, Aldershot: Gower.

Kochan, T. (1996) Presidential address: launching a renaissance in international industrial relations research, *Relations Industrielles/Industrial Relations*, **51**(2): 245–63.

Kochan, T. and Dyer, L. (1995) HRM: an American view. In Storey, J. (ed.) *Human Resource Management: A Critical Text*, London: Routledge.

Kochan, T. and Osterman, P. (1994) *The Mutual Gains Enterprise*, Boston: Harvard Business School Press.

Kochan, T., Batt, R. and Dyer, L. (1992) International human resource studies: a framework for future research. In Lewlin, D., Mitchell, O. and Sterer, P. (eds), *Research Frontiers – Industrial Relations and Human Resources*, Madison, University of Wisconsin: Industrial Relations Association, pp. 309–37.

Kochan, T.A., Katz, H. and McKersie, R. (1986) *The Transformation of American Industrial Relations*, New York: Basic Books.

Kochan, T., McKersie, R., and Cappelli, P. (1984) Strategic choice and industrial relations theory, *Industrial Relations*, **23**: 16–39.

Kolb, D.A. (1984) *Experiential Learning*, Prentice Hall: Englewood Cliffs.

Kotter, J. (1990) *A Force for Change*, New York: Free Press.

Kotter, J. (1996) *Leading Change*, Boston, Mass: Harvard Business.

KPMG (1996) *Learning Organisation Benchmarking Survey*, KPMG: London.

Kruse, D. (1996) Why do firms adopt profit-sharing and employee ownership plans? *British Journal of Industrial Relations*, **34**(4): 515–38.

Kydd, B. and Oppenheim, L. (1990) Using human resource management to enhance competitiveness: lessons from four excellent companies, *Human Resource Management Journal*, **29**(2): 145–66.

Labour Research Department (1988) New wave of union bashing, *Labour Research*, **77**(4): 28–9.

Lash, S. and Urry, J. (1987) *The End of Organized Capitalism*, Cambridge: Polity Press.

Latham, G.P., Saari, L.M., Pursell, E.D. and Campion, M.A. (1980) The situational interview, *Journal of Applied Psychology*, **65**: 422–7.

Lave, J. and Wenger, E. (1991) *Situated Learning*, Cambridge: Cambridge University Press.

Lawler, E. (1986) *High Involvement Management*, San Francisco: Jossey-Bass.

Lawler, E. (1996) Far from the fad in-crowd, *People Management*, 24 October, pp. 38–40.

Lawler, E.E., Mohrman, A. and Ledford, G. (1992) *E1 and Total Quality*, San Francisco: Jossey-Bass.

Leat, M.J. and Lovell, M.J. (1997) Training needs analysis: weakness in the conventional approach, *Journal of European Industrial Training*, **24**(4): 143–53.

Legge, K. (1989) Human resource management: a critical analysis. In Storey, J. (ed.) *New Perspectives on Human Resource Management*, London: Routledge.

Legge, K. (1995) *Human Resource Management: Rhetorics and Realities*, Basingstoke: Macmillan.

Legge, K. (1998) The morality of HRM. In Mabey, C. *et al.*, *Experiencing Human Resource Management*, London: Sage.

Leicester, C. (1989) The key role of the line manager in employee development, *Personnel Management*, March: 53–7.

Levinson, H. (1970) Management by whose objectives?, *Harvard Business Review*, July/Aug: 125–34.

Lincoln, J. and Kalleberg, A. (1992) *Culture Control and Commitment*, Cambridge: CUP.

Littler, C.R. (1982) *The Development of the Labour Process in Capitalist Societies*, London: Heinemann.

Littler, C.R. and Salaman, G. (1984) *Class at Work: The Design, Allocation and Control of Jobs*, London: Batsford.

Lloyd, C. (1997) Microelectronics in the clothing industry: firm strategy and the skills debate, *New Technology, Work and Employment*, **12**(1): 36–47.

Long, P. (1986) *Performance Appraisal Revisited*, London: Institute of Personnel Management.

Long, R.J. (1997) Motives for profit sharing, *Relations Industrielles/Industrial Relations*, **52**(4): 712–31.

Loveridge, R. (1983) Labour market segmentation and the firm. In Edwards, J., Leek, C., Loveridge, R. *et al.* (eds) *Manpower Planning: Strategy and Techniques in an Organisational Context*, Chichester: John Wiley, pp. 155–75.

Lowstedt, J. (1988) Prejudices and wishful thinking about computer aided design: *New Technology, Work and Employment*, **3**(1): 30–7.

Lyon, P. and Glover, I. (1998) Divestment of investment? The contradiction of HRM in relation to older employees, *Human Resource Management Journal*, **8**(1): 56–68.

Mabey, C. and Iles, P. (1991) HRM from the other side of the fence, *Personnel Management*, February: 50–3.

Mabey, C., Skinner, D. and Clark, T. (eds) (1998) *Experiencing Human Resource Management*, London: Sage.

Mabey, C., Salaman, G. and Storey, J. (eds) (1998) *Strategic Human Resource Management*, London: Sage.

McGoldrick, J. and Stewart, J. (1996) The HRM–HRD nexus. In McGoldrick, J. and Stewart, J. (eds) *Human Resource Development*, London: Pitman Publishing.

MacInnes, J. (1987) *Thatcherism at Work*, Milton Keynes: Open University Press.

McGregor, D. (1957) An uneasy look at performance appraisal, *Harvard Business Review*, **35**(3): 89–94.

McGregor, D. (1960) *The Human Side of Enterprise*, New York: McGraw-Hill.

McHenry, R. (1997a) Tried and tested, *People Management*, 23 January, pp. 32–7.

McHenry, R. (1997b) Spurring stuff, *People Management*, 24 July, pp. 28–31.

McIlroy, J. (1988) *Trade Unions in Britain Today*, Manchester: Manchester University Press.

McIlroy, J. (1991) *The Permanent Revolution? Conservative Law and the Trade Unions*, Nottingham: Spokesman.

McKendrick, E. (1988) The rights of trade union members: Part I of the Employment Act 1980, *Industrial Law Journal*, **17**(3): 141–61.

McKenna, L. (1995) Moving beyond adversarial relationships, *Canadian Business Review*, **22**(2), Summer, pp. 25–7.

McKinlay, A. and Taylor, P. (1998) Through the looking glass: Foucault and the politics of production. In McKinlay, A. and Starkey, K. (eds) *Foucault, Management and Organizational Theory*, London: Sage.

McLoughlin, I. and Clark, J. (1988) *Technological Change at Work*, Milton Keyes: Open University Press.

McLoughlin, I. and Gourlay, S. (1992) Enterprise without unions: managing employment relations in non-union firms, *Journal of Management Studies*, **29**(5): 509–28.

McShane, S. (1990) Two tests of direct gender bias in job evaluation ratings, *Journal of Occupational Psychology*, **63**: 129–40.

McShane, S.L. (1995) *Canadian Organizational Behaviour*, 2nd edn, Boston: Irwin.

Malloch, H. (1997) Strategic and HRM aspects of kaizen: a case study, *New Technology, Work and Employment*, **12**(2): 108–22.

Mannion, E. and Whittaker, P. (1996) European Passenger Services Ltd – Assessment centres for recruitment and development, *Career Development International*, **1**(6): 12–16.

Manz, C. and Sims, H. (1989) *Superleadership: Leading Others to Lead Themselves.* Englewood Cliffs, NJ: Prentice-Hall.

Marchington, M. (1980) *Responses to Participation at Work,* Aldershot: Gower.

Marchington, M. (1982) *Managing Industrial Relations,* Maidenhead: McGraw-Hill.

Marchington, M. (1987) A review and critique of research on developments in joint consultation, *British Journal of Industrial Relations,* **XXV**(3): 339–52.

Marchington, M. (1989) Problems with team briefings in practice, *Employee Relations,* **11**(4): 21–30.

Marchington, M. (1995) Involvement and participation. In Storey, J. (ed.) *Human Resource Management: A Critical Text,* London: Routledge.

Marchington, M. and Parker, P. (1990) *Changing Patterns of Employee Relations,* London: Harvester Wheatsheaf.

Marchington, M. and Wilding, P. (1983) Employee involvement inaction?, *Personnel Management,* December: 73–82.

Marchington, M., Goodman, J., Wilkinson, A. and Ackers, P. (1992) *Recent Developments in Employee Involvement,* Employment Department Research Series No. 1, London: HMSO.

Marchington, M., Wilkinson, A., Ackers, P. *et al.* (1993) The influence of managerial relations on the wave of employee Involvement, *British Journal of Industrial Relations,* **31**(4): 553–76.

Marginson, P., Armstrong, P., Edwards, P.K. *et al.* (1993) The control of industrial relations in a large company: initial analysis of the 2nd company-level industrial relations survey, *Warwick Papers in Industrial Relations,* **45**, Warwick, UK: University of Warwick.

Marks, A., Findlay, P., Hine, J., McKinley, A. and Thompson, P. (1998) The politics of partnership? Innovation in employment relations in the Scottish spirits industry, *British Journal of Industrial Relations,* **36**(2): 209–26.

Marsick, V.J. (1987) *Learning in the Workplace,* London: Croom Helm.

Martinez Lucio, M. and Weston, S. (1992) Human resource management and trade union responses: bringing the politics of the workplace back into the debate. In Blyton, P. and Turnbull, P. (eds) *Reassessing Human Resource Management,* London: Sage, pp. 215–32.

Maslow, A. (1954) *Motivation and Personality,* New York: Harper & Row.

Mathias, P. (1969) *The First Industrial Nation,* London: Methuen.

Mayhew, C. and Quinlan, M. (1997) Subcontracting and occupational health and safety in the residential building industry, *Industrial Relations Journal,* **28**(3): 192–205.

Mayo, A. (1991) *Managing Careers,* London: IPM.

Mayo, A. (1998) Memory bankers, *People Management,* 22 January, pp. 34–8.

Meyer, H.H., Kay, E. and French, J.R.P. (1965) Split roles in performance appraisal, *Harvard Business Review,* **43**: pp. 123–9.

Mezirow, J. (1991) *Transformative Dimensions of Adult Learning,* San Francisco: Jossey-Bass.

Michie, J. (1992) Unlucky 13 for the economy, *Observer,* Sunday 5 April, p. 35.

Miles, R. and Snow, C. (1984) Designing strategic human resources systems, *Organizational Dynamics,* Summer: 36–52.

Milkovitch, G.T. and Newman, J.M (1990) *Compensation,* 3rd edn, Boston: Irwin.

Miller, P. (1987) Strategic industrial relations and human resource management – distinction, definition and recognition, *Journal of Management Studies,* **24**(4): 347–61.

Millward, N. and Stevens, M. (1986) *British Workplace Industrial Relations 1980–1984,* Aldershot: Gower.

Millward, N., Stevens, M., Smart, D. and Hawes, W. (1992) *Workplace Industrial Relations in Transition,* Aldershot: Dartmouth Press.

Mintzberg, H. (1976) Planning on the left side and managing of the right side, *Harvard Business Review,* July/August: 49–58.

Mintzberg, H. (1978) Patterns in strategy formation, *Management Science,* **24**(9): 934–48.

Mintzberg, H. (1983) *Power In and Around Organizations,* Englewoods Cliffs, NJ: Prentice-Hall.

Mintzberg, H. (1987) Crafting strategy, *Harvard Business Review,* July/August: 66–75.

Mintzberg, H. (1989) *Mintzberg on Management,* New York: Collier/Hamilton.

Mintzberg, H. (1990) The Design School: reconsidering the basic premises of strategic management, *Strategic Management Journal*, **11**: 171–95.

Mintzberg, H., Ahlstrand, B. and Lampel, J. (1998) *Strategic Safari: A Guided Tour through the Wilds of Strategic Management*, New York: Free Press.

Monks, J. (1998a) Government and trade unions, *British Journal of Industrial Relations*, **36**(1): 125–35.

Monks, J. (1998b) Foreword. In Mabey, C., Skinner, D. and Clark, T. (eds) *Experiencing Human Resource Management*, London: Sage.

Moore, H.L. (1995) The future of work, *British Journal of Industrial Relations*, **33**(4): 657–78.

Moore, L. Devereaux Jennings, P. (eds) (1995) *Human Resource Management on the Pacific Rim*, New York: Walter de Gruyter.

Morgan, G. (1980) Paradigms, metaphors and puzzle solving in organization theory, *Administrative Science Quarterly*, 25: 605–22.

Morgan, G. (1997) *Images of Organization*, London: Sage.

Morgan, J., Pain, N. and Hubert, F. (1998) The world economy, *National Institute Economic Review*, **163**: 37–63.

Mottaz, C. (1988) Determinants of organizational commitment, *Human Relations*, **41**(6): 467–82.

Mowday, R., Porter, L. and Steers, R. (1982) *Employee-Organization Linkages: The Psychology of Commitment, Absenteeism and Turnover*, London: Academic Press.

Munro-Fraser, J. (1971) *Psychology: General, Industrial, Social*, London: Pitman.

Murakami, T. (1995) Introducing team working: a motor industry case study from Germany, *Industrial Relations Journal*, **26**(4): 293–304.

Murphy, C. and Olthuis, D. (1995) The impact of work reorganization on employee attitudes towards work, the company and the union. In *Re-shaping Work: Union Responses to Technological Change*. Toronto, Ont.: Ontario Federation of Labour.

Nahavandi, A. and Malekzadeh, A.R. (1993) Leader style in strategy and organizational performance: an integrative framework, *Journal of Management Studies*, **30**(3): 405–25.

Nanda, A. (1996) Resources, capabilities and competencies. In Moingeon, B. and Edmondson, A. (eds) *Organisational Learning and Competitive Advantage*, London: Sage.

Neher, W.W. (1997) *Organizational Communication*, Boston: Allyn & Bacon.

Newton, T. and Findlay, P. (1996) Playing God? The performance of appraisal, *Human Resource Management Journal*, **6**(3): 42–58.

Nichols, T. (ed.) (1980) *Capital and Labour*, London: Fontana.

Nichols, T. (1986) *The British Worker Question: A New Look at Workers and Productivity in Manufacturing*, London: RKP.

Nichols, T. (1990) Industrial safety in Britain and the 1974 Health and Safety at Work Act: the case of manufacturing, *International Journal of the Sociology of Law*, **18**: 317–42.

Nichols, T. and Beynon, H. (1977) *Living with Capitalism: Class Relations and the Modern Factory*, London: Routledge & Kegan Paul.

Nkomo, S.M. (1988) Strategic planning for human resources – let's get started, *Long Range Planning*, **21**(1): 66–72.

Noon, M. (1992) HRM: A map, model or theory? In Blyton, P. and Turnbull, P. (eds) *Reassessing Human Resource Management*, London: Sage.

Ofsted (1996) *The Appraisal of Teachers*, HMR/18/96/NO, London: Ofsted Publications.

O'Higgins, P. (1986) International standards and British labour law. In Lewis, R. (ed.) *Labour Law in Britain*, Oxford: Blackwell.

Oliver, J. (1993) Shocking to the core, *Management Today*, August 1993, pp. 18–21.

Oliver, N. and Wilkinson, B. (1988) *The Japanization of British Industry*, Oxford: Blackwell.

O'Reilly, J. (1992) Subcontracting in banking: some evidence from Britain and France, *New Technology, Work and Employment*, **7**(2): 107–15.

Osterman, P. (1987) Choice of employment systems in internal labour markets, *Industrial Relations*, **26**(1): 46–67.

Osterman, P. (1995) How common is workplace transformation and who adopts it?, *Industrial and Labor Relations Review*, **47**: 173–87.

Ouchi, W. (1979) A conceptual framework for the design of organizational control mechanisms', *Management Science*, **25**(9): 833–48.

Overbeck, H. (1990) *Global Capitalism and National Decline*, London: Unwin Hyman.

Pahl, R.E. (ed.) (1988) *On Work: Historical, Comparative and Theoretical Approaches*, Oxford: Blackwell.

Parker, B. and Caine, D. (1996) Holonic modelling: human resource planning and the two faces of Janus, *International Journal of Manpower*, **17**(8): 30–45.

Pearson, R. (1991) *The Human Resource*, Maidenhead: McGraw-Hill.

Peck, S. (1994) Exploring the link between organizational strategy and the employment relationship: the role of human resource policies, *Journal of Management Studies*, **31**(5): 715–36.

Pedler, M., Boydell, T. and Burgoyne, J. (1988) *The Learning Company Project Report*, Department of Employment, Sheffield.

Pedler, M., Burgoyne, J. and Boydell, T. (1991) *The Learning Company: A Strategy for Sustainable Development*, Maidenhead: McGraw-Hill.

Pedler, M. and Aspinall, K. (1996) *Perfect PLC?*, Maidenhead: McGraw-Hill.

Pendleton, A. (1997a) The evolution of industrial relations in UK nationalized industries, *British Journal of Industrial Relations*, **35**(2): 145–72.

Pendleton, A. (1997b) What impact has privatization had on pay and employment?, *Relations Industrielles/Industrial Relations*, **52**(3): 554–82.

Penn, R., Lilja, K. and Scattergood, H. (1992) Flexibility and employment patterns in the paper industry: an analysis of mills in Britain and Finland, *Industrial Relations Journal*, **23**(3): 214–23.

Penrose, E.T.. (1959) *The Theory of the Growth of the Firm*, Oxford: Blackwell.

Perkins, G. (1986) *Employee Communications in the Public Sector*, London: IPM.

Pettigrew, A., Sparrow, P. and Hendry, C. (1988) The forces that trigger training, *Personnel Management*, December, pp. 28–32.

Phillips, P. and Phillips, E. (1993) *Women and Work: Inequality in the Canadian Labour Market*, Toronto: Lorimer.

Pickard, J. (1997) Vacational qualifications, *People Management*, 10 July, pp. 26–31.

Piore, M. and Sabel, C. (1984) *The Second Industrial Divide*, New York: Basic Books.

Pitfield, M. (1984) Studying to be a personnel manager, *Personnel Management*, November: 24–9.

Plachy, R.J. (1987) Writing job descriptions that get results, *Personnel*, October, pp. 56–63.

Platt, L. (1997) Employee work-life balance: the competitive advantage. In Hesselbein, F., Goldsmith, M. and Beckhard, R. (eds) *The Organization of the Future*, San Francisco: Jossey-Bass.

Pollard, S. (1969) *The Development of the British Economy, 1914–1967*, 2nd edn, London: Arnold.

Pollert, A. (1988) Dismantling flexibility, *Capital and Class*, **34**: 42–75.

Pollert, A. (ed.) (1991) *Farewell to Flexibility?*, Oxford: Blackwell.

Poole, M. (1980) Management strategies and industrial relations. In Mansfield, R. (ed.) *Managerial Roles in Industrial Relations*, Aldershot: Gower.

Poole, M. and Jenkins, G. (1998) Human resource management and the theory of rewards: evidence from a national survey, *British Journal of Industrial Relations*, **36**(2): 227–47.

Porter, M. (1980) *Competitive Strategy*, New York: Free Press.

Porter, M. (1985) *Competitive Advantage: Creating and Sustaining Superior Performance*, New York: Free Press.

Porter, M. (1990) *The Competitive Advantage of Nations*. London: Macmillan.

Prahalad, C.K. and Hamel, G. (1990) The core competencies of the organization, *Harvard Business Review*, **68**, May–June: 79–91.

Premack, S.L. and Wanous, J.P. (1985) A meta-analysis of realistic job preview experiments, *Journal of Applied Psychology*, **70**(4): 706–19.

Pryce, V. and Nicholson, C. (1988) The problems and performance of employee ownership firms, *Employment Gazette*, **96**(6): 53–8.

Pulakos, E.D. and Schmitt, N. (1995) Experienced-based and situational questions: studies of validity, *Personnel Psychology*, **48**: 289–309.

Purcell, J. (1979) A strategy for management control in industrial relations. In Purcell, J. and Smith, R. (eds) *The Control of Work*, London: Macmillan.

Purcell, J. (1987) Mapping management styles in employee relations, *Journal of Management Studies*, **24**(5): 533–48.

Purcell, J. (1989) The impact of corporate strategy on human resource management. In Storey, J. (ed.) *New Perspectives on Human Resource Management*, London: Routledge.

Purcell, J. (1995) Corporate strategy and its link with human resource management strategy. In Storey, J. (ed.) *Human Resource Management: A Critical Text*, London: Routledge.

Purcell, J. and Ahlstrand, B. (1994) *Human Resource Management in the Multi-Divisional Company*, Oxford: OUP.

Purcell, J. and Sisson, K. (1983) Strategies and practice in the management of industrial relations. In Bain, G. (ed.) *Industrial Relations in Britain*, Oxford: Blackwell.

Quin Mills, D. and Balbaky, M. (1985) Planning for morale and culture In Walton, R. and Lawrence, P. (eds) *Human Resource Management: Trends and Challenge*s, Boston, MA: Harvard Business School Press.

Randell, G. (1994) Employee appraisal. In Sisson, K. (ed.) *Personnel Management*, Oxford: Blackwell.

Rarick, C.A. and Baxter, G. (1986) Behaviourally anchored rating scales (Bars): an effective performance appraisal approach, *SAM Advanced Management Journal*, Winter: 36–9.

Reed, M.I. (1993) Organizations and modernity: Continuity and discontinuity in organization theory. In Hassard, J. and Parker, M. (eds) *Postmodernism and Organizations*, London: Sage.

Reilly, B., Paci, P. and Holl P. (1995) Unions, safety committees and workplace injuries, *British Journal of Industrial Relations*, **33**(2): 275–87.

Reilly, R.R., Smither, J.W. and Vasilopoulos, N.L. (1996) A longitudinal study of upward appraisal, *Personnel Psychology*, **46**: 599–61.

Rendall, P. (1986) Stuck in the middle, *Chief Executive*, September: 333.

Rifkin, J. (1996) *The End of Work*. New York: Tarcher/Putnam Press.

Rinehart, J., Robertson, D., Huxley, C., and Wareham, J. (1994) Reunifying conception and execution of work under Japanese production management? A Canadian case study. In Elger, T. and Smith, C. (eds) *Global Japanization?*, London: Routledge.

Robbins, S.P. (1990) *Organization Theory*, 3rd edn, Englewood Cliffs, NJ: Prentice-Hall.

Robbins, S.P. (1991) *Organizational Behavior*, 5th edn, London: Prentice-Hall.

Robens, Lord (1972) *Report of the Committee on Safety and Health*, Cmnd 5034, London: HMSO.

Roberts, G. (1997) *Recuitment and Selection*, London: Institute of Personnel and Development.

Rodger, A. (1970) *The Seven Point Plan*, 3rd edn, London: NFER.

Rollins, T. (1988) Pay for performance: is it really worth the trouble?, *Personnel Administrator*, **33**(5).

Rose, M. (1988) *Industrial Behaviour*, London: Penguin.

Rothwell, S. (1995) Human resource planning. In Storey, J. (ed.) *Human Resource Management: A Critical Text*, London: Routledge.

Rubery, J. (1992) Pay gender, and the social dimension to Europe, *British Journal of Industrial Relations*, **30**(4): 605–21.

Salamon, M. (1987) *Industrial Relations: Theory and Practice*, London: Prentice-Hall.

Salancik, G. (1977) Commitment and control of organizational behavior and belief. In Staw, B. and Salancil, G. (eds) *New Directions in Organizational Behavior*, Chicago: St. Clair Press

Saporta, I. and Lincoln, B. (1995) Managers' and workers' attitudes towards unions in the US and Canada, *Relations Industrielles/Industrial Relations*, **50**(3): 550–66.

Sapsford, D., Johnes, G., Armstrong, H., and de Kervenoael, R. (1997) British employers and the Social Chapter: some survey evidence, *Industrial Relations Journal*, **28**(3): 236–42.

Sass, R. (1982) Safey and self-respect, *Policy Options*, July–August.

Saul, J.R. (1995) *The Unconscious Civilization*, Concord, Ont.: Anansi Press.

Saxby, M. (1987) Integrated job evaluation, *Management Services*, December.

Sayer, A. (1986) New developments in manufacturing: the just-in-time system, *Capital and Class,* **30**, Winter: 43–72.

Schneider, B. (1987) The people make the place, *Personnel Psychology*, **40**: 437–53.

Schneider, B. and Goldstein, H.W. (1995) The ASA framework: an update, *Personnel Psychology*, **48**: 747–73.

Schonberger, R. (1982) *Japanese Manufacturing Techniques: Nine Hidden Lessons in Simplicity*, London: Collier Macmillan.

Schuler, R.S. (1989) Strategic human resource management and industrial relations, *Human Relations*, **42**(2): 157–84.

Schuler, R. and Jackson, S. (1987) Linking competitive strategies and human resource management practices, *Academy of Management Executive*, **1**(3): 209–13.

Schwab, D. and Grams, R. (1985) Sex-related errors in job evaluation; a real-world test, *Journal of Applied Psychology*, **70**(3).

Scullion, H. (1995) International human resource management. In Storey, J. (ed.) *Human Resource Management: A Critical Text*, London: Routledge.

Selznick, P. (1957) *Leadership and Administration*, New York: Harper & Row.

Senge, P. (1990) *The Fifth Discipline*, New York: Doubleday.

Shalev, M. (1981) Theoretical dilemmas and value analysis in comparative industrial relations. In Dlugos, G. and Weiermair, K. (eds) *Management Under Differing Value Systems*, New York: de Gruyter.

Shenkar, O. (1995) *Global Perspectives on Human Resource Management*, Englewood: Prentice-Hall.

Simpson, B. (1986) Trade union immunities. In Lewis, R. (ed.) (1986) *Labour Law in Britain*, Oxford: Blackwell.

Singh, R. (1997) Equal opportunities for men and women in the EU: A commentary, *Industrial Relations*, **28**(1): 68–71.

Sisson, K. (ed.) (1989) *Personnel Management*, Oxford: Blackwell.

Sisson, K. (1993) In search of HRM, *British Journal of Industrial Relations*, **31**(2): 201–9.

Sisson, K. (ed.) (1994) *Personnel Management*, 2nd edn, Oxford: Blackwell.

Sisson, K. (1995) Human resource management and the personnel function. In Storey, J. (ed.) *Human Resource Management: A Critical Text*, London: Routledge.

Sisson, K. and Temperley, S. (1994) From manpower planning to strategic human resource management. In Sisson, K. (ed.) *Personnel Management*, Oxford: Blackwell.

Smircich, L. and Morgan, G. (1982) Leadership: the management of meaning, *Journal of Applied Behavioral Science*, **18**(3): 257–73.

Smith, A., Craver, C. and Clark, L. (1982) *Employment Discrimination Law*, 2nd edn, London: Unwin Hyman.

Smith, A.R. (1980) *Corporate Manpower Planning*, London: Gower Press.

Smith, I. (1992) Reward management and HRM. In Blyton, P. and Turnbull, P. (eds) *Reassessing Human Resource Management*, London: Sage.

Smith, J.M. and Robertson, I.T. (eds) (1991) *Advances in Selection and Assessment*, Chichester: Wiley.

Smith, P. and Morton, G. (1993) Union exclusion and the decollectivization of industrial relations in contemporary Britain, *British Journal of Industrial Relations*, **31**(1): 97–114.

Sparrow, P. (1996) Too good to be true, *People Management*, 5 December, pp. 22–7.

Sparrow, P.R. and Pettigrew, A.M. (1988) Strategic human resource management in the UK computer supplier industry, *Journal of Occupational Psychology*, **61**(1): 25–42.

Spencer, S. (1990) Devolving job evaluation, *Personnel Management*, January: 15–19.

Spikes, W.F. (ed.) (1995) *Workplace Learning, New Directions for Adult and Continuing Education*, **68**, Winter, San Francisco: Jossey-Bass.

Spychalski, A.C., Quiñones, M.A., Gaugler, B.B. and Pohley, K. (1997) A survey of assessment center practices in the United States, *Personnel Psychology*, **50**: 71–90.

Standing, G. (1997) Globalization, labour flexibility and insecurity: the era of market regulation, *European Journal of Industrial Relations*, **3**(1): 7–37.

Stiles, R., Gratton, L., Truss, C., Hope-Hailey, V. and McGovern, P. (1997) Performance management and the pyschological contract, *Human Resource Management Journal*, **7**(1): 57–66.

Stone, T.H. and Meltz, N.M. (1988) *Human Resource Management in Canada*, 2nd edn, Toronto: Holt, Rinehart and Winston.

Storey, J. (ed.) (1989) *New Perspectives on Human Resource Management*, London: Routledge.

Storey, J. (1992) *Developments in the Management of Human Resources*, Oxford: Basil Blackwell.

Storey, J. (ed.) (1995) *Human Resource Management*, London: Routledge

Storey, J., Cressey, P., Morris, T. and Wilkinson, A. (1997) Changing employment practices in UK banking: case studies, *Personnel Review*, **26**(1): 24–42.

Strebler, M., Robinson, D. and Heron, P. (1997) *Getting the Best Out of Your Competencies*, Report 334, Brighton: Institute of Employment Studies.

Streeck, W. (1987) The uncertainties of management in the management of uncertainty, *Work, Employment and Society*, **1**: 281–308.

Streeck, W. (1996) Comment on Ronald Dore, *Industrielle Beziehungen*, **3**: 187–96.

Streeck, W. and Visser, J. (1997) The rise of the conglomerate union, *European Journal of Industrial Relations*, **3**(3): 305–32.

Tamkin, P., Barber, L. and Hirsh, W. (1995) *Personal Development Plans: Case Studies of Practice*, Report 280, Institute of Employment Studies: Brighton.

Tamkin, P., Barber, L. and Dench, S. (1997) *From Admin to Strategy: the Changing Face of the HR Function*, Report 332, Institute of Employment Studies: Brighton.

Taylor, H. (1991) The systematic training model: corn circles in search of a spaceship?, *Management Education and Development*, **22**(4): 258–78.

Teague, P. and Grahl, J. (1992) *Industrial Relations and European Integration*, London: Lawrence & Wishart.

Teece, D.J. *et al.* (1990) Firm capabilities, resources and the concept of strategy: four paradigms of strategic management, CCC Working Paper, No. 90–8.

Temporal, P. (1978) The nature of non-contrived learning and its implications for management development, *Management Education and Development*, **9**: 20–3.

Terry, M. (1995) Trade unions: shop stewards and the workplace. In Edwards, P. (ed.) *Industrial Relations*. Oxford: Blackwell.

Thompson, P. (1989) *The Nature of Work*, 2nd edn, London: Macmillan.

Thompson, P. (1993) Postmodernism: fatal distraction. In Hassard, J. and Parker, M. (eds) *Postmodernism and Organizations*, London: Sage.

Thomson, A., Storey, J., Mabey, C., Gray, C., Farmer, E. and Thomson, R. (1997) *A Portrait of Management Development*, London Institute of Management.

Thornhill, A., Saunders, M.N.K. and Stead, J. (1997) Downsizing, delayering – but where's the commitment, *Personnel Review*, **26**(1): 81–98.

Thurley, K., and Wood, S. (1983) Business strategy and industrial relations strategy. In Thurley, K. and Wood, S. (eds) *Industrial Relations and Management Strategy*, Cambridge: Cambridge University Press.

Tichy, N. and Devanna, M. (1986) *The Transformational Leader*, New York: John Wiley.

Tichy, N. and Ulrich, D. (1984) The leadership challenge – a call for the transformational leader, *Sloan Management Review*, Fall: 301–22.

Tomaney, J. (1990) The reality of workplace flexibility, *Capital and Class*, **40** (Spring): 97–124.

Torrington, D. and Hall, L. (1987) *Personnel Management: A New Approach*, London: Prentice-Hall.

Towers, B. (1989) Running the gauntlet: British trade unions under Thatcher, 1979–1988, *Industrial and Labor Relations Review*, **42**(2): 296–313.

Towers, B. (1992) Two speed ahead: Social Europe and the UK after Maastricht, *Industrial Relations Journal*, **23**(2): 83–9.

Townley, B. (1989) Employee communication programmes. In Sisson, K. (ed.) *Personnel Management in Britain*, Oxford: Blackwell.

Townley, B. (1994) *Reframing Human Resource Managment*, London: Sage.

Trades Union Congress (1988) *Meeting the Challenge: First Report of the Special Review Body*, London: TUC.

Trethewey, A. (1997) Organizational culture. In Byers, P.Y. (ed.) *Organizational Communication: Theory and Behavior*, Boston: Allyn & Bacon.

Tung, R. (1988) *The New Expatriates*, Boston, MA: Ballinger.

Turnbull, P. (1986) The Japanisation of British industrial relations at Lucas, *Industrial Relations Journal*, **17**(3): 193–206.

Turnbull, P. (1988) The limits of Japanization: 'just-in-time', labour relations and the UK automotive industry, *New Technology, Work and Employment*, **3**(1): 7–20.

Tyson, D.E. (1996) *Profit Sharing in Canada: The Complete Guide to Designing and Implementing Plans that Really Work*, Toronto: John Wiley.

Tyson, S. and Fell, A. (1986) *Evaluating the Personnel Function*, London: Hutchinson.

Tyson, S. and Brewster, C. (1991) Comparative studies and the development of human resource management. In Brewster, C. and Tyson, S. (eds) *International Comparisons in Human Resource Management*. London: Pitman, pp. 257–9.

Tyson, S. (1995a) *Human Resource Strategy*, Pitman: London.

Tyson. S. (ed) (1995b) *Strategic Prospects for HRM*, London: IPD.

Ulman, L. (1992) Why should human resource managers pay high wages?, *British Journal of Industrial Relations*, **30**(2): 177–212.

Ulrich, L. and Trumbo, D. (1965) The selection interview since 1949, *Psychological Bulletin*, **63**: 100–16.

Veres, J. (1990) Job analysis in practice: a brief review of the role of job analysis in human resource management. In Ferris, G. (ed.) *Human Resource Management: Perspectives and Issues*, 2nd edn, London: Allyn & Bacon.

Verlander, E.G. (1985) The system's the thing, *Training and Development*, April: 20–3.

Verma, A. (1995) Employee involvement in the workplace. In Gunderson, M. and Ponak, A. (eds) *Union–Management Relations in Canada*, 3rd edn, Don Mills, Ontario: Addison-Wesley, pp. 281–308.

Visser, J. and Waddington, J. (1996) Industrialization and politics: a century of union structural developments in three European countries, *European Journal of Industrial Relations*, **2**(1): 21–53.

Voos, P.B. (1997) The future of employee representation: discussion, *British Journal of Industrial Relations*, **35**(3): 332–6.

Vroom, V.H. (1964) *Work and Motivation*, New York: John Wiley.

Waddington, J. (1988) Business unionism and fragmentation within the TUC, *Capital and Class*, **36** (Spring): 7–15.

Waddington, J. (1992) Trade union membership in Britain, 1980–1987: unemployment and restructuring, *British Journal of Industrial Relations*, **30**(2): 7–15.

Waddington, J. and Whitston, C. (1994) The politics of restructuring: Trade unions on the defensive in Britain since 1979, *Relations Industrielles/Industrial Relations*, **49**(4): 794–817.

Waddington, J. and Whitston, C. (1997) Why do people join unions in a period of membership decline?, *British Journal of Industrial Relations*, **35**(4): 515–46.

Wageman, R. (1997) Critical success factors for creating superb self-managing teams, *Organizational Dynamics*, **26**(1), pp. 49–61.

Wagner, R.F. (1949) The employment interview: a critical summary, *Personnel Psychology*, **2**: 17–46.

Wajcman, J. (1996) Desperately seeking differences: is managerial style gendered?, *British Journal of Industrial Relations*, **34**(3): 333–49.

Wallace, M. (1989) Brave new workplace: technology and work in the new economy, *Work and Occupations*, **16**(4): 363–92.

Walters, D. (1987) Health and safety and trade union workplace organization: a case study in the printing industry, *Industrial Relations Journal*, **18**(1): 40–9.

Walters, M. (ed.) (1995) *The Performance Management Handbook*, London: IPD.

Walton, R. (1985) From control to commitment in the workplace, *Harvard Business Review*, March/April: 77–84.

Watson, T. (1986) *Management,Organization and Employment Strategy*, London: Routledge & Kegan Paul.

Watson, T. (1994) Recruitment and selection. In Sisson, K. (ed.) *Personnel Management*, Oxford: Blackwell.

Wedderburn, Lord (1986) *The Worker and the Law*, 3rd edn, London: Penguin.

Weick, K.E. (1982) Managerial thought in the context of action. In Srivastva, S. *et al.* (eds) *The Executive Mind*, San Francisco: Jossey-Bass, pp. 221–41.

Wells, D. (1993) Are strong unions compatible with the new model of human resource management?, *Relations Industrielles/Industrial Relations*, **48**(1): 56–84.

West, A.C. (1980) Involving employees – Practical action on Section One, *Journal of Occupational Psychology*, **5**(5): 538–56.

Wheatley, M. (1992) *The Future of Middle Management*, Corby: BIM.

Wheelen, T. and Hunger, J. (1995) *Strategic Management and Business Policy*, 5th edn, New York: Addison-Wesley.

Whipp, R. (1992) Human resource management, competition and strategy: some production tensions. In Blyton, P. and Turnbull, P. (eds) *Reassessing Human Resource Management*, London Sage.

Whittaker, D.H. (1990) *Managing Innovation: A Study of British and Japanese Factories*, Cambridge: Cambridge University Press.

Whittington, R. (1993) *What is Strategy and Does it Matter?*, London: Routledge.

Wickens, P. (1987) *The Road to Nissan*, London: Macmillan.

Wilkinson, A., Allen, P. and Snape, E. (1991) TQM and the management of labour, *Employee Relations*, **13**(1): 24–31.

Wilkinson, B. and Oliver, N. (1990) Obstacles to Japanisation: the case of Ford UK, *Employee Relations*, **12**(1): 17–21.

Williams, A. (1993) *Human Resource Management and Labour Market Flexibility*, Aldershot: Avebury.

Willman, P. (1996) Merger propensity and merger outcomes among British unions, 1986–95, *Industrial Relations Journal*, **27**(4): 331–7.

Willmott, H. (1995) The odd couple?: re-engineering business processes; managing human relations, *New Technology, Work and Employment*, **10**(2): 89–98.

Wilson, F. (1994) Introducing new computer-based systems into Zenbank, *New Technology, Work and Employment*, **9**(2): 115–26.

Wilson, N.A.B. (1973) On the quality of working life, *Manpower Papers*, **7**, London: HMSO.

Witherspoon, P.D. (1997) *Communicating Leadership*, Boston: Allyn & Bacon.

Witz, A. (1986) Patriarchy and the labour market: occupational control strategies and the medical division of labour. In Knights, D. and Willmott, H. (eds) *Gender and the Labour Process*, Aldershot: Gower.

Womack, J., Jones, D., Roos, D. (1990) *The Machine That Changed The World*, New York: Rawson Associates.

Wood, S. (ed.) (1989) *The Transformation of Work*, London: Unwin Hyman.

Wood, S. (1995) The four pillars of HRM: are they connected?, *Human Resource Management Journal*, **5**(5): 49–59.

Woodley, C. (1990) The cafeteria route to compensation, Personnel Management, May: 26–31.

Woodruffe, C. (1992) What is meant by a competency? In Boam, R. and Sparrow, P. (eds) *Designing and Achieving Competency*, Maidenhead: McGraw-Hill, pp. 16–30.

Work in America (1973) Report of a Special Task Force to the Secretary of Health, Education and Welfare, Boston: MIT Press.

Wright, M. (1996) The collapse of compulsory unionism? Collective organization in highly unionized British companies, 1979–1991, *British Journal of Industrial Relations*, **34**(4): 497–513.

Yammarino, F.J. and Atwater, L.E. (1997) Implications of self–other rating agreement for human resources management, *Organizational Dynamics*, **25**(4): 35–44.

Younson, F. (1998) Collective returns, *People Management*, **4**(5): 21–5.

Yukl, G. (1998) *Leadership in Organizations*, 4th edn, New Jersey: Prentice-Hall.

Zuboff, S. (1988) *In the Age of the Smart Machine*, New York: Basic Books.

Index